Mountain Maidu Dictionary

Karen Lahaie Anderson

With much help
from my fellow learners
© Karen Anderson 2015
First Edition
Second Edition 2017
Fish-head Version

In Loving Memory and Gratitude

Farrell G. Cunningham yatám
1976-2013

uním wéye minḱi mákpapaitiwonodi, hónwenuma'aḱan

According to his custom, we avoid saying the names of those who have passed on. If his name must be pronounced, it should be followed by "yatám."

Table of Contents

Introduction 7

Pronunciation Guide 9

How to Use the Maidu-English Section 11

Sources for the Maidu-English Section 12

Maidu-English 15

English-Maidu 301

How to Use the English-Maidu Section 302

Appendices 421

Appendix 1: Maidu Sense of Time 422

Appendix 2: Building Blocks of Maidu Words 423

Appendix 3: Changes Made From Original Sources 428

Appendix 4: About Some of the People Who Preserved the Language 432

Appendix 5: Maps 435

About the Author 449

Bibliography 450

Introduction

Mountain Maidu is a Native American language spoken in Plumas and Lassen counties, California. It is classified as a Maiduan language, closely related to Nisenan and Konkow, all part of the Penutian family in the larger Amerind language family.[1]

There are very few native speakers of Maidu left at this writing. I was privileged to study under Farrell Cunningham, a Maidu who had learned the language from his elders at a young age. He passed away in 2013, leaving his dream of reviving the Maidu language unfinished. My hope is that his dream can edge a little closer to reality with this dictionary.

I have brought together the work of many people into one volume with one orthography. I could not have done this without the fantastic previous work of Roland Dixon and William Shipley, and especially their Maidu informants, Tom Young, Maym Gallagher, Dan Williams, Lena Thomas Benner, Leona Morales, George Peconum, Roxie Peconum, Marie Potts, and Lilly Baker. For a full list of contributors, see the Sources list in the Maidu-English section, and Appendix 4: "About Some of the People Who Preserved the Language." In the years of learning from Mr. Cunningham, another thousand or so words and expressions were added to what was previously recorded. I appreciate the help and support of the other Maidu learners, and the people who supplied me with tapes, papers, maps, and other resources. I wish to thank those who took an interest in this project; if it weren't for their encouragement, this dictionary would not have been completed.

Our teacher considered Shipley's orthography to be confusing, especially using the /j/ for the /y/ sound. Shipley then used the /y/ for the unrounded back vowel (IPA ɯ or ʊ) in Maidu. Mr. Cunningham created his own character, /ᴍ/, for the vowel that Shipley writes as /y/. Although, as I recall, he meant it to represent a hut (hᴍbó), the class began calling it a "fish head" almost immediately, and the name stuck. In the fish-head orthography, a /y/ is written for the English /y/ sound (where Shipley writes /j/) and a fish head /ᴍ/ is written for the unrounded back vowel we don't have in English. In this orthography, we also write Shipley's /ć/ and Dixon's /ts/ as /ch/. This forces us to write the Maidu sound that Shipley writes as /c/ as chh, which is admittedly awkward, but this sound is rare in Maidu. The glottal stop, which Shipley writes as /ʔ/ is written here as an apostrophe, /'/. This glottal stop is not used as frequently in fish-head orthography as in Shipley's orthography, namely, not at the beginning of words which start with vowels. Since all such words really start with the glottal stop, there was no real need to write it. Our teacher wanted to make it easy to read and write the language so that people would not be stumbling over unfamiliar characters. If you would like to install the font that creates the special fish-head character, email the author (see "About the Author" for the email address). For texting in Maidu, the @ sign character could be used for /ᴍ/.

The glottalized characters:

ḱ, ṗ, t́

are found on most computers using "insert symbol" in a word-processing application. I put stress marks /'/ over stressed syllables where word stress is known, although these marks are optional. Accented vowels can also be added to text using "insert symbol."
Although linguists will likely find this book useful, it is primarily written for everyday people wanting to speak, read and write the language. Some quirky humor and silliness have crept in, in remembrance of how our teacher made learning fun.
I am deeply indebted to my fellow students Terry Meekins, Rachel Water, and Eileen Hale for reviewing the manuscript and providing words I didn't have, and to Danny Manning for providing me with important materials. I am grateful to all who shared maps, papers and recordings, as well as those who were supportive and encouraging. The main driving force behind this work is my wish to honor Farrell Cunningham, our Maidu teacher and beloved friend.

---

[1] Ruhlen: 1991:368

I am optimistic that this dictionary will be a helpful tool for those working to revitalize the Mountain Maidu language. It should be considered a work in progress. There will certainly be errors to find and correct, more words to add, and so forth. I would welcome any corrections and suggestions, and hopefully in the future, others will come along to improve on this. Meanwhile, I wish all learners well: yahát mákkitpada!

Note on the Second Edition, 2017

Over the past two years, I have found and corrected numerous typos, a few incorrect or slightly-off definitions, and information that needed clarification. In addition, about 90 missing words have been discovered and added.[2] I have also added more English synonyms to the English-Maidu section, so that students may find their words more easily. In addition, I have entered more grammatical elements in the English-Maidu section, with references to the pages in Mountain Maidu Grammar where they are explained. In this dictionary, only attested words from Maidu speakers are listed, while Modern Maidu invents or borrows new words based on Maidu word-creating techniques.

---

[2] These, with their sources, are described more fully on the Dictionary Errata page in Modern Maidu, which has just been published.

Pronunciation Guide for Maidu Sounds

Consonants:

Imploded consonants (note that Dixon writes that the imploded b and d are only heard before ɯ, while Shipley considers them to always be imploded):[3]

b	intake air as you pronounce a /b/
d	intake air as you pronounce a /d/

Glottalized/ejective consonants:

ćh	a sound between /ts/ and /ch/, pronounced with a gust of breath created by closing off the back of the mouth.
ḱ	a sound between /g/ and /k/, pronounced with a gust of breath created by closing off the back of the mouth.
ṕ	a /p/ sound, pronounced with a gust of breath created by closing off the back of the mouth.
t́	a /t/ sound, pronounced with a gust of breath created by closing off the back of the mouth.

Glottal stop:

' (apostrophe)	a catch in the back of the throat before pronouncing a vowel. All initial vowels are really preceded by a glottal stop.

The other consonants are much like English:

chh is used to represent the English-sounding /ch/. This sound is rare in Maidu.
h, k, l, m, n, p, s (some speakers say /sh/), t, w
y is pronounced as English /y/, as in "yellow."

/m/ before /k/ changes to an /ng/ sound as in "si<u>ng</u>." wóle<u>m</u> kɯlé is pronounced wóle<u>ng</u> kɯlé.
There is no /th/ sound in Maidu. When you see a word with th, pronounce t and h separately: okíthudoi is okít + hudói "barely succeed in arriving;" wehéthachono is wehét + hachóno "take something down and carry it over"
The same goes for ph and sh - if you see these combinations in Maidu, pronounce each consonant separately.

Vowels:

a	/a/ as in "father"
e	/e/ as in "get"
i	ee as in "meet" when in an open syllable (end of word or syllable, like "hiní")
	/i/ as in "with" when in a closed syllable (like "bis")
o	/o/ as in "only"
u	oo as in "food"
ɯ	/u/ sound (oo) without lip rounding
ai, ay	/y/ as in "my" with throat constriction at the end
ei, ey	ay as in "say" with throat constriction at the end
oi, oy	oy as in "boy" with throat constriction at the end

Syllable stress is expressed by an accent over the vowel (ɯ́, á, é, í, ó, ú)

---

[3] See Dixon 1905:3 and Shipley 1963:2

How to Use the Maidu-English Section

The Maidu-English section is listed alphabetically by Maidu, with the fish-head character (ᴍ) first in the alphabet. If you are used to the William Shipley dictionary, please note the following differences: words that start with vowels are listed separately under their vowel, rather than together under glottal stop. We can assume they start with a glottal stop without having to write it. The glottalized consonants are not separated out as in Shipley. In other words, entries starting with k̓ are listed with words starting with k. Again, words are not listed by root as in Shipley. While word roots are interesting, I find that I had to look in several places trying to find a word. So this dictionary is like most language dictionaries, listed alphabetically. In addition, partial words, including affixes, are not listed in the Dictionary, to avoid confusion. Instead, infixes can be found in Appendix 2, "Building Blocks of Maidu Words," and in Mountain Maidu Grammar, Lesson 8.

You will find the entries in six columns. The first column is the Maidu word in fish-head orthography. Verbs are listed without the -dom ending in most cases. -dom is the equivalent of "-ing" in English. I have left the suffixes off of verbs because these are added in context. Please refer to Mountain Maidu Grammar for how to conjugate verbs.

Nouns and adjectives are almost always listed without the -m suffix. A noun can be said with or without the -m; for example, if someone asked you the word for "person," you could either say "máidᴍ" or "máidᴍm." However, in a sentence, the form with -m is the subject, while the form without the -m is the object. In addition, nouns can be used as adjectives. When an adjective modifies a noun, it also has the -m suffix, even if the noun it modifies is not the subject of the sentence. These points are discussed in the first two chapters of Mountain Maidu Grammar. But for this dictionary, expect the forms to be listed without the final -m.

The second column is the English translation, sometimes with an example sentence using the word. If ambiguous, the part of speech is listed (noun, verb, adverb, etc.), and furthermore, verbs are listed as *intransitive* if they cannot take an object. For example, the verb "break" can be either transitive or intransitive in English. When it is transitive, I write "break (something)" to let you know it takes an object. If the verb is intransitive, it cannot take an object (for example: "the glass broke"). In usage, it's important to know whether the verb takes an object or not, so be aware of the "intransitive" notation.

The third column contains initials showing the source of the word. Since the entire Shipley dictionary has been included, you will often see WS in this column, showing this word was found in that dictionary. WST means the word was found in the texts that accompany his dictionary, but was not found in the dictionary section. Another common source is RD, Roland Dixon. These entries were gleaned from his 1912 Maidu Texts. Since he did not write a dictionary, the meanings often had to be inferred from context. Please see Appendix 3 on what I changed from Dixon and Shipley, including modernizing their translations a bit, and making a few other changes. A complete list of sources abbreviated in column 3 of the Maidu-English section follows this section.

In many cases, the word was found in multiple sources, but I only listed WS if it was found in his dictionary. Other times, I listed multiple sources if the spelling, stress, or meanings differed among the sources. If I got an example from another source, I also listed that source even if the sources all agreed on spelling and meaning. FC indicates that Farrell Cunningham was the source of the word. Words that were supplied by his students other than myself have an additional initial after FC. See the source list.

The fourth column is the spelling just the way the source wrote it. This will be helpful to you for several reasons. I have standardized the first column in fish-head orthography, but you can compare how Shipley, Dixon and others wrote the word, using column four. One of the benefits of this column is the insight it gives us on pronunciation. Different sources emphasized different things. Shipley was very careful to always write the glottalized consonants and the glottal stops, while Dixon often did not differentiate these consonants from their non-glottalized counterparts. However, Dixon noticed subtle differences in the vowels that Shipley did not acknowledge. Dixon also carefully noted vowel length, which Shipley didn't. It is known that Nisenan and Konkow have phonemic vowel length, and it may well be that Mountain Maidu does too. You can see the vowel length marked (for example, ā and ē) in the fourth column when RD is the source. These long vowels are just drawn out; they are not pronounced differently the way long vowels are in English. Words that came from FC are not written in this column, since we are using his orthography in the first column. Sources from oral recordings, such as HY (Herb Young), are also not written in the fourth column.

The fifth column is the page number where the word is found in the source. Page numbers are left out for WS because it is easy enough to find them alphabetically in the Shipley dictionary. The words from Farrell Cunningham (FC) have no page numbers because they were from oral lessons, his loose notes, and personal communication. For words coming from RD or WST, it is especially helpful to find the word in context. Not only can you decide for yourself if my interpretation is correct, but you will have a nice example of how to use this word in a sentence. Most of my examples in column 2 can be found on one or more pages listed in column 5.

The sixth column, which does not always have an entry, is an alternate spelling for the word. It's good to see the variation in spellings, as Maidu is not at this time restricted to "correct" and "incorrect" spellings. The alternate spellings can give you more insight into how people are hearing these words. It also shows what phonemes, or sounds, make a difference in meaning - or not. Both Dixon and Shipley, and of course Mr. Cunningham, wrote many words two or more different ways.

Sources for the Maidu-English Section

The Maidu source is the person who originally supplied the word. The non-Maidu source is the person who wrote it down, unless it was also written by the Maidu source. The initials are found in the dictionary to show where each word came from. For more information, see the Bibliography, as well as Appendix 4, "About Some of the People who Preserved the Language."

Initials	Maidu Source	Non-Maidu Source	Bibliography Entry
AK	unknown	A.L. Kroeber	11
BC	Ben Cunningham (typed notes)		1
CM	unknown	Coyote Man (Robert Rathbun)	18
DT	unknown	Dorothea J. Theodoratus, Theodoratus Cultural Research	25
FC	Farrell Cunningham	Karen Anderson	2, 3
FC-E	Farrell Cunningham	Eileen Hale	3
FC-J	Farrell Cunningham	Jesse Sabin	3
FC-JC	Farrell Cunningham	Joyce Cunningham	3
FC-Map	Farrell Cunningham	BethRose Middleton	4
FC-R	Farrell Cunningham	Rachel Water	3
FC-T	Farrell Cunningham	Terry Meekins	3
F-D	unknown	Roland Dixon via Francis Riddell	20
F-Ka	unknown	A.L. Kroeber via Francis Riddell	20
FR	Tom Epperson, Herb Young, Annie Gorbet, and Marie Potts	Francis Riddell	20
FR1	Tom Epperson, Herb Young, Annie Gorbet, and Marie Potts	Francis Riddell	19
FR-AG	Annie Gorbet	Francis Riddell	19
FR-MP	Marie Potts	Francis Riddell	19
FR-TE	Tom Epperson	Francis Riddell	19
FR-HY	Herb Young	Francis Riddell	19
HLME	Leona Morales, Ron Morales, Viola Williams	Simmons and Camacho	24

Initials	Maidu Source	Non-Maidu Source	Bibliography Entry
HM	unknown	C. Hart Merriam	15
HPC	unknown	Arthur W. Keddie	10
HY	Herb Young		29
JD	John Davis, Tom and Sarah Epperson, Emma Evans, Lily and Daisy Baker	John Duncan	8
LM	Leona Morales	Steve Camacho, map on honeylakemaidu.org/creation.html	30
MSOP	Thomas Merino	Maidu Cultural and Development Group	14
PM-D	Frank Joseph, Sara Epperson, Tom Epperson	Mary E. Dunn	9
PM-M	Leona Morales, Lilly Baker, Marie Potts, John Davis	James McMillan	13
RD	Tom Young	Roland Dixon	5
RD-IS	unknown	Roland Dixon	7
RD-NM	unknown	Roland Dixon	6
RM	Ron Morales	Sara-Larus Tolley	26
RR-EP	Edytha Potts		27
RR-SW	Sarah Worth		28
SP	unknown	Stephen Powers	16
SPB	unknown	Stephen Powers	17
WS	Maym Gallagher	William Shipley	21
WS-G	Maym Gallagher	William Shipley	21
WS-MM	Tom Young	William Shipley	23
WS-MP	Marie Potts	William Shipley	21
WST	Maym Gallagher	William Shipley	21
WST-DW	Dan Williams	William Shipley	21
WST-GP	George Peconum	William Shipley	21
WST-LB	Lena Thomas Benner	William Shipley	21
WST-RP	Roxie Peconum	William Shipley	21

Maidu-English

Maidu	English	Source	Source Spelling	Page	Other Spellings
ʔýʔy wa	poisonous mushroom that looks like yomén wa	JD	ɔ'ɔ wa	24	
ʔy'ásito	travel across, go across (farther)	RD	öā'sito	154	ʔyhasito
ʔy'áswodaw	go farther	RD	öās'wodau	230	yʔy'áswodaw
ʔybis	stay, remain, occupy	FC, FC-T			ebis (FC-R)
ʔychák	chance upon, meet by chance	WS	ʔyćák		
ʔychékinu	look down at	RD	ösek'inū	62	
ʔychóno	go over (a mountain, a ridge), go round (in a circle dance) (WS), walk over (to something) (RD)	WS, RD	ʔyćóno (WS), ötson'o (RD)	220	
ʔychónowei	run around	FC			
ʔychópin	come down over towards, go down over towards (WS), go across over (toward something) (RD)	WS, RD	ʔyćópin (WS), ötsop'in (RD)	32, 66, 192	
ʔydá	fade, come off	WS	ʔydá		
ʔydá	go (as footprints or tracks)	RD	ödā'	232	
ʔydáw	go off downhill, go off southward	RD	ödau'	150, 212, 224	
ʔydáw	menstruate	WS	ʔydáw		
ʔydémmai	encounter by accident, with strong emotion	WS	ʔydémmaj		
ʔydémťa	come upon by accident, with strong emotion	WS	ʔydémťa		
ʔydémťahudoi	very nearly come on (someone) by chance	WS	ʔydémťahudoj		
ʔydík	arrive, reach a good sum (cards)	FC			
ʔydíkno	arrive, get to (a place)	WS, RD	ʔydíkno (WS), ödīk'no (RD)	206	
ʔydíknotoye	arrive at a place (plural subject)	RD	ödīk'notō'ye	206	
ʔydíknoweḱoi	come back to where one left (before)	RD	ödik'nowēkoi	150	
ʔydói	ascend, go up, start to go	WS, RD	ʔydój (WS), ödoi (RD)	66, 72	
ʔydóino	go along ascending (WS), go off, start off going, go a little ways off (RD)	WS	ʔydójno (WS), ödoi'no (RD)	230	
ʔydóinoti	cause to go along ascending	WS	ʔydójnoti		
ʔydóiťa	get on top (of something): ódi ʔydóiťaweten bísḱan "after getting on top of a rock, he stayed there"	RD	ödoi'ta	122	
ʔýhʔy	bull-headed, stubborn	WS	ʔýhy		
ʔýhʔy	penis (this is a mild term)	WS	ʔýhy		

Maidu	English	Source	Source Spelling	Page	Other Spellings
ʔyhý	be powerful, be dangerous: ʔyhýkas "I am powerful."	RD	öhö'	130	
ʔyhý	powerful, dangerous: ʔyhým máidy "a powerful man"	RD	öhö'	26, 118, 146	
ʔyháiye	give birth to, groan	RD	öhai'ye	50, 72	
ʔyhákinu	lie sick (WS), lie around moaning (RD)	WS, RD	ʔyhákinu (WS), öhā'kinu (RD)	96, 100	
ʔyhánoye	follow around	WS	ʔyhánoje		
ʔyhé	follow, accompany, go with	RD	öhe'	118, 122, 204	
ʔyhédoi	start going (somewhere) with (someone)	RD	öhe'doi	90	
ʔyhéi	accompany	WS	ʔyhéj		
ʔyhéino	go along with	WS	ʔyhéjno		
ʔyhéḱoi	go around with someone	FC			
ʔyhém	hop	WS	ʔyhém		
ʔyhémno	hop along	WS	ʔyhémno		
ʔyhénoye	go around with someone	FC			
ʔyhéto	go along together with (someone), accompany each other, keep someone company	RD	öhē'to	162	
ʔýhwono	get rid of a penis, get rid of power	WS	ʔýhwono		
ʔýichan	other side: ʔýichan kýsdoina yakwéḱan "it seemed to be coming from the other side of the ridge"	RD	ü'itsan	86	ucháni
ʔý'íto	go across	RD	öi'to	230	
ʔyḱáwche	admire	RD	ökau'tse	100, 176	eḱáwche (WS, FC)
ʔyḱáwchetipe	pretty	RD	ökau'tsetipe	118, 174, 176	eḱáwchetipe (WS, FC)
ʔyḱáwche'us	have self-confidence, have self esteem	RD	ökautseus	52	eḱáwche'us (FC)
ʔyḱáwpinti	to sound nice, sound beautiful	RD	ökau'pinti	86, 120	eḱáwpinti (FC)
ʔyḱoi	journey (PM-D), destination (RD) (noun): niḱí ʔyḱóidi "where I am going"	PM, RD	u-koy (PM-D), ökoi' (RD)	RD 120	
ʔyḱói	go, go away, leave	WS	ʔyḱój		
ʔyḱói'ʔye	go back to where (they) came from	RD	ökoi'öyē	190	
ʔyḱóida	go away from (something) (WS), leave for good (RD)	WS, RD	ʔyḱójda (WS), ökoi'da (RD)	230	
ʔyḱóida	leave-taking (noun), departure (noun)	RD	ökoi'da	98, 162, 230	
ʔyḱóido	traveling	RD	ökoi'do	200	
ʔyḱói'ebís	keep going	FC			
ʔyḱói'idi	go along with (someone)	WS	ʔyḱójʔidi		
ʔýḱoikʔy	Big Dipper constellation	RD-NM			

18

Maidu	English	Source	Source Spelling	Page	Other Spellings
ʔyʔy wa	poisonous mushroom that looks like yomén wa	JD	ɔ'ɔ wa	24	
ʔy'ásito	travel across, go across (farther)	RD	öā'sito	154	ʔyhasito
ʔy'áswodaw	go farther	RD	öās'wodau	230	yʔy'áswodaw
ʔybis	stay, remain, occupy	FC, FC-T			ebis (FC-R)
ʔychák	chance upon, meet by chance	WS	ʔyćák		
ʔychékinu	look down at	RD	ösek'inū	62	
ʔychóno	go over (a mountain, a ridge), go round (in a circle dance) (WS), walk over (to something) (RD)	WS, RD	ʔyćóno (WS), ötson'o (RD)	220	
ʔychónowei	run around	FC			
ʔychópin	come down over towards, go down over towards (WS), go across over (toward something) (RD)	WS, RD	ʔyćópin (WS), ötsop'in (RD)	32, 66, 192	
ʔydá	fade, come off	WS	ʔydá		
ʔydá	go (as footprints or tracks)	RD	ödā'	232	
ʔydáw	go off downhill, go off southward	RD	ödau'	150, 212, 224	
ʔydáw	menstruate	WS	ʔydáw		
ʔydémmai	encounter by accident, with strong emotion	WS	ʔydémmaj		
ʔydémťa	come upon by accident, with strong emotion	WS	ʔydémťa		
ʔydémťahudoi	very nearly come on (someone) by chance	WS	ʔydémťahudoj		
ʔydík	arrive, reach a good sum (cards)	FC			
ʔydíkno	arrive, get to (a place)	WS, RD	ʔydíkno (WS), ödīk'no (RD)	206	
ʔydíknotoye	arrive at a place (plural subject)	RD	ödīk'notō'ye	206	
ʔydíknoweḱoi	come back to where one left (before)	RD	ödik'nowēkoi	150	
ʔydói	ascend, go up, start to go	WS, RD	ʔydój (WS), ödoi (RD)	66, 72	
ʔydóino	go along ascending (WS), go off, start off going, go a little ways off (RD)	WS	ʔydójno (WS), ödoi'no (RD)	230	
ʔydóinoti	cause to go along ascending	WS	ʔydójnoti		
ʔydóiťa	get on top (of something): ódi ʔydóiťaweten bísḱan "after getting on top of a rock, he stayed there"	RD	ödoi'ta	122	
ʔyhʔy	bull-headed, stubborn	WS	ʔýhy		
ʔyhʔy	penis (this is a mild term)	WS	ʔýhy		

Maidu	English	Source	Source Spelling	Page	Other Spellings
ʔyhʔ	be powerful, be dangerous: ʔyhʔkas "I am powerful."	RD	öhö'	130	
ʔyhʔ	powerful, dangerous: ʔyhʔm máidʔ "a powerful man"	RD	öhö'	26, 118, 146	
ʔyháiye	give birth to, groan	RD	öhai'ye	50, 72	
ʔyhákinu	lie sick (WS), lie around moaning (RD)	WS, RD	ʔyhákinu (WS), öhā'kinu (RD)	96, 100	
ʔyhánoye	follow around	WS	ʔyhánoje		
ʔyhé	follow, accompany, go with	RD	öhe'	118, 122, 204	
ʔyhédoi	start going (somewhere) with (someone)	RD	öhe'doi	90	
ʔyhéi	accompany	WS	ʔyhéj		
ʔyhéino	go along with	WS	ʔyhéjno		
ʔyhékoi	go around with someone	FC			
ʔyhém	hop	WS	ʔyhém		
ʔyhémno	hop along	WS	ʔyhémno		
ʔyhénoye	go around with someone	FC			
ʔyhéto	go along together with (someone), accompany each other, keep someone company	RD	öhē'to	162	
ʔyhwono	get rid of a penis, get rid of power	WS	ʔyhwono		
ʔyichan	other side: ʔyichan kʔysdoina yakwékan "it seemed to be coming from the other side of the ridge"	RD	ü'itsan	86	ucháni
ʔy'íto	go across	RD	öi'to	230	
ʔykáwche	admire	RD	ökau'tse	100, 176	ekáwche (WS, FC)
ʔykáwchetipe	pretty	RD	ökau'tsetipe	118, 174, 176	ekáwchetipe (WS, FC)
ʔykáwche'us	have self-confidence, have self esteem	RD	ökautseus	52	ekáwche'us (FC)
ʔykáwpinti	to sound nice, sound beautiful	RD	ökau'pinti	86, 120	ekáwpinti (FC)
ʔykoi	journey (PM-D), destination (RD) (noun): nikí ʔykóidi "where I am going"	PM, RD	u-koy (PM-D), ökoi' (RD)	RD 120	
ʔykói	go, go away, leave	WS	ʔykój		
ʔykói'ʔye	go back to where (they) came from	RD	ökoi'öyē	190	
ʔykóida	go away from (something) (WS), leave for good (RD)	WS, RD	ʔykójda (WS), ökoi'da (RD)	230	
ʔykóida	leave-taking (noun), departure (noun)	RD	ökoi'da	98, 162, 230	
ʔykóido	traveling	RD	ökoi'do	200	
ʔykói'ebís	keep going	FC			
ʔykói'idi	go along with (someone)	WS	ʔykójʔidi		
ʔykoikʔ	Big Dipper constellation	RD-NM			

Maidu	English	Source	Source Spelling	Page	Other Spellings
ʔykóikʉ	usual destination: mʉkí ʔykóikʉna ʔykóikan "he went off towards his usual destination"	RD	ökoi′kö	160	
ʔykóino	move forward (in a board game)	FC			
ʔykóiti	send (a letter, for example)	HY			
ʔykói'ukinu	be traveling continually	RD	ökoi′ūkinu	172	
ʔykóiwo	tell (someone) to go: cháinantedi ʔykóiwokan. "He told (her) to go a different way."	RD	ökoi′wo	160	
ʔykóiye	go towards (something), head towards (a destination)	RD	ökoi′yekoi	216, 236	
ʔykókoi	go off (plural subject) in different directions	WS, RD	ʔykókoj (WS), ökoi′koi (RD)	36	ʔykóikoi
ʔykókoitoye	go away (plural subject) from time to time	WS	ʔykókojtoje		
ʔykókoiyetoye	go away (plural subject) in different directions from time to time (WS), go away (plural subject, each to a different location) (RD)	WS, RD	ʔykókojjetoje (WS), öko′koyetoye (RD)	104	
ýlbʉl	a crying sound made by Coyote's "baby"	WS	ʔýlbyl		
ʉlék	go fast	WS	ʔylék		
ʉlékleki	quickly! Speed up!	FC-T			
ʉléklekno	go along fast, hasten	WS	ʔyléklekno		
ʉlékwochopin	rush up and over towards	WS	ylékwoćopin		
ʉlélem	hurry by, go by rather fast	WS	ʔylélem		
ʉlélemchono	hurry over past	WS	ʔylélemćono		
ʉlém	rush, hurry by	WS	ʔylém		
ʉlémmai	encounter (someone) by chance, with mild emotion	WS	ʔylémmaj		
ʉlémno	rush along past	WS	ʔylémno		
ʉmít	get onto something (like a path), get into something (like a car)	WS, FC	ʔymít		
ʉmítkapin	go down into	RD	ömit′kapin	32	
ʉmmoto	come together (as a group), assemble, assemble, gather (intransitive)	FC, WS	ʔýmmoto		úmmoto
ýmmotope	being held (an event)	FC			
ýmmotope	event, get-together (noun), that which is being held, place where an event is held	WST	ʔýmmotope	44:1	
ʉmmóto	go all around	RD	ömot′o	64	
ýmpin	come down towards	RD	öm′pin	70	ýnpin
ýn	descend	WS	ʔýn, ʔýt		ýt

19

Maidu	English	Source	Source Spelling	Page	Other Spellings
ɱní	travel while doing (+ verb in -dom: lóldom ɱníchoi'a "was grieving as he travelled, travelled with grief")	RD	önī'	232	
ɱnno	go down	WS	ʔýnno, ʔýtno		ɱtno
ɱnnoti	swallow (verb)	WS	ʔýnnoti, ʔýtnoti		ɱtnoti
ɱnnoye	wander around in a generally downhill direction	WS	ʔýnnoje, ʔýtnoje		ɱtnoye
ɱnó	walk, go along, travel, function or run (as a machine)	WS	ʔynó		
ɱnódoi	start up, start off (intransitive)	WS	ʔynódoj		
ɱnódoisma	my departure, my traveling on: ɱnódoisma amám kɱkán "that (previous sentence) is the reason for my traveling on."	RD	önodoisma	134	
ɱnódoiti	start (something) up	WS	ʔynódojti		
ɱnódoiwono	where one started from, the starting off place: mɱkí ɱnódoiwonodi ɱdíknokan "he came back to where he'd started from"	RD	önō'doiwōno	232	
ɱnó'esma	walking around place, territory: nikí ɱno'esmadi "in my territory"	RD	önō'esma	112	
ɱnói	wander around, to range (animals): kɱléni ɱnóidom: "going around with women"	RD	önoi'	90, 146	
ɱnóibenmap	don't wander off	RD	önoi'benmap	218	
ɱnóibenmapa	don't let (someone) wander off	RD	önoi'benmapa	140	
ɱnóibodɱk	not go very far away, not wander far off	RD	önī'bodük	146, 226	
ɱnóibodɱkwet	don't wander too far off, without wandering too far off	RD	önoi'bodukwet	146	
ɱnóimenwet	don't wander off, without wandering off	RD	önoi'menwet	146	
ɱnóinak	a place to go around in	RD	önoi'nak	12	
ɱnókɱ	where one goes, where one travels	RD	önō'kö, ön'ōkö	8	
ɱnókɱdi	on the path of, on the way going along: epínim koyó ɱnókɱdi mɱdí mamákas "on the path of the sky is where I will be"	RD	önō'ködi	150	
ɱnónoi	start to go	RD	öno'noi	138	
ɱnósol	sing to the beat of someone's step	RD	öno'sol	88	

Maidu	English	Source	Source Spelling	Page	Other Spellings
ʌnóti	make (something like a machine) function or run, walk (a child)	WS	ʔynóti		
ʌnótoye	walk off, go off (towards something)- plural subject	RD	öno'toye	202	
ʌnówasa	be hardly able to walk	WS	ʔynówasa		
ʌnówochoi	invite to go along (RD), invite (FC)	RD, FC	önō'wotsoi	68	
ʌnóyaha	want to go, (as a command): you should go	FC			
ʌnóyahape	the place where (someone) wants to go: mínki ʌnóyahape ʌnópada "go wherever you want"	RD	önō'yahape	42	
ʌnóye	walk around (RD), go around, wander around (WS)	RD, WS	önoi'ye (RD), ʔynóje (WS)	30, 148	
ʌnóyekʌ	departure	RD	önō'yekö	11	
ʌnóyek̓oi	go for a walk	WS	ʔynójek̓oj		
ʌnóyeti	to walk (a child)	WS	ʔynójeti		
ʌ́npin	descend down towards, come in	WS, FC-T	ʔýnpin, ʔýtpin		ʌ́tpin
ʌpé	all, just, only, any (RD), just as (WST-DW), only... and no more (WS): k̓ódom yaháma'ak̓an ʌpé yahádom kʌk̓ás "The world will be good; for that, I am being good" ʌpé bísdom "doing nothing, not being too busy" ʌpé bísdom núkti balmádom ka'así "I'm not busy, so I'll write a little."	RD, WS, WST-DW, HY	öpe' (RD), ʔypé (WS)	7, 24, 28, 62	
ʌpé	search for someone	RD	öpē'	122, 142, 146	opé
ʌpé'ʌnoye	go around searching (for someone), go looking around	RD	öpē' önoye	146	
ʌpé'ʌnoyemenkʌ	"no trespassing" area: ʌpé'ʌnoyemenkʌdi kakʌ́ankano "You are in a No Trespassing area"	RD	öpē' önō'yemenködi	146	
ʌpék̓a	the same thing	WS	ʔypék̓a		
ʌpék̓a wiyétidom	by staying away every time (in this case, every year during fall and winter)	RD	öpek'a wiyet'idom	160	
ʌpék̓adom	always (adverb)	RD	öpe'kadom	138, 174	
ʌpék̓ahúyeti	not do anything different, do the same old thing	RD	öpe kahū'yetidom	94	
ʌpék̓akʌm	always, consistently, every time (adverb)	WS	ʔypék̓akym		
ʌpék̓akeno	always be (doing)	RD	öpek'ake'no	104	

Maidu	English	Source	Source Spelling	Page	Other Spellings
ṁpékanbe	all of them, each and every (WS), each and every one (FC)	WS, FC	ʔypékanbe		
ṁpékanbe... waláwpe	exceed everyone in, be the ...est	WS	ʔypékanbe... waláwpe		
ṁpékanbem éki	every day	RD	öpek'anbem ek'i	230, 232	
ṁpékanbenini	always	RD	öpek'anbenini	34, 38, 54, 167, 196	
ṁpékandṁk	all, every last one, every single	WS	ʔypékandyk		
ṁpékandṁkbe	entire, whole	RD	öpek'andökbe	142, 150, 154, 166, 226	
ṁpékani	everyone (RD), all, every (FC), all, every bit (WS)	RD, FC, WS	öpek'ani(m) (RD), ʔypékani (WS)	104	
ṁpékaniluťi	every last one	RD	öpek'aniluti	32	
ṁpékanim	always: ṁpékanim ekí "every day"	RD	öpek'anim	5	
ṁpékanimenwet	not all of it	WS	ʔypékanimenwet		
ṁpékano	always	RD	öpe'kano	13	
ṁpékanohánpin	get all the way down, to land (from the air)	RD	öpek'ano han'pi	82	
ṁpékanu	be continually doing, do over and over	RD	öpek'anu	180	
ṁpékanuhanpin	get all the way down towards	WS	ʔypékanuhanpin		
ṁpékanupe	there, in that very place	WS	ʔypékanupe		
ṁpékape	always (adverb), continuously	RD	öpe'kape(m)	108, 190, 212	
ṁpékapedi	just as it is	WS	ʔypékapedi		
ṁpékapinan	from all directions	RD	öpek'apinan	170	
ṁpékayew	always do, do something for no reason: 'hesádom mayéwḱa?' achói'a. 'ṁpékayewḱas, tetédom,' achói'a. "'Why are you doing (that)?' She said. 'For no reason (or "I always do that"), just playing around,' he said."	RD	öpe'kayēu	90	
ṁpéknim	every one of you	RD	öpek'nim	38	
ṁpénan	from all sides	RD	öpēn'an	190	
ṁpéno	go around searching for	RD	opē'no	144	
ṁpimoto	bring together, bring many together	RD	ö'pimoto	36	
ṁpín	approach (RD), come down towards (WS)	RD, WS	öpin' (RD), ʔypín (WS)	146, 190	
ṁs	dazed, stupefied, somnolent, drunken	WS	ʔýs		
ṁs'ṁno	walk in one's sleep	WS	ʔýsʔyno		
ṁs'ṁnosa	sleep-walker	WS	ʔýsʔynosa		
ṁsáwet	going wherever	FC			
ṁsbokoi	be lost	WS	ʔýsbokoj		

Maidu	English	Source	Source Spelling	Page	Other Spellings
ʔscheheiye	look around with bewilderment (WS), look about absently (WS), have an abstracted air (WS), look all around oneself (RD)	WS, RD	ʔysćehejje (WS), ös′tsehēye (RD)	142	ʔscheheye
ʔscheheyenoye	look and check everywhere about	RD	ös′tsehēyenō′ye	98	
ʔschenusape	one who is always staring off into space	FC			
ʔsíppin	come out towards	WS	ʔysíppin		
ʔsíto	go across (WS), cross over (FC)	WS, FC	ʔysíto		
ʔsíto	mountain pass, river crossing (noun)	WS	ʔysíto		
ʔsítopin	cross down towards	WS, RD	ʔysítopin (WS), ösī′topin (RD)	30	
ʔsítopinim máidʔ	northern people	RD	ösī′topinim mai′dü	30	
ʔsítoye	go all around (inside something)	WS	ʔysítoje		
ʔskʔ	pig	FC			oski
ʔskaye	"devil" in traditional stories	WS	ʔýskaje		
ʔspa	rascal, scoundrel	WS	ʔýspa		
ʔswak	cry in one's sleep	WS	ʔýswak		
ʔswálulu	"devil" in traditional stories (WS), ghost (FC)	WS	ʔyswálulu		uswúlulu (FC)
ʔswálulum wá	poisonous fungus	WS	ʔyswálulum wá		
ʔswelenom yó	mountain lily (MG), snow plant (DW)	WS	ʔýswelenom jó		
ʔsweye	talk in one's sleep	WS	ʔýsweje		
ʔsweyesa	sleep-talker	WS	ʔýswejesa		
ʔt	descend	WS	ʔýt, ʔýn		ʔn
ʔtʔtʔibe	term of affection, translated as "how sweet you look"	WS	ʔytýtýjbe		
ʔtá	be above (something), be on top of	WS	ʔytá		
ʔtái	miss, overlook: homó ʔtáimenwet "without missing any"	RD	ötai′	26, 132	
ʔtno	go down	WS	ʔýtno, ʔýnno		ʔnno
ʔtnoti	swallow (verb)	WS	ʔýtnoti, ʔýnnoti		ʔnnoti
ʔtnoye	wander around in a generally downhill direction	WS, FC	ʔýtnoje, ʔýnnoje		ʔnnoye
ʔtópin	cross over (a river)	RD	ötopin	54	
ʔtpin	descend down towards (WS), cross over (RD)	WS, RD	ʔýtpin (WS), öt′pin (RD)	216	ʔnpin
ʔwáito	separate (verb), part from each other (intransitive): máidʔm wéyebosḱan, ánkanim ʔwáitoḱan. "The people finished talking, then they went their separate ways."	WS, RD	ʔywájto (WS), öwai′to (RD)	32	
ʔwáitoti	separate (things) (verb)	WS	ʔywájtoti		
ʔwála	go past	RD	öwal′a	26	

Maidu	English	Source	Source Spelling	Page	Other Spellings
ṁyé	travel (verb) (RD), come, go towards (WS), come (FC), move (FC-E): hesádom nik mínsṁm wéyemenpem ṁyékṁḱa? "Why didn't you guys tell me you were going?"	RD, WS, FC	öyē' (RD), ʔyjé (WS)	152, 208	
ṁyéwe	turn in one's tracks, go back the same way	RD	öyē'we	76	
ṁyúk	stay overnight	FC-R, FC-E			uyúk
a	be called/named	WS	ʔa		
a	say, do: aḱán niḱí "He said to me;" a niḱí "Tell me;" apáda nik "you may say about me"	WS, RD	ʔa (WS), a (RD)	44, 118	
a niḱí	oh my! (expression of pleasant surprise)	RD	a niki'	44	
a!	Pooh! Baloney! Ridiculous!	RD	a!	112, 114	
a'ṁye	always say	WS	ʔaʔýje		
á'a	crow	WS	ʔáʔa		aha
a'a!	Ouch!	RD	aa	116	
a'ái	stoop down	RD	aai´	62	
achéki	about this time, yet, still, up to now (WS), at this time, right now (FC)	WS, FC, WST-DW	ʔaćék, ʔaćéki	72:3	achék
achékmen	at the time	WS	ʔaćékmen		
achéknu	by this time, by now	RD	atsek'nū	148	
achét	however (WS), that being the case, although, then, meanwhile (RD) (with focus shift, narrative shifts to another character)	WS, RD	ʔaćét (WS), atset (RD)	136, 168, 174, 224	
achétḱan	as for him/her/it - focus shift: In a conversation, shifts to the other person. In narrative, the action shifts to the other character. achétkan aweténkan shows a time and place shift, action that occurs later (new scene if it were a play)	RD	atset'kan	66, 148, 156, 158, 160, 168, 170, 174, 176, 218, 224, 228	
achétḱas	as for me (after talking about someone else)	RD	atset'kas	144	
achétmenim	but it is not the case that... achétmenim ḱódo yahádom ayádom ṁpéḱakenomaḱán "It is not the case that the weather will always be good like this."	RD	atset'menim	104	
achóḱo	both of them, both: achóḱom hiní "both eyes"	WS	ʔaćóḱo		

Maidu	English	Source	Source Spelling	Page	Other Spellings
adᵐ́k	especially, the favorite: mᵐm adᵐ́k "that's my favorite one!" (RD), furthermore (WS)	RD, WS	adök' (RD), ʔadýk (WS)	80	
adá	after a while	RD	ada'	98	
adákan	that being the case	RD	adā'kan	172	
adé	partial word, representing a question: ade ade ade "Where is it?" in a song by FC	FC-T			
adóm	and	FC			
adóm	because, then	WS	ʔadóm		
adóm	saying	FC			
adóm	uh	FC			
adóm 'as	it was said, as (I) told (you before): adóm 'as min kaiyéwḱasi "That's what I've been telling you"	RD	adom as	142	
adóm bei	well, now	FC			
adóm mayé	speaking to: hesásawew epínowet mínchem adóm mayé "speaking to you all, asking how you have been"	HY			
adóm mí?	and you?	FC			
adóm sóldom máiḱade?	what do the lyrics (of the song) mean/say?	RD	adom' sol'dom mai'kade?	94	
adónkan	and so (no focus shift)	RD	adōñ'kan	148, 174, 192	
áha	crow	FC			
ahéset	but (inexplicably)...	RD	ahēset	140	
áho	Western crow	FC			aha
ahóni	pigeon	FC			
ai	or (between two opposite options): wetém chenúnomaḱa ai basápmenḱa? "do you want to watch the dance or are you not well enough?"	RD	ai	100	
ái	invite, request (verb): mínchem áiḱadesi? "Did I invite you (2)?"	RD	ai'	126, 134	
ái	take food from the fire (to eat) (RD), dish up, serve up (WS)	RD, WS	ai' (RD), ʔáj (WS)	234	
ai sᵐ'ᵐi	perhaps, it seems, maybe: unídi ai sᵐ'ᵐi bishelúkmḱas "Maybe I could stay here."	RD, WS	ai'söi (RD), ʔáj syʔyj (WS)	238	
ai sᵐ'ᵐi... ai sᵐ'ᵐi...	or (between two opposites): ai sᵐ'ᵐi min méiḱades ai sᵐ'ᵐi pedádom matíḱa? "Did I give it to you or are you stealing it?"	RD	aisö...aisö...	178	
ai!	oops, sorry! (FC), So! Well! (exclamation) (RD)	RD, FC	ai!	10	

Maidu	English	Source	Source Spelling	Page	Other Spellings
aichénew	to notice all along, be noticing	RD	aitse′neū	78	
áihisáwonoman	"OK" or "Amen" (agreeing with what, for example, the yepóni said. May mean "You have pondered well")	RD	ai′hisa′wonoman	112	
áikakat	wonder (RD), surmise, ponder, think (WS), figure (FC)	RD, WS, FC, WST	aikakat (RD), ʔájk̓akat (WS)	228; 42:2	
áikate	presumably (WS), I figure, it must be (FC)	WS	ʔájk̓ate, ʔájte		áite
áisiye	take food from the fire (to eat), help oneself to food from the fire	RD	ai′siye	214	
áite	presumably	WS	ʔájte		
áite nik̓í	I wonder	RD	ai′te niki′	228	
aiyak	pinyon jay	HM	i-yak		
áiye	take out of the fire, help oneself to food from the fire	RD	ai′ye	216	
akm̓men	at that time	WS	ʔakýmen		
akíchana	raccoon	WS, FC	ʔakícʔana (WS), akíchana (FC)		
akíchanam 'onúknokm̓	coonskin cap	WS	ʔakícʔanam ʔonúknoky		
áli	portable grinding rock	FC			ále (HY)
álim o	pestle	FC			
Am Sewí	Taylor's Creek, which flows through Taylorsville. See map 5 in Appendix 5.	FR1, FR-TE			
amm̓ni	so, and, (or no translation) (RD), thereupon, thereafter, then (WS): focus shift to a different subject follows this.	RD, WS	amön′i (RD), ʔamýni (WS)	136, 148, 154, 156, 192, 194	
amm̓ni	when doing (that), when he did that: om sápam, amm̓ni, wasám máidm̓m machói'am "wood rat, when doing that, was apparently a bad man." (no focus shift to other character with this usage. This type of amm̓ni follows the subject.)	RD	amön′i	222	

Maidu	English	Source	Source Spelling	Page	Other Spellings
amɷnikan	so, but then, or no translation- the main function is a focus shift to the other character, switching speakers in conversation ("then the other one said..."): "méima'ankano," achói'am. "méiluťma'ankano niḱí." amɷniḱan wewémenwet wasóchoi'a. "'Give it,' he said. 'Seriously, give it to me!' but then he (the other character), without saying anything, got mad."	RD	amönikan	136, 150, 152, 154, 156, 172, 174, 180, 222, 224	
amá	that (just mentioned or discussed), that place, that one (RD), then (WS): amá nik yapáitopi! "Tell me where it is!" amá nik méima'ankano "give me that!" Object of sentence.	RD, WS	ama' (RD), ʔamá (WS)	82, 130, 136 142	
amá u	and along with that (referring to what was just discussed), with that added: amá u wónomamɷni "and for that to happen when she was about to die"	RD	amā' ū	74	
amá wóinan	from that point on, from then on, thereafter	WS	ʔamá wójnan		
amádi	there, to that place, at that place	RD	amā'di	48, 218	
amádi'im	from it, from there, its...	RD	amadiim	54	
amádikan	and there, and in that place	RD	amā'dikan	172, 196	
amákan	later, then, after that (focus shift to other character)	RD, FC	amā'kan	146, 168	
amákan niḱí	they will say about me	RD	ama'kan niki'	162	
amám	the latter (referring to the previous sentence), that (refers to a topic just mentioned). because of that (refers to previous sentence) (RD). When used as an adjective: amám máidɷm "the man just mentioned." tetét kakɷánkano éptidom. amám tíkbe min húntas. "You must be very powerful. Because of that, may I hunt you no more."	RD	amām	192, 48, 148, 186, 194, 202	
amám	then, then he/she/they said..., but right now..., then, thereafter, after that (WS):	WS	ʔamám (WS)		

Maidu	English	Source	Source Spelling	Page	Other Spellings
amám bei	after that (referring to what was just told)	WST	amám bej	52:16	
amám ma'át	however, nevertheless	RD	amammaat, amāmaat	58, 228	
amámachet	and yet	RD	amām'atset	34	
áman	you did: part of an expression with áite: hesá áman áite? "I wonder what you did?" uní áite hesí adóm ayáti áman? "I wonder why you did this?" hesátimadom áite ati ťésnopem cha hukítaman "I wonder why you made such a short tree" - The person spoken to is not within earshot. (áman=ámano)	RD	ā'man	64, 66, 232	ámano
amána	to that place (previously mentioned	WST	ʔamána	56:43	
amának	in that direction	RD	amanak		
amánan	from that place (RD), from there (FC)	RD, FC	amānan	54	
amánankan	from that place	RD	amānankan	218	
amánkan	then later, so later, so, meanwhile, in the meantime	RD	amāñkan	66, 154, 174, 176, 190, 218	
amápem	then	FC			
amápem kʌkán	that's the way he/she/it is	RD	amā'peñ kökan', amā'peñkökan'	130, 190	
ámbʌhbʌhpe	which is a little better	RD	ām'böhböhpe'	238	
ámbʌkbʌ	good enough, all right, fair	WS	ʔámbykby		
ámbʌkbʌ	get better (RD), feel better (WS), be all right	RD, WS	am'böxbö (RD), ʔámbykby (WS)	190	
amellʌlʌ	blow fly, shiny metallic blue or green fly, calliphoridae	FC			
amén	not speak, not do: améndom cháinamennimchet, min ʌnnotimakás! "Because you're not doing it, since you won't go away, I will swallow you!"	RD	amen'	178	
amén	without speaking: hʌbóna amén wʌtʌ́swoyekán "without speaking, he came crashing along towards the house."	RD	amen'	216	
aménkʌmse	those who do not speak: aménkʌmse mínchem mawónomano "you have become ones who do not speak"	WS, RD	ʔaménkymse (WS), amen'kömse (RD)	80	
aménwet	not saying anything, without speaking about (something)	RD	amenwet	200	

Maidu	English	Source	Source Spelling	Page	Other Spellings
amét	but (FC), therefore, then (WS)	FC, WS	ʔamét		
amétkan	but	RD	amet'kan	180	
anána	currant, huckleberry (vaccinium)	FC			
ándɨkbe	about this size (showing with hands)	WS	ʔándykbe		
aní	that over there, that (far) (WS), there (FC)	WS	an		an
anídi	in there, on there (FC), over there (RR-EP)	FC, RR-EP			
aním bomó	those, those over there, those yonder	WS	ʔaním bomó		
anímchet	when you do that, since you do... (nim= you): anímchet, min ɨdíknomakás "once you do (that), I will come to you."	RD	anim'tset	88	
anína	that way, in that direction	WS	ʔanína		
ánkabɨḱɨm	but unfortunately for him/her... (RD), just then, just at that moment (WS): ánkabɨḱɨm honí wi'íkan "Unfortunately, he lost his mind." ánkabɨḱɨm mɨchóki wosóm héyukitkan "unfortunately, their skirts fell off."	RD, WS	añ'kabököm (RD), ʔámḱabýḱym (WS)	62, 170, 188, 212	
ánkabɨḱɨnkan	but then	RD	añ'kabököñkan	176	
ánkan	you are (ánkano): unínak ánkano (or unína ka'ánkano) ɨyépem hómpaitoyahadom "You are one who comes to this place wanting to fight."	RD	an'kan	146	
ánkanim	and then (connecting two sentences with the same subject), then, and thereupon, therefore: mɨm máidɨm ɨdíknokan. Ánkanim samo úichan bɨdóikitkan. "the man got there, and then he sat down on the other side of the fire.	RD, WS, FC	añ'kanim (D), ʔánkanim (WS)	174, 222	
ánkaninkan	and therefore, and so	RD	añ'kaniñkan, añkan'iñkan, añ'kaningkan	176, 192, 222	
ánťɨťɨ	this kind of (thing), like this (showing with hands), this size	WS	ʔánťyťý		
ántedi	to/in a faraway place	RD	an'tedi	184	
ántena	away, that way (vaguer than anína)	WS	ʔántena		

Maidu	English	Source	Source Spelling	Page	Other Spellings
ántenántenan	from somewhere in the distance	RD	an'tenan'tenan	120	
ántenantenántedi	(going) all around, here and there	RD	an'tenantenan'tedi	128, 224	
ánwet	paying no attention, without a word	RD	anwet	62	
áp	hoist, lift, carry on the back (something alive)	WS	ʔáp ~ ʔapá ~ háp		apá, háp
ápⱳl	apple (from English)	WS	ʔápyl		
apái	bring (something alive) on the back	WS	ʔapáj ~ ʔapáje ~ ʔapájje		apáye, apáiye
apáno	carry along on the back	RD	apān'o	232	
apá'okit	arrive carrying (something alive) on the back	WS	ʔapáʔokit		
ápbonno	mount for sexual intercourse (as animals)	WS	ʔápbonno		
ápdoi	hoist (something, like a child) up onto one's back (WS), carry (on the back), pick up, carry (someone) (RD)	WS	ʔápdoj (WS), apdoi', ap'doi (RD)	76, 84, 232	hápdoi, apdói
ápe	ask for: húmbotmeni ápemⱳni wíyemenwet méḱan "whatever he asks for/says, they give (him) without saying no."	RD	ā'pe	210	hápe
apém	but then	WS	ʔapém		
apém	such (adjective), that kind of..., those kinds of ... : apém máidⱳ kakḿam "such people they were (then)."	RD	apem'	188	
apém ma'át	in any case, anyway...	RD	apem'maat	130	
apénkan	after: apénkan ⱳḱóida wéyeḱan "after the departure, he spoke."	RD	apeñ'kan	98	apénkan
ápokite	setting someone down (adverb): mⱳkábe wokómⱳni hehe apdóiwonokⱳchoi'a tĭkte apánoweten ápokite. "each time (hehe) when his little sister got tired, he had picked her up; after carrying (her) enough, setting her down."	RD	ap'okite	232	
ás	emphasizes previous word: ni 'as "It is I" (this particle is actually a form of así "I must say, I have to say" and does appear as así in RD, pages 34 and 36)	WS, RD	ʔás (WS), as, asi' (RD)	34, 36	así
ásmⱳni	when I do (it)...: "kⱳlḿlⱳmaḱas," achói'a. "ásmⱳni nik pinma'ánkano." "'I will rumble', he said. 'When I do, you will hear me.'"	RD	asmöni	88, 136, 144	hásmⱳni

30

Maidu	English	Source	Source Spelling	Page	Other Spellings
atá	let them say: atá min wónom máidᴀm betéidom "Let humans say this about you when telling stories."	RD	atā'	8	
atám	hunt, seek out, go looking for	RD, FC	atām', atom	30, 174, 32	
atámᴀkinú	search as one goes along	RD	atam'ökinu'	174	
at'áte	magpie	FC			a'ate (FC-R)
ati	older sister	FC			
ati	such a...: hesátimadom áite atí t́ésnopem cha hukítḱan "I wonder why he made such a short tree."	RD	ati	64	
atóto	say to each other	RD	atōto	66	
a'únodom	and so on, etc.	WS	ʔaʔúnodom		
a'únomapem	etc.	FC			
awaní	big toad	FC-R			
áwasi	hours	FC-E			
awébisim	keep doing, doing over and over (until= verb in -chet): awébisim as nisé wónotiboschet. "He kept doing it to us until he had killed everybody."	RD	awē'bisim	26, 222, 20	
awéḱoi	snicker, make a smug/happy sound: hn-hn	RD	awē'koi	44	
awét	although (an alternative to using -wet on verb, use -dom form of verb followed by awét): hínduschikinodom awét máikᴀḱan. "although his eyes were shut, he still talked."	RD	awet' (RD), ʔawét (WS)	168	
awét mᴀyí	and so (can be at beginning of sentence or phrase)	HY			
awét ma'át	nevertheless	RD	awet' maat	144	
awetén	then (RD), having done so (WS): (focus shift to other character), having done (áweten with verb in -dom: an alternative to verb + weten) (RD)	RD	aweten' (RD), ʔawéten (WS)	224, 228	áweten, awéten
awéten béibᴀ	and again, (sing it) again	FC			
awaténkan	after which, after that, after some time. No focus shift (same subject). Connects two verbs of the same tense but the second one happens later.	RD	aweten'kan	6, 48, 144, 150, 156, 168, 170, 176, 228	
awétkan	after a time	RD	awet'kan	176	
awónom	be left over: sᴀ́ti awónonkan "one was left over"	RD	awōn'om	23	

Maidu	English	Source	Source Spelling	Page	Other Spellings
awónom	it was said, it was called, they were called (named) "emigrants" awónom "they were called 'emigrants'"	WST	ʔawóno	72:3	
ayá	do (this), do like this, be like this: kódom yahádom ayádom "being good weather like it is now"	RD	ayā′	104, 170, 11	
ayán	doing so (adverb): ayán wi'íyaťan "doing so after being without (me)"	RD	ayā′n	96	
ayáno	do (that): unína ayánosi "I ought to do it over here"	RD	ayā′no	70	
ayánu	do (this): nisáḱi ayánuwonodi "because of what we've done" ayánuḱan "that's how they do, that's how it is"	RD, FC	aiyā′nu	228	aiyánu
ayápe	that, that distant (something) (RD), like this (HY)	RD, HY	ayape	46, 72	
ayápedi	in a place like this, this kind of place, that (distant) place	RD	ayā′pedi	72, 162, 226	
ayáti	do like this	RD	ayā′ti	162	
ayáti	like this (adverb): uní áite hesí adóm ayáti aḱán "I wonder why he did it like this here?"	RD	ayā′ti	66	
ayáwe	give a warning, predict an outcome (not necessarily bad)	RD	ayā′wē	72, 148, 102	
ayáwinim	this type of (adj)	RD	ayā′winim	14	
bʌ	poke	FC			
bʌ́	blow, as air or wind, break wind	WS, FC	bý		
bʌ́'áswodóino	a little further along the trail, a little farther beyond the trail	WS	byʔáswodójno		
bʌbʌ́	Jeffrey or Ponderosa pine	WS	bybý		
bʌbʌ́m chá	pine tree (WS), ponderosa pine (FC)	WS, FC	bybým ća		
bʌchekchekʌ	edible mushroom	PM-M	ba-chec-chec-eh		
bʌdʌ́k	seldom	WS	bydýk		
bʌ́da	blow little puffs of air with rounded lips over the surface of someone's body. This is done by shamans in curing.	WS	býda		
bʌ́da	north	RD	bö′da	30	
bʌ́dal	to blow in little intermittent gusts (wind)	WS	býdal		
bʌ́dam máidʌ	a shaman who blows on someone's body to cure them	WS	býdam májdy		
bʌ́dam máidʌ	northern people	RD	bö′dam mai′dü	30	

Maidu	English	Source	Source Spelling	Page	Other Spellings
bᴧdawi	north wind	RD	bö′dawi	132	
bᴧde	weird, evil, criminal, bad	WS	býde		
bᴧdew	to blow gently and coolly (wind)	WS	býdew		
bᴧdíknope	slick	FC-E			bidípnope (WS)
bᴧdói	defecate	RD	bödoi′	36	
bᴧdói	sit	WS	bydój		
bᴧdói′ᴧno	sit around, of several people	WS	bydój?yno		
bᴧdói′ebis	keep on sitting	FC			
bᴧdóihékit	sit down close/next to (someone) (RD), plop down	RD	bödoi′hē′kit	228	
bᴧdóikᴧ	chair	WS	bydójky		
bᴧdóikinu	keep sitting (RD), sit, be sitting down (WS), be sitting around (WST): bᴧdóikinudom sam ínḱidi "sitting around by the campfire"	RD, WS, WST	bödoi′kinu (RD), bydójkinu (WS)	228 (RD), 54:27 (WST)	
bᴧdóikinu′ebismen	to not be (just) sitting around	FC			
bᴧdóikit	sit down	WS	bydójkit		
bᴧdóikitkᴧ	chair	WS	bydójkitky		
bᴧdóinoye	sit around	FC			
bᴧdóiṭa	sit on	WS	bydójṭa		
bᴧdóiṭakᴧ	chair, seat	WS, FC	bydójṭaky		
bᴧdóiṭama	chair	FC			
bᴧdom máidᴧ	Modoc, Modoc people	FR1			
bᴧdonu	stick up, like hair or quills	WS	býdonu		
bᴧdópem	bitter	FC			
bᴧhᴧk	to prick, stab	WS	byhýk		
bᴧhᴧkkᴧ	fork (noun)	WS	byhýkky		
bᴧhᴧknokᴧ	fork (implement)	WS	byhýknoky		
bᴧhᴧm	to prick, stab (WS), stick something (with a fork or spear) (FC)	WS, FC	byhým		bᴧhᴧn
bᴧhᴧnkᴧ	fork (noun)	WS	byhýmky		bᴧhᴧmkᴧ
bᴧhaiye	breathe loudly and heavily	WS	býhajje		
bᴧhehew	blow as a breeze	WS	býhehew		
bᴧhehewi	breeze (noun)	WS	býhehew		bᴧhehew
bᴧhew	to blow (cool breeze)	WS	býhew		
bᴧhewi	cold wind	RD	bö′hewi	130	
bᴧi	feast (noun)	WS	byj		
bᴧi	leach acorns	WS	byj		
bᴧídi	at/to the feast	RD	böi′di	208	
bᴧipe	festival, feast, celebration with eating and acorn leaching: bᴧipena ᴧḱóidom "going to a feast"	WS, WST-LB	býjpe	44:1	
bᴧkᴧḱᴧm sawí	pennyroyal	WS	byḱýkym sawí		
bᴧkᴧ́w	be tight, like a belt	WS	byḱýw		
bᴧkᴧ́wti	tighten, make tight	WS	byḱýwti		
bᴧkᴧ́wtikᴧ	garter, sleeve band	WS	byḱýwtiky		

Maidu	English	Source	Source Spelling	Page	Other Spellings
bɨkkɨk	knock	FC			
bɨkúikɨ	pennyroyal	FC			
bɨkúiti	close, turn off	FC	bukújti (WS)		bukúiti
Bɨlɨkɨ	Willard Creek	FC			
bɨlék	hurry along, go along quickly	WS	bylék		
bɨlékwodoi	get to the top (of a mountain)	RD	bölek'wodoi	46	
bɨlélek	ascend, go up	WS	bylélek		
bɨlélekdoi	get to the top (RD), climb up toward the top of (something) (WS)	RD	bölē'lekdoi (RD), bylélekdoj (WS)	64, 118, 122	
bɨlélekdoichoi	reach the top (of a mountain), get to the top	RD	bölē'lekdoitsoi	118	
bɨlélekdoipoto	be almost to the top (of a mountain)	RD	bölē'lekdoipoto	124	
bɨlók	shove	WS	bylók		
bɨlókdikno	shove (something) all the way in	WS	bylókdikno		
bɨlókdiknoti	shove (something) all the way into	WS	bylókdiknoti		
bɨmɨkɨ	sand (FC, WS), sandy dirt (FC-E)	FC, WS	bymýk		bɨmɨ́k (WS)
Bɨmɨ́kɨm Sewí	place name for Indian Creek. The part of Indian Creek called Sandy Creek was formed by the great snake, while traveling from Soda Rock to Homer Lake (DT). See maps 1, 2 and 5 in Appendix 5.	FR1, FC 2007. DT, FR-HY	bümüküm sewi (FR1), bumukum sewi (FC)	37 (DT)	
Bɨmɨ́kɨm Yamáni Pinem	Babcock Peak	FC			
bɨmhélo	smear (with = ni): chakámni bɨmhélodom "smearing with pitch"	RD	bömhē'lo	92, 98	
bɨ́mheloto	rub, massage, rub on (used for face paint, hair oil, etc., but not for medicine) (WS), smear oneself (RD): chakámni ka'án bɨ́mhelotodom wákdom yepéintimapem. "They will be making a lot of noise, smearing themselves with pitch and crying."	WS, RD	býmheloto (WS), bömhēloto (RD)	52	
Bɨmi	place name for a village east of Quincy. See map 2 in Appendix 5.	AK	Bumi	397	
bɨmí	bone	FC, WS	bym		bɨm (WS)
bɨmím bapáli	marrow	WS	bymím bapáli		
bɨmukɨ	fan (noun)	FC-T			
bɨnó	bump (something)	WS	bynó		
bɨpói	drag oneself around, injured	WS	bypój		
bɨpóipoi	more or less drag oneself around	WS	bypójpoj		

Maidu	English	Source	Source Spelling	Page	Other Spellings
bᴀpupu	sage	FC-E	bupupu		
bᴀsʌ́p	put (something) down	WS	býsýp		
bᴀsʌ́pkit	set (something) in place: uním yamáni bᴀsʌ́pkitchoi'a "these mountains he set in place"	WST-DW	býsýpkit	78	
bᴀsákᴀ	walking stick	FC			basákᴀ
bʌ́sap	blow on (a patient in curing), with the intention of driving the evil spirits away	WS	býsap		
bʌ́sapḱoi	get blown away (This term is used to exorcise evil spirits)	WS	býsapḱoj		
bᴀsápḱoi	cure shamanistically	FC			
bʌ́sapḱoi'us	blow evil from oneself	RD	bö'sapkoiūs'	182	
bʌ́sap'usḱoi	blow on oneself	WST	býsapʔusḱoj	68:43	
bʌ́sasakit	blow gently (not the wind)	RD	bö'sasakit	76	
bᴀsín	machine	WS	býsín		mᴀsín
bᴀtʌ́mi	food scraps on the ground	RD	bötöm'i	190	
bʌ́tchᴀwi	a plant, the aromatic root of which is rubbed on the chest for colds	WS	býtcw (WS perhaps left out a letter)		
bʌ́wo	blow (as wind)	WS	býwo		
bʌ́wo	wind (noun)	WS	býwo		
bʌ́wodoi	start to blow (wind)	RD	bö'wodoi	130	
Bʌ́wom Bom Páidi	place name for Elysian Valley, near Janesville (WS), near Jack Shinn's (Simpanum's) place, near the intersection of East Wingfield Rd and Elysian Valley Rd, #9 on HLME map 3 (HLME). According to Viola Williams, this means "where the wind always blows." See Bʌ́wopo on map 4 in Appendix 5.	WS, HLME	býwopo (WS), Bywom Bom Pajdi (HLME)		
bʌ́wom kaléta	car, automobile	WS	býwom kaléta		
bʌ́wom kalétam bó	highway	WS	býwom kalétam bó		
Bʌ́wom Luku	place name for part of Spanish Creek Canyon below (north of) Keddie. Means "wind canyon" (FR-TE). See map 2 in Appendix 5.	FR1, FR-TE	büwom luku		
bʌ́wopai	blow against (wind)	RD	bö'wopai	130	

Maidu	English	Source	Source Spelling	Page	Other Spellings
Býwopo	place name for Elysian Valley, near Janesville (WS), near Jack Shinn's place near the intersection of East Wingfield Rd and Elysian Valley Rd, #9 on HLME map 3 (HLME). See map 4 in Appendix 5.	WS, HLME	býwopo (WS), Bywom Bom Pajdi (HLME)		
býwowoḱoi	to blow across, to pass by (wind), blow past	WS	býwowoḱoj		
böyök'önoiye	go around gathering (things)	RD	böyök'önoi'ye	148	
böyökdoi	gather (something) up, start to pick up (things)	RD	böyökdoi	44	
böyýksip	select, pick out	WS	byjýksip		
böyýksipdomhehe	gather together a few from among many, select a few from many	RD	böyök'sipdomhehe	166	
bö́ye	feast	RD	bö'ye	26	
böyím motó	festive gathering, feast	WS, FC	byjím motó		
böyím motó	have a feast	WS	byjím motó		
böyó	touch, bump against, bump	RD, WS	böio' (RD), byjó (WS)	68	
böyódatoti	poke (someone) with something (RD), keep bumping (WS)	RD, WS	böiodatoti (RD), byjódatoti (WS)	68	
böyóti	poke with something, cause to poke (RD), bump (someone) with (something) (WS)	RD, WS	böio'ti (RD), byjóti (WS)	68	
bá	dig with paws (RD), paw the ground (WS), dig	RD, WS	bā', bá	98	
bá	get salt	RD	bā	48	
bá	salt	WS	bá		
bá sömí	lunchmeat	BC			
ba'á'aidaw	go down (sun)	RD	baā'aidau	112	
baböm cha	Ponderosa pine tree	JD	babumćom	30	bömböm cha
babáköm cha	rock oak tree, live oak	FC, FC-T			
Bábe	place name, just north of Quincy, #46 on FR map, village with roundhouse south of Sandy Creek, due south of Konkoyo and Kusimen (CM). See map 2 in Appendix 5.	FR, CM	bábe	370-371	
báchawi	feather bunches worn on the head, headstall	RD-NM			bátchawi
bádömdömti	feel around (in the dark, trying to find something)	RD	ba'dömdömti	114	
baheke	trout	HLME	bahekem	20	paliki
bailín	violin	WS	bajlím, bajlín		bailím
baká	branch	RD	bakā'	92	ṕaḱa
báḱocho	scratch noisily with claws	WS	báḱoćo		
baksakala	bobcat	FC, BC	boc-se-caw-la (BC)		paksakala (FC-R)
báku	sharp-shinned hawk	HM	baw'kum		
bákwapa	cattail, flat tule	FC, WS	bákwapa		bakwapö (FC)

36

Maidu	English	Source	Source Spelling	Page	Other Spellings
bákwapai	gather cattails, pull out cattails	RD	ba'kwapai	218	
bál	to write, mark, dye, weave a pattern, paint: lilík báldom - "make a basket design in redbud"	WS, FC	bal (WS), bál (FC)		bál
balbalpe	gray	FC			
balí	writing, design: hóiyam máidᴀm ódi balí "petroglyphs"	FC, FC-T			
bálikᴀ	dye (noun)	FC			
bálim dadáw	erase writing	FC			
bálkᴀ	writing implement, pen, pencil	WS	bálky		
bálkit	write down	FC			
bálti	make designs or pictures, draw	FC			
bám chiti	pine grosbeak	HM	bahm'-shit-tim		bám siti
Bam héli	place name for Ship's Creek, Nevada	WS	bam héli		
bám kúpkᴀ	dwarf salt tule, which is dyed black and used for decorating baskets	WS-MP	bám kúpky		
Bam Ólasi	place name for Soda Rock near Keddie. Deer were attracted here by the salt and the Indians killed them (FR1). See map 2 in Appendix 5.	FR-TE			
bám sᴀmí	corned beef	WS	bám symí		
bám wasása	salt (as an ingredient)	WS	bám wasása		
bamák	grope at (someone) out of sexual interest	WS	bamák		
ban	spread, put over, cover (with a blanket-like object)	WS	ban		
banák	brightness, light (noun)	WS	banák		
banákam pín	to come in (light)	WS	banákam pín		
banákdoi	glow, be brilliant	WS, WST-DW	banákdoj	78	
banákmenpe	darkness: banákmenpedi sólusan "in the darkness they used to sing"	WST-RP	banákmenpe	64	
banákno	lit, bathed in light	WS	banákno		
banákpe	bright	FC			
banának	lighten up (in brightness), get lighter	WS	banának		
bánchik	cover over (with a cloth or sheet): túikᴀm máidᴀm, bánchikma'ankano. "Sleepy person, pull the covers up."	FC, FC-T			
banchik'kᴀm chi	covering cloth (e.g. curtains)	FC			
banchikkᴀ	cover (noun), window blinds	FC			
bánchonoi	wrap up	FC			

Maidu	English	Source	Source Spelling	Page	Other Spellings
bánchonoibos	completely wrap up: dapím sáwni bánchonoiboskan "they wrapped (it) completely in maple leaves"	WST	bánćonojbos	76:1	
bánchonoye	wrap around and cover (with a blanket-like object)	WS	bánćonoje		
banhṁťanu	be flat, thin (as a state)	RD	banhöt'anu	24	
bánkit	spread down (a blanket-like object)	WS	bánkit		
bánḱoi	raise up and turn back (a blanket or quilt)	WS	bánḱoj		
báno	basket for catching fish, polite term for the male genitals, used by old women	WS	báno		
bánťa	put (a blanket-like object) over (WS), put something on (FC): onódi bánťapi "put it on your head."	WS, FC	bánťa		
bapál	marrow	WS	bapál		
basá	cane, walking stick	WS	basá		
basá	make a walking stick out of, use as a walking stick	RD	basa'	76	
basákṁ	walking stick	RD	basākö	198	bṁsákṁ, basáka (FC)
basáp	be strong enough, be healthy enough	RD	basap'	100	
Basíkṁ	place name, west of Lake Almanor Inn	FC			
báslem	stroke affectionately with the hand	WS	báslem		báslam (FC-E)
basánoye	go around with a cane	FC			
báso	spruce, fir	WS	báso		
básom chá	spruce tree, fir tree	WS	básom ćá		
básom chípbṁ	spruce tips, the tender new growth on the extremities of spruce boughs, used for brewing tea	WS	básom ćípby		
bať	flat (adj)	WS	bať		
báť	sift or winnow acorn meal by tossing it on a flat basketry tray so as to remove the larger lumps. This is done after the meal is leached and before it is baked.	WS, FC	bať (WS), bát (FC)		
bátṁtṁnkinu	scowl at angrily	RD	ba'tötöñkinū'	208	
batá	butter (from English)	WS	batá		
batáchonototómen	not chase (people) away (takes plural object)	RD	bata'tsonototōmen	20	
batákinu	take aim, get ready to throw	RD	bāta'kinu	60	
batáḱoi	drive (cattle)	FC			
batám hṁťí	butter	WS	batám hyťí		
batáno	drive (a vehicle)	WS	batáno		
batánokṁ	driver	WS	batánoky		

Maidu	English	Source	Source Spelling	Page	Other Spellings
batáp	throw (something) at (no postposition on either object): wépam ḱaw batápchoi'a hiní "Coyote threw dirt in (their) eyes"	RD	batap'	166	
batápai	catch up with, overtake	WS	batápaj		
batápaihudói	almost catch up with	RD	batā'paihūdoi'	176	
batápaimenchonó	be unable to catch up with	RD	batā'paimentsonō'	54	
batápaipoto	almost catch up: batápaipotóyakkes ái sm'mi "I think I have almost caught up"	RD	batāp'aipoto	176, 236	
batápaipotónanape	close to the place of catching up (with someone)	RD	batāp'aipotō'nannape	234	
batás	edge: momím batásdi "to the edge of the water" (RD), limit (noun), other side, opposite side (WS)	RD, WS	batas' (RD), batás (WS)	32	
batáschono	to the limit, to the far side, a little more than	WS	batáśćono		
batáschonoluť	to the furthest limit, to the furthest extent	FC-E			
batásip	chase out, drive out	RD	bata'sip	19	
batáskinum úyi	the last house	RD	batas'kinum ū'yi	210	
batásluťi	the extreme end, at one end	WS	batásluťi		
batásono	the last (one), the farthest	RD	batās'ono	84	
batátasimotodi	to the very edge	RD	batā'tasimotodi	28	
bátbatpe	flat, planar	WS	bátbatpe		
bátchaw	put on feather headdress	RD	bat'sau	120	
bátchawi	feather headdress (FC), headdress or headstall made of quills and flicker feathers (WS)	FC, WS, RD-NM	batchawi (FC), batćaw (WS)		batchaw (WS), báchawi (RD-NM)
batĭ	powder, sifted material	RD	bati'	78	
bátkm	big twined tightly woven basket (FC), winnowing tray (FC-E), flat basket for sifting acorn meal, about 15 inches in diameter (WS)	FC, WS, FC-E	bátky		
bató	spread out (adjective): lúmlumim sáwim batóm uḱán "there were fir needles spread out there"	RD	bato'	146	
bató'ono	stretched out (skin)	RD	batō'ono	146	batówono
bátpe	flat	FC			
báťti	flatten	FC			
bawá	scratch (the ground)	RD	bawa'	30	
bawbawpe	gray	FC-R	baubaupe		
be	dig	FC			
be cheḱcheke	small yellow mushrooms growing near stumps, which taste sour	JD	be ćek'ćeke	24	

Maidu	English	Source	Source Spelling	Page	Other Spellings
bé hesádom?	now what's going on?	FC			bei hasadom?
bebe	maternal aunt: as a kinship term, this word must have a prefix, either mʌ, nik, or min (see Mountain Maidu Grammar, Lesson 6 for more details)	FC			
bédukan	just as, right when...: bédukan káipe pemádom kan dʌnan yohónkan "just as (they were) about to eat dinner, there was a noise from the bushes"	RD	bē'dukan	216	
béduki	modern	FC-E			béidʌk'i (WS, FC)
bedukto	in a little while (around 20 minutes)	FC			
behék	sift	RD	behek'	234	
behepipo	the period of time before humans, when other beings populated the land	PM-M	be-he-pi-po	3	
bei	now, already (FC), after, then (WS), as soon as (WST): pekʌ yahátibosweten bei, mʌm bomóm ʌyédom bʌdóikitk̓an "as soon as the food was all prepared, the group came and sat down." otódom, mʌkáni bei pedóm, béibʌm tawálk̓oidom usá'es. "As soon as we got up, eating the same thing again, we would go off to work."	FC, WS, WST	bej	78:8, 52:16	be
bei hesádom?	what's new? Now what?	FC			bé hesádom?
bei...bei...	now at last, finally: bei mʌchó'us bei "finally just the two of them;" amá bei mʌ'étim bei makkítk̓an "now at last his sister understood."	RD	bei...bei	140, 208, 8, 144, 142	
béibʌ	also, too	WS	béjby		
béibʌm	again: béibʌm ka'ámenk̓as "I will not do it again"	WS, RD	béjbym (WS), bēi'böm (RD)	44	
béibʌm wéyep	say (it) again, repeat (what you said) - command form	FC			
béidʌk	now	WS	béjdyk		
béidʌkʌm té	newborn infant	WS	béjdyk̓ym té		
béidʌk'i	young, new, modern: béidʌk'im máidʌm madóm "as a young man, when he was a young man"	WS, FC, WST, FC-R	béjdyk?i	54:28	béduki
béidʌkmen	just recently	WS	béjdykmen		

Maidu	English	Source	Source Spelling	Page	Other Spellings
béidmktapo	right now	WS	béjdyktapo		
béidmkto	a short time	WS-MP	béjdykto		
béidmktonanna	just lately, recently	WS	béjdyktonanna		
béikḿ	father: as a kinship term, this word must have a prefix, either mm, nik, or min (see <u>Mountain Maidu Grammar</u>, Lesson 6 for more details)	FC, RD, WS	bē'ikö (RD), béḱy (WS)	136	békm
béikḿwoli	elders, relatives: as a kinship term, this word must have a prefix, either mm, nik, or min (see <u>Mountain Maidu Grammar</u>, Lesson 6 for more details)	RD	bē'iköwoli	184	
bēiki	now	RD	bēiki	94	
béitapo	yet again, yet another, even more so, even more than before (RD), more, more intensely (WS)	RD, WS	bēi'tapo (RD), béjtapo (WS)	176, 194, 214	
béitapoti	give a little more push, do even more	WS	béjtapoti		
béitope	some more of it	WS	béjtope		
béḱm	father: as a kinship term, this word must have a prefix, either mm, nik, or min (see <u>Mountain Maidu Grammar</u>, Lesson 6 for more details)	WS	béḱy		béikm (FC, RD)
beké'chono	tumble over, trip and fall on (something)	RD	beke''tsono	212	
beḱel	hole	RD	bekel (no stress given in Dixon)	36	
beḱúḱuk	stretch up the arms	WS	beḱúḱuk		
Béldmn	place name for Belden, California (from English)	WS	béldyn		
beléw	beside, at the side of	WS, RD	beléw (WS), belē'u (RD)	236	
beléwdi	to the north: ḱódom beléwdi "in the north country"	RD	belē'udi	7, 11, 26	
beléwi	side, side of (but not of a person), the place at the side	WS	beléwi		
beléwlewtodi	beside, along the side of	WS	beléwlewtodi		
ben	do not: wonóben mínsmm! "Don't lose (him)!"	RD	ben	36	
bén	step (verb), take a step	WS	bén		
ben... map	don't do it: wikḿkmi ben map "don't open your eyes!" mnóiben map "don't wander around!" with wíyepada, makes it a stronger command: mdíknoben mapí wíyepada "don't go there, no matter what/or else!"	RD	ben map	12, 122, 192, 218, 136	ben mapi, map ben

Maidu	English	Source	Source Spelling	Page	Other Spellings
béndoi	step up	FC-E			
bené'e	help (verb): nik bené'ebene'e "Please help me."	FC			
bené'ekm	helper	FC			
bénekdi	in the day time	FC			
bénekem mmm béneke	day after tomorrow	WS	bénekem mym béneke		
béneki	tomorrow, morning	FC, WS	bének		bének
bénekto	in the morning (It is obvious from RD p. 196 that bénekto is later morning than ekdá, which is dawn) (RD), tomorrow (FC), morning (WS), days (in counting): sápwim bénektom wosípchet okítkan. "After three days went by, he arrived."	RD, FC, WS	bēn'ekto (RD), bénekto (WS)	34, 196	
bénektodi	in the morning	WS	bénektodi		
bénektonana	towards morning	RD	bēn'ektonana	166	
benékwaito	clearing (noun), open space	RD	benek'waito	142	
benhúye	keep time to the (walking/stepping) rhythm (RD), step in the same manner (as someone else) (WS)	RD, WS	benhu'ye (RD), bénhuje (WS)	86	bénhuye (WS)
benínpin	start to walk down towards	RD	benin'pin	13	
bénkit	step down (WS), step, put down one's foot (FC)	WS, FC	bénkit		
bénno	step (noun), spaces (in a board game)	FC			
bénno	take steps	FC-E			
bénnokm	walker	FC-E			
bénnoye	step around	WS	bénnoje		
bénsip	step out of	WS	bénsip		
bénsito	step across	WS	bénsito		
bénsitoye	step all through	WS	bénsitoje		
bénta	step on	WS	bénta		
Benwawikdowen	Place name for the base of Evans Point, #10 LM map. Evans Point seems to refer to an area in North Arm. See map 5 in Appendix 5.	LM	Benwauwikdowen		
bénye	step (verb), take a step	WS	bénje		
bényepe	step (noun)	RD	ben'yepe	86	
bepélkoi	peck a hole through (something)	RD	bepel'koi	36	
Besapenim	Place name for Big Springs, #21 LM map. May be spelled bmsáppinim, "blowing out evil spirits." See maps 1 and 3 in Appendix 5.	LM			

Maidu	English	Source	Source Spelling	Page	Other Spellings
betá	call (something a name): hesí betámaḱa? "what do you call it?"	FC			
betái	overlook, miss: wólem hesí betáimenmapem "The white man (is) not about to miss a thing"	HY			
beté	ancient, olden times	WS	beté		betéi'i
betéboki	spirit	RD	bete'boki	72	
betéi	beginning of the world	FC			
betéi	legendary being	RD	betē'im	26, 34, 138	
betéi	recount, tell a story	WS	betéj		
betéi	story	FC			betéyi (WS)
betéibok'i	spirit caller, one who raps on the main post of the dance house	WS	betéjbokʔi		
betéiboko	the special shamanistic function of calling spirits by banging cocoon rattles against the main post of the dance house	WS	betéjboko		
betéidom amɷ́ni	when telling the old stories	RD	betēi'dom amön'i	182	
betéihuki	the ancient world, after humans had appeared	FC			
betéi'i	ancient	WS	betéjʔi		beté, betéi
betéim ḱódo	time before this world	FC			
betéinakḱenupe	what goes with storytelling (like songs)	WST-GP	betéjnakḱenupe	70:57	
betéipe	story, stories, what is being told: betéipe pínkinupi! "listen to the story!"	WST	betéjpe	54:27	
betéitai	tell stories about (someone)	FC			
betéito	tell a story	FC			
betéitodi'im	traditional, old-time (adj): solmápem wetémdi betétodi'im solím uním "traditional songs will be sung at dances here."	RD	betē'todiim	102	
betéiyaha	want to tell a story	FC			
beťék	move quickly, spring (verb)	WS	beťék		
betékbono	have the umbilicus healed and the cord lost	WS	betékbono		
beťékchono	jump over (something) to get out (RD), spring over the edge (verb) (WS)	RD, WS	betek'tsono (RD), beťékćono (WS)	74	
beťékda	jump into (boat)	RD	betek'da	58	
beťékdapoto	be just about to jump	RD	betek'dapoto	58	
beťékdaw	jump out	RD	betek'dau	208	
beťékdoi	start off running (RD), bolt and run (WS)	RD, WS	betek'doi (RD), beťékdoj (WS)	212	
betéke	navel, belly-button	WS	beték		
betékem ḱuḱú	umbilical cord	WS	betékem ḱuḱú		

Maidu	English	Source	Source Spelling	Page	Other Spellings
beťékeno	jump into	RD	betek'eno	74	
beťék'inno	spring into	WS	beťék'inno		
betékmitpin	jump down in	RD	betek'mitpin	58	
beťéksip	hop out	RD	betek'sip	30	
beťéksipwew	always hop out, hop out every time	RD	betek'sipwēūkan	222	
betémemenkmdi	in the olden times	RD	betē'memenködi	28, 8	
betémen	be in the olden times	RD	betē'men	28	
betémen	in ancient times, in the olden days, in olden times	RD	betē'men, betē'man	222	
betéyi	story, legend, traditional story, myth	WS	betéji		betéi (FC)
bewés	scratch the ground	RD	bewes'	30	
béwkinu	become a little more: pi béwkinuḱan "they became a little more numerous"	RD	bē'ukinū	20	
bey'í	today	WS	bej?í		
bey'ím 'ekí	today	WS	bej?ím ?ekí		béyim ekí (FC)
bey'ím kulú	this evening, tonight	WS, FC	bej?ím kulú		beyín kulú
bey'ím po	tonight	WS	bej?ím po		
bichí	claw, nail (on finger or toe), hoof, thorn	WS, FC, FC-E	bić		bich
bichí yohónti	snap the fingers	WS	bićí johónti		
bichís	strangle, choke	WS	bićís		
bichísti	strangle (someone)	WS	bićísti		
bichítapope	covered with thorns	FC-E			
bidípno	slick, racer snake, brush snake	WS	bidípno		
bidípnope	slick	WS	bidípnope		
bidít	pierce, stick (with needle-like object)	WS	bidít		bihít
bidítpai	stick (something) on (something), pin (something) on (someone)	WS	bidítpaj		
bidítpaikm	pincushion	WS	bidítpajky		
bihíp	put on (regalia) such as tremblers/feathers	RD	bihip'	120	
bihít	pierce, stick (verb)	WS	bihít		bidít
bihít'inno	stick in (as a splinter)	WS	bihít?inno		
bilísi	speediness, quickness	WS	bilís		bilís
bilísno	quick, fast, speedy	WS	bilísno		
biltitokm	instrument	FC			
biltokm	instrument	FC			
biní	net	FC			
bínisi	beans (from English)	WS, FC	bínis		bínis
bínme	run after (someone)	RD	bin'me	54	
bínmechopin	chase	RD	bin'metsopin	222	
bínmedoi	run after, come after (in anger, to get someone)	RD	bin'medoi	46, 174, 176, 204	
bínmedoipe	pursuer, one who is running	RD	bin'medoipe	46, 180	
bínmeḱoi	go run after, go chase	RD	bin'mekoi	46, 174, 206	

Maidu	English	Source	Source Spelling	Page	Other Spellings
bínmenmímenkm	one who does not go after (someone)	RD	bin′menöi′menköm	178-180	
binmé'okit	come running to (a location), arrive running	RD	binmē′okit	204	
bínmeye	pursue, chase, go after	WS	bínmeje		
bínmeyekto	come after (someone)	RD	bin′mēyekto	170	
bis	stay, remain, dwell, be (somewhere)	WS, RD, FC	bis (WS), büs (RD), bís (FC)		bís
bismkínu	be in an emotional state, be in a situation: pi wasá hubmkdom bismkínu'enkes "We are living in a state of despair"	RD	büsökin′ū	112	
bisál	man whose brother has died	WS	bisál		
bisálbe	little boy whose brother has died	WS	bisálbe		
bíschoi	live over (a hill), live on the other side	RD	büs′tsoi	118, 190	
bísdodo	take custody of, hold (something) for someone temporarily (RD), stay with and take care of (someone) (WS)	RD, WS	büs′dodō (RD), bísdodo (WS)	88	
bísdodoi	stay with and care for (someone), stay awhile, linger	WS	bísdodoj		
bísekoi	be off living somewhere, live somewhere else: pénem ekáwchetipem kmléchom bísekoikan kódom chándi "two beautiful women lived out in the northwest."	RD	büs′ekoi	118	
bíshelu	likely to be (in a certain place)	WS	bíshelu		
bishúkit	make someone stay	RD	büshū′kit	23, 24	
bisí	dwelling (noun), place to live, place	WS, FC	bis		
bískmm kódo	village, residential area	RD	büs′köm kâ′do	26, 214	
bískmmtikoidi	where they were made to live, dwelling-place	RD	büs′kömtikoidi	26, 164	
bísmadom	intending to stay	FC			
bíspem té	newborn infant	WS	bíspem té		
bísta	sit on (something)	WS	bísta		
bístakm	chair, bench	WS	bístaky		
bísti	leave (something) (with someone), leave (something) behind: mmkí wasása hmbódi bístikan "he left his stuff at the house"	WS	bísti		

Maidu	English	Source	Source Spelling	Page	Other Spellings
bístikíye	make (someone) stay, confine, restrict (someone): lʌ́ksiptimenwet hʌbódi bístikíyepem kʌḱán. "Not being allowed to go out, he was was made to stay inside."	RD	büs'tikī'ye	48	
bístisma	the place where I left (someone, something)	RD	büs'tisma	92	
bísto	throughout (adverb), staying through (a time period): mʌm machói'am ḱúmmen bísto "he remained through the winter"	RD	büs'to	150	
bístoto	stay together with (someone) (RD), live together (WS)	RD, WS	büs'todo (RD), bístoto (WS)	146	bístodo
bísyeḱoi	live beyond, live a ways away	RD	büs'ekoi	118	
bísyet	for a while: pedátomenḱan bísyet "he did not answer for a while"	RD	büsyet	48	
bisyéwonope	place where (someone) was	RD	büse'wonopi	110	
bití	thorn	FC			
bití'ukitʌsitopin	use something sharp to grip with (for example, by sticking it into the ground or hillside) to get across	RD	bitiukitösitopin	54	
bíya	beer (from English)	WS	bíja		
bíyam momí	beer	WS	bíjam momí		
bó	road, trail, path, way	WS	bó		
bó	stick (verb), pierce, insert, peck	WS	bó		
bó'	throw (something)	RD	bō'	62	
bo kómbom máidʌ	Yahi, Mill Creek Indians	FC-E			kómbom máidʌ
bóadi	board, whiteboard	FC-T			
bócheye	wait for, await	WS, RD	bōtseye (RD), bóćeje (WS)	198	
bodá	drop from tree or bush, as leaves or fruit	WS	bodá		
bódato	tap (as woodpecker)	RD	bō'dato	36	
bodáw	win in games	WS	bodáw		
bodáwsa	lucky in games	WS	bodáwsa		
bodi	be on the street or in the street	FC			
bodi ʌḱói	hit the road, leave	FC, HY			
bodíkno	hit the target, reach the goal	WS	bodíkno		
bodíknokʌ	target (noun), goal	WS, FC	bodíknoky		
bodói	throw (something) upwards	WS	bodój		
bodóiti	suck (something) out, cause illness to come out	RD	bodoi'ti		
bodúk	deep, as water	WS	bodúk		

Maidu	English	Source	Source Spelling	Page	Other Spellings
bodúkboduk	not very deep	WS	bodúkboduk		
bó'ekmen póḱo	a Mountain Maidu month following the bómhinchulim póḱo	RD-NM			
bohóp	shove (something)	WS	bohóp		
bohópmit	shove (something) in	WS	bohópmit		
bohú'isito	hand over to (object in -na), toss over to: makó mᴎbéikᴎna bohú'isitoḱan "she handed the fish over to her father."	RD	bohū'isito	196	
bokᴎ	hail	FC			
bokɏ́l	be squatting with the weight on the balls of the feet	WS	boḱýl		
bokɏ́lkinu	squat down on the balls of the feet	WS	boḱýlkinu		
bóḱachik	lie in wait along the path (to assault someone)	RD	bō'katsik	180	
bókito	peck each other	WS	bókito		
bóḱkok	knock (verb)	WS	bóḱkok		
bóḱkoḱo	a knock, rap (noun)	WS	bóḱkoḱo		
bóḱkol	peck out, pull out by pecking (This apparently refers specifically to eyes)	WS	bóḱkol		
bokóchono	break (for example, neck)	RD	bokot'sono	212	
boḱói	throw	WS	boḱój		
boḱóiti	lose, misplace	WS	boḱójti		
bokombo	Yahi	FC-T			
boksᴎkᴎla	bobcat, lynx	FC			boksakala
bókweye	invoke (heaven, spirits), ask (spirits) what to do	WS	bókweje		
bokwopu	cattail, bulrush, typha latifolia soft flag	JD, BC	bokwopum (JD), buck wa pum (BC)	76	bakwapᴎ, bakwapa
bol	ball (from English)	WS	bol		
bolákamoto'ino	go up in flames (subject is ḱódom for a large forest fire): ḱódom bolákamoto'inodom tetédᴎḱᴎm yakáchoi'a "the land looked like it was going up in the biggest flames"	RD	bolak'amotoino	64	
bolákdoi	catch on fire, blaze up	RD	bolak'doi	162, 200	
Boléiwi	place name just north of Quincy, #53 on FR map. See map 2 in Appendix 5.	FR	boléywi	370-371	
bolóḱo	shoe, footgear	WS	bolóḱ		bolóḱ
bolóḱom soló	moccasin	WS	bolóḱom soló		
bolóḱti	put on shoes	WS	bolóḱti		
bolóḱtikᴎ	blacksmith	WS	bolóḱtiky		
bolóḱtiwo	have (a horse) shod, put shoes on someone	WS	bolóḱtiwo		
bolóḱtiwoḱoi	go have (a horse) shod	WS	bolóḱtiwoḱoj		

Maidu	English	Source	Source Spelling	Page	Other Spellings
bolóp	jump and run, bolt, rush headlong	WS	bolóp		
bolópchono	jump around behind (something), run around behind (something)	RD	boloptsono	228	
bolóp'inno	bolt into, burst into, pop into (WS), jump back in (RD)	WS, RD	bolópʔinno (WS), bolop'ino (RD)	220	bolópino (RD)
bolópsip	jump out (RD), bolt out, rush out headlong (WS)	RD, WS	bolop'sip (RD), bolópsip (WS)	220, 222	
bóltope	ball game	WS	bóltope		
bom héla	longer version of the grass game	RD-NM			
bom toyakm	street light	FC, FC-T			
bom we'e	edge of the road	FC, FC-T			
bomḿmmkno	pity (someone), feel sorry for (someone)	WS, FC	bomýmykno		
bomḿmmti	suffer	RD	bomöh'möhti	158	
bomḿti	pitiful	WS	bomýti		
bomḿtipe	pitiful, sorry	FC			
bomḿtiti	make pitiful, mistreat, torture (with a plural object): nisé bomḿtitimenma'ankano! "Don't mistreat us!"	WS, RD, FC-E	bomýtiti (WS), bomöt'iti	112	
bomḿtiti	pitiful (adj), made pitiful	WST	bomýtiti	56:41	
bomḿtiweye	say pitifully, talk pitifully	WS	bomýtiweje		
bomákti	measure a distance	RD	bomak'ti	186	
bómhededi	at the side of the road	FC			bomhedi (FC-T)
bómhinchulim póḱo	a Mountain Maidu month following the ḱanáipinom póḱo. "squinting moon or month"	RD-NM			
bomhó	a distant place, faraway place	RD	bomho'	204	
bomhódi'im	in a faraway place: amána uním bomhódi'im máidmm yiláḱoimadom wéyeḱan "to that place the faraway men talked of going courting"	RD	bomhō'diim	118	
bomhóm mmná	a distance from there, at a distance	RD	bomho'm möna'	204	
bomhónan	from the faraway place	RD	bōmhō'nan	118	
bóminki	by the trail, next to the road or path	RD	bōm'inki	84, 86	
bomít	bet (verb), put up a bet	WS, FC	bomít		
bómmo	bet, put up money	WS	bómmo		
bomó	bunch, group, herd, flock, party, gathering (used to form plurals: bomóm máidm "a bunch of people")	WS, FC	bomó		
bomómdi'im	out of the whole group, among the group	RD	bomom'diim	202	

Maidu	English	Source	Source Spelling	Page	Other Spellings
bómtetnom pókʼo	a Mountain Maidu month following the bóʼekmen pókʼo	RD-NM			
bónno	throw in a downhill direction	WS	bónno		
bónnodi	down the hill, in the west (lower elevation) country	WST	bónnodi	42	
bonó	ear: bonóni pínkinupi! "listen with your ears!"	WS, FC	bonó		
bonó	uncle: as a kinship term, this word must have a prefix, either mᴍ, nik, or min (see Mountain Maidu Grammar, Lesson 6 for more details)	WS	bonó		
bóno	drop (something) into (something), put (something) into (something): lolódi úti bónokʼan "she dropped acorns into the basket"	RD	bonʼo	168	
bonó sᴍháwkit	pierce the earlobe, put on ear ornaments	WS	bonó syháwkit		
bonóm chakámi	earwax	WS	bonóm ćakámi		
bonóm chípbᴍ	ear lobe	WS	bonóm ćípby		
bonóm kolókbem	great-grandmother: as a kinship term, this word must have a prefix, either mᴍ, nik, or min (see Mountain Maidu Grammar, Lesson 6 for more details)	FC			
bonóno	uncle (WS), uncle on father's side (FC): as a kinship term, this word must have a prefix, either mᴍ, nik, or min (see Mountain Maidu Grammar, Lesson 6 for more details)	WS, FC	bonóno		
bonóʼolpe	deaf	WS	bonóʔolpe		
bopókno	hit (someone with something)	RD	bopokʼno	114	
bopóťati	put on bands (regalia)	RD	bopotʼati	120	
bós	finish doing: chedá bósweten "having finished breakfast;" bóschet sᴍtim kanίwonom lᴍkchopinkʼan "all but one had finished climbing inside"	WST, RD	bós	62:4 (WST) 108, 200 (RD)	
bóschet sᴍti	all but one	RD	bosʼtset sötʼi	108	
bosíp	be all untied (knots on the invitation string)	RD	bosipʼ	208	
bosíp	jump out, escape	WS	bosíp		
bosó	obsidian, basalt (FC), flint (WS)	FC, WS	bosó		
bosó tawáldom	working obsidian	FC-T			
bosókʼ	freshet, spring (of water)	WS	bosókʼ		

Maidu	English	Source	Source Spelling	Page	Other Spellings
bóstoi	coot (water bird)	HM	bos'-toi		
botó	leaf, clubs (in playing cards): botóm héwdawdom chána "Leaves are falling from the trees."	WS, FC	botó		
botópai	get busy, get working (on something), get to work on: mᴀsém máidᴀ ha'ai botópaiyahakán. "Hopefully they want those people to get busy (on this)."	RD	botop'ai	30	
bowakno	American merganser (duck)	PM-M	bow-wak-nom		
bówochono	gap, pass in the mountains, around the trail	WS	bówoćono		
bówodaw	go along on the trail (like footprints)	RD	bō'wodau	228	
bówokoi	to wind into the distance (trail)	WS-MP	bówokoj		
bówono	to wind along (trail)	WS	bówono		
bú	break wind, pass gas	WS	bú		bᴀ̂
bubúm cha	Jeffrey pine tree, Ponderosa pine	JD	bubumćom, bububća (the last b is probably a typo for m)	28, 30	bᴀbᴀ̂m cha, babᴀ̂m cha
bubúti	yew	HM	boo-boo'-te		
búchᴀli	stink beetle	FC			búchule (FC-R), búchuli (FC-E)
buchí	mountain whitefish (PM-M), whitefish (RR-SW)	PM-M, RR-SW	but-chem		bupchi (BC)
búchilale	wasp	FC			búchailele (RR-SW)
buchiwi	poisonous plant in the carrot/parsley family	JD	bućiwym	77	butchiwi
budawim máidᴀm	Wintun people	FC-T			
budú	bundle, package (noun)	WS	budú		
budú	tie in a bundle, wrap up	WS	budú		
budút	deep, as snow	WS	budút		
budúti	tie (something) up	RD	būdū'ti	132	
budútno	deep everywhere, in all parts	WS	budútno		
budútnoti	cause (something) to be deep	RD	budut'noti	194	
buhúp	ram (something) in	WS	buhúp		bu'úpu
buhúpkoyo	stick some things in there	WS	buhúpkojo		
buhúpno	ram in	WS	buhúpno		
buhúpnobos	get all of them stuck in	WS	buhúpnobos		
buhúpnokᴀ	rammer, something used to ram in	WS	buhúpnoky		
buhúpyo	stick (several things) in	WS	buhúpjo		
buhúpyokᴀ	quiver for arrows	WS	buhúpjoky		
buk buk buk	sound of a hawk	FC-T			
bukᴀ	small sunflower	HLME	bukom	12	
búki	book	FC-T			
bukkuk	knock (verb)	FC			

Maidu	English	Source	Source Spelling	Page	Other Spellings
búklakkm	red-tailed hawk	FC			
Bukom	place name for Rice Canyon, # 6 on HLME map 3. Said to be named for the small sunflowers growing here. Note that túmbakmm is attested for native "sunflower." This may be a different variety, or the name bakmm and bukom could be one and the same. Tum also means "sunflower." See map 4 in Appendix 5.	HLME			bakmm
búksiukm	rattlesnake (black stripe tail)	FC			
bukú	tail (noun)	FC, WS	buk		buk
bukúi	stop burning, go out (as a fire)	WS	bukúj		
bukúibos	be extinguished, go out completely (light or fire)	WST	bukújbos	50:6	
bukúikm	pennyroyal - contraceptive, purple flower	FC			
bukúipoto	be almost out (as a fire)	WS	bukújpoto		
bukúiti	turn off (a light), blow out (a match or candle), extinguish (a fire), close (a door): toyákm bukúitipi! "Turn off the light!"	FC, WS	bukújti		
bukúitida	cause to go out (fire), put out (fire)	RD	būhū'itida	170	
bukúitipi	turn off, close (command): púlkm bukúitipi! "close the door!"	FC			
bukúkuikit	go out completely (fire)	RD	būkū'kuikit	64	
bukúlism	small black ant	PM-M, BC	boo-coo-le-sum		
Bukúlisa Ínkomi	place name, just north of Quincy, #49 on FR map. See map 2 in Appendix 5.	FR	bukúlisa ʔínkomi	370-371	
bukúlusi	big ant	FC			
bukúm yoko	gruel, porridge	FC			
búkwislai	wag the tail	WS	búkwislaj		
bul	bull (from English)	WS	bul		
bulálai	black bear	RD	būlāl'ai	11-12, 192, 236	
búlim kawáyu	stallion	WS	búlim kawáju		
búnoye	blow around (as wind)	FC			bmnoye

Maidu	English	Source	Source Spelling	Page	Other Spellings
Bunúk	place name in Indian Valley, #19 on FR map, a village between Greenville Rancheria and the cemetery a half-mile north of Hunt Canyon. (FR1). According to HY, it means "protected from the wind." According to MP, it means "a place out of the wind." See map 5 in Appendix 5.	FR, FR1, FR-HY, FR-MP	Bunuk	370-371	
búpaito	to rut in mating season (as male animals)	WS	búpajto		
búpaitomenkѡmeni	rutting season, mating season (for animals)	WS	búpajtomenkymen		búpaitomenkѡmen
bupupu	sagebrush, gray sage with big leaves, used for smudges, basin sagebrush	FC, JD	bupupu	44	
búsno	do something continuously or intensely	WS	búsno		
bústoye	coot (water bird), mud hen	PM-M, FC	bus-toi-yem		busdoye (FC)
busúle	acorn cap	FC-T, WS	busúl		busúl
busúlim hámsi	scrub oak	WS	busúlim hámsi		
butchiwi	water hemlock	PM-M	but-chi-wem		buchiwi
butú	hair, fur	WS	butú		
butúipe	hairy, furry	WS	butújpe		
butúitapope	covered with hair, covered with fur	WS	butújtapope		
butúkupem piťí	furry turd (Marvin Cunningham's nickname for a cat)	FC			
butúweh	hairball	FC			
bu'úpu	ram (something) in	WS	buʔúpu		buhúp
bu'úpukѡ	ramrod for a gun	WS	buʔúpuky		
búwo	blow (wind)	FC			bѡwo
búwo	wind (noun)	FC			bѡwo
Buyem Ḱumí	place name for the rocky ridge located on the north side of Highway 89 north of Indian Falls on Indian Creek, with at least 3 split-rock formations. The first formation is Thumb Rock (see Tetém Mamchipbѡm Om), and also includes Búyem Ḱumí. This is on DT map 7. See map 2 in Appendix 5.	DT	Buyem Kume	45	
chѡchѡḱ	wild rhubarb. Stem is round in cross-section	WS	éýcyk		
chѡdoi	grab up (something) in the hand	WS	éýdoj		
chѡdoiťonum	while grabbing continuously in the hand	WS	éýdojťonum		

Maidu	English	Source	Source Spelling	Page	Other Spellings
chʌdonu	hold (something) in the hand	WS	ćýdonu		
chʌi	be unable	WS	ćýj		chui (FC-T)
chʌi	four	WS, RD	ćýj (WS), tsö'yi (RD)	chúiyi	
chʌinini	four times	WS	ćýjnini		
chʌiti	hard (like rock), tough (like meat), strong (like paper, cloth)	WS	ćýjti		
chʌiti	tighten	RD	tsöi'ti	72	
chʌitimen	soft, tender, fragile	WS	ćýjtimen		
chʌititi	make strong, strengthen, make secure, toughen up	WS	ćýjtiti		
chʌkʌťʌ	cricket	WS	ćýkýťy		
chʌlʌ	strainer	WS	ćyl		
chʌlchʌkʌ	wild rose	FC			
chʌlchʌkʌm yó	wild rose flower	WS	ćýlćykym jó		
chʌlchʌl woló	big cone-shaped seining/straining basket, used as a fishing trap or strainer	WS	ćýlćyl woló		
chʌlkʌm woló	basket used as a fishing trap, basket used as a strainer	WS	ćýlkym woló		
chʌmmi	beak	RD	tsümmi	56	
chʌp	spit, expectorate	WS	ćýp		
chʌpátim dʌ	wild lilac, ceanothus, deerbrush	FC-E			chepátim dʌ
chʌpkit	spit, expectorate	WS	ćýpkit		
chʌtʌkʌm cha	red fir tree	HY			
chʌwak	scratch (something) with claws as a cat does	WS	ćýwak		
chʌwakkʌ	claw	WS	ćýwakky		
chʌwikadoi	pick up, scoop/scratch up (dirt)	RD	tsö'wikadoi	166	
chá	tree, wood, stick of wood	WS	ćá		
chá hunékʌ	axe, saw, wood-cutting tool, wood cutter, lumberjack	WS, FC	ćá hunéky		chá hunéikʌ (FC-E)
chá topái	burn off brush or trees	WS	ćá topáj		
chá wulút	pile up wood, stack wood	WS	ćá wulút		
chabába	flying squirrel	FC			
chábe	small tree, stick (noun)	RD, WST	tsā'be (RD), ćábe (WST)	166 (RD), 46:2 (WST	
chacháinoye	wander around in the forest	FC			
cháchato	trees, stand of trees, woods	RD, FC, WS	tsa'tsato (RD), ćáćato (WS)	138	
chacháyi	others (WS), other, various (WST): chacháyim kʌlóknonom wasása yahátiboskan "various women prepared things"	WS, WST	ćaćáji	78:7	
chái	elsewhere, somewhere else, the other one(s)	WS	ćáj		
chái'ʌkoi	go away	WS	ćáj?ykoj		

53

Maidu	English	Source	Source Spelling	Page	Other Spellings
chaicháimeni	acquaintances, not strangers	RD	tsaitsai′meni	136	
chaicháino	all kinds of, any kind of (RD), all different from each other (FC)	RD, FC	tsaitsai′no	134, 190	
cháichainono	all kinds of	WS	ćájćajnono		
cháicheḱonu	stare off in the distance, look elsewhere	WS	ćájćeḱonu		
cháicheḱonuḱuḱus	pretend to be looking elsewhere	WS	ćájćeḱonuḱuḱus		
cháichetipe	odd-looking, different looking	FC			
cháidi	somewhere else	FC			
chái'i	other, something else, someone else (WS), another, different one (RD) (object of sentence): awéten bei chái'i sólḱan "then he sang another one"	WS, RD	tsai'i (RD), ćaj?í (WS)	25	
chái'iḱas	I want a different one, I'm looking for a different one	RD	tsaiī′kas	86	
chái'im	another, different one, different, stranger, next (adj or subject of sentence)	RD, FC	tsai′im	136	
chái'im bének	the next day, the next morning (later than dawn)	RD	tsai′im bēn′ek	110, 222	
chái'im ékda	the next morning, the next day at dawn	RD	tsai′im ekda		
chái'im máidm	foreigner	BC	chi maidum		
cháimen	later, another time	WS, FC	ćájmen		
chaina	be elsewhere, be somewhere else (verb): kmḱás unínan chainadóm bísdom hónwenumaḱas "by staying away from this place I will survive"	RD	tsaina	156	
cháinada	go away from	WS	ćájnada		
cháinakḱenu	do something on the side, incidentally, or in addition to the main thing	WS	ćájnakḱenu		
cháinantedi	in the opposite direction, a different way: cháinantedi mḱóiwoḱan. "He told (her) to go a different way."	RD	tsain′antedi	160	
cháinapi	get out!	WS	ćájnapi		
cháism	the Washo Indians	WS	ćájsy		chai'isim (FC-E)
cháisum máidm	Washo, Washo person	FC			chai'isim máidm (FC-E)
cháitakm	scrub jay	FC-E			
cháitika	be disguised, be different	RD	tsai′tika	40	

Maidu	English	Source	Source Spelling	Page	Other Spellings
cháitikakape	each one different: cháitikakape píkno pedóm "each one eating only a certain/different kind (of food)"	RD	tsai'tikakapepik'no pedom'	188	
cháitikape	different, one that is different: cháitikape yakɯpem máidɯ "people having names that are different"	RD	tsai'tikape	13, 20	
cháitikat	differently (adverb)	RD	tsai'tikat	20, 161	
cháitikawinim	another kind (of)	RD	tsai'tikawinim	16	
cháitikchetipe	different looking	WS	ćájtikćetipe		
cháitiki	different, a different one	WS	ćájtiki		
cháitikkape	different ones, different ...s	WS	ćájtikkape		cháitikape
cháitikkapem wéye	a different language	WS	ćájtikkapem wéje		
cháitikpintipe	different sounding	WS	ćájtikpintipe		
cháitikwinim	another kind (of): cháitikwinim máidɯ "another kind of people"	RD	tsai'tikwinim	15	
chaḱ	fish eggs, roe	WS	ćaḱ		
chaká	pitch, sap (FC), pitch, resin, gum, wax (WS)	FC, WS	ćakám		chak'a (FC-E)
chakáchaka	scouring rushes (equisetum hyemale)	RD	tsakatsaka	52	
Chakám	place name for a site just north of Quincy, #47 on FR map. See map 2 in Appendix 5.	FR	ćakám, ćákim	370-371	Chákɯm
chakámdɯḱɯ	pitch, just pitch	WS	ćakámdyḱy		
Chakámdɯḱɯ	place name in Taylorsville area, #27 on FR map, an old village on the Taylorsville Rancheria at Terry's sawmill (FR1). There was a roundhouse at this village (HY). The name means "pitchy wood" (MP). Does not agree with AK name Kushdu (FR-Ka). See map 5 in Appendix 5.	FR, FC, FR1, FR-HY, FR-MP	ćakámdiḱi (FR), ch'akom duka (FR1)	370-371	chakam dukum (FC), chakom duka (FR1)
Chakámdɯḱɯm Bo	place name of a road going from Chakámdɯḱɯ (across Indian Creek from Taylorsville) to North Arm. See map 5 in Appendix 5.	FC-MAP, MSOP	chakamdi khum bo		
chakámdɯkdɯ́kpe	pitchy, full of pitch	RD	tsakam'dökdök'pe	142, 148	
chakámin	sap of lodgepole or ponderosa pine, used for chewing gum (JD), chewing gum (FC-E)	JD, FC-E	ćakamin	29	
chakámni	pitchy	RD	tsekau'ni	160	
chakámpai	get pitch on (something)	WS	ćakámpaj		
chakámpaiti'us	get pitch on oneself	WS	ćakámpajtiʔus		

Maidu	English	Source	Source Spelling	Page	Other Spellings
chakámťapopem ḱúli	pitch-covered widow(er) (still in mourning)	FC-E			
chakámťapoti	get (something) covered with sap	FC			
chakámti'us	put a mixture of pitch and soot on the cheeks as a mark of mourning	WS	ćakámtiʔus		
chakáti	blackbird	FC, WS	ćakát		chakát
chakom cha	blue oak tree, valley oak	FC-R, FC-E			chakⱮm cha
chalála	fry (intransitive)	WS	ćalála		
chalálati	fry (something)	WS	ćalálati		
chálťáťapi	kingfisher	WS	ćálťáťapi		
Chám Bokini	place name for Nevis Island, now under Lake Almanor, #20 on LM map. See map 3 in Appendix 5.	LM	jambokinee		
Chám Bukúnayim	place name west of Big Meadows, #12 on FR map. See map 3 in Appendix 5.	FR	ćám bukunayim	370-371	
chám hí	species of red (or red orange) fungus parasite which grows on the Douglas Fir, and which was used for face paint	WS	ćám hí, ćám hiní		chám hiní
chám ḱódo	forest	WS	ćám ḱódo		
chám ḱum	hole in a tree: kulúmⱮni ka'ánkano, káinoyeweten, ekímⱮni chám ḱúmdi ma'át bískⱮm. "While it is dark, after flying around, you will be one who stays primarily in a tree hole during the day."	RD	tsañ'kum	214	
chám ṕaḱá	tree branch	FC			
chám piwí	tree roots used in twined baskets, for forming the base of the basket (MP)	WS-MP	ćám piwí		
Chám SⱮdom Pakáni	place name for Homer Lake on the north side of Keddie Peak. This lake had a protruding tree snag that was thought to be a snake's tail, and one could get doctoring powers by swimming out to it, diving all the way down, and opening one's eyes (FR-TE). #25 on LM map. See map 3 in Appendix 5.	FR1, LM, FR-TE	chom-see dohm (LM), ch'amsudonim pakonim (FR1)		Chám SⱮdom
chám sápa	bushy-tailed rat	PM-M	chom-sa-pa		
chám simí	black moss	WS	ćám simí		
chám símpani	lichen	PM-M	sam-sem-pa-ne		sam símpani
chám siwí	black tree moss	WS	ćám siwí		
chám sosó	green or blue-green tree moss	WS	ćám sosó		

Maidu	English	Source	Source Spelling	Page	Other Spellings
chám wulúti	woodpile	WS	ćám wulúti		
chámmi	knife	WS, FC	ćámmi (WS), tsum′mi (RD)	60	chámi (FC), chúmmi (RD)
chan	beside, the place beside: hᴀbóm chándi "beside the house"	WS	ćan		
chan	north, northwest: ḱódom chánna "to the north" ḱódom chándi "in the northwest"	FC, RD	tsan	11, 118	
chanᴀno	travel side by side	RD	tsanyön′o	190	
chánaki	on the other side: chánaki yahátiḱan adóm túimapemnaki wasátiḱan "on the other side, he made it nice, but on the side he was to sleep on, he made it badly"	RD	tsa′naki	70	
chánan... chánan	on one side... and on the other side..., in one hand... in the other hand...: chánan momí chánan makó sódoiḱan "she carried water in one hand and fish in the other"	RD	tsa′nan (noun) (verb)wet tsa′nan (noun) (verb, conjugated)	198	
chani	wild garlic: the leaves are cooked as greens, the bulbs are not eaten	JD	ćani (JD), jaw nem (BC)	34	
chaní	porcupine	FC			chóni
cháni...bei cháneki	on one side...then the other, one of... then the other: ḱódom ékdachet chánim yimí pebóschoi'a. ḱódom kulúlukitchet bei cháneḱi pebóschoi'a. "By morning he had eaten one of his arms. by evening he had eaten the other one."	RD	tsan′i... bēi tsan′eki	190	
chanputi	a type of wild onion, eaten raw	JD	ćanputy	34	
chánwono	one side: chánwono opítsipdom "filling up one side"	RD	tsan′wono	196	
chanyᴀno	going from one side (to the other), going through (something) (adverb)	RD	tsanyön′o	180	
chat	scream or cry loudly or angrily, squeak (like mice)	WS	ćat		
chat	spread (things) out	WS	ćat		
Chatamoto	place name for village with a roundhouse south of Chester, west of Big meadows. See map 3 in Appendix 5.	CM			
chátchat	chatter (like squirrels or monkeys)	WS	ćátćat		
chátchatkᴀ	monkey	WS	ćátćatky		

Maidu	English	Source	Source Spelling	Page	Other Spellings
chátnoye	squeak (verb)	WS	ćátnoje		
chatúti'i	sapsucker (woodpecker)	FC			
cháutata	fish hawk	HM	chow'-tah-tah		
chawá	chin, jaw (WS), teeth (FC)	WS, FC	ćawá		
chawái	chew	WS	ćawáj		
chawám bʌmí	jawbone (WS), chin, jaw (FC)	WS, FC	ćawám bymí		
chawám símpani	beard	WS	ćawám símpani		
cháwo	buckle, brooch	WS	ćáwo		
che	see, be in sight, see (a person's) true worth: mínḱi sʌ cheḱás. "I saw your dog." mínḱi kapótam homóndi maḱáde? mʌm min chedóm kʌḱán. "Where is your coat? It's looking at you (it is within sight)." nik áiḱate cheménkʌm kaḱʌankano. "I guess you must have never seen me."	WS, FC, FC-R, RD	će (WS), tse (RD)	136	
chebʌ́k	have a look at, examine (RD), look at, peer at, read, appear, sprout (WS): chebʌ́kben mapí! "don't peek!" chebʌ́k uní! "Look here!"	RD, WS, FC	tsebök' (RD), ćebýk (WS)	28, 58, 136, 138	
chebʌ́kdoi	begin sprouting, come up (as plants)	WS	ćebýkdoj		
chebʌ́kti	show	RD	tsebök'ti	58	
chebá	miss (someone dead or departed), yearn for (someone): chebáḱas min "I missed you."	WS, FC	ćebá		
chebóḱoi	be unable to see well, fail to recognize (someone)	WS	ćebóḱoj		
chebós	suddenly see, look hard, look closely (RD), recognize (WS): chebósdom yahátidom "looking harder"	RD, WS	tsebos' (RD), ćebós (WS)	32, 76	
chebóye	look for, wait for (RD), watch for, anticipate the arrival of (someone) (WS)	RD, WS	tsebo'ye (RD), ćebóje (WS)	86, 118, 120	
chechʌ́i	be unable to see	WS	ćećýj		
chechʌ́isape	invisible, incapable of being seen	FC-E	chechuisapem		
chechói	find	WS	ćećój		
chedʌ́k	catch fish or animals in a trap	RD	tsedök'	212	
chedʌ́k	trap (noun)	RD	tsedök'	212	
chedá	breakfast, a break	WS, FC-E	ćedá		
chedá	subside (RD), rest, recover, take a break (FC), cease being..., recover from (WS)	RD, FC, WS	tseda' (RD), ćedá (WS)	92	

Maidu	English	Source	Source Spelling	Page	Other Spellings
chedáda	have breakfast	RD	tsedā'da	120, 128, 140, 220, 226, 236	
chedím	be/become arrogant	RD	tsedīm'	174	
chedímti	cause someone to become arrogant	RD	tsedīm'ti	218	
chedónohanoi	to look up at	RD	tsedōnohanoi	66	
chedónuto	gaze up at	RD	tsedōn'uto	184	
che'ésta	personal Indian name of Lena Benner's mother	WS	ćeʔésta		
chehéhechonope	transparent, invisible	RD	tsehē'hetsonope	4	
chehéhedoi	look up	RD	tsehē'hedoi	12	
chehéhekoi	look around	RD	tsehē'hekoi	124	
chehéhekoido	while looking around, looking off in (other = cháidi) directions	RD	tsehē'hekoido	22, 200	
chehéhemitno	look around down into (valley)	RD	tsēhe'hemitno	224	
chehéhenonwet	without looking around	RD	tsehē'hēnonwet	108	
chehéhenoye	look around	RD	tsehē'hēnoē	186	
chehéhesito	look all around across	RD	tsehē'hesito	86	
chehéiheikit	look down at	WST	ćehéjhejkit	72:6	
chehéiheikoi	look across, look across at, go look around	WS, WST	ćehéjhejkoj	78:9	
chehéiheino	look at, inspect	WS	ćehéjhejno		
chehéiheiye	look in the direction of, look toward (object takes -na)	WS	ćehéjhejje		
chehéikoi	look in the direction of	WST	ćehéjhej	78:9	
chehéiye	expect (someone to arrive)	WS	ćehéjje		
chehélu	be able to see	RD	tsehel'u	4	
chehéwodoi	look up, stand up and look around	RD	tsehē'wodoi	12	
chehéye'mno	go along looking at (several)	RD	tsehē'yeöno	92	
chehéye'mnoye	go around looking at (several)	RD	tsehē'yeönoye	92	
chehéyeno	look around	RD	tsehē'yeno	124	
chehéyenoye	look around	RD	tsehē'yenoye	124	
chehéyenoyetiti	have a chance to see: hesím chehéyenoyemenupe, chehéyenoyetitimenwet, kan mmyí dónwikanukan adónkan wónotikan. "Before he had looked around, without having a chance to see anything, something seized him and then killed him."	RD	tsehē'yenoyetiti	124	
chehéyewew	frequently/habitually look back around	RD	tsehē'yewēu	98	
chekḿ	find out	RD	tsekö'	192	
cheká	spy, look secretly	WS	ćeká		
chekákasip	look at repeatedly	RD	tsekā'kasip	42	

Maidu	English	Source	Source Spelling	Page	Other Spellings
chekáta	watch (FC), watch and wait (RD)	FC, RD	tsekāta	56	
chekati	blackbird	FC			
chekáto	watch (someone) secretly, look at secretly	WST	ćekáto	56:40	
chékchekkm	wren	HM	tsek'-tsek-koo		
chekíno	watch (TV), read (a book), look closely at (something)	FC			
chekínokm	book	FC			
chekínu	expect, be watching in expectation	WST	ćekínu	70:58	
chekít	be able to see: kulúdom unídi, min chekítmenḱas "Since it's dark here, I can't see you."	FC-T			
chekíttoto	watch (TV) together	FC			
cheḱói	go see	FC			
cheḱóiboḱói	hardly be able to see (something)	RD	tsekoi'bokoi	130	
cheḱón	look at steadily, gaze at, stare at	RD	tsekōn'	196	
cheḱónu	keep looking that way, stare that way: cháina cheḱónudom "looking the other way"	WS, WST	ćeḱónu	52:22	
chelúṫnak	beautiful place to look at	FC			
chemáka	be unable to see	RD	tsemāka	238	
cheméni	little tiny particles, germs, bacteria: cheméni kapí "bugs you can't see"	FC, FC-T			
cheménḱukus	pretend not to see	WS	ćeménḱukus		
cheménwono'ekm	have never seen: tetéluťi mḱáwchetipem cheménwono'ekmḱas "I have never seen such big beautiful ones"	RD	tsemen'wono'ēkö	176	
chemhúsem	harm (someone), do someone harm	RD	tsemhūs'em	140	
chemhúsemmen	not harm	RD	tsemhū'semen, tsem'hūsemen	160, 194, 222	chémhusemmen
chemínu	gaze into, look into	WS	ćemínu		
chemtaimén	not miss a thing, see everything	RD	tsemtaimen'	168	
chenmḱoi	go visiting, go see	FC			chenoḱoi (FC-E)
chenó	see, meet, encounter	WS	ćenó		
chenói'noye	go take a look around	WS	ćenój?noje		
chenóḱoi	visit, go see (WS), go visit (FC)	WS, FC	ćenóḱoj		
chenóḱoiyahawew	be wanting to go see	RD	tsenō'koiyehāweu	142	
chenóno	have a look, check it out, look for (someone) (RD), go and see, go take a look (WS), investigate	RD, WS	tseno'no (RD), ćenóno (WS)	120, 140, 186	

Maidu	English	Source	Source Spelling	Page	Other Spellings
chenóno'us	appear as oneself, look the same as before: yákadom mᴀkánim chenóno'us "look like himself again"	RD	tsenōn'ous	180	
chenónoye	go take a look around	WS	ćenónoje		
chenó'ohe	look for (someone), try to find (someone missing)	RD	tsenō'ohē	118	
chenó'okit	come to visit (FC), visit	FC, WS	ćenóʔokit		
chenó'okitti	make someone come, get someone to come visit	RD	tsenō'okiti'	38	
cheno'uḱoi	go visit	FC			
chenú	stare, keep looking, watch (verb)	WS, FC, RD	ćenú (WS), tsenū' (RD)	112	
chenúdi	on lookout, on (someone's) watch: niḱí chenúdi kᴀḱán máidᴀ kobéktimenmapem "on my watch, no one will make people scream"	RD	tsenū'di	112	
chenúḱoi	pay attention	FC-E			
chenúḱoimen	not pay attention	FC-T			
chenúno	watch, sit around and watch, be aware	RD	tsenū'no	100	
che'ókole	be reluctant to see (something happen), hate to see (something happen) (RD), be tired of seeing (something or someone) (FC), not want to see	RD, FC, WS	tseo'kolē (RD), ćeʔókole (WS)	130	
che'ókole	be reluctant to watch, not want to watch	RD	tseō'kolet	102	
chepánu	glare at, scowl at (someone)	RD	tsepā'nu	208	
chepátim dᴀ	ceanothus, wild lilac	FC			chᴀpátim dᴀ (FC-E)
chepípitino	look around at, look straight at	RD	tsepipitino	66	
chepítwono	facing towards (as a building) (adv): mᴀḱí hᴀbom chepítwono ḱódom chanantedi kᴀḱán "his house faces towards the north country"	RD	tsepit'wono	172	
ches	I see it! ni ḱuním ḱódo ches! "I saw the land first (just now)!	RD	tses	42	
chesák	recognize	WS	ćesák		
chesákew	recognize now	RD	tsesāk'ēu	98	
chesákmaka	not recognize	RD	tsesak'maka	236	
chesákti	recognizable	WS	ćesákti		
chesáktimen	unrecognizable, disguised	WS	ćesáktimen		
chesáktin	be unrecognizable	RD	tsesak'tin	78	
chesém	be shy of (someone)	WS	ćesém		
chesíto	look across	WS	ćesíto		
chesítonu	gaze across	WST-DW	ćesítonu	80	

Maidu	English	Source	Source Spelling	Page	Other Spellings
chesítope	transparent	FC-E			
cheťá	have a look at (something), check (something) out	WST	ćeťá	56:38	
cheťánu	gaze down from above	WS	ćeťánu		
cheťápai	look around and see something	FC			
chetí	appear to be, seem to, look (in the sense of "look good," "look happy," etc.) (WS), show (FC)	WS, FC	ćetí		
chetímen	not let (someone) see, to hide	RD	tsetī'men	46, 76	
chetínti	be unrecognizable	WS	ćetínti	RD 98	
chetípe	visible, looking like: hesí chetípem makáde? "What does it look like?"	FC, WST-DW	ćetípe	80	
chétnumit	gaze down at	RD	tset'numit	64	
chetó	divide up (something), parcel (something) out	RD	tsetō'	16, 202	
chetókɱ	window, what you look through	WS	ćetóky		
chetól	look through	FC-E			
chewás	see poorly, be partially blind	WST	ćewás	54:24	
chewátai	fail to see, fail to notice	RD	tsewātai	58	
chewé	to witness, talk about (someone or something) one has seen, notice/observe: mi sɱ'ɱi chewé'ano? "Did you notice anything? Did you see anything interesting?" chéwemenpada. "Don't say anything about what you saw."	RD	tsewe'	50, 54, 134, 156, 166, 180-2	
chewéto	testify about, gossip about, notice and talk, comment on, remark on	RD	tsewe'to, tsē'weto	134, 122	chéweto
chewónope	one who has seen	RD	tsewōn'ope	7	
chewúsuktipe	transparent, invisible	RD	tsewu'suktipem	4	
cheyáha	be visible, exposed to view	RD	tseyā'ha	240	
cheyákan	see well	FC			
cheyénu	keep looking towards, stare at	WS	ćejénu		
chhɱkɱ	tickle	WS	cyký		
chhɱkɱchhɱkɱ	tickle	WS	cykýcyky		
chhɱkɱchhɱkɱtoḱoi	go tickling one another	WS	cykýcykytoḱoj		
chhɱkɱchhɱkɱtoto	tickle each other	WS	cykýcykytoto		
chhatáta	rattle (verb), make a rattling sound	WS	catáta		
chhatátaḱa	rattlesnake - note that this word should not be pronounced except at the bear dance ceremony.	WS	catátaḱa		

Maidu	English	Source	Source Spelling	Page	Other Spellings
chhatátakam húskᴍ	rattlesnake - note that this word should not be pronounced except at the bear dance ceremony.	WS	catátakam húsky		
chhatátakatikᴍ	rattles on a snake	WS	catátakatiky		
chhikín	chicken (from English)	WS	cikín		
chhikíni dónkᴍ	chicken hawk	WS	cikíni dónky		
chí	clothing, blanket, clothes: yahát chíkupem "well-dressed, well covered"	WS, FC, WST-DW	ćí	46:1	
chí	wear, put on clothes: chíbospi "get dressed!"	WS, FC-T	ćí		
chí pekᴍm kápuslele	moth	WS	ćí pekým kápuslele		
chí wiyi	naked	FC			
chíbos	be completely dressed	WST	ćíbos	54:23	
Chichi	place name for Feather Falls	FC-T			
chichí	side of the body	WS	ćićí		
chichikᴍ	prairie dog	FC			
chichím bᴍmí	rib	WS	ćićím bymí		
chichím bᴍmím 'ítu	a pain in the side	WS	ćićím bymím ʔítu		
chichim cha	alder, mountain alder	FC, JD			
chidᴍk	to fish with a trap	RD	tsidök'	212	
chídaka	bear grass	JD	ćí·dak	63	chitaká
chídokᴍ	clothespin	FC			
chikáta	focus on, watch intently	RD	tsika'ta	114	
chike	big brown grasshopper, locust	CM		87	chiki
chikí	tooth	FC, WS	ćík (WS), chikí (FC)		chik
chikí 'ítu	have a toothache	WS	ćikí ʔítu		
chikí 'ítu	toothache	WS	ćikí ʔítu		
chikí kᴍkᴍkᴍsti	grind the teeth, grit the teeth	WS	ćikí kykýkysti		
chikím sᴍmí	gums (in the mouth)	WS	ćikím symí		
chikínokᴍ	TV (something you look at)	FC			chekínokᴍ
chikutkᴍ	cricket	FC-R			chukutkᴍ
chillum	tobacco pipe, peace pipe	CM		24, 25	chillem
chílwa	rattlesnake	JD	culuwa		chuluwa
Chílwam Ínkomi (1)	place name for a village just north of Quincy, #50 on FR map, located at Elizabethtown Flat, north of Quincy (FR1). See map 2 in Appendix 5.	FR. FR1	ćílwam ʔínkomi (FR), chilu'am inkomi (2) (FR1)	370-371	

63

Maidu	English	Source	Source Spelling	Page	Other Spellings
Chílwam Ínkomi (2)	place name in Indian Valley, #28 on FR map, a village on the Johnson Ranch between Crescent Mills and Taylorsville. The village site is about ¼ mile off the road back in the hills. Big times were held here (FR1). Chílwam means "rattlesnake." See map 5 in Appendix 5.	FR, FC	ćílwam ínkomi (FR), chiluam inkomim (FC), chilu'am inkomi (FR1)	370-371	
chílwam piwi	snakeroot (root rubbed on legs to repel snakes)	FR1	chilu'am piwi		
chímen	to not own any clothes, not have clothes	FC-E			
chímeni	one who does not own clothes				
chínkuťi	rabbit (WS), jack rabbit (FC)	WS, FC	ćímkuťi		
chínkuťim saláwi	rabbit skin blanket (MP)	WS-MP	ćímkuťim saláwi		
chínu	keep (clothes or coverings) on, have on	WS	ćínu		
chínukm	bedding, sheets and blankets	WS	ćínuky		
chiókoli	chocolate	FC			
chípbm	tip, end, extremity: mam chípbm "finger" pai chípbm "toe"	WS	ćípby		
chípe	garland	FC			
chípi	sheep (from English)	FC-E			
chísml	to shell using the thumb and forefinger	WS	ćísyl		
chísas	Jesus (from English)	WS	ćísas		
chísbmhmlkm	toothpick	WS	ćísbyhylky		
chístatakm	robin	WS	ćístataky		
chíťakm	woman's blouse	WS	ćíťaky		
chíťaka	bear grass (FC, JD), grass for basket weaving (RD), mountain bunchgrass, used for weaving pliable baskets (WS)	RD, FC, WS, JD	tsīt'aka (RD), ćiťák (WS), ći·dak (JD), chítaka (FC)	174, 176	
chiťákam loló	pliable basket, woven of bunchgrass or bear grass	WS	ćiťákam loló		
Chítakam Yamánim	place name for Canyon Dam, #13 on LM map. See map 3 in Appendix 5.	LM	See-tah-kom-yamanim		

Maidu	English	Source	Source Spelling	Page	Other Spellings
Chíṭakam Yamánim	place name for Canyon Dam, #13 on LM map. Means "bear grass mountain." According to AT, the location of Bear grass Mountain is 3.3 miles east of Canyon Dam, a ridge by Hwy 89 where bear grass (white grass) grows. Also place name for Sierra Buttes (FC-E). See map 3 in Appendix 5 for the Plumas County site.	LM , AT, FC-E	ee-tah-kom-yamanim		
Chítani Pakáni	place name for Gold Lake. See maps 1 and 2 in Appendix 5.	PM-D	chee-tani pakanee		
chitatakm	rattlesnake	PM-M	chi-ta-ta-cum		
chitátati	Lewis woodpecker (medium size, dark color, dark red face)	HM	she-tah'-tat-te		
chiṭók	have poison oak rash	WS	ćiṭók		
chiṭók	the small, spriggy variety of poison oak	WS, JD	ćiṭók (WS), ću·toko, ći·toko (JD)	37	
chítosi	Cheetos	FC			
chiṭúṭ	red-shafted flicker	WS	ćiṭúṭ		
chí'uluṭchono	robin (RD), meadowlark (WS-MM), the creature who stretched mud with its foot to make the earth	RD, WS, MM	tsi'ūlutsono	8 (RD), 20 (WS-MM)	
chíwchiwi	clover	WS	ćíwćiwi		
chiwemyo	red maids (plant: calandrinia ciliata)	JD	ći·wemjo	66	
chiwí	clover, clubs (cards), grass	FC, JD	ćywy	59	
chíwi'i	be naked, be lacking clothes, be without clothes	WS	ćíwiʔi		
chíwi'iluṭpe	completely naked, stark naked	WS	ćíwiʔilutpe		
chíwi'ipe	naked, undressed, lacking clothes, without clothes	FC			
Chiwísi	place name for a summer fish camp located near Moccasin Creek on Indian Creek just below Dixie Canyon. It was once a green flat on the right side of the stream (FR). #30 on FR map. DT map 7. See maps 2 and 5 in Appendix 5.	FR1, FR-TE, DT	ch'iwisi (FR1), ćiwisi (FR)	370-371	
chiwíspolótkm	robin (RD), nest-maker, Meadowlark (MM), black-headed grosbeak (HM), oriole (HM), the creature who provided mud to make the earth (RD)	RD, HM, MM	tsiwis'polotkö (RD), se-wis'-po-lōt-kum (HM, black-headed grosbeak), se-wis'-po-lōt-kah (HM, oriole)	9, 25 (RD), 21 (WS-MM)	sewís-polotkm, sewís-polotka (HM)

Maidu	English	Source	Source Spelling	Page	Other Spellings
Chiwítbem Yamáni	place name for Dyer Peak or Dyer Mountain (FC, #24 on LM map), place name for entire Keddie Ridge including Healing Rock (#11-12 on LM map). Note that both FC and LM consider Keddie Ridge and Dyer Peak to have this name. See maps 1 and 3 in Appendix 5.	FC- map, LM	Che-wit-bem Yamani, Ch-wit-bem Yamanim		Chiwítbem Yamáninom
Chiwítbem Yamáninom	place name for Keddie Ridge. Chiwítbem means "little green grass coming up" (FR-TE, FR-HY). See map 1 in Appendix 5.	FR1, FR-TE, FR-HY	ch'witbem yamaninom		Chiwítbem Yamáni
chó	be burned out (middle of log for canoe) (RD), burn, as a fire (intransitive) (WS)	RD, WS	tso' (RD), ćó (WS)	40	
Chóbam Smmtónum	Indian name of Arthur Thomas, Maym Gallagher's uncle	WST	ćóbam symtónum	54-26	
chobót	kiss (verb)	WS	ćopót, ćopót		chopot
chobóttoto	kiss each other	WS	ćobóttoto		
chódoi	flare up (as flames)	WS	ćódoj		
chódoiti	start a fire (WS), cause to flare up (FC)	WS, FC	ćódojti		
choko	both	WS	ćok		chok
Cholcholum	place name for Forgay Point, #8 on LM map. See map 5 in Appendix 5.	LM	Jol-jol-lum		
Choldino	Intake Tower (Lake Almanor	FC			
choní	porcupine	WS, FC	ćon		chon
Choním Yamánim	place name for Porcupine Hill, NE of Susanville, one mile past Antelope Grade on Hwy 139, #17 on HLME map 3. Maidu hunted porcupines here. See map 4 in Appendix 5.	HLME	Ch'onim Yamanim		
chópai	be ignited, start burning	WS	ćópaj		
chópaiti	start a fire	WS	ćópajti		
chópaitikm	kindling, anything to start a fire with	WS	ćópajtiky		
chópoto	be almost burnt out (canoe making)	RD	tsō'poto	40	
chopótpot	kiss (someone)	WS	ćopótpot		
chos	menstruate	WS	ćos		
chosbís	be isolated in menstruation	WS	ćosbís		
chóspe	eat alone in the prescribed manner while in the period of menstruation	WS	ćóspe		

Maidu	English	Source	Source Spelling	Page	Other Spellings
chos'úyi	menstrual hut	WS, FC	ćosʔúji		chosúyi
chotúti	white-headed woodpecker	HM	cho-too'-tim		
chówanoti	red-breasted sapsucker	HM	tsow'-wah-no-te		
chowó	silk tassel bush (Garrya)	HM	tsow-wó		
chówowo	rush out (air) with a whistling sound	RD	tsō'wowobo	138	
chu	melt, as ice or snow	WS	ću		
chu	urine	WS	ćum		
chuᴍkᴍ	spider	HM	choo-ă-kah		
chuchᴍkpe	sour	FC			
chuchú	urinate	WS	ćućú		
chuchú	urine	FC			
Chuchúdom O	place name for Soda Rock, south of Indian Falls on Indian Creek. See maps 2 and 5 in Appendix 5.	FC-MAP, MSOP, DT	Choochoodom Oh, ch'ichuyam bam		Chuchúkᴍm O, Chuchúyem Bam
chuchúi	summit, top, high point of a mountain pass	WS	ćućúj		
chuchúidi	on the top of, at the summit	WS	ćućújdi		chúchuidi
chuchúk	sour	WS	ćućúk		
chuchúkᴍ	Indian rhubarb	FC			
chuchúkᴍ	penis (considered a relatively mild term)	WS	ćućúky		
Chuchúkᴍm O	place name for Soda Rock, south of Indian Falls on Indian Creek. See maps 2 and 5 in Appendix 5.	FC-MAP, MSOP, DT	Choochoodom Oh, ch'ichuyam bam		Chuchúdom O, Chuchúyem Bam
chuchúḱoi	go urinate, go outside to urinate	WS, WST	ćućúḱoj	52:22	
chuchúkpe	bitter	FC			
chuchúku	sour dock (eaten raw)	JD	ću·ćuku	66	
chuchúmme	feel like urinating	WS	ćućúmme		
chuchúno	go urinate	WS	ćućúno		
chuchúsitoye	urinate all over	RD	tsutsū'sitoye	218	
Chuchúye	place name: Soda Springs. See map 2 in Appendix 5.	RD	tsutsuye	54	

Maidu	English	Source	Source Spelling	Page	Other Spellings
Chuchúyem Bam	place name for the soda rock, or salt lick, on Indian Creek below Indian Falls. A small meadow here supports a rank growth of salt grass (FR1). The grass here could be braided into ropes, which were then burned for salt (FR-TE). DT map 7 shows this on Indian Creek near a quarry and Earthmaker's Staff (DT). This site is linked to the traditional story of the women who lived at this spot, and killed people passing by using their urine to wash them into the creek. Worldmaker was able to get by safely using his staff (FR-TE, RD). See maps 2 and 5 in Appendix 5.	FR1, FR-TE, DT, RD	ch'ichúyam bam (DT)		
chudáwileno	run off after. Possibly part of the puberty celebration, after the night of dancing.	RD	tsuda'wileno	182	
chúiyi	four	FC			chḿi
chúkchuk	say ch-ch-ch (like saying "good job!")	RD	tsuk'tsuk	34	
chukú	wash (something)	WS	ćukú		
chukút	wash (something)	WS	ćukút		
chúkuti	cricket	FC			chúkutkm
chúkutkm	cricket	FC			chúkuti (FC), chikutkm (FC-R)
chukútkm witḿtmino	dishrag	WS	ćukútkym witẏṫyjno		
chukútno	go wash	FC			
chulm	sleet	FC			
chulálak	yellow or brown	WS	ćulálak		
chulálakpe	yellow or brown	FC			
chuluwa	rattlesnake	JD	culuwa	77	chilwa
chuluwa piwi	a plant in the carrot/parsley family, used to ward off rattlesnakes	JD	culuwapiwi	77	chilwam piwi (FR1)
chúmbm	mouse	WS	ćúmby (WS), cumbo (SPB) "mouth"		
chúmbmbe	penis (This is a little boy's word, probably involving a pun with chúm, "urine," though the literal meaning is clearly "little mouse")	WS	ćúmbybe		
chúmbitbit	urinate scantily (from some disorder)	WS	ćúmbitbit		
chumí	melt	WS	ćumí		
chumí	urine	RD	tsūmi	50	
chumí donínukm	bladder	WS	ćumí donínuky		

Maidu	English	Source	Source Spelling	Page	Other Spellings
chumíliti	something that can melt, a meltable entity	WS	ćumíliti		
chumilitimotó	be covered all over with a meltable substance	RD	tsūmilitimoto'	172	
chúmlo	kidney	WS	ćúmlo		
chúmmi	knife	RD	tsum'mi	60	chámmi (WS), chámi (FC)
chumú	melt	WS	ćumú		
chupai	urinate against	FC-T			
chupí	willow (WS), gray willow, basket-making willow (FC)	WS, FC	ćup̓		chup̓
chupím chá	willow tree	WS	ćupim ćá		
chutáka	poison oak	HM	tsoo-taw'-gah		
chuwá	snowshoe, ski	WS	ćuwá		
chuwám yúkʉ	ski wax	WS	ćuwám júky		
dʉ́	bush (any kind), bushes, thicket	FC, WS	dý		
dʉ́chik	to close up by stuffing brush in the cracks, lock up (a house or room)	WS, WST	dýćik	58:55	
dʉ́chikchʉi	be unable to lock (something)	WST	dýćikćyi	58:55	
dʉ́chono	cover with brush	RD	dö'tsono	236	
dʉkʉ́	flick (something) with the finger, flick away	RD	dökö'	23, 208	dʉḱ
dʉkʉ́	by oneself (FC), only, alone, just... and no more (WS), than, as (in comparisons) (RD): sʉ́ttim dʉkʉ́ "only once;" mʉm máidʉm dʉkʉ́m etóswalawdom "being stronger than that person" dʉkʉ́m máidʉ "one with no relatives"	FC, WS, RD, FC-T	dyḱ (WS), dökö (RD)	128	
dʉkʉ́m tʉ́sdoi	stand alone	FC-E			
dʉkʉ́toʉsito	snap (someone) with thumb and finger (RD), flick with the finger (WS-MM)	RD	dökö'töusito	RD 23, WS-MM 28	
dʉḱkʉ́	lonely, a loner, alone	FC			
dʉp	slippery, slick	WS	dyp		
dʉ́pdʉp	slippery	WS	dýpdyp		
dʉyʉ́yʉ	shake, tremble (from cold or fright or illness)	WS	dyjýjy		
dʉyʉ́yʉti	vibrate (something), shake (something), cause to shake	WS	dyjýjyti		
dá	wipe	WS	dá		
dadáka	shoulder	WS	dadáka		
dadákase	shoulders	FC-E			dadákasi (FC)
dadakasi	green manzanita, greenleaf manzanita	PM-M, JD	da-da-ka-sem (PM-M), dadakasym (JD)	49	
dádaw	wipe off, erase	WS, FC	dádaw		dadáw (FC)
dádawkʉ	eraser	FC-E			
daḱ	be stuck, get stuck	WS	daḱ		
daḱ	glue, sticky substance	WS	daḱ		

Maidu	English	Source	Source Spelling	Page	Other Spellings
dáḱdikno	get stuck onto (something)	WS	dáḱdikno		
Dakḱa	place name for a village with a large sweat house on the Hunt Ranch, on the back road between Taylorsville and Greenville. It is on a flat where the hill starts up beyond the Hunt Ranch (FR-TE). See map 5 in Appendix 5.	FR1, FR-TE	dak ga		
dáḱpai	stick on, get stuck to	WS, WST	dáḱpaj	56:41	
dáḱpai'i	sticky tape	FC-T			
dáḱpaiti	stick (something) on	WS	dáḱpajti		
dáḱpanu	stuck to, be stuck to	WS	dáḱpanu		
Dáḱpem Sewím	place name for Gold Run Creek in the Susanville area, #12 on HLME map 3. The Indian trail from Susanville to Indian Valley passed through Gold Run Creek (HLME). The name means "sticky creek," which refers to the clay-like mud at the bottom of the creek. There are several old village sites in the area. See map 4 in Appendix 5.	HLME	Dakpem Sewim		
dakú	left (side)	WS-MP	dakú		
dakúna	left hand, to the left (WS), left (side) (FC): dakúna ṁḱói "Go left."	WS, FC, FC-R	dakúna		
dáldal	white	WS	dáldal		
dáldalbene wasása	whiteboard spray	FC-T			
dáldalno	be white	RD	dal'dalno	13	
dáldalpe	white	FC			
dáldalpem bóadi	whiteboard	FC-T	boadi daldal		
dáldalpem koyóm chíwchiwi	white field clover (good to eat)	WS	dáldalpem kojóm ćiwćiwi		
dálkṁ	thimbleberry	PM-M	dal-com		
dálkumsṁmi	jumping mouse	HM	dahl'-kum'-so-mim		
dam	borrow	WS	dam		
dámmai	lend	WS	dámmaj		
daṕí	maple	FC, WS	daṕ		daṕ
daṕím chá	maple tree	WS	daṕím ćá		dopim chom (JD)
daṕím waťá	a flat basketry tray or plate (woven of maple stems and used to eat from)	WS	daṕím waťá		
Dasím Yodá	place name, just north of Quincy, #51 on FR map. May be a typo for Daṕím Yodá. See map 2 in Appendix 5.	FR	dasím yodá	370-371	
debá	iris	FC			
dedébṁl	devil (from English)	WS	dedébyl		

Maidu	English	Source	Source Spelling	Page	Other Spellings
dedempumi	a type of wild celery that is edible	JD	dedempumy	77	
dek	be wet	WS	dek		
dékpe	wet (adj)	FC			
dékti	to water (something), urinate (a mild term used by old ladies and little children)	WS	dékti		
déktikɯ	wet (adj)	RD	dek′tikö	116	
déktino	go urinate, go water (something)	WS	déktino		
démi	counting sticks given to each side in gambling	RD-NM	dē′mi		
demtatoko	squaw carpet (plant)	HM	dem-tah-to-ko		
dí	grow (plants, people, etc.), increase in number (RD)	WS, FC, RD	dí	17	
dí	head louse, lice	WS	dí		
díbos	be ready, be ripe (food), be fully grown	FC			
díchikwonomi	scar	WS	díćikwonomi		
díchulto	meadowlark (FC), species of small gray meadow bird, personal Indian name of Lena Thomas Benner (WS)	FC, WS	díćulto		
dídik	gnat, gnat-like flies	WS	dídik		
díhyo	feather plume stick	RD-NM			
di'ím	in there, within: min kɯkán mɯm di'ím hesíwet "there is something for you in there"	WST-DW	di?ím	72:5	
dímenkɯ	dwarf (noun)	WS	dímenky		
dímoto	grow around (something)	RD	di′moto	36	
dímototi	cause (something) to grow around (something)	RD	di′mototi	36	
dip	slippery, slick	WS	dip		
dísito	grow through (something)	WS	dísito		
dítapope	lousy, full of lice: dítapopem kúli "lice-covered widow" (what the meadowlark's song says)	FC, FC-T, FC-R			
díti	cause to grow, do gardening: dítidom "gardening"	FC-E			
diwó	be caught (in a trap)	RD	diwo	62	
dó	taste (something), bite	WS	dó		
dóbabak	have the mouth hanging open	WS	dóbabak		
dóbap	paint	WS	dóbap		dúbap (RD)
dóchekɯ	delicious	WS	dóćeky		
dóchema	delicious	WS	dóćema		
dódato	keep on biting, bite repetitively	WS	dódato		

Maidu	English	Source	Source Spelling	Page	Other Spellings
dódo	feed a little (food) to (someone)	RD	do'do	158	
dódoi	bite off, start biting (something)	RD	do'doi	190	
dódoi	to hold (something) in the mouth	RD	dō'doi	174, 176	
dohá	carry in the mouth	WS	dohá		
dohádoino	carry uphill in the mouth	WS	dohádojno		
doháḱoi	carry off in the mouth	WS	doháḱoj		
dohánoye	carry around in the mouth	WS	dohánoje		
dohá'okit	bring down (in its mouth) (bird)	FC			
dohátno	carry downhill in the mouth	WS	dohátno		
Dókochok Doyím	place name for a village in Indian Valley, #21 on FR map, located at the mouth of Hunt Canyon, about a mile SE of Bunúk. It means "smeared mouth" (FR-HY, FR-AG). See map 5 in Appendix 5.	FR, FR1	dókoćok doyím (FR), dokochot doyim (FR1)	370-371	dokochot doyim (FR1), Dokochotim (FR-HY)
Dókochom	place name for North Valley (Indian Valley). See map 5 in Appendix 5.	FC-map			
dol	tie (something)	WS	dol		
dólchono	tie (something) around (something)	WS	dólćono		
Doldinom	place name including Humbug, Stover Mountain, Red Mountain to the west, #19 on LM map. See map 1 in Appendix 5.	LM	Dol-de-nome		
dolím motó	tie (things) up together in a bunch	WS	dolím motó		
dólkit	tie up	WS	dólkit		
dólpai	tie (something) onto (something)	WS	dólpaj		
dólsitoye	tie (something) round and round	WS	dólsitoje		
dólwasa	not know how to tie anything	WS	dólwasa		
dólyo	tie several knots	WS	dóljo		
dómaki	have a taste, try some (food): tené mínsᴀm dómaki "Just you try some, just taste it, all of you"	RD	dō'maki	44	
dómi	a girl who has just attained puberty	RD-NM			
dómim uyí	menstrual hut	RD-NM			
dón	grab, catch, hold: nik ma dónpi "hold my hand"	WS, FC, WST	don	54:23	
dónbis	hang onto	WS	dónbis		
dónchmi	be unable to reach	WS	dónćyj		

Maidu	English	Source	Source Spelling	Page	Other Spellings
dónhun	catch, capture	RD	dōn'hun	132	
donhúnbᴧk	try to catch (but not succeed)	RD	dōnhun'bök, dōnhön'buk	212, 224	
doníno	hold	FC			
doнínoḱoi	carry off, take away	FC			
donínoye	carry around	FC			
donínu	hold, hold onto	WS, WST	donínu	58:46	
dónkᴧ	catcher	FC			
dónkᴧm máidᴧ	police (catcher person)	FC			
dónkato	puberty ceremony for girls	RD-NM			
dónomen	to not drop (something): chíťaka dónomenkᴧm kᴧlókbe kᴧkán "she is a woman who never drops bear grass"	RD	dōn'omen	174	
dónwiḱa	grab hold of	WS	dónwiḱa		
dónwiḱachono	jump over into (somewhere) while holding onto (something or someone)	WS	dónwiḱaćono		
dónwiḱadoi	grab (someone or something) and pull (it) up	WS	dónwiḱadoj		
dónwikakit	drag someone to (someplace)	RD	dōn'wikakit	114	
dónwikanu	snatch (someone) and carry them off	RD	dōn'wikanu	124	
dónwiḱatno	reach down and grab hold of (something)	WS	dónwiḱatno		
dónwikatono	drag someone away	RD	dōn'wikatonō'	114	
dópaski	the king in playing cards	WS	dópaski		
dópasno	bearded	WS	dópasno		
dópu	tofu	FC			
dóskol	snore	RD, WS	dos'kol (RD), dóskol (WS)	168	
dóťᴧinope	having a big ugly mouth, prognathous	WS	dóťyjnope		
dóti	to taste (intransitive, as in "tastes good," "tastes bitter," etc.): tetét yahát dóti'usan "it used to taste so good"	WS, WST	dóti	52:13	
dótipe	tasting (good, bad, etc.): mᴧm maháti tetét yahát dótipem kᴧkán "the bread is very good tasting"	FC			
dótodoto	Pleiades constellation	RD-NM			
dúbap	white paint: dúbapni "with white paint"	RD	dū'bap	74	
dúbat	white paint: dúbatni "with white paint"	RD	dū'bat	76	
dúki	sack, small bag with a drawstring	WS	dúki		
duḱulemyo	shooting stars (flower)	JD	duḱu·lemjo	67	
dúpe	be cold (weather)	FC			
dúpe	cold (physically, of a person)	WS	dúpe		

73

Maidu	English	Source	Source Spelling	Page	Other Spellings
dúpeti	cause cold, make (someone) cold	FC			
dúpeti	cold (of the weather, but not freezing)	WS	dúpeti		
dúpetidoi	get cold (of the weather, but not freezing)	WS	dúpetidoj		
dúpeyi	the cold (weather)	FC			
dus	powder	WS	dus		
duschík	close the eyes	RD	dustsik'	122	
duschikíno	have one's eyes closed	RD	dūstsikin'o	168	
duschikínu	keep the eyes closed	RD	dustsikīn'nu	124	
duschikínuwo	tell (someone) to close their eyes	RD	dustsikīn'nuwo	122	
dut	suck (not as an infant)	WS	dut		
dútap	suck	WS-MP	dútap		dúttap
dútdut	suck (as mosquito) (RD), suck, as a curing shaman or on bones while eating (WS)	RD, WS	dut'dut (RD), dútdut (WS)	160	
dúttap	suck in curing	WS-MP	dúttap		dútap
dútwoyo	hire a shaman to suck out a disease	WS	dútwojo		
dúwuwu	shiver	FC			duwu'ul (FC-R)
ebɷ	manzanita	FC			
ebɷ́bɷ	be a long time, be a while	RD	ebö'bö	144	
ebɷ́bɷm	for a long time	HY			
ebɷ́dom	be a long time, be old (as any object which has been around a long time)	WS	ʔebýdom		
ebɷ́m	a long time: ebɷ́m minná pínmenḱas "I haven't heard from you in a long time"	WS, FC	ʔebým		ebum
ebɷ́webismenwet	not long afterwards...	RD	ebö'wēbismenwet	194	
echúktiyo	to partially dry (something)	RD	etsuk'tiō	228	
edáldalnope	whitish, light colored	RD	edal'dalnope	13	
edi	onion	FC			
e'e	a sound a child makes when you needing help going to the bathroom	FC-T			
ehɷ́s	thick in consistency	WS	ʔehýs		
ehɷ́sti	thicken, make thick	WS	ʔehýsti		
ehómi	white pelican	HM	ā-ho'-mim		
éite	younger brother (RD), Nisenan ei= "elder brother"	RD	ēi'te	202	
ekɷ	usually: mɷḱí téchom mɷmɷ́ ekɷ odáto'usan "his two children usually came out to meet him." with negative verb - "never:" cheménwono'ekɷḱas "I have never seen before"	RD	ēkö	228, 176	
ekákasuknope	blue, bluish color	RD	ekā'kasuknope	184, 188	
eḱáw	wonderful, beautiful, excellent	WS	ʔeḱáw		

Maidu	English	Source	Source Spelling	Page	Other Spellings
ekáwche	admire the looks of, look at with wonder or delight	WS	ʔekáwće		
ekáwcheti	look beautiful, look wonderful	WS	ʔekáwćeti		
ekáwchetipe	beautiful, wonderful-looking	WS, FC	ʔekáwćetipe		mkáwchetipe (RD)
ekáwche'us	be conceited, snobbish, stuck up, vain	WS, FC	ʔekáwćeʔus		
ekáwche'us húweye	act like a snob, act conceited	WS	ʔekáwćeʔus húweje		
ekáwche'uspe	uppity, impressed with oneself, vain	FC			
ekáwkinu	silent, quiet (as with spellbound wonder)	WS	ʔekáwkinu		
ekáwpintisape	one who has "attitude," feisty person	FC			
ekdá	day (when counting): helúnini ekdá wosípkan "a few days went by."	RD	ekda'	26	
ékda	dawn, morning (WS) This is earlier morning than bénekto	WS	ʔékda (WS)		
ékda	to dawn, to be (doing) at dawn: okítmenpem ékdakan "at dawn she did not come home." paní pánpedom ékdakas "at dawn I was smoking tobacco." sáichokninima ékdachet okítas "after the sixth (day) has dawned, I should come home."	WS, RD	ek'da (RD), ʔékda (WS)	102, 196, 218	
ékdadakit	be nearly dawn	RD	ek'dadakit	78	
ékdadoi	shine, twinkle (verb)	FC			
ékdadoi	sunrise, dawn (noun)	WS	ʔékdadoj		
ékdadoikm	east	WS	ʔékdadojky		
ékdadoikmdi	to the east	RD	ek'dadoiködi	26, 230	
ékdadoina	to the east (where the sun is rising)	FC			
ekdaipotó	be almost daylight (the subject of this verb is kódom): kódom ekdaipotóchet mkóikan "when it was almost daylight, he left."	RD	ekdaipotō'	70	
ékdakit	be completely light, have dawned	WS	ʔékdakit		
ékdakoi	morning, dawn (noun): yahám ékdakoi nik bei myéma'ankano "a good morning, may you come to me"	WST-RP	ʔékdakoi	66:33	
ékdam lmlḿ	morning star	WS	ʔékdam lylý		
ékdam pokó	sun	WS	ʔékdam pokó		
ékdaye	get to be morning, dawn	WS	ʔékdaje		
ékdoina	to the east	FC-E			
ékdoinan	from the east	FC			

Maidu	English	Source	Source Spelling	Page	Other Spellings
ekí	day, daylight, light: ekí ma'át "all day"	WS, FC, RD	ʔek (WS), eki' (RD)	110	ek
ekím ésto	middle of the day	FC			
ekím éstona	toward midday	FC			
ekím nedí	daydream	FC			
ekím pokó	sun	WS	ʔekím pokó		
ékluť	brightest	FC			
ekókow	grayish	WS	ʔekókow		
ékpm	manzanita, the larger bush-like kind which grows at moderate altitudes	WS	ʔékpy		
ékpe	eat breakfast	RR-EP			
ékpe	lunch (WS), breakfast (FC)	WS, FC	ʔékpe		
ékpe hékitdi	in the afternoon	WS	ʔékpehékitdi		
elák	summer	PM-D	eh-lak		
elákḱoi	start to redden, blush	WS	ʔelákḱoj		
elaḱoiti	make (someone) blush	FC-E			
elákti	cause to blush, make (someone) blush	FC-R			
elálak	reddish	WS	ʔelálak		
elálakpe	reddish	FC-E			
elespúika	dove	WS, FC	ʔelespújka (WS), eléspuikm (FC)		eléspuikm (FC)
eluku	black moss	PM-M	e-lu-coo		
én	wall	RD	en	104	
éni	tongue	FC, WS	ʔen		en
énnan	near the wall (of the house)	RD	en'nan	104	
énto	lick	WS	ʔénto		
épmli	apple (from English)	FC			
epḿ	manzanita	FC, JD	eʔpum	49	
epḿm hini	manzanita berry	FC			
epḿm tm	manzanita powder	FC			
epéni	bumblebee, yellowjacket, bee: epénim wólem "honey bee"	FC, WS, FC-T, FC-R	ʔepén		epén, epine (FC-T), epini (FC-R)
epi	sister-in-law: as a kinship term, this word must have a prefix, either mm, nik, or min (see Mountain Maidu Grammar, Lesson 6 for more details)	FC			
epín	above, over	WS	ʔepín		
epín	ask, question, ask a question	WS, FC	ʔepín		
epínchedónu	be continuously looking up, be looking up the whole time	RD	epin'tsedon'u	212	
epíndom wéye	question words	FC			
epíni	up above	FC			
epínim ḱódo	sky-land, heaven	RD	epin'iñkodo	150	
epínim koyó	heaven, sky	WS, FC	ʔepínim kojó		epínin koyó
epínno	go ask	WS	ʔepínno		

76

Maidu	English	Source	Source Spelling	Page	Other Spellings
epínnoyesakmm máidm	reporter, someone who is always going around asking questions	FC-E			
épti	be strong, healthy, big, powerful	FC			
épti	strong (mentally, spiritually) brave, rough and tough (FC), scary, frightening, awesome, fearful (WS): éptim wasása nisé wéyemmni, yehéptoye'usas "when he told us frightening stuff (stories), we used to get scared."	FC, WS, WST	ʔépti	52:15	
éptito	be strong, be healthy	HY			
éptitoto	be courageous together	FC			
éptito'us	strengthen oneself	FC			
éskocho	gnaw, gnaw on	WS	ʔéskoćo		
éskochowekoi	run around gnawing on things	WST	ʔéskoćo wekój	50:6	
éssem	be cautious, watch out for various dangers (such as snakes, poison oak, etc.) This word is not used for being cautious about people.	WS	ʔéssem		
ésto	be the middle of: ḱúmmen éstodom ka'án. "It's the middle of winter."	HY			
ésto	in the middle, middle: éstom kḿsdi "in the middle of the ridge"	WS, RD	ʔésto (WS), es'to	34	
éstodi	in the middle, in the center, inside	FC, RD		64	
éstoluťi	right smack in the middle	RD	es'toluti	224	
éstom yamáni	Sutter Buttes	FC			
éstoti	put (something) in the middle), put (something) between	WS	ʔéstoti		
éswo	go halfway	RD	es'wo, es'wō	168, 200	
éswokoi	be halfway to, be far from	WS	ʔéswokoj		
éswomit	be half into, come down into the middle of	WS, WST-DW	ʔéswomit	72:1	
éswomitti	have (something) halfway into	WS	ʔéswomitti		
éswowo	be about halfway to (a place): chawatána éswowochet, yohónḱan "when (she was) about halfway to the edge of the forest, it thundered."	RD	es'wowō	200	
éswowodiknoitimáldoi	get about halfway up, get almost all the way up	RD	eswowodiknoitimal'doi	176-178	
éswowokit	be about halfway down	WS	ʔéswowokit		
éswowokoi	be about halfway to	WS	ʔéswowokoj		

Maidu	English	Source	Source Spelling	Page	Other Spellings
éswowosipin	be halfway out of: ḱódo éswowosipiniset yohónḱan "once I was about halfway out of the area, it thundered"	RD	es'wowosipin	200	
éswowotpindi	halfway down	RD	es'wōwōtpindi	128	
éswoye	be nearby	WS	ʔéswoje		
etáp	stop, cease	WS	ʔetáp		
etápkinu	shut up, stop talking: etapkinupi! "shut up!"	WS	ʔetápkinu		
etápmenchono	not stop doing, keep doing on and on	RD	etap'mentsano	202	
etápti	stop (something)	WS	ʔetápti		
etátapkit	stop little by little (rain - subject is ḱódom, or ḱadíkpem ḱódom): ḱadíkpem ḱódom etátapkitḱan "the rain let up, little by little"	RD	itat'apkit	196	
éti	older sister, aunt: as a kinship term, this word must have a prefix, either mm, nik, or min (see Mountain Maidu Grammar, Lesson 6 for more details)	FC, WS	ʔéti		
étikmto	a pair of sisters together, two sisters (WS), pair including older sister (can be a brother and sister) (RD)	WS	ʔétikyto (WS), etī'kötom (RD)	140	etíkmtom
etítit	greenish, bluish	WS	ʔetítit		
etítitpe	greenish, bluish				
etósboduk	be not very strong	WS	ʔetósboduk		
etósi	physically strong	WS	ʔetós		
etósmen	weak	WS	ʔetósmen		
etóspe	strong (physically), muscular	FC, FC-T			
etósti	strengthen, get an erection	WS	ʔetósti		
etóswalaw	be stronger, exceed in strength: ka'ápem máidmm dmḱḿm tetét etóswalawdom ónkomkinuḱan "Being much stronger/more powerful than that other kind of people, he beat them and kept going."	RD	etos'walau	128	
étu	Wait! Stop!	WS	ʔétu		
etúdede	wait a little bit, hold on!	FC			
etúti	cause to wait: etútidom "a break"	FC-E			
etúweti	a break, pause	FC			
e'uschenu	look within oneself	FC-R			uschenu (FC-T)
eymm	freeze	WS	ʔejý		
eymm	ice	WS	ʔejý		
eymkit	be icy	FC			
eymsape	freezing, slow	FC			

Maidu	English	Source	Source Spelling	Page	Other Spellings
eyá	be like this, this way, in this way, do in this way, do like this	FC, WS	ʔejá		ayá (RD)
eyádawinu	be sticking out like this	WS	ʔejádawinu		
eyádom	this way, doing (something) this way	WS	ʔejádom		
eyái	say like this, talk like this	WS	ʔejáj		
eyáiwei	say (it) this way, put (it) this way, say (it) in this manner: eyáiwéiwonom kmkán máisem wulúdoimadom "this is what they said before they started dancing"	WS, WST-GP	ʔejájwej	68:37	
eyánu	stay like this, stay this way (WS), keep on this way (FC)	WS	ʔejánu		
eyáwei	like this (adverb)	WST-DW	ʔejáwje	70:4	
eyáweyeti	do (it) this way, do like this	WS	ʔejáwejeti, ʔejáwjeti		eyáwyeti
eyáwini	this kind, this	WS	ʔejáwini		
Eyolim Ḱoyó	place name for Meadow Valley. See map 2 in Appendix 5.	PM-D	eh-yo-ling-koyo		
hm	house (WS), bark house (FC): nem hmdi máisem lmkmnoḱan. "They went into a great house."	WS, FC, RD	hý (WS), hö' (RD)	208	
hm	pick, gather, collect	WS	hý		
hmbmchik	close up a house	RD	höbö'tsik	216	
hmbmk	have emotion, experience feelings, feel	WS	hybýk		hubuk, hubmk
hmbmkti	to feel a certain way (to the touch, for example: feel warm, feel frozen, feel soft, etc.): yahát hmbmktiḱas "I feel good."	WS, FC	hybýkti		
hmbmkti'us	make oneself feel (a certain way): yahát hmbmkti'us - make yourself happy	FC			
hmbmkto	love (someone)	WS	hybýkto		
hmbmktoto	love each other, be in love	WS	hybýktoto		
hmbmktotopecho	a couple in love with each other	WS	hybýktotopećo		
hmbás	sweep (verb)	FC			hebás (WS)
hmbáskm	broom, sweeper	FC, FC-E			hebáskm (WS)
hmbís	take care of, care for, raise (a child)	WS, WST	hybís	60:63	
hmbó	house; temporary or summer house, as opposed to the winter dug-in bark house (PM-M)	WS, PM-M	hybó (WS), hubo (PM-M)	5	
hmbó húkitmen	homesick	WS	hybó húkitmen		
hmbó wi'ipe	homeless	FC			
hmbóboto	camps, villages, clusters of houses, towns	RD	höbo'boto	174	

Maidu	English	Source	Source Spelling	Page	Other Spellings
hɨbókɨ	have a house, live somewhere	RD	höbō'kö	196, 202, 218	
hɨbókɨpe	homeowner	WS	hybókype		
hɨbókit	bring home	RD	höbo'kit	104	
hɨbóm k̓awí	house dirt, dirt floor	FC			
hɨbóyák̓k̓en	might live (somewhere), might have a house	FC, WST		WST 10:9	
hɨchɨ́	have sex, copulate (This is the most forceful word in the language for sexual intercourse)	WS	hyćý		
hɨchɨ́toya	want to have sex	WS	hyćýtoja		
hɨhá	use (something)	RD	höhā'	234	
hɨhwé	make a speech, exhort	RD	höhwē'	26, 166	
hɨ́hwepai	talk in a loud, shouting voice	WS	hýhwepaj		
hɨ́k̓ɨp	good health, healthiness	WS	hýk̓yp		
hɨk̓ɨ́pi	health	FC			
hɨk̓ɨ́pkupe	healthy	FC			
hɨk̓ɨ́pti	heal (someone)	FC			
hɨk̓ɨ́s	nudge with the elbow	WS	hyk̓ýs		
hɨk̓ɨ́sto	nudge (someone)	WS	hyk̓ýsto		
hɨ́k̓oi	go pick	WS	hýk̓oj		
hɨ́k̓oiti	go pick (something) for (someone), go gather	WS, FC	hýk̓ojti		
hɨ́k̓oiyew	go off to pick (foods) for a while	RD	hö'koiyēu	96	
hɨ́kwo	grouse (bird)	RD, WS, FC	hökwo (RD), hýkwo (WS)	62	hɨ́kwa (FC)
hɨ́lilisno	speed up, do (something) faster, pick up the pace	WS, FC-T	hýlilisno		
hɨlíslisno	hurry	FC			
hɨ́m k̓anáidi	inside the house	RD	höñ'kanaidi	192	
hɨmɨ́smai	charge money	WS	hymýsmaj		
hɨmɨ́smanu	owe	WS	hymýsmanu		
hɨ́mtɨti	rafters, beams of house	RD	höm'töti	114	
hɨ́n	exclamation (used when something cold and wet touches one's skin)	WS	hýn		
hɨ́n adom	say "ew!" (hɨ́n), as in something is gross	FC-R			
Hɨnkɨ	place name for Indian Falls on Indian Creek, several miles upstream from its confluence with Spanish Creek. #5 on LM map. According to Tom Epperson, the name means the sound of an approaching storm. See maps 2 and 5 in Appendix 5.	FR1, LM, DT, FR-TE	Humku-Sewim (LM), Hümkü (FR-TE)	48(DT)	Hɨnkɨ Sewím
hɨ́no	go around gathering, go around picking	RD	hö'no	76, 172	
hɨ́noti	go pick (something) for (someone)	WS	hýnoti		

Maidu	English	Source	Source Spelling	Page	Other Spellings
hɵ́noye	go around picking (foods)	RD	hö'noye	96	
hɵpái	scratch(something) on (something), strike (as a match) (WS), flick with the thumb (FC)	WS, FC	hypáj		
hɵpáikɵ	match, cigarette lighter	WS, FC	hypájky		
hɵpé	have sex, copulate (This is a slightly less forceful word than hɵchɵ́): hɵpé'us ɵkói! "Go fuck yourself!"	WS, FC-R	hypé		
hɵpéto	have sex with, copulate together	WS	hypéto		
hɵpétoḱoi	go have sex with each other, go copulate together	WS	hypétoḱoj		
hɵ́stakobós	scare away all	RD	hös'takobos'	190	
hɵstanóye	go around scaring (something) away	RD	höstanō'ye	216	
hɵ́staye	scare (things) away, shoo (things) off	WS	hýstaje		
hɵ́ťi	fat, grease (noun)	FC, WS	hyť		hɵ́ť
hɵ́ťim maháti	fry bread	FC			
hɵ́ťluťi	a very fat one, the fattest one	WS	hýťluťi		
hɵ́ťpe	fat (adj), obese	WS, FC	hýťpe		
hɵ́tpin	go down (mountain)	RD	höt'pin	126	ɵ́tpin
hɵ́wepaito	make a speech to (people)	RD	höh'wēpaito	80	
hɵwéye	think (a rare variant of húweye)	WS	hywéje		húweye
hɵyá	build, construct (not necessarily a house), spin a web	WS	hyjá		
hɵ́yam wasása	building materials	FC-R			
hɵyámoto	build a house together	RD	höyā'moto	236	
hɵ́ye	pick, gather	WS	hýje		
há	say: nik hásmɵni "when he said to me" (compare: asmɵni - "if I do"); has mɵm wónodom kɵkán "I have to say he is dead"	RD	ha	28, 118	a
ha'ɵkói	go along doing (conjugated, and goes with one or more verbs in -dom)	RD	ha ökoi'	32	

Maidu	English	Source	Source Spelling	Page	Other Spellings
ha'ái	probably do (verb): nik núkpapaimakɱkan ha'áichoi'a "they will probably laugh at me," ha'áiḱan wónom máidɱ wi'ítimapem "he will probably wipe out the humans" ɱpéḱapem húikɱpdom ayádom ha'ái'enḱes hunmoyemapem " while everyone is healthy as we now are, we should probably go hunting"	RD	haai'	32, 104, 156	
ha'ái	probably, likely, hopefully, it seems: kɱkás ha'ái min! "I am likely to do it to you!" mɱm máidɱm ha'ái okítmenkɱḱan "it seems that man didn't come home," tetét ha'ái "It's obvious that..." (RD), nevertheless, on the other hand, really, because (WS)	RD, WS, FC-T	hai, haai' (RD), haʔáj, haj (WS)	72, 142, 156, 170, 178, 206	
ha'ái ka...	be the way (someone) says it	WS	haʔáj ka...		
hachís	sneeze (verb)	FC			
hachóno	go through (RD), come riding over in a vehicle (WS)	RD, WS	hatson'o (RD), haćóno (WS)	30, 32	
hadá	far away, distant, high, tall (RD), deep (FC), a place far away, deep (in water) (WS): hadám ḱódoina ɱḱóidom "going quite a distance" uním tetém cha waláwdɱḱbeḱan hadá "he was taller than these big trees"	RD, FC, WS, WST	hada' (RD), hadá (WS)	46, 234 (RD), 58:50 (WS)	
hadá chódoi	blaze up (as flames)	WS	hadá ćódoj		
hadá chódoiti	make the fire blaze up	WS	hadá ćódojti		
hadá ma'át yɱnɯ́skit	stoop over (like an old person), bend far over	RD	hadā'maat yönös'kitdom	76	
hadádadi	in the distance	FC			
hadádadi'ebis	stay back	FC			
hadádaw	out of reach, far away	WS	hadádaw		
hadádi	far away	RD, WS	hadā'di (RD), hadádi (WS)	136	
hadádoi	far up high, high up (WS), tall (of plant) (FC)	WS, FC	hadádoj		
hadádoiboduk	low (in position)	WS	hadádojboduk		

Maidu	English	Source	Source Spelling	Page	Other Spellings
hadádoiwiyakka	look tall: mᴧm wédam kᴧkán múnmunim sáwim yahát díbosdom hadádoiwiyakkadom. "The spring festival is when the mugwort plant is fully grown and looking tall."	WST	hadádojwijakka	76:4	
hadám k̓ódoidi	long ago	WS-MP	hadán k̓ódojdi		
hadána	off in the distance	FC			
hadánan	from far away	WS	hadánan		
hadánawet	in the distance	FC-R			
hadánk̓oi	be a distance away, be far away	WST-MG	hadánk̓oj	78:10	
hadátok̓oi	go farther, go a distance	RD	hadā'tokoi	232	
hadáw	bring (something) down, across	RD	hadau'	126	
hadáwaito	wide (as a stream)	WS	hadáwajto		
hadáwaitoboduk	narrow	WS	hadáwajtoboduk		
hadíkno	arrive bringing (something)	RD	hadik'no	126	
hádikno	come to the end of: pai hádiknodom "coming to the end of the footprints"	RD	hā'dikno	232	
hadó	load (noun), pack (noun), backpack	RD, WS	hadō' (RD), hadó (WS)	206	
hadói	to load up stuff on one's back, to hoist up on one's back (RD), carry on the back (WS)	RD, WS	hadoi' (RD), hadój (WS)	224	
hádoi	start out following: pai hádoidom "start following tracks"	RD	hā'doi	232	
hadóidi pʌ́tye	untie one's pack: mᴧk̓í hadóidi pʌ́tyek̓an "he untied his pack"	RD	hadoi'di pöt'yedom	206	
hadóikᴧ	suitcase	WS	hadójky		
hadóikᴧm kaléta	truck	FC			
hadóipai	put something on one's back	RD	hadoi'pai	106	
hadónu	wear, have in one's possession (as in one's pocket), have as part of one's equipment	WS	hadónu		
háhadoi	rise, start to rise (sun)	RD	hāhadoi	56	
hai	as, being: ni hai yep̓óni "I, as a headman" "I, being a headman" (In all instances, this is Coyote speaking. It appears Coyote is speaking Konkow "I am a chief.")	RD	hai	52, 132, 134	
hai ak̓án	what they call: wólem hai mᴧm "brake" ak̓án "White people call it 'brake'." mᴧm "key" ak̓án hai "what is called a 'key'."	WST	haj ʔak̓án	58:46, 55	
hai'í	surely, really, actually, currently	RD	haii'	72	

Maidu	English	Source	Source Spelling	Page	Other Spellings
hai'í kᴧḱan	surely it is, surely they are	RD	haii'kökan	72, 136	
hai'i?	what? (if you didn't hear)	FC			
haiyé	come back	RD	haiyē'	32	
haiyéwe	go back taking something, take something back	RD	haiyē'wē	124	
háiyum	yawn	FC			
háiyuyum	yawn a lot, be sleepy	FC			
haḱ	strap, packstrap, carrying strap	WS	haḱ		
hakáka	bitter (adj), gall, bile	WS	hakáka		
hakákakᴧ	gall bladder	WS	hakákaky		
hákalulu	whirlwind	RD	hak'alūlū	132	hákḱalulu
hakélwodoi	raise up (intransitive) a little bit	RD	hakel'wodoi	116	
hakélwodoikato	raise (oneself) up a little bit (off something), lift (oneself) up a bit from (something)	RD	hakel'wodoikato	116	
hakínu	sit, be parked, be in a place	WS	hakínu		
hakít	build (a house)	RD	hakit'	154, 164	
hákḱalulu	dust devil, whirlwind	WS	hákḱalulu		hákalulu
haḱói	push, pull (something) along	WS	haḱój		
hákwowopapai	pack in bundles for carrying	RD	hak'wowopapai'	202	
hal	tell a lie, prevaricate	WS	hal		
halᴧk	pulsate, to beat (pulse, heart)	WS	halýk		
haláp	carry in the hand (RD), drag (something) (WS)	RD, WS	halap' (RD), haláp (WS)	196	
halápdaw	drag (something) out (WS), drag down and out (FC)	WS, FC	halápdaw		
halápdoi	drag (something) upwards	WS	halápdoj		
halápkit	drag (something) down, drag this way	WS	halápkit		
halápḱoi	drag (something) away, drag off	WS	halápḱoj		
halápno	drag (something) along	WS	halápno		
halápnoye	drag (something) around	WS	halápnoje		
halápye	drag (something) towards	WS	halápje		
hálbaḱu	shiner, species of little fish (WS), minnow (HM)	WS	hálbaḱ		hálbukkᴧ
hálbis	outside of marriage (adv): yepíwipem kᴧlém ma'át kᴧḱán hálbis tékᴧdom amᴧni tékᴧmapem. "Even women without husbands are having children outside of marriage, intentionally getting pregnant."	RD	halbüs	50	

Maidu	English	Source	Source Spelling	Page	Other Spellings
hálbisi	virgin (RD), unmarried: hálbisim kᴍlóknonom kᴍḱán yépkᴍdom dᴍḱᴍ yepíḱan wᴍkdimotomapem. "Unmarried women are only marrying (being intimate with) men to form a lasting partnership (being united as one)."	RD	halbüsi	50	
hálbukkᴍ	minnow	HM	hal'buk'-kum		hálbaḱ
hálche	refuse to believe, reject	WS	hálće		
hálcheche	contradict	WS	hálćeće		
hálchecheto	contradict (someone)	WS	hálćećeto		
hálcheto	disagree, be at odds	WS	hálćeto		
hálchetoto	disagree with each other	WS	hálćetoto		
halé	win a game	WS	halé		
haléhudoi	almost win (game)	WS	haléhudoj		
halémmemmoto	be seated and adjusted to begin (game)	WS	halémmemmoto		
hálhudanpe	liar, lying	WS	hálhudanpe		
halíle	concerning, about: halíle adóm "be talking about" "be about" (what a song or story is about)	RD	halī'le	94	
halím máidᴍ	liar	WS	halím májdy		
hálkᴍ	liar	WS	hálky		
hálḱo	carrot	WS	hálḱo		
hálpapai	to trick (someone), deceive: kᴍlóknono hálpapaidom kᴍlékᴍkᴍm ḱódom matá. "Let it be a women-seducing world. Let it be a world where one marries women by tricking them."	RD	hal'papai	196	
hálsa	be dishonest	FC			
hálsa	liar, habitual liar, dishonest person	WS	hálsa		
hálsasape	liar, habitual liar	WS	hálsasape		
halsa'us	lie to oneself	FC			
halúḱup	be clustered on, massed on (as flies on something)	WS	halúḱup		
ham	cook (verb)	FC			
ham	damn!	RD	ham!	178, 220	
ham cha	willow tree	FC			
hamít	soak, douse, immerse	WS	hamít		
hamítyo	soak a bunch of things	WS	hamítjo		
hamóna	to where, toward where, in that/what direction	FC			homónna (WS)
hamónan	from where	FC			homónnan
hamóndi	where, in what place, at what place	FC			homóndi
hamóni	who	FC			homóni
hamónik	whose	FC			homónik

Maidu	English	Source	Source Spelling	Page	Other Spellings
hamónim maḱáde?	who is it (at the door or phone)? who is he/she?	FC			homónim maḱáde?
hamóniwet	someone	FC			homóniwet
hámsi	acorn (WS), black oak acorn (FC)	WS, FC	hámsi (FC, WS), han-shee (PM-D)		hamshi (PM-D)
hámsim baťí	acorn meal	WS	hámsim baťí		
hámsim chá	black oak tree	WS, JD	hámsim ćá (WS), hamsumća (JD	53	
hámsim hómma	acorn soup	WS	hámsim hómma		
hámsim luťí	black oak	WS	hámsim luťí		
hámsim maháti	acorn bread	WS	hámsim maháti		
hámsim soyó	acorn dough	WS	hámsim sojó		
han	gather (something, like acorns)	FC			
hanɨ́	carry (something not alive)	WS	haný		
hanɨ́koi	carry (something) off or away	WS	haný́koj		
hanɨ́koisma	what I am carrying, what is being carried	RD	hanö'koisma	134	
Hanɨ́leke	place name for Honey Lake. Although some say this word was taken from English, the word has Maidu elements and could mean "running off holding something." There is a Maidu story told by Tom Young (RD p. 172-183) about the moon man, who kidnaps children, and runs back carrying the kidnapped child to his home in the Honey Lake valley. See maps 1 and 4 in Appendix 5.	RD	hanöleke	66, 172	Hanílek (WS)
hanɨ́n	haul	WS	hanýn		
hanɨ́nno	haul	WS	hanýnno		
hanɨ́no	carry (something) along	WS	hanýno		
hanɨ́'okit	carry (something) on one's back (RD), bring in, as a crop or game from hunting (WS)	RD, WS	hanö'okit (RD), haný?okit (WS)	228	
hanɨ́okitoyé	bring (something) back	RD	hanö'okitoye'	104	
hanɨ́sito	carry (something) across	WS	hanýsito		
hanɨ́sitopin	carry across towards	WS, WST-DW	hanýsitopin	72:3	
hanɨ́ye	carry in, arrive carrying, bring in, bring	WS, FC	hanýje		
hanána	good (food, etc.)	FC			
hanána yahátidom	making (food) taste good	RD	hanā'na yakā'tidom	110	
hanáni	chokecherry (FC), Western Chokecherry (JD)	FC, JD	hanhanym	71	hanhani (JD)
Hanánim Sewím	place name for Baxter Creek, Buntingville, #4 on HLME map 3. Means "chokecherry creek." See map 4 in Appendix 5.	HLME	Hananam Sewim		

Maidu	English	Source	Source Spelling	Page	Other Spellings
hánbeťek	run away holding (something)	WS	hánbeťek		
hanbeťékchono	flee holding (something) in hands	WS	hanbeťékćono		
hanbeťékdoi	bolt and flee, holding (something) in hands	WS	hanbeťékdoj		
hánchibmi	personal Indian name of Tom Young	WS	hánćibyj		
hané	honey (from English)	WS	hané		hani (FC)
hanéyakmm epéni	honey bee	WS	hanéjakym ʔepéni		
hanháni	western chokecherry	JD	hanhanym	71	hanáni
háni	band-tailed pigeon	HM	hah'nim		
Hanílek	place name for Honey Lake. See map 4 in Appendix 5 under Hanmleke.	WS	hanílek		Hanmleke (RD)
hániyakm	honey bee	FC			
hánno	haul, as with a truck or wagon	WS	hánno		
háno	travel around to, follow (something) to: hánodom bmdam máidmki kódoinantedi "traveling to the land of the northern people;" homo ma'át pai hánomenchoi'a "he did not get anywhere following the tracks."	RD	hān'o	30, 230	
hánokiti	throw (someone) down	RD	han'ōkiti	86	
hanó'ono	look for tracks or footprints, try to follow (tracks)	RD	hanō'onō'	64	
hánpai	quail, valley quail	FC			
hánpi	land on the ground, come down	RD	han'pi	82	
hánwele	run holding something in the arms	WS	hánwele		
hánwelekoi	run off holding (something)	WS	hánwelekoj		
hánwidoi	pull (someone) up by grabbing under the arms	WS	hánwidoj		
hánwilekoi	run off carrying something	RD	han'wilekoi	94	
hánwilekoiye	run off carrying something towards	RD	han'wilekoiye	94	
hánwochono	drag (something) over	RD	han'wotsono	110	
hánwokit	forcefully lay or drag (someone) down (RD), lay (something) down (WS)	RD, WS	han'wōkit (RD), hánwokit (WS)	100, 114	
hánwokitkm	a place where one lays or drags (someone) down	RD	han'wokitkö	114	
hánwokitkmdi	in the place where (someone) is laid down	RD	han'wokitködi	114	
hányewei	return in a vehicle	WS	hánjewej		
hányochono	dive into (somewhere) with (something) in the arms	WS	hánjoćono		

Maidu	English	Source	Source Spelling	Page	Other Spellings
hap	if only: hap nik mᴍkánim ka'abᴍ'ᴍ "if only the same thing would happen to me again." chebᴍ'as hap "if only we (2) could see"	WST, RD	hap	56:36 (WST), 184 (RD)	
háp	hoist, lift, carry on back (something alive)	WS	háp		
hapá	of course, precisely	WS	hapá		hap'á (FC)
hap'á 'as káusas	I am always, of course…, as usual, I am…: wasám hapá 'as káusas wépam "I am always the bad coyote."	RD	hapas' kaū'sas	116	
hápdaw	hand down, take (something) down	WS, WST	hápdaw	74:9	
hápdoi	hoist up onto one's back (as a child) (WS), hoist, lift (RD)	WS, RD	hápdoj (WS), apdoi', ap'doi (RD)	76, 84, 232	apdoi
hápe	ask for (something)	WS	hápe		ápe (RD)
hápeḱoi	go ask for (something)	WS	hápeḱoj		
hapíno	give, hand to: liáni máidᴍna hapínoḱan "he handed money to the man."	RD	hapin'o	210	
hápmit	put down into (by hand)	RD	hap'mit	76	
hápno	hand (something) over to, hand to: sᴍ́ti hápnoḱan sᴍ́ti béibᴍm hápnoḱan "he handed (some) to one (person) then handed (some) to another (person)."	RD	hap'no	44, 60	
hápsip	hand over	WS	hápsip		
hápsipto	hand over to	WS	hápsipto		
hápsiptoti	make (someone) hand (something) over	WS	hápsiptoti		
hápsito	hand (something) across to	RD	hap'sito	198	
hápte	maybe	FC			
hápye	hand (something) to, towards	WS	hápje		
hapyekáka	hurry and bring (something)	RD	hapyeka'ka	220	
has	slip, slide on the feet	WS	has		
hás	urinate (speaking of Coyote) (RD), urinate canine fashion (WS)	RD, WS	has' (RD), has (WS)	30	
hásdoi	slip and lose the balance	WS	hásdoj		
hásdoi	urinate like a dog (lifting leg)	FC			
hásdoihudoi	almost slip	WS	hásdojhudoj		
hasíp	come back to the starting place	RD	hasip'	32	
hasíp	take something out of (RD), push something out (of the water) (WS): yakᴍ́ hasípma'ankano "you will bring the boat out (of the water)"	RD, WS	hasip' (RD), hasíp (WS)	34, 124	

Maidu	English	Source	Source Spelling	Page	Other Spellings
hasíto	bring (something) across	RD	hasī'to	124	
hasítopin	bring (someone) across (in something)	RD	hasī'topin	126	
hasítoye	go across with something, go across taking something	RD	hasī'toye	150	
háskoi	slide away (as on skis or ice skates or on the feet)	WS	hásk̓oj		
hásno	ski, skate, slide	WS	hásno		
hásnom húskm	racer snake	WS	hásnom húsky		
hásnoye	slide around, skid around	WS	hásnoje		
hásnoyekoi	go skating, go skiing	WS	hásnojek̓oj		
háspai	urinate against	WS	háspaj		
hassíno	slip down, slide down	RD	hassīn'o	176	
hástokoi	go skiing, ski	WS	hástok̓oj		
hatám	search for, look for, come looking for, go looking around: mm 'as hatámmenwet "I did not come here looking for that. I did not come here to do that."	WS, RD, FC-E	hatám (WS), hatām' (RD)	144	
hatámmchono	look all over for, hunt down	RD	hatam'ötsono	132	
hatammnóiye	go wandering around looking for	RD	hatāmönoi'ye	90	
hatámkoi	go look for	WS	hatámk̓oj		
hatámnoye	look around for	WS	hatámnoje		
hatámyekinu	to hunt all over	RD	hatam'ekinu	32	
hat'dá	in searching (adv): lmksipmen hátda mkóimenwet uní hedén "don't go outside searching around and don't go far from here."	RD	hatd'a'	142	
hatĭchem	sneeze	WS	hatĭćem		
hawáni	big toad	FC			
hawí	fox	FC, WS	haw		haw
hawíkakit	throw (someone) down	RD	hawi'kakit	110	
háwokit	set down a load	RD	hā'wokit	228	
hayá	put (something), place (something)	RD	hayā'	208	
hayahá	be possible, doable	RD	hayahā'	240	
hayahámen	be impossible	RD	hayahā'men	240	
hayápapai	pack in a sack: smmí hayápapaikan "he packed the meat in a sack"	RD	hayā'papa(y)	228	
hayéwe	come in a vehicle	WS	hajéwe		
Hayino Pakáni	place name for Silver Lake. See maps 1 and 2 in Appendix 5.	PM-D	ha-yi-no pakanee		
háyum	yawn	FC			háiyum
háyuyum	yawn	WS	hájujum		
hé	fall, come loose	WS	hé		
hé'asdaw	slide off (something) (like snow from a roof)	WS	héʔasdaw		héyasdaw

Maidu	English	Source	Source Spelling	Page	Other Spellings
hebás	sweep	WS	hebás		hᴍbás (FC)
hebásdaw	brush off	WS	hebásdaw		
hebásdawkᴍ	whiskbroom, clothes brush	WS	hebásdawky		
hebáskᴍ	broom	WS	hebásky		hᴍbáskᴍ (FC)
hebássip	sweep out	WS	hebássip		
hébe	white lilac	HM	he′-be		
Hébe	place name for a meadow west of Indian Valley. May be Round Valley. The name means "white lilac." See map 5 in Appendix 5.	CM	hebe	22	
Hébem Sewí	Moccasin Creek or Dixie Creek. FR1 does not mention the creek by its English name, but describes Chiwísi as being below Hébem Sewí, just below Dixie Canyon on Indian Creek. Means "white lilac creek." See map 5 in Appendix 5.	FR1	Hébem Sewí		
héchap	dislodge by pulling	WS	héćap		
héchapdaw	pull (something) down (like a hornet's nest)	WS	héćapdaw		
hechíhene	muskrat	WS	hećíhene		
héchiudᴍ	shrew (small mouse-like mammal)	HM	hétchyudu		
héda	old, used, worn out (of things only)	WS	héda, hédak		hédak
hédada	somewhat old, used, worn out (of things only)	WS	hédada, hédakdak		hédakdak
hédakdaw	fall away, come loose and fall	WS	hédakdaw		
hédakpai	persist in being after (someone), pursue persistently	WS	hédakpaj		
hédas	crack (something) open, rip (something)	WS	hédas		
hédasto	crack open, rip open (intransitive)	WS	hédasto		
hédastoti	rape (verb)	WS	hédastoti		
hédatpai	pursue	FC-R			
hédeden	near, close by	RD	hed′eden	202	
hedén	close by, near	WS	hedén		héden (FC)
héden mᴍdí	near here	FC			
hedéndi	right there, at the place (already mentioned)	WS	hedéndi		
hedénim	this (before a noun or adjective): hedénim kódom bískᴍm mama'ánkano "you will be inhabitants of this country."	RD	heden'im	226	
hedénna	nearby	WS-MP	hedénna		
hedénto	nearby	WS-MP	hedénto		
hedéntona	a short distance	WS	hedéntona		

Maidu	English	Source	Source Spelling	Page	Other Spellings
hédikno	arrive at while running away from a pursuer	RD	hē′dikno	224	
hedói	load up (a basket), put (something) in (a container)	RD	hedoi′	198	
hédoi	chase after (with evil intent)	RD	hē′doi	180, 224	
hédoimit	chase up and down (hills)	RD	hē′doimit	224	
hédusimoto	fall in on itself (like a burning house), fall in together	RD	hē′dusimoto′	200	
he'é	yes: he'é maḱáde? "Agreed?" he'e api "say yes"	WS, WST, FC-R, BC	he?é, hehé	10:3	he'éh
hehe	each, each one, every time, every thing: uyúkwonodi hehe "in each place where (they) had camped" kmkán mpéḱanbenini kulúnanammni hehe piyétokm "Every evening she went swimming." mmkábe wokómmni hehe apdóiwonokmchoi'a "every time when his little sister got tired, he had carried her on his back."	RD	hēhē	104, 108, 124, 166, 196, 232, 234, 110	
hehé	hello, goodbye	FC			
hehé'mno	travel in groups	RD	hehē′öno	32	
hehékpe	heavy	WS	hehékpe		
hehénomenwet	without looking at, without paying attention to: mmsambóyewolim mmma'át hehénomenwet heláiḱan "his brothers, without even looking at him, gambled."	RD	hēhē′nomenwet	210	
hehépai	be half gone, be half (of previous): máidmm hehépaiḱan "the people were half gone."	RD	hēhē′pai	140	
hehépaiwiyáka	be few left, less than half left	RD	hehē′paiwiyak'a	146	
hehepiyétono	swim regularly or often, swim routinely	RD	hēhēpiyēt′ono	196	
hehéti	use up half of (something)	RD	hēhē′ti	224	
hei	hey, hi	RD	hēi	220	
hei	with, along with	WS-MP	hej		
héi	chase, follow, pursue	WS	héj		
héidoi	pursue	WS	héjdoj		
héiḱoi	chase	WS	héjḱoj		
heino	go after someone	RD		46	

91

Maidu	English	Source	Source Spelling	Page	Other Spellings
héiwas	not allow hunting: wólem mawé'am nisé sʌmím kaikáino héiwasdom. "The white man is always preventing us from hunting deer and such."	HY			
héiyatokʌm kawáyu	stud stallion	WS	héjjatokym kawáju		
héiyeto	have sex with, copulate with (This is a relatively mild term)	WS	héjjeto		héyeto (RD)
héiyetokʌm kʌlé	prostitute	WS	héjjetokym kylé		
héiyuwaito	open up a place in: mʌm máidʌm sa héiyuwaitoḱan "the man opened a place in the fire (to put something in)"	WS, RD	héjjuwajto (WS), hē'yuwaito (RD)		héyuwaito (RD)
hek	heavy	WS	hek		
hékekkʌ	nuthatch	HM	hā'-kek-kum		
heḱékumsa	soaproot	HM	hā-gā'-kum-sam		
héki	afterwards, later, further into the future: yadʌkdʌkismam héki pukma'ankano "You whom I re-make will produce offspring afterwards."	RD	hē'ki	24	
hékikit	stop, finish up (several people stopping at once) (RD), finish, stop, cease (all with plural subject) (WS)	RD, WS	hē'kikit (RD), hékikit (WS)	210	
hekít	set down, put down (a load or burden)	WS	hekít		
hékit	finish up, stop, quit, cease, be finished (can be verb affix): wéye hékitḱas "I am done talking"	RD, WS, BC	he'kit, hē'kit (RD), hékit (WS) heki (BC)	48, 164	
hekítʌḱoi	go along laying something down	WST-DW	hekít?yḱoj	78	
hekíwno	slide off (as snow from a branch or roof)	WS	hekíwno		
héḱoi	run away (from someone chasing)	RD	hē'koi	224	
heḱóitoye	fetch, go and bring	WS	heḱójtoje		
hekótto	break (intransitive), crack (by itself)	WS	hekótto		
helá	gambling, game (usually the grass game)	WS	helá		
helái	gamble, win: ni heláiḱasi "I won."	WS, FC	heláj		
helái'ekʌm uyí	casino	FC			
heláikʌ	gambler	WS	helájky		
heláikʌm oméiyi	a special fetish for bringing good luck in gambling	WS	helájkym oméjji		
heláiye	gamble	FC			
helám chá	sticks used as counters in gambling	WS	helám ća		

Maidu	English	Source	Source Spelling	Page	Other Spellings
helám oméiyi	a special fetish or charm for bringing good luck in gambling	WS	helám oméjji		heláyim oméiyi
Helám Púksakᴀm Yamani	place name for mountain near Belden. See map 1, Appendix 5.	WST-DW	helám púksakym jamáni	80:6	
heláyim máidᴀ	gambling man	WS	helájim májdy		
heláyim oméiyi	a special fetish or charm for bringing good luck in gambling	WS	helájim oméjji		helám oméiyi, helaiyim oméiyi (FC-R)
helí'eni	wolf	FC			helienᴀ (FC), helíyene (WS), helíane (FC-R)
Helí'enim Sewí	place name for Wolf Creek, just west of Greenville (means Wolf Creek). see maps 1, 3 and 5 in Appendix 5.	FC-map	Heleanam Sewi		
helín	big	SPB	haylin		
helíyene	wolf, timber wolf	WS	helíjene		helienᴀ (FC), heli'eni (FC)
hélmono	high in price, expensive	WS	hélmono		
helú	not much, only a little bit, yet, a few: helúm wasása "a few things"	WS, WST, FC-T	helú	54:29	
helúmeni	not a few, many: tetét helúmenim ekí ᴀnódom "traveling for very many days"	RD	helūm'eni	132	
helúmenini	more than a few times	FC-E			
helúnini	a few, a few times (with -chet construction "after a few..."): helúnini ékdachet "after a few days" helúnini ekdá wosípchet "after a few days had passed"	RD, WS	helū'nini (RD), helúnini (WS)	26, 208	
helúto	only a little bit, a few: wépa helúto méiḱan "he gave Coyote only a little bit"	RD	helū'to	138	
hemé	gopher	RD, WS	hemē' (RD), hemé (WS)	34	
hemí	coals, embers	FC, WS	hem		hem
hémmak	count (verb) (MP, FC), add (BC)	WS-MP, FC, BC	hémmak		hemmák (FC)
hemmák balim	numbers (written)	FC			hémmak balim
hémmakyo	what had been counted: mᴀkí hémmakyo méibosmadom sᴀ́ti awónomchoi'a "when he had about given out all of what he had counted (mᴀkí hémmakyo), there was one left."	RD	hem'makyo	23	
hémmamakno	count (many things), count each of (things)	RD	hem'mamakno	26	
hémno	hop along	RD	hem'no	72	
hémuimu	Delphinus or Job's Coffin constellation	RD-NM			

Maidu	English	Source	Source Spelling	Page	Other Spellings
hénante	beside, in this area, this side of	RD	hen'ante	54, 196	
henó	fetch (water) in a basket	RD	henō'	198	
héno	die (more than one subject) (RD), die in bunches (as in an epidemic or catastrophe) (WS)	RD, WS	heno (RD), héno (WS)	62	
héno	follow (tracks)	RD	hē'no	232	
hénoti	kill (many) (RD), to massacre, kill a bunch of something (like fish or rabbits) (WS), get rid of	RD, WS, FC	hēn'oti (RD), hénoti (WS)	54, 226	
hénoye	chase after	RD	hēn'oiye, hē'noye	54, 170	
hénte	won't you please (with -p imperative), maybe I should (with self-imperative -osi on verb) (RD); well, then, please (WS): hénte tḿskadoiweten uním káiyi hémnosi "maybe I should stand up and hop along this log." hénte unínak wusútkinup "Won't you please lie down here on your belly"	RD, WS	hen'te (RD), hénte (WS)	11, 72	
hénu	keep on running away	RD	hē'nu	224	
hépʌt	come loose, come untied	WS	hépyt		
hépes	part by cracking	WS	hépes		
hépesdaw	crack off (intransitive), fall off by crumbling (as a piece of dough or bread)	WS	hépesdaw		
hépesto	crack open (like bread crust)	WS	hépesto		
hépeswaito	come apart, fall apart, crack wide open	WS	hépeswajto		
hepínḱoi	go back home	WST	hepínḱoj	62:8	
hés eḱáw	how wonderful! (This exclamation may refer to any perceptible quality of a thing - its taste, appearance, feel, sound, etc.)	WS	hés eḱáw		
hés ha'ái	well! How awfully...	WS	hés haʔáj		
hes wi'iye	well, why not	FC			
hés wísse	how tragic! (FC), an exclamation of disbelief, how exaggerated! What a whopper! (WS)	FC, WS	hés wísse		héswise (FC)
hés yehépti	how awful! How frightening!	WS	hés jehépti		

Maidu	English	Source	Source Spelling	Page	Other Spellings
hesá	why? (rude form of hesádom): hesá okítdom makm̓ká? "Why did you come here?" something: hesá hesápedi mak̓áde'as wasá ma'át wónotidom pemápem? "Where will we (2) be able to kill something, even something lousy, in order to eat?"	RD	hesā'	146, 152	
hesá áman áite	I wonder why you did it? (see "áman")	RD	hesā' ā'man ai'te	232	
hesá wise	oh no, yikes!	FC			
hesá!	oh brother! Geez! (FC), What...!, How...! (WS)	FC, WS	hes		hes
hesáchétipe	how someone looks: hesáchétipem áite mayákan chebm̓has hap "if only we (2) could see what he looks like"	RD	hesat'tset'ipe	184	
hesádom	why? (WS), what's the matter, what's going on?, how? (FC)	WS, FC	hesádom		
hesádom [pikno] mayák̓k̓en?	what could be [really] happening/going on?	RD	hesā'dom [pikno] mayā'ken?	140, 228	
hesádom aité	I wonder how (+ verb in yákk̓en): hesádom áite ka'á dm̓km̓ sówodoidom mawewíyakk̓en "I wonder how he always lifts ones like that"	RD	hesa'dom aite'	142	
hesádom máik̓a?	what are you saying? what do you mean?	RD	hesā'dom mai'ka?	228	
hesádom mak̓á?	what's the matter with you? Hesí hesádom mak̓á? "What the heck is the matter with you?"	FC			
hesádom mak̓ádes?	what am I doing?	RD	hesā'dom makā'des?	228	
hesádom mawéw	what's the matter with...(all the time)? hesádom mawéwk̓a? "What is always the matter with you?"	WS	hesádom mawéw...		
hesádom mínsm̓m mak̓á?	what's the matter with you people?	RD	hesā'dom mins'öm makā'?	204, 228	
hesádom nik mínsm̓m wéyemenpem m̓yékm̓k̓a?	why didn't you (pl) tell me you were going?	RD	hesā'dom nik min'söm wēyemenpem öyēköka?	208	
hesádowet ma'át	no matter what cause, no matter how	RD	hesā'dowetmaat	30	
hesádowet mayák̓k̓en	what might be happening? what is going on?	RD	hesā'dowet mayā'ken	122, 140, 146, 206	
hesáhelu	wonder what (someone) will do	WS	hesáhelu		

Maidu	English	Source	Source Spelling	Page	Other Spellings
hesái	do, say, translate: ...hesáiḱa "how do you say...?" "how do you translate..?"	WS	hesáj		
hesáihelukmḱas	What should I do? I should come up with a plan of action.	RD	hesai'helūkökas	156	
hesáiluť	experience the worst case scenario, have the worst luck/outcome: hesáiluťkmḱas achét mínsmm bispadá "if the worst happens to me, you all must carry on."	RD	hesai'lū	96	
hesáḱa?	How's it going?: smʼmi hesáḱa? "what did you do?"	RD	hesā'ka	92, 182	
hesáḱa?	What are you?	RD	hesā'ka	6	
hesáḱade	How are things? How are they? How is he/she/it?	RD, FC	hesā'kade	218	hesásaḱade
hesámmni	due to what was done, when (someone) did that: hesámmni hésmen wónotimenwet mawéam'es chedímtidom "by not killing (him) sooner for what he'd done, we just made (him) arrogant." hesámmni wewémenwet, chenúmenyakḱesi "without speaking when he did that, I should not have watched"	RD	hesā'möni	36, 218	
hesámaka	not be able to do anything to (to punish or stop someone)	RD	hesā'maka	174	
hesámakad	without anything stopping (them) (adv), continuously	RD	hesa'makad	106	hesámakat
hesámakati	without getting caught, getting away with it (doing something bad), without being stopped: hesámakatidom nisé katíḱan "he does it to us without getting caught"	RD	hesā'makati	108	
hesámedas	see "hesámet" (this is hesámet 'as)	RD	hesā'medas	92	
hesámenkm	faultless, stainless, innocent	WS	hesámenky		
hesámet	on the contrary, suppose that..., what if...?: hesámet 'as héyetoḱas "suppose that I was having sex"	RD, WS	hesā'met (RD), hesámet (WS)	34, 82, 92, 96, 114, 146	

Maidu	English	Source	Source Spelling	Page	Other Spellings
hesánbe	how much? (when a question), many, a great number (when not a question): hesánbem k̓úmmenim wosípdom "a great many winters passing" hesánbem liáni mak̓áde? "How much does it cost?" hesánbem k̓úmmenim okítpem mak̓á? "How old are you (how many winters)?"	FC, RD	hesan'be	15, 19, 21, 162	
hesándmkbe ma'át	as many (with negative verb= not many): hesándmkbe ma'át solí makítmenpem kmk̓ás "I don't know very many songs"	RD	hesān'dükbemaat	5	
hesánte	how far, how many (in a question) (FC), far (if not a question)(RD): hesánte kítpemmak̓a? "How old are you?"	FC, RD, BC		230	
hesánte kítade	what time is it?	FC, BC			hesánte kítk̓ade
hesánte ma	far, very far, a far place (with negative verb, "not very far"): hesánte ma pahánomenchoi'a "he did not follow their tracks far"	RD	hesan'te ma	230	
hesánteni	when? at what time? hesánteni sm'mi mawé'am? "When does it usually happen?"	WS, RD	hesánteni	112	
hesánteniwet	whenever	FC			
hesántenuwet	sometime	WS	hesántenuwet		
hesántewet	pretty far: hesántewet k̓uk̓úm piúbonpinyakk̓en adóm. "The rope seems to extend pretty far."	RD	hesan'tewet	186	
hesánudom	how to do	WS	hesánudom		
hesánudowet	in some way or other, no matter what it takes	RD	hesā'nudowet	186	
hesápe	what? (RD) what kind of...? (WS): mi hesápe húheyek̓a? "What do you think about it?" hesápem k̓odóidi mnómmni mayákk̓es cheméndom "to what kind of place could they have gone that I'm not finding them?"	RD, WS	hesā'pe (RD), hesápe (WS)	10, 230	
hesápedi	whereabouts?	WS	hesápedi		
hesápewet	whatever it is	FC			

Maidu	English	Source	Source Spelling	Page	Other Spellings
hesápiknodom	just how (hesádom= how): hesápiknodom mayáiken lɯkdiknomaḱas min "I don't know just how I am going to get up to you"	RD	hesāp′iknodom	176	
hesápḱoi	get out (referring to the departure of spirits when exorcised by the shaman) (WS), chase away bad things (FC)	WS	hesápḱoj		
hesása	how? Be how?	WS	hesása		
hesásaḱa?	how are you?	FC			
hesásaḱade	how are things? How is he/she/it? How are they?	RD, FC	hesā′sakade	174	
hesasawéwḱa?	how have you been?	FC			
hésaswaito	come apart, fall apart, burst	WS	hésaswajto		
hésaswaitoti	cause to burst	RD	hēs′aswaitoti	178	
hesáte	anything, any problem: hesátem honwépepe "surviving anything"	RD	hesā′tem	110	
hesáti	do what? (WS), what (to do): hesáti yaháḱa nik? "what do you want me to do?" (FC)	WS, FC	hesáti	9	
hesáti maḱá?	what are you going to do about it?	FC			
hesáti mi maḱá?	what do you do with (something)?	FC			
hesátichɯi	be unable to do anything to (someone): ɯpéḱanbem máidɯɯ yehéptoyedom hesátichɯidom wónotichɯidom achói'a. "All the people said they were afraid and not able to do anything and not able to kill (him)."	RD	hesā′titsöi	172, 210	
hesátidom	how about...? (with question verb form) (RD), in what manner? by what means? (WS): hesátidom tetébewtimaḱade'as? "How about we make it a little bigger?"	RD, WS	hesā′tidom (RD), hesátidom (WS)	7, 114	
hesátiḱa?	what did you do to (it)?	FC			
hesátimadom	what was the intention/plan for (doing)...? (with question verb form): hesátimadom unína sɯ'ɯi hóiwiaḱa? "What was your intention in bringing (him) here?"	RD	hesāt′imadom	178	

Maidu	English	Source	Source Spelling	Page	Other Spellings
hesátimenkṁ	one who does nothing (no harm) to, one who is harmless to	RD	hesāt'imenkö	180	
hesátimenwet	without doing anything to	RD	hesā'timenwet	48, 172	
hesátimet	why not do...? Hesátimet ka'ánkano "this is what you (should) do"	RD	hesa'timet	114	
hesátimwet	nothing but... what else but...?	WS	hesátimwet		
hesátiyahá	you ought to do it	RD	hesā'ti yahā'	7	
hesátmet	just, only, nothing but	WS	hesátmet		
hesá'usmen	be unable to help oneself, unable to resist: hesá'usmendom, mṁmḿ ónḱoimṁni, méiḱan "unable to help himself, when he was outsmarted, he gave (it) to him."	RD	hesā'ūsmen	138	
hesáwet	whichever	RD	hesā'wet	60	
hesáwinim	what kind of?	FC			
hesáyakḱen	where could __ be?: hesáyakḱen áite nik "I wonder where they could be?"	RD	hesā'yaken	228	
hesbáp	prepare (food)	RD	hesbap'	126	
hésbapin	untie, bring out, get (something) out	RD, WS	hes'bappin (RD), hésbapi (WS)	78	hésbapi (WS)
hésbobopai	gather up one's things, pack up (things) for a journey: mṁchóki wolódi wasása hésbobopaiḱan "the two of them packed up their things in baskets"	RD	hes'bobopai	52, 118, 204	
hésbohamoto	pile (stuff) together	RD	hes'bohamotō	96	
hésboiyoiyo	what-do-you-call-it, thing-a-ma-jig, a playful word for women's genitals	WS, RD	hésbojjojjo (WS), hesboiyoi'yo (RD)		
hésbomoto	get (things) together	WS	hésbomoto		
hésbonoye	poke around in (things) (WS), spread stuff out (FC)	WS, FC	hésbonoje		
hésbopai	pack (things) up (WS), put (something) back in its place (RD)	RD, WS	hes'bopai (RD), hésbopaj (WS)	92	
hésboye	spread (things) out	WS	hésboje		
hésboyoyo	different kinds of things, various things	WS	hésbojojo		
hésdiwet	something, something or other: hutúḱan hésdiwet ma'át wisétpem "he went crazy due to being afraid of something"	WS, RD	hésdiwet (WS), hes'diwet (RD)	190	

Maidu	English	Source	Source Spelling	Page	Other Spellings
hesí	what (in questions) (FC), thing, things (WS) (hesím when subject of the sentence): hesí aká? "what did you say?" hesí betámaka mᴧm? "what do you call it?" hesí ma'át húťamenkasi "I can not even think about such things, it's beyond my imagination" hesím ma'át nik sikálamenkᴧm "nothing is bothering me" wéyekas hesí hesá "I am talking about this and that, talking about nothing"	FC, WS, RD, FC-T	hés (WS), hesī′ (RD)	5, 182, 192	hés
hesí ma'át	anything: hesí máidᴧm ma'át hesátichᴧi "no one (not even one person) could do anything (about it)" hesí ma'át nik ťĭkchemenkan. "He doesn't go along with me in anything. He doesn't trust me (my judgment) in anything" hesí ma'át makítmenpe "not knowing anything"	RD	hesī'maat	28, 32, 172, 190	
hesí máika?	what are you saying? What do you mean?	RD	hesī′ mai′kaa?	206	
hesí mayákken áite?	I wonder what that could be, what could that be?	RD	hesi mayā′ken ai′te	120	
hesí wéyedom?	What are you talking about? What are they talking about?	FC			
hesí yákupem maká?	what is your name?	FC			
hésiki	anything, anyone; nothing (with negative verb or infix): cháichainom máidᴧm hesíki ma'át hesím ma'át káinoyemenchoi'a "no creatures of any kind were flying around."	WS	hésiki	4	
hesím ade?	what is that? What was that?	FC			hesím ma'ade?, hesím makade?
hesím bé?	what now?	FC			
hesím beté	what on earth? (WST), nothing of any kind, nothing at all (WS): hesím beté píkno mawéwyakken mᴧm kᴧlém? "just what on earth could this woman be doing?"	WS, WST	hesím betém	54:32	hesím betém
hesím betéwet	wherever: hesím betéwet ítudom ma'am "wherever (on the body) it hurt"	WS, WST	hesím betéwet	52:18	

Maidu	English	Source	Source Spelling	Page	Other Spellings
hesím máidᴀwet	what kind of creature: hesím máidᴀwet mayákḱen? "what kind of creature could it be?"	RD	hesim' mai'düwet	124	
hesíma'át	no matter what, anything, such a thing (object of a sentence)	RD	hesi'maat	5, 9, 112, 152	
hesímma'át	no matter what, anything, such a thing (subject of a sentence)	RD	hesim'maat	182	
hésippin	chase up out (of a valley), start chasing down into	RD	hē'sipin	224	
hesísi	little thing, distant thing	FC			
hesísi hesa maḱa?	just what are you going to do?	FC			
hesísiwet	anything	WST-LM	hesísiwet	70:60	
hesíwet	something (WS), whatever (FC), in some way (WST), something or other (RD): hesíwet mᴀm máidᴀm ma'át wasádoimᴀni "if that man started to be bad in some way" hesíwet yahádom aním ma'aḱán "whatever you want to do will be fine."	FC, WS, WST, RD	hesíwet (WS), hes'iwet (RD)	60:56 (WST), 9 (RD)	
hesíwetim hesíwetam	maybe this, maybe that	FC-T			
hesíwi	something	FC			
héskᴀ	relative, friend	FC, WS	hésky		
héskᴀto	relatives, friends	FC			
héskᴀtoḱoi	go to make friends, go visit relatives: nikbéiḱᴀm héskᴀtoḱoikan mínḱi mᴀbéiḱᴀdi "my father went to visit relatives in your father's neighborhood"	RD	heskötokoi'	136	
hésmen	already (RD, FC), first (RD), long ago, early, old (of things) (WS): hésmen bénektodi "early in the morning" hésmen peḱás "I've already eaten"	FC, RD, WS	hes'meni, hes'men (RD), hésmen (WS)	28, 46	
hésnama'át	for anything, for even a thing: hésnama'at yahámenpem "not good for anything"	RD	hes'namaat	44	
hésniwet	with something or other	RD	hes'niwet	9	
hesúpai	get dressed up, put on regalia (RD), be dressed up, decked out (WS)	RD, WS	hesū'pai (RD), hesúpaj (WS)	120	
hesúwa?	what next?	FC			
heswéh	an exclamation of amazement or astonishment. what...! what a lot of ...!	WS	heswéh		
héswise	how tragic!	FC			hés wísse

101

Maidu	English	Source	Source Spelling	Page	Other Spellings
hétilkit	be stable (tightened up)	RD	hē′tilkit	24	
héw	yes, OK, good! Thank you, Well...	FC, WS	héw		
héw	support, help, point in the right direction: nik héwma'ankano "Please point me in the right direction (prayer)."	HY			
héw hapá	how true! That's right!	WS	héw hapá		
héw tené	amen!	HY			
héwa(s)	lecture (someone), warn (someone) not to do (something): héwaset nik pínmenkasi "when he told me not to, I didn't listen." (due to the -set ending, not sure if this is actually héwas, "forbid."	RD	hē′wa	164	
hewakaktímoto	make motions in all directions, indicate the surrounding areas	RD	hēwakakti′moto	23	
hewakátnoye	point around at things	RD	hewakat′noye	60	hé'uwakát-noye
héwakátnoye	point around in different directions, point places out	RD	hē′uwakat′noye	60, 128	hewakát-noye
héwdaw	drop down (intransitive), fall down	WST	héwdaw	46:3	
héwi	that one, the one: mꟼm héwim kaiyí mꟼ hai'í hémno'ankano "you - the one who is currently hopping around on a log."	RD	hē′wi	72	
hewíno	fetch (water), go get	RD	hewino	52	
héwkinu	make noise (as children playing)	RD	hēū′kinu	174	
héwkinutimen	not let (someone) make noise, keep (someone) quiet: tét'm'ꟼ mínchꟼm héwkinutimen "don't let the children make noise"	WST-RP	héwkinutimen	64:14	
héwma'aḱade?	Is it OK?	FC			
héwma'aḱan	That will be fine, OK, fine!	FC			
héwpinti	be noisy (WS), cause to be heard (FC)	WS, FC	héwpinti		
héwwelek	beckon with the hand, seduce, entice (someone) sexually	WS	héwwelek		
héwwo	affirm, be verbally supportive	WS	héwwo		
héwwonai	it is good	FC			
héwwonoye	be supportive all around, say "héwwonai"	WS, WST-RP	héwwonoje	64	
heyꟼmpin	plummet, fall (from a height)	RD	hēyöm′pin	186	
heyá	put (something) back in	RD	heyā′	114	
héya	encouraging exclamation: "come on!"	RD	he′a	46	

102

Maidu	English	Source	Source Spelling	Page	Other Spellings
héyap	slide off, slide down	WS	héjap		
héyappin	slide down from above	WS	héjappin	178	héyapin
héyappinpin	slide down one by one from above (WS), slide down little by little (RD)	WS, RD	héjappinpin (WS), hē'apinpin (RD)	178	
héyapyapto	slide down one by one, from out of place	WS	héjapjapto		
heyáwe	support (a cause or actions of others) by providing or doing (something)	RD	heyā'we	8	
héyeto	have sex with	RD	he'yeto	48	héiyeto (WS)
héyetoibisim	have continuous sex with, have sex with over and over	RD	hē'yetobisim	70	
héyetope	one who is having sex	RD	he'yetope	92	
héyu	move vertically	WS	héju		
heyúda	comb the hair	WS	hejúda		
heyúdato	comb someone else's hair	WS	hejúdato		
heyúdatokm	comb (noun)	WS	hejúdatoky		
héyudaw	fall off, as a rock from a high place	WS	héjudaw		heyúdaw (FC)
héyudawkit	fall down	FC			
héyudoi	rise up (as a fish from the bottom of water, or a balloon)	WS, WST	héjudoj, hejúdoj	72:8	heyúdoi
héyukit	fall down (MP), fall down (person or tree) (FC)	WS-MP, FC	héjukit		heyúkit
heyúkiti	drop (something), fell (a tree)	FC			
heyúkitpe	falling-down person, one who falls down	FC			
héyumit	throw down in, land down in (after being thrown or dropped) (RD), fall into (WS)	RD, WS	hē'umit (RD), héjumit (WS)	200	
heyúno	fall down	FC			
héyunpintiyo	throw down many things (from a tree)	RD	heyunpintio	64	
héyup	become detached	WS	héjup		
héyupkit	slip down, as trousers	WS	héjupkit		
héyuwaito	open a place in (the fire), open an oven	RD	he'yuwaito	60	héiyuwaito (WS)
héyuye	drop off (as leaves), run down (as sap down a tree trunk)	WS	héjuje		
heyúyeti	drop (food), let (something) drop	RD	heyuyeti	44	
hí	smell (something), perceive an odor, sniff	WS, FC	hí		
híbmk	sniff, breathe noisily	WS	híbyk		
hibí	birch	WS	hibí		
hibím chá	birch tree	WS	hibím ćá		
hibím dm	birch brush	WS	hibím dý		
hibím loló	a loose-woven birch basket, used for gathering	WS	hibím loló		

Maidu	English	Source	Source Spelling	Page	Other Spellings
hibím patá	a loose-woven birch basket, used for gathering	WS	hibím patá		
hichihi'ina	beaver	FC			hichihihine
hichís	cough	FC			
hihí	pound up dry substance into powder	WS	hihí		
hihíluť	pound up fine	WS	hihílut		
hi'i	hey!	RD	hiī	222	
híky	nose	WS	híky		
híky dyký	snap or flick someone on the nose: híky dykýkan myymý wasódom chepánupe "he snapped them on the nose, being angry that they were scowling at him"	RD	hī'kö dökö'	208	
híky póp	have a nosebleed: myykí tem híky pópḱan "his child had a nosebleed."	WS	híky póp		
híky syháwkit	pierce the septum (of the nose)	WS	híky syháwkit		
híkydakym chi	cloth handkerchief	FC			
híkydakym papéli	handkerchief (paper), Kleenex, tissue	FC			
hiki	the great snake	CM		43	
hil	thrust, pierce	WS	hil		
hílluk	breathe heavily through the mouth, be dry-throated and choky (as children when they run and play too hard)	WS	hílluk		
hiló	ground squirrel	WS	hiló		
híloye	go sniffing around	WS	híloje		
hílpai	thrust many sharp things into (as a porcupine)	WS	hílpaj		
híluk	take a deep breath	WS	hiluk		
hin	float (verb)	WS	hin		
hín duschikkíno	have one's eyes closed	RD	hin'dūstsikin'o	168	
hin'á	wriggle in the shallows (spawning salmon)	WS	hinʔá		
hin'á'etaky	place where it starts going down (sun)	RD	hin'ā'etakö	26	
hin'ápem hiní	crossed eyes	WS	hinʔápem hiní		
hínbochik	have something in the eye	WS	hínboćik		
hínchekoiky	glasses (for the eyes), binoculars, anything to see through	WS, FC-T	hínćeḱojky		
hínchesem	feel strange toward, not know or understand, feel alienated	WS	hínćesem		

Maidu	English	Source	Source Spelling	Page	Other Spellings
Hínchesemim Mómdannim	place name for Eagle Lake, #21 on HLME map 3; "reflection lake (WS-HLME)," "clear sight lake (FC)," This lake is known to be rather haunted, especially at night, as the great snake lives within (HLME). Note the similarity of this name to hínchesem, "feel strange toward." See map 1 in Appendix 5	HLME	Hinch'esimim Momdanim		Hinchesmenim Mómdanni
hinchesmeni	clear sight	FC			
Hinchesmenim Mómdanni	place name for Eagle Lake, north of Susanville (northern-most Mountain Maidu area). "Strange Feeling Lake" based on hínchesem. "Clear-sight lake" according to FC. "reflection lake" according to WS. See map 1 in Appendix 5.	FC, WS			Hinchesemim Mómdannim
hínchetokm	mirror (noun)	WS	hínćetoky		
hínchetoye	float along while looking around (WS-MM), drift about (on water) (RD)	RD, WS-MM	hin'tsetōye, hin'tsetoye	RD 4, 5, 7; WS-MM 18	
hínchik	float over the surface of	WS	hínćik		
hínchikwebis	float over the surface of from time to time	WS	hínćikwebis		
híncho	squint	FC			hínchul (FC-R)
hínchono	go down, set (sun)	RD	hin'tsono	182	
hínchonokmnántedi	towards the place where (the sun) goes down, towards the west	RD	hin'tsono-könan'tedi	212	
hínchukú	sink (verb)	WST	hínćukú	78:10	
hínchukúdaw	sink (verb)	WST	hínćukúdaw	78:11	
hínchul	squint	FC-R			híncho
híndmkm	banded bone in the grass game	WS	híndyký		
hindákm	handkerchief, towel	WS	hindáky		
hindakono	Douglas squirrel	PM-M	hen-da-con-o		
híndiknopoto	be almost sunset	RD	hin'diknopotō'	112	
híndoidoi	show above the edge of something	WS	híndojdoj		
híndukm	unmarked bone in gambling	RD-NM			
hínduschik	close the eyes	WS	hínduśćik		
hinháhadikno	be almost set (sun)	RD	hinhā'hadikno	110	
hiní	eye, berry, seed, face: hiní béibm chakámni bmmhelotodom lólma'akan "also smearing pitch on the face they will grieve"	FC, WS	hin (WS), hinī' (RD)	52	hin
hiní pmpḿi	be dizzy	WS	hiní pypýj		
hiní wichíkkm	sunglasses	FC			

Maidu	English	Source	Source Spelling	Page	Other Spellings
hiním hínyepápalak	blink the eyes repeatedly	RD	hinim' hin'yepāp'alak	178	
hinímotodo	with eyes meeting (adv):	RD	hinim'otodo	182	
hinín	float downstream	WS	hinín		
hinís butu	eyebrow	FC			
hinískᴍlᴍlᴍ	eyelash	WS	hiní skylyly		
hinískwiki	wink	WS	hinískwiki		
hinískwikitkit	blink	WS	hinískwikitkit		
hinískwopai	glance at, take a glance at, catch a glimpse of	WS, WST-DW	hinískwopaj	80	
hiniwáchikkᴍ	eye glasses	FC			
Hinkᴍsimin Mómdannim	place name for Eagle Lake, #39 on LM map. See Hínchesemim Mómdannim on map 1 in Appendix 5.	LM	Hinges sim min mom dahnim		Hinchesmenim Mómdanni
hínkakala	pine cone	FC			hínkak'ala (FC-T)
hínkit	sink (verb), float down (under water)	WS	hínkit		
hínkochik	have (something) in the eye	WS	hínkoćik		
hínkoi	float away (WS), flow (MP)	WS, WS-MP	hínkoj		
hínkoikᴍmnantedi	where it goes down (sun)	RD	hin'koikömnantedi	26	
hínkol	eyeless, with the eyeball missing	WS	hínkol		
hínkolluť	absolutely eyeless	WS	hínkollut		
hínno	float along	WS	hínno		
hínnotikᴍm yaká	boat	WS	hínnotikym jaká		
hínnoye	float around	WS	hínnoje		
hínnoyeti	swirl (something), swish (something) around (as water and gravel in a gold pan)	WS, WST	hínnojeti	52:14	
hínposala	eyelid	WS	hínposala		
hínpupu	go down (sun)	RD	hin'pupu	108	
hínsitoye	float around inside	WS	hínsitoje		
hínsolokᴍ	glasses	FC			
híntata	to drift, float little by little	RD	hin'tata	5	
hinumi	pelican	PM-M	hin-oo-mem		
hínwilok	have a tic in the eye, have an eye twitch	WS	hínwilok		
hínwo	eldest, first (people) (RD), ahead, the place ahead (WS)	RD, WS	hin'wo (RD), hínwo (WS)	106, 140	
hínwono	ahead, in front, older, oldest (person) (WS), eldest (as adjective), already (with a conjugated verb): hínwono ᴍkóidakan hóipaidi "they had already left when..." hínwonomᴍni "when up ahead, when he gets up ahead"	RD, WS	hin'wono (RD), hínwono (WS)	118, 230	
hínwonope	ahead, in front of, older	WS	hínwonope		
hínya	spawn (verb)	WS	hínja		

Maidu	English	Source	Source Spelling	Page	Other Spellings
hínyepápalak	blink repeatedly	RD	hin'yepāp'alak	178	
his	weave	WS	his		
hísam ḱowó	daddy long-legs spider, stinky armpit	FC-E, FC-R	hísam ḱowa (FC-E)		
hīsampᴍno	piss-ant	RD	hīs'ampöno	68	
hisamsaw	mint plant	JD	hisamsaw	57	
hísasape	always smelly, always fragrant	FC			
hísatikᴍ	stinking, stench-causer, stinker, smelly	RD	hīs'atikö	220	
hísatipe	smelly, fragrant: yahát hísatipe "good smelling;" wasát hísatipe "bad smelling"	FC			
híscheno	to space out	FC			
hísdom chuṕí	gray willow, basket-making willow	FC			
hisiswikitkit	blink (eyes)	FC			
hískᴍm bᴍmí	basket-making awl	FC			
hisoche	gopher	PM-M	hi-so-jem		
híssa	stink, smell (good or bad): yahát hísaḱan "It smells good."	WS, FC	híssa		hísa (FC)
híssasa	always stink, normally smell (good or bad)	WS	híssasa		hísasa
híssasakᴍ	always smelly	RD	hīs'asakö	70	
hit	douse, dump liquid on	WS	hit		
hítape	drenched (adjective): mómni hítapem "drenched in water"	RD	hit'apem	170	
híti	cause to smell	FC-R			
hítkit	pour (liquid) in: momí hítkit "Put water in."	FC			
hítpai	throw liquid on, douse	WS	hítpaj		
hítuktukno	sniff along like a dog on a trail	WS-MP	hítuktukno		
ho	"is that so!" "oh." "huh!" after hearing some news	RD	hō	110, 146, 222	
ho	soaproot	FC-J	hom		
hó	follow (someone or something)	WS	hó		
hó	say "oh" or "ho" (verb)	FC			
hó	yes (rare), hey! (not very friendly greeting)	WS, RD	hó		
hódesi	fighter (RD), one who is an expert at dodging arrows (FR1)	RD, FR1	hōd'esi	202	hudesi
ho'ém	gopher snake	FC			
hóhla	badger	WS	hóhla		
hoi'ᴍpai	fall in love (with someone)	RD		88	oi'ᴍpai
hóiche	look back: hóichemen "don't look back"	FC			
hóicheche	glance back	RD	hoi'tsetse	124, 138, 208, 226	

107

Maidu	English	Source	Source Spelling	Page	Other Spellings
hóichenu	look behind (something), gaze past (someone)	FC			
hóipai	follow (in a linear sense)	WS	hójpaj		
hóipai	the place after or behind (in a linear sense), younger, last: sɱti hóipai "one last one"	WS, RD	hójpaj (WS), hoi'pai (RD)	106	
hóipaidɱkɱ	being the very last (adv or rel clause)	RD	hoi'paidökö	114	
hóipaidi	later, afterwards (RD), behind, ago (FC)	RD, FC	hoi'paidi	230	
hóipaikinu	behind, after (in line)	WS	hójpajkinu		
hóipaikinu'ɱsito	follow behind while going across	RD	hoi'paikinuösito	68	
hóipaikit	follow right behind	WS	hójpajkit		
hóipaina	back (going back)	FC			
hóiwi'ai	bring (someone) somewhere	RD	hoiwiai	178	
hóiwiha	bring by leading	WS	hójwiha		
hóiwihachopin	carry (something) over to another place	RD	hoi'wihatsopin	192	
hóiwihadikno	lead (someone) all the way to: momím batásdi hóiwihadiknoḱan. "They led (him) all the way to the water's edge."	RD	hoi'wihadik'no	32	
hóiwihadoinu	be led up to	RD	hoi'wihadoi'nu	90	
hóiwihaḱoi	take (someone someplace)	WS	hójwihaḱoj		
hóiwihamotó	bring (things) together in one place	RD	hoi'wihamotō'	32	
hóiwiháno	lead	FC			
hóiwihapin	bring (someone towards)	WS	hójwihapin		
hóiwihasip	lead away from	FC			
hóiwihasito	lead (someone) across	WS	hójwihasito		
hóiwihatno	take someone along down in (something, like a vehicle)	RD	hoi'wihatno	32	
hóiwihaye	bring towards by leading	WS	hójwihaje		
hóiwihayeti	bring towards by leading	WS	hójwihajeti		
hóiwiḱoi	go get (someone)	RD, WS	hoi'wikoi (RD), hójwiḱoj (WS)	204	
hóiwiḱoiti	go get	WS	hójwiḱojti		
hóiwinotiyá	go get and bring(someone) back	RD	hoi'winoti ā'	204	
hóiwi'okit	get (someone) back, retrieve (someone)	RD	hoiwiokit	178	
hóiwito	copulate, have sex with (This is a mild and genteel term)	WS	hójwito		
hóiwitoto	copulate, have sex with each other (This is a mild and genteel term)	WS	hójwitoto		
hóiyɱ	ancient, last (former)	FC			hóiya
hóiyɱm máidɱ	old-time person	FC			
hóiyɱmmen	last (year, or other time element)	FC			
hóiya	coil foundation for basket	WS-MP	hójja		

Maidu	English	Source	Source Spelling	Page	Other Spellings
hóiya	long ago, formerly	WS	hójja		hóiyᴀ
hóiyam ḱódodi	long ago, once upon a time (This is the conventional opening for a story)	WS	hójjam ḱódodi, hójjam ḱódojdi		hóiyam ḱódoidi
hokót	ridicule, make fun of (WS), argue, call (someone) bad names (RD): tetét nik hokótḱan "they are making fun of me so much"	WS, RD	hokót (WS), hokot' (RD)	220	
hokót'isa	ridiculous	WS	hokótʔisa		
hokótisape	ridiculous	FC			
hokótito	argue with	RD	hoko'tito	30	
hokótitobos	finish arguing with (someone): wépam hokótitobosinkanim ᴍḱóichoi'a "Coyote, having finished arguing, went off."	RD	hoko'titobos	30	
hokótsa	ridiculer, someone who makes fun of	WS	hokótsa		
hokóttipe	ridiculous	WS	hokóttipe		
hokóttisa	nonsense!	FC			
holó	rotten log, dead body	FC-E			
holóhadóikᴍm kaléta	logging truck, hearse	FC-E			
holóḱo	rotten, decayed	WS, FC	holóḱ		holóko
hólsip	bring (something) out, go get (something)	RD	hol'sip	220	
hom	to boil, to stew (intransitive)	WS	hom		
homá	stew, soup, mush, broth	FC			homma (WS)
Homlukbe	place name: north of Yankee Hill, due west of Kunabe, west side of Feather River - borderline Konkow area. See map 1, Appendix 5.	CM			
homó	some, certain (when not a question), which, where? (when a question): homó ᴍḱóiḱade? "where did he/she/it/they go?" homó ᴍḱóiyakḱen? "where could they have gone?" homóm ḱodóidi ᴍnómᴍni mayákḱes cheméndom "to which country could (they) have gone that I can't find (them)?" homóm ḱódonan "from which country"	WS, RD	homó (WS), homō' (RD)	184, 228, 230	
homó ma'át	anywhere: homó ma'át pai hánomenḱan "he was not able to track the footprints anywhere"	RD	homō'maat	230	

Maidu	English	Source	Source Spelling	Page	Other Spellings
homóbokitmeni	every kind of, all kinds	RD	homō'bokitmen	19, 30, 36, 132, 166	homó-bokitmen
homómo	which (of a choice)?	WS	homómo		
homómondiwet	wherever	WS	homómondiwet		
homón	where	WS	homón		
homóna	where to: homóna ꟽnópꟽ'ꟽ "where should we (2) go?" homóna sꟽ'ꟽi ꟽyépema'as "where were we (2) supposed to go (to)?"	FC, RD	homō'na	194	homónna, hamóna
homónan	from where?	FC			
homónante	whereabouts?	RD	hōmō'nante	5	
homóndi	where? Where to?	WS	homóndi		hamóndi
homóni	who? (object of sentence): homóni hatámḱa? "who are you looking for?"	FC, RD	hōmō'ni		hamóni
homónim	who? (subject of sentence): homónim min hatám'ade? "who is looking for you?"	RD	hōmō'nim	130	
homónim aité	I wonder who it is	RD	hōmō'nim aite'	130	
homónim ma'áti	no matter who	RD	homōn'immaati	28	
homónmondiwet	wherever	WS	homónmondiwet		
homónna	to where	WS	homónna		homóna, hamóna
homónnan	from where	WS	homónnan		hamónan
homónte	where in the world, in what area	WS	homónte		
hómpaito	a fight, wrestling match: hómpaito wéyemaḱas "I'll suggest a fight."	RD	hom'paito	130	
hómpaito	fight (someone) physically (verb)	WS	hómpajto		
hómpaitododó	wrestle with (someone)	RD	hom'paitododō'	144	
hómpaitoto	fight each other	WS	hómpajtoto		
hómpaitoyahá	want to fight: hómpaitoyahádom ꟽnoyeménpem ma'át "I am not going around here because I want to fight"	RD	hom'paitoyahā'	146	
hómpilisto	hummingbird	FC			húmpilisto (WS)
hómti	make soup	RD	hom'ti	202	
hónba	put a cover on, put a lid on, cover up	WS	hónba		
hónbakꟽ	cover, lid, top	WS	hónbaky		
honé	tuberculosis	WS	honé		
honém 'ítu	tuberculosis	WS	honém ʔítu		
honépe	tubercular, having tuberculosis	WS	honépe		
honépem máidꟽ	person with tuberculosis	WS	honépem májdy		

Maidu	English	Source	Source Spelling	Page	Other Spellings
hónhukupti	make (someone) healthy, make (someone) live better, make life better: nisé yahát hónhukuptiḱan mínḱi tem "Your son makes us live better."	FC-T, FC-R			
hónhukupti'us	make health for yourself, be healthy	FC			
hónhulu	continue to survive	FC-R			
hónhulu	inspiration	FC			
hónhuluk	keep surviving	FC-E			
hónhulukti	cause to survive	FC-R			
honí	heart, spirit, soul, ace in cards	FC, WS			hon
honí wi'í	lose one's mind: mᴧm kᴧlém honí wi'iḱan "that woman lost her mind."	RD	honī' wīī' (+ conj)	188	
honím lelépe	soft-hearted	WS	honím lelépe		
hónkᴧti	cause to cough, make (someone) cough	RD	hon'köti	130	
hónḱo	cough (verb)	WS	hónḱo		
hónḱo	cold (illness): hónḱo ḱonóitidom "spreading colds"	HY			
hónku	strain while defecating	RD	hoñ'ku	112	
hónkui	strain while defecating	RD	hoñ'kui	112	
hónmak	research (v), find out by investigating	WS, FC-E	hónmak		
hónmakḱoi	go find out	WS	hónmakḱoj		
hónmaknoye	investigate, inquire around	WS	hónmaknoje		
hónmaktin	not hear/detect anything (RD), be deserted, no signs of life (WS): bénekto pinhéyechet, hónmaktinḱas. "In the morning I listened for (him) and didn't hear anything."	RD, WS	hon'maktin (RD), hónmaktin (WS)	34, 90, 140, 150, 228	
hónno	guess (in a game)	WS	hónno		
hónpolpin	defecate (something), push out through the anus	RD	hoñ'polpin	114	
hónpolsip	defecate (something), push out through the anus	RD	hon'polsip	114	
hónsap	moan (verb)	WS	hónsap		
hónsapwebis	be in a coma	WS	hónsapwebis		
hónsaweye	argument	FC-E			
hónsu	get out of a disastrous situation with good luck	WS	hónsu		
hóntos	be strong and stoic, resist temptation, have willpower	RD	hon'tos	42	
hóntustusi	cough (noun), coughing sickness, "coughs and colds"	RD	hon'tustusi	130	

Maidu	English	Source	Source Spelling	Page	Other Spellings
hónwe	breath, speech, words: chái'im máidⱮm nikí hónwe pínyahamⱮni, min yapáitokas "if (you) other people want to hear my words, I am talking to you."	WS, WST-DW	hónwe	74:5	
hónwe	survive, live, get by	RD	hónwe		hónwei (WS)
hónwehelu	survive, be able to live	WS	hónwehelu		
hónwei	breathe	WS	hónwej		
hónwe'i	life	WS	hónweʔi		
hónwe'i	live (verb)	WS	hónweʔi		
hónwe'inu	alive (adj)	WS	hónweʔinu		
hónwe'inu	survive by (doing), make a living by (doing) (RD), be alive, survive (FC)	RD, FC, WS	honwē'inu	216	honwé'inu (RD)
hónwe'inuti	keep (someone) alive	WS	hónweʔinuti		
hónwenu	be alive, survive	WS	hónwenu		
hónwenupe	alive, one who is still living: ni kⱮkas kaním hónwenupem. "I am the last one living."	FC			
hónwenuwéw	survive till now by (doing), stay alive by (doing)	RD	hon'wēnūwē'ū	222	
honwépepe	those who survive: hesátem honwépepe "those who get through anything"	RD	honwē'pepē	110	
hónwesip	exhale	WS	hónwesip		
honwéyepati	survive it, live through it, be brave	RD	honwē'yepati	126	
hónyewei	inhale	WS	hónjewej		
hopítwaito	fill up (something) to bursting	RD	hopit'waito	178	
hópmit	lie on someone	RD	hop'mit	100	
hoṕno	canyon (FC-E), along the creek (Nisenan)	FC-E			
Hóṕnom	place name for the North Arm of Indian Valley. See map 5 in Appendix 5.	FR1, FR-TE, FR-HY	hópenom		
Hóṕnom Bo	place name for North Arm Rd. and Diamond Mountain Rd. See map 5 in Appendix 5.	FC-MAP			
Hóṕnom Sewí	place name for Lights Creek, which flows through North Arm to join Indian Creek. See map 5 in Appendix 5.	FR1, FR-HY	hópenom sewi		
Hóṕnom Ḱoyó	place name for North Arm, Indian Valley (may mean "along the creek meadow" - hoṕ is creek in Nisenan) or "canyon meadow" (FC). See maps 1 and 5 in Appendix 5.	RD-NM, FC			hoṕnom koyo

Maidu	English	Source	Source Spelling	Page	Other Spellings
Hópnomi	place name for Evans Point, #10 on LM map. See maps 1 and 3 in Appendix 5. This is apparently part of North Arm, rather than Evans Peak.	LM	Hope-nomee		
hóte	bead	FC			hóti (FC-E)
hóte hís	do beadwork: wachákɱ níknem hóte hísḱan "my mother wove a beaded belt"	FC			
howáwa	howl	RD	howá'wa	38	
howém	gopher snake	FC			
hóweye	stir a large quantity	WS	hóweje		
hóweyesitoye	stir a large quantity round and round	WS	hówejesitoje		
hówihadoi	lead up, take up (like upstairs)	WS	hówihadoj		
hówihasip	lead out by the hand	WS	hówihasip		
hówikɱp	feel good, be clear (from evil)	RD	hō'wiköp	182	
howówo	make a sound like dragging brush, make a very scary sound	RD	howō'wo, hōwō'wo	214, 216	
hóyyam	once (long ago)	FC			hóiyam
hóyyam ḱodo	ancient land, ancestral land	FC			hóiyam ḱodo
hóyyam ḱododi	in the olden days	FC			hóiyam ḱododi
hóyyam mɱkóto	great grandmother	WST	hójjam mykóto	60:62	
hóyyam máidɱ	ancestor	FC			hóiyam máidɱ
hubɱ́ktiti	make someone feel (wasá "bad"): nik tetét wasá hubɱ́ktitiwe'am "it always makes me feel bad."	RD	hūbök'titi	78	
húboḱoi	not know how to (WS), to make no sense, not be thinking straight (RD), be forgetful or spacey (FC-E)	WS, RD, FC-E	húboḱoj (WS), hū'bokoi (RD)	136	hɱbɱ́ktiti
húboḱoi	nonsense (noun)	FC			
húboḱoipe	having no sense, witless	FC			
húboḱoisape	always witless, never having any sense, one who is always witless	FC-R			
hudán	having (something or someone) in mind: hutákanom paká hudán "I am thinking about a tree branch/sinew." This word is only found once in all the texts we have.	WS, RD	húdan (WS), hudan' (RD)	206	
húdankɱ	thinking about all the time: húdankɱ pedóm "one who thinks about eating all the time"	FC			
hudásu	drunk, intoxicated	WS	hudásu		
hudásuhsuh	tipsy, slightly drunk	WS	hudásuhsuh		

Maidu	English	Source	Source Spelling	Page	Other Spellings
hudáw	cut off a piece (RD), take up a burden (WS)	WS	hudáw		
hudáwdo	a cut-off piece	RD	hūdaudo	68	
hudési	a person expert in dodging arrows, a warrior, man-killer	FR1, CM	hudessi (CM)	25	
hudói	dig up (roots for food)	RD	hūdoi'	232	
huhehé	think about, remember	RD	huhēhē'	176	
huhéhenomen	not think twice about it, not think anything about it	RD	huhe'hēnomen	44	
huhehénonwet	without thinking about it, not giving it any thought: mᴍkí kᴍlé ma'át huhehénonwet ᴍkóikan "without even thinking about his wife, he went off."	RD	huhēhē'nonwet	88, 208	
huhehénumen	not do anything about it: mᴍ wónotichet, chenúwet, huhehénumeneam "after he had killed him, even though they had watched, they didn't do anything about it."	RD	hūhēhē'numen	112	
húheihei	give a thought to	WS	húhejhej		
húheiye	do some thinking	WS	húhejje		
huhéye	imagine	RD	huhē'ye	4	
húheye	think about (an idea), miss (someone) (RD), think about (something) (FC), think (MP): nik níkne húheyedom "I am missing my mother" mi hesápe húheyeḱa? "what do you think (about it)? What's your opinion?"	RD, FC, WS-MP	hū'hēye (RD), húheje (WS)	10, 184	
huhéye'ᴍno	think as one goes along	RD	hūhē'yeöno	124	
huhéyedi	idea, due to an idea: mínḱi huhéyedi "it was your idea. All because of your idea"	RD	hūhē'yedi	184	
huhú	lungs	WS	huhú		
húhuchik	stretch net over/across	RD	hū'hūtsik	222	
húhudoi	wrap (something) up (in a net)	RD	hū'hūdoi	220	
huhúm ítu	lung illness	FC-E			
húikᴍp	be healthy	RD	hū'iköp	104	
húiti	heal	HY			
huk	whistle	WS	huk		
húkes	be wise, be smart (FC), figure out instantly (WS)	WS, FC	húkes		
húkes	wise, clever, smart	WS	húkes		
húkesdom	wisely: húkesdom wéyedom "thinking right"	BC			
húkesi	wisdom	FC			

114

Maidu	English	Source	Source Spelling	Page	Other Spellings
húkeskinu	use correctly, do carefully: yahát wéye húkeskinudom "using correct speech"	WST-LM	húkeskinu	60:1	
húkesmen	foolish, stupid	WS	húkesmen		
húkespe	wise, clever	FC			
húkeswaláwpe	the smartest one(s)	RD	hūk'eswalau'pe	32	
húkesyopaida	be smug, be a know-it-all: m̥pékani wewédi tetét húkesyopaida'ankano, amám unídi okówonodom wónoma'ankano. "In all your speeches, you're such a know-it-all, and because of that you will die here, by starving to death."	RD	hūk'esyopada	32	
húkichik	forget	WS, FC	húkićik		hukichík (FC)
húkinu	remember	WS	húkinu		
hukít	dig down looking for something: uním ḱodo hukíte: digging up this country (looking for gold)	FC			
hukít	create using thought, imagine something into reality	RD	hukit	64, 66, 174, 176	
húkit	lonesome	WS	húkit		
húkit	stop (usually spelled hékit)	RD	hū'kit	232	hékit
hukítimen	be lonely (RD)	RD	hūkit'imen	174	húkitmen
húkitmen	get lonesome, be lonesome	WS	húkitmen		hukítimen
húkitsa	lonely by nature, solitary	WS	húkitsa		
húkḱel	whistle (verb)	WS	húkḱel		
húkḱeltete	whistle tunes	WS	húkḱeltete		
hukói	still do (something) (verb): báldom hukóiḱas "I am still writing."	FC			
húḱoi	still, yet (adverb)	WS	húḱoj		
hukóido	still doing	RD	hakoi'do	42	
huḱóidom	still (adv): huḱóidom, km̥ḱán niḱí! "Still, it is mine!"	FC			
huḱóino	still (do) (adverb)	RD	hūkoi'no	224	
húḱoinum	still, up to now	WS	húḱojnum		
hukót	cut up (wood)	RD	hukot'	172	
hukótchono	cut off (something)	RD	hukot'sono	80	
hukótdaw	cut off	RD	hukot'dau	80	huköt'daw
hukótdoi	start to cut up (small wood)	RD	hukot'doi	172	
hukóto	cut in two	RD	hukoto	56	
húkpai	whistle at, signal by whistling	WS	húkpaj		
húku	leader of a secret society	RD-NM			
húl	cover (with cloth or clothlike material)	WS	húl		

Maidu	English	Source	Source Spelling	Page	Other Spellings
húldoi	pull up one's skirt (WST), get dressed (FC): húldoidom ḱasí "I'm getting dressed."	WS, WST, FC-T	húldoj	54:34	
húldoiti	cover up someone or something, dress someone: tébe húldoitipi "Put some clothes on the baby."	FC, FC-T			
húldoi'us	dress oneself	FC-T			
hulékɱ	covering (noun) (FC), thick heavy bark (as from a pine tree) (WS)	FC, WS	huléky		
hulékɱm hɱbó	bark hut	WS	hulékym hybó		
húlis	stingy, cheap (as a cheapskate), miserly	WS	húlis		
húlissa	miserly by nature, cheapskate	WS	húlissa		
hulmayi	sturgeon	FC			
húlnoye	make a bed, spread a tablecloth, arrange one's clothes	WS	húlnoje		
hulópichi	strawberry	FC			húluṗiti
húluṗiti	blackberry, raspberry (WS), strawberry (FC, JD)	WS, FC, JD	húluṗit (WS), hulumpiti, hulupitem (JD), húlúpiti, hulupite, hulópichi (FC)	JD 70	húluṗit (WS), hulúmpiti (JD)
húmbommoto	ante, put up (money) equally	WS	húmbommoto		
húmbotmeni	every kind of, anything, any (RD), anyone, anytime, sometime, someone, all kinds of (WS): húmbotmeni ápemɱni wíyemenwet médom "giving whatever is asked for, without saying no;" húmbotmeni chema'akas min "I'll see you sometime."	RD, WS, FC	hum'botmeni (RD), húmbotmeni, húmbotmen (WS)	32, 210	húmbotmen (WS)
húmbotmennini	any time	WS	húmbotmennini		
húmbotmenweti	do whatever it takes, do everything you can (expressed as this one word) (RD), anything at all, just anything (WS)	RD, WS	hum'botmenweti (RD), húmbotmenwet (WS)	104, 202	húmbotmenwet
humchi	squaw carpet, mahala mat, prostrate ceanothus	JD	humći	68	
humín	catch fish in a net	RD	humin', hū'min	44, 48, 64	húmin
húmit	remember (what has to be done) (RD), recall, bring to mind (WS)	RD, WS	hūm'it (RD), húmit (WS)	176	
húmitchɱi	be unable to remember	RD	hū'mitchɱi	102	
húmṗilisto	hummingbird	WS, FC	húmṗilisto		hómṗilisto (FC)
húmu	sigh	WS	húmu		
húmusip	sigh (verb) (FC), sigh suddenly and deeply (WS)	WS, FC	húmusip		

Maidu	English	Source	Source Spelling	Page	Other Spellings
humusma	debt: humusma méitimen "not pay back what is owed"	FC			
humusmito	be in debt	FC			
humusmitokm	debtor	FC			
hun	hunt (verb)	WS	hun		
húnmdawtoye	go off hunting	RD	hun'ödautoye	206	
Hunanasim Ḱódom	place name for Mt. Hough, #7 on LM map. See map 1 in Appendix 5.	LM	who-na-na-sim-gohdom		
húnbmk	hunt, kill for food, rape (women)	RD	hun'bök	78, 140, 226	
hundákm	handkerchief, tissue	WS	hundáky		hindákm
huné	cut by sawing, to saw, cut (deck of cards)	WS, FC	huné		
hunékm	woodsaw, saw (noun)	WS, FC	hunéky		
hunhépindikno	arrive home from hunting, come home from hunting	RD	hunhē'pindikno	110, 154	
hunhépinkit	get home from hunting, come home from hunting	RD	hunhē'pinkit	154	
hunhépinḱoi	return home from hunting, come back home from hunting	RD	hunhē'pinkoi	110, 152, 154	
húnhepinye	return from hunting, come back from hunting	WS	húnhepinje		
huní	snot, mucus	FC, WS	hun		hun
húni	occur to (WS), think, consider (FC)	WS, FC	húni		huní (FC)
huní wi'ípe	brainless, stupid	FC			
húnḱoi	go hunting	WS	húnḱoj		
húnḱoido	be on a hunting trip, be in the process of hunting	RD	hun'koido	188	
húnḱoḱoi	go off hunting (plural subject)	RD, WS	hun'kokoi (RD), húnḱoḱoj (WS)	68	
húnmodaw	go hunting	RD	hun'modau	226	
húnmodawtoye	go off hunting (plural subject) together	RD	hun'modautoye	202, 206	
húnmohepínkit	come back from hunting	RD	hun'mohepin'kit	192, 230	
húnmokitpepé	a place to hunt, a place to do a little hunting	RD	hun'mokitpepe'	144	
húnmoḱoi	go off hunting	WS	húnmoḱoj		
húnmoye	hunt around, go around hunting	RD	hun'moye	154	
húno	rely on, bank on, bet on, to sponsor, to back, to support	WS	húno		
Hunódim	place name for Round Valley, which now contains a reservoir, is located two miles south of Greenville (FR1). See map 5 in Appendix 5.	FR1, FR-TE			
Hunódim Mómdanni	place name for Round Valley reservoir. See map 5 in Appendix 5.	FC map, MSOP			

Maidu	English	Source	Source Spelling	Page	Other Spellings
Hunódim Sewí	place name, North Canyon Creek in Round Valley. See map 5 in Appendix 5.	FC map, MSOP			
Hunódim Yamáni	place name for Round Valley Mountain: Green Mountain? See map 5 in Appendix 5.	FC map, MSOP			
hunókit	arrive to hunt	RD	huno'kit	154	
húno'us	have self-confidence	WST-DW	húno?us	70:3	
hunpapus	run (nose)	FC			
hunpapuspe	runny nose	FC-R			
Húntulam Sewí	place name: Butterfly Creek, which flows through Butterfly Valley and joins Spanish Creek a mile upstream from Keddie (FR1). See map 2 in Appendix 5.	FR1, FR-TE	huntulam sewi		
Húntulam Ḱoyó	place name: Butterfly Valley, located about two miles SW of Keddie (FR1). See map 2 in Appendix 5.	FR1, FR-TE	huntulam koiyo		
hunyéhto	hunt (something specific, as a regular thing) (WS), sort of hunt, hunt the lazy way	WS	hunjéhto	RD 94, 98	
húnyeto	hunt here and there (like a mosquito)	RD	hun'yeto, hunye'to	94, 154	
hup	to drink (a thick liquid), slurp	WS	hup		
húpai	foresee, try to figure out (RD), guess (in a game) (FC), guess (WS): homónanten ḱódoidi ḱódom úyakḱen amá húpai "in what place would a land exist - try to figure that out."	RD, FC, WS	hū'pai (RD), húpaj (WS)	5, 24	
húpaikm	guesser (as in the grass game)	WS	húpajky		
húpapai	guess at, not be fluent in: ínyanam wéye húpapaiḱas. "I am not fluent in Maidu."	HY			
hupék	open (something)	WS	hupék		
húsbillaito	snake	WS-MP	húsbillajto		
húsbini	spider web, cob web	FC			
húse	bother, scare (someone)	RD	hūs'e	116	
húselíkm	water snake	HM	hoo'-shel-li-kum		

Maidu	English	Source	Source Spelling	Page	Other Spellings
húsemweteyo	think and talk about together, plan, make plans for (verb): mínchem pénem húkespem máidʍchom uním kódo yamádom húsemweteyodom. "You two wise men are creating and planning for this world."	RD	hū'semweteo	9	
husi	vulture	FC			
husíp	take off clothing, strip, undress	WS	husíp		
húskʍ	snake	WS	húsky		
húskʍm sawí	horsetail, *equisetum*	FC-E			
Húskʍm Yamánim	place name for Worley Mountain, #38 on LM map, # 15 on HLME map 3. Means "snake mountain." A large Maidu village was at the base of this mountain in Húskʍm Ḱoyóm. See map 4 in Appendix 5.	LM, HLME	Huskym Yamanim		
Húskʍm Ḱoyóm	place name for the meadow below Húskʍm Yamánim (Worley Mountain) where a large Maidu village existed (HLME). See map 4 in Appendix 5.	HLME	Huskym kojom		
husók	cut (something like a rope)	RD	hūsok', husok	186, 188	
hutʍkityo	cut to pieces, shred (by gnawing)	RD	hūtök'ityo	168	
húťamen	not think about	RD	hūtamen	5	
hutél	hotel (from English)	WS	hutél		
húti	fat, grease (noun)	FC			
húti	guess	FC			
hútim maháti	fry bread (noun)	FC			
hutiyo	trace (verb)	FC-T			
huťól	spread on (as butter on bread)	WS	huťól		
huťólpi	any spread, like butter or cream cheese	WS	huťólpi		
hútu	crazy (WS), be crazy, act crazy (FC)	WS, FC	hútu		
hútubadoi	go crazy	FC-R			
hútubadoiti	drive someone crazy	FC			
hútudom	being crazy, lunacy	FC			
hútukʍ	lunatic	FC			
hútulʍt	be thoroughly crazy	FC			
hútulʍtti	drive someone thoroughly crazy	FC-E			
hútum sudáka	whiskey	WS	hútum sudáka		
hútupe	crazy	FC			
hútutini	act crazy (as verb), crazily	FC			

Maidu	English	Source	Source Spelling	Page	Other Spellings
húweinonwet	not having anything on one's mind: ni hápte húweinonwet bísyet "For a while I haven't had anything on my mind."	HY			
húweye	think, act like: húweyewe'as min "I'm always thinking about you."	WS, FC	húweje		
húweye	thoughts: yahát húweye kupém ka'ánkano "You have good thoughts, you have a good way of thinking"	FC			
húweyebos	think it all the way through: húweyebos éptito'uspada "May you strengthen yourself in thinking it through all the way."	FC, FC-E			
húweyedoi	start to think about	WST	húwejedoj	76:1	
húweyemeni	one who doesn't think	FC			
húweyepai	think about (someone or something)	WS	húwejepaj		
húweyepepe	having something in mind: wasá húweyepepe kmkán "he was thinking evil thoughts"	WST	húwejepepe	56	
húyeti	intend to, try to do (something) to (RD), do as always (WS)	RD, WS	hūyeti (RD), hújeti (WS)	140	
íchechem	tingle (as when the leg is asleep)	WS	ʔíćećem		
íchem	prickle, sting (intransitive)	WS	ʔíćem		
idát	be sated, full: idátweten, túitoyeḱan "when he was full, he went to sleep"	RD	idat'	152	
ihé	scrape (stems for baskets to make the stems pliable)	FC, WS	ʔihéj		ihéi
ihéluť	to fixate on, focus on: tetéluťi ihéluťweten, méhyotnoḱan "after focusing on the biggest one, he lunged for it."	RD	ihē'lut	80	
ikún	on that side: ikún tehm̃hm̃pḱoiḱan "he stretched it on that side with his feet"	RD	ikun'	11	
ílak	ache	WS	lak		
ílakitó	get injured, get hurt: ílakitóbm̃nm̃'m̃ "you might get hurt"	RD	īl'akito'	142, 148	
ílimto	play the violin	WS	ʔílimto		
ílimtokm̃	violin	WS	ʔílimtoky		
inánas	bear (any species)	WS	ʔinánas		

Maidu	English	Source	Source Spelling	Page	Other Spellings
in'ánto	on either side (one on each side of, for example a person) (RD), between, alongside of, side by side (WS)	RD, WS	in'anto (RD), ʔinʔánto (WS)	192	ínanto
in'ántodi	one on each side	RD	inan'todi	52	
in'ántokit	being one on each side (RD), down between (WS)	RD, WS	in'antokit (RD), ʔinʔántokit (WS)	78	
ínbuki	fisher (animal), pine marten, Martes Pennanti	RD, RR-SW, WS	in'buki (RD), ʔínbuk (WS)	168, 214, 218, 236	ínbuk
inchépi	lynx	FC			
Indak	place name for Placerville	RD-NM			
índakm̥m papeli	toilet paper	FC			
in'ínno	enter, go down into	WS, WST-DW	ʔinʔínno	72:9	
in'ínno	interior, within, inside of, the depths	WS, WST-DW	ʔinʔínno	72:9	
ínkm̥l	waist (of a person), skirt (originally the bark skirt)	WS	ʔínḱyl		
inkasati	type of edible mushroom, big brown mushroom eaten in November	PM-M, JD	in-ca-sa-tee (PM-M), inkasaty (JD)	JD 23	inkasatm̥
ínkayi	mule deer	FC, HY			
ínḱi	beside, the place alongside of, the close place	WS	ʔínḱi		
ínḱidi	alongside of, nearby: sam ínḱidi "by the fire"	WS, WST	ʔínḱidi	54:27	
ínḱiki	next to each other, neighboring	RD	in'kiki	202	
ínḱina	all the way to: púiyam ínḱina "all the way to the door, to beside the door"	RD	in'kina	196	
ínḱinan	close to: km̥lém ínḱinan "close to the woman" lit: "from the woman's next-to place"	RD	in'kinan	196	
ínno	buttocks	WS	ʔínno		
ínnom tuke	asshole (from Nisenan)	FC-T			
ínnoye	go around with one's butt in the air	FC			
ínsep	wildcat	WS	ʔínsep		
íntas	base, hilt	WS	ʔíntas		
íntasluťi	the very base: íntasluťdi hukótdawḱan "he cut it off at the very base"	RD	in'taslut	80	íntasluť (WS)
íntasluťna	to the very hilt, to the very base (of something)	WS	ʔíntasluťna		
ínťa'usto	very fat, covered with fat	WS	ʔínťaʔusto		
ínwok	thrust with the hips (as in sexual intercourse)	WS, WST-LB	ʔínwok	44:11	
ínyambóno	squat down	RD	in'yambon'ō	170	
ínyana	Indian (from English) (noun)	WS	ʔínjana		

Maidu	English	Source	Source Spelling	Page	Other Spellings
ínyanak wéye	Indian language, Maidu language	FC			
ínyanam	Indian (adj): ínyanam wéye "Indian language, Maidu language"	FC			
ínyanam bosó	piece of worked flint (WS), basalt, obsidian (FC)	WS, FC	ʔínjanam bosó		
ínyanam máidm	Indian, Maidu person or people	WS	ʔínjanam májdy		
ínyanam smmí	deer, venison	WS	ʔínjanam symí		
ínyanam smmím té	fawn	WS	ʔínjanam symím té		
ínyanam yó	Indian paintbrush (a species of flower)	WS	ʔínjanam jó		
ínyanam yokóli	traditional Maidu flag or banner	WS	ʔínjanam jokóli		
isádom	variant form of hesádom "why?"	WS	ʔisádom		
íschomi	socks, stockings	WS, FC	ʔísćomi		íssomi
ísdotchono	kick (something) over	RD	is'dotsono	208	
ísdotdoi	kick (something) away	RD	isdotdoi	208	
ísdotmitno	kick down hill	WS, WST	ʔísdotmitno	42:5	
iská	nothing: mmyéchom iská chekán "those two see nothing"	RD	iskā'	166	
íska	arrange (affairs), manage (things)	WS	ʔíska		
íska	thingy, whatchamacallit	FC			
íska	uh, um	FC, WS	ʔíska		
íska	uh-ing, saying "uh"	FC			
ískal	moccasin	WS	ʔískal		
ískalki	moccasin	WS	ʔískalki		
ískalno	moccasin	WS	ʔískalno		
ískadak	trip on something	FC			
ískayaťa	someone who has died (yaťa is also suffixed to a person's name after he dies)	WS	ʔískajaťa		
ískoi	put one's foot into	WS	ʔískoj		
ískoi mákwono	try (footgear) on the feet, try on shoes	WS	ʔískoj mákwono		
íswawakoi	kick away (dirt)	RD	is'wawakoi	232	
íswolak	put a foot rag on	FC			
íswolakm	foot rag	FC			
íswolo	stub one's toe: ódi íswolokas "I stubbed my toe on a rock."	FC, FC-R	íswula		
ísyo	kick (verb)	WS	ʔísjo		
ísyoda	keep on kicking	WS	ʔísjoda		
ítmk	freezing cold	WS	ʔítyk		
ítu	hurt (intransitive), ache, give pain(WS), be sick, be in pain (RD)	WS, RD	ʔítu (WS), ī'tu (RD)	100	

Maidu	English	Source	Source Spelling	Page	Other Spellings
ítu	pain (noun), illness (FC), a "pain" in the shamanistic sense (an object which causes sickness and which is removed by the doctor in curing) (WS)	FC, WS	ʔítu		
ítubodoi	remove the cause of sickness, remove a "pain" (a shamanistic term)	WS	ʔítubodoj		
ítudedes	sickly	WS	ʔítudedes		
ítudoi	start to be sick	WST	ʔítudoj	52:21	
ítuhtu	rather sick	WS	ʔítuhtu		
ítuhtuti	cause a little bit of illness or pain	FC			
ítukɷ	illness, pestilence	RD	i'tukö	130	
ítukpe	pestilential, illness-causing, disease-carrying	RD	ī'tukpe	132	
ítum ḱódo	sickness, the cause of sickness (that has to be removed in curing)	RD	ī'tuñ kâ'do	74	
ítunok	cause of pain (noun)	RD	ī'tunok	74	
ítus	roast (verb)	WS, RD	ʔítus (WS), itus (RD)	234, 216	
ítus	roast, roast meat (noun)	RD	itsu, itus	234, 216	
ítusa	sickly by nature, an invalid	WS	ʔítusa		
ítusape	sickly, someone always sick	FC			
ítusyo	roast (noun), roast meat	RD	ī'tusyo	218	
ítutawal	treat a sick person shamanistically	WS	ʔítutawal		
ítuti	hurt (someone), cause pain	WS	ʔítuti		
kɷ	be (RD, FC), have, possess (WS, RD): kɷyáhadom mamá'ankano ka'átido "if you want to have (it), you will do as told"	RD, WS, FC	kö (RD), ky (WS)	136, 148	ku "have" (FC), ka "be" (WS)
ḱɷ	do, put	WS	ḱy		
kɷ'ḿye	keep on having: téťmťɷ kɷ'ḿye: "keep on having children"	RD	kö'ö'ye	50	
ḱɷchono	sink, go down (as the setting sun)	WS	ḱyćono		
kɷdawe	a turn at something: mi ḱún kɷdawe "your turn"	RD	kö'dawe	6	
kɷdói	sunrise: kɷdoimenupe "just before sunrise"	RD	ködoi'men	34	
kɷháḱoi	carry (something) away	RD	köhāk'oi	136	
ḱɷi	peek, peep, spy	WS	ḱyj		
ḱɷiche	take a peek (WS), glimpse, be able to see (RD): ɷpéḱanim kɷlóknonom mɷ ḱɷichekan "all the women could see it."	WS, RD	ḱyjće (WS), k'ö'itse (RD)	78	

Maidu	English	Source	Source Spelling	Page	Other Spellings
kɵ'ídi	share with (verb)	RD	köi'di	136	
kɵ'ídipe	sharing with, when sharing with (takes -ki on the person shared with): minsámboyeḱi ma'át tibí min kɵídipe ḱúidakmenḱa? "Don't you like to share a little of what you have, even with your brother?"	RD	köi'dipe	136	
ḱɵilulumi	throat	FC			ḱúilulumi
kɵḱás	I am	FC, RD	kökas, kökus (228)	5, 9, 228	kaḱás (WS)
kɵ́ki	cookie	FC			
kɵkít	to bear (children): máidɵm téťɵťɵ kɵkítdom ka'ánkano "you are child-bearing people"	RD	kökit'	22	
ḱɵlɵnoyeti	roll (something) around	WST	ḱylýnojeti	50:6	
ḱɵlɵ́	roll	WS	ḱylý		
ḱɵlɵ́ḱoi	roll away	WS	ḱylýḱoj		
ḱɵlɵ́ḱoiti	roll (something) away	WS	ḱylýḱojti		
ḱɵlɵ́lɵ	roll as thunder	RD	kölöl'ö	144	
ḱɵlɵ́no	roll, roll along	WS	ḱylýno		
ḱɵlɵ́noti	roll (something) along	WS	ḱylýnoti		
ḱɵlɵ́noye	roll around (intransitive)	RD, WS	kölön'oi, kölön'oye (RD), ḱylýnoje (WS)	190	
ḱɵlɵ́plɵlɵp	rumble loudly, to thunder	RD	kölöp'lölöp	150, 158	
ḱɵlɵ́ye	roll toward (intransitive)	WS	ḱylýje		
ḱɵlɵ́yeti	roll (something) towards	WS	ḱylýjeti		
kɵlé	hide (something), bury (a corpse)	WS	kylé		kilé (RD)
kɵlé	woman, wife	WS	kylé		
kɵlécho	two women	FC			
kɵléchoni	with the two women	RD	küle'tsoni	126	
kɵlékɵ	marry a woman	WS	kyléky		
kɵlékɵto	married couple	WS	kylékyto		
kɵlékɵto	marry a woman	FC			
kɵlém kawáyu	mare	WS	kylém kawáju		
kɵlém ṕɵbe	girl	WS, PM-D	kylém ṕybe (WS), kulem buba (PM-D)		
kɵlém sɵmí	doe	WS	kylém symí		
kɵlépeto	marry a woman	FC			
kɵléweye	insult (verb)	WS	kyléweje		
kɵléweyesa	insulting by habit or nature	WS	kyléwejesa		
kɵléwi'ipe	without a woman, bachelor	RD	küle'wipe	50	
kɵléwťi	legal wife	WS	kyléuťi		
ḱɵ́lla	liver	WS	ḱylla		
kɵlókbe	old woman	WS	kylókbe		kolókbe (FC-R)
kɵlókbechu	act like an old woman, be an old woman	FC			
kɵlókbekbe	elderly (of women)	WS	kylókbekbe		
kɵlókbekbedoi	get older, age (of women)	WS	kylókbekbedoj		

Maidu	English	Source	Source Spelling	Page	Other Spellings
kʌlókbepe	elderly (women only)	RD	külok'bepe	82	
kʌlókbepinem póḱo	a Mountain Maidu month following the kónom póḱo. "old-woman dying month? A very hot month of the year"	RD-NM			
kʌlókbetʼʌtʼʌ	old women	FC			
kʌlókbeto	little old lady	WS	kylókbeto		
kʌlóknono	women	WS	kylóknono		kolóknono (FC-R)
ḱʌm	fruit pit, seed	WS-MP	ḱym		ḱomí (WS, FC)
ḱʌmʼʌk	sand	WS	ḱymʔýk		
ḱʌpyeti	leave (something) behind	RD	kö'pyeti	44	
ḱʌsdo	ridge top, crest of the ridge (RD), ridge (WS)	RD, WS	kös'do (RD), ḱysdo, ḱysdoj (WS)	46	
Ḱʌsdu	place name for a village at Taylorsville, later called Telanḱumhʌ (Telan being "Taylors"). May be the same as Chakámdʌḱʌ. See maps 1 and 5 in Appendix 5.	AK	Küshdu	398	
ḱʌsi	sand bar, river bar	RD	kös'	34	
ḱʌsí	ridge, small hill	FC, WS	ḱys		ḱʌs
ḱʌswo	along a ridge: ḱʌswo ʌnódom "going along a ridge"	RD, WS	ḱyswo (WS), kös'wo (RD)	146	
ḱʌswo	ridge	WS	ḱyswo		
ḱʌswodoidi	up at the crest of the ridge	WS	ḱyswodojdi		
ḱʌswodoinodi	along the crest of the ridge	WS	ḱyswodojnodi		
ḱʌswonnodi	down at the lower end of the ridge	WS	ḱyswonnodi		
ḱʌswonó	go along the ridge (verb + conj)	RD	köswono'	148	
ḱʌswowono	along the ridge	RD	kös'wowono	140, 212	
ḱʌswowóno	along the crest of a ridge	RD	köswowon'o	144	
ka	be (according to FC and RD: /a/ changes to /ʌ/ before a /ḱ/: kʌḱán. It remains /a/ before other letters: ka'ánkano)	WS	ka		kʌ (FC, RD) in syllable before glottalized ḱ
ḱá	younger sister: as a kinship term, this word must have a prefix, either mʌ, nik, or min (see Mountain Maidu Grammar, Lesson 6 for more details)	WS	ḱá		
ḱaʼʌkói	go off secretly, sneak off: 'makítdom, kʌḱán nisé ʌhémapem,' aḱán. awéten máisem ḱaʼʌkóiḱan. "'If he finds out, he'll be wanting to go with us,' they said. So they sneaked off."	RD	kā ökoi'	208	

Maidu	English	Source	Source Spelling	Page	Other Spellings
ḱá'ᴍnoye	go around stealthily, sneak around	WS	ḱáʔynoje		
ḱa'ḱa	bald eagle, buzzard	FC			
ka'okít	arrive (as a letter), come to: máise papélim ka'okítkᴍkan. "A letter might come to them."	HY			
ka'á	do like that (RD), do, be (WS): ka'á'as ᴍkóidom "that was how we (2) went, we (2) were doing that when we went"	RD, WS	kaā (RD), kaʔá (WS)	180	
ka'ádᴍtᴍ	single-handedly: hesádom áite teténono ka'ádᴍtᴍ sówodoidom mawewíyakḱen "I wonder how he lifts big ones single-handedly"	RD	kaā'dötö	142	
ka'áhuyeti	do like that, do the same thing, do something	RD, WS	kā'huyeti, kaā'huyeti (RD), kaʔáhujeti (WS)	74, 190	
ka'áhuyetiwomén	tell (someone) not do things like that: mᴍ 'as min ka'ápe ka'áhuyetiwoménḱas "that's just the kind of thing I told you not to do"	RD	kaā'hūyeti-women'	162	
ka'ái	say	WS	kaʔáj, káj		kái
ka'áimape	one who would talk like that, one who talks inappropriately: ka'áimapem sikálamenwet, mínsᴍm ᴍnópi "everybody go on, without someone who would talk like that bothering (you)"	RD	kaai'mapem	206	
ka'áimen	not say such things, not talk like that: ka'áimen! "Don't talk like that!" (when one is talking inappropriately): ka'áimenkᴍm matás "let me never say such things"	FC, RD	kaaimen	54	
ka'áimenwo	tell someone not to say such things	RD	kaai'menwo	148	
ka'áimenwowéw	keep telling someone not to say such things: ka'áimenwowéwkas 'as min! "I keep telling you not to say that!"	RD	kaai'menwowē'u	142	
ka'áimenyahá	what should not be said (noun): ka'áimenyahá káiwonokᴍḱas "I have said what shouldn't be said."	RD	kaai'menyaha'	184	

Maidu	English	Source	Source Spelling	Page	Other Spellings
ka'áinimᴍni	if that's what you mean, if that's what you're saying (nim = "you"): hómpaitoyahadom ᴍnóyemenḱas, ka'áinimᴍni "I didn't come here wanting to fight, if that's what you mean."	RD	kaai'nimöni	146	
ka'ámape	someone who would do something like that	RD	kaā'mape	206	
ka'ámenim máidᴍ	unusual people, strange people, people like that	RD	kaā'menim mai'düm	188	
ka'ámenmapem kᴍḱán	it's not going to be like that	RD	kaamenmapeñ kökan	48	
ka'ámenmapem kano	you should not do like that	RD	kaā'menmapeñ'kano	28	
ka'ánbe	that much, that many (just enumerated)	WS	kaʔánbe		
ka'ánbenini	a certain amount, a certain number of: ka'ánbenini ékdachet okítas "after a certain number of days, I should come home."	RD	kaan'benini	218	
ka'ándukbe	one that size, as much as that: ka'ándukbe sódoiwoḱades? "Did I tell you to bring one that size?"	RD	kaan'dukbe	142	
ka'ánte	showing how much/far, that's how much/far, the size (length, height) of: ka'ánte hóipai wodáwtikᴍḱan "that's how far behind he has left (us) by now"	RD	kaān'te	46, 148, 232	
ka'ánte	so far, up to now	WS	kaʔánte		
ka'ántekit	go a distance, reach (a place) from a distance	RD	kaān'tekit	32, 232	
ka'ántekitchet	after reaching a place from a distance	RD	kaan'tekitset	226	
ka'ántekitdi	in the place reached from a distance	RD	kan'tekidi	232	
ka'ánu	stay, remain in a certain way, stay (at home) like that: ka'ánuḱan "they are staying home." ka'ánup unína "stay around here!"	WS, RD, FC	kaʔánu (WS), kaānu (RD)	68	
ká'anupi	stay here!	RD	ka'anupi	88	
ka'ánuwewol	keep quiet	RD	kaā'nuwēwol	108	
ka'ápaikan	apparently is (inside a quote within a story)	RD	kaā(paikan)	180	
ka'ápe	that kind, that kind of thing	WS, RD	kaʔápe (WS), kaā'pe (RD)	26, 162, 208	
ka'ápe 'as	that's the kind (it was)	RD	kaā'pe as	160	
ka'ápepe	anything like those, things like...	RD	kā'apepe(m), kaā'pepe(m)	30, 214	

Maidu	English	Source	Source Spelling	Page	Other Spellings
ka'ápepem upé	the same eating place, the same place where (someone else) ate	RD	kaā′pe pem ūpe′	234	
ḱa'ás	move (something), slide as a door	WS	ḱaʔás		ka'ás
ḱa'ási	move (noun) as in checkers	WS	ḱaʔási		
ḱa'ásḱoi	open (a door) (DW), move (something) away from, slide	WS, WST-DW	ḱaʔásḱoj	78	ka'ásḱoi
ka'ásḱoikm̥	opening (noun)	FC			
ka'áspin	open inward, as a door	WS	kaʔáspin		
ka'áswosipin	move (something) a little bit towards	RD	kaas'wosipin	58	
ka'át	such, such a	WS	kaʔát		
ka'áti	do, cause to be done	FC			
ka'átido	this way, by doing like this, do like this: ka'átido mm̥m bomó wónotibosma'aḱas "This way, I will kill the whole bunch." km̥yáhadom mamá'ankano ka'átido "if you want to have (it), do like this."	RD	kaā′tido	106, 136	
ka'átik	in such a way	RD	kaā′tik	58	
ka'átimen	don't do	FC			
ka'áwhuyeti	do like that, do this and that, putter around	WS	kaʔáwhujeti		
ka'áwini	alike, same as (RD), in that way (FC), that kind (WS), such-and-such (WST: uním km̥kán ka'áwinim ḱútt̪m̥t̪m̥m "this is such-and-such a bird" ka'áwini wónom máidm̥m adóm uním cham máidm̥ "humans and these tree people are alike"	RD, FC, WS, WST	kaā′wini (RD), kaʔáwini (WS)	162 (RD), 52:17 (WST)	
ka'áyahádom	doing what one wants: go ahead and do what (you) want, "whatever!"	RD	kaā′ yahā′dom	178	
ḱabm̥ḱ	start (verb), begin: wasám ḱabm̥ḱchoi'a "evil had begun"	WS	ḱabým̥ḱ		
ḱabm̥ḱ	start (noun), beginning	WS	ḱabým̥ḱ		
ḱabm̥ḱm̥m	having begun, just as (he/she) started to... (construction is like kaním. Previous word (verb) takes -m ending): ym̥noswoitom ḱabm̥ḱm̥m ḱéndi díwochoi'a "just as she started to bend over, she was caught in the trap"	RD	kabököm	62, 172	
ḱábe	little sister	RD	ka′be	232	
kabíche	cabbage	FC-T			
kachémeni	debris, crumbs	FC			

Maidu	English	Source	Source Spelling	Page	Other Spellings
ḱáchenu	watch secretly	WS	ḱáćenu		
ḱachík	head (someone) off, surround (someone) in order to capture, herd (animals) together by chasing them	RD, WS	katsik′ (RD), ḱaćík (WS)	180	
ḱachíkimotobos	completely surround	RD	katsik′imotobos′	204	
ḱachó	stretch oneself out, lie down	WS	ḱaćó		
ḱachókit	lie down	WS	ḱaćókit		
ḱachókitkm	blanket, ground sheet, anything to lie down on. Sometime used facetiously to mean "wife"	WS	ḱaćókitky		
kadékket	cackle	FC			
kadés	nick, cut by nicking	WS-MP	kadés		
ḱadík kít	rain (verb), come down (rain)	FC			
ḱadíkhekit	stop raining	RD	kadik′hēkit	152	
ḱadíki	rain (noun)	FC, WS	ḱadík		ḱadík
ḱadíkim pibáwi	drizzle (noun), light rain	FC			
ḱadópchik	insert as plug	RD	kadop′tsik	34, 114	
ḱadóschik	choke (someone), strangle	RD	kados′tsik	218	
ḱadót	push, shove (something)	WS	ḱadót		
ḱadótdikno	shove (someone) against (something), stick (something) onto (something), push against	WS	ḱadótdikno	RD 92	
ḱadótkoi	push (something) away	WS	ḱadótḱoj		
ḱadútkit	push (someone) under the ground	RD, WS-MM	kadut′kit	19 (RD), 26 (WS-MM)	
kahás	move, slide as a door	WS	kahás, kaʔás		ka'ás
kahásḱoi	slide, as a door	WS	kahásḱoj		
kaháspin	open inward, as a door	WS, WST	kaháspin (WS), ḱaháspin (WST)	60	
ḱáhḱa	crow (noun)	FC			ḱákḱa (WS)
ḱahúkit	waylay, lie in wait for someone, ambush	WS	ḱahúkit		
ḱahúkittoto	ambush each other	WS	ḱahúkittoto		
ḱahúl	cover (verb), put a cover on	WS	ḱahúl		
ḱahúlchik	cover over	WS	ḱahúlćik		
kahúyeti	cause (something) to happen	RD	kahū′yeti	108	
kai	be lying (like a log) (WS), lie down (FC)	WS, FC	kaj		
kai	fly (verb)	WS	kaj		
kai	log	WS	kaj		

Maidu	English	Source	Source Spelling	Page	Other Spellings
kái	express (feelings) (RD), want, mean, say, signify, refer to (WS): mᴀm kái'usan. "They used to say that." káikas núkti wéwedom. "I am saying just a few words." káikas ka'áwini wónom máidᴀm adóm uním chám máidᴀm "I meant to say, these trees and people are alike."	RD, WS, WST-RP, HY	kai' (RD), káj (WS)	90, 162, 216 (RD), 64:17 (WST)	
k̓ai	evening, twilight: k̓aidi "in the evening"	WS, FC-R	k̓aj		k̓ai'i
k̓ai pakáni	Venus	FC-T			
káichik	fly into	WS	kájćik		
káidoi	fly up	FC			
káidoino	fly up	FC			
káieskᴀ	bluejay, Steller's jay	FC			kaihískᴀ (WS)
káieskᴀm máidᴀ	bluejay man, Steller's jay person	FC, RD	kais'kömmai'düm	102	
k̓aihí	earthworm	WS	k̓ajhí		
k̓aihím ítusi	roasted earthworms	WS	k̓ajhím ítusi		
kaihískᴀ	bluejay, California jay, Steller's jay	WS, RD	kajhísky (WS), kais'kö (RD)	102	káieskᴀ (FC, RD)
kai'im moldo	egret	FC			
kai'ínno	fly into	WS	kaj?ínno		
kái'inpin	swoop down, fly down, land (verb)	FC			
káikᴀm kaleta	airplane	FC			
káikᴀtoto	airline	FC			
kaikáino	and such like: sᴀmím kaikáino "deer and the like"	HY			
káikit	fly down	FC			
k̓aikit	be evening: k̓aikitmᴀni "when evening comes, when it is evening"	FC-T			
kák̓oi	go flying	FC			
káina	somewhat, more or less	WS	kájna		
káinahu	personal Indian name of Dan Williams	WS	kájnahu		
káinokᴀm tᴀlᴀlᴀ	flying squirrel	WS	kájnokym tylýly		
káinoye	fly around	WS	kájnoje		
kai'ókit	arrive by flying	RD	kaio'kit	80	
kái'okitek̓oi	arrive flying	RD	kai'okitekoi	36	
káipaiᴀnoye	fly around from one to another	RD	kai'paiöno'ye	154	
káipai'ᴀtoto	fly from one to another	RD	kai'paiöto'to	152	
k̓áipe	cook dinner (FC), eat lunch (RR-EP), eat dinner, have dinner	FC, RR-EP			
k̓áipe	evening meal, dinner: k̓áipe mádom "setting a meal out, putting dinner on the table"	WS, RD	k̓ájpe (WS), kai'pe (RD)	214	
k̓áipekᴀ	dinner	FC			
k̓áipeti	make dinner for, give dinner to	RD	k!ai'peti	154	

Maidu	English	Source	Source Spelling	Page	Other Spellings
káipewo	give (someone) dinner, tell someone to eat dinner	RD	kai′pe wō	94	
káipewonó	had eaten dinner	RD	kai′pe wonō′	232, 234	
ḱaise	earthworm	PM-M	ki-sem		
káisitoye	fly through, fly around inside	WS	kájsitoje		
kaití	fell (a tree), knock a tree down	RD	kaiti′	138	
kaití′ᴍno	go along knocking down trees	RD	kaiti′öno	138	
kaiwóno	be felled (tree)	RD	kaiwono	66	
káiwono	have said, had said	RD	kai′wonō	184	
káiye	tell (someone), mean: ka'áimenwowet 'as min bístidom káiyeasi "I told you not to talk like that, I should say I'm leaving you."	RD	kai′ye	148	
kaiyéw	be telling (someone), mean: ka'ánte t′ᴍt′ᴍmen ni 'as káiyewḱasi "I have been telling you not (to fetch) sticks like that." "I didn't mean sticks like that."	RD	kaiyē′u	90, 142, 148	
káiyew	keep calling (someone)	RD	kai′yeū	72	
káḱa	eagle, bald eagle, buzzard	WS, FC	káḱ		káḱ (WS)
kakán	it is, he/she is, they are	RD, WS	kakan′	24	kᴍkan (FC, RD)
ḱakánaipin	sneak underneath	RD	kakan′aipin	58	
kakánim po	every night	RD	kakan′im po	196	
ḱákka	crow	WS	ḱákka		ḱahḱa (FC)
ḱákkini	spirit, spirit guide (FC), ḱákkini are the spirits which the shaman evokes in the darkened dance house. They are generally benevolent (WS)	FC, WS	ḱákkin		ḱákkin (WS)
ḱálᴍk	crawl secretly	WS	ḱályk		
ḱálᴍkpai	sneak up on	WS	ḱálykpaj		
kaléta	vehicle, car, wagon, cart (from Spanish carreta "wagon")	WS	kaléta		
kalétam bó	street, auto road, highway, wagon road	WS	kalétam bó		
kalétam uiyi	garage (car house)	FC			
Kalipónia	California	FC-E			
kam	lose hair, lose fur, shed (verb), lose feathers, molt	WS	kam		
ḱámᴍmᴍwet sól	hum (verb)	WS	ḱámymywet sól		
káma	antelope (WS, HY), elk (HM)	WS, HM, HY	káma		kámu (HM)
ḱamák	unripe, not completely cooked, undercooked	WS	ḱamák		
ḱamáka	raw food, uncooked food	RD	kamā′ka	164	

Maidu	English	Source	Source Spelling	Page	Other Spellings
kámda	molt, shed fur, skin, shed feathers	WS	kámda		
kamí	nephew: as a kinship term, this word must have a prefix, either mɷ, nik, or min (see Mountain Maidu Grammar, Lesson 6 for more details)	FC, WS	kam		kam
ḱamí	belly, stomach	FC, WS	ḱam		ḱam (WS), ḱa'mí (FC-T)
kámi'apda	personal name of the canoe thugs' grandmother	RD	kamiapdam	60	
ḱamílák	have a stomach ache, have diarrhea: ḱamílákḱas "I have a stomach ache"	WS	ḱamí lák		
ḱamím betéke	navel	WS	ḱamím betéke		
kamím kɷlé	niece: as a kinship term, this word must have a prefix, either mɷ, nik, or min (see Mountain Maidu Grammar, Lesson 6 for more details)	WS	kamím kylé		
kamím wolí	nephews: as a kinship term, this word must have a prefix, either mɷ, nik, or min (see Mountain Maidu Grammar, Lesson 6 for more details)	WS	kamím wolí		
kamísa	shirt (from Spanish camisa)	WS	kamísa		kamísɷ (FC)
ḱamnak	on the stomach: ḱámnak wusútkinu "lie on your stomach"	RD	kam'nak	12	
kámosi	calf of leg	RD	kam'osi	46	
kampíchulapi	swallow (bird), barn swallow	FC			ḱumpichulipe
ḱampúmpu	tripe	WS	ḱampúmpu		
ḱámtapo	have a big belly	WS	ḱámtapo		
ḱámtapope	big-bellied	WS	ḱámtapope		
ḱan	then, and, and then	WS	ḱan, ḱán		ḱán, kán
ḱan bíschoi'a	there once was..., once upon a time there was...	RD	kan büs'tsoia	104	
kan... kan	just when... then: kan bédukan káipe pemádom yaháhanuchet kan mɷyína yohónchoi'a. "Just when they were about to eat dinner, after it was all prepared, (something) made a loud noise from that direction." kaní batápaipotochet, kan mɷyím máidɷm wilédiknoḱan. "Just as she was about to catch up, that man ran home."	RD	kan...kan	176, 216	kaní...kan

Maidu	English	Source	Source Spelling	Page	Other Spellings
kaná	most certainly (with a future verb) "I WILL" do…, "yes I will!" (RD), a word used at the end of a sentence to announce a resolution of mind (WS): chuchúpaima'aḱas kaná! "I will urinate on it - yes I will!" lᴧkdiknoma'aḱas kaná! "I will climb up there, all right!"	RD, WS	kana' (RD), kaná (WS)	66, 138, 178	
ḱanái	the place beneath	WS	ḱanáj		
ḱanáidi	under, beneath, underneath	WS	ḱanájdi		
ḱanáidi lᴧktik	crawl under	FC			
ḱanái'im	under (adj)	FC			
ḱanái'im kamísa	undershirt	FC			
ḱanái'im ḱódo	another world, lower world	FC			
ḱanáikᴧ	pillow	FC-E			
ḱanáipinom póḱo	a Mountain Maidu month following the tetém chám pautom póḱo	RD-NM			
ḱanáiwositodi	where (it) travels across underneath (like the sun)	RD	kanai'wositodi	26	ḱanáwositodi (RD)
ḱanáyim ínkᴧl	petticoat, slip (undergarment)	WS	ḱanájim ínḱyl		
ḱanáyim símpo	lower lip	WS	ḱanájim símpo		
ḱánbe	all: kanbemᴧni "Out of all the…"	RD	kan'be	100, 104	ka'ánbe
kaní	all, the whole of it, all there is	WS	kan		kan
kaní	finally, because of that, the last (RD), all, the whole of it, all there is (WS), end, only that (FC): sᴧtim kaníwonom lᴧkchopinḱan "the last one climbed in."	RD, WS, FC	kanī', kanim' (RD)	108, 114, 176, 202	kan (WS)
ḱánibem	all, the whole bunch: ᴧpéḱanim niḱi héskatom ḱánibem ínyana wéyepem: "All of my relatives, the whole bunch, (were) speaking Maidu (Indian);" ḱánibem wónobospem sᴧtim hónwenupem "all of them gone (passed away), one still living."	FC			
kaním	last (adj), final	RD	kanim'	24	
kaním ka'am	that's it, that's enough, that was all	FC			
kaním mabó	It shall be so till the end	RD	kanim'abo	182	
kaním maḱade?	is that all?	FC			
kanína	to the end	FC-T			
kaníwoi	final destination	RD	kanī'woi	26	

Maidu	English	Source	Source Spelling	Page	Other Spellings
kaníwoi'ᴍdikno	go as far as that, to reach the destination	RD	kanī'woi ödik'no	26	
kaníwonom	at last, finally	RD	kanī'wonom	166	
kánte	just, indeed, certainly	WS	kánte		
ḱanúkit	waylay, ambush	WS	ḱanúkit, ḱahúkit		ḱahúkit (WS)
ḱa'ó	get up close to	RD, WST	kao	114 (RD), 50:7 (WST)	
ḱa'ódato	get up against (something, someone)	WS	ḱaʔódato		
ḱa'ók	thin, lean (of a person or an animal)	WS	ḱaʔók		
ḱa'okᴍ́kᴍino	peek down quietly and secretly	RD	k!a okö'köino	100	
ḱap	become ripe, get ripe	WS	ḱap		
ḱap	ripe, completely cooked, done	WS	ḱap		
kapá	grizzly bear	FC			
kapáduwa	brown towhee	HM	kah-pah'-doo-wah		
ḱapdói	start to get ripe	FC-E			
kaṕéṕe	generally, in general	WS	kaṕéṕe		
kapí	insect, bug (FC), unpleasant critter (WS): yokᴍ́m kapí nik hédatpaidom kᴍḱán "biting insects are pursuing me."	FC, WS, FC-R	kap		kap, kop (WS), ḱapí (FC-R)
kapíl	squeeze, crush (someone)	RD	kapil'	116	
ḱápkᴍ	baked (adj)	WST	ḱápky	76:2	
ḱápmeninu	unripe, not completely cooked, underdone	WS	ḱápmeninu		
ḱapól	insert	WS	ḱapól		
ḱapólḱoi	shove (something) into (something)	WS	ḱapólḱoj		
ḱapólno	stick (something) into (something)	WS	ḱapólno		
ḱapólsito	stick (something) through (something)	WS	ḱapólsito		
ḱapólyo	keep on shoving (things) in	WS	ḱapóljo		
kapóťa	coat, jacket (from Spanish capote, "cloak")	WS	kapóťa		
ḱáppoto	be almost ripe, be almost cooked	WS	ḱáppoto		
ḱápsito	thoroughly cooked, overcooked, thoroughly ripe, overripe	WS	ḱápsito		
ḱápti	cook, roast (verb), ripen	WS, FC-E	ḱápti		
ḱáptikᴍ	cook (noun)	WS	ḱáptiky		
ḱáptipe	ready (food), ripe	FC			
kapú	thin-layered bark	WS	kapú		
kapúdi	California creeper, a species of small gray bird	WS	kapúdi		
kapúmi	thin-layered bark, bark of a tree	WS	kapúmi		
kapúmim hᴍbó	menstruation hut, bark house	WS	kapúmim hybó		

Maidu	English	Source	Source Spelling	Page	Other Spellings
kapúmim k̓uk̓ú	strings made of bark	FC			
kapúslele	butterfly	FC, WS	kápuslele		kápuslele
kápuslelem kapí	caterpillar	WS	kápuslelem kapí		
kápuslelem mḿkkṁlusi	moth (woodland variety)	WS	kápuslelem mýkkylusi		
k̓asi	wild plum, Sierra plum	WS, JD	k̓as (WS), maidumkasym (JD)	JD 71	maidṁmk̓asi, k̓as
k̓así	I am	FC, RD			k̓as
K̓asím	place name near Susanville #7 on FR map. See K̓asím Yamánim on map 4 in Appendix 5.	FR		370-371	
k̓asím cha	plum tree	FC-E			
K̓asím Yamánim	place name for the mountain immediately to the west of Susanville, above the Roosevelt School swimming pool, #13 on HLME map 3. A large Maidu cemetery is on this hillside (HLME). See map 4 in Appendix 5.	HLME	K'asim Jamanim		K̓asím
k̓ásolto	hum (verb), sing quietly	WS, FC	k̓ásolto		
k̓atá	push (something)	WS	k̓atá		
k̓atáno	push (something) along	WS	k̓atáno		
k̓atáwaito	push (something) apart	WS	k̓atáwajto		
katí	aunt (WS), paternal aunt (FC), woman (SPB): as a kinship term, this word must have a prefix, either mṁ, nik, or min (see <u>Mountain Maidu Grammar</u>, Lesson 6 for more details)	FC, WS, SPB	kat (WS), catee (SPB)		kat (WS)
katí	do to (someone), usually with bad implications, mistreat: nisé katík̓an "he does (this) to us" nisák̓i oiṁpaipem máidṁm ma'át nisá katí'am "Even our beloved men did this to us (2)."	RD	kati'	108, 188	
katída	do (something) to (someone), get back at (someone)	RD	kati'da	54	
kaťot	attach (something) to (something)	WS, RD	kaťot (WS), kat'ot (RD)		káťot (RD)
kaťótyo	attach things to (something) (RD stresses the first syllable)	WS	kaťótjo (WS), kat'otyo (RD)		káťotyo (RD)
káťotyo'us	attach (something) to oneself	RD	kat'otyous	76	
katukpu	huckleberry oak	PM-M	ka-tuc-pum		

Maidu	English	Source	Source Spelling	Page	Other Spellings
ḱa'u	hide (intransitive verb): ni dᴍḱᴍm, ḱa'udom, hónwenuwéwḱas "I alone, by hiding, survived all this time."	RD	kau'	222	
ḱa'uk	hide (oneself) (WS), hide (intransitive) (FC)	WS, FC	ḱaʔuk		
ḱa'ukkinu	crouch down and hide	WS	ḱaʔukkinu		
ḱa'ukḱoi	go and hide	WS	ḱaʔukḱoj		
ka'úsan	it usually is, it used to be	RD	kaūs'an	104	
ḱa'usan	as usual	RD	ka'ūsan	204	
ḱa'úwa	rub	WS-MP	ḱaʔúwa		
ḱaw	be in the dirt, interact with the dirt	FC			
Ḱawa	place name, just north of Quincy, #45 on FR map. See map 2 in Appendix 5.	FR	kawa	370-371	
kawaicho	chopsticks	FC			
Ḱawawtai	place name for Oak Flat, west of Soda Rock (Chuchúyem Bam) right side of Indian Creek, about ½ mile below Indian Falls (FR-TE). DT map #7. see map 2 in Appendix 5.	DT, FR-TE	Ḱow wow tay		Ḱowówtayi
kawáyim bolóḱo	horseshoe	WS	kawájim bolóḱo		
kawáyu	horse (from Spanish caballo)	WS	kawáju		kowayu
kawáyucho	team of horses	WS	kawájućo		
kawáyum té	colt, foal	WS	kawájum té		
ḱáwba	dig a hole	WS	ḱáwba		
Ḱáwbaťi	place name for Butt Valley, meaning "flat ground." Now under Butt Valley Reservoir. See maps 1 and 3 in Appendix 5.	WS	ḱáwbaťi		
Ḱáwbaťim Mómdanni	place name for Butt Valley Reservoir. See maps 1 and 3 in Appendix 5.	FC-map	kowbutim momdani		
Ḱáwbaťim Ḱoyó	place name for Butt Valley, meaning "flat ground valley." Now under Butt Valley Reservoir. See maps 1 and 3 in Appendix 5.	WS	ḱáwbaťim kojó		
ḱáwbe	dig in the dirt	FC-R, FC-E			
ḱáwdaḱa	clay	WS	ḱáwdaḱa		
ḱáwdusi	dust (WS), ashes (MP)	WS, WS-MP	ḱáwdusi		
kawé'am	kept on (doing), continued to (do): niséḱi mᴍbéiḱᴍwoli kawé'am wi'ítidom "they kept on wiping out our elders/fathers"	RD	kawē'am	148	

Maidu	English	Source	Source Spelling	Page	Other Spellings
kawéw	be doing	RD	kawē'u	106	
kawéwkm	always seem to be doing: tetét yahám ḱodóinan kawéwkm'ankano yahám ḱódoidi húnmoyedom "you always seem to be hunting from one good place to another"	RD	kawē'ukö	154	
ḱáweye	whisper: ḱáweye pínsaḱas. "I'm hearing a lot of whispering."	WS, FC-T	ḱáweje		
ḱawéyenoye	go around whispering	FC			ḱawéinoye (FC-E)
ḱawéyetoto	whisper with each other	FC			
ḱáwheheḱoi	leave one after the other (plural subject)	RD	kau'hēhekoi	104, 108	
ḱáwheheḱoḱoi	leave (plural subject, going various ways)	RD	kau'hehēkokoi	104	ḱáwheihei-ḱoḱoi
ḱáwhei	kick up the dust	WS	ḱáwhej		
ḱáwheiheiḱoḱoi	trudge off in all directions kicking up the dust (plural subject)	WS	ḱáwhejhejḱoḱoj		ḱáwhehe-ḱoḱoi
ḱáwheiḱoi	go off kicking up the dust	WS	ḱáwhejḱoj		
ḱawí	dirt, land (property) (FC), ground, earth: ḱawdi tetémen! "Don't play in the dirt!"	FC, WS, SPB, FC-T	ḱaw (WS), caweh (SPB)		ḱaw (WS)
ḱawí dóndom tótto	manzanita (low-growing variety)	WS	ḱawí dóndom tótto		
ḱawí sukdóiti	stir up dirt/dust	RD	kawi' sukdoi'ti	132	
ḱawí yudútkm	groundhog, woodchuck	WS	ḱawí judútky		
ḱawíbano	squaw carpet - wild lilac ground cover, ceanothus	FC, JD	kawybɔno	69	ḱawibono
ḱawíchepe	earth seer, earth finder (according to RD, "robin," according to WS-MM, "meadowlark." the creature that found the dirt which was stretched to make the world.)	RD	kawī'tdepem (d is typo for s)	25	
ḱawídano	ground manzanita, pinemat manzanita	PM-M, JD	ka-we-da-nom (PM-M), kawydano, kawedanom (JD)	49	
ḱawím sá	fireplace	WS	ḱawím sá		
ḱáwmmkkm	shoveler duck	HM	kaw'-muk'-kah		
ḱawná	to the ground	FC			
ḱáwok	thrust secretly	WS	ḱáwok		

137

Maidu	English	Source	Source Spelling	Page	Other Spellings
Ḱáwokum Púlumtom	place name in Indian Valley close to Ḱoyóm Bukúm, across from Moccasin Creek where it comes into Indian Creek (FR1). A divide over which the road now passes just before entering Indian Valley from the south (FR1). The story about the mink brothers trapping the snake occurred here, between the creek and the current railroad tracks. See map 5 in Appendix 5.	DT, FR1, RD	Ḱow Okum Pulumtum		
kawóno	had been, having (done): ínyanam máidɱm kawónom uním ḱódoidi bíspem "Indian people having lived in this land"	WST-DW	kawóno	72:2	
ḱáwono	keep (a secret) from (someone), be silent (finish talking)	WS	ḱáwono		
Ḱáwwati	place name for Butt Lake Valley (according to Lilly Baker, Ḱáwbati was more towards Humbug Valley)	FC			
ḱáwyadom	soil-building	FC-E			
kayi	other	FC			
kayyí	log	FC, RD	kai'yi, kaiyi'	72	kaiyí, káiyi
ḱé	a hillside plant, similar in appearance to the kowá, but the root must be boiled to remove the bitterness.	WS	ḱé		
ḱedé	brother-in-law	WS	ḱedé		
ḱedé	graze, feed (as animals) (WS), scratch the ground (like a chicken) (FC)	WS, FC	ḱedé		
ḱedéhepinkoi	go from feeding, go from grazing	WS	ḱedéhepinkoj		
ḱedékɱto	brothers-in-law, pair of brothers-in-law	WS	ḱedékyto		
ḱedéno	to graze (as animals eat)	RD	kedeno	108	
ḱedétḱet	cackle	WS	ḱedétḱet		
ḱedétonoye	grazing around together	WS	ḱedétonoje		
Kéhemheli Ḱoyó	place name for Sierra Valley	PM-D	kay-hame-heli-koyo		
kéi	old (things), of long ago (people)	WS	kéj		
kéike	shrike (small bird with black eye band)	HM	kā'-ke		
kelé	silent, quiet	WS	kelé		
kelémbo	become silent, stop making noise	RD	kelem'bo	36	
kélikliki	sparrow hawk	HM	kél'-lik-lik-kim		
ḱení	trap, snare	FC, WS	ḱen		ḱen (WS)

Maidu	English	Source	Source Spelling	Page	Other Spellings
kénkiti	make a trap	RD	k'en'kiti	60	
kepḿ	hiccough, hiccup, burp, hack, clear throat	WS, FC-E	kepý		kepú (FC-E)
kétetebo	make a sudden move	RD	ket'etebo	110	
kétetebodom	suddenly	RD	ket'etebodom	110	
kéťi	domestic cat (from English)	WS	kéť, kéti		kéti, kéť
kéy'i	ramshackle	WST	kéjʔi	50:5	
kí	key (from English)	WS	kí		
kí	pinch (verb)	WS-G	kí	8	
kídumchekín	hold on tight to (something), pinch (something) closed	RD	kī'dūmtsekīn'	138	
kíki	domestic cat	WS	kíki		
kikí'usito	go far across	RD	kiki'ūsito	13	
kilé	hide (something): liáni cháina kilépi "hide the money somewhere else"	RD	kilē'	58, 114	kɯlé (WS)
kiléchmi	be unable to hide something: chámmi kilémam kabɯkɯm kiléchmikan "about to start hiding the knife, he couldn't hide (it)"	RD	kilē'tsöi	58	
kiléda	hide (something) for a reason hide (something) "because of that": liáni cháidi kilédakan "so he hid the money in another place"	RD	kile'da	114	
kíloschik	strangle (intransitive)	WS	kílosćik		
kísɯl	to shell (something) with thumb and forefinger	WS	kísyl		
kít	arrive, be (time): hesánte kítade? "what time is it?"	FC			
kítap	squeeze	WS-MP	kítap		
kitkítkɯ	prairie dog	HY			
kiú	also, as well, the same goes for... (kiú follows the noun): kɯlóknono kiú "the same goes for women"	RD	kiū	52	
kíwdi	at the back: hɯbóm kíwdi "at the back of the house"	WST	kíwdi	54:23	
kiwí	back (of a person, of a mountain or of a building), the place behind (something), the other side of (something)	WS, FC	kiw		kiw, kiuí, kiuwí
kiwím bɯmí	spine, backbone	FC			kiwím bɯmí
kiwím bukú	tailbone	WS	kiwím bukú		
kíwna	behind, to the back of: hɯbóm kíwna "towards the back of the house, behind the house"	WST	kíwna	54:23	
kíwna bényewei	walk backwards	WS	kíwna bénjewej		
kíwsukinu	to lie down with one's back to the fire	RD	kīūsukinu	60	

Maidu	English	Source	Source Spelling	Page	Other Spellings
kíwsusukiti	put one's back to the fire while sleeping	RD	kīūsusukiti	60	
kíwwo	thrash, beat, whip, hit someone on the back	WS	kíwwo		
kó	snow (noun)	WS	kó		
kó	snow (verb)	FC			
ḱo	choke (intransitive)	WS	ḱo		
kó kítdom	snow is coming down, it is snowing	FC			
Kóbatas Doyím	place name for a village one mile north of Greenville, #16 on FR map, on the west side of Indian Creek. Means "going up to the edge of snow;" some sources thought this may be the same as Greenville: Kótasi (FR-D, FR-Ka, FR-S). See #10 on map 5 in Appendix 5.	FR1, FR-AG, FR-MP		370-371	Kóbatásdayim
kobébebekchᴍti	whatever caused (someone) to scream (noun), reason for screaming	RD	kobē′bektsöti	106	
ḱobébek	scream (verb), buzz loudly (insects): ḱobébekpem kapí pinḱas. "I hear screaming insects."	WS, FC-E	ḱobébek		
ḱobébeknoti	make (someone) scream	WST-RP	ḱobébeknoti	64:18	
ḱobébekti	make (someone) scream	WS, RD	ḱobébekti	112	
kóchi	pig, bacon (from Spanish cochino)	WS	kóći		
kóchibe	bacon	WST	kóćibe	62:6	
ḱóda	world	RD	kâ′da	28	ḱódo
kodál	bedsheet, sheet	WS	kodál		
kodéle'émto	swing the body from side to side (in dancing)	RD	kode′leem′to	120	
ḱódo	district, country, area, place, time, year, season, TV channel: óktipem ḱódom mamápem kᴍḱán "it is becoming the hungry season"	WS, FC, RD	ḱódo, ḱódoj (WS), kâ′do (RD)	28, 104	ḱódoi
ḱódo ᴍmmoto	travel the world, go all over the land, go all around the world	RD	ko′do öm′moto	230	
ḱódo éstodi	in the middle of the land	RD	kâ′do es′todi	226	
ḱodó topái	set fire to the countryside (to keep vegetation down)	WS	ḱodó topáj		
ḱodódok	gallop	WS	ḱodódok		
ḱódoi	district, country, area, place, time, year, TV channel	WS, FC	ḱódoj		ḱódo
ḱódoi mákpai	learn about the land	RD	ko′doi mak′pai	22	
ḱódoidi	in the country, in the world	FC			

140

Maidu	English	Source	Source Spelling	Page	Other Spellings
ḱodóidi ḱódom	such a world, a world like that	RD	kodoi′di kâ′dom	5, 6	
ḱódoikm	have a land, have a country, have one's own land	RD	kâ′doikö	28, 144	
kodoko	sand-hill crane	HM	ko-do-ko		
kodókoki	fresh-water mussel	HM	ko-do′-ko-ki		
ḱódom	existing as a place, existing as land	RD		4, 6	
ḱódom	weather, wind, weather system: ḱódom mnóchoi'a ḱódom pínkenutihasitochoi'a "the weather went along making noise as it passed over." (see also ḱódo)	RD	kâ′dom	150	
ḱódom bmwochoi'a	the wind blew	RD	kâd′om bö′wotsoia	194	
ḱódom belew	side of the world, part of the world, north	RD	ko′dombelēu	13	
ḱódom bodíkdi	heaven	WS	ḱódom bodíkdi		
ḱódom bodíknokm	heaven	WS	ḱódom bodíknoky		
Ḱódom Bónnodi	place name for Sacramento Valley: west, downhill country (This term is used both for the Sacramento Valley and as a general term for a south-westerly direction)	WS	ḱódom bónnodi		
ḱódom chanantedi	to/in the north, in the northern area, northwest area	RD	kâd′omtsanantedi	140, 172	
ḱódom chándi	the other side of world (FC, RD), to/in the northwest, north, northwest (RD), in the north (WS)	RD, FC, WS	kō′domtsandi, ko′dom tsandi, kâ′domtsandi (RD), ḱódom ćándi (WS)	7, 26, 118, 140, 172, 230	
ḱódom chánna	north, to the north, northwest	WS	ḱódom ćánna		
ḱódom kmlḿlmdom	be thundering, to thunder	RD	kâd′om kölö′lödom	200	
ḱódom kmlḿplmlmpdom	be rumbling, thundering	RD	ko′dom kölöp′lölöpdom	150	
ḱódom kíwdi	heaven	WS	ḱódom kíwdi		
ḱódom yahádom	being good weather	RD	kâd′om yahā′dom	104	
ḱódom yepóni	Creator, headman of the world	PM-D	ko′dom-ye-po-ni		
ḱódomťik	everywhere	RD	kâ′domtik	48, 132	
ḱódoyakm	World-maker, Creator	FC			
ḱódoyape	Earth Maker, the creator, World Maker	WS	ḱódojape		ḱódoyampe
koháḱakoi	flee wildly in all directions (plural subject)	WS	koháhaḱoj		
koháḱoi	flee wildly, be routed	WS	koháḱoj		
koháno	go at utmost speed	WS	koháno		
kóh′bono	a great rain, storm	RD	koh′′bono	170, 152	
kohekíwno	avalanche, snowslide	WS	kohekíwno		
kohíkwm	sage grouse	HM	ko-hik′-wum		

141

Maidu	English	Source	Source Spelling	Page	Other Spellings
kok	soup, broth	WS	kok		
kók chᴍlᴍ́lᴍ	hail, sleet	WS	kók ćylýly		
Kokitbe	place name of old Indian cemetery in a village site between the two Schieser ranches in Indian Valley, #18 on FR map. See map 5 in Appendix 5.	FR1, FR-TE, FR-MP			Kókitpe
Kókitpe	place name of old Indian cemetery in a village site between the two Schieser ranches in Indian Valley, #18 on FR map. See map 5 in Appendix 5.	FR1, FR-TE, FR-MP		370-371	Kokitbe
kókkᴍ	nuts (a general term)	WS	kókky		
kókkok	white	WS-MP	kókkok		
kóko	go, leave (plural subject, a group)	RD	ko'ko	68	
kokó	place, location, site	FC, WS	kok		kok
kokó	seeds, nuts, anything to crack	FC, WS	kok		kok
kókpa	big, watertight, cone-shaped basket made of birch and bunch-grass	WS	kókpa		
kókpam woló	big, watertight, cone-shaped basket made of birch and bunch-grass	WS	kókpam woló		
kolái	orphan boy	WS	koláj		
kolewa	type of edible mushroom, small, slimy, white mushroom eaten in November)	PM-M, JD	ko-la-wa (PM-M), kolewa (JD)	JD 23	
kolóibokit	stop and stand still, stop in one's tracks	RD	koloi'bokit	180, 182	
kolóikinu	stand still, be situated, be standing	RD	kuloi'kinu	230	kulóikinu
kolókᴍ	gull, seagull	HM	ko-low'-kum		
kólokito	to paint (stripes)	RD	kō'lokito	76	
kolóknono	women	FC-R			kᴍlóknono (WS, RD)
kolókolo	turkey	FC			kolókolᴍ
kolulunkᴍ	bell	FC			kolᴍlᴍnkᴍ (FC-E)
kolulunti	to ring (as a bell)	FC-T			
Kólyem	place name in Taylorsville area, #11 on FR map. See map 3 in Appendix 5.	FR		370-371	
kóm chᴍlᴍ́lᴍ	hail, sleet	WS	kóm ćylýly		
kóm káwkit	fall (as snow)	HY			
kóm máidᴍ	Pit River or Atsugewi Indians	WS	kóm májdy		
kóm soló	snowshoe	WS	kóm soló		
kóm wékkesi	snow rabbit, snowshoe rabbit	WS	kóm wékkesi		
Kom Yamánim	place name for Mt. Lassen Ridge, including Mt. Harkness, Mt Hoffman and Crater Mtn. See Map 1 in Appendix 5	LM	Kom-Yamanim	16	

Maidu	English	Source	Source Spelling	Page	Other Spellings
Kóm Ḱoyó	place name for a village in Taylorsville area, which was located in a small meadow behind the Baka Ranch, about a mile below Konók Wusúpa (FR-TE). Means "snow meadow." See map 5 in Appendix 5.	FR, FR1	kong koiyo (FR1)	370-371:32	
ḱomá	father (This term is used only when a member of the family has died): as a kinship term, this word must have a prefix, either mm, nik, or min (see Mountain Maidu Grammar, Lesson 6 for more details)	WS	ḱomá		
ḱomám kmlé	mother (This term is used only when a member of the family has died): as a kinship term, this word must have a prefix, either mm, nik, or min (see Mountain Maidu Grammar, Lesson 6 for more details)	WS	ḱomám kylé		
kombḿ	Sasquatch, bigfoot	FC-JC			
Kómbatasim	place name, meaning "snowline" (MP), which may be another name for Kóbatas Doyím. See #10 on map 5 in Appendix 5.	FR1	ḱombatasim		kobatas doyim
ḱombo	tribal name for the Yana Indians	WS	ḱombo		
ḱómbom máidm	Yahi, Mill Creek Indians ("the enemy, mean" people)	FC			
Komchu	place name for Yankee Hill	FC			
kómchú	thaw	WS-MP	kómću		
ḱomí	seed, seeds	FC, WS	ḱom		ḱómi (FC), ḱom (WS)
komó	south	RD	komō'	42, 48	
kómo	east	SP	ko'-mo	310	komowím (SP, archaic)
komóna	to the south	FC-E			
komónantedi	in the south area, to the south area	RD	kōmō'nantedi, komō'nantedi	150, 212, 230	
komónantenan	from the south area, from the south side	RD	kōmō'nantenan	154	
kómpichilip	barnswallow	WS	kómpićilip		
komt́mt́mkm	chickadee (snow nester)	FC			
ḱómtapope	full of seeds	WS	ḱómtapope		
kómya	snow cloud	FC			
kón	corn (from English): kónim bonó "ears of corn"	WS, FC-E	kón		

Maidu	English	Source	Source Spelling	Page	Other Spellings
Konkoyo	place name for village with roundhouse SE of Big Meadows and north of Sandy Creek, probably near Greenville. See Kóm Ḱoyó on map 5 in Appendix 5.	CM			Kom Ḱoyó
konó	infant	WS	konó, konóḱ		konóḱ
konóbe	infant	WS	konóbe		
ḱonói	go around, go out and about (of people and also illness): wólem hónḱo ḱonóitimmni káwe'as ḱonóinwet bísdom. "Since the white man is spreading colds around, I am always staying (home) without going out and about."	HY			
ḱonóiti	spread around (as illness), cause to go around: wólem hónḱo ḱonóitimmni káwe'as ḱonóinwet bísdom. "Since the white man is spreading colds around, I am always staying (home) without going out and about."	HY			
konóito	be a couple, be together as a couple	WST	konójto	60:63	
konóito	couple, man and woman	WS	konójto		
Konók Wusúpa	place name for a camp site on a flat extending out into the meadow and located about two miles downstream from Taylorsville, #31 on FR map. The name means "baby leaning against" because a baby was accidentally left to die in its cradleboard here (FR-TE). See map 5 in Appendix 5.	FR1, FR		370-371	
konókm	newborn baby, or someone who is addled	FC			
konókḱukus	pretend to be a baby, act childish	FC, WS	konókḱukus		
kónom póḱo	a Mountain Maidu month following the bómtetnom póḱo. "month when babies are born?"	RD-NM			
kopé	pus	WS	kopé		kop'é (FC)
kopé	to form pus, ooze (pus only)	WS	kopé		
kopékit	to form pus, ooze (pus only)	WS	kopékit		
kopí	critter	WS	kop		kop, kapí

Maidu	English	Source	Source Spelling	Page	Other Spellings
ḱós	cut up, butcher, eviscerate (WS), to skin by peeling back (FC)	WS, FC	ḱos		
kósbu	male pubic hair	WS	kósbu		
kosí	penis	FC, WS	kos		kos (WS)
kosím butú	male pubic hair	WS	kosím butú		
kosím 'oḱéli	head of the penis, glans penis	WS	kosím ʔoḱéli		
kosím ṗalá	testicles	FC			
kóspumi	foreskin	WS	kóspumi		
Kótasi	place name for Greenville, or just east of Greenville. Means "snowline" (FR-TE). See map 5 in Appendix 5.	RD-NM, FC, FR1			kotassi
Kótasim Sewí	place name for Wolf Creek, which flows through Greenville. See maps 3 and 5 in Appendix 5.	FR1			
ḱótchonokachopin	turn back towards	RD	kot'sonokatso'pin	228	
kotó	grandmother: as a kinship term, this word must have a prefix, either mm, nik, or min (see Mountain Maidu Grammar, Lesson 6 for more details)	WS	kotó		
kotókmto	a pair including a grandmother, for example, grandmother and grandchild	RD	kotok'öto	222	
kotóto	grandmother	WS	kotóto		
ḱotwélemtodo	while turning from side to side in dancing (adv)	RD	kotwel'emtodo	126	
ḱótwochono	go back and forth across, crisscross: máisem ḱódo ḱótwochonoḱan. "They crisscrossed the country."	RD	kot'wochono	212	
ḱótwochonoye	turn in one direction and then another (in dancing)	RD	kot'wochonoye	120	
ḱótwoḱoi	turn and face away from	WS	ḱótwoḱoj		
ḱótwoye	turn and face toward	WS	ḱótwoje		
ḱowḿtḿtkm	killdeer (FC), meadowlark (WS)	FC, WS	ḱowýtýtky		
kowá	brodiaea, purple (FC) edible bulb and flower, Golden brodiaea (JD), species of wild field plant with white flowers and a thumb-sized, turnip shaped, edible white root (WS)	FC, JD, WS	kowam (JD), kowá (WS)	JD 35	
kowáiyo	horse	FC			kawáyu
kowékesi	jackrabbit, snow shoe rabbit	FC			kówwekkesi (WS)
ḱowekkesi	rabbit, jackrabbit, (WS) snowshoe rabbit (FC)	WS, FC	kówwekkesi		kówwekesi (WS)

Maidu	English	Source	Source Spelling	Page	Other Spellings
kówkow	gray	WS	kówkow		
Kówkowki Yakḿm	place name in Taylorsville area, #17 on FR map, for a village near the Milt Gott Ranch, about two miles NE of Greenville towards the Rancheria (FR-HY). The village was on a hillside, where house pits may still be visible. Yakḿm means "boat" or "canoe." See map 5 in Appendix 5.	FR, FR1, FR-HY, FR-MP	Kówkowki yakɨm (FR), kow kok yakum (FR1)	370-371	
kowkowtiche	get gray	FC-E			
ḱowó	armpit, underarm	WS, FC	ḱowó, ḱowój		ḱowói (WS), ḱowá (FC-R)
ḱowóidi	in the armpit	WS	ḱowójdi		
ḱowóm bḿmí	rib	WS	ḱowóm bymí		
ḱowóm ḱumí	armpit	WS	ḱowóm ḱumí		
ḱowóm pḿnno	armpit, the hole in the armpit	WS	ḱowóm pýnno		
Ḱowówtayi	place name for a village at Oak Flat occupied in pre-contact times. Located on the right side of Indian Creek, about a half-mile below Indian Falls (FR1), #34 on FR map. See map 2 in Appendix 5	FR, FR1	Kowówtayi (FR), k'ow u'ow tay (FR1)	370-371	Ḱawawtai (DT)
kówukm	grebe (freshwater diving bird) (HM), lesser scaup (duck), nyroca affinis (PM-M)	HM	ko'-woo-kum (HM), ko-woo-cum (PM-M)		
kówwil	thick in dimension	WS	kówwil, kowwíl		kowwíl
kóyekini	avalanche of snow, rocks, etc.	WS	kójekini		
koyó	make up for, pay for (crime)	RD	koyō'	204	
ḱoyó	valley, meadow, field	WS	kojó		
ḱoyói	stranger	RD, WS	koioi' (RD), ḱojó, ḱojójo (WS)	94	ḱoyó, ḱoyóyo
Ḱoyóm	place name for the valley area below Susanville, #29 on HLME map 3. Means "valley." See map 4 in Appendix 5.	HLME	Kojo, koyom		
Ḱoyóm Bo	place name for North Valley Rd. (the road that runs along the north side of Indian Valley from Greenville to North Arm Rd.); see map 5 in Appendix 5	MSOP			

Maidu	English	Source	Source Spelling	Page	Other Spellings
Ḱoyóm Bukúm	place name in Indian Valley, #29 on FR map; for Crescent Mills (FC), village on the west side of Indian Creek, just upstream from the mouth of Moccasin creek (FR) where Moccasin Creek comes into Indian Creek (DT Map7). Means "valley tail" or "end of meadow" (MP). See map 5 in Appendix 5.	FR, FC, DT, FR1, FR-MP, FR-AG		370-371	
Ḱoyóm Bukúm Sewíno	place name for Indian Falls on Indian Creek, several miles upstream from its confluence with Spanish Creek. See maps 2 and 5 in Appendix 5.	FR1	Ḱoiyumbokum Sewino		Ḱoiyom Bokum Sewino
Ḱoyóm Bukúm Sewíno	place name for Indian Falls on Indian Creek (FC, FR-HY), DT map 7: See maps 2 and 5 in Appendix 5.	FC-MAP, DT, MSOP, FR-HY	koiyombokum sewino (FR-HY)		
Ḱoyóm Ḱawi	place name in Konkow area "meadowlands" (FR), Oroville (FC-T)	FR-Ka, FC-T	kóyo·mḱawi	370-371	Konkau (Ka)
ḱoyóm títtitkm	species of ground squirrel	WS	kojóm títtitky		
ḱoyóm upedi	into a valley or meadow area	RD	koyom'upedi	224	
ḱoyōwaťa'ɱno	walk along the edge of a meadow	RD	koyō'watāta'öno	8	
ḱoyóyo	stranger	WS	ḱojójo		ḱoyó
koyúmsiti	cedar bird, cedar waxwing	HM	koi-um'-sit-tim		
ku	become empty of liquid, drain	WS	ku		
kú	have	FC			kɱ (WS)
kúchilili	golden-crown sparrow	HM	koo'-she-lil'-le		
Kúduidɱm	Stover Mountain	FC			
ḱui	neck	WS	ḱuj		ḱuyí
ḱúidak	to like (someone or something)	WS	ḱújdak		
ḱúidakboduk	not care much for (something or someone)	WS	ḱújdakboduk		
ḱúidakmen	dislike, dislike it	WS	ḱújdakmen		
ḱúidakwiyakka	to sort of like (someone or something)	WS	ḱújdakwijakka		
ḱúila	necklace, beads	WS, FC	ḱújla		ḱɱila (FC-E)
ḱúilai	wear a necklace	WS	ḱújlaj		
ḱuilái ḱúilaipe	necklace-wearing	RD	k!ūila' k!ūi'laipem	168	
ḱúilaimape	be decked out, be wearing jewelry	FC			
ḱúilaiti	put beads, necklace on someone, make (someone) wear a necklace	RD	k!ū'ilaiti	164	

Maidu	English	Source	Source Spelling	Page	Other Spellings
k̓úilam loló	trinket basket, necklace box	WS-MP	k̓újlam loló		
k̓úilam patá	trinket basket	WS-MP	k̓újlam patá		
k̓úilulumi	throat	WS	k̓újlulumi		k̓úlulumi, k̓ᴀilulumi (FC)
k̓úilulumim pú	have the voice break (as at puberty)	WS	k̓újlulumim pú		
k̓úiwitubil	twist (something) around (someone's) neck	WS	k̓újwitubil		
kuiyí	neck	FC-E			k̓ui (WS)
kúkú	burrowing owl	HM	koo'-koo'		
k̓ukú	make rope	WS	k̓ukú		
k̓ukú	rope, string, twine, wire	FC, WS	k̓uk̓		k̓uk̓ (WS)
k̓ukú pán	make rope: mᴀm kᴀléchom k̓ukú pánk̓an "the two women made rope"	WS	k̓ukú pán		
kul	fiddleneck (plant) - may be from Nisenan	FC-T. FC-E			kᴀl
k̓úl	be widowed, be bereaved	RD	kūl'	52	
k̓ulái	orphan	WS	k̓uláj, k̓oláj		k̓olái
k̓uláiwoli	orphans	WS	k̓ulájwoli		
kulanabeli	pomegranate	FC			
k̓úli	widow	FC			k̓úlu
Kulkumik	place name for Colfax	RD-NM	kulkumic		
kulómum	Susanville people	SP			
kulú	be dark (verb)	FC			
kulú	dark, night	WS, FC	kulú		
k̓úlu	be orphaned	WS	k̓úlu		
k̓úlu	widow	WS	k̓úlu		k̓úli (FC)
kulúchet	once it was dark, once it gets dark: kulúchet k̓úmlaidom mᴀm kᴀlóknonom kᴀk̓án "once it was dark, the women were dancing in the roundhouse"	RD	kūlū'tset	56	
kulúdi	yesterday (WS), last night, at night, tonight (use verb tense to show past or future): chemá'ak̓as min kulúdi "I'll see you tonight." chek̓ás min mᴀ kulúdi "I saw you last night." min chekᴀ'ᴀm ma'ás kulúdi "I saw you at night."	FC, WS	kulúdi		
k̓uluibe	widow	FC			
kulúkit	get dark	WS	kulúkit		
kulúlukit	be just before dark	RD	kūlū'lūkit	190, 204	
k̓ulúlumi	throat, neck	FC			k̓úilulumi (WS)
kulúm bénekto	yesterday morning	RD	kulum' bēn'ekto	128	
kulúm ekí	night	WS	kulúm ekí		
kulúm ésto	middle of the night	FC			
kulúm kapúslele	moth	FC			
kulúm k̓ódom	the spirit land	WS	kulúm k̓ódom		
kulúm máidᴀ	spirit person	WS	kulúm májdy		

Maidu	English	Source	Source Spelling	Page	Other Spellings
kulúm pokó	moon	WS	kulúm pokó		
kulúm ya	dark cloud	FC			
kulúma	Susanville people	SP	kulómum		
kulúmeni	at dusk, at twilight	WS	kulúmen		
kulúmenpe	just before dark	RD	kūlū′menpe	98	
kulúmi	at evening time	RD	kūlūm′i	102	
kulúnan	towards evening	RD	kūlū′nan	228	
kulúnanna	evening (RD), along toward dusk (WS), nightfall, towards dark (FC)	RD, WS, FC	kūlū′nana (RD), kulúnanna (WS)	196	
kulúnanna	get to be dark, get to be night-time	RD	kūlū′nana	56, 206	
ḱúlupem té	orphan child	WS	ḱúlupem té		
ḱúlusa	orphan girl	WS	ḱúlusa		
kulúwoye	get to be dark	WS	kulúwoje		
kum	strangle, choke	WS	kum		
ḱumbe	dig a hole	FC			
ḱumhṁ	bark house, sweathouse, roundhouse	RD, WS, FC	kumhöm′ (RD), ḱumhý (WS)	154	ḱumhú (FC), ḱumú (WS)
ḱumhṁ púiya	door to the house (not the smoke hole)	RD	kumhöm′ pū′iya	220	
ḱumhṁkṁ	have a bark house	RD	kumhö′kö	192	
ḱumhṁm hṁbo	dwelling house	PM-D	k'umu-ng-hubo		ḱumhúm hṁbo
ḱumí	hole	FC, WS	ḱum		ḱum (WS)
ḱumlái	dance around the fire in the dance house (WS), dance in the roundhouse (FC), dance in the sweathouse, sweat and dance (RD)	WS, FC, RD	ḱumláj (WS), kum′lai (RD)	56	ḱúmlai
ḱúmlai	hibernate	WS	ḱúmlaj		
ḱumle	type of edible mushroom, brown mushroom eaten in the Fall	PM-M, JD	kum-lay (PM-M), k'umle (JD)	JD 24	
ḱúmmemenkitpoto	be almost another winter	RD	kum′memen′-kitpotō′	40	
ḱúmmen	through the winter	RD	kum′men, k!um′men	156, 158, 228	
ḱúmmen bísdom	wintering over	RD	kum′men büs′dom	150	
ḱumménchik	be the winter season: uním máidṁm ka'án díwebisim díwebisim pínini ḱumménchikdom pínini ékdadom "this people is growing and growing, over many winter seasons, over many day dawnings"	RD	kumen′tsikom	14	
ḱúmmenda	become winter	RD	kum′menda	150	
ḱúmmenheki	when winter ends: ḱúmmenheki, ḱódom wṁsṁmṁni, eptitoma'enḱesi. "At the end of winter, when the weather clears up, we will be strong."	HY			

149

Maidu	English	Source	Source Spelling	Page	Other Spellings
ḱúmmeni	winter, year (in counting years): hesánbem ḱúmmenim okítpem maḱá? "How old are you?"	WS	ḱúmmeni		
ḱúmmenkit	wintertime	WS	ḱúmmenkit		
ḱúmmenna	for the winter, (in preparation) for the winter	RD	kum'mena	104	
ḱúmmenowet	winter house	RD	kum'menowet	228	
ḱúmmenwi	dugout granary for storing pine nuts in winter	JD	kumenwym	29	
ḱumpᴧdónu	continue to go down (a hole)	RD	kumpödon'u	232	
ḱumpᴧnno	hole, cavity in the ground	WS	ḱumpýnno		
ḱumpichilipe	swallow (bird)	FC			kompichiliṕ (WS)
ḱúmpiťi	mud	WS	ḱúmpiťi		ḱum piti
ḱumtapo	be full of holes	FC-E			
ḱumtapoti	make a bunch of holes	FC			
ḱumú	dance house, community dwelling, round house	WS, HY	ḱumú		ḱumhᴧ, ḱumhú
ḱún	smother	FC			
Kunabe	place name northeast of Yankee Hill, due east of Homlukbe, east side of Feather river - borderline Konkow area. See map 1, Appendix 5.	CM			
ḱuní	first, next: mí ḱuní "you first" ni ḱuní "me first"	FC			
ḱúpa	father-in-law: as a kinship term, this word must have a prefix, either mᴧ, nik, or min (see <u>Mountain Maidu Grammar</u>, Lesson 6 for more details)	WS	ḱúpa		
kupé	having	FC			kᴧpé
kúpkᴧ	round green tule, deergrass, bulrush, scirpus	WS, FC, JD	kúpky (WS), kupʔkum, kuʔpku (JD)	JD 47	kupkᴧ (FC), kuṕku
ḱusem	enemy, someone you don't like: as a kinship term, this word must have a prefix, either mᴧ, nik, or min (see <u>Mountain Maidu Grammar</u>, Lesson 6 for more details)	FC			
Kusim	place name in Indian Valley. See map 5 in Appendix 5.	FC, MSOP			Kusimen

Maidu	English	Source	Source Spelling	Page	Other Spellings
Kusim Bo	place name for road going between Kusim/Tam Kusim and Nadam Ḱoyó all the way to Indian Creek (Sandy Creek). See map 5 in Appendix 5.	FC-MAP, MSOP	Kusi Bo		Ḱᴍsim Bo
Kusimen	place name for village with roundhouse in Indian Valley; may be the same as Kusim. See map 5 in Appendix 5.	CM			Kusim
kúsu	blind	WS	kúsu		
kúsuboswedoi	be almost blind	WS	kúsuboswedoj		
kúsuhsu	rather blind, partially blind	WS, WST	kúsuhsu	52:22	
kúsupe	blind	FC			kúsᴍpe
kúsuti	to blind (someone)	WS	kúsuti		
ḱútᴍtᴍ	bird, animals (any size animal): pekᴍm ḱútᴍtᴍ "game, food animals" cháichainom ḱútᴍtᴍ "all kinds of animals" ḱútᴍtᴍk sólnip. "Use the song of a bird."	RD, FC-E	ku'tötö, kut'ötö, kutöti	10, 28, 140, 192, 216	ḱúttᴍtᴍ, kᴍtᴍtᴍ (FC-E)
kutí	drain (something), empty (something)	WS, WST-DW	kutí	74:13	
ḱutí	creature, animal, four-legged creature	FC, WS	ḱut		ḱut
ḱutíbe	small animal	FC			
Ḱutím Sewi	Deer Creek	FC			
ḱútḱut	cluck	WS	ḱútḱut		
ḱútḱutnoye	go around clucking	WS	ḱútḱutnoje		
ḱúttᴍtᴍ	bird, creature that hops around (WS), any animal (including large game) (RD)	WS, FC	ḱúttʸtʸ		ḱútᴍtᴍ
kuwitiktikᴍ	killdeer (one is not allowed to kill this bird)	FC, PM-M	coo-wit-tit-tit-cum (PM-M)		kuwittititkᴍ
ḱuyi	neck	FC			ḱui
lᴍk	crawl, climb	WS	lyk		
lᴍkᴍ́i	cut into strips	RD	lököi'	110	
lᴍkᴍ́nno	crawl down inside (RD), enter, (as into a bark house) (WS)	RD, WS	lökön'o (RD), lyḱýnno (WS)	70	
lᴍkᴍ́nnomakwonowo	tell (someone) to try to crawl down into	RD	lökö'nomakwono'wo	166	
lᴍkᴍ́nnombos	crawl all the way in	RD	lökön'ombos	200	
lᴍkᴍ́no	go inside: lᴍkᴍ́nodom bᴍdóitapᴍ'ᴍ "Let's (2) go in and sit down."	RD	lökön'o	126, 168, 194, 208, 230	
lᴍ́kabis	still be lying down	RD	lök'abis	100	
lᴍ́kdaw	come down, climb down	WS	lýkdaw		
lᴍ́kdikno	reach (somewhere) by crawling (RD), crawl under (something) (WS), crawl in (FC)	WS, FC, RD	lýkdikno (WS), lök'dikno (RD)	176, 222	

Maidu	English	Source	Source Spelling	Page	Other Spellings
lʌkdoi	crawl up, climb up	RD, WS	lök'doi, luk'doi (RD), lýkdoj (WS)	64, 176	
lʌkdoichʌi	be unable to climb up, be unable to crawl up	RD	lök'doitsöi'	172	
lʌkdónu	keep crawling	RD	lökōn'u	198	
lʌkḱoi	crawl away	WS	lýkḱoj		
lʌkmit	crawl into (as an animal into a hole)	WS	lýkmit		
lʌkmitpin	approach crawling, come crawling out	RD	lök'mitpin	222	
lʌksip	crawl out, climb out, exit, go out of a building	FC			
lʌksipbodʌkkʌ	one who hardly ever gets out (of the house)	RD	luk'sipbodökö	126	
lʌksipbos	crawl all the way out	RD	lök'sipbos'	196	
lʌksipebisim	keep crawling out	RD	lök'sipebisim, lök'sipebusim	196	
lʌksipmenew	not be crawling out, not be coming out: cheménewḱas, lʌksipmenewḱan 'as "I haven't seen (any) all this time; they have not been coming out"	RD	lök'sipmeneū	222	
lʌksipno	climb out of	FC			
lʌksipti	make (someone) go out: mʌḱí te lʌksiptimenḱan. "He did not let his child go outside."	RD	lök'sipti	48	
lʌksipwono	excrement, that which had come out	RD	lök'sipwono	34	
lʌksitoye	scamper across, crawl or scamper all around	WST	lýksitoje	50:6	
lʌksu'ano	goshawk, bird of prey which can fly through small openings	HM	look'-soo-ah-no		
lʌkťa	ride on (a horse), climb on top	WS	lýkťa		
lʌkťakʌ	horseman, horse rider	WS	lýkťaky		
lʌkťakʌm sʌ	horse	WS	lýkťakym sý		
lʌkťano	ride a horse	FC-E			
lʌkťaye	come on horseback	WS	lýkťaje		
lʌktik	crawl	FC			
lʌkwebis	pulsate, beat (as pulse or heart)	WS	lýkwebis		
lʌkyewei	come back, crawl back	WS	lýkjewej		lʌkyewe
lʌlʌ	star: lʌlʌm máidʌdi "at the star men's (place)"	WS, RD	lylý (WS), lölö' (RD)	184	
lʌlʌkbomo	flock of wild geese (used as a model for basket designs)	WS	lýlýkbomo		
lʌlʌku	snow goose (FC), wild goose (according to DW, lʌlʌḱ means a flock of geese, with lo as the singular) (WS)	WS, WS-DW	lýlyḱ		lálaku (FC), lʌlʌḱ (WS)
lʌlí	redbud	WS	lyl		lilí (FC), lʌl (WS)
lʌp	be warm	WS	lyp		
lʌpkit	sweat (verb)	WS	lýpkit		

Maidu	English	Source	Source Spelling	Page	Other Spellings
lʌpkitti	sweat (noun)	FC			
lʌpkittiti	make (someone) sweat	FC-E			
lʌpúpu	rabbit sage (flowers like marigold) (FC), rabbit brush (PM-M)	PM-M	la-poop-pum		lapuṕu, lupúpu
lʌt	bake by burying in the ashes	WS	lyt		
lʌtím húti	baked fat	FC			
la	be suspended, hang	WS	la		
lachḿi	wilt	WS	laćyj		
láda	shorter version of the grass game	RD-NM			
lái	warm (of weather)	WS-MP	láj		
láidamlʌlʌm bo	Milky Way	RD-NM			
láimeni	summer	FC, WS	lájmen		láimen (WS)
láimenkit	summertime	WS	lájmenkit		
láino	be warm, heat (as fire): hesádom nik makáde sam láinomendom? "Why isn't the fire warming me?"	RD	lai'no	168	
láisi	rice	FC			
lakít	wash (something), bathe (something) (RD), bind (a child) into the cradle (WS) - WS and RD translated the same story differently (Coyote and his mother-in-law)	RD, WS	lakit' (RD), lakít (WS)	70	
láklak	red	WS	láklak		
láklaḱam piwí	beet, red root	WS	láklaḱam piwí		
láklakluťpe	very red	RD	lak'laklutpem	188	
láklakpe	red	FC			
láklakpem ékpʌ	red bushlike manzanita with small berries	WS	láklakpem ékpy		
láklakpem hiní	red berry, raspberry	FC-E			
láklakpem ťókpem honí	ace of hearts	WS	láklakpem ťókpem honí		
láklakpem tótto	manzanita (low-growing variety)	WS	láklakpem tótto		
lákono	pileated woodpecker	FC			
lalám	long	WS	lalám		
lalám kiwíkupem	station wagon (car)	FC-T			
lalám tólkupe	having long legs	FC			lalám tólkʌpe (RD)
lalámpe	long	FC			
lalámpem tólkʌpe	long-legged	WS	lalámpem tólkype		lalámpem tólkupe
lam	long, tall	WS	lam		
lámlam	rather long, longish	WS	lámlam		
lanchelía	rancheria	FC			
lánḱeḱét	stand on tiptoe	WS	lámḱeḱét		
lanóye	be around, be in the vicinity, hang around	WS	lanóje		
lap	sit on the buttocks with legs sticking out	WS	lap		
lapchikínu	sit on (something), covering it	RD	laptsikīn'u	178	
lapin lolo	basket	PM-D	la-pin-lo-lo		

153

Maidu	English	Source	Source Spelling	Page	Other Spellings
lápkinu	sit down (RD), sit on the ground on the buttocks, with the legs crossed or stretched out in front (WS)	RD, WS	lap'kinū (RD), lápkinu (WS)	228	
lápsito	move over in a sitting position, scoot over	WS	lápsito		
lápťanu	be perched on, be sprawled out on	WS	lápťanu		
láptikinu	sit down close to	RD	lap'tikinu	84	
lapúpu	rabbit brush, rabbit sage	JD	lapup'um	45	lupúpu, lᴍpúpu
lat	drip (verb)	WS, FC	lat		
látdaw	drip away	WS	látdaw		
láťinpin	drip down	WS	láťinpin		
látkit	drip down	FC-T			
latomi	stalk (of a plant), stalks of mule's ear plant	JD	latomym	45	latumi
látpe	leaky	WS	látpe		
látsape	be leaky (like a faucet), that which keeps dripping	FC-T			
latumi	plant part, stalk	FC			latomi
láwa	flour (from English)	WS	láwa		
láwam wadápi	flour sack	WS	láwam wadápi		
lawáni	flour	FC			
lawióli	ravioli	FC			
lédi	next to, close to, by the side of: ḱumhᴍ́ lédi "by the side of the bark house"	RD	lē'di	166	
léhle	pant (as a dog)	WS	léhle		
léiwo	some (RD), some of a larger whole, a part of (WS): léiwom ínyanam "some Indians, some of the Indians" yahát eḱáwchetidom léiwom "some of them being very beautiful"	RD. WS, WST, WST-RP	lēiwo (RD), léjwo (WS)	50 (RD), 52:19, 68:42 (WST)	léwo
léiwonini	sometimes, once in a while	RD	lēi'wonini	180	
lelé	fragile	WS	lelé		
leléchopin	go along on the side of a hill	RD	lelētsopin	54	
lelédikno	get halfway up (a hill)	RD	lelē'dikno	118	
leléimpini	hillside, slanted roof	RD	lelē'impini	214	
lélemchono	move past quickly	RD	lel'emtsono	86	ᴍlélemchono (WS)
lelépe	fragile	FC			
lemít	roll (something fragile, as a cigarette)	WS	lemít		
lénki	blanket	RD	len'ki (RD), lémki (WS)	218	lemki
lenó	garden, cultivated plot	WS	lenó		
lenóm koyó	garden	WS	lenóm kojó		
lepípi	five-finger fern, maidenhair fern	FC			lopípi
leťá	to cover up (with ashes for cooking)	RD	leta	60	

Maidu	English	Source	Source Spelling	Page	Other Spellings
leťábos	completely cover over (with ashes, for example)	RD	letā'bos	60	
léwo	some of a larger whole, a part of (WS), the rest, leftovers (RD): peyáťan léwo sodóidom mkóikan hmbóna mmkí. "After eating for a while, he took the leftovers to his house."	RD, WS	lē'wo (RD), léwo (WS)	214	léiwo
léyi	slope (noun)	RD	lē'yi	176	
liáni	money, clamshells	FC			líyani (WS)
liánim uiyi	bank	FC			
líham cha	Douglas fir	FC			
likm	pintail (duck), dafila acuta tzitzihoa	PM-M	lee-com		
líki	teal duck	HM	le'-kem		
lílchiche	rosa califonica, wild rose	FC, JD	lilćićym	71	lilchichi
lilí	pine nut	WS	lilím		
lilí	redbud	FC			lmli (WS)
lilim cha	black cottonwood tree	JD	lylym	72	wililim cha
lillil cha	madrone tree	FC			
líllilta	mountain maple, Torrey maple	HM	lil'-lil-tah		
linó	plant (general term for any plant)	FC			
Líno	Reno	FC-T			
linóditi	to rake	FC-E			
lismwi	reserve	FC-E			
liuwí	eel	FC, RR-SW, FC-E			luwu, liwi
líyani	money	WS, FC	líjan		liáni (FC)
ló	wild goose, Canadian goose	WS, FC	ló		
lokbó	angelica - ferny leaves at base, 4' tall stalks, for tea that heals the throat (FC), plant used similarly to bḿtchmwi (WS); a tea that is boiled for stomach ailments (HLME)	FC, WS, HLME	lokbó		
lokbóm piwí	medicinal root of angelica	WS, FC	lokbóm piwí		
lokbóm sawí	edible greens on top of angelica	WS, FC	lokbóm sawí		
lokéket	sort of tiptoe	WS	lokéket		
lokét	tiptoe, go on tiptoes	WS	lokét		
lokétdoi	creep up slowly	RD	lōke'tdoi	168	
lokéťinno	tiptoe into	WS	lokéťinno		
lokétkoi	go on tiptoe (WS), creep up, sneak (FC), creep away slowly (RD)	WS, FC. RD	lokétkoj (WS), lōke'tkoi (RD)	168	
lokétnoye	tiptoe around	WS	lokétnoje		
lokétsito	tiptoe across	WS	lokétsito		
lokó	elderberry plant	HM	lo-ko		
lokó	many, cluster, a cluster of, myriad	FC, WS	lok		lok (WS)

155

Maidu	English	Source	Source Spelling	Page	Other Spellings
lokóm	tiger lily	WS	lokóm		
lokóm hiní	elderberry	FC, JD, WS	lokomhenim (JD), lokóm hiní (WS)	42	
lokómim yó	tiger lily flower	WS	lokómim jó		
lokómini	tiger lily (FC), leopard lily, panther lily (JD)	FC, JD	lokomyn	62	lokomin (JD)
lóksu	seed beater basket (RD), type of basket, shallow with handle (FC)	RD, FC	lok'sum	234	lóksm (FC), lókse (FC-T)
lól	grieve, mourn, weep, cry in mourning	WS, FC	lól		
lólmkoi	go weeping, weep as one goes	RD	lō'lökoi	184	
lólekoi	go out crying	RD	lolekoi	202	
lólnino	go around crying, go around grieving	RD	lol'nino	230	
loló	basket, bowl, cup, container: tí'im loló "tea cup"	WS, FC, FC-E	loló		
loló bálkm	material woven into a basket to make the design	WS	loló bálky		
lolosi	toyon (from Konkow)	FC-E			tolosi (FC-E)
lóm cha	valley oak (long side limbs)	FC			
lóm káidom	geese flying (basket design)	FC			
lop	eat something soupy with the hands (WS), eat with the fingers (FC-E)	WS, FC-E	lop		
lopbm	wild carrot, Lomatium	PM-M, JD	lop-bum (PM-M), lop'bum (JD)	77	
lopípi	five finger fern, maidenhair fern (MP)	WS-MP, FC	lopíp		lepípi
lópkoi	go to a feast	WS	lópkoj		
lópkokoi	go off to a feast (plural subject)	RD	lop'kokoi	208	
lopom kidi	elderberry	FC			
lowí	valley oak, white oak	WS	low		low (WS)
lowím chá	valley oak, white oak tree	WS	lowím ćá		
lúklukto	river canyon	RD	luk'lukto	116	
luksíto	go across, crawl across	RD	luksī'to	228	lmksíto
lukú	spring of water, brook: sewí lukú píkno "right in the middle of the stream"	FC, WS, WST-DW	luk	74:12	luk (WS)
lukúbe	little brook, freshet	WS	lukúbe		
lukúm momí	spring water	WS	lukúm momí		
lukúm tímsawi	wild peppermint	WS	lukúm tímsawi		
lukúm wélketi	brook frog, little green frog	WS	lukúm wélketi		
lukúmbe	small brook, freshet	FC			
lulí	redbud	JD	luly	58	lilí
lulú	torso, body, waist	RD, FC-E	lulu	56	
lúlukm	snow goose (FC), white-fronted goose (HM)	HM	loo'-lo-kum		lúlokm
lulúmi	torso, body, narrow part (RD, FC), waist (WS)	RD, FC, WS	lulūm'i (RD), lulúmi (WS)	142, 190	

Maidu	English	Source	Source Spelling	Page	Other Spellings
lulúmwochono	hug (verb)	WS	lulúmwoćono		
lumí	fishhook	WS	lum		lum
lumí	stem, tube, waist	FC, WS	lum		lum (WS)
lúmi	room (from English)	WS	lúmi		
lumím chá	fishing pole	WS	lumím ćá		
lumít	to fish	WS	lumít		
lumit'ṃkói	go fishing, go fish (card game)	FC			
lumítkṃm chá	fishing pole	FC-E			
lumítḱoi	go fishing	WS	lumítḱoj		
lúmlumi	Douglas fir or spruce	HM	loom'-loom-me		
lúmlumi kuiyó	small fir trees	HY			
lúmlumim sáwi	fir needles	RD	lum'lumim sā'wi	146	
lunu	wild carrot, lomatium	FC, PM-M	lun-um		
lupúpu	gray sage brush with big leaves	FC			lṃpúpu
lút	bake in ashes	RD	lut'	76	lṃt
lúťi	real (adj)	WST		62:9	
lúťna	right (hand)	FC			
lúťpeḱanim	every single one (of), all (adj): lúťpeḱanim téťṃťṃ kṃkán yakṃpem "all children have names"	RD	lut'pekanim	15	
luwú	eel, fresh-water eel	FC			lowá (FC-T), liuwí (FC-E), lou-wom (BC)
Luwú Humenim	place name for the rapids where Indian Creek joins the Feather River, DT map 7 (may mean "catching freshwater eel in nets"). See map 2 in Appendix 5.	DT			
mṃ́	shoot, spear (something)	WS	mý, mú		mú
mṃ́	that one, there, he, she, it, the, that	WS	mý		
mṃ'ṃi	away, across: hadádi mṃ'ṃi "far away"	WST-DW	myʔyj	70:4	
mṃcha'i	difference	FC			
mṃchó	the two who... (RD), those two (WS)	RD, WS	mötso' (RD), myćó (WS)	78	
mṃchó'us	those two by themselves	RD	mötso'us	142	
mṃ dṃkṃ	by himself, herself	FC			
mṃ́dato	keep on shooting (WS), spray (as skunk), shoot all (arrows) (RD)	WS, RD	mýdato (WS), mö'dato (RD)	170, 210, 224	
mṃ́de	bear, brown bear	WS	mýde		
mṃdí	there	WS	mydí		
mṃ ekídi	yesterday	FC			
mṃhéwi	that same one (WS), those things (WST)	WS, WST	myhéwi	56:42	
mṃhúnḱói	go hunting	FC			mohunḱói (RD), muhunḱói (WS)
mṃ́kṃli	mercury (metallic element)	FC			
mṃkṃlúsi	big owl, Great Horned Owl	FC			mṃkkṃlṃsi (WS)

157

Maidu	English	Source	Source Spelling	Page	Other Spellings
mʌkʌlúsim sawí	cat's breeches (hydrophyllum capitatum)	FC			
mʌkahúlkʌ	American Bittern (bird) (FC, PM-M), heron, bittern, shitepoke (WS)	FC, PM, WS	muk-a-hol-cum (PM-M), mykahúlky (WS)		mʌkaholkʌ, mʌkahʌlkʌ
mʌkámimwoli	nephews	WS	mykámimwoli		
mʌkán(im)	the same as before, the same place where one started out, this country (with words like kódo or kʌsdo)	RD	mökan'(im)	48, 134, 146, 152, 180, 232	
mʌkándi	in the same place as before, just as before	RD	mökandi	198	
mʌkáni	the same thing, the same place (WS), something, the same (FC)	WS, FC	mykáni		makán (RD)
mʌkito	shoot at each other	WS	mýkito		
mʌkkʌlʌsi	owl, big owl, Great Horned Owl	WS, FC	mýkkylysi		mʌkʌlúsi (FC)
mʌkúni	that one first: hésmen mʌkúnim ʌdíknokan "he got there first"	WS, RD	mykúni (WS), mökū'ni (RD)	206	
mʌkúnim máidʌ	that man first, him first	WS	mykúnim májdy		
mʌkúnin kʌlé	that woman first, her first	WS	mykúnim kylé		
mʌl	roll the eyes	WS	mýl		
mʌldoi	roll, stretch up the eyes in anger	WS	mýldoj		
mʌlokʌ	blue heron	FC			
mʌm bének	the next day	WS	mym bének		
mʌm bomó	all of the people	FC			
mʌm bomó	those, all those	WS	mým bomó		
mʌmʌ́	him, her (object of sentence): mʌmʌ́ yákkadom hapá "doing precisely like him or her"	WS, FC	mymý		
mʌmʌ́m	he, she (subject of sentence)	WS, FC	mymý		
mʌmʌ́m hapá	of course it was he/she	WS	mymým hapá		
mʌmʌ́t	anything belonging to, anything associated with: mʌmʌ́t wépam máidʌ dónbosdom hóiwihamotochoi'a. "Anything of Coyote Man's, grabbing all of it, they brought it together in one place."	RD	mömöt'	32	
mʌmʌ́weti	as for him, as for her: mʌmʌ́wet machói'am uním wélketim kʌlókbeki ʌnnotiwonom madóm ʌpékadom machói'am "as for him, he remained being repeatedly swallowed by this old frog woman"	RD, WS	mömö'weti, mömö'wet (RD), mymýwet (WS)	180, 204	mʌmʌ́wet
mʌmbʌdʌnkʌ	spotted sandpiper	HM	mum'-bud'-dun'-ka		

Maidu	English	Source	Source Spelling	Page	Other Spellings
mᴧmén	at that time, at that point in time	WST-GP, RD	mymén (WST), mömmen' (RD)	68:39 (WST), 144 (RD)	mᴧmmén
mᴧméntapo	eventually, somehow, one way or another, at some point (in time), over time	RD	mömen'tapo	30, 186	
mᴧmméndᴧkᴧ	only then	RD	mömmen'dökö	136, 218	
mᴧná	that way, to there	WS	myná		
mᴧná'anwet	without talking about it, ignoring it	RD	möná'anwet	108	
mᴧnáki	to him/her for it: mᴧnáki pakálpi "pay for it"	FC			
mᴧnámenwet	without talking about it	RD	möná'menwet	106	
mᴧnán	from there	WS	mynán		
mᴧnándi	at that place, from in that place	FC			
mᴧnéwoli	mother and other relatives, female elders	RD	möne'woli	188	
mᴧnmᴧni	silver wormwood, western mugwort (medicinal plant)	FC			múnmuni
mᴧpéne	those two	FC			
mᴧpulíto	a woman and her second husband as a pair	FC			mᴧ pulíto
mᴧsámboye	brother, the brother	RD	mösam' bōye	136	mᴧ-sambᴧyi (FC)
mᴧsámboyekᴧtoto	brothers: mᴧsámboyekᴧtotom bíschoi'a tetét pim. "There once were very many brothers living together."	RD	mösam' bōyekötotom	118, 136	
mᴧ sámboyem kᴧlé	sister	RD	mösām' bōyeñ küle'	150	
mᴧsap	shoot entirely through (something)	WS	mýsap		
mᴧséna	those people there	FC			
mᴧséwet	by themselves (WS), however many there are (FC)	WS, FC	myséwet		
mᴧsín	machine (from English)	WS	mysín		
mᴧsito	shoot through	WS	mýsito		
mᴧskᴧt	shotgun (from English "musket")	WS	mýskyt		
mᴧso	spear	PM-M	musho		
mᴧtᴧnbe	her younger brother, his younger brother, the younger brother or little brother: mᴧtᴧnbe cha woiyókan "she sent her little brother for firewood."	RD, FC	mötön'be	148, 224	
mᴧ'úsi	by himself, by herself	RD	möū'si	128	
mᴧwet	to himself/herself: mᴧwet áiḱaḱatchoi'a "he thought to himself"	RD	mö'wet	124	

Maidu	English	Source	Source Spelling	Page	Other Spellings
mᴍwéti	that person, the other one: mᴍwét bistá "Let him stay by himself!"	FC, RD	möwet'	204	mᴍwét
mᴍyák	be like	FC			
mᴍyák	the same	FC			
mᴍyáka	do likewise, do the same	RD	möyāk'a	152	
mᴍyákaka	be about the same, be similar, be well matched (opponents)	RD	möya'kaka	212	
mᴍyákape	the same (adj)	FC-R			
mᴍyákat 'as	the same way (adverb)	RD	möyak'adas	98	
mᴍyákati	repeat (action), do (something) the same way as before, do the same again (RD), do equally, to the same degree, to the same amount (WS): béibᴍ mᴍ mᴍyákatipi! "do it the same way again! do it the same as before!"	RD	möyak'ati (RD), myjákati (WS)	64, 234	
mᴍyákatini	simultaneously	RD	möyak'atini	64	
mᴍyákbe	an equal amount	RD	möyak'be	138	
mᴍyákbebe	equally, to the same degree, to the same amount (WS), half and half (RD)	RD, WS	möyak'bebe (RD), myjákbebe (WS)	136	
mᴍyákchetipe	resembling, looking like	FC			
mᴍyákdᴍkbe mᴍyákbe	exactly half, exactly the same portions	RD	möyak'dökbe möyak'be	138	
mᴍyákkᴍti	be the same as each other	RD	möyaköt'i	162	
mᴍyáktitiluťi	be exactly the same: hómpaitopᴍ'ᴍ mᴍyáktitiluťi ka'ánḱas "Let's wrestle since we're exactly the same size"	RD	möyak'titiluti	130	
mᴍyákwiyeti	force (someone) out again, cause (someone) to leave again	RD	möyak'wiyeti	216	
mᴍyé	that (thing), that (one)	RD	möye	92	
mᴍyésᴍ	those people	RD	möyē'sö	112	
mᴍyí	there (a place just mentioned)	RD	möi		mᴍi
mᴍyídi	in that same place, at that same place	RD	möi'di	148	
mᴍyím	that (previously mentioned person), that person	RD	möim'	234, 236	mᴍyim
mᴍyím	that person, that (just mentioned). Subject of sentence (mᴍyím) or modifier: mᴍyím máidᴍ "that (just mentioned) man"		möim		
mᴍyína	from that same place: mᴍ'ína yohónchoi'a "a sound came from the same place/direction as before"	RD	möi'na	214, 216	

Maidu	English	Source	Source Spelling	Page	Other Spellings
ma	be, accomplish, do, make: mapí! "do it!"	WS, FC	ma		ma'á
ma	rule (noun), law, regulation	FC			
má	hand, paw, paw-print: má chukútpi! "wash your hands!"	WS, RD, SPB, FC	má (WS), ma (RD), mamah (SPB)	230	
má dóntoto	grasp hands	WS	má dóntoto		
má 'etósti	double up the fist, make a fist	WS	má ʔetósti		
má leléwaito	open up the hand	WS	má leléwajto		
ma sᴧ́tikᴧ	one-handed	FC			
má wátdan	clap the hands	WS	má wátdan		
má welék	wave the hand in the air	WS	má welék		
má weléknoye	wave the hand idly in the air	WS	má weléknoje		
ma'a	people	FC, RD	maa		ma (as suffix)
ma'á	do, be, accomplish: ma'ákᴧḱan "I guess it is, I guess it does"	WS, RD	maʔá (WS), maā (RD)	44	ma
ma'ái	sound (good, loud, terrible, etc.)	WS	maʔáj		
ma'áiḱan	apparently will be, apparently will do/perform (the verb form -áiḱan is used in quotes within stories): kolóknonom pelípchoi'a, 'mᴧkótoki pᴧ́sbutu silépaipem máidᴧm, ma'áiḱan kái'eskᴧm máidᴧm.' "The women shouted, 'A man decked out in his grandmother's pubic hair, now performing: Bluejay Man!" Speculative or Conjecture future tense	RD	maai'kan	102	
ma'ákᴧ	doer	WS	maʔáky		
ma'ákᴧḱan	it's true, it is the case	RD	maā'kökan	44	
ma'ákᴧm	that's the way it always is	RD	maa'köm	68	
ma'ám	was, were, part of past tense, 3rd person: kᴧ'ᴧm ma'am "they were" or "he/she/it was" (see <u>Mountain Maidu Grammar</u>, Lesson 9 for more details)	RD	mām (köm mām)	84	
ma'ámᴧni	the reason why: ma'ámᴧni káiyewḱas yówochikdom min "the reason why I kept calling you was to ask you to cure (someone)"	RD	maa'möni	72	
ma'ándᴧkbe	so large, as big as that, as long/far as that	RD	maā'ndükbem	23	
ma'ánte	this far, so far (ma.. + ante)	WS	maʔánte		
ma'ántekit	get this far	WS	maʔántekit		
ma'ántem ḱódo	as far as this country	RD	maān'teñ ko'do	238	

Maidu	English	Source	Source Spelling	Page	Other Spellings
ma'ánteni	the first time doing something: ma'ánteni kʌkasí. "This is my first time doing it."	HY			
ma'ápe(ni)	(with) this sort of thing	RD	maape(ni)	58	
ma'át	even (after a noun or wií): mʌki mʌm ási ma'át wónotichoi'a "he killed even his own sister-in-law." mʌki hʌbóm ma'át hísatikʌ "even his house stinks." chedá wií ma'át "without even any breakfast;" as for (after verb in -dom): wíyekan hómpaitodom ma'át "as for fighting, the answer is no." although might be (after an adjective): tibíbe ma'át chenókoimaḱas "although I might be small, I will go see." yépḱʌpem ma'át chai yépḱʌmapem "although they might be married, they will take another husband." not even one/not any (with a negative verb): sʌtim ma'át wonómenwet "without missing any" máidʌ ma'át chémhusemenwet "without bothering any people;" maybe/could be: hesánbem ḱúmmenim ma'át wosípchet "maybe after a few years" lulúmi ma'át 'as ílakito'usan "Usually it is the torso that could get hurt." in case (with verb in -mʌni): hésiwet mʌm máidʌm ma'át wasádoimʌni "in case that man starts doing anything bad;" homó ma'át: anywhere, hesí ma'át: anything.	RD, WS, FC, WST	maat (RD), maʔát (WS)	8, 17, 130, 138, 142, 144, 148, 152, 156 170, 190, 196, 202, 204, 214, 216, 222, 228, 230 (RD), 60:56 (WST)	
ma'át 'as	even (after a noun or adverb): betémen ma'át 'as "even back in the old days..."	RD	madas'	228	
ma'át...ma'át...	or: hiló ma'át ítusdom makó ma'át ítusdom "roasting ground squirrel or fish"	FC, RD	hilom'aat it'usdom makom'aat it'usdom	214	
ma'áti	cause to do	FC			
ma'áwew	be normal, usually be	RD	maā'wēu	68, 78	

162

Maidu	English	Source	Source Spelling	Page	Other Spellings
ma'áwewḱan	it is always like that, that's the way it usually is, is normal	RD	maā'wēukan	68, 78	
mábichí	fingernail	WS	mábićí		
mabó	it shall be so, it will be (no conjugation. Does not imply that the speaker wants it to be so)	RD	mabo	52	
mábo	have something stuck in the hand	WS	mábo		
machói	be coming up, be in the future	FC			
machói'am	apparently was, apparently stayed, apparently remained (conjecture past tense): dáldalpem pánom mᴀm machói'am pusúnem máidᴀm. "the silvertip man was apparently a white grizzly bear." (with action verb in -dom): mᴀm nénom hᴀbó machói'am tochíldom "the old man was apparently burning down the house." (Note that WS and RD both translate this as "they say," but my interpretation is different. machói'am is actually the main verb in these sentences. maichoi'am does mean "they apparently said." For more on this, see Mountain Maidu Grammar Lesson 9)	RD	matsoi'a(m)	48, 150, 202, 224, 230, 234	machói'a
machóiḱan	apparently is, apparently are. This verb is used within quotes in stories already using the conjecture or speculative verb tense (such as -choi'a): 'mᴀm máidᴀm pi ḱuťmťm wónotipem máidᴀm machóiḱan,' achói'am símmakdom "'that man is a prolific game-killing man,' they apparently said, gossiping." Speculative or conjecture present tense.	RD	matsoi'kan	192	
machókito	be under the impression that, believe that	WS	maćókito		maichákito (RD)

Maidu	English	Source	Source Spelling	Page	Other Spellings
machókito	being under the impression that, believing that: húboḱoidom ka'ánkano chái'im machókito nik méimendom. "You are not being sensible, being under the impression that (I am) a stranger, and not giving (it) to me."	RD	mastso'kito	136	
máchoḱo	ten	FC			máischoko
madí dón	take (someone) by the hand: nik ma dónpi! "take my hand!"	WS	madí dón		
madóm ᴍpéḱadom	over and over, continue repeatedly	RD	madom' öpek'adom	180	
madóntoto	shake hands with (someone)	FC			
mahá	bring, fetch	WS	mahá		
maháchono	carry (something) over	RD	mahā'tsono	128	
mahádikno	arrive carrying	RD	mahā'dikno	56	
mahádoi	bring (something) up from (somewhere)	WS	mahádoj		
maháiye	bring (something): maháti maháiyekas minna "I brought bread for you."	FC			
maháiyeti	cause to bring: papéli min maháiyetiḱas "I had the paper brought to you."	FC			
maháḱoi	go carrying	RD	mahā'koi	56	
mahámoto	bring to one place	RD	maha'moto	32	
mahá'okit	arrive bringing	WS	maháʔokit		
mahát	make bread	WS	mahát		
maháti	bread	WS	mahát		mahát
mahá'uḱoi	take away (something)	FC			
maháwkit	arrive bringing (something)	RD	mahau'kit	208	
maháye	carry towards (RD), bring (WS)	RD, WS	mahā'ye (RD), maháje (WS)	128	
mahélu	to happen to be (RD), happen, occur, eventuate, come out (WS)	RD, WS	mahel'u (RD), mahélu (WS)	82	
mái	to mean, speak about, indicate, sing lyrics (RD), speak, quote, say (WS): hesádom máiḱa? "what do you mean?" ᴍpé mái'usan máisᴍm "that's what they used to say, that's what they used to talk about" uní maiḱá? "Do you mean this (showing something)?"	RD, WS, WST	mai' (RD), maj (WS)	5, 88, 148, 208, 206, 228 (RD), 52:21 (WST)	
maichákito	be under the impression	RD	maitsak'ito	188	machókito (WS)
máicho	those two, they (2)	WS	májćo		

Maidu	English	Source	Source Spelling	Page	Other Spellings
máidm	become a man, pubesce (verb) (of boys only)	WS	májdy		
máidm	person, people (including trees, birds, and all creatures), man: wépam máidm "coyote man" bḿwokmpem máidm "the man who had possession of the winds"	FC, WS, RD, SPB	májdy (WS), mai′dü, mai′dö (RD), midoo (SPB)	48, 144, 166	
máidm donkm	people catcher, police	FC			
máidm homím sewí	creek running into Spanish Creek at Dublin Jack Ravine. meaning: "people-cooking creek"	FC			
máidmbe	a small man, a legendary man; a young man	RD, BC	mai′dübe	150	
máidmhehe	every one of the people	RD	mai′döhehe	166	
máidmm pípenak	a place where there are many people, a city: máidmm pípenak mnódom ka′ánkano pénem mnópem kmkán wémt'ikpem "you are traveling in a populated area, two who travel is just the right number."	RD	mai′düm pi′penak	122	
máidmmenim	a different man, not the same man: obḿchopindi kmkán wasám máidmmenim "next door is a bad, different man"	RD	mai′dümmenim	192	
máidmmnono	a lot of men or people (subject of sentence. Object would be máidmnono)	FC			
máidmse	Man, Mankind, menfolk, men: máidmsem kódo chehéyechoi'a, sámsuku chemádom, cheménchoi'a. "The men-folks looked all around the land, hoping to see smoke from the fire, (but) they didn't see (it)."	WS, RD	májdyse (WS), mai′düse (RD)	166	
máidmwet	some kind of creature	RD	mai′düwet	112	
maihí	salmon	WS	majhí		maiyí (RD)
mái'odikno	lean against (something) with the palms of the hands or arms extended	WS	máj?odikno		
mái'odiknonu	stand leaning against (something) with the palms of the hands or arms extended	WS	máj?odiknonu		
máism	those three or more, them	WS	májsy		
máischokna péne	twelve	FC			
máischoko	ten	FC			máchoko
máischokom máischoko	one hundred, hundred	FC			

Maidu	English	Source	Source Spelling	Page	Other Spellings
máiye	to mean, talk about, refer to	RD	mā'ye	148	
máiyew	keep trying to say	RD	māi'yeu	186	
máiyewyakken	he/she/they could be been talking about: áite máiyewyakken: I wonder what he/she/they could be talking about?	RD	mai'yeūyaken	138	
maiyí	salmon	RD	maiyi'	44, 48, 64	maihí (WS)
mák	try: wépam mákchoi'a, sólebisim "Coyote tried, singing on and on"	RD	mak'	6	
máḱ	dance at the girls' puberty rites (verb)	WS	máḱ		
makm̈ká?	what might you be doing? What do you think you're doing?	RD	makökā'	146	
makm̈	afraid of, leery of	WS	maký		
makm̈	turn out to be: ym̈sípmm̈ni, mm̈'étim makm̈kan: "when she went out, it turned out to be his sister." wónonkm̈ makm̈! "turn up as a corpse!" (insult)	WST, RD	maký, makö'	56:40, 64	
makm̈mm̈ni	if it is (speculation), if it turns out to be: m̈hm̈m ḱódom kakm̈kan. Hesápem ḱódowet makm̈mm̈ni, ni béi'im okítmentasi. "It might be a dangerous land. If it turns out it is that kind of country, then let me not come back as well."	RD, WST	makö'möni (RD), makýmyni (WST)	146 (RD), 56:40 (WST)	
makm̈no	become like	RD	makö'no	38	
maḱá	girls' puberty rites	WS	maḱ		maḱ
makáchipa	personal name of John Meadows	WS	makáćipa		
makalúsim sawi	hydrophyllum capitatum, ballhead waterleaf	JD	makalusimsawym	56	mm̈km̈lúsim sawí
maḱám solí	girls' puberty rite song	WS	maḱám solí		
makán	right there	RD	makan'	170	mm̈káni (WS, FC)
makáťi	spider: makáťim nik dómen! "spider, don't bite me."	FC, WS, RD, FC-T	makáť (WS), makad' (RD)	216	makáť
makáťim hm̈bó	spiderweb	WS	makáťim hybó		
makít	understand, know, remember (a person): mi ka'ánkano nik mákitmenpem "You are one who doesn't remember me." makítḱa? "Do you understand?" ni km̈kás hesíma'at makítmenpem máidm̈m. "I am somebody who doesn't know anything."	FC, RD	mā'kit	9, 136	mákkit (WS), mákit (RD)

Maidu	English	Source	Source Spelling	Page	Other Spellings
makiti'us	understand for oneself	FC			
makitḱukus	pretend to know	FC			
makítpe	knowledgeable, acquainted with (information): uním ḱódo mínchem makítpem mayákḱeno. "You might be knowledgeable about this country." pi makítpem ka'ánkano "You are so smart/knowledgeable"	RD, FC	makit'pe	60	
makitsa	understand, have an understanding of	FC			
makítto	learn together	FC			
mákkinu	be aware of	WS	mákkinu		
mákkit	know, understand	WS	mákkit		makít (FC, RD)
mákkitdoi	learn	WS	mákkitdoj		
makkíti	have a plan	FC			
makkítti'us	understand for yourself	FC			makiti'us
mákkityaha	want to learn, want to know	WS	mákkitjaha		
mákmakɱ	pileated woodpecker (RD), cormorant (double-crested) (PM-M), yellowhammer, flicker (WS)	RD, PM-M, WS	mak'maköm (RD), mak-mak-cum (PM-M), mákmakkɱ (WS)	RD 36	
mákmakitmen	not know, not know much about: ni hesí mákmakitmenḱas. "Me, I don't know much of anything."	RD	mak'makitmen	11	
makó	fish (noun)	WS	makó		
makó hilóm ka'ápepekan	things like ground squirrel as well as fish	RD	makō' hilom' kaā'pepekan	214	
makóm	catch fish (by basket)	FC			
makóm báno	fishing basket	WS	makóm báno		
makóm biní	fish net	FC-E			
makóm onóm balí	fish-head font, fish-head orthography	FC			
makóm patá	fishing basket (MP)	WS-MP	makóm patá		
makóm sɱkɱ́ni	fishing basket	WS	makóm sykýni		
makóm tétɱtɱ	minnows	FC			
mákpai	find out, learn: wémťiki makpái "find out what happened"	WS, RD	mákpaj (WS), mak'pai (RD)	118	
mákpaipe	expectation: mákpaipe mákpaidom "having expectations" wépam mákpaipe mákpaidom chɱ́iyim ekí pelípmenta. "The expectation was that Coyote would not howl on the fourth day"	RD	mak'paipe	34	
mákpaiti	instruct, direct, order	WS	mákpajti		
mákpaitipedi	to the place (he was) directed to, in the place (he was) told about	RD	mak'paitipedi	84	

Maidu	English	Source	Source Spelling	Page	Other Spellings
mákpapai	learn	WS	mákpapaj		
mákpapaiti	teach, instruct, explain: mᴀkí okítmape mᴀm bomó mákpapaitiḱan "he explained to the group when he would come home."	WS, RD	mákpapajti (WS), mak'papaiti (RD)	218	
mákpapaitikᴀ	teacher	FC			
mákpapaitikᴀm uiyí	school house, school (building)	FC			
mákulu	wrist	WS	mákulu		
mákulum bᴀmí	wrist bone	WS	mákulum bymí		
mákupe	rule-maker, lawmaker	FC			makᴀpe
mákwono	try to, try: mákwonop béibᴀ "try again."	WS, FC	mákwono		
mákwonohóiye	start to learn, begin trying	RD	mak'wono hoi'yedom	82	
mákwonopi	try!	FC			
mákwonoyaha	want to try, ought to try	WST	mákwonojaha	52	
málbᴀ	marsh hawk	HM	mahl'-bum		
mám bichí	fingernail(s)	FC			
mám chípbᴀ	finger(s)	WS	mám ćípby		mám chipᴀ
mam ḱadátim honí	ace of diamonds	WS	mam ḱadátim honí		
mám ťáťa	palm of the hand	WS	mám ťáťa		
mamá	advise, mentor (verb)	FC			
mamámen	advise not to, warn	WS	mamámen		
mamánkano	you shall be	RD	manāñ'kano	216	
mamáwet	although it will be so	RD	mamā'wet	104	
mamchuiyi	nine	FC			
maméni	one who is not	RD	mamen'i	134	
maní	cedar	WS	man		man (WS), máni (FC)
máni	rub in the hands, manipulate, "by hand"	FC			
maní sínto	mix by hand, shuffle cards: papélimbe maní síntop! "shuffle the cards!"	FC			
máni tawál'us	masturbate	WS	máni tawál?us		
Maním Báldᴀkᴀ	place name near the south of Big Meadows, #13 on FR map. See map 3 in Appendix 5.	FR	maním báldikɨ	370-371	
maním chá	cedar tree, incense cedar: lalám maním cham kᴀḱán "It is a tall cedar tree."	WS, JD, FC, FC-E	maním ćá (WS), manymća (JD)	31	mánim cha (FC)
maním sawí	cedar leaves, cedar tree needles	FC			
máno	go get (something)	FC			
mántedoi	high up	RD	mān'tedoi	64	
mapa	have someone do it (negative with "ben"): mᴀkí te ᴀnóiben mapá "Don't let his child wander far!"	RD	mapa	140	

Maidu	English	Source	Source Spelling	Page	Other Spellings
mapém mᴧkan	being the same as before, just like (they were) before: hesádom uním wónokᴧm k̓út̓m̓ᴧm mapém mᴧk̓an pok̓ᴧkinumak̓ade? "Why should these dead animals come back to life being just like before?"	RD	mapem' mökan	28	
mapí	do it!: unína mapí! "Come here!" (negative with "ben" - see also "ben... map" for examples): teté map sódoiben "don't pick up big ones" hadá map ᴧkóiben "don't go far!"	RD, WST		54:32 (WST), 142 (RD)	map
masᴧ́	and, both of them (WS), plural marker following a noun (WST): nikkotó masᴧ́ nikópa ᴧhénoye'usas "I used to go with my grandmothers and grandfather"	WS, WST	masý, masým	60:1	masᴧ́m
masá'a	wild celery, eaten raw in early spring (FC, JD), species of plant with an edible root, similar to the sok̓ómi, or Queen Anne's Lace (WS)	FC, JD, WS	masam (JD), masá (WS)	77	masá
másc̓okna sᴧ́tti	eleven	WS	másćokona sýtti		
másc̓oko	ten	WS	másćoko		máischoko
másc̓okom másc̓oko	one hundred, hundred	FC			
mási	brother-in-law, sister-in-law: as a kinship term, this word must have a prefix, either mᴧ, nik, or min (see Mountain Maidu Grammar, Lesson 6 for more details)	FC, WS, RD	mas (WS), möm ā'si (RD)	202	mas (WS), masá (FC)
masím kᴧlé	sister-in-law: as a kinship term, this word must have a prefix, either mᴧ, nik, or min (see Mountain Maidu Grammar, Lesson 6 for more details)	WS	masím kylé		
masím máidᴧ	brother-in-law: as a kinship term, this word must have a prefix, either mᴧ, nik, or min (see Mountain Maidu Grammar, Lesson 6 for more details)	WS	masím májdy		
matakúpno	glove	FC			
matí	bring about, intentionally cause (RD), do (something) to (someone) (WS)	RD, WS	matī' (RD), matí (WS)	176	

Maidu	English	Source	Source Spelling	Page	Other Spellings
matíwe	always cause (problems), always do (something) to (someone), usually do (something to)	RD	matī'we	142	
matíwe'aman	you keep causing (problems), you keep intentionally doing to (someone): hesím aité matíwe'aman "I wonder what you are, (who) keep causing problems" - see áman.	RD	matī'weaman	142, 214, 218	
matíwewi	do to (someone) again	RD	matī'wewī'	106	
matíwi'ano	you did it: homóndi sꟽ'ꟽi matíwi'ano? "where did you do it?"	RD	matī'wiano	84	
máwꟽḱꟽ	five	WS, RD, FC	máwyḱy	RD 32	máwike, máwꟽkkꟽ
máwꟽḱꟽ péne	seven (this is a rare variant form for sáichoḱona sꟽtti)	WS-LB	máwyḱym péne		
máwꟽḱꟽ sꟽtti	six (this is a rare variant form for sáichoḱo)	WS-LB	máwyḱym sýtti		
máwꟽknini	five times	WS	máwyknini		
máwa	thigh, hip	WS	máwa		
máwam bꟽmí	hipbone	WS	máwam bymí		
máwam pulúmto	between the legs, between the thighs	WS	máwam pulúmto		
mawé'aman	you are: hesím áite mawé'aman "I wonder what you are!" see áman. These questions are out of earshot of the person asked.	RD	mawē'aman	216	
mawé'uḱa	have you been doing (something)?: hesátidom sꟽ'ꟽi wónotidom mawé'uḱa? "how have you been killing (them)?" without sꟽ'ꟽi: "how do you usually kill them?"	RD	mawē'uka	84	
mawewí	can, always be able to do, always do, be able to do: hesádom áite ka'ádꟽtꟽ sówodoidom mawewíyakḱen "I wonder how he can carry ones like that."	RD	mawēwi'	142	
mayá	save back, conserve	WS	majá		
mayáikḱen	it might be possible	RD	mayāiken (no stress marks in Dixon)	176	

Maidu	English	Source	Source Spelling	Page	Other Spellings
mayákḱen	somehow, at last, to his/her surprise, suddenly, unexpectedly, not knowing what was about to happen. This verb has many meanings. It is used in story telling, apparently as a foreshadowing technique ("without knowing what was about to happen"). It also occurs in a series of three or more at the most exciting part of a story. the first in a series can often be translated "suddenly," and the following occurrences as "subsequently". Alternatively, "at last" can be translated. With question words like hesádom, hesádowet, hesím, ai sm'mi, áite, etc. it means "could it be?" hesádowet mayákken "What is going on?" With forms of yakát, it translates as "seems like." There is an overall feeling of being vulnerable, not knowing what to do, or being surprised, that doesn't directly translate into English.	RD	mayā'ken, mayā'kan	60, 78, 80, 138, 140, 144, 146, 184, 196, 200, 206, 208, 214, 216, 228	
mayákḱeno	you might be: uním ḱódo mínchem makítpem mayákḱeno. "You might be knowledgeable about this country."	RD	mayā'keno	60, 88	
mayákḱes	without my knowledge	RD	mayā'kes	230-232	
mayéwḱa	were you doing (that) to (something or someone)?: hesádom mayéwḱa? "Why were you doing that (to someone)?"	RD	mayē'uka	90	
mayhí	salmon	FC			maihí, maiyí
mé	take, get, take along: yálulu méḱan "they took along a flute"	WS, RD	mé (WS), mē' (RD)	168	
me'ahemi	gooseberry	PM-M	mea-hem-em		
méchms	matches (from English)	WS	méċys		
méda	take (something) from (someone)	WS	méda		
médato	take (something that is handed over or offered)	RD, FC	mē'dato	60, 104, 198, 220	
méhťakit	assault, rape (verb)	RD	mē''takit	180	

Maidu	English	Source	Source Spelling	Page	Other Spellings
méhyo	lunge and grab	WS	méhjo		
méhyodoi	start to grab (someone), bite (as a snake) (RD), make a lunge for and grab (WS)	RD, WS	mehyodoi, meh'yodoi (RD), méhjodoj (WS)	54, 92	
méhyotno	spring down onto suddenly and grab	WS	méhjotno		
méi	give, allow: mᴍ nik méima'ankano "give it to me!" hesádom maká yepónim máidᴍm wónom máidᴍki kᴍlékan ma'át sikásaitodom méimenmapem? "why do you, the chief, not allow for humans to have a little fun with women?"	WS, RD, SPB	méj (WS), mē'i (RD), meëy (SPB)	48, 136	
méibono	not give, hoard	WS	méjbono		
méibonosa	miserly, stingy	WS	méjbonosa		
méikᴍ	generous	WS	méjky		
méikᴍsa	generous, free-handed	WS	méjkysa		
méiluť	really/seriously give (something): nik méiluťma'ankano "seriously, give it to me!"	RD	mē'ilut	136	
méimenkᴍ	never giving to	RD	mē'imenköm	202	
méiti	being given away (verb), be free of charge	FC			
méiťi	stingy	WS	méjťi		
méiťipe	stingy	FC			méiťipe (WS)
méiťisa	miserly, stingy	WS	méjťisa		
méito	deal (cards), buy, give out (for example, múnmuni at the bear dance)	FC, WS	méjto		
méitokᴍm hᴍbó	store, shop (noun)	WS	méjtokym hybó		
méitokᴍm uiyí	store, shop (noun)	FC			méitokᴍm uyí
méitokoi	go shopping	WST	méjtokoj	54:30	
méitom hᴍbó	store, shop (noun)	WS, WST-DW	méjtom hybó	74:8	
méitowokᴍ	salesman	WS	méjtowoky		
méiwo	ask someone to give, ask someone for: mᴍyákdᴍkbe mᴍyákbe méiwochet, wíyedom helúto méikan. "When she asked (him) to give her half, he said 'No', and only gave a few."	RD	mēi'wo	134, 138	
méiyewe	give (something) back, return (something): ᴍkóikᴍ'ᴍm ma'ás, hesím ma'át mᴍm nikí liáni méiyewemenwet "I left without him giving me back any of my money"	FC, WS, WST	méjjewej	60:58	méiyewei
memé	take (something) back, get (something) back, recover (something)	RD, WS	memē' (RD), memé (WS)	166, 172	

Maidu	English	Source	Source Spelling	Page	Other Spellings
méni	season, period of time	WS	mén		mén
mením kʌkán	be irrelevant to, be meaningless, nothing to: nik mením kʌkán "it doesn't matter to me" mením kʌkán "it's not that"	FC			
méno	take (something) over or across: yak ménop "take the canoe across (the river)" as command, go get (FC)	RD, FC	mēn'o	124	
ménu	hold	WS	ménu		
me'ókole	be reluctant to give, not want to give	RD	meō'kolē	134	
mépai	start on, get started on	WS	mépaj		
mépbo	assail, attack (as an evil spirit)	WS	mépbo		
mépbodoi	start to attack (someone)	WST-RP	mépbodoj	66:30	
méwikadoi	pick (something) up (off the ground)	RD	mēwikadoi	60	
méyodoi	seize, start to seize, jump at to seize	RD	mē'yodoi	106, 110, 208	
mi	you (subject of sentence)	FC			
mí hapá	of course it was you, you, of course	WS	mí hapá		
mihasi	vulture	FC			
mikchíkti	to stretch a net over (something) as a trap	RD	miktsik'ti	220	
míkki	fish trap	WS	míkki		
míkkit	set a fish trap	WS	míkkit		
míknoye	lounge around lazily	WS	míknoje		
míkuni	you first: míkun kʌdawe "your turn, you go next"	WS, RD	míkuni (WS), mīk'un' (RD)	6	
míkyosippin	move slowly up towards by seeping	WS	míkjosippin		
mil	be heavy	FC			
mílda	metal	FC			
míldan kúk	telephone wire, phone call	FC			
míldan kúkti	make a phone call: míldan kuktidom Lilly "calling Lilly"	FC			
mími	mommy	FC			
mimíwet	you yourself	WS	mimíwet		
mín	you (object of a sentence), to you, for you: oméidom kʌkán min "it is a good-luck charm for you"	WS, FC, WST-DW	mín	70:5	
min chai'í	someone other than you (object of sentence)	RD	min tsaiī'	114	
min káikasi	I'm talking to you! I mean YOU	RD	min kai'kasi	72	
min yákkadom hapá	doing precisely like you	WS	min jákkadom hapá		
mínchʌ	you (three or more), all of you	WS, FC	mínćy		

Maidu	English	Source	Source Spelling	Page	Other Spellings
mínchᴧwet	you (three or more) yourselves	WS	mínćywet		
mínche	you two	WS	mínće		
mínchewet	you two yourselves	WS	mínćewet		
míncho	you two	WS	mínćo		
mínchowet	you two yourselves	WS	mínćowet		
miní	milk, woman's breast	FC, WS	min		min (WS)
miní	suck (as verb - a mosquito sucking blood) (RD), suckle (WS)	RD, WS	miní' (RD), miní (WS)	152	
miníhusi	buzzard	FC-T			miní'usi
Miníhusim O	place name for Buzzard Rock. This may be the same as Mínminim Om. See map 2 in Appendix 5.	WS	miníhusim ʔó		
miním onó	nipple	WS	miním ʔonó		
miním óschumi	nipple	WS	miním ʔósćumi		
miníti	breastfeed, cause to suck	WS	miníti		
miní'usi	buzzard, vulture	WS, FC	miníʔusi		miníhusi
mínḱi huhéyedi	this was your idea, all because of your idea	RD	min'ki hūhē'yedi	184	
mínḱini	with yours (your thing), using yours	RD	min'kini	92	
mínmeni	not you	WS	mínmeni		
mínmeni ka'as	I don't mean you, I am not picking you	RD	min'meni kaas	86	
mínmini	drops of milk or white liquid	RD	minmini	56	
Mínminim Om	place name for Snake (milk) rock, #4 on LM map. See map 2 in Appendix 5.	LM	mem-men-nam-ohm		
mínobe	everyone, everything, every	WS	mínobe		
mínono	fantasizing, kidding around, "in fun" (adverb)	RD	mī'nono	188	
mínsᴧ	you all, everybody, all of you (object of sentence)	FC			
mínsᴧm	you all, everybody, all of you (subject of sentence): mínsᴧm káipe pedóm mapí "all of you, be eating your dinner!"	RD, FC	min'söm	46	
mínsᴧm sᴧ́ti	one of you: hesádom mínsᴧm sᴧ́ti ma'át opénomendom maḱá? Why doesn't one of you go search?				
minṭáp	to milk (verb), nurse (verb)	FC			
mi'úsi	you alone (subject of sentence)	FC			
míwet	you, just you (subject of sentence): míwet ma'át "by yourself"	RD	mi'wet	100	
mo	drink (verb)	WS	mo		

174

Maidu	English	Source	Source Spelling	Page	Other Spellings
mó'aka	cormorant	HM	mo'-ah-kah		
mobɨ́dɨk	seldom drink	WS	mobýdyk		
mobúdɨkɨ	light drinker	WS	mobúduk		
modá	brown the outer bark of sticks over the fire, as a part of the basketmaking process	WS	modá		
móda	bury in ashes	WS	móda		
mohɨ́hɨt	do (something) louder and faster	WS	mohýhyt		
mohɨ́hɨtdoi	resume (any activity) more loudly and at a faster rate	WS	mohýhytdoj		
mohɨ́hɨtnoti	perform louder and faster	WS	mohýhytnoti		
mohɨ́twono	be loud (RD), be loud and fast (WS)	RD, WS	mohöt'wonō (RD), mohýtwono (WS)	126	
mohɨ́twonowiḱoi	make a lot of noise	RD	mohöt'wono'wikoi	72	
mohunkoḱói	go off hunting (plural subject)	RD	mōhunkokoi'	214	muhunkoḱói, mɨhunkoḱói
móilompani	lizard (RD), a kind of big green lizard (WS)	RD, WS	moil'ompani (RD), mójlompan (WS)	142, 144	
mói̓yu	burn hair off (something)	RD	moi'yu	62	
mokɨ́	beverage, drink (noun)	WS	moký		
mokɨ́m loló	drinking container, drinking glass (MP)	WS-MP	mokým loló		
mokúla	coax a disease out of the patient's body by means of singing, shaking rattles, etc.	WS	mokúla		
mólbiti	leech	WS	mólbiti		
móldo	egret	FC			
Molma	place name for Auburn	RD-NM			
molókɨ	blue heron, condor	FC			mɨlokɨ (FC)
molpeti	water beetle	PM-M	mul-be-tem		
moluku	golden eagle	FC			
móm	rise (water in a river), fill with water	RD	mom'	194	
momɨ́	drinker	WS	momý		
mombobónpin	start to flow down into (water) (verb)	RD	mombobon'pin	194	
mómbochono	flow over, flow around	RD	nom'botsono	28	
mombomínu	be filled up (with a lot of water)	RD	mombomin'u	200	
mombomít	to flood down into	RD	mombomit'	40	
mombóno	to flow, flood	RD	mombon'o	194	
mombudútchono	be flooded with water, covered with water	RD	mombudutsono	60	
mombudútchonoti	cause water to cover over	RD	mombudut'sonoti	40	
mombudútḱoi	rise (as water in a flood)	RD	mombudut'koi	40	
momchúiti	make more watery	WS	momćújti		
mómdani	lake	WS	mómdani		
mómdo	under water, covered with water (adverb)	RD	mom'do	42	
momhɨ́ḱoi	go fishing with nets	RD	momhökoi'	214, 216	momhɨ́ḱoi (WS)
momhɨ́	fish by using nets	WS	momhý		
momhɨ́koi	go fishing with nets	WS	momhýḱoj		momhɨḱói (RD)

Maidu	English	Source	Source Spelling	Page	Other Spellings
momhʌkokoi	catch in nets	RD	momhök'okoi	216	
momí	water, stream	WS, FC, SPB	mom (WS), momeh (SPB)		mom
mómi wowáka	salamander	HM	mum'-me wo-wah'-kah		
momím chetókʌ	window glass, glass (as a material)	WS	momím ćetóky		
momím húskʌ	water snake	WS	momím húsky		
momím loló	water bucket (MP)	WS-MP	momím loló		
momím taméli	watermelon	WS	momím taméli		
momím yó	water lily	WS	momím jó		
momípispisto	water ouzel, American Dipper (bird)	RD	momi'pispisto	212	mompíspisto
momít	put on: chám sádi momítdom "putting wood on the fire"	FC			
mómkiwi	watercress	FC			
mómlolo	drinking cup, water cup	FC			
mómni hítpaino	go douse with water, go immerse in water	WS	mómni hítpajno		
mompáno	otter	WS	mompáno		
mompíspisto	water ouzel (bird)	WS, FC	mompíspisto		mompispísto (FC)
mómpoldoi	swirl and bubble (water)	WS, WST-DW	mómpoldoj		70:4
mómpoldoitikʌ	Jacuzzi pump	FC-E			
mómpoyoi	yellow pond lily, cow lily	JD, PM-M	mompojoym (JD), mom-po-yol-em (PM-M)	64	mompoyoli (PM-M)
momsík	thirsty	WS, FC	momsík, momsýk		mómsuk (FC), momsʌk (WS)
momtátati	wild water rhubarb	WS	momtátati		
momwasipťa	pour water out on: epʌm momí yamádom, mʌm epʌm tʌdi momwasipťama'ankano. "To make manzanita cider, pour water over the manzanita powder."	FC-T			
momwasó	water parsnip (poisonous), Lomatium	JD	momwaso, momwasom	15, 77	mowasó
mómwiyakti	make more watery, thin up by adding water	WS	mómwijakti		
momyodádanu	shimmer, quiver	RD	momyodā'danu	226	
monkʌdati	ring (noun)	FC			monkadati (FC)
monkʌlío	red-winged black bird	FC			monkoli'o (FC), mʌnkʌlio (FC-R)
monkoba	raccoon	FC			
monkolí'o	red-winged blackbird	FC			monkʌlío
mosápe	one who frequently drinks, always drinking	FC-E			
mósda	spread open, spread apart, of the legs (intransitive)	WS	mósda		
mósdada	spread open, spread apart, of the legs (intransitive)	WS	mósdada		
mósdadati	spread the legs apart (transitive)	WS	mósdadati		

Maidu	English	Source	Source Spelling	Page	Other Spellings
mósdawaito	spread wide open, of the legs (intransitive)	WS	mósdawajto		
mósdawaitoti	spread the legs wide apart, (as when changing an infant's diaper)	WS	mósdawajtoti		
mósťapin	sit astraddle, gripping with the legs	WS	mósťapin		
mósťapinhanóye	put one's legs over someone in a sexual way	RD	mōs'tapinhanō'ye	90	
motápai	be courageous	RD	motā'pai	46	
motápai	invest with courage	WS	motápaj		
moti	water (verb), cause to drink	FC			
motó	gather together, assemble, put together (WS), mix ingredients (WST)	WS, WST	motó	76:1	
motópe	a go-round (in dancing), wetémim motópe - dance (n), round dance	WST-LB		42:1,2,3	
mowasó	wild parsnip	RD	mowasō' (RD), mówaso (WS)	118	mówaso (WS)
mówinᴧnkᴧ	water bug	WS	mówinymky		
moyáha	like to drink	WS	mojáha		
moyó	elbow	FC			
moyó	to elbow (someone)	FC			
mú	shoot	WS	mú, mý		mᴧ́
múhun	hunt with guns or arrows	WS	múhun		
múhunepínimoto	come back from hunting together	RD	mū'hune-pin'imoto	214	
muhúnḱoi	go hunting	RD	mūhun'koi	204	mohúnḱoi
múhunkoḱói	go hunting (plural subject)	RD	mū'hunkokoi	214	mohúnkoḱoi
muhúnmitno	go down into (valley) to hunt	RD	mūhun'mitno	224	
múi	crouch down and put something like a basket or cloth over the head (for father-in-law avoidance)	WS	múj		
muiyukᴧ	yellow fritillaria	FC			muyuko
mukálkᴧ	bittern (a wading bird in the heron family)	HM	mu-kahl'-kah		
mukédewowe	goldfinch, yellow bird	HM	muk-ked'-de-wow'-we		
muku	wild bulb, yellow star tulip, eaten as a potato	JD	mukuʔ	60	
muli	second husband	FC			
múnmuni	wormwood, mugwort	WS, FC, JD	múnmuni (WS), munmunum (JD)	44	mᴧnmᴧni
múnmunim sawí	wormwood leaves, mugwort leaves	WS	múnmunim sawí		
muntu	type of edible mushroom (PM-M), poisonous red mushroom (JD)	PM-M, JD	moon-too (PM-M), muntu (JD)		
muso	spear	PM-M	musho		mᴧso
mussú	cheek, face	WS, FC	mussú		musú (FC)
mútmutpe	soft-textured, fine (like hair)	WS	mútmutpe		

Maidu	English	Source	Source Spelling	Page	Other Spellings
mutútu	master of a pet	WS	mutútu		
mu'ús	alone	WS	muʔús		mᴧ'úsi
muyuko	fritillaria pudica, yellow fritillaria	JD	muju·kom	61	muiyukᴧ
nᴧnholwa	blue currant	PM-M	nun-hol-wam		nunholwa
nᴧs	short, low	WS	nys, nus		nus
nᴧ́wᴧn	swing (verb)	WS	nýwyn		
nᴧ́wᴧnto	rock back and forth, as in a chair	WS	nýwynto		núwunto
nᴧ́wᴧntokᴧ	a child's swing	WS	nýwyntoky		
nᴧ́wᴧntokᴧm bísťakᴧ	rocking chair	WS	nýwyntokym bísťaky		
nᴧ́wᴧntowebis	sit and rock, keep rocking	WS	nýwyntowebis		
nada	this place	FC-R	nadan		
Nadam Ḱoyó	place name for Indian Valley, or the southern part of Indian Valley. See maps 1 and 5 in Appendix 5.	PM-D, MSOP	na-dan-koyo		
nak	vicinity, near, nearby	WS	naḱ		
nak dó	grab at (do is conjugated) a certain part of someone: búknak dóndom "grabbing the tail"	FC			nakí do
Náka Yáni	Mt. Dyer	FC			
naḱám ḱódo	from the nearby country	WST-DW	naḱám ḱódo	74:6	
Náḱam Mómdanni	Lake Almanor	FC			
Náḱam Sewí	Big Meadows river (FC), Hamilton Branch, which ran through Big Meadows. #22 on LM map. See map 3 in Appendix 5.	RD, FC-map, LM	nāʼkam sēwimʼ (RD), Nakam Sewi (FC), Nah-kohm-sewi (LM)	212	Nakom Sewi
Naḱám Ḱoyó	place name for Big Meadows (under Lake Almanor) (WS), place name for village south of Óidim Ḱoyó (RD-NM), #15 on LM map. See maps 1 and 3 in Appendix 5.	WS, RD-NM, FC, LM, RD	naḱám kojó (WS), nakankoyo (RD-NM), nog-kom-kojom (LM)	56	naḱóm ḱoyó (FC)
nakí	place	WS	nakí		
nákweye	talk through a door, window, or any opening, talk into a microphone, talk on the telephone	FC, WS, FC-T, FC-E	nákwej		nakwei (WS)
naná	chest of body: naná banchíkpi! "Cover your chest! Put on a shirt!"	WS, FC-E	naná		
nanám miní	woman's breast	WS	nanám miní		
nawási	skirt (FC), woman's dress (from Spanish naguas "petticoats") (WS)	WS, FC	nawás		nawás (WS)
nawáspe	the queen in cards	WS	nawáspe		
ne	big	RD	ne	208	
né	hen	WS	né		

Maidu	English	Source	Source Spelling	Page	Other Spellings
né	mother: as a kinship term, this word must have a prefix, either mʌ, nik, or min (see Mountain Maidu Grammar, Lesson 6 for more details); tetét yahám nem ekím "Happy Mother's Day." mʌnándi ʌdíkma'adom, mínne hehé yapáito nikí "When you get there, tell your mother Hi from me."	WS, BC, FC	né		
nécho	a mother and another person, mothers: as a kinship term, this word must have a prefix, either mʌ, nik, or min (see Mountain Maidu Grammar, Lesson 6 for more details): mʌnécho	RD	mö nē'tsom	98	
nedí	dream (noun): nedídi nik kaimákpapaiti'ankano "in a dream you taught me how to fly."	FC, FC-T			
nedí	dream (verb)	WS, FC	nedí		
nedím ḱódo	dream land	WS	nedím ḱódo		
nedísape	dreamy, dreamer	FC			
nedí'us	dream to oneself	RD	nedī'us	196	
nékʌto	doing with their mothers	RD	nē'kötodom	182	
Nem Tonna	Lake Tahoe	FC			
nenasíno	move down across	RD	nenasī'no	154	
néndoi	pull up and leave (a place)	WS	néndoj		
nénḱoi	move, change place of residence	WS	nénḱoj		
nénnoye	travel around	WS	nénnoje		
nénnoyebokuk	seldom change habitats	WS	nénnojebokuk		
nénnoyesape	nomadic, always moving around	WS	nénnojesape		
nenó	grow old, be old	RD	nenō'	236	
nenó	old (of people)	WS	nenó		
nenóhno	elderly, sort of old	WS	nenóhno		
nénoḱoi	move away, relocate	FC			
nenóluť	eldest	WS	nenóluť		
nenómen	young, not old	WS	nenómen		
nenópe	old (person)	FC, BC	na nom pem		
neyé	middle-aged: neyé máidʌ "middle-aged man"	RD	nēye'	126	
ni	I	FC			
ní haṕá	of course it was I, I as usual	WS	ní haṕá		
ni!	oops, sorry, my bad	FC			
niḱ	me	WS	niḱ		
níḱ yákkadom haṕá	doing (something) just like me	WS	níḱ jákkadom haṕá		

Maidu	English	Source	Source Spelling	Page	Other Spellings
níkdi	at my house: níkdi bísdom "staying at my house, staying with me"	WST	níkdi	60:63	
niḱi	my (+ noun), mine (when not followed by a noun)	FC			
níḱmeni	not me	WS	níḱmeni		
niku	foolish	FC			
níḱuni	me first	WS	níḱuni		
niníwet	I myself	WS	niníwet		
nisá	us two	WS	nisá		
nisá'usi	us two alone	WS	nisáwʔusi		
nisáwet	us two ourselves	WS	nisáwet		
nisé	us (three or more)	WS	nisé		
niséma	our people	RD	nisē'ma	140	
nisé'usi	we alone (3 or more)	WS	niséʔusi		
niséwet	we ourselves (3 or more)	WS	niséwet		
niu	canoe made from hollowed-out cedar log	JD	niu	31	
ní'usi	I alone	WS	níʔusi		
níwet	by myself	RD	nī'wet	120	
noká	quiver (for arrows)	RD	nokam'	236	
noḱó	arrow, bullet	FC, WS	noḱ		noḱ (WS)
noḱóm hiní	elderberry	JD	nokomhyni	42	
noḱóm noká	quiver for arrows	RD	nokom' noka'	224	
Noḱóm Pino	place name NW of Quincy between American Valley and Butt Valley #37 on FR map. See map 2 in Appendix 5.	FR		370-371	
nóto	north	SP	nó-to	310	
notom ma'a	Northern people	FC			Notoma
nowim cha	white fir tree	JD	nowymća	28	
nuk	laugh (verb)	WS	nuk		
núkbosno	laugh really hard	FC			
núkbusno	laugh very hard, keep laughing	WS	núkbusno		
núkbusto	laugh very hard about (something)	WS, WST	núkbusto	56:36	
núkcheche	smile	WS	núkćeće		
nukchetípe	cute	FC			
núkdowéye	laugh and say	RD	nukdoweye	66	
nukí	laugh!	WS	nukí		
núknoye	have a good time, have fun	WS	núknoje		
núkpapai	laugh at	RD	nuk'papai	28	
núksa	smile, laugh (verb)	WS, FC	núksa		
núksasa	smile, always laugh, laugh a lot, be silly, giggle	FC			
núksasati	cause fun, be fun	FC			
núksasatipe	fun	FC			
núkti	a little bit, somewhat: núkti cháitikape "one that is somewhat different"	WS, RD	núkti		
núktiluťi	tiny, very tiny	WS	núktiluťi		

Maidu	English	Source	Source Spelling	Page	Other Spellings
núktina	for a little while, after a while	WS	núktina		
Nukuti	place name for a village in present-day Quincy. see map 2 in Appendix 5.	AK	Nukuti	397	
núkyahape	absurd, rather silly: núkyahape tawáldom kawéwḱas ínyana wéye nikí wéyedom. "I have been working all this time speaking my own Indian language, which is kind of silly."	HY			
nunholwa	ribes cereum, squaw currant, wax currant, golden current	JD, FC	nunholwam	73	nᴧnholwa
nupᴧm	youth, adolescent, pubescent	FC			
nus	short, low	WS	nus, nys		nᴧs
núsnusi	personal name of a brother of Tom Young	WS	núsnusi		
nútbem	little boy	FC			
núti	pet name for referring to any little boy	WS	núti		
nútipe	baby boy	FC			
nuwim	eel	FC-T			
núwunto	to rock (verb)	FC			nᴧwᴧnto (WS)
o	be left behind (the thing left is subject): mᴧm pándakam okᴧḱan "the bow was left behind, they left the bow behind."	RD	o, okö (kö probably an infix)	234, 236	okᴧ
ó	rock (noun), stone	WS, SPB, FC	ʔó (WS), ohm (SPB)		
O Buwuwum Ḱumí	place name for Wind Hole. See O Wichono.	DT	Abuwu wum kumi	45	
ó chawáidom	mining, hard rock mining	FC-R, FC-E			
ó 'opánokᴧ	turtle	WS	ʔó ʔopánoky		

Maidu	English	Source	Source Spelling	Page	Other Spellings
O Wichono	place name for Wind Hole, Thumb Rock and Split Rock, on Indian Creek, NE of Indian Falls, DT map 7. According to DT, it means Wind Rock. Other names DT lists for this rock (part of a rocky ridge formation) are: Split Rock, O Buwuwum Ḱumí (which probably does mean Wind Hole), muyen pa'pah pitoui yem-sit tem (according to DT, this means "where the wind begins"). This formation is located on the north side of Highway 89 north-east of Indian Falls on Indian Creek, with at least 3 split-rock formations. including Tetém Mámchipbᴍm Om and Búyem Ḱumí. See map 2 in Appendix 5.	DT	O Witchono	45	
o'ᴍ'ᴍlim	shake the head	RD	oö"ölim	122	
obᴍ'aschono	opposite from, across from	RD	obö'astsono	192, 210	
obᴍ'asdoino	opposite: mᴍnán obᴍ'asdoinonan "on opposite sides" or "on both sides"	RD	obö'asdoino	122	
obᴍ'asino	across from	RD	obö'asino	25	
obᴍ'asito	opposite: obᴍasitona "from the opposite side" (RD), a little further across (WS)	RD, WS	obö'asito (RD), ʔobýʔassito (WS)	88	obᴍ'assito (WS)
obᴍchono	across, opposite (RD), further on over (WS)	RD, WS	obö'tsono (RD), ʔobýćono (WS)	194, 218	
obᴍchopindi	on the opposite side, on the other side, next door	RD	obö'tsopindi	192	
obᴍdaw	be from far away, be from somewhere else. "outsider:" obᴍdawim máidᴍ	RD	obö'dawi	134	
obᴍdawnan	from a distance	RD	obö'daunan	216	
obᴍdoyim símpo	upper lip	WS	ʔobýdojim símpo		
obᴍichonodi	to the place opposite, to the place across from	RD	oböi'tsonodi	192	
obᴍnno	lower, below, down	WS	ʔobýnno		
óbᴍno	mallard duck	HM	o'-boo-no		óbunu (PM)
obᴍno	along there	WS	ʔobýno		
óbetᴍ'ᴍ	pebble	WS	ʔóbeťyťy		
obúdoi	the place above	WS	ʔobúdoj		
obúdoidi	on top, atop	WS	ʔobúdojdi		
óbunu	mallard (duck)	PM-M	o-bun-um		óbᴍno (HM)
obúschono	go over the top (of)	RD	obus'tsono	46	

182

Maidu	English	Source	Source Spelling	Page	Other Spellings
Ochó	place name in Indian Valley, #23 on FR map, a village on the southern tip of Forgay Point (FR-AG). place name for Forgay Point (FC). According to Roxie Peconum, it was called Ochomis and Servilicn used to live here (FR1). See map 5 in Appendix 5.	FR, FR1, FC, FR-AG	ʔoćó (FR), ooho (FC)	370-371	Ochomis
ochúlak	swarthy, dark complexioned	WS	ʔoćúlak		
odá	encounter (verb)	WS	ʔodá		
odáto	come towards each other and meet (can be strangers or not, by accident or not) (RD), encounter, meet (someone someplace) (WS)	RD, WS	odā'to (RD), ʔodáto (WS)	130, 144, 228	
odátoto	come towards each other, meet each other in passing	RD	odā'toto	182	
ódi dí	grow in the rocks: mᴧm yom ódi díḱan. "The flower is growing in the rocks."	FC			
ódo	gold (from Spanish oro)	WS	ʔódo		
ódo tawál	to mine gold, to pan for gold	WS	ʔódo tawál		
odóko	fresh-water clam, mussel	WS, FC	ʔodóko		odokᴧ (FC), odakᴧ (FC-R)
odókom posála	clam shell	WS	ʔodókom posála, ʔodókom posáli		odókom posáli
odókpepe	Achomawi, Pit River ("clam eaters")	WS	ʔodókpepe		
odókpepem máidᴧ	an Achomawi person, Pit River person	WS	ʔodókpepem májdy		
ódom piláto	gold pan	WS	ʔódom piláto		
ohaibuldᴧ	redhead (duck), nyroca americana	PM-M	o-hi-bul-dum		
ohé	be there, mix in (with people), be in a crowd: sᴧ́tim kᴧlém ᴧkáwchetiluṯpem ohékᴧḱan "one exceptionally beautiful woman was among the crowd at that time."	RD	ohē	40, 100, 202	
ohéti	cause to mix, mix (transitive) in, infuse	RD	ohe'ti	10	
oi'ᴧpai	love (someone)	RD	oiö'pai	52	
oi'ᴧpaipe	beloved, loved one, spouse, lover	RD	oiö'paipem	188	
óichei	be dirty	FC			
óichei	dirty	WS	ʔójćej		
óichepe	dirty	FC			

Maidu	English	Source	Source Spelling	Page	Other Spellings
óidi	top part (óidiim waḱám: "the top part of the meat")	RD	oi'di	164	
Óidim Ḱoyó	place name for Big Meadows (P, RD-NM), Chester (FC), for the Chester area, near Lassen Park (WS). see maps 1 and 3 in Appendix 5.	PM-D, RD-NM, FC, WS	oi-do-ing-koyo (PM-D), oidoingkoyo (RD-NM), ʔójdim kojó (WS)		óidoim koyó (PM-D, RD-NM)
óidoina	to the top, at the top	FC-E, FC-R, RD	odo'ina	120	odoina (RD)
óidon	grab (something) out of the air, catch (something)	WS, RD	ʔójdon		
oiwɘ	balsam root, arrowleaf balsam root	PM-M, JD	oi-wum (PM-M), ojwəm (JD)	JD 44	
ók	be hungry: tetét óḱkasi "I am really hungry"	WS, FC	ʔók		
ók	begin the menstrual period	WS	ʔók		
okɘ́	be left behind (RD), be located, be left, remain, be left over (WS)	RD, WS	okö' (RD), ʔoký (WS)	66, 176, 236	
okɘ́i	peek, peep through (something)	WS	ʔoḱýj		
okɘ́ikinu	have the head bowed	WS	ʔoḱýjkinu		
okɘ́inoye	spy around	WS	ʔoḱýjnoje		
okɘ́isito	peek through (a hole)	WS	ʔoḱýjsito		
okɘ́kɘin	peek down (through)	RD	okö'köïn	72	
okɘ́kɘino	look in, peek in	RD	okö'köïno	228	
okɘ́kɘinpin	look down in, peek down in	RD	okö'köïnpin	196	
okɘ́kɘsip	peek out of (of a door/smoke hole)	RD	okö'kösip	222	
okɘ́ḱoidikno	go right up to and look: híndi okɘ́ḱoidiknoḱan "he went right up and looked in (her) eyes."	RD	okö'koidikno	168	
okɘ́nɘni	a mass, glob	RD	okö'nöni	114	
okɘ́tno	piece (noun): sɘmím okɘ́tno "piece of meat"	RD	okötno	152	
okɘ́tnobe	small piece	RD	okötnobe	160	
ókda	get hungry	HY			
oḱéli	knob, finial, head, head of a penis, garden hose, etc.	WS	ʔoḱéli		
oḱénkɘ	pillow	WS	ʔoḱénky		
oḱénkum wadápi	pillow case	FC			
okíkit	to arrive or come home one by one (RD), arrive (plural subject), arrive from time to time (WS)	RD, WS	okī'kit (RD), ʔokíkit (WS)	202, 206, 214, 218	
okít	arrive (WS), come down, come (as a season) (FC)	WS, FC	ʔokít		
okíthudoi	barely succeed in arriving	WS	ʔokíthudoj		

Maidu	English	Source	Source Spelling	Page	Other Spellings
okítkɯ	arrival, homecoming: mɯséḱi okítkɯ "their arrival"	RD	okit′kö	110	
okítmeniseti	if I don't come back, if I don't come home: yahát bíspada okítmeniseti "If I don't come back, stay well."	RD	okítmeniset	140, 146	
okítnoye	be present	WS	ʔokítnoje		
okítpoto	almost reach	RD	okit′boto	186	
okíttoye	arrive from time to time	WS	ʔokíttoje		
okítweḱoi	come along	WST	ʔokít weḱój	56	
óḱket	be careful, cautious, leery (especially of other people), watch out, doubt, don't trust	WS, FC, RD	ʔóḱket	78	okét
óḱketwono	take special precautions, be extra vigilant: ɯhɯ́m máidɯm káiḱan; t́ótimenwet mínsɯm okkétwonopi. "He is a powerful man; without being weak, take extra precautions!" óḱketwonoma'ankano! "You watch out!"	WS, RD, FC	ʔóḱketwono (WS), oket′wono (RD)	28, 40, 126, 140	okétwono
óḱmeni	springtime	FC, WS	ʔóḱmen		yóḱmeni
óḱmenkiti	springtime	FC, WS	ʔóḱmenkit		
óḱmolaḱa	rainbow	WS	ʔóḱmolaḱa, ʔóḱwilaḱa		óḱwilaḱa (WS), óḱmolakɯ (FC)
óḱmolakkit	stretch down (rainbow)	WS	ʔóḱmolakkit, ʔóḱwilakkit		óḱwilakkit
okóle	be reluctant, be unwilling to, be lazy (WS, FC), be bored (FC)	WS, FC	ʔokóle		
okóleboduk	not be very lazy	WS	ʔokóleboduk		
okóleḱas	I am reluctant	RD	okâl′ikas	158	
okólesa	lazy by nature, indolent	WS	ʔokólesa		
okólesape	lazy	FC			
okóleti	cause laziness	FC			
Okóno	place name in Indian Valley, #22 on FR map, a village with a roundhouse on Forgay Point, where a cemetery is now located. (FR-AG). See map 5 in Appendix 5.	FR, FR1, FR-AG	ʔokóno	370-371	
okówono	starve to death, die of hunger	RD	okō′wōnō	5, 32	
óḱpai	sunlight	FC			óḱpayi (WS)
óḱpai ochónodom	sun is going down	FC			
óḱpai waḱítdom	sun is shining, it is sunny	FC			
óḱpai wochónodom	the sun is going down	FC			
óḱpayi	sunlight, sun rays, sunshine	WS	ʔóḱpaji		óḱpai
óḱpayim pín	come in (sunlight)	WS	ʔóḱpajim pín		
óḱsa	hunger (noun)	FC			
óḱti	cause hunger	RD	ok′ti	104	

Maidu	English	Source	Source Spelling	Page	Other Spellings
óktipem ḱódo	hungry season, food shortage time of year	RD	ok'tipeñkâd'om	104	
ókwa	blue grass, a tall grass, seeds are good roasted	FC			
ókwilaḱa	rainbow	WS	ʔókwilaḱa, ʔókmolaḱa		ókmolaḱa
ókwilakkit	stretch down (rainbow), descend (rainbow)	WS	ʔókwilakkit, ʔókmolakkit		ókmolakkit
ókwono	starve	FC			
ól	be deaf	FC			
ól	deaf	WS	ʔól		
ólbadoi	become deaf	FC-E			
ólboswedoi	become completely deaf	FC-E, FC-R			
olé	incline the head	WS	ʔolé, ʔolék		olék
olé	man's netted cap, any hat	WS, FC	ʔolé		
olékɱ	put on a hat	FC			
olékinu	have the head bowed	WS	ʔolékinu, ʔolékkinu		olékkinu
olékinuhudansa	having the head always more or less hanging	WS	ʔolékinuhudansa, ʔolékkinuhudansa		olékkinuhudansa
olékinusa	having the head always hanging	WS	ʔolékinusa, ʔolékkinusa		olékkinusa
oléli	coyote	FC, WS	ʔolél		
oléspuikɱ	dove	FC			ɱléspuikɱ
Olílimbe	place name in Indian Valley, #20 on FR map, presumably a village located about one mile east of Greenville (FR-AG), place name near Greenville (FC). See map 5 in Appendix 5.	FR, FR1, FC, FR-AG	ʔolílimbe	370-371	olelim (FC)
ólḱuḱus	pretend to be deaf	FC-E			
Ólla	place name and people on the Feather River, opposite the mouth of the Bear River	SP			
óloli	big black ant	PM-M	oh-lo-lem		
ólolokó	smoke-hole entrance to the bark house	WS, RD	ʔóllolók (WS), âl'oloko (RD)	218	óllolok
ólolokóm chuchúi	the top of the smoke hole	RD	âl'olokom tsutsū'i	218	
ólpe	deaf, one who is deaf	FC-E			
olupkɱ	teal (duck)	PM-M	o-lup-cum		
ólwedoi	become deaf	FC-E, FC-R			
óm bomó	rocks (as a feature of the landscape)	WS	ʔóm bomó		
Om Chatim Sewi	Squaw Queen Creek	FC			
Om Chatim Yamáni	Squaw Peak	FC			
Om Chatim Ḱoyóm	Squaw Valley (Plumas County)	FC			
Óm Chumí	place name for Dixie Peak on a map from the 1800s. "Mt. Urine." See map 1 in Appendix 5.	HPC	omjumi		

Maidu	English	Source	Source Spelling	Page	Other Spellings
Óm Hʌbe	place name, just north of Quincy, #46 on FR map, a village northeast of Quincy (AK). See map 2 in Appendix 5.	FR-Ka, AK	omhübe ? (FR), omhübe (AK)	FR 370-371, AK 397	
óm hámsim cha	live oak, interior live oak, quercus wislizenii	FC, JD	omhamsymća	53	
óm ḱʌikʌ	hellgrammite, Dobsonfly or its larvae	WS	ʔóm ḱyjky		
Óm Kulúdoiwem	place name for Fredonyer Mountain (HLME), or Coppervale Mountain (LM), #24 on HLME map 3; #28 on LM map. The Indian trail from Big Meadows and Westwood to Honey Lake Valley passed by this mountain. See Map 1 in Appendix 5.	HLME, LM	Om Kuludojwem (HLME), omkuluday-wem (LM)		
óm ḱumí	cave	WS	ʔóm ḱumí		
óm ḱúmpiťi	clay, clay soil	FC-E			
Óm Lolóm Yamáni	place name for Kettle Rock Mountain. See map 1 in Appendix 5.	FC-E			
Óm Lulʌlʌ	place name for Diamond Mountain, #35 on LM map; Diamond Mountain range, # 11 on HLME map 3 (HLME). See maps 1 and 4 in Appendix 5.	LM, HLME	omlulyly (LM), Om Lu lyly		
óm pítchaḱa	any small lizard	WS	ʔóm pítcaḱa		pítchaḱa
óm sʌmí	mountain goat	FC			om sʌmí
óm sá	stove, fireplace, fire pit	WS	ʔóm sá		
óm sá bodóitikʌ	stovepipe	WS	ʔóm sá bodójtiky		
óm sápa	wood rat, pack rat	WS	ʔóm sápa		
óm sewówokit	rocky river bed	RD	ōm sewō'wokit	212	
óm sulú	good luck fetish pebble, good luck charm (found by a man in his youth and kept permanently for good luck)	WS, WST-DW	ʔóm sulú	72:6	ómsulu
óm tʌlí	caseworm	WS	ʔóm tylí		
Óm Willium Kasdoi	place name for Mountain Meadows, #14 on LM map. See maps 1 and 3 in Appendix 5.	LM	Om-willium-casdoi		
óm yʌyʌko	rock-strewn place, rocky place	RD	om yöyö'ko(i)	222	
Óm Yamáni	place name for Rocky Mountains or Sierra Nevada Mountains	WS, WST-DW	ʔóm jamáni	74:4	
Óm Yawken	place name for Clear Creek or Clear Creek Canyon, #26 on LM map. See maps 1 and 3 in Appendix 5.	LM	omyow-ken		

Maidu	English	Source	Source Spelling	Page	Other Spellings
Óm Yepónim Yamánim	place name for Antelope Mountain, #37 on LM map, #16 on HLME map 3. If this spelling is correct, it means "rock-chief mountain." See maps 1 and 4, Appendix 5	LM, HLME	omeponom yamanim		
Óm K̓oyó	place name in Taylorsville area, #25 on FR map, a village at the Forman place, at the Forman's ravine off the North Arm of Indian Valley (FR-TE). There was a large roundhouse here, doctors held power matches, football games and foot races and arrow-dodging contests (FR1). See map 5 in Appendix 5.	FR1, FR-TE	Óm K̓oyó		Óm K̓oyó
Óm K̓oyódikno	place name for a village about 3 miles from Taylorsville (FR-Ka) at the old Patton ranch (FR-HY). Possibly the same as Óm K̓oyó. See map 5 in Appendix 5.	FR-Ka, FR-HY	Ong-koyo-diknom	398	
Óm K̓umím	place name for Tommy Tucker Cave. Located east of the hot springs north-east of Honey Lake, it was named for the first Lassen County man (a Maidu) to be killed in WWI. He was from the DeHaven family in Susanville. The place name means "rock hole," or "cave."	HLME	Om K'umim		
oméikʌ	gambling charm	FC-T			
oméiyi	fetish, good-luck charm of bone or stone	WS	ʔoméjji		
omenani	camp	PM-D	oh-men-a-nee		
ómkanai	turtle	FC-T			ónkanai
ómpʌnno	cave, rock cavity	WS	ʔómpynno		
Ómpʌnno	place name for a natural amphitheater in the mountains north of Susanville, said to be caused by a meteorite. This is apparently seen from Antelope Grade near Antelope Mountain. Om pʌnno means "rock hole." See #15 on map 4, Appendix 5.	WS, RM	ʔómpynno		
ómpu	purple milkweed (isclepias cordifolia)	JD	ʔompuʔ	39	
ómsʌ	an edible plant in the carrot/parsley family	JD	ʔomsuʔ	77	

Maidu	English	Source	Source Spelling	Page	Other Spellings
ómsulu	small pebble, kept for good luck	FC			óm sulú
ómteni	canyon dudleya (plant), which was eaten	JD	omteni	46	
ómtitiwi	canyon wren	HM	om'-te-te-we		
onᴀ́nkiti	bend (something) over	RD	onön'kiti	60	
ónanai	argh! god dammit! ónanai, ódi íswolokḱas "dammit, I stubbed my toe on a rock."	FC-R			
ónkᴀsdobe	little ridge, small island, sand bar	RD	on'kösdobe	32	
ónkoi	overcome, come out on top, beat someone, outsmart, thwart, vanquish, conquer. be victorious (if no object), drive out (spirits)	RD, WS	on'koi (RD), ʔónḱoj (WS)	28, 72	
ónkoi'ᴀkinu	beat someone and keep on going, overcome something and keep on going	RD	on'koiökin'u	128	
ónḱoiti	get beaten, lose (in a contest), cause (someone) to win	WS	ʔónḱojti		
ónḱoiti'us	cause oneself to lose (by one's own actions), play the victim (RD), get (oneself) beaten (WS)	RD, WS	on'koitius (RD), ʔónḱojtiʔus (WS)	28, 102	
ónḱoito	in order to beat (someone) (in a competition) (adverb)	RD	on'koito	102	
ónḱoito	overcome, beat, outsmart (someone)	FC-E			
ónḱokoi	compete	WS	ʔónḱoḱoj		
ónḱoḱoito	contest (noun): sol ónḱoḱoito "singing contest"	RD	on'kokoito	98	
ónḱoḱoito	overcome (several things or several times), outsmart (several people) (RD), clash with, disagree/argue among themselves (FC)	RD, FC	on'kokoito	54, 120	
onó	be on the head: chakám onódom: "pitch being on the head"	RD	onō'	52	
onó	head (noun)	WS, SPB	ʔonó (WS), onum (SPB)		
onó bᴀnó	bump the head	WS	ʔonó bynó		
onó o'ᴀ́'ᴀlᴀm	shake the head	RD	onó' öö'ölöm	30	
onó sᴀḱáw	massage and press the head (for headache)	WS	ʔonó syḱáw		
onódᴀkᴀ	the head only	WS	ʔonódyḱy		
onóm butú	hair of the head	WS	ʔonóm butú		
onóm butú podápe	bald	WS	ʔonóm butú podápe		
onóm huní	brain	WS	ʔonóm huní		
onóm ṕibáwi	dandruff	WS	ʔonóm ṕibáwi		
onóm sᴀdóldol	curly-haired	WS	ʔonóm sydóldol		

Maidu	English	Source	Source Spelling	Page	Other Spellings
onóm ťadákɯm máidɯ	Chinese person	WS	ʔonóm ťadákym májdy		
onóspatpatto	slap water on top of the head	WS	ʔonóspatpatto		
onotḿitɯikɯ	curly-haired (adj), rolling head man	RD	onōtöi′töiköm	188	
onúk	put (something) under the head while lying down	WS	ʔonúk		
onúkno	put on a hood	WS	ʔonúkno		
onúknokɯ	hood, winter cap	WS	ʔonúknoky		
Opɯle	place name just north of Quincy, #53 on FR map, a village northwest of Quincy (AK). See map 2 in Appendix 5.	FR-Ka, AK	opüle ? (FR), ophüle (AK)	FR 370-371, AK 397	
ópa	grandfather: as a kinship term, this word must have a prefix, either mɯ, nik, or min (see Mountain Maidu Grammar, Lesson 6 for more details)	WS	ʔópa		
opáno	carry (something) on the back	WS	ʔopáno		
opékoi	go to look for (someone), search	RD	opē′koi	140, 146	ɯpékoi
opékoipe	one who looks for, searcher	RD	opē′koipem	146	
opéno	search around (for someone)	RD	opē′no	144	
opín	gush out, run out, be disgorged	WS	ʔopín		
opíninu	be hanging out, be sticking out	WS	ʔopíninu		
opínti	cough up (for example, blood or some object, as a shaman does when curing)	WS	ʔopínti		
opít	full, fill up (intransitive)	WS	ʔopít		
opítino	completely fill up by going down into	RD	opit′ino	196, 198	
opítkinu	fill up (intransitive)	RD	opit′kinu	66	
opítlɯťpe	full to the max	FC			
opítsip	completely fill up from one end to the other	RD	opit′sip	198	
opítti	fill (something) up	WS	ʔopítti		
opók	have a headache	RD	opok′	198	
opókti	cause a head ache, give someone a headache	RD	opok′ti	198, 200	
osɯ	bunches (of grass)	RD	osö(m)′	30	
osákɯ	mint plant	JD	osa·kom	57	osokɯm bukuikɯ
oschúmdi	to the top, at the top of (object precedes and ends in -m): basákɯm oschúmdi "at the top of the walking stick"	RD	ostsūm′di	82, 198	
óschumi	tip, topmost extremity	WS	ʔósćumi		

190

Maidu	English	Source	Source Spelling	Page	Other Spellings
óschumluťdi	at the pinnacle, at the very top	WS	ʔósćumlutdi		
óschumnaki	end piece, tip	RD	os'tsūmnaki	80	
ósdal	bald	WS	ʔósdal		
osímno	dark complected, swarthy	WS	ʔosímno, ʔosíwno		osíwno
osíwno	dark complected, swarthy	WS	ʔosíwno, ʔosímno		osímno
Óskꟺpe	place name name of a mountain in the Honey Lake area, probably Bald Mountain: Óskꟺpem Yamáni mentioned in Maidu Texts. Coyote urinated on this mountain and caused it to fall and spill water into the great snake's house, forming a lake. See maps 1 and 4 in Appendix 5, under Yóskopem Yamáni.	RD	osköpim, osköpem	66	
óski	pig (Genesee dialect)	FC			ꟺskꟺ
óskoko	top of the head	WS	ʔóskoko		
óskoni	gray hair	WS	ʔóskoni		
óskonpe	gray-haired	WS	ʔóskonpe		
oskúni	stump of a tree	FC, WS	ʔoskún		oskún (WS)
osókꟺ	spring of water (WS), bog, marshy area (FC)	FC, WS	ʔosók		osók (WS)
osókꟺm bukúikꟺ	herb, Maidu mint tea	FC			osákꟺ (JD), asalkꟺm bꟺkuikꟺ (FC-R)
osókbe	little spring (of water)	RD	osok'be	118	
osóksokto	spring (of water) area, area of several springs	RD	osok'sokto	182	
óspo	tadpole	WS	ʔóspo		
ostu	burning (cremation)	PM-D	o'stu		
Oťa Yakꟺ Yamáni	place name: may be Coyote Peak; important for a cave where special mano/metate rocks could be obtained. Said to be near Yakꟺkim Yamáni (FR-TE). See map 1 in Appendix 5.	FR1, FR-TE	oťa yaku yamani		
oťámoto	on the top of a bark house where it comes together	RD	otam'oto	114	
Otem Pakáni	place name for Crystal Lake. See map 1 in Appendix 5.	PM-D	o-tem pakanee		
otó	arise, get up	WS	ʔotó		
ótokma	oven	RD	ōtokma	60	
ótoto	rocky place: ótotodi "in a rocky place"	FC-E			
ow	semen	WS	ʔow		
owánchi	orange (fruit) (from English)	FC, WS	ʔówenći		ówenchi
owílliw	toss the head	WS	ʔowílliw		

191

Maidu	English	Source	Source Spelling	Page	Other Spellings
owólak	tie (something) on the head	WS	ʔowólak		
owólakkʌ	scarf, anything tied on the head	WS	ʔowólakky		
oyʌ́pai	love in a light-hearted way, play around with (someone) in a silly, affectionate way, be infatuated with (someone)	WS	ʔojýpaj		oi'ʌ́pai
pʌ́be	boy, child, young man (plural: pʌ́ʌ́mʌ́ʌ́m): mʌʌm yahám pʌ́bem mʌʌkí "that good boy of his" ínyanam pʌ́be "young Indian man"	FC, WST, RD	pýbe	54:34 (WST), 52	
pʌ́bebe	little boy (under 2 years old)	BC	pooh beh bem		
pʌchʌ́	ant	WS	pyćý		
pʌchʌ́lale	wasp	WS	pyćýlale		
pʌchʌ́m úyi	ant hill (ant house)	RD	pötsöm' ū'yi	230, 232	
pʌchʌ́mi	piss ant	FC			
pʌdónu	keep going down and down (hole)	RD	pödon'u	232	
pʌkʌ	red columbine	PM-M	peu-cu		
pʌkʌ́	plants, any small edible (violets, etc)	FC			
pʌkáni	water pool, spring	FC			pakáni
pʌkkʌ́	wild pansy	WS	pykký		
pʌkónu	have the anus open and looking around (sic)	WS	pykónu		
pʌ́ksalew	stumble and fall fast, stagger and fall	WS	pýksalew		
pʌlʌ́	grinding hole	FC			
pʌlʌ́lʌmpe	spherical	WS	pylýlympe		
pʌlʌ́m	plum (from English)	WS	pylým		
pʌlʌ́m	round	WS	pylým		
pʌlʌ́t	a small plant with a white edible root, probably a variety of Queen Anne's Lace	WS	pylýt		
pʌlástiki	plastic	FC-E			pilástiki
pʌ́mbel	peep-hole	RD	pömbel	72	
pʌ́n	untie	WS	pýn, pýt		pʌ́t
pʌní	pimple	WS, FC-T	pyn		puní (FC-T)
pʌním 'ítu	smallpox	WS	pyním ʔítu		
pʌ́nḱel	cranny, chink, hole, peephole, cranny to peek through	WS	pýnḱel, pýnḱeli		pʌ́nḱeli
pʌ́nno	hole, cavity	WS	pýnno		
pʌno	ant: hísam pʌno "piss ant"	RD	pöno	68	pʌchʌ́
pʌ́no	hole, cavity, cave	WS	pyn		pʌ́nno (WS)
pʌ́ntapo	pimply, covered with pimples	WS	pýntapo		
pʌ́p	bounce, jump, pop up (small nonliving objects)	WS	pýp		

Maidu	English	Source	Source Spelling	Page	Other Spellings
pÿpḱoi	jump abruptly (as popcorn or beans)	WS	pýpḱoj		
pÿpnoyeokit	bounce along until arriving	RD	pöp'noyeokit	190	
pÿpsip	pop out, jump out (as popcorn out of a pan)	WS	pýpsip		
pÿpyewé	bounce off	RD	pöpyēwē'	86	
pÿpyewei	bounce back, rebound	WS	pýpjewej		
pÿsbÿ	pubic hair	RD	pös'bö	102	
pÿsbu	female pubic hair	WS	pýsbu		
pÿsbutu	female pubic hair	FC			
pÿsí	vagina, female genitals	FC, WS	pys		pÿs (WS)
pÿsím butú	female pubic hair	WS	pysím butú		
pÿsím ení	clitoris	WS	pysím ení		
pÿsím ḱumí	vagina	WS	pysím ḱumí		
pÿskusum máidÿ	"pussy-whipped" man ("blinded by the vagina")	FC			pÿskusim máidÿ
pÿstÿ	have an inflamed vagina, inflammation of the vagina	WS	pystý		
pÿstapo	have a large vagina	WS	pýstapo		
pÿt	untie	WS	pýt, pýn		pÿn
pÿṱ	wart	WS	pyṱ		
pÿṱÿṱÿ	boys, children, young people: kÿlém pÿṱÿṱÿ "girls"	WS, WST	pýṱyṱy		
pÿtno	step into water	RD	pöt'no	68	
pÿtwaito	untie a knot	WS	pýtwajto		
pÿtye	untie (the item with the string takes -di): mÿḱí solódi pÿtyeḱan "he untied his shoe"	RD	pöt'ye	206	
pÿtyo	untie several knots	WS	pýtjo		
pÿya	the place in front of	WS	pýja		
pÿyé	sew: pÿyém kÿlé "stitching woman"	WS, FC-E	pyjé		
pÿyékÿ	needle (WS), basketry awl (FC)	WS, FC	pyjéky		
pÿyékÿ bidítpaikÿ	pincushion	WS	pyjéky bidítpajky		
pÿyékÿm ḱuḱú	thread	WS	pyjékym ḱuḱú		
pÿyéto	swim (of people)	WS	pyjéto		
pa	to stand (as a tree)	WS	pa		
pá	thicket, bushes (WS), a general term for willow (FC)	WS	pá		
pá'im chípbÿ	toe	FC			paiyím chipbÿ
pachititi	Oregon junco (bird)	FC			
padí	in the brush	WS	padí		
pahádaw	follow tracks, to track	RD	paha'dau	230	
paháno	follow tracks going along (object pai or ma (paw))	RD	pahā'no	230	
pahánoye	track, trace, follow tracks	WS	pahánoje		
pahéḱoi	to follow tracks	RD	pahē'koi	46	
pahḱuts	buffalo	FC			
pai	foot	WS	paj		paiyí
pai chekátḱoi	find (someone) by tracking	RD	pai tsekat'koi	184	

193

Maidu	English	Source	Source Spelling	Page	Other Spellings
pai háchono	follow someone's tracks	RD	paihā′tsono	174	
pai hánochmi	be unable to find footprints, be unable to track	RD	pai hā′notsöi	184	
pai kanái'i	floor	FC			
pai wochík	look for tracks	RD	pai wotsik′	184	
pái'im bichí	toenail(s)	FC			paiyím bichi, páibichí
páibichí	toenail, hoof	WS	pájbićí		pái'im bichi, paiyím bichi
páibo	have something stuck in the foot	WS	pájbo		
páikmtḱmt	hobble along, tiptoe along with hurt feet	WS	pájḱytḱyt		
páikulu	ankle, small of ankle	WS	pájkulu		
páikulum bmmí	ankle bone	WS	pájkulum bymí		
páini	on foot, afoot	WS	pájni		
páisuku	heel of foot	WS	pájsuku		
páitolo	pants, trousers (from Spanish pantalon)	WS	pájtolo		
páitolo	put on pants	WS	pájtolo		
páitolom lulúmi	waist of pants, waistband	WS	pájtolom lulúmi		
páiwilok	have the leg twitch involuntarily	WS	pájwilok		
paiyí	foot	FC			pai
paiyím kulú	ankle	FC			páikulu
paiyím ťáťa	sole of foot	FC			payím ťáťa (WS)
paḱ	gristle	WS	paḱ		
paká	sinew	FC, WS	pak		pak (WS)
ṕaká	limb of a tree, branch, stick	FC, WS	ṕaḱ		ṕaḱ (WS)
pakál	pay (from Spanish pagar)	WS	pakál		
pakályewei	repay	WS	pakáljewej		pakályewe
ṕaḱán tú	branch fence	FC			
pakáni	pond, bog, swamp, pool (especially those found in high mountain meadows)	FC, WS	pakán		
pakánkanto	springs (of water)	RD-IS			
ṕákchik	get stuck together (as canine animals in sexual intercourse)	WS	ṕákćik		
pákpa	egg	FC			
pákpaka	egg	WS	pákpaka		
pákpakam posála	eggshell	WS	pákpakam posála, pákpakam posáli		pákpakam posáli
pákpakam púmpu	eggshell	WS	pákpakam púmpu		
ṕáktapopem chá	limby tree, tree with a lot of limbs	WS	ṕáktapopem ćá		
ṕála	testicles	WS	ṕála		
ṕalaḱ	headdress, headstall (characteristically made of quills and flicker feathers)	WS	ṕálaḱ		
ṕálam wadápi	scrotum	WS	ṕálam wadápi		
paláwaikm	great snake	RD, WS	palā′waikö (RD), paláwajky (WS)	66, 196	

194

Maidu	English	Source	Source Spelling	Page	Other Spellings
Paláwaikmnundun	place name for Wasám Pool, on Indian Creek between Chiwísi and Sandy Beach: considered a haunted and dangerous place. Big snake is in the name (DT). See map 5 in Appendix 5.	DT	Palo Why-cunun Dune	45	
pále'oyo	large bird, bird of prey: pále'oyom we'ékan, ťúnodi nisáki wókmḱan. "the bird is circling; something must be caught in our trap."	RD	palē'oyo, pāl'eoyo	56	
palíki	trout (FC), rainbow trout (RR-SW), shiner, a kind of small fish (WS)	FC, RR-SW, WS	palík (WS), ba-lee-kem (BC)		palík (WS)
palíkukuté	whippoorwill	FC			
palo	snake	DT		45	
palúťi	yampa, perideridia (eaten raw), (JD), a kind of bulb plant, camassi quamash (FC)	JD, FC	palutym	77	palute (FC)
pam beché'okm	black phoebe (a small flycatcher bird, black on top, white underneath)	HM	pahm-bā chā-o-kum		
pám cha	willow	FC			
pám hiní	buckberry, currant (MP)	WS, WS-MP	pám hiní		
Pám Sewím	place name for Susan River, #19 on HLME map 3, #31 on LM map. Means "willow creek." See maps 1 and 4 in Appendix 5.	HLME, LM	Pam Sewim		Pom Sewim (LM)
Pám Sewím Ḱódom	place name for the Susanville area, including Inspiration Point, #13 on HLME map 3. Means "willow creek country." The remains of the lower village are still visible below Thumper Hill Rd. outside Susanville (HLME). See map 4 in Appendix 5.	HLME	Pam Sewim K'odom		
pám wáksi	brush crane	WS	pám wáksi		páwaksi (WS)
pám wékkesi	brush rabbit	WS	pám wékkesi		
pama	male salmon	FC			
pámbiche'okm	chipping sparrow	HM	pahm'-bet-tsā-o-kum		
pámchmkm	willow branch (big part)	FC			
pamíni	gooseberry (HM), wild currant (WS)	HM, WS	pah-me'-nim (HM), pamín (WS)		pamín (WS)
pámyoli	Mexican, Spaniard (from Spanish espanol)	WS	pámjoli, pámwili, pámwolo, pánwyli		pámwili, pámwolo, pánwmli

Maidu	English	Source	Source Spelling	Page	Other Spellings
pán	make rope, roll strands of bark, deer sinew or other similar material on the thigh in order to make rope	WS, RD	pán (WS), pan' (RD)	186	
panaḱ wa	a type of mushroom growing in groups of four near brush, red in color, and not eaten	JD	panak'wa	24	
panáka	acorn woodpecker	FC			
pándaḱa	bow, gun, rifle	FC, WS	pándaḱ		pándaḱ (WS)
pándaḱam cha	yew tree	FC			
paní	tobacco	FC, WS	pan		pan (WS)
paní chawái	chew tobacco	WS	paní ćawáj		
pani'ini	raspberry	FC			
Paním Bisím Yamáni	place name near Belden, CA. The name means "tobacco dwelling mountain." See map 1 in Appendix 5.	WST-DW	paním bisím jamáni	80:6	
páno	grizzly bear	WS	páno		
páno wetemmi	bear dance	FC			
pánpe	smoke tobacco	WS	pánpe		
pánpekᴎm papéli	cigarette papers	FC			
pánpesape	chain smoking, chain smoker	FC			
pánpetokᴎ	smoking pipe (noun)	FC			
panú	be standing	WS	panú		
papᴎle	onion	FC			papúle
Papá	place name where Worldmaker stopped to eat papá (yampa), and scattered seeds and bulbs to grow for the people. Could be the same as Papáikᴎdi, Willards Ranch area along Hwy 36. See map 1 in Appendix 5.	RD, AT, PM-M	papa	66	
papá	yampa, a little white edible root	WS, FC	papá		papo
papái	lead (verb), as in dancing	WST	papáj	78:6	
papáidi	in the vicinity of	FC			
Papáikᴎdi	place name, Fredonyer and Willard Creek, #29 on LM map. Could be the same as Papá. Probably Willards Ranch area near Hwy 36 today. See map 1 in Appendix 5.	LM, AT	pa-pie-ka-dee		
papám piwí	edible root, yampa	FC			
papáyi	path, way	WS	papáji		
papél	write	WS	papél		
papéli	paper (from Spanish papel)	FC, WS	papél		papél (WS)
papéli hanᴎnokᴎm máidᴎ	postman, mail man	WS	papéli hanýnokym máidy		
papélim uiyí	post office	FC			papélim uyí
papélim wa'áitikᴎ	paper shredder	FC-E			

Maidu	English	Source	Source Spelling	Page	Other Spellings
papélim yepóni	manager, boss (paper chief)	FC			
papélimbe	playing cards	FC			
papélkɰ	pencil, pen	WS, FC	papélky		
papélkɰm kɰlé	journalist (female)	FC			
papélkɰm máidɰ	journalist (male)	FC			
papélkit	write (something) down	WS	papélkit		
papélkítkɰ	pen, pencil	FC			
papélkitti	cause to be written down, to record on a recording device: min papélkittima'akan "he will record you."	WS, WST-LM	papélkitti	62:3	
papélni	use paper	FC			
papuli	onion, wild onion	FC, JD	papulɔm (JD)	34	papulɰ (JD)
pasali	beetle	HM	pah-sah-le		
pát	slapping or flopping motion	WS	pát		
patá	tray basket (for sifting or serving) (RD), loose-woven gathering basket (WS)	RD, WS	patā' (RD), patá (WS)	234	
patáidi	on a (flat) basket, on a tray	RD	patai'di	234	
patáimi	using a flat basket, using a tray	RD	patā'imi	234	
ṗatátaka	raccoon	FC			ṗataktaka (FC)
pátkadoi	get up, get back up	RD	pat'kadoi	178	
pátkoi	flip away, jump out of reach	WS	pátḱoj		
pátnoye	flop around, as a fish out of water	WS	pátnoje		
patpát	to boil, to bubble: patpátkɰm momí "bubbly water"	FC-R, FC-T			
patpátkɰ	bubbly	FC-E			
páwaksi	brush crane	WS	páwaksi		pám wáksi (WS)
payím chípbɰ	toe	WS	pajím ćípby		paiyím chípbɰ, pa'ím chípbɰ
payím ťáťa	sole of the foot	WS	pajím ťáťa		paiyím ťáťa
Payím Yáhni	place name for Mt. Jura east of Taylorsville. See maps 1 and 5 in Appendix 5.	MSOP	Payum Yahni		
pe	eat	WS	pe		
pebɰ́dɰk	seldom eat	WS	pebýdyk		
pebós	eat (something) up, eat all up	WS, FC	pebós		
pebóslew	eat up all the rest (of the food)	RD	pebos'leu	62	
pebós'us	eat oneself up	RD	pebos'us	190	
Pecháma	place name, just north of Quincy, #48 on FR map. See map 2 in Appendix 5.	FR	pećáma	370-371	
pechí	bite (only of fish when fishing)	WS	pećí		
pedɰ́kɰ	just eat	FC			

Maidu	English	Source	Source Spelling	Page	Other Spellings
pedá	steal	WS	pedá		
pedá'ᴍkinu	habitually kidnap, keep on kidnapping	RD	pedā'ökinu	172	
pedá'ᴍkoi	go off taking what was stolen, carry off stolen goods	RD	pedā'ökoi	162	
pedáhaḱoi	kidnap and carry off	RD	pedā'hakoi	174	
pedáhamoto	add to cache of what was stolen, bring home more stolen property	RD	pedā'hamoto	172	
pedá'i	theft	FC			
pedákᴍ	thief	WS	pedáky		
pedáḱoido	in order to steal	RD	pedā'koido	174	
pedápe	what to steal: pedápe bᴍyᴍksipdom "picking out what to steal"	FC			
pedása	thief (habitual)	WS, FC	pedása		
pedásape	thief (habitual)	RR-SW			
pedáto	answer, reply, echo	RD	pedā'to	34, 153	
pedáyeto	go around stealing, kidnap (children)	RD	pedā'yeto	172	
pedési	louse (body), lice	FC, WS	pedés		pedés (WS)
pedésťapope	full of lice	WS	pedésťapope		
pédowal	federal	FC-E			
pedú	bait	WS	pedú		
pedúsi	ashes	RD	pedūsi	76	pidúsi
pedúti	bait (a hook)	WS	pedúti		
pehéipe	clown	RD-NM	pehei'pe		
pei	grandchild: as a kinship term, this word must have a prefix, either mᴍ, nik, or min (see Mountain Maidu Grammar, Lesson 6 for more details)	WS	pej		peyí
pe'ídi	eat with (someone)	RD	peī'di	96	
péine	daughter-in-law: as a kinship term, this word must have a prefix, either mᴍ, nik, or min (see Mountain Maidu Grammar, Lesson 6 for more details)	WS	péjne		
pekᴍ́	food	FC, WS	peký		
pekᴍ́m ťoló	spoon	WS	pekým ťoló		
pekᴍ́m uyí	restaurant	FC-T			
pekᴍ́ti	feed, provide food for	FC			
pekᴍ́tikᴍ	scissors	FC			
pékuchi	package, pack (from English)	WS	pékući		
péḱuḱus	pretend to eat	FC			
pekúla	be inquisitive, inquisitive, curious	WS	pekúla		
pekúni	mountain lion	FC, WS	pekún		pekún (WS)
pelílipno	howl (like Coyote)	RD	pelil'ipno	36	
pelíp	yell, shout, howl (like a coyote)	WS, RD	pelíp (WS), pelip' (RD)	34	
pelíppai	yell at, shout at	WS	pelíppaj		

Maidu	English	Source	Source Spelling	Page	Other Spellings
pelíptonu	plead loudly	WS	pelíptonu		
pemén	be on her period, be menstruating	WS	pemén		
pemén	not eat	FC			
penʌ́	bend	WS	pený		
penʌ́kit	bend down under weight (as branches under snow, ice, or fruit)	WS	penýkit		
pená	meal, serving (pen "eat" according to SPB)	RD, SPB	penā' (RD), pin (SPB)	152	
pénchuiyi	eight	FC			
péne	two: péne pénekan yáchoi'a "he created two of each"	WS, RD	péne, pénej (WS), pēn'e (RD)	13	pénei
péneinini	twice	WS	pénejnini		pénenini
pénem máschoḱo	twenty	WS, FC	pénem másćoḱo		pénem maischoḱo (FC)
pénemte	two children	FC			
pénene	by twos: pénene píkno yáchoi'a "only by twos he created them."	RD	pēn'ene	13	
penówei'us	brag, boast	WS	penówejʔus		
penóweye	support, praise (verb)	WS	penóweje		
pé'okit	come and eat: ʌyépi pé'okit "come and eat!"	FC			
pepáno	give verbal support to the shaman during a ceremony, say "amen" to	WS	pepáno		
pepáno	swim alongside	WS	pepáno		
pepánototo	smoke tobacco together	WST	pepánototo	76:5	
pepánu	be smoking tobacco	WST-RP	pepánu	64:13	
pepéne	second	WST-LB	pepéne	42:3	
Pepépem Ḱum	place name for a site in Mountain Meadows where Leona Morales' grandfather collected food for winter (PM-M), #8 on FR map. See map 3 in Appendix 5.	FR, PM-M	Pepépem ćum (FR), pe-pe-pem-cum (PM-M)	370-371	Pepépem Cham (FR)
pepí	eat!	FC			
pepímen	don't eat	FC			
pesíto	swim across	WS	pesíto		
pesítopin	swim down across	WS	pesítopin		
petí	poison, venom	WS	pet		pet (WS)
péti	mother-in-law, father-in-law (WS translates "son-in-law"). As a kinship term, this word must have a prefix, either mʌ, nik, or min (see Mountain Maidu Grammar, Lesson 6 for more details)	WS	pet		
petílkit	be stable	RD	petil'kit	24	

Maidu	English	Source	Source Spelling	Page	Other Spellings
pétim kᴧlé	mother-in-law: as a kinship term, this word must have a prefix, either mᴧ, nik, or min(see <u>Mountain Maidu Grammar</u>, Lesson 6 for more details)	RD	pet'iñ küle'	68	
petím wá	poisonous toadstool	WS	petím wá (WS), petymwam (JD)		
péto	eat with, join people eating	FC			
pétoto	eat together	FC			
péwᴧnto	seesaw	WS	péwynto		
pewéḱoi	go around eating	WST	pe wéḱoj	50:7	
pewíhakit	prepare food, cook	RD	pewī'hakit	132	
pewíkakit	prepare food, cook	RD	pewī'kakit	112	
pewó	give food to someone, feed, offer food, tell to eat	RD	pewo'	126, 152	
pewóťakᴧ	table	WS	pewóťaky		
péya	pear (from English)	WS	péja		
peyáche	save back some food for (someone)	WS	pejáće		
peyáha	like to eat	WS	pejáha		
peyí	grandchild: as a kinship term, this word must have a prefix, either mᴧ, nik, or min (see <u>Mountain Maidu Grammar</u>, Lesson 6 for more details)	FC			pei
peyím kᴧlé	granddaughter: as a kinship term, this word must have a prefix, either mᴧ, nik, or min (see <u>Mountain Maidu Grammar</u>, Lesson 6 for more details)	FC			
pí	be many, be a lot, multiply (i.t.): 'ḱawím dékmᴧni pídom ma'aḱás,' achói'a sᴧhᴧ́lim. "'When the ground is wet, I will be many,' said Mosquito."	RD	pī'	160	
pí	lots of, many (FC), group, crowd, bunch (WS): tetét pim "a great many" pim wasása "a lot of stuff"	FC, WS, RD	pí (WS), pī' (RD)		pi'i (FC)
pí epínsa	inquisitive, curious, asking many questions	WS	pí epínsa		
pí yawí	be expensive	WS	pí jawí		
ṗibáw	fade	WS	ṗibáw		
ṗibáwi	tiny particles, dust, drops	FC			
píboduk	scarce, not very many	WS	píboduk		
ṗibú	be charred, blackened, burnt	WS	ṗibú		
ṗibúti	black person	WS	ṗibúti		

Maidu	English	Source	Source Spelling	Page	Other Spellings
p̓ibútim máidm	black person	WS	p̓ibútim májdy		
p̓íchms	peaches (from English)	WS	p̓ićys		
p̓ichádaito	mink	WS, RD	p̓ićádajto (WS), pitsadaito (RD)	RD 54	p̓icháditu (RR-SW)
p̓ichík̓uk̓u	fly (insect)	WS	p̓ićík̓uk̓u		p̓ichikikm (FC), p̓ichitikm (FC-E)
p̓íchilipe	swallow (bird)	AT, LM, FC			k̓ump̓íchilipe (FC)
Pichilipem	place name for Devil's Corral, #30 on LM map. Means "swallows." See map 1 in Appendix 5.	LM	Pit-chee-lip-pem		
pichititi	mountain chickadee	HM	pe-tse'-te-te		
p̓íchuchu	melt (as fat or butter) (intransitive)	WS	p̓ićuću		
pichum cha	white fir tree	JD	pyćumćom	28	
p̓ídati	full	FC			
p̓idúsi	ashes, fire pit	WS, FC	p̓idúsi		pedúsi (RD)
pi'eto	swim	FC			piyeto
p̓íhol	char	WS	p̓íhol		
p̓íholkit	burnt and charred	WS	p̓íholkit		
p̓íkmsma	what I have a lot of, my having a lot of: tetét chek̓ínuk̓an nik̓í solí p̓íkmsma "they really expect me to have a lot of songs"	WS, WST-RP	p̓íkysma	70:58	
p̓ik̓ál	dried out, dry	WS	p̓ik̓ál		
p̓ik̓ál	dry (intransitive)	FC			
p̓ik̓álchiki	scab	WS	p̓ik̓álćiki		
p̓ik̓álpe	dry (adj)	FC			
p̓ik̓álti	dry (something) (verb)	FC			
p̓ík̓itpmnk̓elpe	having many holes	WS	p̓ík̓itpynk̓elpe		
pikno	only, just (follows word: mín pikno "just you," dmdi pikno "only in the bushes") (RD), much, lots of (WS)	RD, WS	pikno (RD), p̓íkno (WS)	40, 164	
p̓íknodom	all the time	FC			
p̓íknona	much: tetét p̓íknona "too much"	FC			
pik̓ói	swim away	WS	pik̓ój		
p̓ik̓ói	burn out (fire), burn over (an area)	RD	pikoi	64	
p̓ik̓ókolauk̓oi	become a little warmed up (meat), get only slightly cooked (meat)	RD	piko'kolaukoi	164	
p̓ilái	hot (of weather) (MP)	WS-MP	p̓iláj		
pilástiki	plastic	FC			pmlastik
piláto	gold pan (from Spanish plato)	WS	piláto		
p̓ilís	be hot	FC			
p̓ilís	hot (of things)	WS	p̓ilís		
p̓ilísbos	be excessively hot	FC-E			
p̓ilut̓i	a great number, a lot, a huge amount	WS	p̓ilut̓i		
pím pok̓ó	a long time "many months"	FC			pi'ím pok̓ó

Maidu	English	Source	Source Spelling	Page	Other Spellings
pímeli	grape	FC			pimili, pímmili
pímelim sudákm	wine	FC			
pímmili	wild grape	WS, JD	pímmil (WS), pimily (JD)	78	pimeli
pímmilim ṕikáli	raisin	WS	pímmilim ṕikáli		
pin	come into, enter, merge with	WS	pin		
pin	eat	SPB	pin		
pín	hear, understand, obey	WS, RD	pin (RD), pín (WS)	208	
ṕináw	have an erection	WS	ṕináw		
ṕináwtipe	sexually arousing (to a man), erection-causing	FC-E			
pínchmi	be deafened	WS	pínćyj		
piné	lunch	WS	piné		
pinéti	fix lunch	WS	pinéti		
pinhássito	to come across (sound), be heard across	WS	pinhássito		pinhásito
pinhéhenon	not listen, not take (someone's words) seriously, not pay attention to, tune (something) out: nik wéyechet pinhéhenonismmni, ha'ái kmkán wasódom. "When he talked to me, I didn't listen, so he is probably angry."	RD	pinhē'henon	106, 164	pínheiheinon
pínheiheino	listen	WS	pínhejhejno		pinhéheno (RD)
pinhéye	listen for: bénekto pinhéyechet, hónmaktinḱas. "In the morning I listened for (him) and didn't hear anything. In the morning, after listening for (him), I didn't hear anything."	RD	pinhē'ye	34, 36	
piní	riverbed	WST-DW	piní	74:12	
píninu	so many times	RD	pī'ninu	54	
pínkenu	keep listening (RD), listen (WS)	RD, WS	pin'kenu (RD), pínḱenu (WS)	118	pínkanu (RD), pínḱeno (RD), pinkinu (FC)
pínkenutihadáw	cause to listen far away, be heard in the distance: witḿmtmmim máidmm pínkenutihadáwchoi'a komónantedi mdáwchoi'a. "Thunder Man was heard in the distance (as) he went down in the southern area."	RD	pin'kenutihadau'	150	
pínkinu	listen	FC			pínḱenu (WS)
pínluť	hear with comprehension, listen carefully	WS, WST	pínluť	54:27	
pínmakit	hear of, know about by hearing	FC			
pínmenpe	heedless, one who doesn't listen	WS	pínmenpe		

Maidu	English	Source	Source Spelling	Page	Other Spellings
pínno	swim downstream	WS	pínno		
pínnoti	sound like...	WS	pínnoti		
pinó	swim upstream	WS	pinó		
pínokole	be reluctant to hear, not want to hear (something)	FC-E			
pinópininu	listen and listen, keep listening and listening	RD	pinop'inīnū'	190	
pinóweye	brag, boast	WS	pinóweje		
pinóweyesa	braggart, boaster	WS	pinówejesa		
pinóye	swim around	FC			
pintái	mis-hear	FC			
pínti	cause to hear, sound	FC			
píntikⰀ	radio	FC			
píntikⰀm wasása	radio	FC			
píntimen	not let someone hear about it: mⰀyím wasám máidⰀ mínsⰀm píntimenma'ankano. "Don't you let that bad man hear about it."	RD	pin'timen	208	
píntiti	sound (good, bad, clear, etc.)	WS	píntiti		
píntitini	-sounding (e.g. good-sounding, clear-sounding, etc.)	WS	píntitini		
pintitinini	resoundingly	FC			
pinwéye	hear, listen to: pinwéyesmⰀni, méima'ankano nik "If you hear me, you will give it to me"	RD	pinwē'ye	136	
pinwoyénu	listen for a while from a distance	RD	pinwoyen'ū	216	
pípai	spring into flame	WS	pípaj		
pípaiti	light (a fire or cigarette): pípaitipi! "spark it up! Light it!"	WS	pípajti		
pípe	full of (adj)	RD	pī'pem	148	
pípem ḱódo	throughout the land, everywhere around: ⰀhⰀm ka'án pípem ḱódo "danger is everywhere."	RD	pī'peñ kâdo	148	
pípenak	full of: máidⰀm pípenak "a place full of people"	RD	pī'penak	122	
pis	be leached (stress is on the next syllable)	RD	pis	202	
pís	peas (from English)	WS	pís		
pisíp	swim out	WS	pisíp		
pisíto	swim across	WS	pisíto		
písto	pet name for any little girl	WS	písto		
pístobe	girl, small girl, a pet name for any little girl (WS), little girl (under 2 years old (BC)	WS, FC, BC	pístobe		
pístola	pistol (from Spanish pistola)	WS	pístola		
písum cha	white fir	FC			

Maidu	English	Source	Source Spelling	Page	Other Spellings
piť	defecate	WS	piť		pitǐ (FC)
ṗiťákitti	burn (something, like a house) down	RD	pitak'iti	228	
pi'taloka	wild garlic, considered too strong tasting to eat	JD	pi'taloka	34	
ṗiťápkít	burn to the ground (intransitive)	RD	pitap'kit	56	
ṗiťápkítwono	having burned down (intransitive)	RD	pitapkit'wono	200	
pítchakm	lizard	FC, WS	pítcak		pítchaḱ
pitchoti	put a diaper on	WS	pitćoti		
Pitelim	place name for a village north of Quincy. See map 2 in Appendix 5.	AK	Piteli	397	
pitǐ	excrement: mm̌dek pitǐnip! "Use bear manure!"	FC, WS, FC-E	piť		piť (WS)
pitǐ	to defecate	FC			
pitǐ ḱatanokm	small, yellow-striped, manure-rolling beetle	WS	pitǐ ḱatanoky		
pitǐkm	anus, rectum, asshole	WS, FC	pitǐky		
pitǐm uyí	outhouse, bathroom, privy	FC, WS	pitǐm ují		
pitǐsitoye	defecate all over	RD	pitī'sitoye	218	
pitǐyo	defecate on	RD	pitī'yo	218	
pitkml	be constipated	WS	pitkyl		
pitḱol	gut an animal	WS	pitḱol		
pítkololo	guts, intestines	WS	pítkololo		
píto	too many	RD	pī'tom	23	
Píttelim	place name, just north of Quincy, #41 on FR map. The same as Píttelim.	FR-R, FR-Ka	píttelim	370-371	Pitelim
ṗiťúk	be disgusted with (someone or something), dislike, hate (WS), be angry (RD)	WS, RD	pituk' (RD), ṗiťúk (WS)	166	
ṗitúḱoi	pass through burning (as forest fire)	RD	pitukoi	64	
ṗitúḱoido	be burned up	RD	pitukoido	64	
ṗiťúp	burn up completely	WS	ṗiťúp		
ṗiťúpti	burn (something) up completely	WS	ṗiťúpti		
píuboduk	not extend all the way	RD	pi'ūboduk'	186	
píubokiti	make (something) hang down to, make (something) extend down reaching (something)	RD	pi'ūbokiti	186	
píuboḱoiti	stretch a rope, extend a rope	RD	pi'ubokoiti	7	
píuboḱoitibos	get (something like a rope) all the way stretched	RD	pi'ubokoitibos	7, 8	
piúbonpin	extend down: hesántewet piúbonpinyakḱen adóm? "it seems to hang down quite a ways."	RD	piū'bonpin	186	

Maidu	English	Source	Source Spelling	Page	Other Spellings
piúbonpininu	hang down (intransitive), extend down	RD	piū'bonpinin'u	186	
píubonpinti	let something (like rope) extend down towards, hang (something) down towards	RD	pi'ūbonpinti	7, 8, 186	
piwí	root	FC, WS	piw		piw (WS)
piwímduki	bag of roots	RD	piwim'duki	200	
ṗiyé	forest fire, burn as forest fire	RD	piye	64	
piyéto	swim (humans), bathe	FC			
ṗiyú	get singed	WS	ṗijú		
ṗiyúhissa	smell of singeing	WS	ṗijúhissa		
ṗíyuno	what hummingbird says	RD	pī'ūno	80	
ṗiyúti	singe	WS	ṗijúti		
ṗiyútidaw	singe off	WS	ṗijútidaw		
ṗíyutkɯ	a species of bird, native to the California Sierras, designated as a "nightingale"	WS	ṗíjutky		
po	animal hide, skin	RD	po	192	
po	soaproot	FC			
pó	daughter: as a kinship term, this word must have a prefix, either mɯ, nik, or min (see Mountain Maidu Grammar, Lesson 6 for more details)	WS	pó		
pó	night	WS	pó		
pó	wade	WS	pó		
po wáksi	night heron	HM	pow wahk-sim		
póchode	bat (animal)	RD, PM-M, FC	potsō'de, pots'ode, pots'odep (RD), por-che-nem (PM-M)	202, 210, 212	pochóde, póchodep (RD), póchene (PM-M), pochéde (FC)
podá	barren of vegetation, desert	WS	podá		
podáti	strip, make barren	WS	podáti		
pódatihudoi	virtually stripped of vegetation and life (as barren desert country)	WS	pódatihudoj		
pódaw	wade into	WS	pódaw		
pó'esto	midnight	WS	póʔesto		
pó'estodi	at midnight, in the middle of the night	WS	póʔestodi		
Poidowin	place name for Bill's Place, #23 on LM map. See map 2 in Appendix 5.	LM	Poi-doh-win		
pókɯto	mother and daughter	WS	pókyto		
pókɯtoto	mother and daughter as a pair	WS	pókytoto		pókitoto

Maidu	English	Source	Source Spelling	Page	Other Spellings
pokŕkinu	come (back) to life (wade out of the water after death): hesádom uním wónokɐm ḱutt́ɐt́ɐm pokŕkinumaḱade? "Why should these dead animals come back to life?"	RD	pōkö′kinu	28	
pokŕs	hunch the back	WS	poḱýs		
pokŕsnu	hunchbacked	WS	poḱýsnu		
pókitoto	a pair that includes a daughter	RD	pō′kitoto	96	
poḱó	large heavenly body such as sun or moon, month	FC, WS	poḱ (WS), pocum (SPB)		poḱ (WS)
poḱóki ḱɐchonokɐdi	towards the west, towards where the sun sets	RD	pokō′ki kö′tsonoködi	7, 11, 210	
poḱóki ḱɐchonokɐnantedi	in the area where the sun sets, in the western region	RD	pokō′kikötsonokönan′tedi	230	
poḱóm hínkitkɐdi	west	WS	poḱóm hínkitkydi		
poḱósi	knee	FC, WS	poḱós		poḱós (WS)
poḱósyokinu	kneel sitting on the heels with the knees and the tops of the feet touching the ground	WS	poḱósjokinu		
poḱósyokit	kneel	RD	pokos'yokit	138	
ṕóksino	personal Indian name of Cap Singer	WS	ṕóksino		
ṕoléwḱuti	whippoorwill	WS	ṕoléwḱuti		
polko	type of edible mushroom, a brown Springtime mushroom	PM-M, JD	pol-ko (PM-M), polko (JD)	JD 24	
poló	buckeye	FC			
polóm cha	buckeye tree	FC			
polópokanda	propaganda	FC-E			
polówa	floor (from English)	WS	polówa		
pólpol	to steam, boil, bubble (verb)	WS	pólpol		
pólpolchenopem momí	rapids waterfall	WS	pólpolćenopem momí		
Pólpolim Yamánim	place name for Hot Springs Mountain, #41 on LM map, Skedaddle Range, Omkumi Yamani and Amadee Mountain, #40 on LM map; #2 on HLME map 3. See map 1 in Appendix 5.	LM, HLME	Polpolim Jamanim, Pol-polmi Yamanim (LM)		
Pólpolpolim	place name for Hot Springs near Amadee Mountain, # 23 on HLME map. See map 1 in Appendix 5.	HLME			
póm poḱó	moon	WS	póm poḱó		
Pom Sewím	place name for Susan River, #31 on LM map	LM	Pom-see-wim		Pam Sewim (HLME)
pómolmoli	wet and slick, slimy, slippery	WS	pómolmol		pómolmol

Maidu	English	Source	Source Spelling	Page	Other Spellings
pompomi	barberry (mahonia pinnata), Oregon grape	JD	pompomy	39	
pónoye	walk around in water	FC			
póp	shoot out, emerge suddenly and forcefully	WS	póp		
ṗopó	hay, dry grass	WS, FC	ṗopó		
popoka	raven	FC			
ṗopóm kaléta	haywagon	WS	ṗopóm kaléta		
popópkm	screech owl	FC			
popósi	poison oak (FC, JD), poison oak (the large bushy variety) (WS)	FC, JD, WS	nikposym (JD), popós (WS)	37	popós (WS)
popósim pá	poison oak bush	WS	popósim pá		
pópti	shoot (as a gun), ejaculate (semen) (WS), pop, shoot a gun, explode (FC)	WS, FC	pópti		
póptino	go shoot (a gun)	WS	póptino		
póptipoto	be about to ejaculate	WS	póptipoto		
póptiweḱoi	sound like there's someone shooting	WS	póptiweḱoj		
ṗopún	sparks	WS	ṗopún		
ṗopúnḱoi	drop sparks	WS	ṗopúnḱoj		
ṗopúnti	sparks	FC			
posála	hide, skin, shell	WS	posála		
posí	cousin (FC, WS), poison oak (JD): when used as a kinship term, this word must have a prefix, either mm, nik, or min (see Mountain Maidu Grammar, Lesson 6 for more details)	FC, WS, JD	pos (WS), nikposym (JD)		pos (WS)
pósip	wade out	WS	pósip		
pósito	wade across	WS	pósito		
posól	blister	WS	posól		
Potádi	place name south of Big Meadows, #15 on FR map. See Map 3 in Appendix 5.	FR		370-371	
pótapo	all night long	RD	pō′tapo	44	
potáyamno	big-bellied, bloated, pregnant	WS	potájamno		
pótchode	bat (animal)	WS	pótćode		pochóde, póchodep (RD), póchene (PM), pochéde (FC)
potéto	potato (from English)	WS	potéto		
póti	bands (as part of regalia), some part of regalia	RD	pât′i	120	
potókbe	small tree	RD	potok′be	206	
pówo	come out (smoke)	WS	pówo, pówow		pówow
pówowochono	blow over (smoke)	WS	pówowoćono, pówowwoćono		pówowwochono
pójmt	split (intransitive)	WS	pójyt		
pójmtwaito	split (intransitive)	WS	pójytwajto		
poyó	blue camas, Indian potato - blue-flowered plant	FC			poya

Maidu	English	Source	Source Spelling	Page	Other Spellings
poyoli	false hellebore, corn lily, cow cabbage, skunk cabbage; veratrum californicum	PM-M, JD	po-yo-lem (PM-M), pojoly (JD)	62	
pu	wild hemp	FC, PM-M	poom		
pú	swell up	WS	pú		
puchᴍlule	wasp	FC			
púchik	swell shut, swell over	WS	púćik		
pui	the place outside: púina tetét p̓ilísk̓an "it's really hot outside"	WS, BC	puj, pújja		púiya
púidi	outside	WS	pújdi		
puisla	white camas	FC			
Púislam Ḱoyó	place name for a village located about two miles below (north of) Keddie, on Spanish Creek. Tom Epperson's maternal grandparents lived here, and he lived here with them as a child. There is a bedrock mortar with 4-5 pits. #35 on FR map. The name means "white camas valley" (MP). See map 2 in Appendix 5.	FR1, FR, FR-TE, FR-MP	Púslem Koyo, Puslam Ḱoiyó	370-371	Púislam Ḱoiyó
púiyadi	outside	RD	pū'iyadi	230	
púiyam ínkina	by the door, the area by the (side) door	RD	pū'iyam in'kina	196	
púiyam sá	campfire	WS	pújjam sá		
púiyana	to the outside, towards the outside, towards the side door	FC			púina
púiyanaki	the area by the (side) door	RD	pū'iyanaki	198	
púiyanan	from outside the (side) door, from outside	RD	pū'iyanan	196	
puḱ	give birth, produce offspring, reproduce: yadᴍ́kdᴍkismam pukma'ankano "you, who I have perfected, will produce offspring." ka'as ḱódom yohméndadom yohménkitmᴍni pukmápem. "during springtime, when spring comes, I will produce offspring."	RD, WS, FC	puk (RD), puḱ	10, 14, 24, 160	
pukᴍ́	lupine, columbine	JD	puk, puku	59	puk (JD), pᴍkᴍ́ (FC)
pukét	touch (someone)	WS	pukét		
pukétkachono	almost touch (something) as it goes over, brush over (something)	RD	puket'katsono	212	
pukétkakachono	touch as it goes over/by, to brush someone	RD	puket'kakatsono	124	
púḱsakᴍ	Creator, birth-giver	WS	púḱsaky		

Maidu	English	Source	Source Spelling	Page	Other Spellings
púksito	bring about	WST-DW	púksito	72:10	
púkta	be created	RD	puk'ta	10	
púkti	be born, cause to give birth (FC), cause to come into being (WS)	FC, WS	púkti		
púkwono	be born	FC			
púkwonom ekí	birthday	FC			
púl	open (something)	WS	púl		
pulí	spouse previously married	FC, WS	pul		pul (WS)
púli	marry again	RD	pūl'i	52	
púlito	a woman and her second husband as a pair	FC			
púlkɯ	door	WS	púlky		
púlkɯ bukúitipi	close the door	FC			
púlkɯ púlkitpi	open the door	FC			
púlkɯdi	through the door	RD	pul'ködi	92	
pulkati	type of edible mushroom	PM-M	pul-ka-tee		
púlkinu	be left open	WS	púlkinu		
púlkit	open (verb)	FC			
pulót	stick (mud) on, stretch (something), stitch a nest together with mud	RD	pulot'	8	polot
pulpkɯ	raven	PM-M	pulp-ka		popoka (FC)
pulúm	flume (from English)	WS	pulúm		
púlumto	the place between	WS	púlumto		
pum	peel (verb)	WS	pum		
pumdum	spreading dogbane (plant)	JD	pumdum	38	pum
pumi	peel, peeling, membrane (noun)	WS	pum		
pumí	milkweed, showy milkweed	FC, JD	pumym	39	
pumlénki	blanket, quilt	WS	pumlémki		
púmpu	skin, peeling	WS	púmpu		
púmpumi	membrane, skin, peeling (noun)	WS	púmpumi		
púmsalawi	burlap	WS	púmsalawi		
púmsalawim wadápi	gunnysack	WS	púmsalawim wadápi		
pun	make knotted strings (for invitations), tie knots	RD	p'un	26	
púnto	tie (rope, string, etc), tie up	FC			
púnya	knot	WS	púnja		
púnyapem walási	knotted string used for day-counts. One knot was untied each day. When all the knots were untied, the designated day had arrived.	WS	púnjapem walási		

Maidu	English	Source	Source Spelling	Page	Other Spellings
púnye	tie a knot for each one: hesánbem ḱodóidiwet máidmki bíspem ḱódoidi púnyemadom púnchoi'a. "however many countries, which are men's dwelling places, he tied knots, intending to make a knot for each one."	RD	p'un′e	26	
púppup	dull grayish color	WS	púppup		
púppupmape	becoming gray, getting gray as hair in old age (adj)	WST-DW	púppupmapem	80	
Pupuwelim Sewí	place name for creek going northeast from Genesee. May be Hosselkus Creek. See map 5 in Appendix 5.	MSOP			
púsle	redbell, a species of plant with an edible bulb. The flowers are red with yellow centers.	WS	púsle		
púslem yo	redbell flower	WS	púslem jo		
pusúne	silver tip bear	RD	pusūn′e	224	
pu'u	together	FC			
pu'u	wild hemp	FC			
púya	stitch (verb), sew	FC			pmyé (WS)
púyate	"blue stars" brodiaea, brodiaea minor (poisonous)	PM-M	poo-ya-tem		
puyí	door (not the smoke hole)	RD	pūyi′	220	
sm	insert	WS	sy		
sm	meat, animal carcass	RD	sö	192	
sm	protrude	WS	sy		
sm	dog, any pet	RD, WS, SPB	süi, sö (RD), sý (WS), seyu (SPB)	58	
sm'ḿi	changes a question to past tense. with ai-words, translates as "I wonder"	WS	sy?ýj		
sm'á'asdoi	raise a bow up to shoot, aim	RD	söä′asdoi	46	
sḿche	turn the head towards, look at (RD), look upon with affection (WS)	RD, WS	sö′tse, sýće	76	
smdáldalino	paint white stripes with fingers	WS	sydáldalino		
smdáw	protrude	WS	sydáw		
smdáwwinu	be sticking outwards (like porcupine quills)	WS	sydáwwinu		
smdétno	stick into (as a sliver), run a sliver into the hand	WS	sydétno		
smdói	stick up vertically	WS	sydój		
smdóko	main post of the house or roundhouse	RD	södâk′o	110	sudoḱo (WS)
smdóldol	curly	WS	sydóldol		

Maidu	English	Source	Source Spelling	Page	Other Spellings
sýdon	make a pet of, keep as a pet	WS	sýdon		
sɨhýli	mosquito	FC, WS	syhýl		sɨhýl (WS), sɨhúli (RR-SW)
Sɨhýlim Sewí	place name for Mosquito River, where Caribou and Mosquito Creeks join together	WS, WST-DW	syhýlim sewí		74:12
sɨháw	pierce	WS	syháw		
sɨháwkit	pierce earlobe or septum of nose	WS	syháwkit		
sɨhehéhno	be alongside of, the place alongside of	WS	syhehéhno		
sɨhehéiḱoi	go alongside of	WS	syhehéjḱoj		
sýheheino	alongside	RD	söheheino	66	
sɨhehéinodi	alongside of	WS	syhehéjnodi		
sɨhéheno'ɨno	pass along very close to	RD	söhē'henoönō	92	
sɨheihéino	be alongside of	WS	syhejhéjno		
sɨhékachono	spring to one side (WS), spring to someone's side (RD)	WS, RD	syhékaćono (WS), söhē'katsono (RD)	80	
sɨhésip	come back out (of water)	RD	söhē'sip	116	
sɨhóp	stick into (as a sliver)	WS	syhóp		
sɨhópḱoi	insert, stick into	WS	syhópḱoj		
sɨhópwokit	aim down at	RD	söhop'wokit	202	
sɨk	dig plants with a digging stick	WS	sýk		
sýk	dig up plants	FC			
sɨḱɨ	paternal grandfather: as a kinship term, this word must have a prefix, either mɨ, nik, or min (see Mountain Maidu Grammar, Lesson 6 for more details)	FC			
sɨḱýi	scratch with hand, itch	WS, FC-T	syḱýj		sukúi (FC)
sɨḱýi'ɨno	go along scratching (oneself)	RD	sököi'öno	80	
sɨḱýitoto	scratch each other	WS	syḱýjtoto		
sɨḱýi'us	scratch oneself	WS	syḱýjʔus		
sɨḱýni	fish basket	WS	syḱýn		sɨḱýn
sɨḱýnyo	put everything in the sɨḱýni (fish basket)	WS	syḱýnjo		
sɨkála	bother, annoy	WS	sykála		sakála, sikála
sɨkála'us	masturbate	WS	sykálaʔus		
sɨkála'usmen	not be bothered with	FC			
sɨkásai	engage in foreplay, hug, tickle, pinch, whisper in ear, etc.	WS	sykásaj		
sɨḱáw	feel the pulse, palpate, diagnose by feeling the patient (this is a term used for certain shamanistic curing procedures)	WS	syḱáw		
sɨkdói	dig up (roots)	RD	sökdoi'	234	

Maidu	English	Source	Source Spelling	Page	Other Spellings
sʌkéketkit	point down (at something): 'unídi 'as hánwokiteam,' achói'a, sʌkéketkitdom "'Here is where he was dragging (them) down,' she said, pointing."	RD	sökē'ketkit	112	
sʌkés	prepare (something) in cooking	WS	sykés		
sʌkéswo	prepare	FC			
sʌkét	point with the finger	WS	sykét		
sʌkétnoye	point here and there with finger	WS	sykétnoje		
sʌ́kkoi	go off to dig (something) up	RD	sök'oi	182	
sʌkói	stick (something) into an orifice (híkʌdi múnmunim sawí sʌkóidom, mʌsék bonódi béibʌm "sticking wormwood in their noses and in their ears too"); WS translates as "rub on"	WST	sykói	76:5	
sʌkóiti	stick (something) into an orifice on someone else (see sʌkói for example and comment)	WST	sykóiti	76:5	
sʌkúl	school (from English)	WS	sykúl		
sʌkúla	bother, annoy	WS	sykúla		sʌkála, sakála, sikála
sʌkúla'us	masturbate	WS	sykúlaʔus		
sʌkúlḱoi	go to school, attend school	WS	sykúlḱoj		
sʌkúm	get in a circle	FC			
sʌlát	shape the skull of an infant by massaging and rubbing	WS	sylát		
sʌlékwono	step up quickly	WS	sylékwono		
sʌlékwopin	to rush in, come running in (to a room)	RD	sölek'wopin	116	
sʌlékwotpin	rush out	RD	sölek'wotpin	204	
sʌlépai	stick feathers in the hair, put on feather regalia	WS	sylépaj		
sʌlépai'i	regalia: sʌlépai'im wasása mʌsék yáḱan "he made his regalia."	WST	sylépaji	76:2	
sʌlépaipem máidʌ	warrior, man wearing feathers	WS	sylépajpem májdy		
sʌlépaiti'us	put on feather regalia	WS	sylépajtiʔus		
sʌlépe	abalone shell	FC			
sʌ́m bomó	dogs, pack of dogs	WS	sým bomo		
sʌ́mbe	little dog	FC-T			
sʌmbó	deer trail, trail for large animals	WS, RD	symbó (WS), sömbō' (RD)	RD 84	
sʌmhún	hunt deer	WS	symhún		
sʌmhúnḱoi	go hunt deer	WS	symhúnḱoj		
sʌmhúnḱoḱoi	go off hunting deer (plural subject)	WST	symhúnḱoḱoj	WST 10	

Maidu	English	Source	Source Spelling	Page	Other Spellings
sɤmí	deer, meat	FC, WS	sym	sɤm (WS), sumí (FC)	
sɤmím te	fawn	FC			
sʌ́mpaito	play horseshoes	WS	sýmpajto		
sʌ́mpitï	cascara buckthorn	WS	sýmpitï		
sʌ́mpitïm chá	buckthorn tree (the bark of this tree was used as a laxative)	WS	sýmpitïm ća		
sʌ́mpupa	night hawk	RD	söm'pupa	192	
sʌ́mtonu	personal Indian name of Fred Thomas, Lena Benner's father	WS	sýmtonu		
sʌ́nche	look (in some direction)	WS	sýnće		
sʌ́nchechopin	look over and down towards	WS	sýnćećopin		
sʌ́nchedónu	be facing towards, stare at continuously	RD	sön'tsedōn'u	56, 196	
sʌ́nchetutumoto	stand around together glowering at (someone)	RD	sön'tsetutumoto, sön'tsetutūmot'o	208	
sʌ́nchewodoi	turn upside down (RD), look back up (WS)	RD, WS)	sön'tseodoi' (RD), sýnćewodoj (WS)	82	
sʌ́nchewono	look back at	WS	sýnćewono		
sʌ́ncheye	look toward	WS	sýnćeje		
sʌ́ndaka	forehead	WS	sýndáka		
sɤné	pestle	FC			suné
sɤnóye	handle things, work around with things	WS	synóje		
sɤnpányɤtim máidɤ	Spaniard, Mexican	WS	synpánjytim májdy		
sʌ́nwokoi	be headed (in a certain direction), have the head turned toward (a certain direction)	WS	sýnwokoj		
sɤpá	groundhog	HM	sŭpah		supú (FC), supo (HLME)
sʌ́pa	porcupine, woodchuck	RD, AT	sü'pa	60	
Sɤpám	place name for a village and burial site three miles NE of Susanville, about one mile NW of Center Rd past Brockman Slough and the RR tracks, # 18 on HLME map 3. Name means "groundhog" or "woodchuck." See map 4 in Appendix 5.	HLME	Supom		Supóm
sʌ́pam sɤ	porcupine pet, woodchuck pet	RD	sö'p'amsö	58	
sɤpányeti	Spaniard	FC-E			
sɤpó	grass	WS	sypó		
sɤpó helá	grass game	WS	sypó helá		
sɤpól	thrust (something) into (something)	WS	sypól		
sɤpólno	thrust (something) into (something)	WS	sypólno		
sɤsɤ́	fire poker, poker, stick for stirring the fire	RD, WS	sösö' (RD), sysý (WS)	216	

Maidu	English	Source	Source Spelling	Page	Other Spellings
sᴧsᴧ́	moss	FC			sosó
sᴧsínu	be protruding	WS	sysínu		
sᴧssᴧ	paternal grandmother: as a kinship term, this word must have a prefix, either mᴧ, nik, or min (see <u>Mountain Maidu Grammar</u>, Lesson 6 for more details)	FC			
sᴧ́ssᴧ	prefer, be partial to	WS	sýssy		
sᴧ́ssᴧmen	not like much, not be partial to	WS	sýssymen		
sᴧ́tᴧni	once in a while	RD	sö'töni	172	
sᴧtápó	ready, done (as food, water boiling, etc.): sᴧtápo kᴧkán "It's done. It's ready."	FC			
sᴧtéchi	stagecoach (from English)	WS	sytéći, sytéjći		sᴧtéichi
sᴧ́ti	one, one of them, a certain, a single, each (with negative verb means "no one": sᴧ́tim nenóm máidᴧm anídi bísḱan "a certain old man lived there." lᴧ́ksipḱan sᴧ́ti "one of them climbed out" sᴧ́tim pínmenḱan "no one heard." (when sᴧ́ti means "one of them," it does not take the -m ending even as subject of the sentence)	RD, FC	söt'i	140, 166, 196, 218	sᴧ́tti (WS)
sᴧ́ti béibᴧm	in turn (do to) another: sᴧ́ti hápnoḱan sᴧ́ti béibᴧm hápnoḱan "he handed some over to one person, then handed some to another."	RD	sö'ti bei'böm	44	
sᴧ́ti béi'im	another one	RD	söt'i bēim	144	
sᴧ́ti yónnope	unicorn	FC-E			
sᴧ́tibe	once	RD	sötibe	11, 16	
sᴧ́tidi	together, in one place	RD	söt'idi	136, 180	
sᴧ́tim ma'át	every single one, even a single one, one of: mínki tét'ᴧt'ᴧm sᴧ́tim ma'át ᴧpéḱanim ka'án yakᴧ́pem mamápem. "your children, every single one, all will be ones with names." mínsᴧm sᴧ́tim ma'át "one of you"	RD	söt'immaat	20, 144	
sᴧ́titi	for each one	RD	söt'iti	186	
sᴧ́tti	one	WS	sýtti		sᴧ́ti
sᴧ́ttim dᴧḱᴧ́	only once	WS	sýttim dyḱý		
sᴧ́ttim máschoḱo	ten	WS	sýttim másćoḱo		

Maidu	English	Source	Source Spelling	Page	Other Spellings
sɨ́ttini	once, one time, at one time, once upon a time, for once	WS	sýttini		
sɨ́tunima'át	even one time (with a negative verb, means "never once")	RD	sut'ūnimaat	38	
sʍwái	open up (as the hand)	WS	sywáj		
sʍwáiti	open up the hand	WS	sywájti		
sʍwédoi	stand up	RD	söwē'doi	178	
sʍwéikadoi	jump up from a prone position	WS	sywéjkadoj		
sʍwéiweidoi	creep, crawl	WS	sywéjwejdoj		sʍwéwedoi (FC-R)
sʍwékadoi	stand up, get up	RD	söwē'kadoi	13, 168	
sʍwéwe	look down into, go head first into	RD	söwē'we	108	
sʍwéwedoi	peer down into an opening, start entering head-first	RD	söwē'wedoi	232	
sʍwéweimpin	slither down into (head first, as a reptile)	RD	söwē'weimpin	228	
sʍwéwikadoi	get up to a standing position	RD	söwē'wikadoi	13	
sɨ́ya	make a pet of, keep as a pet	WS	sýja		
sʍyáwkito	insert (ear) ornaments, quills	RD	söiau'kito	182, 184	sʍi'áwkito
sá	fire	WS, SPB	sá (WS), sum (SPB)		
sa ku	build a fire, have a fire: mínḱi innóm ḱanáidi sa kúma'aḱasi "I will light a fire under your butt"	FC			
sa kupai	keep a fire going	BC			
sa wó	build a fire	FC			
sa yá	build a fire	FC			
sa yewé	go back home (return to the fire)	RD	sa yewē'	186	
sa'á	in that case (RD), so then... (WS): ʍnóbene'e sa'á "in that case, you'd better go." ʍnó sa'á! "go ahead (and do it)!"	RD, WS	saa (RD), saʔá (WS)	94, 198	
sáchoḱo	six	FC			
sáichoḱna sɨ́ti	seven	RD	sai'tsokna söti	118	
sáichoḱninima	the sixth one	RD	sai'tsokninima	100	
sáichoḱo	six	WS	sájćoḱo		
sáichoḱom sɨ́ti	seven (American Valley dialect)	FC			
sáichoḱonini	six times	WS	sájćoḱonini		
sáine	Chinese (from English)	WS	sájne		
sáinem kapí	a species of fat beetles, something like a turtle in appearance, called locally a "bottleneck beetle"	WS	sájnem kapí		
sáinem máidʍ	Chinese person (from English)	WS	sájnem májdy		
sakɨ́	make a fire, build a fire	WS	saký		sa ku (FC)
sakɨ́minu	have a fire going inside (something)	RD	sā kö'minu	60	

Maidu	English	Source	Source Spelling	Page	Other Spellings
sakᴧnno	put (wood) in a fire (in a stove)	WS	sakýnno		
sakᴧťa	put (wood) on a (camp) fire	WS	sakýťa		
sáḱa	grandchild, specifically son's child: as a kinship term, this word must have a prefix, either mᴧ, nik, or min (see Mountain Maidu Grammar, Lesson 6 for more details)	FC, WS	saḱ		saḱ (WS)
saláwi	blanket, cover, cloth (WS), rabbit-skin blanket or cloak (RD)	RD, WS	salā'wi (RD), saláw (WS)	116	saláw (WS)
saláwi	rabbit skin blanket	FC			
sállaito	vest	WS	sállajto		
salwétas	baking soda (from English saleratus)	WS	salwétas		
sam hómpaitokᴧm bomó	firefighters	FC			
sam ó	fire pit, fireplace	RD	samō	198	
sam símpani	lichen (alternate spelling makes more sense)	PM-M	sam-sem-pa-ne		cham símpani
sam sukú	smoke from a fire	RD	samsukū'	166	
sámboye	elder brother, elder first cousin: as a kinship term, this word must have a prefix, either mᴧ, nik, or min (see Mountain Maidu Grammar, Lesson 6 for more details)	FC, RD	sambúyi (FC), sām'bōye, sam'bōye (RD)	202	sambúyi (FC), mᴧsámboye (RD)
sámboyem kᴧlé	older sister: as a kinship term, this word must have a prefix, either mᴧ, nik, or min (see Mountain Maidu Grammar, Lesson 6 for more details)	PM-D, RD	ma-sam-boi-kule (PM-D), mösām' bōyeñ küle' (RD)		mᴧ sámbᴧyem kᴧlé
San Wan Ḱᴧsí	San Juan Ridge	FC			
sánodi	behind the fire	RD	sā'nodi	230	
sápᴧ	three	WS	sápy		
sápᴧinini	three times	WS	sápyjnini		
sápᴧm máischoḱo	thirty	FC			
sápa	rat	WS	sápa		
sapí	spawn	WS	sapí		
sápwi	three	RD	sāp'wi	34	
sásaḱa	slang for "hesásaḱa"	FC			
sásasi	marten (animal)	HM	sásasim		
sáteki	Saturday	FC-T, FC-R			
Sátkini Waťám Ḱumhú	place name, just north of Quincy, #43 on FR map. See map 2 in Appendix 5.	FR, AK	Satkini(AK), sátkini waťám ḱumhú (FR)	370-371, AK 397	Sátkini
sátodep	ignite, catch fire	WS	sátodep		
sátoyo	falling star	RD-NM			

Maidu	English	Source	Source Spelling	Page	Other Spellings
sáuko	Clark Crow, a type of nutcracker, gray with black wings and part of tail	HM	saw′ko		
sáwa	sour (from English)	WS	sáwa		
sáwali	gray squirrel	FC			sáwwali
sáwalim payí	gray squirrel foot (basket design)	FC			
sawáwa	make a sound like dragging brush, make a very scary sound in the brush	RD	sawā′wa	214	
sáwdoi	leaf out	RD	sau′doi	152	
sawí	greens, vegetation, edible greens, foliage	FC, WS	saw		saw (WS)
sáwinkotutu	yellow warbler (bright yellow bird with olive green)	HM	sow′-win-ko-too-too		
sáwno	go to seed, pass maturity (of plants)	WS	sáwno		
sawó	fire drill, buckeye	RD, WS	sāwō′ (RD), sawó (WS)	172	
sáwom cha	buckeye (fire drill) tree	FC			
sáwono	other side of fire pit (away from door)	RD	sāwon′o, sā′wono	104, 196, 222	sawóno (RD)
sawónonaki	the place behind the fire pit	RD	sāwon′onaki	198	
sáwsip	leaf out (in spring)	WS	sáwsip		
sáwwali	gray squirrel	WS	sáwwali		sáwali
sáwwalim sínkᴍpe	having a squirrel-like mouth, a protruding jaw	WS	sáwwalim símkype		
sáwwono	go to seed	WS	sáwwono		
sáwwonom máidᴍ	Snake-eater man. A bad legendary person to whom are sent the symbols which are thrown into the creek 4th day of yom wéda (spring big-time).	WS	sáwwonom májdy		
sedé	blood	WS	sedé		
sedém paká	vein	WS	sedém paká		
sedétapo	having too much blood (a term used in shamanism)	WS	sedétapo		
sekés	jackass (from English)	WS	sekés		
Sekumne	place name for Sacramento	RD-NM			
sél	sell (from English)	WS	sél		
seléwwa	a mountain bush, resembling a chokecherry, with red inedible berries, bitter cherry (prunus emarginata)	WS, FC	seléwwa		selewa (FC), siliwa (JD)
sém kᴍs	river sandbar	RD	señ′kös	30	
seméni	autumn, seeds	RD, WS, RDNM	semen′i (RD), semén (WS)	150	semén (WS)

Maidu	English	Source	Source Spelling	Page	Other Spellings
sémenim póḱo	a Mountain Maidu month following the kɱlókbepinem póḱo. In autumn - "seed month"	RD-NM			
seménkit	autumn	WS	seménkit		
seménkit	become autumn	RD	semen'kit	150	
seménkit kɱmén	during the fall	WS	seménkit kymén		
seménkitti	fall, autumn	FC			
sessessilkɱm dɱ	chinquapin bush	PM-M	ses-ses-sil-cum-dum		
séwbonpini	river bed	WS-DW	séwbonpini	74:12	
sewí	river, creek	FC, WS	sew		sew (WS)
sewí ɱdói	upstream	FC			
sewí'ɱno	go to the river's edge	FC			
sewím bo	creek bed, river bed	FC			
sewím piní	confluence of rivers	WS	sewím piní		
sewíno	waterfall, rapids	FC, FC-E			
sewíspolotkɱ	black-headed grosbeak	HM	se-wis'-po-lōt-kum		
sewíspolotka	oriole	HM	se-wis'-po-lōt-kah		
séwḱoi	river current	RD	seu'koi	212	
séwsewto	rivers	HY, RD	sēu'sēuto	180	
séwsewtodi biskɱ	one who lives in the rivers	RD	sēu'sēutodi büsköm	180	
séwwonpini	river bed	WS, WST-DW	séwwonpini	74:6	
si	Hey, Say!	RD	sīi, sī	142, 220, 222	
siɱhékachono	follow closely over or around	RD	siöhek'atsono	114	
si'ɱne	Jerusalem Cricket	FC, RR-SW			shíne (RR-SW)
Siápkɱ	place name for Westwood. See map 3 in Appendix 5.	FC			Sihápkɱ
Siápkɱm Ḱoyóm	place name for Westwood Mill pond area, #27 on LM map. See map 3 in Appendix 5.	LM	see-up kohm koyom		
sidádalino	put on white ceremonial paint	RD	sidā'dalino	76	
sidétno	run a sliver into the hand	WS	sidétno		
sidí	city (from English)	WS	sidí		
sidóp	shove	WS	sidóp		
sidópsip	push out, shove forward	WS	sidópsip		
Sihápkɱ	place name for what was formerly called Nevis Island, now under Lake Almanor near Canyon Dam Store (WS); where Creator left his footprint (WST-DW), Westwood (FC), Westwood Mill pond area (LM), Mountain Meadows (PM-M). See map 3 in Appendix 5.	WS, WST-DW, FC, LM, PM-M	sihápky	80:7	Siápkɱ
si'ítku	western scrub jay	HM	si-ē't-koo		
sikála	bother	FC			sakála, sɱkála

Maidu	English	Source	Source Spelling	Page	Other Spellings
sikásai	engage in foreplay with (someone)	RD	sikas'ai	90	
sikásaito	have fun (sexual sense) (with = "kan"): hesádom maká yepónim máidᴧm wónom máidᴧki kᴧlékan ma'át sikásaitodom méimenmapem? "why do you, the chief, not allow for humans to have a little fun with women?"	RD	sikas'aito	48	
sikáta	be on the lookout	RD	sikat'a	40	
sikés	work on, make, create, prepare (food, for example by skinning and gutting an animal) (RD), prepare (something) in cooking (WS)	RD, WS	sikes' (RD), sikés (WS)	28, 40, 214, 220, 8	
sikéstido	to prepare food for	RD	sikes'tido	110	
siḱét	point with the finger, motion with the finger	WS, WST	siḱét	54	
sikéyo	hang (meat) up to dry, prepare	RD	sikē'yo	108	
sila	violet (plant)	PM-M	se-lam		
silépai	put on feather ornaments (intransitive)	RD	silē'pai	102	
silépaiti	put feather ornaments on (someone)	RD	silē'paiti	102	
sililikᴧm cha	Quaking Aspen tree	PM-M, JD	se-le-le-cum-chom (PM-M), sylylykumća	72	
siliwa	bitter cherry	PM-M, JD	se-le-wa (PM-M), siliwa (JD)	JD 70	seléwwa (WS)
Silóm	place name for Quincy, #2 on LM map. See map 2 in Appendix 5.	LM	seeloom		
Silóm ma'a	Quincy area people	FR1	silom ma'a		
Silóm Sewí	Spanish Creek	FC			
Silóm Ḱoyó	place name for Quincy (FC), American Valley (WS), Quincy, or just south of Quincy (RD-NM). See maps 1 and 2 in Appendix 5.	FC, WS, NM	silóm kojó (WS), silongkoyo (RD-NM)		
silsilwape	silvery	FC-T			
sílwa	silver (from English)	WS	sílwa		
sím watámchik	smack the lips	FC			
símbᴧnno	put the mouth down close to someone else's, with unpleasant connotations	WS	símbynno		
símbachaminu	have the mouth closed primly, with the lips pursed and set	WS	símbaćaminu		
símdadaptonu	have the mouth hanging open	WS	símdadaptonu		
símdakᴧm chi	cloth napkin	FC			
símdakᴧm papéli	paper napkin	FC			
símdoi símkit	one face up, one face down (card games)	FC			

Maidu	English	Source	Source Spelling	Page	Other Spellings
simí	mouth, face (playing cards, face up or down)	FC, WS	sim		sim (WS)
simí waťánchik	slap in the face	WS	simí waťánćik		
símimpo	lip	FC			
símmak	gossip, chat, talk idly	WS	símmak		
símmaksa	gossiper, idle talker	WS	símmaksa		
símmakto	gossip together, gossip to each other, gossip with	RD, WS	sim'akto (RD), símmakto (WS)	192	
símmolus	translate: helú símmoluskasi. "I am translating some (words)."	HY			
símmoluschmi	be hard to translate, not easy to translate: wólem wéye símmoluschmiwet káikasi "although English is hard to translate, I say it."	HY			
símni sóltikm	harmonica	WS	símni sóltiky		
símpani	beard, mustache	WS	símpani		
símpani wmkḿsto	shave	WS	símpani wykýsto		
símpo	lip	WS	símpo		
símwilok	twitch at the corner of the mouth	WS	símwilok		
sín	mix, make with ingredients (as in cooking), contain (as an ingredient): bám wasásani síndom "made with salt"	WS, WST	sín	52:13	
sínkm	baking powder	WS	sínky		
sinóyewew	move around a certain way: mmyákat 'as sinóyewewkan. "He has been moving around the same way (as someone else)."	RD	sinō'yewēu	98	
sisisilchmm dm	bush chinquapin (castanopsis sempervirens or chrysolensis sempervirens)	JD	sysysylcumdum	49	
sitái	grab at and miss, guess wrong in the grass game, miss a shot with bow or gun	WS	sitáj		
sitápin	hug (verb)	WS	sitápin		
sitápintoto	hug one another	WS	sitápintoto		
sítek ́	precipice, cliff	WS	sítek ́		
siťiw	grasp, hold tight with the hand	WS	siťiw		
sito	cross over	FC			
sitók	to dry something (like meat)	RD	sitok'	110	
siwáwawaito	dig (something) open, dig apart (ant hill)	RD	siwā'wawaito	230	
siwéwedoi	climb up an icy slope	RD	siwē'wedoi	176	
siwí	digging stick, root digger (tool)	RD	siwī, siwi'	62, 234	

Maidu	English	Source	Source Spelling	Page	Other Spellings
siwím cha	Mountain Mahogany	FC			
síwsium hiní	blackberry	FC-E			
síwsiw	black	WS	síwsiw		siusiu
síwsiwhudoipe	almost black, dark	RD	si'ūsiūhudoipe	13	
síwsiwpe	black	FC			síwsiwpe
síwsiwpem botóm honí	ace of clubs	WS	síwsiwpem botóm honí		
síwsiwpem chakáti	blackbird	WS	síwsiwpem ćakáti		
síwsiwpem chíwchiwi	black clover, used as medicine and for dyeing in basket making	WS	síwsiwpem ćíwćiwi		
síwsiwpem ékpm	black bushlike manzanita with large berries	WS	síwsiwpem ékpy		
síwsiwpem húlupiti	blackberry	WS	síwsiwpem húlupiti		
síwsiwpem ťókpem honí	ace of spades	WS	síwsiwpem ťókpem honí		
síya	saddle (from Spanish silla)	WS	síja		
siyawkit	baptize	FC			
sobá	serviceberry (The stems of the plant were used to make arrows for small game)	WS	sobá		
sódoi	carry, bring, lift up, pick up (and go off) (RD), grab up, pick up (WS): péyaťan, léwo sodóidom ᴍkóiḱan "after eating for a while, he went off carrying the leftovers." (Negative command with ben map): tetém cha sódoiben map "don't carry big firewood"	RD, WS	sōd'oi, sa'doi, sodoi' (RD), sódoj (WS)	84, 128, 142, 188, 214	sodói (RD)
sódoipai	lift (someone) on one's shoulder (RD), clutch to oneself (WS)	RD, WS	sâ'doipai (RD), sódojpaj (WS)	236	sódopai
sódoiti	make someone carry	RD	sö'doiti	208	
sódoiwo	send (someone) to fetch (wood), tell someone to go get (something): ka'ándukbe sówodoiḱades? "Did I tell you to bring one like that?"	RD	sōd'oiwo	142, 148	
sódoiyew	keep lifting (multiple times), keep on carrying: tetét hai tibím ma'át teténono sódoiyewḱan "even being very small, he keeps on lifting big ones."	RD	sō'doiyēu	142	
sódopai	lift (someone) onto the shoulder	RD	sō'dōpai	100	sódoipai
soduwḿpkm	snipe (bird)	FC			
sohá	carry something alive in the arms	WS	sohá		

Maidu	English	Source	Source Spelling	Page	Other Spellings
soháchono	carry (something) across, carry (something) over	RD	sōhā'tsono	220	
soháchopin	bring in the arms down towards	WS	sohaćopin		
soháchopinyo	keep on carrying (something alive) in	WS	sohaćopinjo		
sohádoi	carry (something alive) upwards	WS	sohádoj		
sohádoino	pick up and carry (someone)	RD	sōhā'doino	86	
sohái	bring (something) back	RD	sōhai'	188	
soháḱoi	carry (someone) off, kidnap (RD), carry in the arms to... (WS)	RD, WS, WST	sohā'oi (RD), sohaḱoj (WS)	174, 42:3	
sohá'okit	come back carrying (wood), bring back (wood)	RD	sohā'okit	142, 148, 220, 236	
sóhasipin	carry (something) down into	RD	so'hasipin	236	
sohásito	carry across in the arms	WS	sohásito		
sohátno	carry (someone) off (RD), carry downwards in the arms (WS)	RD, WS	sohat'no (RD), sohátno (WS)	100	
soháye	bring (something) back, carry (something) back (RD), bring (something) alive) in the arms (WS)	RD, WS	sōhā'ye, sōhai'ye (RD), soháje (WS)	142, 148	
sóhino	go off to gather (wood)	RD	sō'hino	142	
sohún	go get	FC			
sohúnbʌk	try to catch (someone) to kill them	RD	sohun'bök	224	
sohúnbʌkʌsipin	try to catch (someone) while chasing, to kill them	RD	sohun'bökösipin'	224	
sohúnpin	go get, bring in	FC			sohonpin
sóiba	California Bay. The branches of this tree were whipped around inside the house to drive out Bad Coughing Man, the causer of respiratory ailments. A medicinal tea was made with the leaves. WS: pepperwood	WS	sójba		
sóibam chá	pepperwood tree, Bay tree	WS	sójbam ća		
sóisup	lift out with the hand	WS	sójsup		
sóiwino	fetch, bring (wood, for example)	RD	soi'wino	142	
sóiyo	fetch, go get: chá sóiyopi! "go get firewood!"	RR-SW			sóyo
sókit	set (something) down	RD	sō'kit	198	
sókiti	set (something, like food) down (for someone)	RD	sō'kiti	208	
sokólwolwoli	snail	WS	sokólwolwoli		

Maidu	English	Source	Source Spelling	Page	Other Spellings
sokómi	a variety of Queen Anne's Lace with a small white root about the size of a little finger. These were peeled and sun dried, or were ground in a mortar into a kind of flour or paste. They have a bland flavor and a crisp texture.	WS	sokóm		sokóm
sokómim hómma	broth made of sokómi	WS	sokómim hómma		
sokóti	rattle made of cocoons, maple bark tassles on the flag (FC), Attacus cocoon (These were gathered dry and filled with little pebbles to make shaman's rattles) (WS)	FC, WS	sokót		sokót (WS)
sokótkmpem húskm	rattlesnake	RD	sokotköpem huskö	56	
sokúmbibi	small tule	HM	so-kum'-be-bim		
sol	sing, run or function (as a machine)	WS	sol		
solamwene	a plant in the carrot/parsley family used for rattlesnake bites "rattlesnake medicine"	JD	solamwene	77	
sólbusno	sing wildly, emotionally	FC			
sóldoi	start singing, start running (as a machine)	RD, WS	sol'doi (RD), sóldoj (WS)	102	
solé	bleeding heart (plant)	FC			
sólebisim	keep singing	RD	sol'lebisim	72	
sólekoi	to be singing away	RD	sol'ekoi	74, 86, 94, 194	
sólekwono	drop (something) quickly, let go of (something) immediately	RD	sol'ekwono	116	
solém pmkm	edible greens of bleeding heart	FC-T			
solí	song	FC, WS	sol		sol (WS)
solí solé'uskm wasása	radio, "the thing that sings songs to itself"	FC			
sól'idi	sing along with (someone)	WS	sólʔidi		
solím motó	songfest	WS	solím motó		
solím wókm	drum	WS	solím wóky		
sólkm	song	HY			
sólmakito	learn songs	FC-T			
sólmakwono	try to sing	WST-GP	sólmakwono	66:35	
soló	put on shoes: solópi! "put on your shoes!"	FC-T			
soló	shoe, footprint	WS	soló		
solóm bolóko	shoe	WS	solóm bolóko		
solónkokoito	compete in singing (pl. subject), win song competitions, win singing contests	RD	solon'kokoito	100, 102	

Maidu	English	Source	Source Spelling	Page	Other Spellings
sólpai	sing about: tetétikʌm k̓ódo sólpaidom "singing about a great country"	HY			
sólti	play (music), run (a machine) (WS), make (someone) sing, cause singing (FC): nisé yáluluni sólti'usan "he used to play the flute for us."	WS, FC, WST	sólti	52:15	
sóltikʌ	musical instrument, musician	WS	sóltiky		
sóltiwasa	not know how to play (musical instrument)	WS	sóltiwasa		
sóltoto	sing together	FC-R			
sóltotokʌ	harmonica	WS	sóltotoky		
sólwasa	not know how to sing, sing poorly	WS	sólwasa		
sólwebis	keep on singing	FC			
sólwet	a different song	RD	sol'wet	88	
sólwo	ask (someone) to sing	RD	sol'wō	102	
sólwon	song which had been sung: ékdachoi'a sóldom yúhbodom mʌyím mʌkʌ́lʌsik sólwon. "At dawn he was singing and dancing that great owl's song (the song which had been sung by the great owl)."	RD	sol'won	190	sólwono
sólwoyo	hire (someone) to sing	WS	sólwojo		
sopó	grass	FC			
sopóm helá	grass game gambling	FC-T			sʌpó helá (WS)
sopóm helám sól	sing grass-game songs: sopóm helám sólk̓an "he sang a gambling song."	WS	sopóm helám sól		
sopóm helám solí	grass-game song	WS	sopóm helám solí		
sopóť	froth, foam	WS	sopóť		
sosó	moss	WS	sosó		sʌsʌ́
soťálkʌ	spread: butter, jelly, etc.	FC			
sótto	a kind of gambling game, played at night over an upturned basket	WS	sótto		
sowáiti	open up (something): mínk̓i ma sowáiti "open up your hand"	WST	suwájti	72:8	suwáiti
sówek̓adoi	grab up something quickly and run	WS	sówek̓adoj		
sówik̓achono	lift and carry (something) over the shoulder	RD	sō'wikatsono	110	
sówik̓adikno	lift and carry (something) all the way	RD	sō'wikadikno	138	
sowík̓ado	lift (someone) up, pick (someone) up	RD	sowi'kado	100	
sówik̓adoi	grab up (something) with the arms and run	WS	sówik̓adoj		
sówik̓oi	go to fetch, go get (wood, for example)	RD	sō'wikoi	142	

Maidu	English	Source	Source Spelling	Page	Other Spellings
sówino	bring (firewood)	RD	sō'wino, sowin'o	148	sowíno (RD)
sówodoi	lift (something) up	RD	sō'wodoi	142	sówwodoi
sówokit	set or lay (someone) down, let someone get down	WST	sówokit	42:3	
sówono	let someone go, let someone get away, hand someone over to someone else (RD), release with the hand (WS): batápaimenchonódom, sówonoḱan "because he couldn't catch up with him, he let him get away."	RD, WS	sō'wono, sōwon'o (RD), sówono, sówwono (WS)	54, 130, 170, 220	sowóno (RD), sówwono (WS)
sówoťa	lay out, set out (food)	WST	sówoťa	78:8	
sówoťayo	set out many things	WST	sówoťajo	78:7	
sówwodoi	lift up with the hands	WS	sówwodoj		sówodoi
sówwokit	set (something) down	WS	sówwokit		
sówwosip	carry out by hand, take out by hand	WS	sówwosip		
soyá	pass (something) to (someone): bá nik soyáp "pass me the salt."	FC			
sóye	pass, hand (something)	WS	sóje		
sóyewe	push (things) back, set (things) back	WS, FC	sójewej		sóyewei
soyó	acorn dough, any dough	WS, FC	sojó		
sóyo	fetch, go get: chá sóyopi! "go get firewood!"	RR-SW			sóiyo
su	enough, that's enough (FC), Well! OK! (RD)	FC, RD	sū	68	
su	coffeeberry, California buckthorn	HM	shoom		
sú	go ahead and..., right now!, "OK"	WS, WST	sú	10	
sú	show, circus (from English)	WS	sú		
sudá	be delicious, be tasty: tetétluťi sudáḱan "it is very tasty."	RD	sudā'	44	
súda	soda	FC			súdi (WS)
sudábe	sweet-tasting, savory tasting	RD	sudabe	46	
sudák	sugar, sweet	WS	sudák		
sudákm	wine, whiskey, hard liquor	FC			
sudákm momí	whiskey, hard liquor	FC-T			
sudákpe	sweet	WS	sudákpe		
súdam wasása	baking soda (as a cooking ingredient)	WS	súdam wasása		
súdi	soda (from English)	WS	súdi, súda		súda
sudoḱo	the main post of the dance house, against which the shaman struck his rattles during a séance	WS	sudoḱ		
suhúli	mosquito	FC			sm̥húli

Maidu	English	Source	Source Spelling	Page	Other Spellings
súk	smoke (intransitive verb - as a fire smokes)	FC-T			
súka	sugar	FC			
súkam maháti	cake, sweet baked items	FC			
súkam momí	sweet drink, soda	FC			
súkda	make smoke	FC			
súkdaw	drift away (smoke) (verb)	WS	súkdaw		
súkdawi	drifting-away smoke (noun)	WS	súkdawi		
súkdoipeti	rise (smoke)	RD	suk'doipeti	164	
sukdóiti	stir up (dirt or dust), raise dust: ḱawí sukdóitiḱan "it stirred up dirt"	RD	sukdoi'ti	132	
suklí	smoky	RD	suklī'	166	
sukmítti	blow dust or dirt down into	RD	sukmit'ti	132	
súknoti	make dust fly	RD	suk'noti	134	
súkpai	to get on (someone) (smoke)	WS	súkpaj		
súksipmape	smoke hole, chimney	WS	súksipmape		
sukú	heel, butt (of something, like a gun)	WS	suk		
súku	smoke (noun): súkum tibitikᴧm cha "wood that makes very little smoke (manzanita)" súku nik méi "Give me a smoke"	FC, WS, FC-T	suḱ		suḱ (WS)
sukúi	scratch (verb), itch	FC			sᴧkḿi
sukun	bark storage bin for winter food storage	JD	sukun	11	
súllala	bracken fern (The central peeled stem was dyed black and used for making the black designs in baskets)	WS, FC	súllala		súlala
súlu	marked bone in gambling	RD-NM			
sum pekim yehi	snowberry	FC			
sumbíli	wild lobelia	WS	sumbíl		
Súmbilim	place name for Susanville, #5 on FR map; place name for Indian Heights in Susanville, CA. (WS), an old village site west of the rancheria near the Indian Heights Mission Church, # 28 on HLME map 3 (HLME). The name means "lobelia." See maps 1 and 4 in Appendix 5.	FC, FR, HLME	sumbílim	FR 371	
sumbilnandi	from around Susanville	FC			
sumpiti	cascara sagrada (plant), cascara buckthorn, bearberry (used as a laxative), coffeeberry	JD	sumpiti	69	
súmpupa	nighthawk	HM	soom'-poo'-pah		

Maidu	English	Source	Source Spelling	Page	Other Spellings
sumú	sugar pine, pine nut	WS	sumú		sumɨ́
sumúm chá	sugar pine tree	WS, JD	sumúm ćá (WS), su·mu·mća (JD)	JD 29	
suné	pestle	WS	suné		sɨné
súneki	Sunday	FC-T, FC-R			
suném o	pestle	FC			
súpa	ground squirrel	FC			
Supóm	place name for a village site three miles NE of Susanville, about one mile NW of Center Rd past Brockman Slough and the RR tracks, # 18 on HLME map 3. See map 4 in Appendix 5.	HLME	Supom		Sɨpám
supú	groundhog	FC			sɨpá
supút	sop up, dip in a liquid	WS	supút		
supútput	sop (something) about in this and that liquid	WS	supútput		
supútputtonu	be sopping or dipping in this and that liquid from time to time	WS	supútputtonu		
supútsitoye	scoop (something) around in (something)	WS	supútsitoje		
supúttonu	sop up/dip in liquid from time to time	WS	supúttonu		
supwa	marmot	PM-M	soop-wa		
susu	valley quail	HM	soo-soo		
susúpdoi	let (something) slip and fall, knock (something) off	WS	susúpdoj		
sut	dig	FC			
sútto	play hand game in winter without grass	WS	sútto		
sútumi	centipede	HM	soo'-too-mim		
tɨ	powder	FC			
tɨ́	burn (not as a fire, but as the object that burns)	WS	tý		
tɨ́i	be sleepy, be lying down (RD), recline, lie down (WS)	RD, WS	tö'i (RD), týj (WS)	80	tɨ́i (WS)
tɨ́iha	coiling around (like a snake)	RD	t!öi'ha	196	
tɨ́ikinu	be lying down	WS	týjkinu		
tɨ́ikit	lie down	WS	týjkit		
tɨ́ikiti	hunker down, squat down	RD	töi'kiti	226	
tɨ́inoye	lie around	WS	týjnoje		
tɨi'tánu	be lying on (something)	RD	töitā'nu	58	
tɨ́kɨma	people living in the Sacramento Valley	RD-NM	tö'köma		
tɨkɨ́s	flea	WS	tyḱys		
tɨ́ktɨ́k	kindling	FC			
tɨlɨ́lɨ	small gray pine squirrel with tufted ears and brown sides	WS	tylýly		tulúli (FC)
Tɨldino	Prattville	FC			Táldinom (FR)

Maidu	English	Source	Source Spelling	Page	Other Spellings
t꞉lí	grasshopper	FC, WS	tyl		t꞉l (WS), tulí (FC-R)
t꞉lím homí	grasshopper stew	WS	tylím homí		
t꞉mét꞉	tomato (from English)	FC			tumétu
ť꞉n	rot, rotten	WS, FC-E	ťyn		
t꞉n	growl (verb)	WS, FC-R, FC-T	tún (FC-T), tyn		tún
t꞉n꞉p	turnip (from English)	WS	týnyp		
t꞉ní	younger brother: as a kinship term, this word must have a prefix, either m꞉, nik, or min (see Mountain Maidu Grammar, Lesson 6 for more details)	FC, WS	tyn		t꞉n (WS)
t꞉nk꞉to	pair of brothers	WS	týnkyto		
ť꞉nti	be rotten: aním ṕakám ť꞉ntikan "that branch is rotten."	FC-T	tumti		
t꞉p	jump, leap (verb)	WS	typ		túp (RD)
t꞉pchopin	jump off towards	WS	týpćopin		
t꞉pínpin	come jumping down, jump off	WS, FC	týpínpin, týpýnpin		t꞉ṕ꞉npin, tupinpin
t꞉pmitno	go jumping in, jump or dive in	WS, RD	týpmitno (WS), tup'mitno (RD)	80	túpmitno
t꞉pmitpin	jump down into	RD	töpmitpin	58	
t꞉pnoye	jump or hop around	WS, FC, RD	týpnoje		tupnoye (RD)
t꞉ppin	jump towards	WS	týppin		
t꞉psito	jump across	WS	týpsito		
t꞉s	stand, be vertical	WS	tys		
t꞉sape	violet (plant)	FC			
t꞉sbokit	stand by (something), stand inside or on (something) (RD), stop in one's tracks (WS)	RD, WS	tös'bokit (RD), týsbokit (WS)	34, 36, 110	
t꞉sbokitno	stand up and watch for	RD	tös'bokitno	30	
t꞉sboťa	stand on top of	WS	týsboťa		
t꞉sda	be standing, be poised at	RD	tösda	198	
t꞉sdanu	be continually standing next to (smoke-hole, for example)	RD	tös'danu	164	
t꞉sdikno	stand in a certain place	WS	týsdikno		
t꞉sdiknoti	stand (someone) in a certain place, position (someone)	WS, WST	týsdiknoti	54:23	
t꞉sdoi	rise (from sitting to standing), stand up	WS	týsdoj		
t꞉skadoi	get up, stand up, get to one's feet	RD, WS	tös'kadoi (RD), týskadoj (WS)	194, 104	
t꞉skinu	stand	WS	týskinu		
t꞉skit	stop, stand still	RD	tös'kit	180	

Maidu	English	Source	Source Spelling	Page	Other Spellings
tʉskitwonodi	where stopped, where (they) had been stopped: ʉpéknudom mʉm lʉlʉm máidʉm tʉskitwonodi mʉséki sʉtídi wálukinuḱan. "Forever those star men are immobilized together in the place where they had been stopped"	RD	tös'kitwonodi	180	
tʉsťa	stand on	WS	týsťa		
tʉsweye	stand	WS	tyswéje		
tʉswonoye	stand around	FC			
tʉswoye	stand (permanent object), stand up, get to be in a standing position, come to a stop: anídi 'as sʉdókom tʉswoyeḱan "there is where the main house post stands."	RD, WS	tös'woye (RD), týswoje (WS)	80, 110	
tʉswoyeyaťan	after having stood around	RD	tös'woyeetan	194	
ťʉťʉti	to build nests	FC			
tʉtʉ	be apart from, stay away from (someone): tʉtʉp niḱí! "let go of me! get away from me!" wónom máidʉ map sikálaben! tʉtʉpada! "Don't bother humans! Stay away from them!" ka'ánte ʉḱóiwet tetébe tʉtʉwonokʉḱan "showing how much they had grown up since they went away"	RD	tötö', töt'ö	160, 200, 232	tʉtʉ
tʉtʉ	cradle basket, cradleboard	WS, FC	tytý		
ťʉťʉ	nest	FC			ťuťú (WS)
ťʉťʉ	twig	RD	tötö'	90	ťʉtťʉ (WS)
ťʉťʉ	gather kindling	RD	tötö'	148	
tʉti	burn (something) (WS), cause to burn (FC)	WS, FC	týti		
ťʉttʉ	a kind of manzanita	PM-M	thot-tom		tátum (HM)
ťʉttʉ	twigs, wood chips, kindling	WS	ťýtťy		
tachípi	big brown-headed chipmunk, bigger chipmunk	FC, WS	taćip		tachip (WS)
ťadá	braid, plait (verb)	WS	ťadá		
ťadákʉm máidʉ	person with braided hair	WS	ťadákym májdy		
tahohoni	sucker fish	PM-M, BC	ta-ho-hon-em (PM-M), ta hawn nim (BC)		
tái	west	WS, FC	táj		tái'i (FC)
Tái Yamáni	place name for Mount Lassen (WS), Coast Range (RD). See map 1, Appendix 5	WS, RD	tájjamani (WS), tai'yamani (RD)	166	

Maidu	English	Source	Source Spelling	Page	Other Spellings
tái'epeni	species of big hornet with a spot on the head (WS), type of bee (PM-M)	WS, PM	tájʔepeni (WS), tie-e-pen-em (PM-M)		
tái'i	Konkow	WS	tájʔi		
tái'idi	in the twilight	FC-E			
tái'im máidm	Konkow person, Konkow people (WS), West People - from Oroville area, Berry Creek (FC)	WS, FC	tájʔim májdy		táiyima
táina	towards the west, to the west	FC-E			tái'ina
Táisida	place name for Marysville, or just south of Marysville	RD-NM			
taiyái'aluť	pelt down (rain) on the roof	RD	taiyai'alut	194	
táiyima	western people, people living to the west of the Mountain Maidu, Konkow people	RD-NM	tā'yima		tái'im máidm
tákakabo	jump suddenly, jump quickly (because of something)	RD	tak'akabo	108, 114	
ťákkaka	jump and make a tapping sound	WS	ťakkaka		
takósi	taco	FC			
takúpno	glove	FC			
Táldinom	place name between Big Meadows and Butt Valley, #14 on FR map. See map 3 in Appendix 5. Prattville (FC)	FR, FC		370-371	Tmldino (FC)
tállala	the unbanded bone used in the grass game	WS	tállala		
tallóli	brush rabbit	PM-M	tall-lo-lem		telóli
talóp	spring, jump (verb)	WS	talóp		
talópsip	jump out of	WS	talópsip		
tam	bury	WS	tam		
tambini	net trap	FC			
Tám Kusim	place name of a site south of Kusim in Indian Valley, Tankusim Hill. See map 5 in Appendix 5.	MSOP			Tankusim
Tam Sewí	place name for North Fork of the Feather River. See maps 1, 2 and 3 in Appendix 5	PM-D	tam-say-we		
ťamámi	buttercup	FC, WS	ťamám		ťamám (WS)
ťamámim yó	buttercup flower	WS	ťamámim jó		
taméli	watermelon (from English)	WS	taméli		támeli (FC)
támlelep	do very quickly	RD	tam'lelep	106	
támlelepno	go at utmost speed	WS	támlelepno		
támlep	very fast	RD	tam'lepe	46	
támlepluť	move at the greatest speed	RD	tam'leplut	212	

Maidu	English	Source	Source Spelling	Page	Other Spellings
támlepti	send (something) at great speed, make (something) go fast	RD	tam'lepti	46	
támpipidikno	go up quickly (hill slope), slope up steeply	RD	tampipidikno	66	
támṗiṗítḱoi	go very fast	WS	támṗiṗítḱoj		
támṗit	swoop	WS	támṗit		
támṗiťin	swoop down, dart down fast	WS	támṗiťin		
támṗiťinpin	swoop down towards	WS	támṗiťinpin		
tánkɷ	burial ground	WS	támky		
tánkɷ	Nisenan	WS	tánky		
Tánkɷ	place name for Auburn, or between Nevada City and Auburn, down to the north fork of the Consumnes River	FC, FC-T	tonkɷ		
tánkɷdi	at a burial place	WS	támkydi		
tánkɷm ḱawí	burial ground	WS	támkym ḱawí		
tánkɷm máidɷ	Nisenan person	WS	támkym májdy		
tánkɷma	Nisenan	RD-NM	tan'köma		
tánkit	bury	WS	támkit		
Tánkusim	place name of a site south of Kusim in Indian Valley, Tankusim Hill. See map 5 in Appendix 5.	MSOP			Tam Kusim
ťápɷ	juniper	PM-M, JD	tha-pom (PM-M), tapom (JD)	JD 30	
ťápɷm cha	juniper tree	FC			
tapɷ́kɷ	California poppy	FC			
tapewe	seven (dialectal)	FC			
tapó	do all that (verb): ham! mi tapóm kaná hónwema'ankano! "Damn! After intentionally doing all that, you will survive!"	RD		62	
tapó	with everything done, with all that done (adverb): tapó mayákḱen máisem ɷnódoiḱan "with all that done, subsequently they started off."	RD	tapō'	36	
tás	gag, strain, retch, moan	WS	tás		
Tasíkoyo	place name for Taylorsville. See Tosí Ḱoyó	RD-NM			Tosikoyo, Tosí Ḱoyo, Tosím Ḱoyo
Tásma	place name for Humbug Valley, CA (WS), main village of Humbug Valley (FC). See map 1 in Appendix 5.	WS, FC	tásma		
Tásmam Ḱoyó	place name for Humbug Valley. See maps 1 and 3 in Appendix 5.	FC			
tásti	make (someone) moan (with pleasure)	RD	tas'ti	90	

Maidu	English	Source	Source Spelling	Page	Other Spellings
ťát	tight (of shoes), lame	WS	ťát		
táta	papa, daddy	FC			tátta
ťaťá	dogwood	WS	ťaťá		
ťáťa	palm, sole	WS	ťáťa		
ťaťákam wétemi	the sound of (people) dancing	WS	ťaťákam wétemi		
ťaťám cha	dogwood	FC			
ťaťám yó	dogwood flower	WS	ťaťám jó		
tatámɱ	cricket	FC			
ťátate	sucker fish (FC), carp (RR-SW)	FC, RR-SW			ťóttadi (PM-M)
tatókum cha	snowberry bush	HM	taw-to'-kum chah		ťɱťɱm cha
tátta	father	WS-MP	tátta		táta
tátum cha	whiteleaf or sticky manzanita tree	HM	taw'-tum chah		ťɱttɱ (PM-M)
tawál	make, build, work on (something): ódo tawálmamɱni "when he would pan for gold..."	RD, WS, WST	tawal' (RD), tawál (WS)	40 (RD), 52:11 (WST)	
tawálɱsip	work one's way outward	WST-DW	tawál?ysip	74:13	
tawálbos	complete work, finish work, accomplish	RD	tawal'bos	68	
tawáldɱkdɱk	work over, revise, rectify, repair, fix up	WS	tawáldykdyk		
tawálhekitbos	finish all the work, wind up the job, be all done working (for the day)	WST	tawálhekitbos	52	
tawáli	work (noun)	FC, SPB	tawale (SPB)		
tawálihape	job, mission, goal: mɱkí tawálihape tawálbosweten, ɱkóiḱan. "His job being all done, he left.	RD	tawal'lihape	68	
tawálkɱ	get a job: tawálkɱpi! "get a job!"	FC			tawalku
tawálnoye	work around, go around working	WS	tawálnoje		
Tawkusim	place name for a site south of Kusim in Indian Valley, NW of Taylorsville. Could be the same as Tam Kusim.	RD-NM	taukusim		Tam Kusim, Tankusim
táwlikkɱ	mountain tanager (bird)	HM	tawl'-lik-ku		
té	child, son	WS, FC, RD	té (WS), tē (RD)	140	
té bísti	give birth to a child	WS	té bísti		
ťe'áswaito	stretch with foot	RD	teās'waito	11	
tébɱli	table (from English)	FC, WS	tébyl		tébɱl (WS)
tébe	baby	FC			
tébeťɱťɱ	babies	FC			
tebíbe	seven (Indian Valley dialect)	FC			
ťedátdikno	using feet, stretch (something) all the way (to)	RD	tedat'dikno	12	
ťedís	slip, lose balance	WS	ťedís		
ťédisdaw	slip down	RD	yed'isdau	176	ťédisdaw
ťedísdoi	start to slip	WS	ťedísdoj		

Maidu	English	Source	Source Spelling	Page	Other Spellings
ťédisdoihudódoiye	almost start to slip while going up towards	RD	t!ed'isdoihudō'doiye	178	
ťedísim	slipping	FC-E			
ťehᴂhᴍpḱoi	stretch (something) out gradually using one's foot	RD	tehö'höpkoi	11	
ťehᴂp	stretch using foot	RD	tehöp'	11	
ťehᴂpḱoi	stretch (something) out using one's foot	RD	tehöp'koi	11	
téha	be pregnant	WS	téha		
téhadoi	be pregnant	WS	téhadoj		
ťehul	stomp on (something): hᴍbó mayákḱen ťehuldom yepíntiḱan. "Suddenly he made a loud noise, stomping on the house."	RD	te'hul	216, 222	
ťehús	step into (something like mud)	WS	ťehús		
tékᴍ	be pregnant, give birth, have a child	WS	téky		téku (FC)
tékᴍma	be pregnant	WS	tékyma		
tékᴍti	get (someone) pregnant, impregnate	WS	tékyti		tékuti (FC)
tékᴍto	parent and child	WS	tékyto		
téku	be pregnant	FC			tékᴍ (WS)
tékupe	pregnant	FC			
tela	wood rat	FC			
telólele	cottontail rabbit	WS-MP	telólele		
téloli	cottontail rabbit	RD, HM, WS	telâl'i, te'loli (RD), tel'-lo'-le (HM), télol (WS)	88, 218	telóli (RD), télol (WS)
tem chám pautom póḱo	a Mountain Maidu month following the sémenim póḱo. little tree-freeze moon or month - late Fall.	RD-NM			
tem chipbᴍ	thumb	FC			
tem kᴍlé	daughter	FC			
tém púḱti	fetus, embryo	WS	tém púḱti		
tém uyí	uterus	WS	tém ují		
témbini	net	RD	tem'bini	220	
tené	the same, the very one, the one referred to (WS), exactly (FC): tené makwónoma'ankano "Just try doing the same thing."	WS, FC, RD	tené (WS), tene' (RD)	160	
tení	wood tick	HM	te-nim'		
té'oluťkᴍ	bluebird	HM	tā'-o-lut-kah		
teṕ	the banded bone in the grass game	WS	teṕ		
tépkᴍ	flint flaker (tool)	RD	tepkö	54	
ťes	short in stature, brief	WS	ťes		
ťesnono	shortish	RD	tesnono	64	
téspe	short	FC			
ťéstimen	prolong	WS	ťéstimen		

Maidu	English	Source	Source Spelling	Page	Other Spellings
tétᴧtᴧ	children, young people (more than two)	WS, FC	tét̯yt̯y		
tétᴧtᴧkᴧ	bear a litter (WS), be a parent of, have a child (RD): wépam machói'am tétᴧtᴧkᴧpem sᴧtim pᴧbe. "Coyote had one son. Coyote was the parent of one son."	WS, RD	tét̯yt̯yky (WS), tē′tötökö	48, 228	
tétᴧtᴧkᴧpe	parent, mother, father: kᴧlé wásak̯an, tétᴧtᴧkᴧpe ma'át "they were bad to women, even mothers."	RD	tē′tötököpem	48, 228	
ťeťálak	grind (something) underfoot	WS	ťeťálak		
teté	big	WS	teté		
teté	greatly, tremendously, extremely (adv), a great deal: teté yehéptoyek̯an. "They were greatly afraid."	RD	tete′	210	
téte	play (children), hang out (adults) ("with" = kan): wépam máidᴧm, cháitikadom, uním máidᴧm bomók̯an tétechoi'a "Coyote Man, being disguised, hung out with this group of people." mᴧm téchom hᴧbódi tétek̯an "the two children played in the house."	RD, WS, FC	tē′tē (RD), téte (WS)	40, 228	
teté sínkᴧpe	big-mouthed, having a big mouth	WS	teté símkype		
tetébe	bigger, largest	RD, WS	tetē′be (RD), tetébe (WS)	9, 232	
tetébe	get a little larger, grow, be growing up, get a little older, make (something) a little larger: popósim, tetébe ma'át bek̯el "Cousin, make the hole a little bigger." ka'ánte ᴧk̯óiwet tetébe tᴧtᴧwonokᴧk̯an "showing how much they had grown up since they had left"	WS, RD	tetébe (WS),	36, 232	
tetébetᴧtᴧ	get a little bigger, get a little older: mínk̯i tétᴧtᴧ, tetébetᴧtᴧᴧni, uním k̯ódo mák̯paima'ak̯an. "Your children, when they are a little older, will learn about this country."	RD	tetē′be tötö′	22	
tetébetᴧtᴧwono	had grown a little bigger	RD	tetē′be tötö′wono	232	

234

Maidu	English	Source	Source Spelling	Page	Other Spellings
tetébew	be a little larger, get a little larger (WS), become a little bigger, a little bigger (adj)	RD, WS	tetē′beu (RD), tetébew (WS)	7	
tetébewti	make a little bigger: hesátidom tetébewtimakade'as "how about we (2) make it a little bigger?"	RD	tetē′beuti	7	
tetéboduk	be not very big, be not big enough, be not big enough for	WS	tetéboduk		
tetéboduk... na	be not big enough for: tetébodukkas ka'ápem tawálna "I'm not big enough for that kind of work."	WS	tetéboduk... na		
tetédmḱm	by being loud, with a loud noise (adv): tetédmḱm wisétyahátpintiwe'am "by being loud, he always causes panic."	RD	tetē′dökö	214	
tetédmḱm	the very loudest (sound), the heaviest (rain): tetédmḱm yákakan: "it made the loudest sound, it was like the biggest..."	RD	tetē′dökö	150, 152, 170, 200	
tetékm	junco (bird)	HM	te-te′-kum		
tétekmm	great, mighty	HY			
tétekoi	go play	WS	tétekoj		
tetéluťi	enormous, biggest	WS	tetéluť		tetéluť
tetéluťi mḱáwchetipe	biggest and most beautiful	RD	tetē′luti ökau′tsetipem	176	
tetém chám pautom póko	a Mountain Maidu month following the tem chám pautom póko. Big tree-freeze moon or month. Winter	RD-NM			
tetém mám chípbm	thumb	WS	tetét mám ćípby		
Tetém Mamchipbmm Om	place name for the rocky ridge located on the north side of Highway 89 north of Indian Falls on Indian Creek, with at least 3 split-rock formations. The first formation is Thumb Rock (Tetém Mámchipbmm Om), and this ridge also includes Búyem Kumí and O Wichono. This is on DT map 7. See map 2 in Appendix 5	DT	temtemmom chip boom om	45	

Maidu	English	Source	Source Spelling	Page	Other Spellings
Tetém Mómdanni	place name for Lake Tahoe (FC), ocean (MP), Honey Lake (LM), #33 on LM map. Means "big lake." For Honey Lake, see maps 1 and 4 in Appendix 5.	FC, WS-MP, LM, HLME	tetém mómdani (MP), tetem momdanim (LM, HLME)		
tetém momíki yochónonupe	great waterfall	RD	tetēm′ momi′ki yotson′onupe	212	
Tetém Sewí	Feather River	CM			
tetém té	big child	WS	tetém té		
Tetema	place name for Nevada City	FC			
teténa	more	FC-E			
teténak tibínak	more or less	FC-R			
téteno	go play	WS	téteno		
teténono	a lot of big ones	WS	teténono		
teténoye	play (verb)	RD	tetēn′oe	142	
teťép	pepper	WS	teťép		
tetét	very, very much, really, so: tetét min yoyáhakas. "I really want to hit you. I so want to hit you."	WS, FC	tetét		
tetét pí yawí	be very expensive	WS	tetét pí jawí		
tetét pídom	by very much (with a negative verb in -men- "not by very much"): póchodem máidᴧm tetét pídom tókdatiusmenchoi'a "Bat Man did not get himself beaten (in a race) by very much. Bat Man was not outrun by very much."	RD	tetet′ pī′dom	212	
tetét píkno	very much, so much, too much, excessively	WS	tetét píkno		
tetét yahám kayí	very big load of logs	WS	tetét jahám kají		
tetétbewto	harder: tetétbewto kadíkchoi'a "it rained harder"	RD	tetet′beuto	194	
tetéte	higher level	WST	tetétom	56:43	
tetétluťi cheyáha	to so want to see, to want so much to see	RD	tetet′luti tseyā′ha	124	
tetétluťim mómdanni	ocean	FC-R			
tetétse	certainly, surely	WS	tetétse		
téteweḱoiyew	hear (a child) playing	RD	tēt′ēwekoiyeu	174	
tétpikno	too much	FC			
tétyol	stomp on (something)	RD	tet′yol, tetyol′	220	tetyól
teyá	coil (like a snake)	WS	tejá		
téyaťa	dead child	WS	téjaťa		
ťeyó	kick backwards (like a mule)	WS	ťejó		
ťeyóyewei	kick (something) backwards	WS	ťejójewej		ťeyóyewe

Maidu	English	Source	Source Spelling	Page	Other Spellings
ti	to cause (something) (rare as verb): yahát 'as tené hésmen tikasí. "Mission accomplished, I already made that happen."	RD	ti	62	
tí'i	tea	FC			
tibí	be small	FC			
tibí	small	WS	tibí		
tibí yawí	be cheap	WS	tibí jawí		
tibíbe	playmate (as children)	RD	tibī'be	136	
tibíbew	dwindle, get fewer or smaller	WS	tibíbew		
tibíbi	tiny ones, small: tibínonom méitokmm hmbókmpem "having several small shops"	WS, WST	tibíbi	54:29	
tibíbinono	several tiny ones, small ones	WS, WST	tibíbinono	54:29	
tibíbiti	cause to be in many small pieces	WS	tibíbiti		
tibíbitidom wiyńl	cut up into small pieces	WS	tibíbitidom wijýl		
tibíluti	the smallest	WS	tibíluti		
tibím chábe	splinter	WS	tibím ćábe		
tibím kówekkesi	cottontail, small rabbit	WS	tibím kówekkesi		
Tibím Sewím	place name for Smith Creek/Piute Creek, #20 on HLME map 3. North of the Susanville area. The name means "little creek." See map 4 in Appendix 5.	HLME	Tibim Sewim		
tibím uyí	outhouse	FC			tibím uiyi
tibíma'át	small, indefinite amount (FC-T), although small (RD)	FC-T, RD			
tibína	for a bit, for just a moment	WS	tibína		
tibína	less	FC-E			
tibínak	a little bit	FC-R	tebinak		
tibínak	in a little bit, soon	FC			
tibíti	make small, make smaller	FC			
tĭk	enough, sufficient	WS	tĭk		
tĭk	woodtick	WS	tĭk		
tíkbe	no more, no longer: tíkbe min huntás: "may I hunt you no more."	RD	tik'be	42	
tĭkche	believe, trust, trust (someone's) judgment, go along with (someone's ideas): hesí ma'át nik tĭkchemenkan. "He doesn't go along with me in anything. He doesn't trust me (my judgment) in anything;" yahát tĭkchepi "you'd better believe it!"	WS, RD	tĭkće (WS), tik'tse (RD)	28, 124	

Maidu	English	Source	Source Spelling	Page	Other Spellings
t̆ikchelelepe	gullible, one who easily believes: ᴍpéḱani t̆ikchelelepem ḱasí "I am so gullible! I believe anything!"	RD	tik′tselelepe	116	
tíkisuwi	Atsugewi/Pit River name for the Northeastern Maidu	WS	tíkisuwi		
t̆ikḱói	be just enough for	RD	tikoi′	152	
t̆iknan	from every: ḱódom t̆iknan "from every country"	RD	tik′nan	48	
t̆iḱói	all over, every place: ḱódom t̆iḱóidi "all over the land"	RD	tikoi′	172	
t̆ikpin	believe (what you hear), believe by hearing: t̆ikpinma'ankano nik "Believe what you hear from me!"	RD	tik′pin	40	
t̆ikte	a short ways, a little ways along, a little bit (adverb)	WS, FC	t̆ikte		
t̆iktedoi	a certain distance upwards	RD	tik′tetedoi	176	
t̆iktein	by a little bit: bénekto poḱóm t̆iktein háhadoichet, ᴍyéḱan. "In the morning when the sun had risen a little bit, he came."	RD	tiktein	56	
t̆ikteḱóidi	in a place a certain distance away: ᴍḱóiyebisim ᴍḱóiyebisim t̆ikteḱóidi noḱóm noḱá wehétkitḱan "he kept going, kept going, and then hung up a quiver of arrows in a place a distance away."	RD	tik′tetekoidi	224	
t̆iktenaki	for a short time, for a certain time, after a little while	RD	tik′tenaki	176	
t̆ikteno	a ways, some distance, a certain distance: ᴍnóm kaním t̆ikteno, ᴍᴍḱí hᴍbó okítḱan. "after having gone a ways, he arrived at his house."	RD	tik′teno	224	
t̆iktete	a little way	WS	t̆iktete		
t̆iktetedikno	to be almost there	RD	tik′tetedikno	120	
t̆iktetedoinodi	after a little distance on the way up: t̆iktetedoinodi 'donínup niḱí wachákidi,' achói'am. "On the way up, he said 'hold on to my belt!'"	RD	tik′tetedoinodi	122	
t̆iktsteḱoi	go a little way, go off a certain distance	WS, RD	t̆ikteteḱoj		

Maidu	English	Source	Source Spelling	Page	Other Spellings
t̆ıktetek̇óidi	in a place a little further away	RD	tik'tekoidi	224	
t̆ıktetenan	from a distance, from a certain distance	RD	tik'tetenan	216	
t̆ıktetepin	go a little ways	RD	tik'tetepin	168	
t̆ıktetepindi	a little further on	RD	tik'tetepindi	170	
t̆ıktetéye	be a little ways out on one's way (toward), be just starting along on one's way (toward): ᴍnóyedom t̆ıktetéyechet wokók̇an "After going a little ways, she got tired."	RD	tiktete'ye	84	
tilítili	katydid	WS	tilítili		
tímsawi	wild peppermint	WS	tímsawi		
tipi	Fall mushroom (JD), type of edible mushroom (PM-M)	JD	typi (JD, tee-pee (PM-M)	23	
tisák	recognize	RD	tisak'	42, 116	
t̆ısíp	go out in a bunch or flock	WS	t̆ısíp		
t̆ısíye	emerge, come out in a bunch	WS	t̆ısíje		
tíswili	low-limbed	RD	tiswili	64	
tít	green, blue	WS	tít		
titipi	pepper, spice: síwsiwpem titipi "black pepper"	FC-E, FC-R			tetipi (FC-R)
títtit	green, blue	WS	títtit		
títtitkᴍ	Belding squirrel (PM-M), a kind of ground squirrel (WS)	PM-M, WS	títtitky (WS), ti-tit-cum (PM-M)		
títtitpe	green	FC			
t̆ıw	fog, mist (noun)	WS	t̆ıw		
t̆ıwdoi	rise (as fog) from the ground	RD	ti'udoi	34	
tiwí	TV	FC			
tiwí wat̆á	satellite dish	FC			
tiwít̆ati	turn on the TV	FC			
t̆ıwki	foggy	RD	tīu'ki	6, 34	
t̆ıwkit	fog up	WS	t̆ıwkit		
t̆ıwkiti	fog (noun)	WS	t̆ıwkiti		
t̆ıyᴍk	move, shake (intransitive): nidᴍkᴍm, t̆ıyᴍkmendom, hónwenuwéwk̇as "I alone, by not moving, managed to survive all this time."	RD, WS	tiyök (RD), t̆ıjýk (WS)	24, 42, 222	
t̆ıyᴍkti	make (something) move around	RD	tiyökti	24, 134	
t̆ıyᴍyᴍk	move a little, shake (as the earth)	WS, RD	t̆ıjýjyk (WS), tiyöyök (RD)	160	
tíyani	king snake, milk snake	HM	ti'-yah-ne		
tochíl	burn (something) down, like a house	RD	totsil'	230	
tochóno	set fire to the land (as a controlled burn)	FC			
to'éskᴍ	towhee (bird)	HM	to-es'-kum		

Maidu	English	Source	Source Spelling	Page	Other Spellings
Tohánom	place name NE of Quincy between American Valley and Butt Valley, #36 on FR map. Along the East Branch of N. Feather River. See map 2 in Appendix 5.	FR		370-371	
ťohóni	sucker fish (HM), sucker (RR-SW), a kind of fish with many bones (WS)	WS, HM, RR-SW	ťohón (WS), to-ho-nim (HM)		
ťoi	be weak	RD	toi	100	
ťoi	physically weak	WS	ťoj		
tóihlalaino	dance and prance around	RD	toih'lalaino	86	
ťoiyí	weakness, illness	RD	t!ōiyi'	130	
ťok	sharp	WS	ťok		
tókda	to outrun, beat (in a race), leave (someone) behind, take off without someone	RD	tok'da	46, 128, 176, 210	
tókdati'us	be outrun, lag behind, be beaten in a race: póchodem máidⱥm tetét pídom tókdati'usmenchoi'a "bat man did not lose the race by very much"	RD	tok'datius	212	
tókdato	foot race (noun)	RD	tok'dato	210, 212	
tókdato	race (verb), race against, run a race	WS, RD, FC	tókdato		
tókdatokⱥm	racer	WS	tókdatoky		
tókdatokⱥm kawáyu	racehorse	WS	tókdatokym kawáju		
tókdatoto	outrun each other	RD	tok'datoto	212	
tókdoi	raise	WS	tókdoj		
ťókmen	dull, blunt	WS	ťókmen		
ťókmul	be dull (knife)	RD	tok'mul	58	
tókno	have the hand under (someone), reach under	WS	tókno		
ťókpem bosó	sharp obsidian	FC			
ťóktiti	sharpen (something) a little	RD	tok'titi	58	
tókwaito	open up (as the hand)	WS	tókwajto		
tolí	leg	FC, WS			tol (WS)
tolím bⱥmí	shinbone	WS	tolím bymí		
tólkupem	having legs: lalám tólkupem "long-legged"	FC			
tóllalaino	take longer strides	WS	tóllalajno		
ťoló	shovel, spoon	WS	ťoló		
ťoló eskochim máidⱥ	Paiute	FC-E			
ťolóma	bobcat	FC-E			
tólomma	Paiute	FC			
ťolómmam máidⱥ	Paviotso, Paiute	WS, FC	ťolómmam májdy		
tómdan	clang, hit with a bonking sound	WS	tómdan		
tóni	basket, container (could be a mortar), for ritual items: ítum tóni "illness container"	RD-NM, PM-M	tō'ni		

240

Maidu	English	Source	Source Spelling	Page	Other Spellings
topái	set fire to (something)	RD, WS	topai' (RD), topáj (WS)	204, 228	
tópanu	attend to (work): kᴧlóknonom mᴧséki tawáli tópanuḱan "the women attended to their work."	RD	top'anū	108	
tosáidom máidᴧ	tall-standing people (from Indian Valley) (FC), Indian Valley people (FR1)	FC			tasaidum, tosaidum
tosí	north	FC-E, FC-T			
Tosí Ḱoyó	place name for Taylorsville (FC), Indian Valley (WS, LM), #9 on LM map. See maps 1 and 5 in Appendix 5.	WS, FC, LM, MSOP	tosím kojó (WS), tosinkojo (LM), Tosi Koyo (MSOP)		Tosíkoyo, Tasíkoyo, Tosím Ḱoyó
Tosí Ḱoyóm Sewí	place name for the part of Indian Creek passing through Taylorsville (DT). See map 5 in Appendix 5.	DT		37	
Tosím Bo	place name for a trail going east-west along the southern end of Indian Valley between Crescent Mills and Taylorsville. Arlington Rd. See map 5 in Appendix 5.	MSOP, FC	Yosim Bo		Yosim Bo
tosína	to the north	FC-E			
tosopim piwí	a medicinal root that could be smoked for headaches or depression. Could be inserted into gambling bones. Also used to make storms go another way.	HLME	tosopim pewim		
ťoť	thin (in dimension)	WS	ťoť, ťoťó		ťoť, ťóťťoť (WS)
ťotimén	don't be weak, be brave, be strong	RD	totimen'	46	tóttimen (WS)
ťotimenwetí	without being weak, don't be weak	RD	totimenweti'	46	
ťóttati	carp (fish)	PM-M	thot-ta-tem		tátate
tótto	the small, low-growing variety of manzanita which is found in the high mountains	WS	tótto		
ťóťťoť	thin (in dimension)	WS	ťóťťoť		ťoťó (WS)
towáni	gray pine, digger pine, pinenuts from the gray pine tree	FC, WS, FC-E	towán		
towánim chá	gray pine ("nut tree"), digger pine tree	WS, FC	towánim ćá		
towndi	into town, in town	FC			
towóikit	to reach, get as far as	RD	towoi'kit	46	
toyá	candle, lamp, light, flame	WS, FC	tojá		
toyá	illuminate, light a light	WS	tojá		
toyákᴧ	be lighted	FC			

Maidu	English	Source	Source Spelling	Page	Other Spellings
toyákm	candle, lamp, light fixture	WS, FC	tojáky		
toyákm toyákmti	turn on a light	FC			
toyákmtikm	light switch, pilot light, etc. (that which causes light)	FC			
toyákmtipe	lights, headlights: mínki kalétam toyákmtipem bukúitipem kmkán "your headlights are (turned) off"	FC			
toyákit	light a candle, lamp, light	WS, FC	tojákit		
toyés	be awakened by something, have sleep disturbed	WS	tojés		
tu	burn	FC			
tú	native sunflowers (wyethia)	FR1	tu		tm
ṭú	fence, dam, barrier: ṕakám ṭú "barrier made of brush"	WS, FC-T	ṭú		
ṭú tawál	build a fence	WS	ṭú tawál		
ṭúchik	dam up, dam (a river)	WS, WST-DW	ṭúćik		
túi	sleep (verb)	WS	túj		
túiboduk	sleep lightly, hardly be able to sleep	WS, RD	tújboduk (WS), tū'ibodök	RD 96	túibodmk
túibosno	sleep soundly	FC			
túibusno	be sound asleep	WS	tújbusno		
túicheno	wake up: túichenoḱa mínsmm? "Are you all awake?"	WS, RD	tújćeno (WS), tū'itseno	38	
túichenonommni	wake-up time	FC-E			
túichenonomawe	let's be alert and aware	RD	tū'itsenō'nomawe	110	
túichenonopai	be awake, be alert and aware	RD	tū'itsenopai'	110	
túichenotoye	go around half-asleep	RD	tū'itsenotoye	218	
túichikm	nightgown	WS	tújćiky		
túichinukm	bedcovers	WS	tújćinuky		
túikm	bed	WS, FC-R	tújky		
túikmm butú	eyebrow	WS	tújkym butú		
túikmm máidm	sleepy person	FC-T			
túikinu	be sleeping	RD	tū'ikinu	70	
túikit	go to sleep, go to bed	WS	tújkit		
túikitbos	be in bed for the night, be all tucked in	WST	tújkitbos	52:15	
túiḱoi	go off somewhere to sleep	RD	tū'ikoi	78	
túimape	lodging, place to sleep, where (someone) will sleep	WS	tújmape		
túimehme	be somewhat sleepy	WS	tújmehme		
túimei	be sleepy: túimeiḱas "I am sleepy"	FC			túime
túimeninu	doze	WS	tújmeninu, tujmenínu		tuimenínu (WS)

Maidu	English	Source	Source Spelling	Page	Other Spellings
túiti	put to sleep, put (children) to bed	WS, WST	tújti	52:15	
túitoye	go to sleep	RD	tū'itoye	104, 206	
túitoyewéḱoi	go off to sleep	RD	tūi'toyē'wekoi	168	
túiyidi	sleep with (someone)	RD	tū'yidi	84	
tuiyím mé	be sleepy	WS	tujím mé		
túiyiwol	go to sleep sitting up, try to sleep, sleep uncomfortably: káipe wi'í ma'át, túiyiwolchoi'a "without any dinner even, they slept poorly."	RD	tū'yiwol	216	
tuk	hole (from Nisenan)	FC			
tulí	shrimp	FC-T			tⱮlí
tulúli	pine squirrel	FC			tⱮlᴧlⱮ (WS)
tulúpi	pintail duck	HM	too-loo'-pim		
Túm Ḱoyó	place name for a small valley at the head of Clear Creek, a tributary of Spanish Creek. Named for the sunflowers (wyethia) that grow here (FR-TE). See map 2 in Appendix 5.	FR1, FR-TE			
túmbakⱮ	mule's ear (plant), sunflower, wyethia mollis (can eat seeds)	FC, JD	tu·mbokon, tu·mbokum	45	tumboko, tumboku, tumbaka
TúmbakⱮm	place name for Shaffer Mountain, #36 on LM map, # 35 on HLME map 3. The name refers to sunflowers (túmbakⱮ). See map 1, Appendix 5.	LM, HLME	tambaken (LM), Tymbakam (HLME)		tᴧmbakⱮ
tumétu	tomato (from English)	WS	tumétu		tⱮmétⱮ (FC)
túmilmili	dragonfly	HM	too'-mil-mil'-lim		
tumímya	rain cloud	RD	tumim'ya	210	
tumyedói	drift, move as a cloud	RD	tumyedoi'	210, 212	
tún	growl (verb): aním wépam sⱮm nik túndom kⱮḱán "That dog is growling at me."	FC-T			tᴧn (FC-R), tⱮn (WS)
ťúno	trap (noun)	RD	t'ū'no	56	
ťúp	spit (verb)	WS, FC	ťúp		
túpinpin	jump off	FC	tupinpin		tᴧpinpin (WS)
túpmitno	dive in	RD	tup'mitno	80	tᴧpmitno
túpno	hop along	RD	tup'no	72	tᴧpno
túpnoye	hop around	FC-E, RD	tup'noye		tᴧpnoye (WS)
túpnoyetikⱮ	what makes (someone) hop around	FC-E			
ťúppai	spit on	WS	ťúppaj		
ťúppaito	spit on one another	WS	ťúppajto		
ťúpsip	spit out	WS	ťúpsip		
túptupe	Cooper hawk	HM	toop-too-pe		
túpyewe	jump back, jump backwards	FC			
ťuťú	bird's nest	WS, RD	ťuťú, tūtū'	7	ťᴧťᴧ (FC)

Maidu	English	Source	Source Spelling	Page	Other Spellings
tutukⱭm cha	red fir tree, silvertip fir tree	JD	tu·tukumćam	28	
túwei	preach, orate, tell stories of long ago	WS	túwej, tújwej, túweje, tújweje		túywey, túweye, túyweye
túweikⱭ	prayer, orator, storyteller	WS	túwejky		
túweye	pray	FC			
túweye	prayer	FC			
ťúye	set a trap	RD	t'ū'ye	54	
ťúyeti	fix a trap	RD	tūyeti	54	
ťúyetiti	fix/repair a trap, set up a trap (for someone)	RD	t'ū'yetiti	54	
u	other, opposite	WS	ʔu		
ú	and also, too, accompanying: kⱭlóknono yépsⱭ u "women and men too"	WS, RD	ʔú (WS), ū (RD)	102	
ú	be located, be somewhere, be there, exist there (things): solím úma'aḱan "there will be songs" pⱭlᴧm om bᴧdóikitkⱭdi uḱán "A round rock, on which he sits, is located there."	RD	ū	25, 60, 114	
uchándi	on the other side	WS	ʔućándi		
ucháni	the other side, the opposite side	WS	ʔućáni		
udó	in these times, even now, to this day (adverb): machói'am uním bᴧwom máidⱭm uním ḱódoidi udó "apparently this wind man remains in this country to this day"	RD	ūdo'	138	
Úho	place name for area near Indian Creek, NW of Nadam Ḱoyó: Forgay Point. This was written ooh-ho, which might have been a mistake for Ochó. See map 5 in Appendix 5.	MSOP	ooh-ho		
ú'ichan	other side: ú'ichan béibⱭ mⱭ mⱭyákatimaḱán "they will also do it the same way on the other side"	RD	ū'itsan	64	
ú'ichan...ú'ichan	on the other side of: ú'ichan sewí ú'ichan hⱭbóm kⱭḱán "on the other side of the river is a house."	RD	ū'itsan...ū'itsan	124	
uiyí	house, building	FC			uyí
úkit	abandon (something), leave behind: yak úkitḱan. "They abandoned the boat."	RD	ukit	60	
úk'uk	whine, whimper (as a dog)	WS	ʔúkʔuk		

Maidu	English	Source	Source Spelling	Page	Other Spellings
úm	together, together with: nik mᴧném níkdi úm bísdom kᴧkán "My mother is living with me."	WST		10:1, 60:64	
umén	not exist: ka'áwinim kútt'ᴧt'ᴧm uményakken. "that kind of bird might not exist."	RD	ūmen'	6	
úmmoto	come together, gather (intransitive), join a gathering	FC			ᴧmmoto
úmmototo	come together (group), meet together	FC			ᴧmmototo
umpétililla	small brown lizard	HM	um-pe'-til-lil-la		
una'inu	chokecherry	FC			
uní	place (noun), this place, here, the place where the story character is	RD, FC	ūni'	30, 86	
uní	this, this one	WS	ʔuní		
uní maiká?	Do you mean this? (showing something)	RD	ūni maika'	206	
uní wóinan	from now on, henceforth	WS	ʔuní wójnan		
uní woyím	from now on, henceforth	WS	ʔuní wojím		
unícho	these two	WS	ʔuníćo		
unídi	here (FC), right here (RR-EP)	FC, RR-EP			
uním bomó	these (people), this bunch, this group	WS	ʔuním bomó		
uním kulúdi	tonight	WS	ʔunim kulúdi		
unína hedénna	nearby: unína hedénna yakwékan "it seemed to come from close by"	RD	uni'na heden'na	86	
unína mapí	come here!	WST	ʔunína mapí	54	
unínan	from here on	FC			
unínandi	from in this place	FC			
unínante	from/around this place (RD), around here (WS)	RD, WS	ūnī'nante (RD), ʔunínante (WS)	26, 21	
úno	divorce (noun)	FC			ýᴧno
upédi	in this place	RD	upē'di	28	
upupupe	blue currant, ribes nevadense	PM-M	u-poop-poop-em		yu'pupᴧ
uschenu	look into oneself, look inside oneself	FC-T			
úspᴧdu	bull frog	FC			
ustabaku	black wasp	FC, PM-M	usta-bacum		
ustu	cemetery	FC			
Ustuma	place name for Nevada City	FC			
úsu	elder brother: as a kinship term, this word must have a prefix, either mᴧ, nik, or min (see Mountain Maidu Grammar, Lesson 6 for more details)	WS	ʔúsu		
uswúlulu	ghost (FC), devil (WS)	FC			ᴧswálulu (WS)

Maidu	English	Source	Source Spelling	Page	Other Spellings
utí	put, relocate (something), leave (something somewhere): yákni hasípdom, utíkan. "Getting out of the boat, they left it there."	RD	ūti'	60, 136, 168, 17	
úti	acorn	FC			
utíbos	put out the last: wéye utíbosweten "having spoken the last words"	RD	utī'bos	192	
útim cha	oak tree	FC			
utípedi	where something was put: mínḱi utípedi "the place where you put it"	RD	ūti'pedi	114	
utíyo	to place (something), put: 'nik mínḱi wólsadi utíyopi,' aḱán aním ḱuḱúm wéyedom. "'Put me in your pocket,' said that string, speaking."	FC, FC-T			
uyí	house, shed, small structure (WS), modern house, building (FC): úyi bísk ͏mm máidm͏m "stay-at-home man"	WS, FC, RD	ʔuj (WS), úyi (RD)	108	uy (WS), uiyí (FC), úyi (RD)
úyina	toward the house	FC, RD	ū'ina (RD)		ú'ina
uyúk	stay overnight, spend the night	WS, FC	ʔujúk		m͏yúk (FC-R)
uyúkakitk͏m	camping place	RD	ūyūk'akitkö	120	
uyúkit	camp for the night	RD	ūyū'kit	230	
uyúkk͏mm kaléta	RV, camping car	FC			
uyúkkakit	set up camp, camp for the night	RD	ūyūk'akit	68, 120, 188, 226, 232	
uyúkkakitwonodi	at the place where they had camped: m͏kóichoi'a m͏ḱóiyebisi uyúkkakitwonodi m͏díknochoi'a. "He left and kept going until he arrived at the place where they had camped."	RD	ūyūk'akitwonodi	236	
uyúkkit	camp for the night (in a place)	WS	ʔujúkkit		
w͏mchadai	twist (verb), braid (verb)	FC			
w͏md͏ḿm	a throw (noun)	WS	wydým		
w͏md͏ḿm	toss, knock down (RD), throw (WS)	RD, WS	wödöm' (RD), wydým (WS)	118	
w͏md͏ḿm'͏mheyno	throw (something) along after (someone)	WS	wydýmʔyhejno		
w͏md͏ḿmchono	throw (someone) off (as a horse would do)	WS	wydýmćono		
w͏md͏ḿmdadawino	throw (this and that) off	WS	wydýmdadawino		
w͏md͏ḿmdaw	cast (something) off, toss (something) away (RD), throw (something) off (as clothes) (WS)	RD, WS	wödöm'dau (RD), wydýmdaw (WS)	80, 170	
w͏md͏ḿmdawino	throw (something) off	WS	wydýmdawino		
w͏md͏ḿmdawto	throw (something) down	FC-E			

Maidu	English	Source	Source Spelling	Page	Other Spellings
wɤdɤmdo	throw (something) towards, into	RD	wödöm'do	170	
wɤdɤminnokakínu	knock (something big) down, blow over a tree (wind)	RD	wödöm'inokakīn'u	138	
wɤdɤmino	throw (something) down into	RD	wödöm'ino	198, 204	
wɤdɤmit	throw down in	RD	wödöm'it	200	
wɤdɤmkit	throw (something) down	RD, WS	wödöm'kit (RD), wydýmkit (WS)	198	
wɤdɤmḱoi	throw away	WS	wydýmḱoj		
wɤdɤmḱoino	throw (something) down an incline	WS	wydýmḱojno		
wɤdɤmmit	throw (something) into	WS	wydýmmit		
wɤdɤmmitno	throw (something) down an incline	WS	wydýmmitno		
wɤdɤmno	go along throwing (something)	RD	wödöm'no	170	wɤtɤmno
wɤdɤmsito	throw (something) across	WS	wydýmsito		
wɤdɤmsitopin	throw (something) across towards	WS	wydýmsitopin		
wɤdáktemáldoi	cause to slip and fall, throw (someone) off balance	RD	wödak'temaldoi	58	
wɤhúlpe	heavy	FC			
wɤḱɤk	scatter (dry material), sprinkle (dry material)	WS	wyḱýk		
wɤkɤ́mchik	tie shut with: ḱuḱú wɤkɤ́mchikpe "tied shut with string"	RD	wököm'tsik	128	
wɤḱɤ́s	cut	WS	wyḱýs, wyḱýt		wɤḱɤ́t
wɤḱɤ́skɤ	scissors	WS	wyḱýsky		
wɤḱɤ́sto	cut (something), shave	WS	wyḱýsto		
wɤḱɤ́stokɤ	razor	WS	wyḱýstoky		
wɤḱɤ́stokɤm máidɤ	barber	WS	wyḱýstokym májdy		
wɤḱɤ́t	cut, slice	WS, FC	wyḱýt, wyḱýs (WS), wököt' (RD)	60	wɤḱɤ́s
wɤḱɤ́tchono	cut off the end of (something), cut through (something cylindrical, like a neck)	WS	wyḱýtćono (WS), wököt'sono (RD)	60	
wɤḱɤ́tdaw	cut off	WS	wyḱýtdaw		
wɤḱɤ́tyo	slice (verb)	WS	wyḱýtjo		
wɤ́kdi	together, in one place, as one	WS, RD, FC	wýkdi (WS), wök'di (RD)	RD 78	
wɤkdi maháye	bring together in unity	FC			
wɤkdimoto	marry, come together (as a couple)	RD	wök'dimotō, wökdi'moto	50	wɤkdímoto
wɤkdimotolut'	gather (things) together in one place	RD	wök'dimotōlut	32	
wɤkkánuhadóino	become one with (something) and let it carry along upwards	RD	wökan'uhadoi'no	34	
wɤ́n	turn (verb)	WS	wýn		
wɤnɤ́doi	travel around in a circle	RD	wönö'doi	230	
wɤnɤ́inɤichono	travel back and forth, travel in a zigzag	RD	wönöi'nöitsono	8	

Maidu	English	Source	Source Spelling	Page	Other Spellings
wʌ́ndʌ	patch	WS	wýndy		
wʌ́ndʌi	change directions, go in another direction (WS), change one's ways (FC)	WS, FC	wýndyj		
wʌ́ndoi	turn off (from a road), turn aside	WS	wýndoj		
wʌ́ndoikʌ	turning off place	WS	wýndojky		
wʌ́nnʌnʌi	turn around (in an axis-like sense)	WS	wýnnynyj		
wʌ́nnʌnʌiḱoi	turn around toward (something)	WS	wýnnynyjḱoj		
wʌ́nnʌnʌiḱoiti	turn (something) around toward (something)	WS	wýnnynyjḱojti		
wʌ́nnʌnʌinoye	turn around and around (as a windmill)	WS	wýnnynyjnoje		
wʌ́nnoye	turn around	WS	wýnnoje		
wʌ́nnoyeti	turn (something) around (as a vehicle)	WS	wýnnojeti		
wʌ́nťeťenoye	swing round and round, curl	FC-T, FC-E			wánťeťe-noye (WS)
wʌpʌ́lʌmnoye	whirl (oneself) round and round	WS	wypýlymnoje		
wʌpʌ́lam	whirl oneself around	WS	wypýlam, wypýlym		wʌpʌ́lʌm
wʌpʌ́lamnoye	whirl oneself round and round	WS	wypýlamnoje, wypýlymnoje		wʌpʌ́lʌmnoye
wʌpʌ́lamto	roll over and around (like a horse)	WS	wypýlamto, wypýlymto		wʌpʌ́lʌmto
wʌpʌ́pʌlamto	roll (on the ground)	RD	wöpö'pölamto	38	
wʌsʌ́	clear up (weather) (No subject noun. ḱodo is object of this verb rather than subject): ḱodo wʌsʌ́dom, yahálutḱan "clearing up, it was beautiful weather."	RD	wösö'	170, 196	
wʌ́sʌḱoi	"go away" to a dog, shoo!	FC			
wʌsʌtikʌ	lid	FC-R			
wʌ́sdoino	float up, lift (like fog)	RD	wös'doino	34	
wʌsíp	float out	RD	wösī', wös'ip	38	
wʌ́skʌtḱʌt	hop with a certain skipping movement, said to be characteristic of Coyote; swing the tail while hopping Coyote-style	WS	wýskytḱyt		
wʌ́slʌ	sucker fish	WS	wýsly		
wʌ́ssa	depart in haste	WS	wýssa		
wʌ́ssasip	get out, exit hastily as a result of having been ordered to leave	WS	wýssasip		
wʌsuisúikit	deflate, lose momentum, run out of energy	FC, FC-E			wusuisúikit
wʌsuiťakʌ	a shade	FC, FC-E			
wʌťʌ́i	tear, rip	WS	wyťýj		
wʌťʌ́ikitbos	tear to pieces	WS	wyťýjkitbos		
wʌťʌ́iwaito	tear apart	WS	wyťýjwajto		

Maidu	English	Source	Source Spelling	Page	Other Spellings
wᴧtᴧ́mi	thundering: wᴧtᴧ́mi waisím wéyechoi'a. "Thundering, the old man spoke."	RD	wötöm'i	156	
wᴧtᴧ́mtᴧmi	thunder	RD	wötöm'tömi	156	wutúmtumi (FC)
wᴧtᴧmwidótnoye'ᴧno	go tossing debris around (like wind would do)	RD	wötömwidot'noyeöno	134	
wᴧtᴧ́swoye	noisily make one's way towards (somewhere)	RD	wötös'woye	216	
wᴧtᴧ́'uchono	fly off with something	RD	wötö'utsono	56	
wá	fungus, mushroom, toadstool	WS	wá		
wá	throw a lot of material	WS	wá		
wa dáte	large, tender white mushroom which tastes like pork, bracket fungus (polyporaceae)	JD, PM-M	wa'date (JD), wa-dá-te (PM-M)	24	
wa wuku	shelf fungus that grows on white fir and black oak trees	JD	wawuku	24	
wa'á	scrape the outer surface of stems to prepare them for basket-weaving	WS	waʔá		
wa'ái	break (verb)	FC			wáye (WS)
wa'áipe	broken	FC			
wa'áiti	break, split (the sucker for baskets)	FC			
wa'áti	to "size" sticks for basket-making	FC			
wabálto	personal Indian name of a brother of Tom Young	WS	wabálto		
wachákᴧ	belt	FC			wicháka
wacháki	belt: wachákidi "in or under the belt"	RD	watsa'ki	58, 62	
wachákinu	be belted on: saláwi mᴧkí wachákinupe déktikᴧm "his rabbit-skin blanket, which was belted on, was wet."	RD	watsa'kinu	116	
wáchopin	throw (a lot) over into	WS	wáćopin		
wádᴧm	throw a lot of material	WS	wádym		
wadᴧ́m	a throw (noun)	WS	wadým, wydým		wᴧdᴧ́m
wadᴧ́m	throw (verb)	WS	wadým, wydým		wᴧdᴧ́m
wádᴧm'ᴧheyno	throw (things) along after; throw (something) along after (someone)	WS	wádymʔyhejno, wadýmʔyhejno		wadᴧ́m'ᴧheyno
wadᴧ́mchono	throw (someone) off (as a horse would do)	WS	wadýmćono		
wadᴧ́mdadawino	throw (this and that) off	WS	wadýmdadawino		
wádᴧmdaw	throw (a lot) out	WS	wádymdaw		
wadᴧ́mdaw	throw (something) off (as clothes)	WS	wadýmdaw		
wadᴧ́mdawino	throw (something) off	WS	wadýmdawino		
wádᴧmit	throw/pour down into	RD	wādömit	66	wadᴧ́mmit (WS)
wádᴧmkit	throw (a lot) down	WS	wádymkit		wadᴧ́mkit
wadᴧ́mkit	throw (something) down	WS	wádymkit		wᴧdᴧ́mkit
wadᴧ́mḱoi	throw (something) away	WS	wadýmḱoj		
wádᴧmḱoi	throw (a lot) away	WS	wádymḱoj		wadᴧ́mḱoi

Maidu	English	Source	Source Spelling	Page	Other Spellings
wadᴧmkoino	throw (something) down an incline	WS	wadýmkojno		
wádᴧmmit	throw (a lot) into	WS	wádymmit		
wadᴧmmit	throw (something) into	WS	wadýmmit		wádᴧmmit (RD)
wadᴧmmitno	throw (something) down an incline	WS	wadýmmitno		
wádᴧmpai	throw (a lot) on	WS	wádympaj		
wádᴧmsito	throw (a lot) across	WS	wádymsito		
wadᴧmsito	throw (something) across	WS	wadýmsito		
wadᴧmsitopin	throw (something) across towards	WS	wadýmsitopin		
wádᴧmye	throw away	RD	wā′dömye	146	
wadá	health	FC			weda
wadá	healthy, well, get well	WS	wadá		
wadá	to dodge, get away, stay alive: hútuwonom ma'át wadádom anídi bísk̓an. "Even having gone crazy, staying alive, he lives there." hénuk̓an wadák̓an mᴧ́'am. "He ran away, dodged, shooting the whole time."	RD	wadā′	190, 208, 224	
wadáhuye	dodge (a pursuer) as one runs	RD	wada′hūyē	224	
wadáhuye'ᴧpin	dodge (a pursuer) as one runs	RD	wada′hūyeöpin′	224	
wadákdakᴧ	miner's lettuce	FC			
wadámenhelu	perhaps not get well	WS	wadámenhelu		
wádamino	spill out	RD	wā′damino	66	
wadán	fall forward headlong	WS	wadán		
wadánkit	fall forward headlong	WS	wadánkit		
wadápᴧno	go along carrying a sack	RD	wadap′öno	132	
wadápi	sack, bag	WS, FC	wadápi		
wadápyo	sack up (things), put up or can (fruit)	WS	wadápjo		
wadásto	split a long object	WS	wadásto		
wadáti	cure, make well	WS	wadáti		
wadáti'us	make oneself healthy, cure oneself	FC-E			
wádaw	dump, throw out (as garbage or dirty water)	WS	wádaw		
wádikno	throw onto	WS	wádikno		
wahéno	waste (verb)	RD	wahe′no	44	
wahík̓ᴧ	river hawthorn (crategus rivularis)	HM	wah-hi′-kum		
wai	a wild potato ("Indian potato") which was roasted and eaten	JD	waj	36	
waihá	a kind of berry resembling the serviceberry, but much rarer. The bush has many black thorns	WS	wajhá		
wáiheno	wasteful, extravagant	WS	wájheno		

250

Maidu	English	Source	Source Spelling	Page	Other Spellings
wáihenosape	one who is habitually extravagant, habitually extravagant (adj)	FC-E			
wai'ó	skunk	WS	wajʔó		wái'o (FC), woiyó (RD)
wáipolo	a mountain plant with dark, marble-shaped roots and white flowers. The roots must be boiled before they are edible.	WS	wájpolo		
waisí	old man	FC, RD	waisim'	156	wáisi (FC)
wáiwotopin	pour over towards by magic power	WS	wájwotopin		
wáiyo	throw (things) into (somewhere)	RD		64	wáyo
wáiyuyuk	yip (as a dog or coyote)	FC-E			
wak	cry, weep	WS, FC	wak		wák (FC)
Wakmdat	place name for Grass Valley	FC			
wakmdíkno	arrive crying	WST-RP	wák ʔydíkno	66:30	
waká	meat, muscle	FC, WS	waḱ		waḱ (WS)
wakbósno	cry continuously	FC			
wakdm	pied-billed grebe (water bird)	PM-M	wak-dum		
wákda	to dry (meat)	RD	wak'da	106, 228	
wákinu	be thrown down	RD	wā'kinu	126	
wákit	put down into, throw down (WS), come down: ókpai wákitdom "sunshine coming down" (FC)	WS, FC	wákit		
wakkmléw	keep crying over a woman	RD	wak küle'u	204	
wáknoyesa	go around wailing, go around complaining all the time	FC			
wákpai	to bark (like a dog)	FC			wékpai
wákpai'us	cry to oneself	FC			
wáksape	crybaby, always crying	FC			
wáksapem hámsim chá	valley oak tree	WS	wáksapem hámsim ćá		
wáksi	crane	FC			
wákti	make (someone) cry	FC			
wáktihudoi	almost make (someone) cry	RD	wak'tihūdoi	92	
wákwakno	cry out repeatedly	RD	wak'wakno	108	
wákwaknonu	keep crying	WS	wákwaknonu		
wákwaknu	keep crying out	RD	wak'waknu	104	
walád	personal Indian name of Cap Singer. He was also called póksino	WS	walád		
walási	buckskin knotted string for keeping a day-count	WS, RD	walás (WS), walas'i (RD)	208	walás (WS)
walátkm	rock roller (for grinding)	WS	walátky		
waláw	exceed, be more than	WS	waláw		
waláwdmkbe	more than: hadá waláwdmkbe: "taller than"	RD	walau'dökbe	46	

Maidu	English	Source	Source Spelling	Page	Other Spellings
waláwti	more than	WS	waláwti		
walét	winnow	WS	walét		
walétkṁ	winnowing basket	WS	walétky		
wálim cha	lodgepole pine tree	JD	walyméa	29	wálum cha (FC)
walú	sterile, incapable of reproduction	WS	walú		
wálukinu	be immobilized, be impotent, be incapacitated	RD	wal'ukinū	180	
wálum cha	lodgepole pine tree	FC			
wámit	pour (dry material) into (a container)	WS	wámit		
wanṁn	roll of maple, redbud or fern roots, rolled up like a doughnut for use in weaving. Material for making baskets is stored in this form.	WS	wanýn		
wáno	spill (verb)	WS	wáno		
wánpin	throw down into	WS	wánpin		
wánťeťenoye	swing round and round in dancing (like Coyote)	WS	wánťeťenoje		
wapṁn	hopper basket	WS-MP	wapýn		
Wapúnbem	place name for Wapúnbem Hill in Indian Valley. See map 5 in Appendix 5.	FR1, MSOP			
wás	be angry, growl, forbid	WS, HY	wás, wasó		wasó
wás	do (something) poorly, be doing poorly: kṁkás máisem nik chebṁ wásdom "they might see me, that I am doing poorly"	WST	wás	54:23	
wasṁdaw	go off angry	RD	wasö'dau	162	
wasṁkoi	go away angry	RD	wasö'koi	28, 98, 162, 230	
wasṁkoiwonoda	angry departure (noun): wi'ípedi okítḱan mṁposíki wasṁkoiwonoda okítḱan "he came home to an empty place, he came home after his cousin's angry departure."	RD	wasö'koiwonoda	164	
wasá	bad, evil, harmful: hesí wasá "something that is bad, something that is evil" wasám máidṁ "a bad man"	WS	wasá (WS), wasā (RD)	130	
wasá	be bad, be (morally) wrong: wasáḱan "it's no good."	RD, FC	wasā'	48	
wasá	wrong: mṁ ka'ánkano wasá wéyedom. "You are saying it wrong. You are speaking of it incorrectly. You are wrong on that."	RD	wasā	48	

Maidu	English	Source	Source Spelling	Page	Other Spellings
wasá'ape	ugly	RD	wasā'apem	84	
wasácheda	regain one's temper, stop being angry	WS	wasáćeda		
wasácheti	look bad, be ugly	WS, FC	wasátćeti		wasátcheti
wasachetípe	ugly	FC			wasát-chetipe
wasáchetípe	bad-looking, ugly	WS, FC	wasátćetipe		wasát-chetipe
wasádoi	get tired, get worn out	WS	wasádoj		
wasám chewé	not like much	WS	wasám ćewé		
wasám kᴍlé	wild woman	BC			
wasám máidᴍ	wild man	BC	wa sem ka lem		
wasám nedí	bad dreams	FC	wa sem maidum		
wasám yomém kᴍlé	witch	FC			
wasánu	be bad, wrong: wasánukan "It's not right."	RD	wasā'nu	9	
wasánu	evil (noun)	WS	wasánu		
wasása	some kind of (follows noun): kútťᴍťᴍm wasása chedóm, nisé níkopam wéyekan, 'uním kᴍkán ka'áwinim' "Seeing some kind of bird, my grandfather said, 'this is such-and-such.'"	WST	wasása	52:17	
wasása	thing(s), stuff, materials, ingredients, food, something	WS, RD, FC	wasása (WS), wasā'sa (RD)	154, 194	
wasásoti	cause strife	FC-E			
wasát	badly	WS	wasát		
wasát che	dislike: mᴍm máidᴍ wasát chekás "I don't like that guy."	WS	wasát će...		
wasát chenó	be ugly	WS	wasát ćeno		
wasát hᴍbᴍk	grieve, feel bad	WS	wasát hybýk		
wasát yatí'us	do badly for oneself, mess up one's life	WS	wasát jatí?us		wasáyati'us
wasáti	ruin, mess up (something)	FC			
wasáya	get the better of (someone), defeat (someone), beat	RD	wasā'ya, wasai'a	32, 46, 144	
wasáyati	make (something) bad for (someone)	WS	wasájati		
wasáyati'us	make (something) bad for oneself	WS	wasájati?us		wasát yatí'us
wáschᴍ	mad, quick tempered	FC			
wásekinu	look angry	RD	was'ekinu	92	
wásip	pour (dry material) out of (a container)	WS	wásip		
wás'isyo	kick angrily	WS	wás?isjo		
wáskato	be displeased with, irritated	WS	wáskato		
wáskatope	acting angry	RD	was'katope	134	
wasó	angry	FC			
wasó	be angry, get angry (RD), growl, forbid (WS)	RD, WS	wasō' (RD), wasó, wás (WS)	162, 164	wás
wasóhati	bring wrath down upon	FC			
wasói	get poisoned	WS	wasój		

Maidu	English	Source	Source Spelling	Page	Other Spellings
wasóiti	poison	WS	wasójti		
wasóitikm	poisoner	WS	wasójtiky		
wasó'ituti	anger making (someone) sick, be angry till it hurts	FC			
wasópai	be angry at (someone): wasópaiḱa niḱí? "Are you mad at me?" wasópaimenḱas min "I am not mad at you."	RD, FC	waso'pai	162	
wasópaito	be mad at each other	FC			
wasósa	be grouchy	FC-E			
wasósape	hot-tempered	RD	wasō'sape	202	
wasósati	get (someone) riled up, get (someone) angry about something	FC			
wasóso	get angry	RD	wasō'so	136	
wasóti	make angry (RD), poison (someone) (FC)	RD, FC	wasō'ti	28	
wáspololo	pygmy owl	HM	was'-po-lo-lo		
wáswewe	speak angrily to (RD), curse out, swear at (WS)	WS, RD	wáswewej (WS), was wēwē'	166	wáswewei, waswewé
wáswewé'us	swear at oneself, curse oneself	RD	was'wēwē'us	116	
wásweye	talk bad, say bad things, swear	FC, WST-LB	wásweje	42:5	
waswéye'us	swear at oneself	RD	waswē'yeus	116	
watá	plate, dish, any flat object used to eat from	WS	watá		
watá	shore, bank of stream, margin, edge	WS	watá		
wáta	throw on (WS), cover up (FC)	WS, FC	wáta		
watá dákm	dishtowel	WS	watá dáky		
watáito	throw at and miss	WS	watájto		
waták	throw (something pliable, like cloth or rope)	WS	waták		
watákkoi	throw (a pliable thing) away	WS	watákkoj		
watákmit	throw (something) down into	WST	watákmit	78:10	
watáksitopin	throw (a pliable thing) across towards	WS	watáksitopin		
watákye	throw (a pliable thing) towards	WS	watákje		
watám chetípe	round, disk shaped	WS	watám ćetípe		
watán	slap, hit with the flat of the hand	WS	watán		
watánan	from the shore, from the water (coming out)	RD	wata'nan	80	
watánchik	slap in the face	WS	watánćik		
wátayo	cover up well by tossing things on, cover up (several things)	WS, FC	wátajo		watáyo (FC)
wátdakm	clapper stick	RD-NM			
wátdan	clap (verb): ma wátdanḱas "I clapped my hands"	WS, FC	wátdan		

Maidu	English	Source	Source Spelling	Page	Other Spellings
wati	catch fish with hook and line	BC	wahteka		wóti (WS)
wátkm	duck, mallard duck	WS	wátky		
watoktiti	pine tree	FC			
waťokťoko	sour dock (eaten raw)	JD	wadokdoko	66	woťokťok (WS)
wawi	lesser snow goose	HM	wah-weem		
waymymk	yelp with pain	WS	wajýjyk		
Wayápom Momí	place name in the Taylorsville area, #24 on FR map. See map 5 in Appendix 5.	FR		370-371	Wépam Momí
Wayápom Momí	place name, just north of Quincy, #40 on FR map. See Wépam Momí on map 2, Appendix 5.	FR	wayápom momí	370-371	Wépam Momí
Wayápom Momím Cháťá Hmbé	place name, just north of Quincy, #39 on FR map. See Wépam Momí Cháťá Hmbé on map 2, Appendix 5.	FR	wayápom momím ćáťá hibé ?	370-371	Wépam Momím Cháťá Hmbé
Wayápom Momím Ustu	place name, just north of Quincy, #38 on FR map. See Wépam Momí Ustu on map 2, Appendix 5.	FR	wayápom momím ʔústu	370-371	Wépam Momím Ustu
wáye	break	WS	wáje		wa'ái (FC)
wáyo	throw (something) in (RD), toss a lot of times (or a lot of things) (WS)	RD, WS, WST-DW	waio (RD), wájo (WS)	64 (RD), 74 (WST-DW)	wáiyo (RD)
we	speak: yépsmm máidmm mmyák wékan "The menfolks said the same thing."	RD	wē	28, 106	
wé	vomit: min wétikan "it makes you barf"	WS, FC	wé, wem		wem
wé'aka	close to, near: ésto wé'aka close to the middle (RD), out to the middle (of a lake, for example)	RD	wē'aka	32	
wébelbel	see something moving through a hole, speak through a hole	RD	wē'belbel	36	
wéda	big time, celebration (noun): wédam solí "celebration song"	FC			
wéda	celebrate the big time (verb)	FC			
wedaka	small	SPB	wedaka		
wédam buyi	main day of the big time	FC			
wédamape	upcoming feast, upcoming big time	WST	wédamape	76:1	
we'e	edge	FC			wehé
we'é	to circle (bird of prey)	RD	wē'ē	56	
wéh	exclamation of pleasure (WS), self-satisfaction. "so there!"	WS	wéh	64	
wehé	edge, margin, border	WS	wehé, wohó		wohó (WS), we'e (FC)

Maidu	English	Source	Source Spelling	Page	Other Spellings
wehé'no	skirt, go along the edge of (something)	WS	wehé?no		
wehépti	misfortune	FC			yehépti (FC)
wehétda	take down (something hung up)	RD	wehet'da	224, 234	
wehétdaw	take down (something hung up)	RD	wehet'dau	234, 236	
wehéthachono	take down (something hung up) and carry across	RD	wehet'hatsono	192	
wehéthachopin	take down (something hanging) to carry to another place	RD	wehet'atsopin	192	
wehétkinu	be hanging, be hung up	RD	wehet'kinu	194, 206, 234, 236	
wehétkit	hang (something) up	RD	wehet'kit	192, 224, 234	
wehétyo	hang up multiple things	RD	wehet'yo	194	
wehétyodi	at the place where things were hung up	RD	wehet'yodi	224	
wehétyonutohelu	be likely to be hanging up	RD	wehet'yonū'tohelu	192	
wéhyakbedom	be very many (-dom is part of the verb stem): wéhyakbedomchoi'a "there were very many"	RD	wehyakbe	104	
wéido	go around outdoors, go out and about: nisám smbekan wéidonwet kúmmen bísyet. "My little dog and I don't go out and about while it is winter." (n in wéidonwet is negative marker)	HY			
wékm	vomiter	FC			
wékmm kutí	vulture	WS	wékym kutí		
wékkesi	rabbit	FC, WS	wékkes		wékkes
wekói	run around	FC			
wékpai	bark (of dogs)	WS	wékpaj		wákpai (FC)
wékweke	kingfisher (WS) (RD doesn't translate) we:kwek is chicken hawk in Nisenan	RD, WS	wek'weke (RD), wékweke (WS)	100	
welé	a run, test, instance, "trial run"	WS, WST-DW	welé	72:9	
welé	lodgepole pine	WS	welé		
welé	run (verb)	FC			
welé'mkoi	run away	FC			
weledaw	flee from, run away from	WS	weledaw		
weledoi	run up (a hill, a staircase)	WS	weledoj		
weledoino	run up (a hill, a staircase)	WS	weledojno		
welék	wave (something)	WS	welék		

Maidu	English	Source	Source Spelling	Page	Other Spellings
welékoi	run off, go off running: séwna welékoikan "They ran off to the river."	WST	welékoj	78:8	
welele wa	type of edible mushroom	PM-M	we-le-le-wam		
welém chá	lodgepole pine tree	WS	welém ćá		walum cha
weléno	run, run along, run away	WS, FC	weléno		
welénokm	runner	WS	welénoky		
welénokmm kmlé	prostitute	WS	welénokym kylé		
welénoye	run around	FC			
welésito	run across	WS	welésito		
weléye	run back (to where one started)	RD	welē'ye	56	
wélketi	frog	WS	wélketi		
wélketim chaká	frog eggs	WS	wélketim ćaká		
Wélketim O	place name west of Hwy 147, East Lake Almanor. #18 on LM map. See map 3 in Appendix 5.	FC-map, LM	welketim Oh (FC-map), Welketom (LM)		
wéllep	fan (verb)	WS	wéllep		
wéllepkm	fan (noun)	WS	wéllepky		
wem	maggot	WS	wem		
wem	vomit	WS	wem, we		we
wém	enough, surfeit	WS	wém		
wém memé	feel nauseated	WS	wém memé		
wémchmchmkti	bad cause-to-vomit man, a mythical and evil being, bad vomity man	WS	wémćyćykti		
wémchichmkpintipe	sounding awful	FC			
wemchichmktiti	dirty-acting, disgusting, revolting	RD	wēmtsitsök'titi	218	
wémchik	get enough	WS	wémćik		
wémmuk	gag, retch	WS	wémmuk		
wesiki	big-mouthed	FC			
wemtichmkti	ugly	RD	wēmtitsök'ti	218	
wemtichúti	dirty, ugly	RD	wēmtitsū'ti	220	
wémtik	have enough (WS), be enough for (RD): smtim penádmkm wémtikchoi'a "there was enough for just one meal"	WS, RD	wémtik (WS), wem'tik (RD)	152	
wémtik wéye	to have talked enough, be finished talking	FC			
wémtikbo	be enough	WS	wémtikbo		
wémtikdmkbe	be just (big) enough, be the right size: uním kódom ai sm'mi mnóinak wémtikdmkbedom yahánachen. "Perhaps this land being just big enough to wander around would be good."	RD	wem'tikdök'be	12	
wémtiki	enough, just enough, (with motion verbs) as far as possible, all the way: wémtiki péweten, mkóikan. "When he had eaten enough, he left."	RD	wem'tiki	154, 158, 230	

Maidu	English	Source	Source Spelling	Page	Other Spellings
wémtiki	true words, the truth: wémtiki makpáidom, okítmaḱas "When I learn the truth, I will come home."	RD	wem′tiki	38, 118	
wémtiki káiḱas	I'm telling the truth	RD	wem′tiki kai′ḱas	98	
wémtikiti	be sufficient	RD	wem′tikiti	186	
wemtikḱás	that's enough, I have said enough, I have had enough	FC			
wémtikluťpe	exactly enough, just right: teténonom kᴍlóknonona kᴍḱán wémtikluťpem "It is just right for big women."	RD	wem′tiklutpe	92	
wémtikpe	enough, just right: yaha wémtikpe "good enough," minná wémtikpe "enough for you"	RD	wem′tikpe	92, 160	
wené	medicine, good (thing), good (adj): yahát wené ma'át sudáḱade? "Although it's good, is it delicious?"	WS, FC, RD	wené (WS), wene (RD)	44	
wene'ᴍnó	doctor (people) while traveling, go doctoring	RD	weneöno′	72	
wenépᴍkᴍ	medicine plant	FC			
wépa	coyote	WS	wépa (WS, FC, RD), wē′ba (RD)	38	
wépa te	coyote's baby	FC			
Wépa Usitom	place name near Crescent Mills, "coyote crossing"	FC			Wepasito (FC)
wépam máidᴍ	Coyote Man	WS	wépam májdy		
Wépam Momí	place name for a village apparently located on the west side of Forgay Point in Indian Valley (FR-AG), #24 on FR map. The name means "coyote water." See map 5 in Appendix 5.	FR1, FR, FR-AG	wayapom momi		Wayápom Momí
Wépam Momí	place name for a village in American Valley - not the same as the one on Forgay Point. See map 2 in Appendix 5.	FR1	wayapom momi		
Wépam Momím Chaťá Hᴍbé	place name for a site in the northern part of American Valley. #39 on FR map. See map 2 in Appendix 5.	FR-D, FR-Ka	wayápom momím ćaťá hibé		
wépam sᴍ́	dog	WS	wépam sý		
wépam wáisi	Old Man Coyote	WS	wépam wájsi		
Wépam Yamáni	place name for Coyote Mountain, which was in the middle of Mountain Meadows (now a reservoir). See map 3, Appendix 5.	RM	wepum yamani	233	

Maidu	English	Source	Source Spelling	Page	Other Spellings
wéppem	strum	WS	wéppem		
wéppemto	strum away idly	WS	wéppemto		
wéppenkʌ	any stringed instrument, especially a guitar	WS	wéppemky		
wétʌk	gnaw (something) to cut it	RD	wē'tök	168	
Wetáyam	place name for an area about five miles southeast of Susanville, CA (WS), Sand Slough, #10 on HLME map 3. This was a Maidu village and burial site. See map 4 in Appendix 5.	WS, HLME	wetája (WS), Wetajam (HLME)		
Wetáyam	place name for a large Maidu village in southwestern Susanville, #30 on HLME map 3 - apparently this is a different place from the Sand Slough Wetáyam. Roxie Peconum was born here; the location was on the Hulsman property. Wetáyam was the name of a head man for this village, and there were two other villages with the same name.	HLME	Wetajam (HLME)		
wetém	dance (noun)	WS	wetém		
wetém	dance (verb)	FC			
wetémchono	dance in a circle	WS	wetémćono		
wetémchonom sóldom	round-dance singing	RD	wetem'tsonom sol'dom	88	
wetémdodo	dance with (someone), dance around	RD	wetem'dodo	100	
wetémdodoi	dance around, dance with (someone)	WS	wetémdodoj		
wetémdoi	start dancing	FC			
weteméw	always dance, be always dancing	RD	wetemē'u	88	
wetémhoiyapa	puberty dance age	RD	wetem'hoiyapa	182	
wetémim motó	a get-together for the purpose of dancing, a dance (as an event)	WS	wetémim motó		
wetémḱoi	go dancing, go to a dance	RD	wetem'koi	94	
wetémno	go to a dance, go dancing	RD	wetem'no	88, 94, 182	
wetémpe	dance place	WST		42:1	
wetémti	make (someone) dance	WS	wetémti		
wétetepdaw	keep tearing with the teeth	RD	wē'tetepdau	190	
wéti	cause (someone) to vomit	FC			
wétpeikʌ	banjo	FC			
wéttito	in a little bit, soon	FC			

Maidu	English	Source	Source Spelling	Page	Other Spellings
wéw	do (habitually), do again and again: wéwwonokᴍchoi'a: "They had done again and again"	RD	wē ū'	232	
wewé	speech, (sound of) talking: wewédi tetét húkes'ankano "You are so clever in (your) speech, you are so clever at speaking."	WS	wewé (WS), wēwē' (RD)	32, 214	
wewé	talk or speak (not converse), deliver a speech: kulúchet wewéchoi'a. 'túimenkᴍm ni,' achói'a. "Once it was dark, he spoke. 'I am one who never sleeps,' he said."	RD, FC	wewē'	168	
wewéi	say (especially for the utterances of legendary figures), say softly, orate (WS), talk through doctors (as spirits) (WST)	WS, WST	wewéj	64:15	
wewém sᴍdói	increase of speech volume and pitch during a shamanistic séance	WS	wewém sydój		
wewémen	not answer, not say anything	RD	wewē'men	230	
wewémenwet	without speaking, without answering	RD	wewē'menwet	56, 152	
wéwetoto	tell each other	RD	wē'wētoto	106	
wewéyebis	deliver a monologue, keep up a speech	RD	wewē'yebis	168	
wewéyedoi	start to give a speech	FC			
wewéyekᴍ	speaker	FC			
wewéyekoi	begin to speak (not converse), start talking away	RD	wewē'yekoi	168	
wéye	speech: yahát pinḱás mínḱi wéye "Good to hear your news."	WS	wéj, wéje		wéi (WS)
wéye	tell, talk, say, speak, talk about, suggest, discuss: hómpaito wéyema'aḱas "I'll suggest a wrestling match."	WS, FC, RD	wéj, wéje (WS), wē'ye (RD)	130	wéi (WS)
wéye kaní	end of talking, "the end"	FC			
wéye wí'iḱas bei	I have nothing to say, I have no words	FC			
wéye'ᴍsip	go through (a place) telling about: ᴍpéḱanim ḱódoidi wéye'ᴍsipḱan "through every land he went telling about (it)"	RD	wē'yeösip	38	
wéyebe	brief message	FC			
wéyebis	keep talking	FC-E			
wéyebos	finish talking	FC			

Maidu	English	Source	Source Spelling	Page	Other Spellings
wéyechmi	be mute, be unable to talk, be speechless	WS	wéjećyj		
wéyedoi	start talking	WS	wéjedoj		
wéyedom kai	give advice: min yahát wéyedom kai'ás "I gave you good advice"	RD	wē'yedoñ kai (+ conj)	162	
wéyekmm máidm	speaking person, speaker	FC			
wéyeḱoi	go telling about: mpéḱanim ḱódoidi wéyeḱoidom "in every land going and telling about (it)"	RD	wē'yekoi	38	
wéyemasma	what I would say about, what I might say about, my report about: tetét wisétdom mm wéyemasma kmkán "He was very much afraid of what I would say about him"	WST	wéjemasma	58:51	
wéyenoyesakm	gossiper, someone who goes around talking all the time	FC-E			
wéyes min	I must tell you, I have to tell you (something), I ought to tell you: etú! ka'ánupi! wéyes min, unína bísbene'e. "Wait! Stay here. I have to tell you, please stay where you are."	RD	wē'yes min	88	
wéyet	after saying it, after saying this speech: yokóschononudom wéyet ammnikan mmm kmlé wewémenchoi'a. "Lying down beside her after saying this speech, he spoke no more to the woman."	RD	wē'yet	230	
wéyetai	misspeak	FC			
wéyeti	make (someone) talk	WS	wéjeti		
wéyeto	(in) speaking (to). This adverb can be used to clarify who just spoke (subject) or who was spoken to (object): mm éti wéyeto "speaking to her sister;" yepónim máidmm wéyeto "the headman speaking"	RD	wē'yeto, wē'yet	112, 186, 226, 230	wéyet
wéyetodom	outreach	FC			
wéyetoti	practice (verb)	FC			
wéye'us	talk to oneself	FC			
wi'í	lack, not have	WS	wiʔí		

Maidu	English	Source	Source Spelling	Page	Other Spellings
wi'í	to not be, not exist, disappear, be destroyed: wónom máidᴧm wi'ímenkᴧm matá "May human beings never be destroyed." ka'ápe wéyedom, uním ḱódoidi wi'íma'ankano. "Talking like that, you will not be in this world."	RD, FC	wīī'	26, 30, 180, 206	
wi'í ma'át	without any, with nothing: chedá wi'í ma'át "without any breakfast"	RD	wīī' maat	170	
wi'íhudai	palpitate, beat violently (heart)	WS	wiʔíhudaj		
wi'ímen	not be destroyed, not be lacking	RD	wīī'men, wīīmen	23, 25, 30	
wi'ínit	pretty soon	RD	wīī'nit	116	
wi'ípe	empty, abandoned, deserted	RD	wīī'pe	164	
wi'ípedi	to the deserted place, in the deserted place	RD	wīī'pedi	98	
wi'íti	wipe out, destroy, cause to not exist	RD	wīī'ti	148, 156	
wi'ítid	in wiping out, in destroying	RD	wīītid	108	wīī'tidi
wi'ítida	be wiping (someone) out, be destroying	RD	wīī'tida	142	
wi'ítisa	destroy over time, kill one by one	RD	wīī'tisa	140	
wi'íwonope	which had been destroyed, which had disappeared	RD	wīī'wonopem	138	
wi'íye	not be there, be missing, fail	RD	wīī'ye	148	
wi'íyemen	not fail, succeed: wi'íyemenma'aḱan. "It shall not fail. It shall succeed."	RD	wīī'yemen	40	
wi'áswaito	stretch (something)	RD	wiās'waito	7, 9	
wibák	detach from a flat surface	WS	wibák		
wibákdoi	pull (something) up from a flat surface	WS	wibákdoj		
wibát	break with the hands, break by snapping with the hands	WS	wibát, wibátto		wibátto
wíbusi	weasel	FC, WS	wíbus		wíbus (WS)
wichák	encircle (something) with (something)	WS	wićák		
wichákᴧ	belt (noun)	WS, FC	wićák		wacháka
wichákiti	belt (noun)	WS	wićákiti		
wicháp	dislodge	WS	wićáp		
wichápdaw	pull (something) down from a high place	WS	wićápdaw		
wichík	cover something over, obscure (something), obliterate	RD	witsik'	64	
wichúmᴧl	stir a small quantity	WS	wićúmyl		

Maidu	English	Source	Source Spelling	Page	Other Spellings
widmktotó	take hold of each other's hands	RD	widöktotō'	230	widóktoto
widák	pull loose from a permanently fixed surface	WS	widák		
widákdaw	detach from a permanently fixed surface	WS	widákdaw		
widán	pull (something flat and clothlike), pull on (something flat and clothlike)	WS	widán		
widándoi	pull up (something like a blanket)	WS	widándoj		
widás	rip	WS	widás		
widásdo	rip, split, split open	WS	widásdo		
widátpai	tie on (to something), attach (something to something): piwí kan basákmm oschúmdi widátpaichoi'a "then he tied a root to the end of the walking stick."	RD	widat'pai	198	
widói	pull (something) up	WS	widój		
Widóikmm	place name for Janesville (HLME), #5 on HLME map 3. A large old Maidu burial ground is here in Janesville. According to LM, this refers to the mountain range including Omkumi Mountain and Amadee Mountain, #45 on the LM map. See maps 1 and 4 in Appendix 5.	LM, HLME	widojkym range		
Widóikmm Yamánim	place name for Thompson Peak, #34 on LM map, # 22 on HLME map 3. See maps 1 and 4 in Appendix 5.	LM, HLME	widojkym yamanim (LM), Widojkym Jamanim (HLME		
widók	grasp with the hand, holding (someone's) hand: mínḱi widókpe nik "holding your hand in mine"	WS, WST	widók, widýk	54:24	
widókdaw	pull off, pull loose with the hand	WS	widókdaw		
widókdoi	grasp with hand and pull (something or someone) up	WS	widókdoj		
widókhaḱoi	lead (someone) by the hand	WS, WST	widókhaḱoj	54:23	
widóknoye	lead (someone) around by the hand	WS	widóknoje		
widókpai	break (something) off	WS, RD	widókpaj (WS), widok'pai (RD)	74	
widóktoto	hold hands with each other	WS	widóktoto		widmktotó (RD)
widóktotonu	hand-in-hand	WS	widóktotonu		

Maidu	English	Source	Source Spelling	Page	Other Spellings
widóktotopepe	dancing in a circle holding hands	WS	widóktotopepe		
widópo	blackberry (HM), wild raspberry (PM-M)	HM, PM-M	we-do'-po (HM), we-do-po (PM-M)		
widót	shove (someone) with the hand or arm	WS	widót		
widótk̓oi	shove (someone) aside, elbow (someone) out of the way	WS	widótk̓oj		
widú	contract the muscles spasmodically, draw up (as in convulsions)	WS	widú		
widúmmoto	be tied around	WS	widúmmoto		
wihɨ́l	be heavy	WS	wihýl		
wihɨ́p	stretch by pulling	WS	wihýp		
wihɨ́pkɨ	elastic	WS	wihýpky		
wihɨ́pk̓oi	stretch by pulling	WS	wihýpk̓oj		
wihám cha	mountain live oak	HM	wi-hahm' chah		
wiháp	pull (a long, stemlike object)	WS	wiháp		
wihápdoi	pull up (a long, stemlike object)	WS	wihápdoj		
wiháwtokɨ	accordion	WS	wiháwtoky		
wihópdoi	take out (of a pocket)	RD	wihopdoi	60	
wihúl	pull up over (someone), as bedcovers, pull (anything)	WS	wihúl		
wihúldoi	pull (something) up	WS	wihúldoj		
wihúlt̓a'us	pull (something) over oneself	WS	wihúlt̓aʔus		
wíhya	make imperfect, introduce imperfections into	RD	wi'hya	26, 66	
wi'íwo'us	deny oneself, go without	FC-R			
wíiye	no: wíiye api! "Say No!"	WS	wíjje		wíye
wikɨ́kɨi	open the eyes	RD	wikö'köi	122	
wikɨ́p	extract	WS	wikýp		
wikɨ́pdoi	extract, pull out (for example, nails from a board)	WS	wikýpdoj		
wiká	netted cap worn by men	RD-NM	wīka'		
wiká	put on a netted hat	RD	wika'	120	
wik̓éidoi	lift up one's skirts	WS	wik̓éjdoj		
wik̓éik̓eidoi	lift up one's skirts (high)	WS	wik̓éjk̓ejdoj		
wik̓él	perforate	WS	wik̓él		
wikú	tug at, pull at (something)	WS	wikú		
wikúku	pull now and then, pull here and there (RD), sort of pull on (WS)	RD, WS	wikū'ku (RD), wikúku (WS)	24	
wikútui	squinting (RD), tugging, pulling (based on other similar words). (adv)	RD	wikū'tui	218	
wíl	wheel (from English)	WS	wíl		
wilɨ́lwo'aito	open eyes a little	RD	wilöl'woaito	124	
wilák	turn red	WS	wilák		
wilákk̓oi	blush	WS	wilákk̓oj		
wilákno	flush with anger, blush	WS	wilákno		

Maidu	English	Source	Source Spelling	Page	Other Spellings
wiláknope	ruddy of complexion	WS	wiláknope		
wiláwsip	pull (something) off	RD	wilausip	60	
wílba	wheelbarrow	WS	wílba		
wilémkoitikm	one who makes people run away	FC			
wilédaw	run out and away	RD	wile'daw	238	
wiledíkno	run up to, arrive at (a place) running, run home: kaní batápaipotochet, kan mmyím máidmm wilédiknoḱan. "Just as she was about to catch up, that man ran home."	RD	wiledik'no	176	
wilédoino	go running up(hill)	RD	wile'doino	90	
wilék	hurry, go fast	WS	wilék		
wilékleki	hurry! go fast, quickly	FC, WS	wiléklek		wiléklek
wilékleknini	quickly	WS	wilékleknini		
wilékni	quickly	RD, WS	wilek'ni (RD), wilékni (WS)	92	
wiléknoye	rush around, hurry around	WS	wiléknoje		
wilékoi	run off, start off running	RD	wile'koi	176	
wilékoiye	run off towards	RD	wile'koiye	176	
wilékokoi	run away (plural subject)	RD	wilek'okoi	216	
wiléle	tremblers, feather plumes	RD	wile'le	120	
wiléno	run, run on	FC, RD	wilen'o	176	
wilésito	run across	RD	wile'sito	88	
wiléspuikm	dove (bird)	FC			wieléspuikm (FC-E)
wiléw	be running all that time, be running along	RD	wilē'u	176	
wiléwkit	run along arriving in (a place)	RD	wilē'ukit	176	
wiléwkittikoi	be causing (someone) to run away	RD	wilē'ukitikoi	216	
wiléye	run back (to where one started)	RD	wilē'ye	56	
wilíl	tremble, flutter	WS	wilíl		
wilílim chá	cottonwood tree, black cottonwood, quaking aspen	WS, JD	wilílim ćá (WS), wylylymća (JD)	72	wmlílim chá
wilíliwa	cottonwood mushroom	JD	wylylywam	24	
wilíliwimoto	twist together	RD	wilil'iwimoto	62	
wílliw	twirl (for example, a rope), toss (something) around	WS	wílliw		
wilók	twitch	WS	wilók		
wimík	recover consciousness, come to life	WS	wimík		
wimíkekoi	wake up (intransitive)	RD	wimī'kekoi	168	
wimíkhudanpe	easily awakened	WS	wimíkhudanpe		
wimú	itch (verb)	FC-R			
wimúmu	itch	WS	wimúmu		

Maidu	English	Source	Source Spelling	Page	Other Spellings
wínit	might or might not: wákdom tásdom awébisim ka'án wínit tétʼmʼtʼm kʼmmápem "crying and moaning on and on in order to give birth to children, they might or might not (succeed)."	RD	wī'nit	50	
wínťu	tribal name for the Wintu Indians	WS	wínťu		
wínťum máidm	Wintu person	WS	wínťum májdy		
winú	be slow: winúmenwet "Don't be slow!"	RD	winū'	178	
wípe	acorn-leaching festival, a celebration with feasting	WS	wípe		
wiṗélki	cottontail	WS	wiṗélki		
wiṗélkim hiní	beady eyes	WS	wiṗélkim hiní		
wiṗélno	a kind of rabbit	WS	wiṗélno		
wiṗíl	be lightning	WS	wiṗíl		
wiṗíli	lightning	FC, WS	wiṗíl		wiṗíl (WS)
wipól	pluck, pull, extract	WS	wipól		
wipólsip	pull out, pluck out	WS	wipólsip		
wiṗún	tie (verb)	WS	wiṗún		
wiṗúnkit	tie (something) down	WS	wiṗúnkit		
wipúppu	dismal, dull, gray	WS	wipúppu		
wisɨ́	clear up (of weather), abate (of a storm)	WS	wisý		
wisɨ́sɨ	quake, shake (of the earth)	WS	wisýsy		
wisét	be scared, frightened	WS, FC	wisét		
wisétboduk	not be very frightened	WS	wisétboduk		
wisétikm	one who scares someone	FC			
wisétpe	scared	FC			
wisétsapem kilím bomó	a bunch of scaredy cats	FC			
wisétset	frightened	WS	wisétset		
wisétsetpinti	to cause fear by scary sounds (to plural object)	RD	wiset'setpin'ti	214	
wisétti	frighten (someone)	WS	wisétti		
wisétyahátpinti	to cause panic by making noise	RD	wiset'yahat'pinte	214	
wisílsilchono	shake off: makád wisílsilchono "spider, shake off" (RD), alternative interpretation: cover something with a web	RD	wisil'siltsono	216	
wískaye	a devil, something evil	FC			
wísla	chipmunk	WS	wísla		
wíslai	wag (tail), flick (tail), swish (tail), sway (branch)	WS, FC	wíslaj		
wíslam bukú	yarrow (chipmunk tail)	FC, JD	wislumbucu	43	
wíslam pa	mountain willow (high altitude)	HY			
wíslam yo	yarrow flower	JD	wislamjo	43	

Maidu	English	Source	Source Spelling	Page	Other Spellings
wisóp	break by snapping suddenly (intransitive)	WS	wisóp		
wisópinpin	break by jerking down suddenly (for example, a light cord from the ceiling)	WS	wisópinpin		
wisópsa	prone to break (as string), always breaking, delicate	WS	wisópsa		
wisópti	break (something) by snapping suddenly	WS	wisópti		
wisótpin	dislike the sound of (WS), yank down (WST-RP)	WS, WST-RP	wisótpin	65:20	
Wisótpinim	place name for Big Springs, #10 on FR map. See Maps 1 and 3 in Appendix 5.	FR, RD	wisot'pini (RD)	RD 196, FR 370-371	
wistátak	robin	FC-T			chistatak
wisúp	snatch	WS	wisúp		
wisúpno	snatch away from	WS	wisúpno		
witɥ'ú	wring out (something)	RD	witöu'	116	
witɥm	run away	RD	witöm'	214	
witɥmino	run going downhill (RD), run down (a hill) (FC)	RD, FC	witōm'ino, witöm'ino	46, 56	
witɥmit	run down towards	RD	witöm'it	46	
witɥmkokoi	go running away (plural subject)	RD	witöñ'kokoi	216	
witɥmtɥm mé	give a stroke of lightning to	RD	witöm'töm mē'	162	
witɥmtɥmi	thunder	WS, FC	witýmtym		witɥmtɥm (WS), witúmtumi (FC)
witɥswitɥsnói	go along breaking off (something like bear grass) one after another	RD	witös'witösönoi'	176	
witʼɥtʼmino	piece of cloth: chukútkɥm witʼɥtʼmino "dishrag"	WS	witýtyjno		
witái	exaggerate in talking	WS	witáj		
witáka	prostitute	WS	witák		
witákam kɥlé	prostitute	WS	witákam kylé		
witákam máidɥ	pimp	WS	witákam májdy		
witákana yépsɥ hóiwihayetikɥm máidɥ	pimp	WS	witákana jépsy hójwihajetikym májdy		
witám	cinch, tighten	WS	witám		
witámdoi	cinch up (a belt, a saddle)	WS	witámdoj		
witámmoto	cinch together, tighten with laces	WS	witámmoto		
witámmotokɥ	corset	WS	witámmotoky		
witámto	cinch	WS	witámto		
witáye	put hitches on (a packsaddle), cinch up (a saddle)	WS	witáje		
witáyeyo	tie and cinch up a bunch of things	WS	witájejo		
Witáyim	place name, Susanville area, #1 on FR map	FR		370-371	

Maidu	English	Source	Source Spelling	Page	Other Spellings
witípwai	to spread out (intransitive) (as a search team)	RD	witip'wai	32	
witókʌm cha	young pine trees	HY			
witóktʌtʌ	young trees	HY			
witúbil	twist, wind on	WS	witúbil		
witúbil'us	to coil (as a snake)	WS	witúbilʔus		
witúl	roll (something) up in a roll	WS	witúl		
witúlkit	roll (something) up and tie (like a sleeping bag)	WS	witúlkit		
witúlkityo	roll (things) up and tie (them)	WS	witúlkitjo		
witúlyo	roll (several things) up	WS	witúljo		
witúmtumi	thunder (noun)	FC			witʌmtʌmi
wiwái	divide (something)	WS	wiwáj		
wiwáito	divide (something) with someone, divide (something)	RD, WS	wiwai'to (RD), wiwájto (WS)	136	
wiwó	lift, raise	WS	wiwó		
wiwódoi	lift up, raise up	WS	wiwódoj		
wiyʌl	split, divide up (something)	WS	wijýl		
wiyʌt	split	WS	wijýt		
wiyʌtto	split (something) open	WS	wijýtto		
wiyák	somewhat, sort of	WS	wiják		
wíye	no	FC			wíiye (WS)
wíye	refuse, say "no", be missing, to not do, to not be like that (verb): wíyema'aḱan "It's not going to be like that." mʌyádʌkbe mʌyákbe méiwochet, wíyedom, helúto méiḱan. "When she asked (him) to give half, refusing, he gave (her) just a few." mʌḱí téchom, mʌmʌ́ ekʌ odátokʌm ma'át, wíyeḱan. "Even his two children, who usually came out to meet him, were missing."	RD	wī'ye	5, 138, 228	
Wiyekʌm	Almanor Inn area	FC			
wíyeḱan	no, the answer is no	RD	wī'yekan	122	
wíyeḱan ʌpé	it is nothing	RD	wī'yekan öpe	90	
wíyekana	say "hell, no!" answer "absolutely not!"	RD	wī'yekana	70	
wíyepada	no matter what! (used with negative commands): wikʌ́kʌiben map wíyepada! "Don't open your eyes, no matter what!"	RD	wī'yepada	12, 122	
wiyéti	force (someone) to be gone, make (someone) leave	RD	wiyet'i	160	

Maidu	English	Source	Source Spelling	Page	Other Spellings
wo	tell (someone) to (do something), have (someone) do (something)	WS	wo		
wó	be caught (in trap or net)	RD	wo'	56, 212, 220	
wó	call out, whoop, howl, crow (as a rooster)	WS, FC, RD	wo (WS), wō' (RD)	38	
wó	stab (someone) (RD), hit (WS): mᴎm sáwim botópem niḱí híndi wóḱan "the leafy foliage hit me in the eyes"	RD, WS, WST-DW	wō (RD), wó (WS)	60 (RD), 70:4 (WST)	
wó	start a fire using a fire drill	RD	wo'	172	
wó'ᴍhadoito	go at it fast and strong	WS	wó?yhadojto		
wó'ᴍhanoye	perform with maximum (spiritual) vigor (as a shaman)	WS	wó?yhanoje		
wó'a	hit	FC			
wó'akᴍ	clapper stick	FC			
wo'áswono	on the edge, outskirts of: hanᴍlekem ḱoyóm wo'áswono "on the outskirts of Honey Lake Valley"	RD	woas'wono	172	
wob	weep, cry (verb)	WS	wob		
wobí	tears (from the eyes)	WS	wob		
wobítapo	filled with tears, tearful	WS	wobítapo		
wobúno	mash, roll around roughly, smash	WS	wobúno		
wóchedai	drill a hole	WS	wóćedaj		
wochík	ask (someone) to (do something)	WS	woćík		
wochík	look for, follow (tracks): tétewonopem yᴍnóyedi pai wochíkchoi'a. "Where they had gone around playing, he looked for their footprints."	RD	wotsik'	230	
wochíkimoto	go all around looking for	RD	wotsik'imoto	64	
wochóno	be in the vicinity of	WS	woćóno		
wochóno	go up and over, go over something, encircle: ókpai yamáni wochónodom "sun coming up over the mountain" lulú wochóno "encircle the waist, go around the waist"	FC, FC-E			
wochóno	path, trail	FC			
wochónodi	in the vicinity of	WS	woćónodi		
wochót	small piece of board	WS	woćót		
wodá	fall (verb), fall down	RD, WS	wodā' (RD), wodá (WS)	58	
wodá	recover from an illness, get well	WS	wodá		wadá
wodák	stick close to	RD	wodak'	110	

Maidu	English	Source	Source Spelling	Page	Other Spellings
wodákdonu	to keep very close to (something)	RD	wodak'donu	110	
wódato	to hit (RD), hit with an instrument (WS), hit others (FC)	RD, WS, WST	wō'dato (RD), wódato (WS)	102 (RD), 78:8	
wodáwti	leave (someone): hóipai wodáwti "leave (someone) behind"	RD	wodau'ti	46	
wodíkno	get ahead, get beyond: uním tétem cha waláwdᴍbedom hadá aní wodíknoweten ᴍnóchoi'a. "He went along, having gotten ahead, being taller (or farther) than these big trees."	RD	wodik'no	46	
wodíkno	throw (something) up to (somewhere)	WS	wodíkno		
wodói	fly like a bat, to flap	RD	wodoi'	210, 212	
wodóino	beyond	WS	wodójno		
wodónbis	remain standing: ni piyém pikóiwono hóipaidi wodónbisusas "I usually remain standing after a forest fire has burned through."	RD	wodōn'bus	64	
wodónu	be standing (as a tree)	RD	wodōn'ū	160, 166	
wodót	fling with a stick	WS	wodót		
wodótḱoi	fling (something) away with a stick	WS	wodótḱoj		
wodótmit	knock (something) into (something) with a stick	WS	wodótmit		
wodótmityo	knock (a lot of things) into (something) with a stick	WS	wodótmitjo		
wóhᴍ	knock off (something like berries or caterpillars) (FC), put a container (patá) under a bush and knock the berries off into it with a stick (WS)	WS, FC	wóhy		wohᴍ́ (FC)
wohᴍ́kᴍm patá	gathering basket, especially for berries	WS	wohýkym patá		
wóha	cow	WS	wóha		
wohadóimakat	not being up to, not being in any shape for: wíyekan, hómpaito ma'át wohadóimakat; wokókas. "The answer is No. Not being up to even a wrestling match, I am tired."	RD	wohadoi'makat	130	
wóham bomó	cattle, herd of cattle	WS	wóham bomó		
wóham pití	bullshit	FC-R			
wóham sᴍmí	cattle, beef	FC			wóham sumi
wohó	edge, margin, border	WS	wohó		
wohó'ᴍno	skirt, go along the edge of (something)	WS	wohó?yno		

Maidu	English	Source	Source Spelling	Page	Other Spellings
wohóholodoi	break into pieces (intransitive)	RD	woho'holodoi	46	
wohóp	perform an action with the hands	WS	wohóp		
wohópmit	insert (something)	RD	wohop'mit	116	
wohópmithudódoito	try to insert (something) into, almost insert (something) into	RD	wohop'mit hūdō'doito	116	
wohópno	stick (something) into a hole, to fit and close it up, cork (something) up	WS	wohópno		
woi	outer limit, extent: wónom máidⴟki bísmape woi ⴟdíknoweten kan yasánchoi'a. "After he had arrived at the outer limit of where humans were to live, then he stopped." kaní woi ⴟdíknoꝁan "That's as far as he went."	RD	woi	18, 26	
woiyó	select, pick (someone to do a job), hire: máidⴟ woiyómadom hatámꝁan. "He was looking for a man to hire, he was searching in order to hire a man."	RD	woiō', woiyō'	164, 166	woyó (WS)
woiyó	send (someone) outside (for something), send outside for: mⴟtⴟnbe cha woiyóꝁan. "She sent her little brother out to get firewood."	RD	woiō', woiyo'	52, 142, 148, 166	woyó (WS)
woiyó	skunk	RD	woio'	168, 170	wai'ó (WS), wái'o (FC)
woiyókoi	send (someone) away, drive (people) out	RD	woiō'koi	226	
wókⴟ	club, stick, anything to hit with	WS	wóky		
wokⴟ́	Adam's apple	WS	woký		
wokⴟ́chono	hit with a club or stick	RD	wokö'tsono	194	
wokⴟ́kⴟsitoye	scatter (something) about, sprinkle (something like a powder) around	RD	wokö'kösitoye	78	
wokⴟ́m chhikíni	rooster	WS	wokým cikíni		
wokíkit	set down (food for a meal) for (plural subject and object)	RD	wokī'kit	214	
wokít	put (something) down	WS	wokít		
wókit	squabble, fight from jealousy	WS	wókit		
wokkadássikka	a very strong expletive, expressing anger, said to be borrowed from Atsugewi/Pit River	WS	wokkadássikka		
wókkolo	small seashell punched with a hole, acquired by trading	WS	wókkolo		

Maidu	English	Source	Source Spelling	Page	Other Spellings
wókkolom ḱúila	necklace of seashells	WS	wókkolom ḱújla		
wokó	be tired, weary	WS	wokó		wokó (FC-E)
wokócheda	take a break due to fatigue, rest, get rested	RD, WS	woko'tseda (RD), wokóćeda (WS)	208	
Wokodot	place name for village south of Nevada City: Grass Valley	RD-NM			wakadat
woḱói	go have (something) done	WS	woḱój		
woḱói	wind into the distance (as a road or stream)	WS	woḱój		
wokópe	tired	FC			
wokóti	tire out, make (someone) tired	FC			
wokótito	quarrel	WS	wokótito		
wolabɤkɤ	type of wild onion, eaten raw	JD	wolabəkə	34	
wóldokkɤ	wild swan (WS), sand hill crane, swan (FC)	WS, FC	wóldokky		
wóle	white person, Caucasian	WS, FC	wóle		
wóleimen	during the time of the white men	WS	wólejmen		
wólek bosó	glass	FC			
wólek dɤ	scotch broom, non-native plant	FC			
wólek túmbakɤ	sunflower	FC			
wólek wéye	English (language)	FC			
wólek yodáwi	roll (for example, of tape) (noun)	FC			
wólem chakámi	chewing gum	WS	wólem ćakámi		
wólem kɤlé	white woman	WS	wólem kylé		
wólem maháti	wheat bread, loaf bread	WS	wólem maháti		
wólem máidɤ	white man	WS	wólem májdy		
wólem poyó	potato	WS	wólem pojó		
wólem sɤmí	beef	WS	wólem symí		
wolkinú	be sitting down	RD, WS	wolkinū' (RD), wólkinu (WS)	202, 218	wólkinu (WS)
wólkinudompenan	from where (they were) sitting	RD	wol'kinūdompenan	208	
wólkit	sit down	RD, WS	wol'kit (RD), wólkit (WS)	168	
woló	burden basket, conical basket (FC), any large cone-shaped watertight basket, made of birch and bunchgrass (WS)	FC, WS	woló		
wolóllokɤ	flicker (bird)	FC, WS	wolóllok		wolúlukɤ (FC)
Wolóllokɤm	place name in Milford, #3 on HLME map 3. The name means "flicker." a big roundhouse was once here, whose remnants can still be seen above the old bed of Mill Creek. See map 1 in Appendix 5.	HLME	Wolollok'om		
wolólo	trill, gargle	WS	wolólo		
wolósi	leather, animal skin (FC), buckskin, deerskin (WS)	FC, WS	wolós		wolós (WS)

Maidu	English	Source	Source Spelling	Page	Other Spellings
wolósim ʼískali	buckskin moccasins	WS	wolósim ʔískali		
wolósim ʼískalki	buckskin moccasins	WS	wolósim ʔískalki		
wolósim ʼískalno	buckskin moccasins	WS	wolósim ʔískalno		
wolósim ḱuḱú	buckskin string	WS	wolósim ḱuḱú		
wólsa	pocket	FC			wólsm
wólṭa	sit on	WS	wólṭa		
wólṭanu	be sitting on	WS	wólṭanu		
wólṭanutono	sit in a row on (something)	RD	wolʼtanūtono	92	
wolúlukm	flicker (bird)	FC			wolóllok (WS)
wom	tears (from eyes)	WS	wom		
wom	weep, cry (verb)	WS	wom		
womákti	measure (verb)	WS	womákti		
womáktichonoye	take various measurements	WS	womáktićonoje		
wómbusno	cry continually, weep continually	WS	wómbusno		
womít	put (something) down into, record (verb): aním cha sa womítpi "Put that wood in the fire."	FC, FC-T, WST-LM	womít	62:1	
wónmidoikapin	make a circuit going around	RD	wōnʼöidoikapin	128	
wónmidoiwonope	where one had started: mmkí wónmidoiwonopem ḱódoidi mdíknoḱan "He came back to where he had started."	RD	wōnʼöidoiwonope	13	
wonó	get into, fall into, get underway	WS, WST-GP	wonó	68:37	
wonó	lose, suffer the loss of, be deprived of	WS, FC	wonó		
wóno	die	WS	wóno		
wónoʼmḱoi	travel as a spirit	WS	wónoʔyḱoj		
wónobos	die off, be all gone (dead)	FC			
wónoda	pass away, die, be dead	RD	wōnʼoda	78	
wónodawono	death	RD	wōnʼodawono	78	
wónohudoi	almost die	WS	wónohudoj		
wónokm	mortal, resulting in death (adj): wónokmm ḱódo mabó. "It shall be a mortal world."	RD	wōʼnōkö	52	
wónokinu	be laid out, as a corpse	WS	wónokinu		
wónoʼḱoikmm solí	elegy, requiem, song sung after the funeral oration	WS	wónoʔḱojkym solí		
wónom máidm	mankind, mortal man, human	WS, FC	wónom májdy		
wonómen	not miss, not skip (doing): smtim kulúnana maʼát wonómenḱan. "She did not miss even a single night."	RD	wonōʼmen	20, 196	
wónomen	be deathless, immortal	WS	wónomen		
wónomenkm	an immortal, immortal	WS, FC	wónomenky		
wónomenkmm ḱódo	heaven	WS	wónomenkym ḱódo		
wonónan	from the beginning	WST-GP		68:37	

Maidu	English	Source	Source Spelling	Page	Other Spellings
wonónomen	not overlook	RD	wonō'nomen	30	
wónoti	kill	WS	wónoti		
wónotikm	murderer	FC			
wónotimeninu	not be killing: ni 'as tetét húnmoyewet, húḱoinum hesíma'at wónotimeninuḱas. "In spite of hunting a lot, I myself still am not killing anything."	RD	wōn'ōtimeninū	152	
wónotito	make war, kill one another	WS	wónotito		
wónoti'us	kill oneself	FC			
wónotiwe	be obliged to kill (someone): bínmedoipe wónotiwedom "(we) must kill the one who is running away!"	RD	won'otiwe	46	
wónotiwew	keep killing	RD		222	
wónotiwono	something killed	FC	wōn'ōtiwēū		
wónotiya	want to kill (someone), feel like killing (someone): yahát ka'ánte min wónotiyakmḱas. "I have a good mind to kill you. I could just kill you."	RD	wōn'ōtiya	92	
wonóto	trade (verb): solóna wónotodommni ka'as min médom. "I am giving you (this) in trade for the shoes."	WS	wonóto		
wónotodo	trade for (something)	RD	won'otodo	210	
wónowono	corpse, something dead	WS	wónowono		
wónowonom máidm	corpse	WS	wónowonom májdy		
wónowonom máidm tánkm	burial ground	WS	wónowonom májdym támky		
wo'ó	howl	WS	woʔó		
wopók	hit with a club	WS	wopók		
wopókkit	knock down	FC			
wopókno	knock (someone) over, knock (someone) down, hit with a club (RD), club to death (WS), fight (FC)	RD, WS, FC	wōpok'no	86, 102, 216	
wopóldoi	uproot with a digging stick	WS	wopóldoj		
wopólno	uproot with a digging stick	WS	wopólno		
wósdok	hop, limp	WS	wósdok		
wósdoknoye	hop around	WS	wósdoknoje		
wósdot	hop on one foot	WS	wósdot		
wósdotno	lame	WS	wósdotno		
wósdotnoye	hop around on one foot	WS	wósdotnoje		
wosíkmtoto	cousins (RD), those who go way back together, those who used to spend time together growing up, childhood friends	RD	wosī'kötoto	136	posi

Maidu	English	Source	Source Spelling	Page	Other Spellings
wosíp	spend (time), go by, pass (time): pim kúmmeni wosípmʌni "when (someone) has spent many winters," helúnini ekdá wosípchet "after a few days had gone by," tetét pim ekím wosípdom "while very many days are going by"	RD	wosip'	19, 20, 26	
wosíppini	just above, a little further up	WS	wosíppini		
Wóslum Ḱoyóm	place name, "red ants," #3 on LM map. See map 2 in Appendix 5.	LM	wohs-loom-koyom		
wosó	bark skirt, skirt, apron, genitals	RD, RD-NM, WS	woso' (RD), wosó (WS)	76, 168, 170	wossó
wosó	match (for fire)	FC			
wosóťa	woman's bark apron, man's loincloth	WS, WST	wosóťa	54	
wosóťadʌk	having only a loincloth	WS	wosóťadyk		
wóspoi	walk with one leg short	WS	wóspoj		
wóspoiki	clubfooted	WS	wóspojki		
wóspoino	walk along with one leg short	WS	wóspojno		
wóswosi	some kind of bird or animal which does not sleep, and is constantly saying "woswoswos;" Konkow: special night hawk	RD	wos'wosi	164, 168	
woťá	lay (something) down on top of (something)	WS	woťá		
wotí	catch a fish	WST-LB	wotí	44:12	
wótno	ante, place a bet	WS	wótno		
wótno	downward	WS	wótno		
wótnomeninu	have not yet placed a bet	WS	wótnomeninu		
wótnopi	ante, bet	FC			
wótnoti	put chips in (in card games)	FC-R			
wotók	cause (something) to come out (of a container) by hitting with a stick	WS	wotók		
woťókťok	plant called wild dock, with red streaks in the leaves and stems. Cooked like rhubarb, it has a sour taste.	WS	woťókťok		wadokdoko (JD)
wotón	button (from Spanish boton); to button	WS, FC	wotón		
wowáka	salamander	HM	wo-wah'-kah		
wowéw	keep telling (somebody), tell (someone) all the time: ka'áimen, wowéwḱas 'as min. "Don't say stuff like that, I keep on telling you."	RD	wowē'u	142	
wowó	be lying (somewhere), staying, lay (something)	FC			

Maidu	English	Source	Source Spelling	Page	Other Spellings
wowóchono	lay (something) down: sohá'okitweten mómdi wowóchonok̓an. "After carrying them back, they laid them in the water."	RD	wōwō'tsono	188	
wowói'onuto	lie scattered around	RD	wowoi'onuto	148	
wowókinu	be lying (someplace)	WS	wowókinu		
wowómit	put or lay (something) in (somewhere): nik̓í wasása nik̓í hadóikʌdi wowómitbos kʌ'ʌm ma'ás. "I laid all my things in my suitcase."	WS, WST	wowómit	60:56	
wowót̓a	lay (something) down on top of (something)	WS	wowót̓a		
wowót̓anu	be lying on top of (something)	WS	wowót̓anu		
wowóti	catch fish one after another	WST	wowóti	44:10	
woyé	get to be (some way)	WS	wojé		
woyó	hire (someone) to (do something), send (someone) to (do something)	WS	wojó		woiyó (RD)
wóyo	hit all around (as with a stick)	WS	wójo		
woyók̓oi	send (someone) to (go do something), send (someone) away	WS	wojók̓oj		
woyók̓oiwono	be driven out	RD	woiō'koiwono	226	
woyóno	send (someone) inside	RD	woyon'o	176	
woyónute	be scattered around	RD	woion'ute	146	
woyósip	send (someone) out	WS	wojósip		
wu	to pile up	RD	wū	104	
wubúno	roll around roughly under the hand or foot	WS	wubúno		
wuchulus	curl up, fold up (like a dry leaf)	FC-T			
wudúmkit	throw down (cards), throw (it) down	FC			wʌdʌ́mkit
wuiléspuikʌ	mourning dove	FC			
wuiléspuikʌm yo	mariposa lily (FC), Indian potato, calochortus (JD)	FC, JD	wulys pujkomjom	60	wuilespuikʌm yo
wulú	dance at the wéda	WS	wulú		
wúlu	dance in a circle	FC			
wulúdoi	start dancing	WST	wulúdoj	68:42	
wulúi	roast in ashes	RD	wulū'i	234	
wuluku	white snow goose	FC			
wulúlukʌ	flicker (bird)	FC			
wulul utikʌ	St John's wort	FC			wulutikʌ (FC-T)
wulumoto	go around while dancig in a circle	FC			
wulút	pile, stack (verb)	WS	wulút		
wulútdoi	pile (something) up	WST-DW	wulútdoj	74:12	
wulúti	big pile	RD	wūlū'ti	104	
wúni	slowly, with difficulty	RD	wū'ni	178	
wunúnoye	stagger, be unstable	FC			

Maidu	English	Source	Source Spelling	Page	Other Spellings
wusíp	float out	RD	wusip', wusī'	38	
wusuisuikit	deflate, lose motivation	FC			wᴧsuisuikit
wusutikᴧ	bottle cap, stopper: bíyam lolóm wusutikᴧ "beer bottle cap"	FC-T			
wusútkinu	lie on the belly, lie face down	RD	wusut'kinu	12	
wutúl	pile, stack	WS	wutúl		
wutúlkit	throw into a pile	WS	wutúlkit		
wutúlyo	pile up (a bunch of things)	WS	wutúljo		
wutúmtumi	thunder	FC			wᴧtᴧ́mtᴧmi (RD)
Wuwáyonoktom Sewí	Middle Fork of the Feather River	FC			
yᴧ́	go	WS	jý		
yᴧ́'asᴧsip	start to bulge out, start to come back out	RD	yöas'ösip	178	
yᴧ́'asdaw	move down and off, move aside, move over! get out of the way	RD	yö'āsdau	178	
yᴧ'ástaino	stagger around	FC			
yᴧ'áswodaw	go farther (downhill-ish)	RD	yöās'wodau	230	ᴧ'áswodaw
yᴧ'áswodikno	move close to each other	RD	yöās'wodikno	168	
yᴧ'áswodoi	go further (uphill-ish)	RD	yöās'wodoi	230	
yᴧ'áswokityochono	dive further down	WST-DW	jyʔás wokit jóćono	70:4	
yᴧ'áswokoi	go off farther	RD	yöās'wōkoi	142	
yᴧ'aswono	be a torrential rain, come down in buckets (rain): tetét kadíkebisim bei yᴧ'aswonokan. "It kept raining hard, then it came in buckets."	RD	yö'āswōno	194	
yᴧ'áswopai	move closer to (someone), be getting closer (a pursuer)	RD	yö'āswōpai'	224	
yᴧchóno	exist everywhere	RD	yötsóno	4	
yᴧdᴧ́mitno	put (something) down into (something)	RD	yödömitno	60	
yᴧdᴧ́mno	toss (something) while going along	RD	yödöm'no	170	
yᴧdᴧ́msitodo	while throwing (something) across	RD	yödöm'sitodo	60	
yᴧ́di	at a place, in a location: ᴧdíknokan mᴧm hómpaitokᴧm yᴧ́di. "He arrived at the place where they had fought."	RD	yö'di	146	
yᴧdónu	be in a vertical position (like posts, trees, lumber)	WS	jydónu		
yᴧhémi	gooseberry	FC, WS	jyhém		yᴧhém (WS)
yᴧ́kkᴧk	shake, tremble (only of a person)	WS	jýkkyk		
yᴧmᴧ́	put (something), lay (something)	WS	jymý		
yᴧmᴧ́'asito	put/bring over on other side, bring across	RD	yömö'asito	44, 62	
yᴧmᴧ́chono	put over into, put into	WS, RD	jymýćono (WS), yömö'tsono (RD)	RD 74	

Maidu	English	Source	Source Spelling	Page	Other Spellings
ymmḿdoi	pick (something) up	RD	yömö'doi		
ymmḿkit	put (something) down, lay (something) down	WS	jymýkit		
ymmḿkitcho	lay (something) down	RD	yömö'kitso	60	
ymmḿkiti	set (something) down	RD		76	
ymmḿtno	put (something) down into	RD	yömöt'no	76	
yḿmmoto	surround, encircle, enclose	WS	jýmmoto		
ymn	elsewhere	WS	jyn		
yḿnmnmschopin	start to climb down in (RD), come over towards while crouched or bent at the waist (WS)	RD, WS	yön'önöschopin (RD), jýnynyscopin (WS)	106	
ymnḿs	be stooped, stooped over	WS	jynýs		yḿnos (RD)
ymnḿskit	be bent over, stooped	WS	jynýskit		
yḿnan	from a place: ḱódom yḿnan: ínyanam wi'ípem ḱódoidi ḱódom yḿnan msitopinḱan "They crossed over here from a land where there were no Indians."	WST-DW	jýnan	72:1	
yḿnno	go down into	WS	jýnno		
yḿno	separate, split, divorce	FC			yúno, úno (FC)
ymnó	thin, slim (as a man, a tree, etc.)	WS	jynó		
ymnó	go	WS	jýno		
yḿnope	divorced, separated	FC-E			
yḿnoswoito	bend over towards (something)	RD	yönoswoito	62	
yḿnoye	make a circuit, go around	WS	jýnoje		
ymnóye	go around (same as mnóye)	RD	yönō'ye, yöno'e	226	mnóye
ymnóyedi	in the place where (someone) travels: mmkánim ymnóyedi "in the same area (he) goes around in," at the place where (someone) is going around: tétewonopem ymnóyedi "at the place where (they) had been going around playing"	RD	yöno'yedi	90, 230	mnóyedi
yḿnpin	come into (a room or building)	WST	jýnpin	56:41	yúnpin, yínpin (FC-R)
yḿpm	pubesce (girls only), have the first menstrual period, menstruate	WS	jýpy		yúpu (FC)
yḿpmhekiti	menopause	WS	jýpyhekiti		
yḿpmkato	puberty ceremony for girls	RD-NM			
yḿpmm solí	girls' puberty ceremony song	WS	jýpym solí		
yḿpe	young people, teenagers	FC			
ymsáno	stop (intransitive)	RD	yösā'no, yasa'no	176	
yḿsip	go out of, go out	WS, WST	jýsip	56:40	

Maidu	English	Source	Source Spelling	Page	Other Spellings
yṁsito	go across	WS	jýsito		
yṁsíto	go across	RD	yösī'to	13	
yṁtḿi	rip	WS	jytýj		
yṁtḿito	rip open	WS	jytýjto		
yṁtḿiwaito	rip wide open	WS	jytýjwajto		
Yṁtámoto	place name for Genesee. See Yetomoto on map 5 in Appendix 5	FC			
Yṁtámoto ma'a	Genesee/Taylorsville people	FR1	yetameto ma'a		Yatamoto, Yotamoto
yṁt́ano	ride on top (of a horse)	FC			
yḿwaitokṁdi	in every place: ḱodom yḿwaitokṁdi "everywhere in the world"	RD	yö'waitoködi	132	
yṁwáitokṁdi	everywhere the world extends	RD	yöwai'toködi	132	
yṁwáitokṁnan	from everywhere: ḱodom yṁwáitokṁnan - from the far reaches of the world	RD	yöwai'tokönan	28, 38	
ya	make, construct, do, build, shape (something): ṗidúsdi maháti yawéten, lḿt'usan "After making bread, they used to bake (it) in the ashes." kṁkás yadóm. "That's why I'm doing this."	WS, FC, WST, FC-E, HY	ja	52:12	
yá	cloud, sky	WS	já		
yá	good, like to, want to (short for yahá)	WS	já		
yá	name (noun): niḱi yam kṁkán "my name is..." yákudom "having a name" hesí yákupem maḱá? "What is your name?"	WS, FC, FC-T	já		
yá	swim (for fish only)	WS	já		
ya'ati	create	FC			
yabát	break by snapping	WS	jabát		
yabáti	broken - personal Indian name of John Meadows' younger brother who had a broken arm	WS	jabáti		
yabátyo	break, snap (things)	WS	jabátjo		
yabós	finish, complete (something)	WS	jabós		
yabóspe	pre-made	FC			
yabóspem bosó	arrowhead	WS	jabóspem bosó		
yáchachái'inpin	trot down over towards	RD	yā'tsatsai'inpin	120	
yáchaichai	trot, as a horse	WS	jáćajćaj		
yáchaichaino	trot along	WS	jáćajćajno		

Maidu	English	Source	Source Spelling	Page	Other Spellings
yaché	keep, keep back, hold back, save back, reserve: hesíma'at yachémenwet, ᴍpéḱaniluťi mahámotoḱan. "without withholding anything, they brought every last one together." búknakim mᴍdᴍ́kᴍ yachéḱan. "Only the tail part did they keep."	RD, WS	yatsē' (RD), jaće (WS)	32, 56	
yachépe	that which was saved, that which was held back	RD	yatsē'pe	170	
yadᴍ́kdᴍ́k	revise, fix up, rectify, repair, work over, adjust (something out of whack), re-make	WS, RD	jadýkdyk (WS), yadök'dö (RD)	24	yadᴍ́kdᴍ
yadᴍ́kdᴍkisma	that which I have repaired	RD	yadök'dökis (a)mam	24	
yaha	we/you should, we/you ought to, it ought to be done (suffixed to another verb stem but not conjugated): bályaha "we ought to paint," hesátiyaha "we ought to make something" ka'áimenyaha "what should not be mentioned" (noun)	RD	yaha	7, 9, 184	
yahá	be good, do good, be blessed: yaháḱan "that's good." yahá yahá'ankano "You are doing good things. You will do great things." yahádom, helám oméikᴍ min méidom. "You are blessed, since a gambling charm is being given to you." yaháluťkas "I am doing great." yahámenḱan "It's not right."	FC, WST, RD, BC		72:6, 9, 10	yá
yahá	good (adj): yahám ekí "a good day"	WS	jahá		
yahá	good thing, good idea (noun): etú! yahá wéyesi. "Wait! I must tell you a good idea!"	RD	yaha	9	
yahá	right, well (adv), the right way: yahá húheyedom kakᴍ́'ankano. "Now you might be thinking right."	FC, RD	134	134	

Maidu	English	Source	Source Spelling	Page	Other Spellings
yahá	want to (do), like to (do) (can be suffixed to another verb stem, and conjugated): ꟽnóyahanimmꟽni, mínsꟽm ꟽnóma'enkes bénekto. "If you want to go, let's all go tomorrow." ꟽnóyahaḱas "I want to go."	WS, FC, RD, WST-DW	jahá (WS), yaha (RD)	68	
yahá'ade?	Is it good? Are things good?	FC-T			
yahácheti	look good, be likeable, be attractive	WS	jaháćeti		
yaháchetipe	good-looking, pretty, handsome	WS	jaháćetipe		
yaháchetí'uspe	beautiful to oneself, narcissistic	FC			
yahádi	for good, securely, safely, with certainty: hesápem ḱodóidiwet utimádom bístimadom, yahádi bístimadom dꟽkꟽ pꟽ́tma'ankano. "In whatever country you are going to put it and leave it, to leave it safely, being all alone, you will untie it."	RD	yahā'di	136	
yahádikꟽ	superb one	WS	jahádiky		
yahádoiti	start doing good (things): mi yahádoiti "you, do better! Start doing better!"	FC			
yaháha	good (making the modified noun plural), good ones, the better (of two): póchodem máidꟽm yaháham máidꟽdi sꟽ́ti wasósapem ohéchoi'a. "Bat Man was the only bad-tempered one out of (all) the good men." hesáwet mínchem mayákḱen yaháha chámikꟽpem? "I wonder which of you two has the best knife?"	WS, RD	jaháha (WS) yahā'ha (RD), RD-IS	60, 202	
yaháhaluťi	very good, the best	RD	yahā'haluti	60	
yaháhanu	be prepared, cooked for a while	RD	yahā'hanu	216	
yaháhati	prepare (something), prepare meat after skinning, get a bow ready to hunt, pack belongings	RD	yahā'hati	140, 146	
yaháhati'us	fix oneself up, get clothes on, get ready to go out	RD	yahā'hatius'	170	

Maidu	English	Source	Source Spelling	Page	Other Spellings
yahákan	good, great, that's good. Can also be used sarcastically, "Oh, great!" 'wónom máidm̓ sa pedákas,' achói'a wm̓tm̓mim máidm̓m. am̓m̓nikan sm̓hm̓lim wasóchoi'a. 'Ho,' achói'a. 'yahákan!' "'I stole fire from the humans,' said Thunder Man. Then Mosquito was angry. 'Oh,' he said. 'Great!'	RD, FC	yahā'kan	162	
yaháluť	be great, be awesome	RD	yahā'lut	164, 170	
yahámakit	be skilled at, talented at, know how to do something well	RD	yahā'makit	80, 82	
yahámakitpe	one who is skilled: tetét yahámakitpem kakm̓'ankano "You must be very skilled"	RD	yahā'makitpe	80, 82	
yahámeni	reject (noun), not a good one	FC			
yahánu	do good (in the world)	FC			
yahápada	behave yourself!	FC			
yahápe	good	FC			
yahát	very: yahát wené ma'át, sudákade? "Although it's very good (healthy?), is it tasty to you?"	WS, WST-RP, FC-E	jahát	44	
yahát	well, good: yahát chíkm̓pem "well-dressed" yahát bíspada "may you stay well, stay calm, stay safe" Note: the translation as "good" is with certain verbs, for example: yahát dótipem "tasting good" yahát hm̓bm̓kdom "feeling good" yahát hísatipe "good-smelling"	WS, WST-RP, FC-E	jahát	146	
yahát 'as	mission accomplished, it went well, I did it well	RD	yaha'das	200	
yahát bis	be safe, stay well, stay safe: yahát bíspada "may you stay safe."	FC-E, FC, RD		146	
yahát hapá	how true! That's right! Amen!	WS	jahat hapá		
yahát hísatipe	smelling good, smelling sweet	FC			
yahát hubúk	feel good, feel pleasant	FC			yahát hm̓bm̓k
yahát hubúktipe	good-feeling, pleasant, which is pleasant	FC-E			
yahát hubúkti'us	make yourself happy	FC			yahát hm̓bm̓kti'us
yahát ka'ánte	I have a good mind to..., I could just... right now!: yahát ka'ánte min wónotiyakm̓kás! "I have a good mind to kill you!"	RD	yahat' kante	92	

Maidu	English	Source	Source Spelling	Page	Other Spellings
yahát yatí'us	do well for oneself	WS	jahát jatí?us		
yahátche	like (verb)	WS	jahátće		
yahátcheno	handsome, pretty, good-looking	WS	jahátćeno		
yahátchetiboduk	be not so very good-looking	WS	jahátćetiboduk		
yaháti	prepare (food), get food ready to cook (RD), get things in order, organize things (WS), make something good/better (FC, HY): nik yaháti'ankano "you make me better" "thank you;" mᴍdí'im wéye yahátimabᴍs ebᴍ́bᴍm wéyedom. "By speaking this language for a long time, I might get better (at it)."	RD, WS, FC, HY	yahā'ti (RD), jaháti (WS)	164	
yahátkana	for sure, surely, definitely: yahátkana uním kulúdi mᴍyák wéyechet pínma'aḱas. "For sure, if he says the same thing tonight, I will listen."	RD	yahat'kana'	216	
yahátupe	safely: yahátupe mᴍkí tépkᴍni bitíukitᴍsitopinḱan. "He came across safely, sticking his flint-flaker in the ground to grip on."	RD	yahatupe	54	
yáhni	hill	FC			
yahóiyape	first one created, first one to create	RD	yahoi'ape(m)	25	
yáhpat	come after, go after, run after (someone)	RD	yāh'pat, ya''pat	164, 170	
yáhpatchono	go over to attack someone, go after someone (in anger)	RD	yā''patsono	222	
yáhpatdoi	start pursuing (someone)	RD	yāh'patdoi, ya''patdoi	32, 170	
yáhpatḱoi	go off after (someone or something)	RD	ya''patkoi	164	
yáhpatyeweḱoi	come back after someone, come after someone again (to attack them): ḱáipe mádom ma'át wokítchet, máidᴍm yá'patyeweḱoichoi'a. "Just as they were setting dinner out, a man came back after them."	RD	ya''patyewēk'oi	214	yá'patyeweḱoi
yáhule	cloud cover (noun)	FC			
yáhule	cover over (as clouds) (verb)	FC-E			
yáiṭapada	in covering (his) tracks	RD	yai'tapada	64	

Maidu	English	Source	Source Spelling	Page	Other Spellings
yáiyochopin	pile things up by throwing over or through something	RD	yai'yotsopin	110	
yaiyókit	pile (things) up	WS	jajókit		yayókit (WS)
yaiyókitye	pile up (things, firewood)	RD	yaiokitye	100	
yaiyókityo	stretch (things) out, spread (things) out: humíndom unídi yaiyókityodom ka'án wáyomapem. "Catching fish in nets, here they are stretching out (the nets), getting ready to throw them in the water."	RD	yaiyokityo	64	
yaiyóno	lay (something) down	RD	yaiyono	60	
yaiyónpin	throw in (firewood), stack (something)	RD, WS	yaion'pin (RD), jajónpin (WS)	100	yayónpin (WS)
yak	be like, be as if, resemble	WS	jak		yáka (RD)
yákm	cloud up, cloudy	WS	jáky		
yákmdoi	blow over the sky (clouds)	WS	jákydoj		
yakm	be named	WS	jaký		
yakm	boat, canoe, bridge (WS): yaḱ mep nik. "Bring me the canoe." mmyákapem yakḿdi ká'enḱasi "We (2) are in the same boat"	FC, WS, FC-R, RD	jaḱ (WS), yakā' (RD)	58	yaḱ (WS), yaká (RD)
Yakḿki	place name for mountain called Canoe's (RD), may be Hamilton Mountain (FR1), features in the flood story (FR-TE). See also Yakḿm Yamani and Yakḿm O. Several mountains have similar names. See map 1 in Appendix 5.	RD, FR1, FR-TE	yakū'ki	42	yakúkim yamani (FR1)
Yakḿm O	place name for Big Boat Mountain, #1 on LM map. Possibly Coyote Peak or Hamilton Mountain. See map 1 in Appendix 5. See also Yakḿm Yamáni (possibly Keddie Peak or Keddie Ridge).	LM	Yakomov		
Yakḿm Yamáni	place name for Keddie Peak. See maps 1, 3 and 5 in Appendix 5.	FC-map, MSOP			
yakḿti	to name (cause to have a name)	RD	yakö'ti	14	
yaká	saliva	FC			
yaká	boat, canoe	RD	yakā'	40	yakḿ
yáka	be like, seem like: achét ḱódo ayádom mpéḱake'nomapem yákade? "But will the weather always be like it is (now)?	RD	yāk'a	104, 152, 234	yak (WS)

Maidu	English	Source	Source Spelling	Page	Other Spellings
yakán	saliva	WS	jakán		
Yakani	place name for Buck's Ranch. See map 2 in Appendix 5.	PM-D			
Yakani Pakáni	place name for Buck's Lake. See map 1 in Appendix 5.	PM-D	yakani pakanee		
yakánu	seem like, look like	RD	yakan'u	48, 160, 166, 170, 224	
yákanudo	resemble	RD	yak'anudo	62	
yakát	like (adverb), similarly: luťim yakát "just like," kᴧlóknonom yakát wéyeḱan "he talked like a woman"	RD	yakat'	76, 78	yákkat (WST)
yákati	seem to cause, cause what seems like: kóh'bonom mᴧ mómni hítapem yákkatichoi'a. "The storm seemed to drench it with water."	RD	yak'ati	170	
yakawéw	look like (someone), look more and more like someone	RD	yakawē'u	98	
yakbé	to look like, seem like, be like (analogy): okítebisim okítebisim uním chám yamánim yakbéchoi'a "They kept coming and coming (until) they were like this tree-covered mountain."	RD	yakbe'	38	
yákcheti	look like, resemble	WS	jákćeti		
yákchetiluť	look just like (something or someone): wónom máidᴧm yákadom, mayákḱen péne tólkᴧdom péne yímkᴧdom wónom máidᴧm yákchetilútweten, ᴧnóchoi'a. "Looking like a human, having two legs and two arms, once he looked exactly like a human, he travelled."	RD	yak'tsetilut'	200	
yakchetípe	resembling	FC			
yákdᴧkbe	be just like, same as: tetém máidᴧm nik yákdᴧkbe máidᴧm "a man the same size as me, a big man like me"	RD	yak'dükbe, yak'dökbe	130, 152	

285

Maidu	English	Source	Source Spelling	Page	Other Spellings
yákhubᴧk	feel like, feel as if: nenónopem máidᴧm ma'át béidᴧkim kᴧlé oiᴧpaidom, ka'án pᴧbem máidᴧm yakhubᴧkmapem "Even an old man, falling in love with a young woman, will feel like a teenager."	RD	yak'hubök (RD), jákhybyk (WS)	52, 92	yákhᴧbᴧk (WS)
yákit	get cloudy	WS	jákit		
yakka	spear	FC-E			
yákka	do like (someone does), seem like (in the speculative sense, for example, "he must be home by now.")	WS	jákka		
yákkasma	what seems like to me, what I consider to be: amá kᴧkán nik hútupem yákkasma. "That, to me, is what I consider crazy."	WST-RP	jákkasma	66:29	
yákkat	like (adverb): yákkat píntiam "it sounded like"	WST	jákkat	60	
yákkatcheti	looks as if (it) might be...	WS	jákkatćeti		
yákḱen	I don't know (the answer), I'm not sure (about something proposed) (RD), seem like (FC), seem to be... might be... (WS)	RD, FC, WS	yā'ken (RD), jákḱen (WS)	9, 156	yatken (FC)
yákkit	know (something)	WS	jákkit		
yaḱói	go to call (someone), go get (someone) to come	RD	yakoi'	92	
yakpínti	sound like	RD	yakpin'ti	86	
yaktekít	same time of year, same season	RD	yak'tekit	150	
yaktekítpedi	in a short time, in the same season	RD	yaktekit'pedi	150	
yáku	be gray and overcast, cloud up	FC			yákᴧ
yakwé	seem like, sound like, talk as if: hedénna yakwéḱan "It sounded close by." ḱódom kᴧlᴧplᴧlᴧpdom tetédᴧkᴧm yakwéḱan. "Rumbling, it sounded like the loudest (noise)." mᴧm máidᴧm hesíma'at makítmenpem yakwédom kᴧkán. "That man sounds like he doesn't know a thing (=one who doesn't know anything)."	RD	yakwē'	28, 72, 86, 150, 200	
yákwei	talk as if	WS	jákwej, jákweje		yákweye

Maidu	English	Source	Source Spelling	Page	Other Spellings
yákweḱelkm	canoe thug, someone up to no good in a boat, canoe striking (RD), ones who stab people in boats (MM)	RD, WS-MM	yak'wekelkö	RD 58, WS-MM 55	
yakwéto	echoing, resounding: wépa wómmni pim yakwéto pedátochoi'a. "When he howled, echoing, many answered Coyote."	RD	yakwē'to	38	
yalálapdoi	reach up	WS, WST-DW	jalálapdoj		
yaláp	reach for	FC			
yállal	board (of wood)	WS	jállal		
yállalati	make a sound like boards banging together	WS	jállalati		
yálulu	elderberry flute	WS	jálulu		
yálulu	play the flute	RD	yāl'ulu	192	
yálulum dm	elderberry bush	FC			
yáluluwebis	keep playing the flute, play the flute on and on	RD	yāl'uluwēbis	192	
yamái	shade, shadow: nik yamái chíkmenma'ankano "don't stand in my shadow" (standing in someone's shadow is considered rude)	WS, FC	jamáj		yamái'i, yamái (FC)
yamáichik	be in the shadow of someone else's body (FC), be in someone's light, cast a shadow (WS)	WS, FC	jamájćik		
yamáichik ḱúmhm	willow shaded shelter	FC			
yamáitototi	shelter each other: yahát yamáitototima'ankano nisé "Let us be good to each other."	FC			
yamánbe	little mountain	RD	yamanbe	66	
yamándato	mountains	RD	yaman'dato	8	
yamáni	mountain	FC, RD, WS	yaman'i (RD), jamán (WS)	118	yamán
yamánim bmkúike	a mountain herb	FC			
yamánim chupí	red-barked willow	FC			
yamánim kiw	behind the mountain, at the back of the mountain	RD	yamān'im kiū'	84	
yamánim pinim	from top to bottom of a mountain	FC			
yamánim sedém	lava	FC-E			
yamánim tótto	manzanita (low-growing variety)	WS	jamánim tótto		
yamánmanto	mountain range	FC			
yamánmantono	mountain ranges: yamándatom yamánmantono: "mountain range after mountain range"	RD	yaman'mantono	8	
yamánnodi	along in the mountains	WS	jamánnodi		
yami'i	sucker fish	FC			

Maidu	English	Source	Source Spelling	Page	Other Spellings
yámli	shiner, a small shiny sardine-like fish	WS	jámli		
yámmoto	get even with, get revenge on	WS	jámmoto		
yámmotopai	get even, retaliate	FC			
yan	hillside	FC			
yanái	tremble, quake (as earth)	WS	janáj		
yanáinaito	tremble, quiver, as an earthquake	WS	janájnajto		
yanáito	tremble, quiver (as an earthquake)	WS	janájto		
yanánaito	earthquake	FC			
yánikútakuta	butterfly	HM	yah'-ne-kut'-tah-kut'-tah		
yánno	swim downstream (fish only)	WS	jánno		
yáno	swim, swim upstream (fish only)	WS, FC	jáno		
yánoye	swim around (fish only)	WS	jánoje		
yánta	badger	WS	jánta		
yánto	create	RD	yan'to	25	
yányanto	foothills	FC			
yapái	demonstrate, show	WS	japáj		
yapáiḱoi	go show (someone something)	WS	japájḱoj		
yapáino	go show (someone something)	WS	japájno		
yapáisitoye	show (someone) all around inside	WS	japájsitoje		
yapáito	talk (noun), conversation: yahám yapáitoni "with good conversation"	RD	yapai'to	134	
yapáito	talk to, converse with, chat: : níknedi yapáitodom "in conversing with my mother"	WS, WST	japájto	50:4	
yapáitodo	speaking to (multiple people): mᴧkí mᴧnéwoli ᴧpéḱani yapáitodo "speaking to her female elders"	RD	yapai'todo	188	
yapáitoto	converse, talk together, chat with each other	WS, FC	japájtoto		
yapáitotokinu	say to each other	RD	yapai'totokinu	36	
yapáito'us	talk to oneself	RD	yapai'tous	192	
yapát	pursue, chase	WS	japát, jáppat		yáppat, yáhpat
yapáti	ceanothus, native lilac	JD	japatym	68	chapati (FC)
yapátḱoi	chase	WS	japátḱoj		
yápoḱno	rape (v)	FC			
yáppatdoi	take off after	WS	jáppatdoj		
yasáno	give up, stop	RD	yasāno, yasānu	54, 88	yasánu, yᴧsano
yásḱakno	a skinny man, the jack in cards	WS	jásḱakno		

Maidu	English	Source	Source Spelling	Page	Other Spellings
yasmá	what I am doing, what I did: núkmakas wólem ínyana wéyemmni ayápem hesísiwet yasmá pínkenudom. "I will laugh when the white people are speaking Maidu anything like this, from listening to what I am doing."	HY			
yásmaye	stumble around	FC			
yásnoye	stumble around	FC-E			
yát	well, very much (variant of yahát)	WS, WST-DW	ját	70:4	
yaťa	peel or skin off a thin membrane (as from a potato or vegetable)	WS	jaťa		
yaťá	former, the late, deceased (always suffixed to the verb ("formerly ...") or noun ("late"))	WS	jaťa		
Yatámoto	place name for Genesee, Coppertown. See map 5 in Appendix 5, under Yetomoto.	FC			Ymtámoto, Yetámoto, Yotámoto
Yatámotom Ma'a	place name for Genesee	FC-E			Ymtámoto Ma'a, Yetámoto Ma'a, Yotámoto Ma'a
yatí	create (FC), make (something) for (someone) (WS)	FC, WS	jatí		
Yatim	place name for Salmon Falls, #17 on LM map. Waterfall on the Feather River near Seneca (4 miles south of Lake Almanor), where salmon could be speared (PM-M). See map 3 in Appendix 5.	LM, PM-M			
yátken	don't know	FC			yákken
yaw	stir	WS	jaw		
yawi	miner's lettuce	JD	jawy	66	
yawí	cost	WS	jawí		
yawí	mention, call by name, talk about	RD, WS	jawí (WS), yawi' (RD)	RD 78	
yawí	name (noun), word: hesí yawíkmka? "What name do you have?"	FC-T			
yawí	read, say a word	WS	jawí		
yawíd	by that word, in saying that word: 'yóno' máikmchoi'am yawíd achét máisem pínmenkmchoi'a. "He meant 'antler' by that word, but they didn't understand."	RD	yawīd'	208	
yawíkukus	pretend to read	FC			

Maidu	English	Source	Source Spelling	Page	Other Spellings
yawíti	teach school	WS	jawíti		
yawítikm	schoolteacher, teacher	WS	jawítiky		
yawítikm hmbó	school, schoolhouse	WS	jawítikym hybó		
yawítikm kmlé	female teacher, schoolmarm	WS	jawítikym kyle		
yawítikm máidm	male teacher	WS	jawítikym májdy		
yawónope	that which was created/made	RD	yawo'nope(m)	28, 172	
yáwsitoye	stir all around	WS	jáwsitoje		
yayó	do something with several things	WS	jajó		
yayókit	pile things up, put things down	WS	jajókit		yaiyókit (RD)
yayónpin	throw things down in (to somewhere)	WS	jajónpin		yaiyónpin (RD)
yayópin	throw things in	WS	jajópin, jajówpin		yayówpin
yé	feather, wing of an insect	WS	jé		
yé	invite	WS	jé		
yebúbuchik	be gradually covered over	RD	yebūb'utsek	180	
yedát	be hung up, stuck together	WS	jedát		
yedáttoto	be hung together, as dogs in intercourse	WS	jedáttoto		
yedúdutkit	crawl flat along the ground, to avoid detection	RD	yedu'dutkit	58	
yedúwokit	crawl flat along the ground, to avoid detection	RD	yedū'wokit	58	
yehéhedoi	look up	RD	yehē'hedoi	12	
yehép	afraid, timid, shy, hesitant	WS	jehép		
yehéppinti	sound frightening	WS	jehéppinti		
yehépti	misfortune: hes yehépti! "What a tragedy"	FC			
yehéptoye	be afraid of (RD), be afraid, frightened (WST) timid, shy, hesitant (WS)	WS, RD, WST	jehéptoje (WS), yehep'toye	106 (RD), 52:15 (WST)	
yehéptoyehye	be uneasy, be a little worried	WST	jehéptojehje	60	
yehéptuye	be afraid or worried	RD	yehep'tuye	112, 152, 228	
yehéptuyetipe	dangerous, scary	RD	yehep'tuyetipe	138	
yehétchono	put under/behind (belt)	RD	yehetsono	58	
yehétdoi	stick (something) in a belt	RD	yehet'doi	60	
yehétdonupe	which was carried under the belt	RD	yehetdonupe	60	
yéi	fly (verb)	WS	jéj		
yéi 'mdíkno	fly to (some goal)	WS	jéj ʔydíkno		
yéi 'mwódoi	fly upward	WS	jéj ʔywódoj		
yéidíkno	hover	RD	yē'idik'no	80	
yéiwodoi	swoop upwards	RD	yē'iwodoi'	80	
yekói	go off to tell about (something), go off to round people up	RD	yekoi'	166	

Maidu	English	Source	Source Spelling	Page	Other Spellings
yékoi	invite (someone) to go, summon	WS, RD	jékoj (WS), yekoi' (RD)	38	yekói
yelábito	reach out and grab	RD	yelāb'ito	178, 200	
yelákoi	go off courting	RD	yelāk'oi	202	yilákoi (RD)
yelálapdoi	reach up and grab	RD	yelā'lapdoi	58	
yelápwo	grab at	WS	jelápwo		
yelápwo'ṁheno	reach down in	RD	yelap'woöhēno	92	
yéltutu	wild rose	HM	yel'-too-too		
yem	hawk	FC-T			
yem oḱen	feather pillow	FC-T			
yémba	wing of a bird	WS	jémba		
yemík	set a fish trap	WS	jemík		
yenḿnnokṁ	wheel, something that turns	WS	jenýnnoky		
yé'okít	invite (someone) to come	WS	jé?okít		
yepaisolo	glasses	FC			
yépcheti	be quite a few, be a lot, do a lot, do intensively, provide a lot	RD	yep'tseti, yeptset'i	56, 78, 80, 90, 142, 146, 148, 202, 208, 214	yepchéti
yépchetiti	make quite a few pieces	RD	yep'tsetiti	110	
yepéinti	make a lot of noise, do a lot of	RD	yepeinti	52	
yepésto	intromit vigorously, used to describe the initial action of the male in copulation	WS	jepésto		
yepí	be embarrassed, ashamed	WS	jepí		
yepí	man, male, male animal, husband (plural yépsṁ)	FC, WS	jeṕ		
yepíbem te	boy	PM-D	yeṕ ebenta		
yepím chhikini	rooster	FC			
yepím kawáyu	stallion	WS	jepím kawáju		
yepím sṁmí	buck deer	WS	jepím symí		
yepím wóha	bull	FC			
yepín	ask	RD	yepin'	152	epin
yepínti	make a lot of noise, be very loud	RD, WST-LB	yepin'ti (RD), jéppinti (WST)	108, 158, 168, 216 (RD), 42:5 (WST)	yéppinti (WS)
yepíntiti	cause (someone) to make a lot of noise, cause it to be very loud	RD	yepin'titi	114	
yepísape	shameful	FC			
yepíti	embarrass (someone), cause shame: nik yepíti'ankano "You are the cause of my shame. You are embarrassing me."	WS, FC-R	jepíti		

Maidu	English	Source	Source Spelling	Page	Other Spellings
yépkm	marry a man	RD	yep'kü	228	
yépkmlele	take another husband, marry many men	RD	yep'kölēle	52	
yépkmpe	have a husband, be married (to a man)	RD	yep'küpem	228	
yepkmto	couple of men	FC			
yepóni	head man, chief	FC, RD	yepōn'i	28	yopóni
yepónim kmlé	the queen in cards	FC-T			
yepónim máidm	head man, chief, king in cards	FC-T			
yepónim te	the jack in cards	FC-T			
yepsḿ	men	WS	jepsý		
yépsabe	man: bam yépsabe "salt man"	RD	yepsabe	46	
yépti	accident, misfortune, tragedy, bad luck "something that comes up that isn't good"	FC			yehépti
yépti'us	embarrass oneself: yépti'uskas "I embarrassed myself"	FC-T			
yesáno	halt, stop, cease moving (intransitive)	WS	jesáno		yasáno, yasánu, ymsano
Yetámeto	place name for Genesee	MSOP, FR, FR-HY	yoťamoto, yetameto		Yoťámmoto
Yetámeto ma'a	people of Yetámeto, Genesee people	FR1, FR-HY			
Yetámeto non	place name for Genesee, a village at the confluence of Grizzly and Indian Creek in Genesee Valley. Big times were held here and there was a large sweat house (FR-HY). The pioneer settlement of Coppertown was located on this site (FR-TE). According to Herb Young, Yetameton is Genesee Valley. See Yoťámmoto Ḱoyó on map 5 in Appendix 5.	FR1, FR-TE, FR-HY	yetameto non		
Yetámeto Ḱoyó	place name for Genesee Valley. See map 5 in Appendix 5.	MSOP			
Yetámetom Bo	place name for Genesee Rd (road going from Taylorsville to Genesee). See map 5 in Appendix 5.	MSOP			
Yetámeton	place name for Genesee Valley. See map 5 in Appendix 5.	FR-HY			Yotamoto, Yatamoto
yewé	back, in return (adv)	FC			
yewé	come back, give back, return	FC, WS	jewéj		yewéi (WS)
yewé'iti	recycle	FC			

Maidu	English	Source	Source Spelling	Page	Other Spellings
yewékit	take (something) back out	FC			
yewéto	returning from, on (his) return from. This adverb clarifies the subject or object: at'átem máidᴀ yewéto "returning from Magpie Man's" (if Magpie Man were the subject, it would be at'átem máidᴀm)	RD	yewē'to	126	
yilák̇oi	go courting	RD	yila'k̇oi	118	yelák̇oi (RD)
yímbᴀmi	elbow	WS	jímbymi		
yímdᴀk̇ᴀ	right (side)	WS-MP	jímdyk̇y		
yímdᴀk̇na	to the right	WS-MP	jímdyk̇na		
yímdi dón	grab by the arm: yelábitodom, yímdi dónk̇an. "Reaching out, he grabbed her by the arm."	RD	yim'di dōn'	200	
yímdukna	to the left	WS	jímdukna		
yímduku	left (side)	WS	jímduku		
yimí	arm	FC, WS	jim		
yimí hadóikᴀm wáisi	personal Indian name: "Old man Carries His Arm"	WS	jimí hadójkym wájsi		
yímluťi	right hand, right arm	WS	jímluťi		
yímluťna	to the right, right hand	WS, FC	jímluťna		
yímwilok	have the arm twitch involuntarily	WS	jímwilok		
yínpin	come down, come in, come down in, welcome!	FC-R, FC-T, FC-E			yᴀ́npin
yíwoye	swing arms (while dancing)	RD	yi'woye	190	
yo	hit with the hand, bite, sting (insects only): tetét min yoyáhak̇as. "I really want to hit you."	WS, WST-LB	jo	44:6	
yó	flower	WS	jó		
yó	move through water	WS	jó		
yo'ᴀ́hésitoye	dive in after someone and pursue in the water	RD	yoöhē'sitoye	116	
yo'ᴀ́'ᴀsk̇oi	get along toward twilight	WS	joʔýʔysk̇oj		
yo'ᴀ́'ᴀsno	get along toward twilight	WS	joʔýʔysno		
yo'ái	take (food) off the fire	RD	yōai'	216	
yóchono	dive, dive in	WS, WST-DW	jóćono	70:4	
yodᴀ́msito	toss back across (used with wᴀdᴀ́m: "toss" for tossing back and forth): mᴀm bol wᴀdᴀ́msitok̇an. Achét mᴀkán yodᴀ́msitopink̇an. Achét béibᴀm yodᴀ́msitok̇an. "He threw the ball across. Then she threw it back. Then again he threw it (to her)"	RD	yodömsito	60	

Maidu	English	Source	Source Spelling	Page	Other Spellings
yodᴧ́msitodo	while throwing (something) across	RD	yodöm'sitodo	60	
yodᴧ́msitopin	throw (something) back across (towards someone) - this form and yodᴧ́msito are used for throwing something back and forth. The first throw uses wᴧdᴧ́msito: mᴧm bol wᴧdᴧ́msitokan. Achét mᴧkán yodᴧ́msitopinkan. Achét béibᴧm yodᴧ́msitokan. "He threw the ball across. Then she threw it back. Then he threw it again (to her)"	RD	yodöm'sitopin	60	
yodá	make a hit, hit the mark, as with a bullet or an arrow	WS	jodá		
yodá	split maple sticks lengthwise after heating them over the fire (This is part of the preparations for basketweaving)	WS	jodá		
yodádalchopin	start to get white (sky in the morning)	RD	yodā'daltsopin	38	
Yodati	place name for a village with a roundhouse. This may be in the North Arm area of Indian Valley, or may be the same as Yodáwim. FR1 mentions yodadim "shoot" as the origin of the place name of Yodáwim. The word yodadi(m) is very similar to Yodati. See map 5 in Appendix 5.	CM, FR1	yodawim (FR1)		
yódaw	dive off	FC			
yodáwi	coil (of basket material)	FC			
Yodáwim	place name in Taylorsville area, #26 on FR map, place name for a village 1-1/2 miles from Taylorsville, across the stream, with the largest sweathouse (AK). A village in the North Arm of Indian Valley, near the electric substation (FR-HY), means "basketry coil" (FC). See map 5 in Appendix 5.	FR-R, FR-Ka	Yodawi (FR-AK), yodawim (FC)	370-371	

Maidu	English	Source	Source Spelling	Page	Other Spellings
Yodáwim Ustu	place name for a village located in North Arm of Indian Valley near the electric substation. There was a large roundhouse here. Now there is a cemetery, so it is called Yodáwim Ustu (FR-HY). See map 5 in Appendix 5.	FR1	yodawim üstu		
yodói	jump out of water (fish)	RD	yodoi'	212	
yódoi	come up to the surface in water (WS), dive up, swim up to surface (WST), jump out of water (fish) (RD)	WS, RD, WST-DW	jódoj (WS), yodoi' (RD)	212 (RD), 70:4 (WST)	yodói (RD)
yodót	tie (verb)	WS	jodót		
yodótpai	fasten, secure one end of something (like a rope), attach (something) to (something) (RD), tie up (WS)	RD, WS	yodot'pai (RD), jodótpaj (WS)	186, 192	
yodótpaikᴍm ḱuḱú	tie-rope	WS	jodótpajkym ḱuḱú		
yodótpaitino	tie up (something) for (someone)	WS	jodótpajtino		
yodótpaititi	tie up (something) for (someone)	WS	jodótpajtiti		
yodótpanu	be secured to, be attached (by rope)	RD	yodot'panu	194	
yodótpanuto	be hanging up from, be tied to	RD	yodot'panuto	192	
yodúk	hit the mark	RD	yoduk'	46	
yóhmenda	become Spring, get to be Spring: ḱódom yóhmendamᴍni ᴍnóma'enḱes "When it becomes Spring, we will travel."	RD	yōh''menda, yoh'men'da	150, 154, 160	
yóhmendapoto	be almost spring	RD	yōh''mendapoto	156	
yóhmeni	Springtime	RD	yōh''meni	150	yókmeni (WS)
yohón	noise (noun)	WS	johón		
yohón	thunder (verb), make a noise, beat (as the heart)	WS	johón		
yohónnoye	buzz around (like a fly)	WS	johónnoje		
yohónti	cause a loud sound: bichí yohónti "snap fingers"	FC			
yohónto	be loud, noisy	FC			
yohóp	insert, stab	WS, WST-LB	johóp	44:11	
yohópḱoi	stick (something) into (something)	WS	johópḱoj		
yohópmit	stick (something) down into	WS	johópmit		
yóiyoi	coarse, stiff (like a broom)	WS	jójjoj		
yók	pound dry material to powder, grind	WS, FC	jok		
yókᴍchipe	flowery, which is decorated with flowers: yókᴍchipem kamísa	FC-E			

Maidu	English	Source	Source Spelling	Page	Other Spellings
yokḿm kapí	biting varmint, anything that stings	WS	jokým kapí		
yókit	dive, dive down deep	WS	jókit		
yokíto	fight with the fists	WS	jokíto		
yokítoto	to box, fight each other with fists	FC			
yókkm 'ó	grinding rock (FC), mortar (WS)	WS, FC	jókkym ?ó		
yókmendadi	in the springtime	WS	jókmendadi		yóhmendadi (RD)
yókmeni	springtime, year (for counting age years when someone is born in spring): kmkḿm ma'ás tibím tem, sápmm yókmenim okítpem tem. "I was a little child, a three-year-old child (a three-springtimes-passing child)."	WS	jókmeni		yóhmeni (RD)
yókmenkitdi	in the springtime	WS	jókmenkitdi		
yókoi	dive	WS	jókoj		
yókoli	traditional flag or banner, any flag	FC, WS	jokól		yók'oli, yókoli (FC-E), yokól (WS)
yókolkm	deer-hoof rattle	RD-NM			
yók'olťanu	flag on top	FC			
Yokólťanum Yamáni	place name for flag-on-top mountain, past Belden. See map 1 in Appendix 5.	WST-DW	jokólťanum jamáni	80:6	
yokós	lie down, recline	WS	jokós		
yokóschononu	be lying on top of, be lying down with (someone), be sleeping with (in a sexual sense)	RD	yokos'tsononu	228, 230	
yokóskinu	lie on the back, lie down	RD, WS, WST	yokos'kinū (RD), jokóskinu (WS)	184, 104 (RD), 52:20 (WST)	
yokóskinuto	lie down together, lie down next to	WS, RD	jokóskinuto	90	
yokóskit	lie down outstretched	RD, WST	yokos'kit (RD), jokóskit (WS)	11, 12, 236 (RD), 54:34 (WST)	
yokósmit	lie between	WS	jokósmit		
yokóspanúto	lie close to, be lying close to	RD	yokos'panū'to	166	
yokósťaheyto	lie all over (someone), wallow in (something) (WS), straddle (RD)	WS, RD	yokos'taheyto (RD), jokósťahejto (WS)	90	
yokósti	make (someone) lie down	FC-T			
yokóstimen	don't make (someone) lie down	FC-T			
yokóstonu	be lying on top of	RD	yokostonū	11, 12, 48, 184, 228, 236	
yolílim cha	yew tree (Nisenan)	FC			

Maidu	English	Source	Source Spelling	Page	Other Spellings
yolók	mash (wet material) into a mush, mash up	WS	jolók		
yolós	stumble	WS	jolós		
yolósḱukus	pretend to stumble	FC			
yolósno	stumble	WS	jolósno		
yom	practice shamanism, doctor in the traditional way	WS	jom, jow		
yóm wéda	spring festival	WS	jóm wéda		
yomḿsitoye	go around doctoring across an area	RD	yomö'sitoye	72	
yomá	get ready to hit	WS	jomá		
yómbos	completely cure	FC			
yómdo	practice doctoring, cure	RD	yōm'do	76	
yomé	shaman, traditional doctor	FC, WS, RD	jom, jow		yow, yomí
yomén wa	type of edible mushroom (PM-M), spring mushroom (JD)	PM-M, JD	yoh-men-wa (PM-M), jomenwa (JD)	23	
yómetsusu	moth	HM	yo'-met'-soo-soo		
yomí	doctor	WS	jomi		yomé
yomím kḿlé	female shaman	WS	jomím kylé		yomém kḿlé
yomím máidḿ	shaman, doctor	WS	jomím májdy		
yomímeni	layman, one who is not a doctor	WS	jomímeni		
yómkit	set out to doctor (someone)	RD	yoñ'kit	72	
yómkit	treat shamanistically, suck	WS, RD	jómkit (WS), yōñ'kit (RD)	74	
yómkiteḱoi	go to doctor, set about doctoring	RD	yoñ'kitekoi	72	
yómkiti	cure (someone)	RD	yoñ'kiti	72	
yómnono	doctors	WST-RP	jómnono	64:12	
yomó	call to (someone) to come, invite (someone)	WS	jomó		
yomó	wish for, pray for: mḿyí chebóschoi'a mḿḱi yomópe "He saw there all that he prayed for"	RD	yōmō'	76	
yomó'ḿnoi	wander around calling (someone)	RD	yōmō'önoi	90	
yómpa	sorcery, witchcraft	WS	jómpa		
yómpom saiwí	yerba santa	JD	jompomsaywy	56	
yómpom sawí	tarweed (has yellow flowers, seeds eaten)	FC, JD	jompomsawy	JD 45	
yómye	invite to doctor	WS	jómje		
yómyemai	invite to doctor	WS	jómjemaj		
yómyemaisma	being hired by me to doctor	RD	yom'yemaisma	74	
yómye'ókit	approach someone asking them to cure (someone)	RD	yōm'yeo'kit	74	
yónno	antler, horn	WS	jónno		
yónnowḿkḿ	unicorn	FC-E			
yonó	gush forth, as a spring of water	WS	jonó		
yóno	dive	WS	jóno		
yo'ó	honk (as goose)	FC			

Maidu	English	Source	Source Spelling	Page	Other Spellings
yopípilipe	bright	RD	yopī'pilipe	184	
yopóni	important man, head man, chief	WS	jopón		yepóni
yopónim húskm	kingsnake	WS	jopónim húsky		yepónim húskm
yosáno	halt, stop, cease moving (intransitive)	WS	josáno		yesáno
yosánoti	stop (a car, a horse, etc.)	WS	josánoti		
Yosim Bo	place name for road skirting the south end of Nadam Koyo (Indian Valley) going East-West, may be a typo for Tosím Bo.	MSOP			Tosim Bo
yósip	emerge from water	WS	jósip		
yóskope	gray or red fox	FC			yóskopi (WS)
yóskopem hawí	gray or red fox	FC-E			
Yóskopem Yamánim	place name for Bald Mountain near Janesville, #42 on LM map; #7 on HLME map. yóskope means "fox." See also Oskmpe, which may refer to the same mountain. In HLME, Ron Morales tells the story of how Coyote kicked this mountain over and broke it into three parts. This is very similar to the story in RD, except that in that case, Coyote urinated on the mountain (called Oskmpe) until it fell over. See maps 1 and 4 in Appendix 5.	LM, HLME	Joskopin Yamanim (LM), joskopim yamanim (HLME)		Oskmpe, Yóskopi, Yóskopim Yamáni
yóspem hawí	red fox	FC			
yossó	field mouse	WS	jossó		
yoťá	get on top of, mount for sexual intercourse (said only of humans)	WS	joťá		
Yoťámmoto	place name for Genesee, #33 on FR map, a village at the confluence of Grizzly and Indian Creek in Genesee Valley. Big times were held here and there was a large sweat house (FR-HY). The pioneer settlement of Coppertown was located on this site (FR-TE). According to Herb Young, Yetameton is Genesee Valley. See maps 1 and 5 in Appendix 5.	FR-R, FR-D, FR-Ka, FR-HY, RD-NM	Yoťám moto	370-371	Yetámeto, Yetamoto, Ymtamoto
Yoťámmoto Ḱoyó	place name for Genesee Valley. See maps 1 and 5 in Appendix 5.				

Maidu	English	Source	Source Spelling	Page	Other Spellings
Yóti	Big Springs Village (Hamilton Branch area)	FC			
Yoťĭm	place name for town of Clear Creek, # 9 on FR map. see maps 1 and 3 in Appendix 5.	FR		370-371	
Yoťĭm Sewí	place name for Clear Creek, according to Shipley. May refer to Hamilton Branch or Clear Creek going through Clear Creek town. See maps 1 and 3 in Appendix 5.	WS	joťĭm sewí		
Yoťĭm Yamáni	place name for Keddie Ridge, according to Shipley. See map 1 in Appendix 5.	WS	joťĭm jamáni		
yótitdoi	bloom and leaf out (WS), flower (verb), bud out, become green (FC) (as plants in springtime)	WS, FC	jótitdoj		
yotótchik	separate, divide, compartmentalize	WS	jotótćik		
yowa	poisonous mushroom which grows in the Fall	PM-M, JD	yo-wa (PM-M), jowa (JD)	24	
yowáwi	the one who carries the rattle in ceremonies (RD), singers (WS-MM)	RD, WS-MM	yōwā′wi	RD 182 WS-MM 141	
yówwochik	ask to cure, diagnose, doctor by sucking, suck (as a shaman)	WS	jówwoćik		
yu	stick on, sting (as an insect)	WS	ju		
yú	luck: helám yúdi "in gambling luck"	WST-DW	jú	72:9	
yú	rub, rub on	WS	jú		
yudáto	sting persistently, keep stinging	WS	judáto		
yudúdutkit	duck down	WS	judúdutkit		
yudúdutḱoi	crouch down, go along crouched	WS	judúdutḱoj		
yudút	root (verb) with snout (as a pig)	WS	judút		
yúhbo	to dance (including, but not only, the bear dance)	RD	yūh′bō′, yūh″bo	56, 188, 190	
yúhbod	in dancing (adverb), while dancing	RD	yūh″bod	190	yúhbodi
yúhyu	quail, California quail	WS	júhju		
yúkm	wax	WS	ćuwam júky		
yúkbo	dance (noun), a romping dance, bear dance	WS, FC	júkbo		
yúkbositoye	to dance around	WS	júkbositoje		
yulúmdaweyo	always break (things)	RD	yūlūm′dawe′o	54	
yúmotodi	all around: ḱódom yúmotodi "all around the world"	RD	yū′motodi	28	

Maidu	English	Source	Source Spelling	Page	Other Spellings
yúmotokmdi	wherever one meets (people), all around: kódom yúmotokmdi "all around the world"	RD	yū'motoködi	132	
yunemi	gooseberry, canyon gooseberry	JD	junemim	73	
yúno	separate, divorce (as a couple)	WS, FC	júno		ymno (FC)
yunókmdi	wherever one goes	RD	yūnō'ködi	132	
yúnototo	separate from each other	WS	júnototo		
yúnpin	come on down	FC			ymnpin (WST)
yunúk	crouch down before springing at someone	RD	yunuk'	58	
yúnunu	mole (animal)	WS	júnunu		
yúnunukm	mole (animal)	WS	júnunuky		
Yupu	place name for a village at the confluence of the Feather and Yuba Rivers	RD-NM			
yúpu	adolescent girl	FC			ympm
yupupi	Sierra currant	JD	ju'pupym	73	yu'pupm, upupupe
yupúppupi	a rare bushy plant with pink flowers in clusters and gray berries	WS	jupúppupi		
yúsasaswaito	break to pieces (intransitive)	RD	yūsasaswaito	62	
yúsasaswaitoti	break (something) to pieces	RD	yūsasaswaitoti	62	
yuťa	ride or mount a horse	FC			
yútduli	mole (animal)	FC			
yúto	rub in	WS	júto		
yútokmm wené	liniment, medicinal fluid rubbed on the skin	WS	jútokym wené		
yuťúchik	shut up a house, seal up	RD	yūtū'tsik	72	yuťúichik
yuťúi	seal, close up	WS	juťúj		
yuťúichik	seal up	WS	juťújćik		yuťúchik
yutúp	shoot all of one's arrows	RD	yutūp'	210, 224	
yutúpotonan	shoot almost all of one's arrows (see hehéti)	RD	yutūp'otonan'	224	
yuwáwaito	open up a place in	WS	juwáwajto		
yúyu	quail	FC			
yúyulu	quail	FC			

English- Maidu

How to Use the English-Maidu Section

The English-Maidu side of the dictionary should be used to find Maidu words via English, and then from there look them up in the Maidu-English section for more information. The English-Maidu section does not include examples, source information, or details of translation that can be found in the Maidu-English section.

The first definition listed in the second column is the word that most closely matches the English in the first column. There may be more than one Maidu word that matches, separated by commas. After a semicolon (;) these may be followed by words with more specific meanings.

For best results, search for the main word of a phrase, for example, if searching for "in that case," look up "case." For negatives such as "not know," look under "know."

The list of words under each English term may sometimes be daunting - which one should you choose? In many cases, you can choose any of them, and have the same type of variety in your Maidu speech as you have in English. But it helps to know the Maidu word building blocks, or infixes, which can be found in Appendix 2. Each infix adds some flavor and nuance to a word. The infixes can be combined to convey very intricate meanings. If you know that -doi, for example, means either "start to" or "do upwards" you can already guess the difference between words like ᴍnó and ᴍnódoi. If you know that the -ti- infix means "cause," you can guess the difference between wóno and wónoti. Knowing these infixes will also help you create missing words, since I have only included attested words in this dictionary, that is, words that were written down as spoken by a native Maidu speaker.

You will notice that for some English words there are many Maidu words with various shades of meaning. Pay attention to the word roots. For example, under "carry" there are Maidu words for "carry in the arms," "carry in the mouth," or "carry on the back." The more specific meanings, involving coming or going away, going up or down, or diving in while carrying, still have the meaning of their root - how the item is carried. There is almost too much nuance to a Maidu word to express easily in a definition.

In many cases, you will see a mixture of spelling, since I chose to keep the spellings of the main sources (other than changing the orthography, which does not change the pronunciation). For example, you will find both "ekáwchetipe" and "ᴍkáwchetipe" listed under "beautiful." The former was written by Shipley and the latter by Dixon. Both scholars wrote it the way they heard it from native speakers, and yet the /e/ and /ᴍ/ represent slightly different sounds. I did not attempt to choose one or the other. For more information about the source of each word and how they spelled it, look the word up in the Maidu-English section.

For the Second Edition, I have added more words to the English-Maidu section. These are either synonyms of words we already had (making it easier to find your word) or grammatical elements of Maidu and how to find them in the grammar book. The abbreviation MMG stands for <u>Mountain Maidu Grammar</u>.

English	Maidu
-'s	possessive ending, belonging to, of: MMG p. 23, -k or -ki on noun
a lot	excessively, hard (like "work hard"), too much: MMG p. 55, -luťinfix on verb
a or an	MMG p. 12, not expressed
a pair of	MMG p. 75, -cho dual ending on nouns
abalone shell	sᴍlépe
abandon	úkit
abandoned (place)	wi'ípe
abate	wisᴍ
abduct	pedáyeto, sohákoi - kidnap
abhor	kúidakmen - dislike (v)
abode	hᴍbó - house
about	be about, mean: halíle
above	epín, óidoina; up above: epíni; the place above: obúdoi; just above: wosíppini; be above: ᴍťá
above (being)	do "on:" MMG p. 56, -ťa infix on verb
absent	make someone absent: ᴍpéka wiyétidom
absurd	núkyahape - silly; hokótisape - ridiculous
abuse (v)	bomᴍtiti - mistreat
abuse verbally	wáswewe, wásweye
accelerate	wilék - hurry (v)
accept (believe)	tíkche - believe, trust
accept (condone)	méi - allow
accept (tolerate)	kúidakwiyakka - sort of like
acceptable	ámbᴍkbᴍ - good enough, OK (adj)
access (v)	lᴍkᴍnno - enter, go in
accident	yépti
accompanied by	with (someone else), and (along with): MMG p. 23, -kan on the first noun
accompany	ᴍhéi; accompany or follow: ᴍhé; go along with: ᴍhéino; go along together: ᴍhéto
accomplice	bené'ekᴍ - helper
accomplish	ma, ma'á; accomplish a job/project: tawálbos; yabós - finish, complete
accordion	wiháwtokᴍ
accumulate (tr)	hᴍ - collect, gather
ace	honí
ace of clubs	síwsiwpem botóm honí
ace of diamonds	mam kadátim honí
ace of hearts	láklakpem ťókpem honí
ace of spades	síwsiwpem ťókpem honí
ache	ítu, ílak
achieve	ma - accomplish; yahát yatí'us - succeed
Achomawi	odókpepe, odókpepem máidᴍ
acknowledge	méi - allow, accept, permit (v), condone
acknowledge	héwwonoye - be supportive towards
acorn	hámsi, úti
acorn bread	hámsim maháti
acorn cap	busúle
acorn dough	soyó, hámsim soyó
acorn festival	wípe
acorn meal	hámsim baťí
acorn soup	hámsim hómma
acorn woodpecker	panáka
acquaintance	héskᴍ - friend; chaicháimeni - not strangers
acquainted with	makítpe
acquire	mé - get, take; méito - buy
acquit	sówono - let someone go
acreage	kawí - land
across	obᴍchono, ᴍᴍ'ᴍi; travel across: ᴍ'ásito
across (going across)	over (going over): MMG p. 56, -sito infix on verb
across from	obᴍ'aschono, obᴍ'asino; to the place across from: obᴍi'chonodi
act (n)	ma - law (n), measure (n), deed, statute, ordinance, guideline
act like	húweye
action	What action should I take?: hesáihelukᴍkas?
actual	béidᴍktapo - right now, current (adj)

English	Maidu
actually	hai'í
Adam's apple	wokṁ
address (n)	wewé - speech, message, dispatch (n), announcement
address (v)	wewé - deliver a speech; hṁhwé, wewéi, túwei - make a speech
adequate	t'ík - enough (adj), sufficient
adhere	dák'pai - stick on
adhesive	dak' - glue
adjust (something)	yadṁkdṁk'
admire	ek'áwche (WS), ṁk'áwche (RD)
adolescents	yṁpe - young people, teenagers
adorable	nukchetípe - cute
adore	k'úidak - like (v)
advance ($) (v)	dámmai - lend
advent	okítkṁ - arrival
adversity	wehépti
advice	give advice: wéyedom kai
advise	mamá; give advice: wéyedom kai
advise not to	mamámen
affection	term of affection: ṁt'ṁt'ṁibe
affirm	héwwo
affix	hook (v), hitch: yodótpai - fasten
afraid	yehép; afraid of: makṁ; be afraid: yehéptuye; be afraid of: yehéptoye
after	apénkan; after that: amám bei, amákan, aweténkan, bei; after a while: awétkan; after in position/behind: hóipai, hóipaikinu
after	since (something happened), once: MMG p. 85, -chet or -weten suffix on verbs. -chet changes the subject in the next clause, -weten keeps the same subject
after (in distance)	wodóino - beyond, other side of
after while	cháimen - later
afterlife	wónomenkṁm k'ódo - heaven
afternoon	in the afternoon: ékpe hékitdi
afterwards	héki, hóipaidi
again	béibṁm, béitapo; and once again: awéten beibṁ
against	get up against: ka'ódato; "against" is usually expressed with the -pai infix on verbs.
against (do against or to)	MMG p. 56, -pai infix on verb
age	nenó (to get old); to get old (women only): kṁlókbekbedoi; what is your age: hesánbem k'úmmenim okítpem maká?
age (n)	méni - period of time
aged	nenópe - old (person)
aggravate	sṁkála - bother
agitate (tr)	dṁyṁyṁti - shake
ago	hóipaidi
agonize	bomṁṁmṁti, ítu - suffer, be in pain
agree	t'íkche - go along with (ideas)
agreeable	yahát hubúktipe - pleasant
agreed	yahát hapá
ahead	hínwo, hínwono, hínwonope; be ahead of or older: wodíkno
ahead of time	hésmen - early
aid (v)	bené'e - help (v)
aide	bené'ekṁ - helper
aim (i.t.)	sṁnwok'oi - be headed (a certain way)
aim (n)	bó - way, orientation, bearing, inclination, track, direction
aim (tr)	batákinu, sṁ'á'asdoi, sṁhópwokit
air	air being let out with a whistling sound: chówowo
air out	wéllep - fan (v)
airline	káikṁtoto
airplane	káikṁm kaléta
alarm (tr)	wisétti - frighten
alcohol	hútum sudáka - whiskey
alcoholic (n)	mosápe - one who is always drinking
alder tree	chichim cha
alert	be alert and aware: túichenonopai
alienated	hínchesem
alight	hánpi - land on the ground

English	Maidu
alike	ka'áwini
alive	hónwe'inu; be alive: hónwe'inu, hónwenu; stay alive: hónwenuwéw, wadá; keep someone alive: hónwe'inuti
all, every	mpékani(m), mpékanbe, tíkói, kánibem; every single: mpékandmk, lúťpekanim; all over/around: yúmotodi; the whole bunch: mmm bomó; out of all: kánbe; from every: tíknan; all kinds: homóbokitmeni, húmbotmeni; all kinds of: chaicháino, cháichainono; all of you: mínsmm; Is that all? kaním makáde?; all done/the end: kaní; all right (adj): ámbmkbm; all that: tapó; not all of it: mpékanimenwet
allocate	wiyḿl, chetó - divide up, split, parcel out
allow	méi
almost (do)	MMG p. 56, -poto infix on verb
alone	dmkḿ, mu'ús; loner: dmkkḿ; stand alone: dmkḿm tḿsdoi
along (going)	go along doing: MMG p. 56, -no infix on verb
along with	with (doing with): MMG p. 55, -idi on verb
alongside	beside: ínki, in'ánto, obḿno, beléwlewtodi, ínkidi, sḿheheino, smhehéinodi; along with: hei, kan; be alongside of: smhehéhno/smheihéino; go alongside of: smhehéikoi; pass very close to: smhéheno'mno
already	hésmen, bei, hínwono
also	béibm; the same goes for: kiú; accompanying: ú
altercation	hónsaweye - argument
although	achét, awét, ma'át; although it will be: mamáwet; "although" is expressed by the -wet suffix on verbs
although	even though, in spite of: MMG p. 87, -wet suffix on verb
always	mpékanbenini, mpékano, mpékadom, mpékakmm, píknodom; continuously: mpékape; always be: mpékakeno; always seem to be: kawéwkm; it is always that way: ma'áwewkan; "always" is also expressed by the -we- or -sa- infix on verbs
always (doing)	habitually, by nature: MMG p. 56, -sa infix on verb
am	kmkás, kasí
am	MMG p.29, -kas(i) verb ending. p. 34 for "am I?" questions, use "did I?/do I?" form, -(k)ades on verb.
amass	hḿ - collect, gather
amassed	sḿtidi
amazing	ekáw or mkáw- wonderful
ambush	kahúkit; ambush each other: kahúkittoto
amen	áihisáwonoman, yahát hapá, hew tené, héwwonai
American bittern	mmkahúlkm
American dipper	mompíspisto, momípispisto
American merganser	bowakno
American Valley	Silóm Ḱoyó
ammunition	nokó - bullets, arrows
among	"among" is expressed by -di on the noun
amount	ka'ánbenini; an equal amount: mmyákbe
amount	ka'ánbe - that much, that many
amount ($)	yawí - cost
Amtrak	train
amulet	óm sulú, oméiyi - good-luck charm (n)
ancestor	hóyyam máidm
ancestors	hínwo hóyyam máidm - first people, ancestor
ancestral time	hóyyam ḱódo
ancient	betéi'i, hóiym, beté; ancient times: betéim ḱódo, betémen, betéihuki; ancient land/world: hóyyam ḱódo
ancient times	betéihuki - the ancient world, after humans had appeared
and	ḱan, adóm; and so: ánkaninkan; and along with all that: amá u
and (along with)	accompanied by, with (someone else): MMG p. 23, -ḱan on the first noun
and (connecting 2 simultaneous verbs)	"and" is not needed between two verbs in the same tense and person.
and (connecting two non-simultaneous verbs)	MMG p.84-86. Verbs must take different forms depending on the sequence of actions. Only the main verb (last thing in the sequence of events) is conjugated. "And" is not needed to connect these verbs.
and (connecting two nouns)	"and" is not needed between two nouns in the same form (both subject or object)
angel	ḱákkini - spirit
angelica	lokbó; angelica root: lokbóm piwí; angelica greens: lokbóm sawí

English	Maidu
angle	wᴀndoikᴀ - turning off place
angry	wasó; be angry: wasó, wás, píťúk; get angry: wasóso; be angry at: wasópai; make angry: wasóti, wasósati; look angry: wásekinu; act angry: wáskato; be mad at each other: wasópaito; bring wrath down upon: wasóhati; go off angry: wasᴀdaw; go away angry: wasᴀkoi; get over anger: wasácheda; speak angrily to: wáswewe; hot-tempered: wasosape; illness-causing anger: wasó'ituti; angry departure: wasᴀkoiwonoda; roll the eyes in anger: mᴀldoi; flush with anger: wilákno; acting angry: wásekinupe
animal	ḱutí, ḱúťᴀḿ/ḱúťᴀḿ; small animal: ḱutíbe
ankle	páikulu, paiyím kulu; ankle bone: páikulum bᴀmí
annihilate	wi'íti
annihilate	wi'íti - destroy
announce	wéye - tell
announcement	wewé - speech
announcer	wewéyekᴀ - speaker
annoy	sᴀkála/sakála
annoyed	wasó - angry
another	chái'im, chái'i; then another: sᴀti béibᴀm; another one: sᴀti béi'im; another kind: cháitikawinim, cháitikwinim; another time: cháimen; another (not the same) man: máidᴀmenim
answer	pedáto; not answer: wewémen; without answering: wewémenwet
ant	pᴀchᴀ́, pᴀno; big ant: bukúlusi (FC), óloli; piss-ant: pᴀchᴀ́mi, hísam pᴀno; small black ant: bukúlisᴀ (PM-M)
ante	wótno, húmbommoto
antelope	káma
Antelope Mountain	Óm Yepónim Yamánim
anthill	pᴀchᴀ́m úyi
anticipate	chehéiye - expect (someone to arrive)
anticipate	húpai - foresee
antique (adj)	betéi'i - ancient (adj)
antiquity	betéihuki - the ancient world, after humans had been created
antler	yónno
anus	piťíkᴀ
any	ᴀpé
any kind of	chaicháino
anyone	húmbotmeni
anything	hesí ma'át, húmbotmeni, hesísiwet, hesáte; for anything: hésnama'at
anytime	húmbotmennini
anyway	apém ma'át
anywhere	homó ma'át
apart	be apart from: tᴀtᴀ́
apart	MMG p. 57, -wai infix on verb
aperture	ka'ásḱoikᴀ - opening (physical)
apparently	apparently is: ka'ápaikan, machóikan; apparently was: machói'am, machó'a; apparently will be: ma'áiḱan
apparently did or was	MMG p.66, use -choi'a verb suffix if telling about anything you don't know first-hand (in the past tense)
apparently is or does	MMG p.67, use -choikan verb suffix if telling about anything you don't know first-hand (in the present tense)
appeal (v)	hᴀhwé, wewéi, túwei - make a speech
appealing	yaháchetipe - pretty
appear	chebᴀ́k; appear to be: chetí
applaud	má wátdan - clap the hands
apple	ápᴀl (WS), épᴀli (FC)
appliance	ma'ákᴀ - doer
appoint	woiyó - select, pick for a job
apportion	wiyᴀ́l, chetó - divide up, split, parcel out
appreciate	ḱúidak - like (v)
approach	ᴀpín; approach each other: odáto, odátoto; go right up to: okᴀ́ḱoidikno; approach crawling: lᴀ́kmitpin
approach (time)	ḱit - arrive
apron	wosó, wosóťa; note this is a genitals-covering apron, and can also mean "genitals"
apt to be	probably be, liable to be: bíshelu - likely to be

English	Maidu
archaic	betéi'i - ancient (adj)
arduously	wúni
are	they are: kmkán/kakán; you are: ka'ánkano; we (2) are: ká'anḱas; we (3 or more) are: ká'enḱes
are	MMG p. 29, depends on meaning, "you are" -ka'ankano on verb, "we (2) are" -ka'anḱas, we (3+) are" -kaenḱes on verb.
area	ḱódo, ḱódoi; my area: mnó'esma; territory: mnóinak; -place: nak; in the vicinity of: papáidi, wochónodi; in this area: hénante, unínante; be in the vicinity of: wochóno
argue	hokót; argue with: hokótito; finish arguing: hokótitobos
argument	hónsaweye
arid	ṕiḱálpe - dry (adj)
arise	otó
arise	tḿsdoi - rise, stand up
arm (n)	yimí; stretch up the arms: beḱúkuk
armpit	ḱowó, ḱowóm ḱumí, ḱowóm ṕmnno; in the armpit: ḱowóidi
aromatic	yahát hísatipe - fragrant
around	go around/out and about: ḱonói, wéido; all around: ántenantenántedi. "around" can be expressed by the -noye infix on the verb
around (action going over or around an obstacle)	over MMG p. 55, -chono infix on verb
around (going)	go around doing: MMG p. 56 -noye infix on verb
around (time)	during: MMG p. 23, -mmni on noun
arousing (sexually)	ṕináwtipe
arrange	íska, yaháti
arrange	yaháti - organize
arrest (v)	dón - catch; dónhun - capture
arrival	okítkm
arrive	okít, mdíkno; plural subject: mdíknotoye, okíkit; arrive carrying/bringing: mahádikno, maháwkit, mahá'okit; hanḿye, hadíkno, apá'okit; arrive running: wiledíkno, wiléwkit, binmé'okit, hédikno; arrive flying: ḱái'okiteḱoi, kai'ókit; arrive crying: wakmdíkno; reach the final destination: kaníwoi'mdikno; barely succeed in arriving: okíthudoi; be almost there: ťíktetedikno; arrive from time to time: okíttoye; arrive at a good sum (games): mdík; arrive home from hunting: hunhépindikno; arrive to hunt: hunókit; arrive (as a letter): ká'okit
arrogant	be arrogant: chedím; make someone arrogant: chedímti
arrow	noḱó
arrowhead	yabóspem bosó
arrowleaf balsam root	oiwm
Arthur Thomas	Chóbam Smmtónum
article	wéyebe - brief message
article	wasása - thing
articulate (v)	ḱái - refer to, mean
articulately	yahát wéye húkeskinudom - using correct speech
artist (music)	performer (music): sóltikm - musician
as	dmḱḿ; as big as: ma'ándmkbe; as far as this land: ma'ántem ḱódo; I as a headman: ni hai yepóni; as for: ma'át; as for me: achétḱas; as for him: achétḱan, mmmḿweti; as soon as: bei
as a result	adóm - because, then; -di on verb
as typically done	ká'usan - as usual
ascend	mdói, bmlélek; go along ascending: mdóino; move vertically: héyu; cause to ascend: mdóinoti
ascertain	hónmak, mákpai - find out
ashamed	be ashamed: yepí
ashes	ṕidúsi (WS), pedúsi (RD)
asinine	húkesmen - foolish, stupid
ask	yepín, epín; go ask: epínno; invite: ái; invite to go along: mnówochoi; ask to do: wochík; ask around: hónmaknoye; ask a lot of questions: pekúla; ask spirits what to do: bókweye; ask for: hápe/ápe; ask to give: méiwo; go ask for: hápeḱoi
asleep	go around half asleep: túichenotoye
aspen tree	sililikmm cha, wilílim chá
assail	méhťakit - assault, rape
assassin	wónotikm - murderer
assassinate	wónoti - kill

English	Maidu
assault (v)	méhťakit
assemble	ᴍmmoto; assembly: ᴍmmotope; put together: motó; bring together: ᴍpimoto; get things together: hésbomoto;; pre-made: yabóspe
assembly	ᴍmmotope - get-together
assert	wewé - speak
assess	áikakat - figure, surmise
asshole	piťíkᴍ, ínnom tuke
assignment	tawáli - work
assist	bené'e - help (v)
associate with	ohé - mix in (with people), be in a crowd
assortment	cháitikkape - different ones
at	on, to (place), in: MMG p. 23, -di on noun or pronoun
at last	kaníwonom, bei...bei...
at times	léiwonini - sometimes, once in a while
at whatever time	hesántenuwet - sometime
athlete	tókdatokᴍ - racer
atone for	koyó - make up for, pay for
Atsugewi Indians	kóm máidᴍ
attach	kaťót; attach things to: kaťótyo, attach things to oneself: káťotyo'us; attach one end/tie to: yodótpai, widátpai; be attached to: yodótpanu
attack	go over to attack: yáhpatchono; come after to attack: yáhpatwékoi; start to attack: mépbodoi; attack as an evil spirit: mépbo
attack (v)	méhťakit - assault, rape
attain	bodíkno, ᴍdík
attempt (n)	welé - test, trial run
attempt (v)	mák, mákwono - try, try to
attend	ohé - be there
attend to	tópanu
attend to	chikáta - focus on, watch intently
attention	pay attention: chenúkoi; not pay attention: chenúkoimen; without paying attention: hehénomenwet
attire (n)	outfit (n), garment: chí - clothes
attitude	have "attitude: " ekáwpintisa
attractive	yaháchetipe; be attractive: yahácheti
Auburn	Molma (RD-NM), Tánkᴍ (FC)
aunt	katí, éti, bebe
authority	mákpapaitikᴍ - teacher
automobile	kaléta, bᴍwom kaléta
autumn	seméni, seménkit, seménkitti; become autumn: seménkit; during autumn: seménkit kᴍmén
avalanche	kohekíwno, kóyekini
avenue	bó - road
avert	wadá - dodge, get away
avoid	pátkoi; wadá - dodge, get away
await	chehéiye - expect (someone to arrive)
awake	be awake: túichenonopai; be awakened: toyés; easily awakened: wimíkhudanpe; let us be wide awake: túichenonomawe
aware	be aware: chenúno; be aware of: mákkinu; be alert: túichenonopai
away	ántena, mᴍ'ᴍi
away	off (as in go off): MMG p. 55, -daw or -koi infix on verb
awe	be in awe: ekáwkinu
awesome	épti; be awesome: yaháluť
awful	sounding awful: wemchichᴍkpintipe
awl	hískᴍm bᴍmí, pᴍyékᴍ
axe	chá hunékᴍ
Babcock Peak	Bᴍmᴍkᴍm Yamáni Pinem
babe	ᴍťᴍťmibe - term of affection
baby	tébe, konó, konóbe; newborn baby: konókᴍ, bíspem té, béidᴍkᴍm té; babies: tébeťᴍťᴍ; baby boy: nútipe; act like a baby: konókkukus
babysit	bísdodo
bachelor	kᴍléwi'ipe

English	Maidu
back	kiwí; at the back of: kíwdi; to the back of: kíwna; backbone: kiwím bʌmí; load something on the back: hadóipai; go back: yewé; going back in time: hóipaina; to back someone/back a cause: húno
back (adj)	kíwdi - at the back
back (do something "back")	MMG p. 57, -yewe infix on verb
back country	cham ḱódo - the woods
backbone	kiwím bʌmí
background	ḱódo - place
backpack	hadó
backwards	walk backwards: kíwna bényewei
backwoods	cham ḱódo - the woods
bacon	kóchi, kóchibe
bacteria	cheméni
bad	wasá, bʌ́de; a bad one: yahámeni; be bad: wasá, wasánu; bad dream: wasám nedí
bad (n)	wasánu - evil
badger (n)	hóhla, yánta
badger (v)	yáhpat - chase, follow, pursue, go after
badly	wasát; do badly: wás; do badly for oneself: wasát yatí'us
badly	poorly: MMG p. 57, -was infix on verb
bad-tempered	wasósape - hot-tempered
bag	wadápi, dúki; bag up: hayápapai, wadápyo
bag-full	dúki, wadápi - sack, bag
bait	pedú; to bait: pedúti
bake	lʌt (WS), lút (RD); bake bread: mahát; baked: ḱápkʌ; baked fat: lʌtim húti
baking powder	sínkʌ
baking soda	súdam wasása, salwétas
balance	lose balance: hásdoi
bald	ósdal, onóm butú podápe
bald eagle	ḱáḱa
Bald Mountain	Yóskope, Yóskopem Yamáni, Óskʌpe
ball	bol; ball game: bóltope
ball (dance)	wetém - dance (n)
ballhead waterleaf	makalúsim sawí
balsam root	oiwʌ
band (tribe)	ma'a - people
bandana	owólakkʌ - scarf
banded bone in gambling	teṕ, híndʌkʌ
bands, part of regalia	póti
bang (v)	yállalati, tómdan (hit making a sound); wó, wódato -hit with an instrument
banish	batásip - drive out, chase out
banjo	wétpeikʌ
bank	liánim uiyí (for money); river bank: waťá
banner	yókoli, ínyanam yokóli
banquet	bʌi - feast (n)
baptize	siyawkit
barbecue	bʌi - feast (n)
barber	wʌḱʌ́stokʌm máidʌ
barberry	pompomi
bare	chí wiyi - naked
barf	wé - vomit
bark (like a dog)	wékpai (WS), wákpai (FC)
bark (n)	thin-layered tree bark: kapúmi, kapú; thick bark: hulékʌ
bark house	hʌ́, ḱumhʌ́, hulékʌm hʌbó
barn swallow	kómṕichiliṕ (WS), ḱumpichilipe (FC)
barren	podá, pódatihudoi; make barren: podáti
barrier	ťú; én - wall
BART	train
basalt	bosó; worked basalt: ínyanam bosó
base	íntas; the very base: íntasluťi; to the very base: íntasluťna
bashful	yehép - shy
basic	tibíluťi - smallest, bare minimum
basically	hesátmet - just, only, nothing but

English	Maidu
basket	loló; big cone-shaped basket: woló, kókpam woló, chᴍlkᴍm woló, chᴍlchᴍl woló, kókpa; flat basket/tray: bátkᴍ, dapím waťá, patá; gathering basket: hibím loló, wohᴍkᴍm patá; fishing basket: báno, makóm báno, makóm patá, makóm sᴍkᴍni, sᴍkᴍni; seed-beater basket: lóksu; beargrass basket: chiťákam loló; trinket basket: kúilam loló, kúilam patá, tóni; hopper basket: wapᴍn, winnowing basket: walétkᴍ, bátkᴍ; unknown basket type: lapin loló; coil foundation for basket: hóiya; basketry materials coil: yodáwi, wanᴍn; on a flat basket: patáidi; using a flat basket: patáimi
bassinet	tᴍtᴍ - cradleboard
bat (n) (animal)	póchode (RD), pótchode (WS), póchene (PM-M), pochéde (FC)
bathe	bathe someone: lakít; take a bath/swim: piyéto
bathroom	piťím uyí
battalion	bomó - group
batter	kíwwo - beat, whip, beat up
battle	hómpaito - fight (n)
bawl	wak - cry
bay tree	sóiba, sóibam chá
be	ka, kᴍ, ka'á, ma, ma'á; you shall be: mamánkano; although it will be: mamáwet; it shall be forever: kaním mabó; apparently will be: ma'áikan; be in a situation: bisᴍkínu; be around: lanóye; be in a group/crowd: ohé; become: woyé; bring into being: púkti; I wonder what it could be? hesí mayákken áite? be left: okᴍ; not be: wi'í; not be there: wi'íye
be	MMG p. 29 for all forms
be a waste of time	hayahámen - be impossible
be able to	depends on meaning: can you do me a favor? use future tense -ma-; can you count (do you know how), use mákkit; can you walk (are you physically able to), use mawéw. cannot: use -chᴍi or -maka infix on verb for inability; use -men on verb for "do not do."
be absentminded	húbokoi - be forgetful
be against	ónkokoi, ónkokoito - compete, disagree with each other
be aggressive	ťotimén - be strong
be airborne	yéi, kai - fly (v)
be apprehensive	ókket - be careful
be at	ohé - be there
be available (person)	okítnoye - be present
be averse to	okóle - be reluctant, be unwilling
be balmy	kódom yahádom - be good weather
be behind	tókdati'us - lag behind
be busy	botópai - get busy, attend to work
be courageous	ťotimén - be strong
be crabby	wasósa - be grouchy
be creeped out	hínchesem - feel strange toward
be dangling	wehétkinu - be hanging
be determined to	húyeti - intend to
be developed	díbos - be fully grown
be done (doing)	finish doing, completely do: MMG p. 54, use -bos infix on verb
be dormant	kúmlai - hibernate
be dressed	hesúpai
be established	hakínu - be parked, be in a place
be fair (weather)	kódom yahádom - be good weather
be fashionable	yahát chíkupem - be well-dressed
be fierce	ťotimén - be strong
be flustered	yepí - be ashamed, embarrassed
be fond of	kúidak - like (v)
be forced	force oneself, have to (do): MMG p. 54 and 56, -ti infix on verb for being forced to do, use -ti'us (ti + 'us infixes) on verb for forcing oneself
be forceful	ťotimén - be strong
be found	ú - be located
be gone (v)	wi'í - disappear
be gone!	cháinapi - get out!
be good for	yaháti - make (something) good
be grumpy	wasósa - be grouchy
be happy	yahát hubúk - feel good, feel pleasant

310

English	Maidu
be helpless	wálukinu - be impotent
be hopeless	hayahámen - be impossible
be humiliated	yepí - be ashamed, embarrassed
be identical	mmyáktitiluŕi - be exactly the same
be ignorant	mákmakitmen - not know, not know much about
be in style	yahát chíkupem - be well-dressed
be in the neighborhood	éswoye - be nearby
be indebted to	hmmḿsmanu - owe
be ineffective	wálukinu - be impotent
be inept	wálukinu - be impotent
be loath to	okóle - be reluctant, be unwilling
be microscopic	chechḿisape - be invisible
be mortified	yepí - be ashamed, embarrassed
be naughty	wasá - be bad
be no more	wi'í - disappear
be oblivious	chenúḱoimen - not pay attention; húboḱoi - be forgetful
be occupied (with)	botópai - get busy
be on one's period	mdáw, chos - menstruate
be pleased	yahát hubúk - feel good, feel pleasant
be positioned	hakínu - be parked, be in a place
be possible	hayahá - be doable
be powerless	wálukinu - be impotent
be present	ohé - be there
be proud	mḱáwche'us - have self confidence
be proud of	mḱáwche - admire
be prudent	ókket - be careful
be rowdy	wasá - be bad
be self-confident	mḱáwche'us - have self confidence
be situated	ú - be located
be skeptical	ókket - doubt
be sorry	yepí - be ashamed
be stuck on oneself	eḱáwche'us - be conceited
be successful	yahát yatí'us - do well for oneself
be sunny	ḱódom yahádom - be good weather
be supine	wusútkinu - lie face down, lie on the belly
be suspended	la; wehétkinu - be hanging
be tenacious	t́otimén - be strong
be truant	wi'íye - not be there, be missing
be unable to do	can't, cannot: MMG p. 55, -chmi infix on verb
be unseen	chechḿisape - be invisible
be useless	hayahámen - be impossible
be vigilant	ókket - be careful
be workable	hayahá - be doable
beach	wat́á - shore
bead	hóte; put beads on: ḱúilaiti; do beadwork: hóte hís; baked beads: ḱáptipem hóte
beady eyes	wipélkim hiní
beak	chḿmmi
beam (of a house)	hḿmtmti
beam (ray)	ókpayi - ray of sunshine
beans	bínisi
bear (animal)	inánas, mḿde; brown bear: mḿde; black bear: bulálai; grizzly bear: páno, kapá; silver-tip bear: pusúne
bear (children)	kmkít, té bísti; bear children/a litter: tét́mt́mkm; give birth - puḱ
bear (v)	honwéyepati - survive something, endure, stand (tr)
bear dance	pánom wéda, páno wetémmi
bear grass	chít́aka, chídaka
bear with	ḱúidakwiyakka - sort of like
bearberry	sumpiti
beard	símpani, chawám símpani: bearded: dópasno
bearing	inclination: bó - way

English	Maidu
beat	defeat (v): ónḱoi, ónḱoito, wasáya; beat several others: ónkoḱoito; beat in a race: tókda; in order to beat/win: ónḱoito; get beaten: ónḱoiti, ónḱoiti'us; get beaten in a race: tókdati'us; beat someone on the back: kíwwo; beat as the heart: lm̑kwebis, yohón, wi'íhudai
beat a retreat	wm̑ssasip - leave, be forced to leave
beat it!	cháinapi - get out! chái'm̑koi - go away!
beat up	kíwwo - beat, whip; bomm̑titi - mistreat
beautician	wm̑km̑stokm̑m máidm̑ - barber
beautiful	eḱáwchetipe (WS), m̑ḱáwchetipe (RD); look beautiful: eḱáwcheti; sound beautiful: m̑ḱáwpinti
beaver	hichihi'ina
because	adóm; because of that: amám, kaní
because	while, when: MMG p. 84, 86, -mm̑ni or -dom suffix on verbs. -mm̑ni changes the subject in the next clause, -dom keeps the same subject.
because of	due to, in doing: -di on abstract noun - see huhéyedi in Maidu-English section.
beckon	siḱét (motion with the finger), héwwelek (seduce, entice)
become	-woyé on verb; -doi on verb; makm̑no - become like; -da or -kit on noun - become a season or time of year; have become: mawónom
become angry	wasóso - get angry
bed	túikm̑; go to bed: túikit; put to bed: túiti; be in bed for the night: túikitbos; bedcovers: túichinukm̑, chínukm̑, bedsheet: kodál
bee	epéni, tái'epeni
beef	wóham sm̑mi, wólem sm̑mí
been	had been: kawóno
beer	bíya, bíyam momí
beet	láklakam piwí
beetle	pasali; stink beetle: búchm̑li; water beetle: molpeti; manure-rolling beetle: pití katanokm̑; bottleneck beetle: sáinen kapí
before	hínwo, hínwono; already: hésmen; before doing x: add -menupe to verb x
beforehand	hésmen - early
beg (v)	hápe, ápe - ask for
begin	ḱabm̑ḱ; beginning: ḱabm̑ḱ; from the beginning: wonónan; beginning of the world: betéi
beguile	héwwelek - seduce
behave towards	katí - do to (with negative connotations)
behave well towards each other	yamáitototi - shelter each other
behave yourself	yahápada
behind	behind something: kiwí, kíwna, kíwdi; behind/after: hóipai, hóipaidi, hóipaikinu; behind the fire pit: sánodi, sawónonaki
being, as	hai
belch (n)	ḱepm̑ - burp (n), hiccup (n)
Belden	Béldm̑n
believe	tǐkche; believe what you hear: tǐkpin; be under the impression that: maichákito; one who believes anything: tǐkchelelepe; refuse to believe: hálche
believe in	húno - rely on, back
bell	kolúlunkm̑
belly	ḱamí; big bellied: ḱámtapope, potáyamno; have a big belly: ḱámtapo
belly button	beték, ḱamím betéke
belonging to	of, 's, possessive ending: MMG p. 23 -k or -ḱi on noun
belongings	wasása, hesí - things
beloved	oi'm̑paipe
below	obm̑nno
belt	wichákm̑, wachákm̑, wicháḱiti; belt on: wacháḱinu; carried under the belt: yehétdonupe; in or under the belt: wacháki
bench	bísťakm̑
bend	penm̑; bend down (by itself): penm̑kit; bend/stoop over: a'ái; bend over towards: ym̑noswoito; bend something over: onm̑nkiti; be bent/stooped over: ym̑nm̑s, ym̑nm̑skit, hadá ma'át ym̑nm̑skit
beneath	ḱanái, ḱanáidi
benefactor	bené'ekm̑ - helper
benefit (v)	yaháti - make (something) good

English	Maidu
bereaved	bereaved brother: bisál, bisálbe; bereaved father: ḱomá; bereaved mother: ḱomám kᴀlé;
berry	hiní
beside	ínḱi, beléw, beléwlewtodi, chan, chándi, hénante
besides	kiú, béibᴀ - also
best	yaháhaluťi; be the best: ᴀpéḱanbe yahawaláwpe
bet	bomít, bómmo, wótno; bet equally: húmbommoto; bet on: húno; to not yet place a bet: wótnomeninu
better	yaháha; get better (health): ámbᴀḱbᴀ; make someone better (health): hónhukupti; do better/improve: yahádoiti; yaháti - make (something) good/better
between	in'ánto; the place between: púlumto; down between: in'ántokit; put between: éstoti
beverage	mokᴀ
bewildered	be bewildered as one looks around: ᴀscheheiye
beyond	wodóino; a little further: bᴀ'áswodóino; get beyond: wodíkno; hadá - distant (adj)
bide one's time	étu - wait
big	teté, ne; big ones: teténono; not big enough: tetéboduk... na; bigger: tetébe; biggest: tetéluťi, tetédᴀḱᴀ; be big/strong: épti; get a little bigger: tetébe, tetébew; had grown bigger: tetébe tᴀtᴀwono; make a little bigger: tetébewti; be not very big: tetéboduk
Big Boat Mountain	Yakᴀᴀ O
Big Dipper	ᴀḱoikᴀ
Big Meadows	Naḱám Ḱoyó, Óidim Ḱoyó
Big Meadows River	Náḱam Sewím
big rig	kaléta - truck
Big Springs	Besapenim, Wisótpinim
Big Springs Village	Yóiti
big time	wéda; upcoming big time: wédamape
bighearted	méikᴀ - generous
bills (n)	humusma - debt
Bill's Place (Big Meadows)	Poidowin
binoculars	hincheḱoikᴀ
birch	hibí: birch tree: hibím chá; birch bush: hibím dᴀ; birch basket: hibím loló, hibím patá
bird	ḱuťᴀťᴀ (WS), ḱuťᴀťᴀ (RD); California creeper: kapúdi; cedar bird: koyúmsiti; swallow: ḱumpichilipe; bittern/heron: mᴀkahúlkᴀ; goldfinch: mukédewowe; large bird of prey: pále'oyo; nightingale: ṗíyutkᴀ; Clark crow: sáuko; yellow warbler: sáwinkotutu; snipe: soduwᴀpkᴀ. See also: dove, meadowlark, hawk, eagle, crow, raven, robin, etc.
birth	give birth: puḱ, té bísti, tékᴀ; be born: púḱti; keep on giving birth: kᴀ'ᴀye
birthday	púḱwonom ekí
bit	for a little bit: tibína, tibínak
bit (n)	hudáwdo, okᴀtno - a cut-off piece
bite	dó; start to bite/bite off: dódoi; keep on biting: dódato; bite as fish: pechí; bite as snake: méhyodoi; bite as insect: yo; biting insect: yokᴀm kapí
bitter	chuchúkpe, bᴀdópem, hakáka
bittern	mᴀkahúlkᴀ, mukálkᴀ
black	síwsiwpe, síwsiw; dark/almost black: síwsiwhudoipe
black (swarthy)	ochúlak - swarthy, dark complexioned
black bear	bulálai
black magic	yómpa - sorcery
black oak	hámsi, hámsim luťi; black oak tree: hámsim chá
black person	ṗibúti, ṗibútim máidᴀ
blackberry	widópo, húluṗiti, síwsium hiní, síwsiwpem húluṗiti
blackbird	chakáti, síwsiwpem chakáti; red-winged blackbird: monkᴀlío/monkolí'o
blacksmith	bolóḱtikᴀ
bladder	chumí donínukᴀ
blameless	hesámenkᴀ
blank	wi'ípe - empty, abandoned
blanket (n)	chí, lénki, pumlénki, saláwi, ḱachókitkᴀ, chínukᴀ, túichinukᴀ; rabbit-skin blanket: chínkuťim saláwi
blanket (v)	layer (v), overlay: húl, ban - spread, put over, cover over
blather	húboḱoi wéyedom - make no sense

English	Maidu
blaze	bolákdoi; blaze up: hadá chódoi; make blaze up: hadá chódoiti
bleeding heart	solé; bleeding heart greens: solém pmkm
blend (v)	motó, ohéti, sín - mix (v)
blessed	be blessed: yahá
blind	kúsu, kúsupe; be almost blind: kúsuboswedoi; be partially blind: chewás, kúsuhsu; to blind someone: kúsuti
blink	hiníswikitkit, hisiswikitkit; blink repeatedly: hínyepápalak, hiním hínyepápalak
blister	posól
bloated	potáyamno
block (n)	bo - road, city block
block (v)	etápti, yosánoti - stop something
blood	sedé; having too much blood: sedétapo
bloom	yótitdoi
blouse	chíťakm
blow	bḿwo (WS), búwo (FC), bḿ; blow gently: bḿsasakit, bḿdew; blow as a breeze: bḿhehew, bḿhew; start to blow: bḿwodoi; blow around: búnoye; blow over (like smoke): pówowochono; blow over (like a tree): wmdḿminnokakínu; blow over (like clouds): yákmdoi; blow in little gusts: bḿdal; blow across: bḿwowoḱoi; blow against: bḿwopai; blow past: bḿwowoḱoi; blow stuff around: wmtmmwidótnoye'mno; blow down into; blow out (a candle): bukúiti; blow shamanistically to cure: bḿsap, bḿsapḱoi'us, bḿsap'usḱoi, bḿda; be blown off shamanistically: bḿsapḱoi
blow out	pópti - explode
blow past	mwála - go past
blow up	pópti - explode
blowout	wéda - big time, gala, festivity, festival
blue	títtit, tít, ekákasuknope; bluish: etítit, etítitpe
blue currant	nmnholwa, upupupe
blue grass	ókwa
blue heron	mmlokm/molókm
blue oak	chakom cha
bluebird	té'oluťkm
bluejay	káieskm (FC), kaihískm (WS), káieskmm máidm
bluff (n)	síteḱ - precipice, cliff
blunder (v)	sitái - miss a shot, grab at and miss
blunt	ťókmen
blush	wilákḱoi, wilákno; start to blush: elákḱoi; make someone blush: elákti, elaḱoiti
board	yállal, wochót, bóadi
boast	pinóweye, penówey'us; boaster: pinóweyesa
boat	yaḱḿ, hínnotikmm yaḱá; boat-riding killer: yákweḱelkm
bobbin	wanḿn - roll of basketry materials
bobcat	baksakala/boksmkmla, ťolóma
body	lulú; torso: lulúmi; dead body: holó
bog	osóḱm, pakáni
bogey man	uswúlulu - devil
boil	pólpol, patpát; cook soup or stew: hom
bold	épti - brave
bolster	etósti, chḿititi - strengthen
bolt (v)	bolóp; bolt and run: hanbeťékdoi, beťékdoi; bolt out: bolópsip; bolt in: bolóp'inno
bone	bmmí; marked gambling bone: súlu, teṕ; unmarked bone: tállala, híndukm
bonehead	húboḱoisape - one who is witless
bonk	tómdan
book	búki, chekínokm
booze	hútum sudáka - whiskey
border	wehé, wohó
bored	be bored: okóle; be boring: okóleti
born	be born: púḱti; was born: púḱwono
borrow	dam
boss	papélim yepóni
botch	sitái - miss a shot, grab at and miss; wasáti - mess up, ruin
both	choḱo; both of them: achóko, -masḿ
bother	smkála/sikála/smkúla; bother/scare: húse; not be bothered with: smkála'usmen
bottle	mokḿm loló

English	Maidu
bottle cap	wusutikm
bottom (n)	k̓anái; base: íntas
boulevard	bó - road
bounce	pm̓p; bounce back: pm̓pyewei; bounce off: pmpyewé; bounce along until it reaches somewhere: pm̓pnoyeokit
bounce back	pokm̓kinu - come back to life
bound (v)	welé - run (v)
boundary	wehé - border, edge; woi, batáslut̓i
bow for hunting	pándak̓a
bow the head	bow the head: olékinu; have the head bowed: okm̓ikinu; incline the head - olé
bowels	pítkololo - guts
bowl	loló
box	loló; budú - package; jewelry box: k̓úilam loló, k̓úilam patá
box (v)	bánchonoi - wrap up
boxer	hódesi - fighter
boy	pm̓be, yepíbem te; boys: pm̓t̓m̓t̓m̓; baby boy: nútipe; pet name for boy: núti, nutbe
brace (v)	etósti, chm̓ititi - strengthen
bracken fern	súllala
bracket fungus	wa dáte, wa wuku
brag	pinóweye, penówey'us; braggart: pinóweyesa
brag about (someone)	penóweye - praise (v)
braid hair	t̓adá, wmchadai: person with braided hair: t̓adákmm máidm
brain	onóm huní
brainless	huní wi'ípe
brainy	húkes - smart, clever
branch	pak̓á/baká, chám pak̓á; willow branch: pámchmkm
brandish	welék - wave (tr)
brave	épti; be brave: t̓otimén, honwéyepati; being brave about it: t̓otimenwetí
bravo!	hés ek̓áw - (how wonderful)
bread	maháti; loaf bread: wólem maháti; make bread: mahát
break (v)	wáye, wa'ái; cause to break: wa'áiti; break something cylindrical: bokóchono: break/crack by itself: hekótto; break by snapping: wisóp, wisópinpin, wisópti, yabát, yabátyo, wibát; break into pieces: wohóholodoi, yúsasaswaito, yúsasaswaitoti; break off: widókpai, witm̓switm̓snói; prone to break: wisópsa; always break: yulúmdaweyo; break (as a boy's voice): k̓úilulumim pú; take a break: chedá, wokócheda; a break/rest: chedá, etúweti; break wind: bm̓/bú
break (lucky)	yú - luck
break down (v)	mákpapaiti - explain, teach
break open	hédas - crack open
breakable	chm̓itimen - fragile
breakfast	chedá; have breakfast: chedáda, ékpe
breakup (n)	úno - divorce (n)
breast	miní, nanám miní
breastfeed	miníti
breath	hónwe; take a deep breath: híluk
breathe	hónwei; breathe heavily: hílluk, bm̓haiye; breathe noisily: híbmk; breathe on (unpleasantly): símbmnno
breathe out	hónwesip - exhale
breed (i.t.)	puk̓ - give birth
breed (tr)	púk̓sito - bring about
breeze	bm̓hehewi
bridge	yakm̓
brief (adj)	t̓es
brief (n)	wéyebe - brief message
bright	banák̓pe, yopípilipe; be bright: banák̓doi; brightest: éklut̓
brightness	banák̓
brilliance	banák̓ - brightness

English	Maidu
bring	mahá, maháiye/maháye, sódoi; go get/fetch: hekóitoye, hewíno, sóiwino/sówino, sóiyo/sóyo, sówikoi, (water:): henó; bring someone: hóiwi'ai, hóiwiha: arrive bringing: hadíkno, mahá'okit/maháwkit, hanmye; bring back: hanmokitoyé, sohái, sohá'okit, soháye; bring home: hmbókit; bring over/across: hadáw, hasíto, ymmm'asito, hasítopin, soháchopin, ymmm'asito; bring in: sohúnpin, hanm'okit; bring something down: hadáw; hurry and bring: hapyekáka; bring on the back: apái; bring someone towards: hóiwihapin, hóiwihaye, hóiwihayeti; bring up(wards): mahádoi; bring out: hasíp, hólsip; bring out of a tied bag: hésbapin; bring together: mpimoto, hóiwihamotó, mahámoto, wmkdi maháye; bring about: matí, púksito
bring forth	puk - give birth
bring up the rear	tókdati'us - lag behind
brittle	chmitimen - fragile
broad	hadáwaito - wide
brodiaea	kowá; blue stars brodiaea: púyate
broken	wa'áipe, yabáti
bronchitis	hóntustusi - coughing sickness
brooch	cháwo
brook	lukú; small brook: lukúbe, lukúmbe
broom	hebáskm (WS), hmbáskm (FC)
broth	kok, homá/hómma
brother	sámboye, úsu, éite; younger brother: tmní, mmtmnbe; pair of brothers: tmnkmto
brother-in-law	kedé, mási, masím máidm; pair of brothers-in-law: kedékmto
brow	smndaka - forehead
brown	chulálak, chulálakpe
brown (skin)	ochúlak - swarthy, dark complexioned
brown bear	mmde
brush	dm, pa; in the brush: padí; cover with brush: dmchono; clothes brush: hebásdawkm; scouring brush: chakáchaka
brush by	pukétkakachono, pukétkachono
brush off	hebásdaw
brush snake	bidípno
bubble (v)	pólpol, patpát, mómpoldoi
bubbly	patpátkmm
buck	yepím smmí
buckberry	pám hiní
bucket	momím loló
buckeye	poló, sawó; buckeye tree: polóm cha, sáwom cha
buckle	cháwo
Buck's Lake	Yakani Pakáni
Buck's Ranch	Yakani
buckskin	wolósi
buckthorn	su, smmpiťi/sumpiti, smmpiťim chá
bud (v)	yótitdoi
buddies	wosíkmtoto - cousins, associates
budge	ťiymk - move (v - i.t.)
buffalo	pahkuts
bug (insect)	kapí; biting bug: yokmm kapí
build (n)	lulú - body, physique, shape, figure
build (v)	ya, hmyá, tawál; build a house: hakít; build a house together: hmyámoto; build a fence: ťú tawál; build a fire: sa ku/sakm, sa wó, sa yá; building materials: hmyam wasása
building	uyí/uiyí
bulb	Indian potato: wai, muku, wuiléspuikmm piwí; wild onion: wolabmkm; yampa: palúťi, papa; brodiaea with edible bulb: kowá
bull	bul, yepím wóha
bull frog	úspmdu
bullet	nokó
bullshit	wóham piťí
bulrush	bokwopu, kúpkm
bumblebee	epéni
bump	bmnó; bump against: bmyó; poke with: bmyódatoti, bmyóti; bump the head: onó bmnó
bumper	én - wall

English	Maidu
bunch of	bomó, pí
bunches of grass	osᵐ
bundle	budú; pack in bundles: hákwowopapai
bungle	wasáti - mess up, ruin
burden (n)	hadó - load
burden basket	woló
burglar	pedákᵐ - thief
burglary	pedá'i - theft
burial ground	tánkᵐ, tánkᵐm ḱawí, wónowonom máidᵐm tánkᵐ; at a burial ground: tánkᵐdi
burlap	púmsalawi
burn	tᵐ/tu (burn of itself); burn something: tᵐti; start burning: chópai; burn off brush or trees: chá topái, ḱódo topái; burn up (like a big fire): ṗiṭúp, ṗiṭúpti; burn over: ṗiḱói, ṗitúḱoi; burn down: ṗiṭákitti, ṗiṭápkít; having burned down: ṗiṭápkítwono, tochíl; be burned out (canoe log): chó; burn hair: móiyu; be burned up: ṗitúḱoido; burnt: ṗíholkit; be burnt: ṗibú
burn out (i.t.)	bukúi - go out (fire)
burn out (tr)	wokóti - tire out (tr)
burning (cremation)	ostu
burp	ḱepᵐ
burr	bichí - thorn
burrowing owl	kúkú
burst	hésaswaito; cause to burst: hésaswaitoti; burst into: bolóp'inno
burst out	bolákdoi - catch on fire, blaze up
bury	tam, tánkit, kᵐlé (WS), kilé (RD); bury in ashes to cook: móda, lᵐt
bush	dᵐ, pá
bushy tree	ṗáktapopem chá
bushy-tailed rat	chám sápa
busy	be busy with: tópanu; not be busy: ᵐpe bísdom
busybody	símmaksa
but	amét, amétkan, amᵐnikan; but then: ánḱabᵐḱᵐnkan, apém; but inexplicably: ahéset; but unfortunately: ánḱabᵐḱᵐm; but it is not the case that: achétmenim
butcher (v)	ḱós
butt	ínno; heel/butt of something: sukú
Butt Lake Valley	Ḱáwwati
Butt Valley	Ḱáwbaṭi, Ḱáwbaṭim Ḱoyó
Butt Valley Reservoir	Ḱáwbaṭim Mómdanni
butter	batá, batám hᵐṭí, soṭálkᵐ, huṭólpi
buttercup	ṭamámi; buttercup flower: ṭamámi yo
butterfly	kapúslele, yánikútakuta
Butterfly Creek	Húntulam Sewí
Butterfly Valley	Húntulam Ḱoyó
buttocks	ínno
button	wotón (noun and verb)
buy	méito
buzz	ḱobébek; buzz around: yohónnoye
buzzard	káḱa/ḱa'ḱa, miníhusi/miní'usi
Buzzard Rock	Miníhusim O
by	done by: -ḱi on noun; located by: ínḱidi (follows the noun, which ends in -m)
by and by	after while, consequently, subsequently: hóipaidi - afterwards
by nature	always (doing), habitually: MMG p. 56, -sa infix on verb
bygone	betéi'i - ancient (adj)
cabbage	kabíche
cable	ḱuḱú - rope
cackle	kadékket (FC), ḱedétḱet (WS)
cafeteria	pekᵐm uyí - restaurant
cake	súkam maháti
calamity	wehépti - misfortune
calculate	húkes - figure out
calf (of leg)	kámosi
California	Kalipónia
California poppy	tapᵐkᵐ
call	kái; keep calling: káiyew; call by name: yawí; call something: betá, hai aḱán; be called: a, awónom; call out/howl: wó, pelípto; call to invite: yomó

English	Maidu
call (on phone)	míldan k̓úk̓ti - make a phone call
call for	ápe - ask for
call names (ridicule)	hokót, hokótito
call on	chenók̓oi - visit (v)
call out (v)	pelíp - shout
call to mind	húmit - recall
call up	míldan k̓úk̓ti - make a phone call
camas	poyó (blue), puisla (white), palút̓i (quamash)
camouflage (v)	kilé - hide (something)
camp (v)	uyúk; camp for the night: uyúkit/uyúkkit; set up camp: uyúkkakit; camps: hꟺbóboto; camping place: uyúkakitkꟺ, campfire: púiyam sá; camper (vehicle): uyúkkꟺm kaléta; camp (noun): omenani (PM-D)
campaign (n)	tókdato - race
camper	mobile home, motorhome: uyúkkꟺm kaléta - RV
can (container)	loló; to can (food): wadápyo
can (v)	depends on meaning: can you do me a favor? use future tense -ma-; can you count (do you know how), use mákkit; can you walk (are you physically able to), use mawéw. cannot: use -chꟺi or -maka infix on verb for inability; use -men on verb for "do not do."
can (v)	be able to: Maidu expresses "can/be able to" either by "know how" (makkit), or a verb without "can:" "I can see it" = "I see it," or by the future tense "Can you mow the lawn?" = "Will you mow the lawn?"
can't	cannot, be unable to do: MMG p. 55, -chꟺi infix on verb
Canadian goose	ló
canal	sewí - river, creek
candle	toyá, toyákꟺ
cane (walking)	basákꟺ (RD), bꟺsákꟺ (FC), basá (WS); go around with a cane: basánoye
cannot	be unable to do, can't: MMG p. 55, -chꟺi infix on verb
canoe	yakꟺ́, niu
Canoe Mountain	Yakꟺ́m O
canyon	lúk̓lukto, hop̓no
Canyon Dam	Chítakam Yamánim
canyon dudleya	ómteni
canyon wren	ómtitiwi
cap (hat)	olé; netted cap: wiká; winter cap: onúknokꟺ, coonskin cap: akíchanam 'onúknokꟺ; lid: wꟺsꟺtikꟺ/wusutikꟺ; put on a netted cap: wiká
Cap Singer	p̓óksino, walád
caper (v)	cavort: tóihlalaino - prance
capture	dónhun
car	kaléta, bꟺ́wom kaléta
carcass	sꟺ
card	postcard: papélimbe - playing cards, papélbe - card
care for	hꟺbís
career	tawáli - work
careful	be careful (about people): ókket, (about other dangers): éssem; do carefully: húkeskinu
caress	sꟺkásai - hug, engage in foreplay
caress	báslem - stroke with the hand; chobót - kiss (v)
cargo	hadó - load (n)
carp	t̓óttati
carport	kalétam uiyí - garage
carried (by me)	hanꟺ́k̓oisma
carrot	hálk̓o; wild carrot: lop̓bꟺ, lunu, ómsꟺ, solamwene

English	Maidu
carry	sódoi, hanʌ́; carry in arms: sohá, soháchopinyo, sohásito; carry in the hands: haláp; carry on the back: áp, apáno, hanʌ́'okit, opáno; hoist/load up onto the back: háp, hadói, ápdoi; pick up and carry: sohádoino, sówiḱachono, sówiḱadikno; arrive carrying: mahádikno, apá'okit, hanʌ́ye; carry around: donínoye; carry along: hanʌ́no; carry in the mouth: dohá, dohánoye, dohá'okit, dohádoino, doháḱoi, dohátno; carry across/over: hanʌ́sito, soháchono, hanʌ́sitopin, hóiwihachopin, maháchono, soháchono; carry upward: sohádoi; make someone carry: sódoiti; carry away: kʌháḱoi, donínoḱoi, hanʌ́ḱoi, pedáhaḱoi, soháḱoi, sohátno; carry off stolen goods: pedá'ʌḱoi; carry back: soháye; go carrying: maháḱoi; carry downwards: sóhasipin, sohátno; carry out: sówwosip; carry towards: maháye; carry a sack/bag: wadápʌno; keep on carrying: sódoiyew
carrying weight	ʌhʌ́ - powerful
cart	kaléta
cart (tr)	hanʌ́n - haul
carton	budú - package
cascara sagrada	su, sʌ́mpiťi/sumpiti, sʌ́mpiťim chá
case (box)	budú - package
case (legal)	hónsaweye - argument
case (n)	in that case: achét, sa'á; adákan; it is the case that: ma'ákʌkan; in any case: apém ma'át; it is not the case: achétmenim
caseworm	óm tʌlí
cash (n)	liáni - money
casino	helái'ekʌm uyí
cast (v)	wʌdʌ́m - throw
cast (v) (cast off)	kam - shed, molt
cast off (throw down)	wʌdʌ́mdaw
cast out (tr)	batásip - drive out, chase out
cat	kíki, kéťi, butúkupem piťí
catastrophe	wehépti - misfortune
catch	dón, dónhun; catch in the air: óidon; catch fish in nets: momhʌ́koḱoi; catch fish: wotí; catch fish one after another: wowóti; try but fail to catch: donhúnbʌk; try to catch in order to kill: sohúnbʌk, sohúnbʌkʌsipin; catch in a trap: chedʌ́k; catcher: dónkʌ
catch fire	sátodep
catch on	makít - understand
catch up	batápai; almost catch up with: batápaihudói, batápaipoto; be unable to catch up with: batápaimenchonó; close to where one will catch up: batápaipotónanape
cater an event	pekʌ́ti - feed
caterpillar	kápuslelem kapí
cat's breeches	mʌkʌlúsim sawí
cattail	bákwapa (WS, FC), bokwopu (JD); gather cattails: bákwapai
cattle	wóham sʌmi, wóham bomó
Caucasian	wóle
caught	be caught in a trap or net: wó, diwó
cause (n)	bodíknokʌ - goal, target
cause (v)	cause to do: ma'áti, cause to be done; ka'áti; intentionally cause: matí; cause to happen: kahúyeti, ti; keep causing problems: matíwe
cause (v)	get (someone to do), make (someone do), force: MMG p. 56, -ti infix on verb
cause problems	matí - cause, do (something) to
cautious	ókket (about people), éssem (about other dangers)
cave	óm ḱumí, ómpʌnno, pʌ́no
cave in	hédusimoto
cavern	óm ḱumí, ómpʌnno - cave
cavity	pʌ́nno/pʌ́no
cavort	tóihlalaino
ceanothus	chepátim dʌ/chʌpátim dʌ (FC), yapáti (JD); squaw carpet: ḱawíbano
cease	hékit
cease (tr)	etápti - stop something
cease moving	yesáno/yosáno
cease to exist	wi'í - disappear
cedar	maní
cedar leaves	maním sawí
cedar tree	maním chá

English	Maidu
cedar waxwing	koyúmsiti
celebrate	wéda; have a feast: bʌyím motó
celebration	wéda, bʌyím motó, bʌ́ipe
celery	masá'a, dedempumi
cemetery	tánkʌ, ustu, wónowonom máidʌm tánkʌ
center	ésto - middle
centipede	sútumi
central (topic)	tetébe - bigger, largest
CEO	yepóni - chief
ceremony	wéda - celebration
certain (one)	sʌ́ti, homó
certainly	kánte, tetétse, kaná
chair	bʌdóikʌ, bʌdóikitkʌ, bʌdóiťakʌ, bʌdóiťama, bísťakʌ
chairman	yepóni - chief
challenge (n)	ónkoḱoito - contest (n)
challenge (v)	hálcheche - contradict
chamber	lúmi - room
change (classes, jobs)	nénḱoi - change residence
change directions	wʌ́ndʌi
channel (TV or radio)	ḱódo, ḱódoi
char	píhol
characterize	mákpapaiti - explain
charge (battery)	hónwe'inuti - keep (someone) alive
charge money	hʌmʌ́smai
charm (n)	good luck charm: óm sulú, oméiyi; for gambling luck: heláikʌm oméiyi, helám oméiyi, heláyim oméiyi, oméikʌ
charred	píholkit; be charred: píbú
chase	yapát, héiḱoi, bínmechopin, yapátḱoi; pursue: héi, bínmeye; chase after: hédoi, hénoye; try to catch in order to kill: sohúnbʌk, sohúnbʌkʌsipin; go chase: bínmeḱoi; chase in water: yo'ʌhésitoye; chase out: batásip, hésippin; chase up and down (hills): hédoimit; not chase away: batáchonototómen
chat	yapáito; chat with each other: yapáitoto; chat idly: símmak, símmakto
chatter	yapáito - chat (v)
chatter like a squirrel	chátchat
cheap	stingy: húlis; cheapskate: húlissa; be cheap in price: tibí yawí
check all around	ʌ́scheheyenoye
check in	okít - arrive
check out (from the library)	dam - borrow
check out (look at)	chenóno, cheťá; chebʌ́k - have a look at
cheek	mussú
cheer (v)	má wátdan - clap the hands; ho - say "oh" or "ho" (verb)
cheer up	yahát hubúkti'us
cheerful	yahát hubúktipe - pleasant
Cheetos	chítosi
cherish	ḱúidak - like (v)
cherry (bitter)	siliwa (PM-M, JD), seléwwa (WS)
cherub	ḱákkini - spirit
chest (of body)	naná
Chester	Óidim Ḱoyó
chew	chawái
chew tobacco	paní chawái
chewing gum	wólem chakámi
chickadee	komťʌ́ťʌkʌ, pichititi
chicken	chhikín
chicken hawk	chhikíni dónkʌ (WS); Cooper's hawk: túptupe; sharp-shinned hawk: báku; red-tailed hawk: búklakkʌ
chief (dominant)	tetébe - bigger, largest
chief (foremost)	hínwom - first, ahead of, older (adj)
chief (n)	yepóni (FC, RD), yopóni (WS), yepónim máidʌ

English	Maidu
child	té; children (more than 2): téťmťm; two children: pénemte; boy/child: pḿbe; boys/children: pḿťmťm; big child: tetém té; dead child: téyaťa; childhood friends: wosíkmtoto; child and parent (pair): tékmto; have a child: tékm, téťmťmkm; act childish: konókḱuḱus
chimney	súksipmape
chin	chawá, chawám bmmí
Chinese	sáine; Chinese person/people: sáinem máidm, onóm ťadákmm máidm
chink (hole)	pḿnḱel
chinquapin	sisisilchmm dm (JD), sessessilkmm dm (PM-M)
chip in	méi - give
chipmunk	wísla; brown-headed: tachípi
chips (poker)	put chips in (to bet): wótnoti
chirp	tweet, warble: sol - sing
chocolate	chiókoli
choke	ḱo; choke someone else: ḱum, ḱadóschik, bichís
chokecherry	hanáni/hanháni, una'inu; bitter cherry: seléwwa
chomp	chawái - chew
choose	woiyó, bmyḿksip; select from many: bmyḿksipdomhehe
chop (n)	hudáwdo - a cut-off piece, cutlet, steak
chopsticks	kawaicho
chore	tawáli - work
chow	pekḿ - food
chowder	homá - soup
CHP	dónkmm máidm - police (n)
chuck roast	ítus - roast (n)
chuckle	nuk - laugh
churn	dmyḿymti - shake
cigarette papers	pánpekmm papéli
cinch (v)	witám, witámto; cinch things together: witámmoto; cinch up: witámdoi, witáyeyo, witáye
circle (n)	wichákm - belt (noun) (wichákm means encircle)
circle (v)	get in a circle: smkúm; to circle (like bird of prey): we'é; travel around in a big circle: yḿnoye, wónmidoikapin
circle around	wmnḿdoi - travel in a circle
circulate	wmnḿdoi - travel in a circle
circumference	wichákm - belt (wichák means encircle)
circus	sú
city	sidí, máidmm pípenak
city block	bo - road
clam	odóko
clam shell	odókom posála, liáni
clamor	yohón - noise
clamp (v)	ḱítap - squeeze
clang	tómdan
clap	wátdan; clap hands: má wátdan
clapper stick	wó'akm (FC), wátdakm (RD-NM)
clarify	mákpapaiti - explain, teach
clarinet	yálulu - elderberry flute
clash	hómpaito - fight; hálchetoto - disagree with each other
claw	bichí, chḿwakkm
clay	ḱáwdaḱa, óm ḱúmpiťi
clear (adj)	chehéhechonope - transparent
clear (clean)	be clear from evil: hówikmp
Clear Creek	Óm Yawken (LM), Yoťim Sewí (WS)
clear up (weather)	wmsḿ (RD), wisḿ (WS)
clear view	hinchesmeni
clearing (in woods)	benékwaito
clerk	méitowokm - salesperson
clever	húkes
cliff	síteḱ
climate	ḱódom - weather
climax (v)	pópti - ejaculate

English	Maidu
climb	lᴍk; climb up: lᴍkdoi; get to the top: bᴍlékwodoi, bᴍlélekdoi; be almost to the top: bᴍlélekdoipoto; climb down: lᴍkdaw; start to climb down: yᴍnᴍnᴍschopin; climb on top (horse, etc): lᴍkťa; climb out of: lᴍk'sipno; be unable to climb: lᴍkdoichᴍi
cling (i.t.)	dákpai - stick on
cling to	dón - catch
clique	bomó - group
clitoris	pᴍsím ení
clockwise	lúťna - right (hand)
close (eyes)	duschík, hínduschik; keep the eyes closed: duschikínu; have the eyes closed: hín duschikkíno/duschikíno; tell someone to close their eyes: duschikínuwo
close (near)	hedén, hédeden; near here: unína hedénna; close to: ínkinan, lédi; the nearby place: ínki; get close to: k̓a'ó; stick close to: wodák, keep close to: wodákdonu; pass close to: sᴍhéheno'ᴍno
close (shut)	bᴍkúiti/bukúiti; close the door: púlkᴍ bukúitipi; close up/seal: yuťúi; close up a house: hᴍbᴍ́chik; close up with brush: dᴍ́chik
cloth (rag)	witᴍ́ťᴍino
clothes	chí; put on clothes: chí; keep clothes on: chínu; one who doesn't own any clothes: chímeni
clothespin	chídokᴍ
cloud	yá; rain cloud: tumímya; snow cloud: kómya; dark cloud: kulúm ya; cloud cover: yáhule; cloud up: yákᴍ/yáku, yáhule, yákit; blow over the sky (clouds): yákᴍdoi
cloudless	chehéhechonope - transparent
clover	chiwí, chíwchiwi; white clover: dáldalpem k̓oyóm chíwchiwi; black clover: síwsiwpem chíwchiwi
clown	pehéipe
club (stick)	wókᴍ
clubfooted	wóspoiki
clubs (cards)	botó, chiwí
cluck	k̓útk̓ut; go around clucking: k̓útk̓utnoye
cluster	lokó
clutch (something)	sódoipai
coach (n)	mákpapaitikᴍ - teacher
coals	hemí
coarse	yóiyoi
coast (n)	waťá - shore
Coast Range	Tái Yamani (RD)
coat (jacket)	kapóťa
coax	héwwelek - seduce
cobweb	húsbini
cocky	ek̓áwche'uspe - uppity
coffeeberry	su (HM), sumpiti (JD)
coil (n)	wanᴍ́n - roll of basketry materials; yodáwi - coil; coil foundation for basket: hóiya
coil (v)	coil like a snake: witúbil'us, teyá; coiling around (snake): tᴍ́iha
coin (v)	púk̓sito - bring about
coke	súda - soda
cold	cold (weather): dúpeti; the cold: dúpeyi; freezing cold: ítᴍk; be cold: dúpe; make someone cold: dúpeti; get cold (weather): dúpetidoi; a cold (illness): hónk̓o
Colfax	Kulkumik
collapse (v)	hédusimoto - fall in on itself
collect	hᴍ́; start to collect: bᴍyᴍ́kdoi; go around collecting: bᴍyᴍ́k'ᴍnoiye
color (n)	balikᴍ - dye
colt	kawáyum té
columbine	pᴍkᴍ (PM-M), pukᴍ́ (JD)
coma	hónsapwebis
comb	heyúdatokᴍ; to comb: heyúda, heyúdato
combat	hómpaito - fight
combatant	warrior, boxer, soldier: hódesi - fighter
combine	motó, ohéti, sín - mix (v)
come	ᴍyé; come in a vehicle: hayéwe; come here! unína mapí!, ᴍyépi!
come (ejaculate)	pópti - ejaculate
come (time)	kit - arrive
come across	ᴍchák, chenó, odáto - chance upon, meet

English	Maidu
come across (as sound travels)	pinhássito
come after	hóipai - follow
come after, chase	bínmedoi, bínmeyekto, yáhpat, yáhpatwéḱoi
come all the way out	lᴀ́ksipbos
come along	okítweḱoi
come and get it	pé'okit - come and eat
come apart	hépeswaito, hésaswaito
come back	yewé, haiyé; come back in a vehicle: hányewei; crawl back: lᴀ́kyewei, lᴀ́kmitpin; come back from hunting: húnmohepínkit, húnhepinye; come back to the starting place: hasíp, ᴍdíknoweḱoi; come back carrying: sohá'okit; come back out: sᴍhésip; if I don't come back: okítmeniseti
come down	ᴀ́n, okít; come on down: yúnpin/yínpin; come down towards: ᴀ́mpin, ᴍchópin; to land: hánpi; climb down: lᴀ́kdaw; come down as rain: ḱadík kít; come down as sunshine: ókpayim pín, wákit
come face to face with	odáto - meet, encounter
come home	okít; come home (plural subject): okíkit; come home from hunting: hunhépinḱoi, hunhépinkit, hunhépindikno
come in (light)	banákam pín
come into	pin, yᴀ́npin
come near	ᴍpín - approach
come off	ᴍdá
come on! (cheer)	héya
come out	come out towards: ᴍsíppin; come out in a bunch: t̓isíye; come out of water: yósip; come out as smoke: pówo; come out suddenly: pop; not be coming out: lᴀ́ksipmenew
come over (the horizon, like the sun)	wochóno
come to mind	húmit - recall
come together	úmmoto/ᴀ́mmoto, úmmototo; come together as one: wᴀ́kdimoto
come towards	ᴍpín; come over towards: yᴀ́nᴍnᴍschopin
come up (plants)	chebᴀ́kdoi
come up to surface	yódoi
come upon	ᴍchák, ᴍlémmai, ᴍdémt̓a, ᴍdémmai; nearly come upon/meet: ᴍdémt̓ahudoi
come visit	chenó'okit
coming (n)	okítkᴍ - arrival
command (v)	mákpaiti - instruct, direct, order
commemorate	bᴍyím motó - celebrate
commemoration	wéda - celebration
commencement	ḱabᴀ́ḱ - start (n),beginning (n)
comment (n)	wéye; no comment: wéye wí'ikas bei, wewémenwet ḱasí; wéyebe - brief message
comment (v)	chewéto - testify about
commotion	yohón - noise
compact (adj)	nᴍs - low (adj)
companion	héskᴍ - friend
companions	wosíkᴍtoto - cousins, associates
compartment	lúmi - room
compartmentalize	yotótchik
compensate (with wages)	pakál - pay (v)
compensate for	ḱoyó
compete	ónḱoḱoi; compete in singing: solónḱoḱoito
complain	go around complaining: wáknoyesa
complete	to complete something: yabós
completely	totally, finishing off: MMG p. 54, -bos infix on verb
comply	t̓íkche - go along with (ideas)
component	wasása - ingredient
compound (n)	ḱoyó - field
comprehend	makít - understand
compress	ḱítap - squeeze
comprise	sín - contain (as ingredient)
compromise (v)	t̓íkche - go along with, trust
compromise with	t̓íkche
compute	húkes - figure out

English	Maidu
conceal	kilé - hide (something); kiléda -conceal for a reason; chetímen - not let (someone) see; be unable to conceal something: kiléchmi
conceited	eḱáwche'us; act conceited: eḱáwche'us húweye
conceive	huhéye - imagine; púḱsito - bring about
concern (tr)	sm̥kála - bother
concerning	halíle
conclude (tr)	etápti - stop (something)
concur	ťíkche - go along with (ideas)
condemn	ḱúidakmen - dislike (v)
conditions	ḱódom - weather
condone	méi - allow
condor	molókm̥
conductor	batánokm̥ - driver
conference	m̥mmotope - event, get-together
confident	be confident: húno'us, m̥ḱáwche'us
confine (someone)	bístikíye
conflict (n)	hómpaito - fight
conflict (v)	hálchetoto - disagree with each other
confluence (rivers)	sewím piní
congratulate	héwwonoye - be supportive towards
congratulations!	hés eḱáw - (how wonderful)
congregate	m̥mmoto - assemble, come together
congregation	m̥mmotope - get-together
conical basket	woló
conquer	ónḱoi
consequently	adóm - because, then; -di on verb; hóipaidi - afterwards
conserve	mayá
consider	húni
consist of	sín - contain (as ingredient)
constipated	be constipated: pitkm̥l
construct	hm̥yá, ya; build a house together: hm̥yámoto
construction materials	hm̥yam wasása
consume (eat)	pe - eat
consume (waste)	wahéno - waste (v)
contact	post-contact times: wóleimen
contain	ym̥mmoto - enclose, encircle
contain as ingredient	sín
container	loló; budú - package; container for ritual items: tóni
contamination	petí - poison (n)
contemplate	húni - consider
contemplate (doing)	húyeti - intend to
contemporary	béduki - modern
contend	hokótito - argue with
content (adj)	yahát hubúktipe - pleasant
contented	yahát hubúktipe
contest (competition)	ónkoḱoito
continue doing	awébisim, madóm m̥péḱadom; continued doing: kawé'am
continuously	m̥péḱape; do continuously: m̥péḱanu, búsno
contradict	hálcheche; contradict someone: hálchecheto
contrary	on the contrary: hesámet
contribute (money)	méi - give
contribute towards	heyáwe - support by doing something
control (someone)	bístikíye - restrict, confine
convene	m̥mmoto - assemble, come together
convenient (close by)	hedénna - nearby
convention	m̥mmotope - event, get-together
conventional	betéitodi'im- traditional, one who is traditional
conversation	yapáito
converse with	yapáito, yapáitoto
convey	ḱái - refer to, mean
cook	ham; cook dinner: ḱáipeti; make soup/stew: hómti; roast: ḱápti; prepare food: sm̥kés, yaháti, pewíkakit; cook for: sikéstido; a cook: ḱáptikm̥

English	Maidu
cooked	k̓ap; be almost cooked: k̓áppoto; be overcooked/completely cooked: k̓ápsito; be cooked for a while: yaháhanu
cookie	kṁki
cooking (n)	pekṁ - food
cool off (from anger)	wasácheda
cooperate with	t̓ı̆kche
Cooper's hawk	túptupe
coot	bóstoi, bústoye
Coppertown	Yetámeto non, Yatámoto
Coppervale Mountain	Óm Kulúdoiwem
copulate	hṁpé, hṁpéto, héiyeto, hóiwito, hóiwitoto; hṁchṁ; go copulate with each other: hṁpétok̓oi
copy (someone)	yakka - do like
cord	k̓uk̓ú - rope
cork (n)	wusutikṁ - stopper
cormorant	mó'aka, mákmakṁ
corn	kón
corn lily	poyoli
corned beef	bám sṁmí
corner	wṁndoikṁ - turning off place
corpse	wónowono; dead person: wónowonom máidṁ
correct (adj)	yahá - right (adj)
correctly	do correctly: húkeskinu
corset	witámmotokṁ
cosmos	k̓ódo -world
cost	yawí
costly	hélmono
cottontail	téloli, telólele, tibím kówekkesi, wip̓élki
cottonwood mushroom	wilíliwa
cottonwood tree	lilim cha, wilílim chá
cougar	pekúni
cough	hónk̓o; cause a cough: hónkṁti; coughing sickness: hóntustusi; cough up: opínti
could be	mayákk̓en; -yákk̓en suffix on verbs
couldn't	temporarily could not: MMG p. 55, use -men infix on verb + imperfect verb ending (p. 64)
couldn't	was unable to: MMG p. 55, use -chṁi infix on verb with a past tense ending (p. 63-66)
counsel (v)	mamá - advise, tell
count (v)	hémmak; count many: hémmamakno; what had been counted: hémmakyo
count on (someone)	húno - rely on, back (v)
count on (something)	tetétlut̓i yahá - so want to (verb before yaha)
counterclockwise	dakúna - to the left
country	k̓ódo, k̓ódoi; in the country: k̓ódoidi
county (n)	k̓ódo - district, area
couple	konóito (man and woman); married couple: kṁlékṁto; a couple in love with each other: hṁbṁ́ktotopecho; a woman and her second husband: mṁpulíto, púlito; a couple of guys: yep̓kṁto; be a couple: konóito
courageous	be courageous: motápai; be courageous together: éptitoto; invest with courage: motápai; épti - brave
course (meal)	pená - serving
courting	go courting: yilák̓oi/yelák̓oi
courtyard	koyó - field
cousin	posí; older cousin: sámboye; childhood friends/cousins: wosíkṁtoto
cover	kahúl, hónba, k̓ahúlchik; cover with cloth-like object: húl, ban, bánchik, bánt̓a, húldoiti; completely cover over: let̓ábos; cover with water: mombudútchonoti; cover with brush: dṁ́chono; cover as clouds: yáhule; cover with ashes: let̓á; cover up: wát̓a, wát̓ayo; cover one's tracks: yáit̓apada; lid/cover: hónbakṁ, wṁsṁtikṁ; cloth cover (blanket, curtain, etc): chí, saláwi, banchikkṁ, banchik'kṁm chi; bark covering: hulékṁ
cover up	chetímen - not let (someone) see

English	Maidu
covered with	be covered with water: mombudútchono, mómdo; be gradually covered over: yebúbuchik; be covered with flies: halúkup; "be covered with" is expressed by adding -tapo to the end of the noun: butúitapo "be covered with hair," pʌ́ntapo "be covered with pimples"
cow	wóha
cow cabbage	poyoli
cow lily	mómpoyoi
coyote	wépa, oléli, wépam máidʌ; Coyote's baby: wépa te
Coyote Crossing	Wépa Usitom
Coyote Peak	Oťa Yakʌ́ Yamáni, Yakʌ́m O
crack	crack by itself: hekótto; crack something: hépes; crack off: hépesdaw; crack open by itself: hépesto, hépeswaito; crack something open: hédas, hédasto
cradleboard	tʌtʌ́
crag	síteḱ - precipice, cliff
crane	wáksi; sand-hill crane: kodoko, wóldokkʌ, brush crane: pám wáksi/páwaksi
cranny	pʌ́nkel/pʌ́nḱeli
crate	budú - package
crater	pʌ́nno - cavity
crawl	lʌk, lʌkdónu, sʌwéiweidoi; crawl to avoid detection: yedúwokit, yedúdutkit; crawl secretly: ḱálʌk; approach crawling: lʌ́kmitpin; crawl across: luksíto; crawl around: lʌ́ksitoye; arrive by crawling: lʌ́kdikno; crawl back: lʌ́kyewei; crawl out: lʌ́ksip; keep crawling out: lʌ́ksipebisim; crawl all the way out: lʌ́ksipbos; not be crawling out: lʌ́ksipmenew; crawl away: lʌ́kḱoi; crawl down in: lʌkʌ́nno; tell someone to try to crawl down into: lʌkʌ́nnomakwonowo; crawl down into: lʌ́kmit; crawl all the way down into: lʌkʌ́nnombos; crawl under: ḱanáidi lʌktik; crawl up: lʌ́kdoi; be unable to crawl up: lʌ́kdoichʌi
crazy	hútu, hútupe; be crazy: hútu; go crazy: hútubadoi; be thoroughly crazy: hútulʌt; drive someone crazy: hútubadoiti; drive someone thoroughly crazy: hútulʌtti; crazily: hútutini; lunacy: hútudom
cream cheese	huťólpi
create	ya, ya'ati/yatí, yánto; create using thought: hukít; create/work on: sikés; be created: púḱta; that which was created: yawónope
Creator	ḱódoyape, ḱódoyakʌ, ḱódom yepóni, púḱsakʌ
creature	máidʌ, ḱutí; some kind of creature: máidʌwet
creek	sewí, momí
creek bed	sewím bo, séwwonpini
creep up	loḱétḱoi, sʌwéiweidoi; creep up slowly: loḱétdoi
creeper (bird)	kapúdi
cremation	ostu - burning
Crescent Mills	Ḱoyóm Bukúm
crest	kʌ́sdo; at the crest of the ridge; kʌ́swodoidi; along the crest of the ridge: kʌ́swodoinodi, kʌswowóno
crib	bassinet: tʌtʌ́ - cradleboard
cricket	chukútkʌ/chikútkʌ (FC), chʌḱʌ́tʌ (WS), tatámʌ; Jerusalem cricket: si'ʌne
criminal	bʌ́de
crimp (n)	kink, wave (in hair), coil (v), spiral: wʌ́nťeťenoye - curl
crippled	wósdotno; walk with one leg short: wóspoi, wóspoino
crisscross	ḱótwochono
critter	kopí
crook	pedákʌ - thief
cross over	ʌsíto, ʌtópin; go across down towards: ʌsítopin; cross back and forth: ḱótwochono
crossed eyes	hin'ápem hiní
crossing (mountain or river)	ʌsíto
crosspiece	hʌ́mtʌti - beam (n), rafter
crouch down	yudúdutḱoi; crouch down and hide: ḱa'ukkinu; crouch down before springing at someone: yunúk
crow	áha/áho/á'a; ḱáhḱa/ḱákḱa; Clark crow: sáuko; to crow: wó
crowd (n)	bomó - group
crumbs	kachémeni
crunch (v)	chawái - chew
crush	kapíl

English	Maidu
cry	wak, wob, wom; cry due to grieving: lól; make someone cry: wákti: almost make someone cry: wáktihudoi; cry continuously: wakbósno, wómbusno; keep crying: wákwaknonu; go around crying/complaining: wáknoyesa; keep crying over a woman: wakkmléw; arrive crying: wakmdíkno; cry in one's sleep: mswak; cry loudly/angrily: chat; go out crying: lólekoi; go around grieving: lólnino; grieve as one goes: lólmkoi; cry out: wákwakno, wákwaknu, cry to oneself: wákpai'us; crybaby: wáksape
cry for joy	ho - say "oh" or "ho" (verb)
crypt	tánkm - burial ground
Crystal Lake	Otem Pakáni
cuisine	pekm - food
cup	loló; drinking glass: mómlolo, mokmm loló; tea cup: tí'im loló
cure (v)	wadáti; cure shamanistically: bmsápkoi, yom, yómdo, yómkiti; completely cure: yómbos; suck out the illness: bodóiti; remove the illness: ítubodoi; approach a doctor asking them to cure: yómye'ókit; ask someone to doctor: yómye, yómyemai, yówwochik; a place where I was asked to doctor: yómyemaisma; cure oneself: wadáti'us
curious	pí epínsa, pekúla
curl	wmnťeťenoye; curl up (like a leaf): wuchulus
curly	smdóldol; curly-haired: onóm smdóldol, onotmitmikm
currant	pám hiní/pamíni, anána; blue currant: nmnholwa, upupupe; Sierra currant: yupupi; golden currant: nunholwa
currency	liáni - money
current (adj)	béidmktapo - right now; béduki - modern
current (river)	séwkoi
currently	hai'í
curse (v)	wáswewe, wásweye - swear
curtail	tibíti - make smaller
curtain	banchik'kmm chi
curve (v)	wmn - turn (v)
customarily	ká'usan - as usual
customary	betéitodi'im- traditional, one who is traditional
cut	wmkms, wmkmsto; cut in two: hukóto; cut off: hukótchono, hukótdaw, wmkmtdaw, hudáw; cut off the end: wmkmtchono; slice: wmkmt; cut by sawing: huné; cut into strips: lmkmi; cut up wood: hukót; start to cut up wood: hukótdoi; nick: kadés; cut by chewing: wétmk, hutmkityo; cut up (meat): kós; cut (something like a rope): husók; a cut-off piece: hudáwdo
cut down	tibíti - make smaller
cute	nukchetípe
cutlet	hudáwdo - a cut-off piece
cylinder	lumí - tube
dab	kachémeni - crumb
daddy	táta
daddy long-legs spider	hísam kowó
daily	mpékanbem ekí - every day
dainty	nukchetípe - cute
dam	ťú; dam up: ťúchik
Dan Williams	káinahu
dance	wetém, yúhbo; always dance: weteméw; dance and sweat: kumlái; turning/swinging from one side to the other: kodéle'émto, kotwélemtodo, kótwochonoye; dance around: wetémdodo, wetémdodoi, yúkbositoye; dance at the wéda/feast: wulú; go dancing: wetémkoi, wetémno; dance in a circle: mchóno, wetémchono, wúlu; dance in a circle holding hands: widóktotopepe; make someone dance: wetémti; start dancing: wetémdoi, wulúdoi; dance at the girls' puberty ceremony: mák; a dance: wetémmi, yúkbo; a dance get-together: wetémim motó; dance house: kumú; round dance singing: wetémchonom sóldom; the sound of dancing: ťaťákam wétemi; while dancing: yúhbod
dandruff	onóm pibáwi
dangerous	mhm, yehéptuyetipe
dangle	la - be suspended, hang

327

English	Maidu
dark	kulú; be dark: kulú; get dark: kulúkit; get to be dark: kulúnanna, kulúwoye; be just before dark: kulúlukit; darkness: banákmenpe; just before dark: kulúmenpe; once it is dark: kulúchet; almost black: síwsiwhudoipe; dark-skinned: ochúlak, osímno, osíwno
dark-skinned	ochúlak - swarthy, dark complexioned
darling	oi'ɱpaipe; mʼɱmʼibe - term of affection
darling (adj)	yaháchetipe - pretty
dart (n)	nokó - arrow
dart (v)	hɱlíslisno, wilék - hurry
dart ahead	ɱwála - go past
dash (n)	tibínak - a little bit; kachémeni - crumb
daughter	pó, tem kɱlé; daughter-in-law: péine; a pair that includes a daughter: pókitoto
dawn	ékda, ékdadoi, ékdakoi; to dawn/be doing at dawn: ékda; be nearly dawn: ékdadakit; get to be dawn: ékdaye; the next morning at dawn: chái'im ékda
day	ekí; days (when counting): ekdá; the next day: chái'im bének, mɱm bének; the next day at dawn: chái'im ékda; day after tomorrow: bénekem mɱm béneke; every day: ɱpékanbem éki; middle of the day: ekím ésto; to this day: udó; main day of the wéda: wédam buyi; in the daytime: bénekdi
daydream	ekím nedí
daylight	ekí; be almost daylight: ekdaipotó; be completely daylight: ékdakit
dazed	ɱs
dead	wónowono; be dead: wónoda; dead person: ískayaťa; dead child: téyaťa
dead end	batásluťi - the extreme end
deaf	ólpe, ól, bonó'olpe; be deaf: ól; become deaf: ólwedoi, ólbadoi; become completely deaf: ólboswedoi; be deafened: pínchɱi; pretend to be deaf: ólkukus
deal (cards)	méito
deal (v)	wonóto - trade (v)
deal with	katí - do to (with negative connotations)
dear (n)	oi'ɱpaipe; mʼɱmʼibe - term of affection
death	wónodawono
deathless	wónomen
debate (n)	hónsaweye - argument
debilitated	etósmen - weak
debris	kachémeni
debt	humusma; be in debt: humusmito
decayed	holóko
deceased	yaťa
deck	polówa - floor
declaration	wéye - speech
declare	wéye - tell, wewé - speak
decline (go down)	tibíbew, wɱsuisúikit - dwindle, get fewer, deflate
decline (say No)	wíye - refuse (v)
decomposed	holóko
decrease (v)	tibíbew, wɱsuisúikit - dwindle, get fewer, deflate
decrepit	kéy'i; feeble, frail: ťoi, etósmen - weak
deed	ma - law (n)
deep	hadá; deep as water: bodúk; deep as snow: budút; be deep everywhere: budútno; be not very deep: bodúkboduk; cause to be deep: budútnoti
deer	sɱmí; deer meat: ínyanam sɱmí; mule deer: ínkayi
Deer Creek	Kutím Sewí
deer hoof rattle	yókolkɱ
deer trail	sɱmbó
deerbrush	chɱpátim dɱ
deerskin	wolósi
defeat (v)	wasáya, ónkoi, ónkoito
defecate	piť, piťí, bɱdói; strain while defecating: hónku, hónkui; push out while defecating: hónpolpin, hónpolsip; defecate on: piťyo; defecate all over: piťísitoye
defect (v)	pull out, forsake, walk out on: wasɱkoi - go away angry
defile	wasáti - mess up, ruin
define	mákpapaiti - explain
definitely	yahátkana, kaná
deflate	wɱsuisúikit/wusuisuikit
degree	bénno - step

English	Maidu
dehydrate	ṗikálti - dry (tr)
dehydrated	ṗikál - dried out
delay (tr)	etúti - cause to wait
delete	balím dadáw - erase
deliberate	húni - consider
deliberately	wúni - slowly
delicate	wisópsa; delicate health: ṫoi, etósmen - weak
delicious	yahát dótipe, dóchekm, dóchema; be delicious: yahát dóti, tetétluṫi sudá
delight in	ḱuidak - like (v)
deliver	soyá - pass (by hand)
Delphinus constellation	hémuimu
deluge (n)	kóh'bono - a great rain, storm
deluge (v)	mombóno - to flood, flow
demand (v)	méiwo - tell someone to give; ápe - ask for
demolish	wi'íti - destroy
demon	uswúlulu - devil
demonstrate	yapái
dent (n)	pḿnno - cavity
deny	hálcheche - contradict
deny oneself	wi'íwo'us
depart	mḱoi, mḱoida; plural subject: ḱawhehekoi, ḱawhehekokoi; depart quickly: wḿssa
departure	mḱoida, mnóyekm; angry departure: wasmḱoiwonoda; my departure: mnódoisma
depend on	húno - rely on, back
deplete	wahéno - waste (v)
depleted	hehépai
deplore	ḱuidakmen - dislike (v)
deport	woiyóḱoi - send (someone) away
depression	pḿnno - cavity
deprived	be deprived of: wonó
descend	ḿn, ḿnno, ḿt, ḿtno; hike down: hḿtpin; go down towards: ḿtpin, ḿnpin; go down over towards: mchópin; get all the way down towards: mpéḱanuhanpin; get all the way down: mpéḱanohánpin; go off downhill: mdáw; wander in a downhill direction: ḿnnoye; come down towards: ḿmpin
describe	mákpapaiti - explain; a, wéye - talk about, discuss
desecrate	wasáti - mess up, ruin
desert (barren area)	podá
desert (v)	bosíp, wadá - escape (v), get away
deserted	wi'ípe; to/in a deserted place: wi'ípedi; be deserted: hónmaktin
desertion	mḱoida - departure
desiccate	ṗikálti - dry (tr)
design	bal, balí; to make designs: bálti; basket design material: loló bálkm
designate	mmyákkḿti - be the same as each other
desolation	podá - desert
despise	ḱuidakmen - dislike (v); hokót - ridicule
destination	mḱoi; usual destination: mḱoikm
destroy	wi'íti; destroyed: wi'ípe, wi'íwonope; be destroying: wi'ítida; be destroyed: wi'í; destroy over time: wi'ítisa; in destroying: wi'ítid; not be destroyed: wi'ímen
detach	wibák; detach from a fixed surface: widákdaw; become detached: héyup
detain	bístikíye - confine, restrict
detect	not detect anything: hónmaktin
deter	hḿstaye - scare away
detest	ṗiṫúk - hate (v)
devastate	wi'íti
develop	dí - grow
developed	ḱap - ripe
deviate	wḿndoi - turn aside
device	ma'ákm - doer
devil	ḿsḱaye, wísḱaye, mswálulu, dedébml
devil	ḿsṗa - rascal
Devil's Corral	Pichilipem
diagnose	smḱáw
dial (n)	yenḿnnokm - wheel, something that turns
Diamond Mountain	Óm Lulmlm

English	Maidu
diaper	put a diaper on: pitchoti
diarrhea	ḱamílak have diarrhea: ḱamílak
dictate	mákpaiti - instruct, direct, order
did (helping verb)	MMG p. 28, verb ending depends on subject. p. 34, "did" for asking questions, verb ending depends on subject
die	wóno; plural subject: héno; almost die: wónohudoi; be dead: wónoda; die off, be all (of them) passed on: wónobos
die down	bukúi - go out (fire)
die out	wi'í - disappear
differ (disagree)	hálcheto - disagree
differ (vary)	cháitika - be different
difference	mᴧcha'i
different	chái'i (object), chái'im (subject/adjective), cháitiki, cháitikape; all different: chaicháino; each one different: cháitikakape; different-looking: cháichetipe, cháitikchetipe; I want a different one: chái'iḱas; be different: cháitika; a different language: cháitikkapem wéye; a different (not the same) man: máidᴧmenim; different ones: cháitikkape; different kinds of things: hésboyoyo; different sounding: cháitikpintipe
differently	cháitikat
differing (adj)	chái'im - different
dig	sut, be; dig with paws: bá; dig a hole: ḱáwba; dig in the dirt: ḱáwbe; dig up plants: sᴧk; dig up roots: sᴧkdói, hudói; go off to dig: sᴧḱḱoi; dig up plants/roots with a tool: wopóldoi, wopólno; dig something open or apart (like an ant-hill)
digger pine	towáni, towánim chá
digging stick	siwí
dilapidated	kéy'i
dilute	mómwiyakti, momchúiti - make more watery, thin up
diminish (tr)	tibíti - make smaller
diminutive	nᴧs - low (adj)
dim-witted	húboḱoipe - witless
dining room	pekᴧm uyí - restaurant
dinner	ḱáipe, ḱáipekᴧ; make dinner for: ḱáipeti, ḱáipewo; had eaten dinner: ḱáipewonó
dip in	supút; dip in this and that: supútputtonu; dip in from time to time: supúttonu
direct (v)	mákpaiti; yaháti - organize things
direct oneself	sᴧnwoḱoi - be headed (a certain way)
direct to	héw - point in the right direction
directed	where (one is) directed: mákpaitipedi
direction	bó - way; in that direction: anína, amának, hamóna; in the opposite direction: cháinantedi; change direction: wᴧndᴧi
director	yepóni - chief
dirt	ḱawí; be in the dirt: ḱaw; stir up dirt: ḱawí sukdóiti; dirt floor: hᴧbóm ḱawí
dirty	óichei, óichepe, wemtichúti; be dirty: óichei
dirty looks	give someone dirty looks together: sᴧnchetutumoto
disabled	wósdotno
disagree	hálcheto; disagree with each other: hálchetoto
disappear	wi'í; that which had disappeared: wi'íwonope
disapprove	ḱúidakmen - dislike (v)
disaster	wehépti; get out of a disaster with good luck: hónsu
disbelieve	hálche - reject (v)
disburse	pakál - pay (v)
discharge	pópti - explode
disco	wetém - dance (n)
discontinue (tr)	etápti - stop something
discontinued (adj)	hésmeni, kéi - old
discourage from	héwa, mamámen - warn not to do
discover	hónmak, mákpai - find out
discuss	wéye; mention: yawí
disease	ítu; disease-carrying: ítukpe
disembark	ᴧdíkno, okít - arrive at, arrive
disgorged	be disgorged: opín
disguised	chesáktimen; be disguised: cháitika
disgusted	be disgusted: ṗiťúk
disgusting	wemtichᴧktiti; sounding disgusting: wemchichᴧkpintipe
dish	waťá; dish up: ái, áiye; help oneself to food: áisiye

330

English	Maidu
dishonest	hálsa; be dishonest: hálsa
dishrag	chukútkᴍm witʼᴍtʼᴍino
dishtowel	waťá dákᴍ
disk	waťá; disk-shaped: waťám chetípe
dislike	ḱúidakmen, wasát che; hate: píťúk; not like much: ḱúidakboduk
dislodge	wicháp; dislodge by pulling: héchap
dismal (weather)	wipúppu
dismiss (reject)	hálche - reject (v)
dismiss (send away)	woiyóḱoi - send (someone) away
dispatch (n)	wewé - speech
displace	force out of place: batásip, hᴍbónan batásip - chase out, drive out; wiyéti - force someone out
displeased	be displeased with: wásḱato
dispose of	remove, eliminate, get rid of: wiyéti or wiyéti - cause to be missing/gone - make someone leave
dispute (v)	wokótito - quarrel (v); hokótito - argue with; hálcheche - contradict
disregard	chenúḱoimen - not pay attention
dissent (v)	hálcheto - disagree
dissimilar	chái'im - different
dissolution	úno - divorce (n)
dissolve	kómchú - thaw
dissolve	mómwiyakti - make more watery
distance	ťíkteno; in the distance: hadánawet, hadá, hadána, hadádadi; at a distance: bomhóm mᴍná; a short distance: ťíkte, hedéntona, ťíktete; from a distance: ťíktetenan, obᴍdawnan; a certain distance upwards: ťíktedoi, ťíktetedoinodi; from somewhere in the distance: ántenántenan; in a place a certain distance away: ťíkteḱóidi; in a place reached from a distance: ka'ántekitdi; after reaching a place from a distance: ka'ántekitchet; be a distance away: hadánḱoi; go a distance: ka'ántekit, hadátoḱoi, ťíkteteḱoi
distant	hadá; a distant place: bomhó; in a distant place: bomhódi'im
distant past	betéihuki - the ancient world, after humans
distinct	chái'im - different
distort	witúbil - twist
district	ḱódo, ḱódoi
distrust	ókket - doubt
disturb (person)	sᴍkála - bother
disturb (shake)	dᴍyᴍyᴍti - shake
dive	yóno, yóḱoi, yóchono; dive down deep: yókit; dive in: túpmitno/tᴍpmitno, yóchono; dive into while holding something: hányochono; dive off: yódaw; dive farther down: yᴍ'áswokityochono; dive in after someone to chase: yo'ᴍhésitoye; dive up/come up to the surface: yódoi
divide	wiwái, yotótchik
divide up	chetó, wiyᴍl
divide with	wiwáito
divorce	úno; to divorce: yᴍno; divorcé(e): yᴍnope
divvy up	wiyᴍl, chetó - divide up, split, parcel out; kᴍ'ídi - share
dizzy	be dizzy: hiní pᴍpᴍi
do	ma, ma'á, ya, ka'áti, hesái, kᴍ; do with the hands: wohóp; be doing: ayáno, ayánu, kawéw; do like that: ka'á; do like this: ayá, ayáti; cause to do: ma'áti; always do: mawéw; always seem to be doing: kawéwkᴍ; do this and that: ka'áwhuyeti; doing what one wants: ka'áyahádom; probably do: ha'ái; go along doing: ha'ᴍḱói; do habitually: wéw; tell someone to do: wo; go have something done: woḱói; do something with several things: yayó; not do: wíye, ka'átimen; without doing anything to: hesátimenwet; doing so: ayán; when doing that: amᴍni; do it!: mapí; do better/do good things: yahádoiti; do to intentionally: matí; always do (intentionally): matíwe; do to (someone) again: matíwewi; do whatever: húmbotmenweti; do well for oneself: yahát yatí'us; what I am doing: yasmá
do (helping verb)	MMG p. 34, verb ending depends on subject. p. 34 "do" for asking questions, verb ending depends on subject

331

English	Maidu
do (in questions)	Just what are you going to do? hesísi hesá maká?; What do you want me to do? hesáti yaháka nik?; What do you think you're doing?: makmká?; What should I do?: hesáihelukmḱas?; Why were you doing that?: hesádom mayéwḱa?; What are you going to do about it?: hesáti maká?; what did you do to it?: hesátika?; What do you do with it?: hesáti mi maká?
do business	deal (v): wonóto - trade (v)
do something about	hesáti - do something
do something about it	húmbotmenweti; not do anything about it: huhehénumen; be unable to do anything about it: hesátichmi, hesámaka
do to again and again	matíwe - always do, keep causing (problems)
do to/for oneself	self-, oneself: MMG p. 54, -'us infix on verb
do without	wi'í - lack
dock (plant)	woťókťok (WS), waťokťoko (JD)
doctor	yomé, yomí, yomím máidm, yomém máidm; doctors: yómnono; female doctor: yomím kmlé/yomém kmlé; doctor who blows to cure: bḿdam máidm; one who is not a doctor: yomímeni; to doctor: yom; practice doctoring: yómdo; invite to doctor: yómye, yómyemai; approach asking to doctor: yómye'ókit; ask to doctor: yówwochik; set out to doctor: yómkit; go to perform doctoring: yómkiteḱoi; go around the land doctoring: yomḿsitoye; doctor people while traveling
dodge	wadá; dodge as one runs: wadáhuye, wadáhuye'mpin; an expert in dodging arrows: hódesi/hudési
doe	kmlém smmí
doer	ma'ákm
does (helping verb)	MMG p. 34, "does" for asking questions -(ḱ)ade on verbs. For negatives "does not," use -menḱan ending on verbs.
dog	sḿ, wépam sḿ; little dog: sḿmbe; pack of dogs: sḿm bomó; small dog: sḿbe
dogbane	pumdum
dogwood	ťaťá; dogwood tree: ťaťám cha; dogwood flower: ťaťám yó
doing	in so doing: hesámmni
domestic (adj)	bískmm - residential
domesticate	sḿdon - make a pet of
dominant	tetébe - bigger, largest
dominate	ónḱoi - come out on top, beat, outsmart
donate	méi - give
done	done as food: ḱap, smtápó; had done: kawóno
don't do	ben... map/ben mapí
door	púlkm, ḱumhḿ púiya, puyí; by the door: púiyam ínkina, púiyanaki; through the door: púlkmdi; from outside the door: púiyanan; towards the door: púiyana; open the door: púlkm púlkitpi; close the door: púlkm bukúitipi
doorknob	oḱéli - knob
dope	húboḱoisape - one who is witless
dopey	húboḱoipe - witless
double (adj)	péne - two
double (v)	onḿnkiti - bend something over
doubt	ókket
dough	soyó
Douglas fir	líham cha, lúmlumi
Douglas squirrel	hindakono
douse	hit, hítpai; soak: hamít, hamítyo; go douse something: mómni hítpaino
dove (bird)	wiléspuikm, wuiléspuikm, elespúika, oléspuikm
down	obḿnno; downward: wótno
down (action going down)	MMG p. 55-56, -mit, -daw, -n, or -t infixes on verb
downhill	bónnodi; go off downhill: mdáw; wander around downhill: ḿnnoye, ḿtnoye
downpour	kóh'bono - a great rain, storm
downtown	town
downy	butúipe - furry
doze	túimeninu
drag	haláp; drag down: halápkit; forcefully drag down: hánwokit; drag along: halápno; drag around: halápnoye; drag away: dónwikatono, halápḱoi; drag out: halápdaw; drag over: hánwochono; drag towards: halápye, halápdoi; a place where one drags someone down: hánwokitkm; in the place where someone is dragged down: hánwokitkmdi; drag somewhere else: dónwikakit
dragonfly	túmilmili

English	Maidu
drain (energy)	wokóti - tire out (tr)
drain (liquid)	ku; drain something: kutí
drapery	banchik'ᴍm chi - curtains
draw (a picture)	bálti
draw (cause)	ti - cause
draw (pictures)	bálti - make pictures
draw a blank	húkichik - forget
draw near	ᴍpín - approach
dread (v)	yehéptoye, wisét - be afraid of
dream	nedí; to dream: nedí; dream to oneself: nedí'us; dreamer: nedísape, ᴍschenusape; bad dreams: wasám nedí; dream land: nedím ḱódo
drench	to drench: hit; drenched: hítape
dress	get dressed: chí, húldoi'us, húldoi; be completely dressed: chíbos; get dressed up: hesúpai, yaháhati'us; dress someone: húldoiti; a woman's dress: nawási
dress up (i.t)	hesúpai
drift	as a cloud: tumyedói; drift away (smoke): súkdaw; drift little by little: híntata
drill	to drill: wóchedai; fire drill: sawó
drink	mo; drink something thick: hup; seldom drink: mobᴍdᴍk; like to drink: moyáha; cause to drink: moti; a drink/beverage: mokᴍ; drinker: momᴍ; light drinker: mobúdᴍḱᴍ; heavy drinker: mosápe
drinker (habitual)	mosápe - one who frequently drinks
drip	lat; drip away: látdaw; drip down: láťinpin, látkit
drive	batáno; driver: batánokᴍ
drive out	batásip, woiyóḱoi, wiyéti; drive out spirits: ónḱoi; be driven out: woyóḱoiwono
drizzle (n)	ḱadíkim pibáwi
droop	la - be suspended, hang
drop (v)	as leaves: bodá, héyuye; drop by itself: héwdaw; drop something: heyúkiti; let something drop: heyúyeti; drop quickly from the hand: sólekwono; drop something into: bóno; not drop: dónomen
drop in on	chenóḱoi - visit (v)
drop the ball	sitái - miss a shot, grab at and miss
drops	pibáwi; drops of milk or white liquid: mínmini
drug (n)	wené - medicine
drum	solím wókᴍ
drunk	hudásu; slightly drunk: hudásuhsuh
dry	piḱálpe, piḱál; dry by itself: piḱál; dry something: piḱálti; to partially dry something: echúktiyo dry meat: wákda, sitók
Dublin Jack Ravine creek	máidᴍ homím sewí
duck	wátkᴍ; mallard: wátkᴍ, óbunu/óbᴍno; teal: líki, olupkᴍ; pintail: tulúpi, likᴍ; scaup: ḱówukᴍ; shoveler: ḱáwmᴍkkᴍ; merganser: bowakno; redhead: ohaibuldᴍ
duck down	yudúdutkit
dudleya	ómteni
due to	in doing, because of: -di on abstract noun - see huhéyedi in Maidu-English section.
dull	ťókmen; gray/dismal: wipúppu; be dull (as a knife): ťókmul
dummy	húboḱoisape - one who is witless
dump (v)	wádaw
dupe (v)	hálpapai - trick, deceive
during	around (time): MMG p. 23, -mᴍni on noun
dusk	kulúnanna; at dusk: kulúmeni
dust	pibáwi, ḱáwdusi; dust-devil: hákḱalulu; stir up the dust: ḱawí sukdóiti, sukdóiti; kick up the dust: ḱáwhei; make dust fly: súknoti
duty	tawáli - work
dwarf (n)	dímenkᴍ
dwell	bis; dwelling: bisí; dwelling place: bísḱᴍmtiḱoidi
dwelling (n)	hᴍbó - house
dwindle	tibíbew
dye	balikᴍ; to dye something: bal
Dyer Mountain	Chiwítbem Yamáni, Náka Yáni
each	ᴍpéḱanbe, sᴍ́ti; each one: hehe; for each one: sᴍ́titi
each other	MMG p. 56, -toto infix on verb
eagle	káḱa, moluku

English	Maidu
Eagle Lake	Hinkɨsimin Mondámim (LM), Hinchesmenim Mómdanni (FC), Hínchesemim Mómdanni (HLME)
ear	bonó; ear lobe: bonóm chípbɨ; pierce the ear: bonó sɨháwkit
early	hésmen
earth	dirt: k̓awí; world: k̓ódo
Earth Maker	k̓ódoyape, k̓ódoyakɨ
earthquake	yanánaito
earthworm	k̓aihí, kaise; roasted earthworms: k̓aihím ítusi
earwax	bonóm chakámi
ease up	chedá - rest
east	ékdadoikɨ; to the east: ékdadoikɨdi, ékdadoina, ékdoina; from the east: ékdoinan
eat	pe; eat with the fingers: lop; go around eating: pewék̓oi; eat all up: pebós; eat all the rest: pebóslew; just eat: pedɨ́kɨ; pretend to eat: pék̓uk̓us; come and eat! pé'okit; eat! pepí; like to eat: peyáha; not eat: pemén; seldom eat: pebɨ́dɨk; don't eat! pepímen! eat together: pétoto; eat with someone: pe'ídi, péto
eats (n)	pekɨ́ - food
eccentric (n)	ka'ámenim máidɨ - strange people
echo (v)	pedáto; echoing: yakwéto
economy size (adj)	tetébe - largest
-ed ending	past tense: MMG p. 28, 63-67 - depends on tense and subject
edge	batás, we'e, wehé, wohó, wat̓á; edge of the road: bom we'e; edge of the water: wat̓ánan; go along the edge: wehé'no, wohó'ɨno; walk along the edge of the meadow: k̓oyówat̓a'ɨno; to the very edge: batátasimotodi; on the edge: wo'áswono; show above the edge: híndoidoi
edifice	uyí - building (n)
edit out	balím dadáw - erase
eel	liuwí, luwú, nuwim
eerie	bɨ́de - weird, evil
egg	pákpaka, pákpa
eggshell	pákpakam posála, pákpakam púmpu
egotistical	yaháchetí'uspe
egret	kai'im moldo, moldo
eight	pénchuiyi
either	meaning "also:" béi'im or béyim; on either side: in'ánto; see also "or."
ejaculate	pópti; be about to ejaculate: póptipoto
elapse	pass (time): wosíp - spend (time)
elastic	wihɨ́pkɨ
elbow	moyó, yímbɨmi; to elbow someone: moyó; elbow someone out of the way: widótk̓oi
elderberry	lokó, lokóm hiní, nok̓óm hiní, lopom k̓idi; elderberry bush: yálulum dɨ; elderberry flute: yálulu
elderly	nenóhno; elderly (of women): kɨlókbekbe, kɨlókbepe; nenópe - old (person)
elders	male elders: béikɨwoli; female elders: mɨnéwoli
eldest	hínwo, hínwono, nenólut̓
elect	woiyó - select, pick for a job
elegy	wóno'k̓oikɨm solí
element	wasása - ingredient
elevate	hoist: wiwó - lift, raise
elevated	hadádoi - high up
eleven	máschok̓na sɨ́tti
eliminate	wiyéti - cause to be missing/gone - make someone leave
elk	káma
else (who else, etc.)	chái'im - other
elsewhere	chái, yɨn, cháidi; be elsewhere: chaina
elude	wadá
elude	wadá - dodge, get away
Elysian Valley	Bɨwopo
embarrass	yepíti; be embarrassed: yepí; embarrassing: yepísape; embarrass oneself: yépti'us
embed	yɨmɨ́chono - put into
embers	hemí
embrace (v)	sitápin, lulúmwochono - hug (v)
embryo	tém púkti

English	Maidu
emerge	msíppin; emerge in a bunch: ťisíye; emerge from water: yósip, smhésip; emerge suddenly: pop
emit	hónwesip - exhale
employ	woiyó - hire
empty	wi'ípe; in/to an empty place: wi'ípedi
en route	mnókmdi - on the way going along
encircle	wichák; enclose: ymmmoto; go around (waist, etc): wochóno
enclose	ymmmoto
encore (adj)	béibmm - again
encounter	odá, chenó, odáto; encounter by chance: mdémmai, mdémťa, mlémmai
encourage	pepáno - give verbal support
encumbrance	hadó - load
end (n)	end piece, tip: chípbm, óschumnaki; the extreme end: batásluťi; end of talking: wéye kaní; the end: kaním ka'am; end of (a hose): oḱéli; to the end: kanína; come to the end of: hádikno
end (tr)	etápti - stop something
end of the line	batásluťi - the extreme end
end up doing	MMG p.65, -wono on verb
endorse	héwwo, húno - be verbally supportive
endure (i.t.)	mbis - remain, last
endure (tr)	honwéyepati - survive something, stand (tr), bear (v)
enduring (adj)	wónomen - immortal
enemy	ḱuse
energetically	do energetically: wó'mhanoye, wó'mhadoito
energy	run out of energy: wmsuisúikit
engine	ma'ákm - doer; mmsín - machine
English	wólek wéye
enjoy	núknoye; ḱuidak - like (v); enjoyable: yahát hubúktipe
enjoyable	yahát hubúktipe - pleasant
enlarge (i.t.)	tetébe - get larger
enlightened one	húkespe - wise, clever
enormous	tetéluťi
enough	ťik, wém, wémťiki; exactly enough: wémťikluťpe; that's enough: kaním ka'am, su; be enough: wémťik, wémťikbo, wémťikiti, wémťikpe; be just enough for: ťikḱói, wémťikdmkbe; get enough: wémchik; enough talking: wémťik wéye; I have talked enough: wemťikkás
enroll	papélkitti, womít - record (v)
ensue	hóipai - follow
enter	ymnpin, in'ínno, lmkmnno; enter a car or path: mmít; go down into: mmítkapin
enter one's mind/head	húmit - recall
entice	héwwelek
entire	mpéḱandmkbe
entrails	pítkololo - guts
environment	ḱódoi - area
envisage	húpai - foresee
envision	huhéye - imagine
epoch	méni - period of time
equal	equal amount: mmyákbe; do equally: mmyákati
equally	mmyákbebe, mmyákdmbe mmyákbe
-er (comparison - like bigger or better)	MMG p. 74
era	méni - period of time
eradicate	wi'íti - destroy
erase	dádaw; erase writing: balím dadáw
eraser	dádawkm
erection	have an erection: pináw; get an erection: etósti; erection-causing: pináwtipe
erroneous	mistaken, in error, improper: wasá - wrong
erroneously	inaccurately, mistakenly, incorrectly: wasá
erupt	pópti - ejaculate
escape	bosíp; flee wildly: koháḱoi; flee wildly in all directions: koháhaḱoi
escape one's memory	húkichik - forget
escarpment	síteḱ - precipice, cliff
escort (v)	hóiwiháno - lead

English	Maidu
esophagus	kḿilulumi - throat
especially	adḿk
essentially	hesátmet - just, only, nothing but
-est (comparison - like best or most)	MMG p. 74: use forms of waláw ("exceed") or use the -luťinfix on the verb.
establish	bᴍsḿpkit - set in place
esteem	have self-esteem: ᴍkáwche'us
estimate (v)	áikakat - figure, surmise
etc.	a'únodom, a'únomapem
eternal	wónomen - immortal
eternity	wónomenkᴍm kódo - heaven
ethical	yahá - good
eulogize	penóweye - praise (v)
evacuate (i.t.)	wḿssasip - leave, be forced to leave
evade	wadá - dodge, get away
Evans Point	Hópnomi
evaporated	pikálpe - dried out
even	ma'át, ma'át 'as
even though	in spite of, although: MMG p. 87, -wet suffix on verb
evening	kai, kulú, kulúnanna; at evening: kulúmi; in the twilight: tái'idi; towards evening: kulúnan; be evening: kaikit; get along towards evening: yo'ḿᴍskoi, yo'ḿᴍsno; this evening: bey'ím kulú
event	ḿmmotope
eventually	mᴍméntapo - over time
eventually	ultimately: MMG p. 65, -wono on verb
everlasting	wónomen - immortal
every	ᴍpékani(m); every single one: sḿtim ma'át, ᴍpékanbe, ᴍpékandᴍk, ᴍpékaniluťi, lúťpekanim; every place: tikói; from every place: tiknan; every kind: homóbokitmeni; every day: ᴍpékanbem éki; each and every: hehe
everyone	ᴍpékani(m), mínobe, mᴍm bomó; every one of the people: máidᴍhehe; every one of you: ᴍpéknim
everything	mínobe
everywhere	kódomťik; in every corner of the world: yḿwaitokᴍdi; all around: yúmotodi; wherever one meets people: yúmotokᴍdi; wherever one goes: yunókᴍdi; throughout the land: pípem kódo; from all directions: ᴍpékapinan; from all sides: ᴍpénan; from everywhere: yḿwáitokᴍnan; to exist everywhere: yᴍchóno
evict	wiyéti - force someone out
evil (adj)	wasá - bad
evil (n);	wasá, bḿde; something evil: wískaye
eviscerate	kós; pitkol - gut (v)
exact	that exact place: ᴍpékanupe
exact (v)	méiwo - ask someone to give
exactly	tené
exaggerate	witái
examination	welé - test, trial run
examine	chebḿk; examine oneself: uschenu; chehéiheino - inspect
exasperated	wasó - angry
excavate	káwba, sut - dig a hole, dig
exceed	waláw; be the best or most: ᴍpékanbe... waláwpe
excellent	ekáw
excerpt	léiwo - part
excessively	tetét píkno
excessively	hard (like "work hard"), too much, a lot: MMG p. 55, -luťinfix on verb
exclamations	pleasant surprise: a nikí; "How wonderful!" hés ekáw; "Nice:" wéh; unpleasant surprise: "ouch!" a'a!; "ew!" hḿn; "damn!" ham!; "Oh, no! How awful!" hesá wise/hés wísse!; "argh! dammit!" ónanai; "how awful!" hés yehépti!; "damn it!" wokkadássikka; agreeing with someone: "how true! amen!" héw hapá, héw tené; "good luck to you, come on!" héya; "OK:" ho, hew; disagreeing with someone: "baloney!" a!; "oh, brother!" hesá!; "nonsense!" hokóttisa!; greetings: "hello:" he'é ho; "hey!" hi'i, si'í; miscellaneous: "oops! sorry!" ai!; "well!" hés ha'ái!; "that's enough!" su!; "well, why not..." hes wi'iye; "wow!" heswéh; "help me to the bathroom (child)" e'e; To make any of these into a verb, add "adóm" after it, for example: hḿn adóm "say 'ew!'"

English	Maidu
excrement	pití
excursion. sightseeing	ṁkóido - traveling
excuse (v)	sówono - let someone go
execute	wónoti - kill
executive (n)	yepóni - chief
exfoliate	kam - shed (v)
exhale	hónwesip
exhaust (v)	wokóti - tire out (tr)
exhibit (v)	yapái - show (v)
exhort	hṁhwé
exist	ú; exist everywhere: yṁchóno; not exist: umén, wi'í
exit (v)	yṁsip - go out
expand (i.t.)	tetébe - get larger
expect	chekínu; expect someone to arrive: chebóye, chehéiye
expedition	ṁkóido - traveling
expel	woiyókoi - send (someone) away
expensive	hélmono; be expensive: pí yawí; be very expensive: tetét pí yawí
experience (v)	hṁbṁk - feel
experiment (n)	welé - test, trial run
experiment (v)	mákwono - try to
explain	mákpapaiti
explanation	ma'ámṁni - reason why
explode	pópti; bolákdoi - catch on fire, blaze up
explode at (in anger)	wasóhati
exploit (v)	hṁhá - use
explore	hónmaknoye - investigate
express	kái
expression	yawí - word
extend	extend something: píubokoiti; make something extend down: píubokiti; let something extend down: píubonpinti; hang down/extend down by itself: piúbonpininu, piúbonpin; not extend all the way: píuboduk
extend	overhang, stick out, project (v), jut out: sṁ, sṁdáw - protrude
extend (i.t.)	tetébe - get larger
extend (tr)	t́éstimen - prolong
extend to (i.t.)	stretch to: towóikit
extent	woi
exterior (n)	púidi - outside
exterminate	wi'íti - destroy
extinguish	bukúitida, bukúiti
extinguished	be extinguished: bukúibos, bukúkuikit; be almost extinguished: bukúipoto
extort	demand (v), exact (v): méiwo - ask someone to give
extra	do something extra: cháinakḱenu
extract	wikṁp; pull out: wikṁpdoi, wipól
extravagant	wáiheno; one who is always extravagant: wáihenosape
extremely	tetét pikno - too much
extremely	really, a lot: MMG p. 55, -luť infix on verb
extremity	íntas - base (n), hilt; chípbṁ - tip
extricate	wikṁp - extract (v)
eye	hiní; have something in the eye: hínbochik, hínḱochik; have an eye twitch: hínwilok; crossed eyes: hin'ápem hiní; beady eyes: wipélkim hiní; have the eyes closed: hín duschikkíno; roll the eyes: mṁl, mṁldoi; with eyes meeting: hinímotodo; eyeless: hínkol; absolutely eyeless: hínkolluť
eyebrow	hinís butú, túikṁm butú
eyelash	hinískṁlṁlṁ
eyelid	hínposala
fabled	betéi - legendary
fabricate (build)	yatí - create
fabricate (lie)	hal - tell a lie
face	mussú, hiní, simí; turn and face toward: ḱótwoye; turn and face away: ḱótwokoi; face up: sṁnchewodoi; be facing towards: sṁnchedónu; facing towards: chepítwono; one face down, one face up (as in card games): símdoi símkit
facing	chepítwono - facing towards
faction	bomó - group

English	Maidu
fade	pibáw, ṁdá
fail	wi'íye; to not fail: wi'íyemen
fail to (do)	MMG p. 54, -boḱoi infix on verb
fair (adj)	yahá - good
fair (light)	off-white: edáldalnope - light (colored)
fair, good enough	ámbṁkbṁ
fall (autumn)	seméni, seménkit, seménkitti; become fall: seménkit; during the fall: seménkit kṁmén
fall (down)	wodá, heyúno, héyukit, héyudawkit, hé; fall off (by itself): hédakdaw, hépesdaw; fall from above: heyṁmpin, héyudaw; fall down (by itself): héwdaw; trip and fall: pṁksalew, beké'chono; fall down (as pants): héyupkit; one who always falls down: heyúkitpe; fall forward headlong: wadán, wadánkit; fall into: wonó, héyumit; fall in on itself: hédusimoto; fall apart: hépeswaito, hésaswaito
fall asleep	túikit - go to sleep
fall silent	kelémbo - become silent
falling star	sátoyo
false hellebore	poyoli
familiar spirit	ḱakkini - spirit guide
family size (large)	tetébe - largest
fan	bṁmukṁ, wéllepkṁ; to fan: wéllep
fang	chikí - tooth
fantasizing	mínono
fantastic	eḱáw - wonderful
far	hadá, hadádi, hadádaw, hesánte; from far away: hadánan; a far-away place: hesánte ma, bomhó; from a faraway place: bomhónan; to/in a faraway place: ántedi, bomhódi'im; how far?: hesántewet?; This far/so far: ma'ánte; as far as this country: ma'ántem ḱódo; far up/high up: hadádoi; be far away: hadánḱoi; get this far: ma'ántekit; farthest: batásono; not far: t̆ikte, t̆iktein
fare (food)	pekṁ - food
farewell	yahát bíspada - stay well
farm (n)	ḱawí - land
farm (v)	díti
far-off	hadá - distant (adj)
farther	go farther: hadátoḱoi, yṁ'áswodaw; go farther downhillish: yṁ'áswodaw; had gotten a little farther: tetébe tṁtṁwono; a little farther: t̆iktetepindi; a little farther up: wosíppini; a little farther along the trail: bṁ'áswodóino; in a place a little farther away: t̆iktetekóidi
farther than	after (in distance), past (in distance): wodóino - beyond, other side of
fashion (v)	form (v), shape (v): yatí, yánto, ya'ati - create
fast	wilékni, wilékleknini, bilísno; very fast: támlep; go very fast: támlelepno; go faster: hṁlilisno
fast (v)	pemén - not eat
fasten	yodótpai
fat	hṁt̆i/húti (noun); hṁt̆pe (adj); very fat: ínt̆a'usto; the fattest one: hṁt̆lut̆i
father	béikṁ/békṁ, tátta; parent: tét̆ṁkṁpe; bereaved father: ḱomá; father-in-law: ḱúpa, péti
fatherland	hóyyam ḱódo - ancestral land
faultless	hesámenkṁ
favor (v)	sṁssṁ - prefer
favorite	adṁḱ
fawn	sṁmím te, ínyanam sṁmím té
fear (v)	yehéptoye, wisét - be afraid of
feast (n)	bṁi, bṁipe, bṁyím motó, wéda; upcoming feast/big time: wédamape; main day of the feast/big time: wédam buyi; at the feast: bṁídi; to the feast: bṁipen; have a feast: bṁyím motó; go to a feast: lópḱoi; go off to a feast (plural subject): lópkoḱoi
feast (v)	wéda - celebrate the big time
feather	yé; feather plume stick: díhyo, wiléle; feather headdress/headstall: báchawi/bátchawi/bátchaw; put on feather regalia: bihíp
Feather Falls	Chichi
feather pillow	yem oḱén
Feather River	Tam Sewí, Tetém Sewí
features	mussú - face
federal	pédowal

English	Maidu
feeble	ťoi, etósmen - weak
feed (n)	pekm̓ - food
feed (v)	pekm̓ti, pewó; feed a little food to someone: dódo; graze/feed (as animals): ḱedé; go from grazing: ḱedéhepinḱoi
feel (a certain way)	hm̓bm̓k; cause to feel: hm̓bm̓kti; make oneself feel: hm̓bm̓kti'us; be made to feel: hubm̓ktiti; feel better: ámbm̓kbm̓; feel strange toward: hínchesem; feel bad: wasát hm̓bm̓k/hubúk; feel good: yahát hm̓bm̓k/hubúk; feel clear (from evil): hówikm̓p; feeling good: yahát hubúktipe
feel (with hands)	pukét - touch (v)
feel around (to find)	bádm̓md m̓mti
feel creepy	hínchesem - feel strange toward
feel happy	yahát hubúk - feel good, feel pleasant
feel like (one is)	yákhubm̓k/yákhm̓bm̓k
feel like doing	yahát ka'ánte
feel pain	bomm̓mm̓ti, ítu - suffer, be in pain
feel sorry for	bomm̓mm̓kno
feisty	eḱáwpintisape
fell (a tree)	heyúkiti, kaití; be felled: kaiwóno
fence	ťú; branch fence: ṕakán tú; build a fence: ťú tawál
ferment	patpát - boil (i.t.), bubble (v)
fern	bracken fern: súllala; five finger/maidenhair fern: loṕíṕi/leṕíṕi
festival	wéda - big time; bm̓ipe
festivity	wéda - big time
fetch	sóiyo, sóyo, sohún, mahá; go fetch: sówiḱoi, sóhino, sóiwino, heḱóitoye, hewíno; fetch (water): henó
fete (n)	feast, celebrate, observe: wéda - celebrate the big time
fetus	tém púḱti
few	a few: helú, helúnini, helúto; be few left: hehépaiwiyáka; be fewer: tibíbew; not a few: helúmeni; more than a few times: helúmenini
few and far between	píboduk - scarce
fiddle (n)	bailín - violin
fiddle (v)	ílimto - play violin
fiddleneck	kul
field	ḱoyó
field mouse	yossó
fiend	uswúlulu - devil
fight	fight someone: hómpaito; fight each other: hómpaitoto; want to fight: hómpaitoyahá; fight with the fists: yokíto; squabble: wókit; a fight: hómpaito; fighter: hódesi
figure (n)	lulú - body
figure (think)	áiḱaḱat; I figure: áiḱate
figure out	figure out fast: húkes; try to figure out: húpai
file (v)	hésbopai - pack things up, put back in its place
fill up	fill up by itself: oṕít, oṕítkinu; (like a river): móm; fill up from one end to the other: oṕítsip; be filled with water: mombomínu; fill something up: oṕítti; fill something up to bursting: hoṕítwaito; completely fill up by going down into: oṕítino
filter (n)	chm̓lm̓ - strainer
final	kaním
finalize	yabós - finish, complete
finally	kaní, kaníwonom; now finally: bei...bei...
finance (v)	heyáwe - support by doing something; húno - sponsor (v)
find	chechói; find by tracking: pai cheḱátḱoi
find a way	figure out how: húpai - try to figure out
find out	máḱpai, chekm̓; go find out: hónmakḱoi; find out by investigating: hónmak
fine (hair)	mútmutpe
fine (OK)	héwma'aḱan; is it fine with you? héwma'aḱade?
finest	yaháhaluťi - the best
finger	mám chípbm̓
fingernail (s)	mábichí, mám bichí
finish	yabós, bós; finish up: hékit; finish up (plural subject): hékikit; finish all the work: tawálhekitbos; finished: kaním
finishing	completely, totally: MMG p. 54, -bos infix on verb

English	Maidu
fir	báso; fir tree: básom chá, tutukʌm cha; Douglas fir: lúmlumi; small fir trees: lúmlumi kuiyó; red fir: chʌtʌkʌm cha
fir needles	lúmlumim sáwi
fir tips	básom chípbʌ
fire	sá; build a fire: sa ku/sakʌ́, sa yá; start a fire using a fire drill: sa wó; forest fire: pʼiyé; set fire to the land (as in a controlled burn): kódo topái, tochóno; start a fire: chódoiti, chópaiti; catch on fire: bolákdoi; go up in flames: bolákamoto'ino; have a fire going inside something: sakʌ́minu; behind the fire: sánodi; lie down with one's back to the fire: kíwsukinu; sleep with one's back to the fire: kíwsusukiti
fire drill	sawó; start a fire using a fire drill: wó
fire pit	óm sá, sam ó, pʼidúsi (ashes); other side of the fire pit: sáwono; place behind the firepit: sawónonaki
firearm	pándakʼa - gun, rifle
firefighters	sam hómpaitokʌm bomó
fireplace	óm sá, sam ó, kʼawím sá
firm (adj)	chʌ́iti - hard, tough
first	hésmen, hínwo; first one created: yahóyape; me first: níkʼuni; you first: míkʼuni; that one first: mʌkʼúni; that man first: mʌkʼúnim máidʌ; that woman first: mʌkʼúnim kʌlé; do for the first time: ma'ánteni
first-rate (adj)	yaháhalutʼi - the best
fish	makó (noun); to fish: lumít; go fishing: lumítkoi; catch fish: wotí; to fish with a trap/basket: chidʌ́k, makóm; to fish with nets: momhʌ́, humín; go fishing with nets: momhʌ́koi/momhʌkʼói; catch fish one after another: wowóti; set a fish trap: míkkit; fish trap or basket: makóm patá, makóm sʌkʌ́ni, míkki, báno, chʌ́lkʌm woló, chʌ́lchʌl woló, yemík, sʌkʌ́ni; put everything in the fish basket: sʌkʌ́nyo; go fish (card game): lumít'ʌkói; a small fish or minnow: yámli, hálbakʼu
fish eggs	chakʼ
fish hawk	cháutata
fisher (animal)	ínbuki, sásasi
fish-head orthography	makóm onóm bálni
fishhook	lumí
fishing pole	lumím chá, lumítkʌm chá
fist	má 'etósti; fight with the fists: yokíto
fitness	hʌkʼʌ́pi - health
five	máwʌkʼʌ́; five times: máwʌknini
fix (in place)	bʌsʌ́pkit - set in place
fix (v)	tawáldʌkdʌk, yadʌ́kdʌkʼ - repair (v)
fix oneself up	yaháhati'us
fix up	yadʌ́kdʌkʼ, tawáldʌkdʌk; get something working: ʌnóti; that which I have fixed up: yadʌ́kdʌkisma
fixate on	ihéluť
fizzle out	bukúi - go out (fire)
flag	yókoli, ínyanam yokóli; flag on top: yók'olťanu; maple bark strips on the traditional flag: sokʼóti
Flag-on-top Mountain	Yók'olťanum Yamáni
flake (v)	kam - shed (v)
flame (n)	toyá (n)
flame (v)	bolákdoi - catch on fire, blaze up, spring into flames: pʼipai
flank (n)	chichí - side of body, ribs
flap (wings)	wodói
flare (v)	bolákdoi - catch on fire, blaze up
flare up (fire)	chódoi
flat	baťʼ, bátbatpe, bátpe; be flat: banhʌ́tanu; flatten: báťti
flatulate	bú/bʌ́
flea	tʌkʌ́s
flee	kohákʼoi; flee wildly in all directions: koháhakʼoi; flee from: weledaw; flee holding something: hánbeťek, hanbeťékchono, hanbeťékdoi; bosíp, wadá - escape (v), get away
flick	flick with the finger: dʌkʌ́, dʌkʌ́tomsito; flick with the thumb: hʌpái; flick the tail: wíslai
flicker (bird)	wolóllokʌ/wolúlukʌ/wulúlukʌ; red-shafted flicker: chiťúť; yellowhammer/flicker: mákmakʌ (WS)
flicker (v)	wilíl - flutter, tremble

English	Maidu
fling with a stick	wodót, wodótḱoi
flint	bosó; worked flint: ínyanam bosó; flint flaker tool: tépkm
flip through	hiníswopai - glance at, catch a glimpse of
float	hin; float along: hínno; float along while looking: hínchetoye; float away: hínḱoi; float downstream: hinín; float little by little: híntata; float around: hínnoye; float around inside: hínsitoye; float down into water: hínkit; float out: wmsíp/wusíp; float over the surface: hínchik; float over the surface from time to time: hínchikwebis; float like fog: wmsdoino; float like clouds: tumyedói
flock	bomó
flog	kíwwo - beat, whip, beat up
flood (v)	to flood: mombóno; flood down into: mombomít; be flooded with water: mombudútchono; mómbochono - flow over
floor	pai kanái'i, polówa
floor (1st or 2nd)	polówa - floor
flop around	pátnoye; flopping motion: pát
flora	linó
flour	lawáni, láwa; flour sack: láwam wadápi
flourish	yahát yatí'us - do well for oneself
flow (v)	yonó, opín - gush forth, gush out; mombóno, hínḱoi; flow around or over: mómbochono; start to flow down into: mombobónpin
flow in (v)	mombomít - flow, flood (v), flow down into
flower	yó; to bloom: yótitdoi; flowery/flower-decorated: yókmchipe
flub	sitái - miss a shot, grab at and miss
fluctuate	dmymym - shake, tremble (i.t.)
fluent	not be fluent (in a language): húpapai
fluffy	butúipe - furry
fluid	momí - water
fluke	yú - luck
flume	pulúm
flunk	wi'íye - fail
flush with anger	wilákno
flute	yálulu; play the flute: yálulu
flutter	wilíl
fly	insect: ṗichíkuḱu, amellmlm, óm ḱmikm; to fly: kai, yéi; go flying/fly off: káiḱoi; arrive flying: kai'ókit, kái'okiteḱoi; fly around: káinoye,; fly around from one to another: káipaimnoye, káipai'mtoto; fly down: kái'inpin, káikit; fly into: káichik, kai'ínno; fly to: yéi 'mdíkno; fly off with: wmtḿ'uchono; fly up: káidoi, káidoino, yéi mwódoi; fly through/fly around inside: káisitoye; fly like a bat: wodói
fly by	mwála - go past
flycatcher (bird)	pam beché'okm
flying squirrel	chabába, káinokmm tmlḿlm
foal	kawáyum té
foam	sopóṫ
focus on	chikáta, ihéluṫ
fog	t̃iw, t̃iwkiti; to fog up: t̃iwkit; foggy: t̃iwki
fold (v)	onḿnkiti - bend something over
fold up	bukúiti - close (v), turn off
fold up (like a leaf)	wuchulus
foliage	sawí
folklore	betéi - story
follow	héi, mhé, hó; follow in a sequence or series: hóipai; follow around: mhánoye; follow right behind: hóipaikit; follow behind while going across: hóipaikinu'msito; follow closely over or around: simhékachono; follow tracks: pai háchono, héno, pahádaw, pahánoye, pahéḱoi, hanó'ono; follow tracks to: háno; start out following tracks: hádoi; follow tracks going along: paháno
fondle	smkásai - hug, engage in foreplay; báslem - stroke with the hand
food	pekḿ; food scrap: bmtḿmi
fool (v)	hálpapai - trick, deceive
fool around	sikásaito
foolhardy	hokótisape - ridiculous
foolish	húkesmen, niku
foot	pai, paiyí; footprint: soló, pai; foot rag: íswolakm; on foot: páini; have something stuck in the foot: páibo; put one's foot into: ísḱoi; put a foot rag on: íswolak; be unable to find footprints: pai hánochmi

English	Maidu
foot (base)	íntas - base (n), hilt
foot the bill	pakál - pay (v)
foothills	yányanto
footstep	bénno - step (n)
for	MMG p. 23, -ki or -na on noun or pronoun
for it	mᴍnáki
forbid	was, ka'áhuyetiwomén; forbid someone to say: ka'áimenwo; keep forbidding someone from saying: ka'áimenwowéw; that which is forbidden to say: ka'áimenyahá
force	cause, get (someone to do), make (someone do): MMG p. 56, -ti infix on verb
force oneself	have to (do), be forced: MMG p. 54 and 56, -ti infix on verb for being forced to do, use -ti'us (ti + 'us infixes) on verb for forcing oneself
force open	hédas - crack open
force out	wiyéti
force out of place	batásip, hᴍbónan batásip - chase out, drive out
forebears	hínwo hóyyam máidᴍ - first people, ancestor
forecast (v)	ayáwe - predict; húpai - foresee
forefathers	hínwo hóyyam máidᴍ - first people, ancestor
forehead	sᴍndaka
foreigner	ḱoyói - stranger
foreman	yepóni - chief
foremost	hínwom - first, ahead of, older (adj)
foreplay	engage in foreplay: sᴍkásai/sikásai
foresee	húpai
foreskin	kóspumi
forest	chám ḱódo; woods: cháchato
forest fire	ṗiyé
foretell	húpai - foresee; ayáwe - predict
forever	kaním mabó; ᴍpéḱnudom - continually
Forgay Point	Cholcholum, Ochó, Úho
forget	húkichik
forgetful	húboḱoi
forgive	sówono - let someone go
fork	bᴍhᴍkkᴍ/bᴍhᴍnkᴍ, bᴍhᴍknokᴍ
fork of a river	sewím piní - confluence
form (v)	yatí, yánto, ya'ati - create
former	hínwom - ahead; yaťa
former times	hóiya - formerly
formerly	hóiya
forsake	wasᴍḱoi - go away angry
fortify	etósti, chᴍititi - strengthen
fortune	yú - luck
found (v)	bᴍsᴍpkit - set in place
four	chᴍi/chúiyi; four times: chᴍinini
fox	hawí, yóskopem hawí, yóskope
fraction	léiwo - part of
fragile	lelé, lelépe, chᴍitimen
fragrant	hísatipe, hísasape, yahát hísatipe
frail	ťoi, etósmen - weak
fraternize	ohé - mix in (with people), be in a crowd
Fred Thomas	sᴍmtonu
Fredonyer Butte	Om Kulúdoiwem (see also Coppervale Mountain)
free (tr)	sówono - let someone go
free of charge	méiti
free time	ᴍpé bísdom - doing nothing
freedom	ka'áyahádom - doing what one wants
freeway	bᴍwom kalétam bó
freeze	eyᴍ; freezing: eyᴍsape, ítᴍk
freight	hadó - load (n)
frequently	ekᴍ - usually
freshet	lukúbe, lukúmbe, bosóḱ
friend	héskᴍ; friends: héskᴍto; go make friends: heskᴍtoḱoi

English	Maidu
frighten	wisétti; be frightened: wisét, wisétpe, yehéptoye; be not very frightened: wisétboduk; frightened: wisétset; frighten with scary sounds: wisétsetpinti; to sound frightening: yehéppinti; make people run away: wiléwkittiḱoi; one who scares people: wisétikm; one who makes people run away: wilémḱoitikm
frighten off	hḿstaye - scare away
frightening	épti
fritillaria	muiyukm/muyuko
frizzy	onotḿitmikm - curly-haired
frog	wélḱeti; little green frog: luḱúm wélḱeti; bull frog: úspmdu; frog eggs: wélḱetim chaká
from	MMG p. 23, -nan on noun or pronoun
from then on	amá wóinan
from there	amádi'im
front	pḿya; in front of: hínwono, hínwonope
froth	sopóť
frown at (v)	bátmtmnkinu, chepánu - scowl at (v)
fry	chalála (by itself); fry something: chalálati
fry bread	hḿtim maháti
fulfill	yabós - finish, complete
full	pídati, opít; full of: pípe; a place full of: pípenak; full to the max: opítlmťpe; be full/satisfied (of food): idát
fumble	sitái - miss a shot, grab at and miss
fume	wasó'ituti - be angry till it hurts
function (v)	mnó, sol; make something function: mnóti
fund (v)	húno - sponsor (v)
funeral song	wóno'ḱoikmm solí
fungus	wá; a red or orange fungus that grows on Douglas Fir: chám hí
funny story	mínono - in fun, kidding
fur	butú; furry: butúipe; covered with fur: butúitapope
fur (from skinned animal)	po - hide, skin
furious	wasó - angry
furnish	méi, méito - give, give out
furthermore	admḱ
furthest	batásono
future	be in the future: machói
future tense	will (do or be): MMG p. 47, -ma on verb + verb endings
gag (n)	mínono - in fun, kidding
gag, retch	tás, wémmuk
gait	bilísi - speediness
gala	wéda - big time
galaxy	lmlḿm máidmdi - at the home of the star men
gall bladder	hakákakm
gallop	ḱodódok
gamble, gambling	helái, heláiye; play hand games in winter: sútto; gambling: helá; grass game gambling: sopóm helám; basket game: sótto; grass game: helá; long version of grass game: bom héla; short version of grass game: láda; gambler: heláikm, heláyim máidm; be seated and ready to gamble: halémmemmoto
gambling bone	banded bone: teṕ, súlu; unbanded bone: tállala
gambling charm	oméikm
gambling sticks	helám chá, démi
game	ónkoḱoito - contest (n)
game (ball game)	bóltope
gang	bomó - bunch, group
gap or mountain pass	bówochono
gape	cheḱón - gaze at
gape (mouth open)	símdadaptonu, dóbabak
garage	kalétam uiyí
garden	lenó, lenóm koyó; do gardening: díti
gargle	wolólo
garland	chípe
garlic	wild garlic (not eaten): chani, pi'taloka
garment	chí - clothes
garter	bmḱḿwtikm

English	Maidu
gather	gather something: hḿ, hḿye, han; gather up: bmyḿkdoi; go around gathering (things): bmyḿk'mnoiye, hḿno, hḿnoye; gather a few from many: bmyḿksipdomhehe; go gather: hḿḱoiti, sóhino; go gather for someone: hḿnoti; gather things together in one place: wḿkdimotoluť; gather up one's things: hésbobopai; gather/assemble together as people: motó; come together: úmmoto, ḿmmoto
gathering	ḿmmotope - get-together
gathering (n)	ḿmmotope; a gathering of: bomó
gauge (v)	womákti - measure (v)
gawk at	cheḱón - gaze at
gaze across	chesítonu
gaze at	cheḱón; gaze up at: chedónuto
gaze down	cheťánu, chétnumit
gaze into	chemínu
gaze past	hóichenu
gear	wasása - stuff
geese	lḿlmḱbomo; geese flying (as basket design): lóm káidom
gem	om - rock
general	in general: kaṕéṕe
generous	méikm, méikmsa
Genesee	Yetámeto/Yoťámmoto/Yatámoto/Ymtámoto
Genesee people	Yetámeto ma'a/Yatámotom Ma'a/Ymtámoto ma'a
Genesee Rd.	Yetámetom Bo (south of Taylorsville), Chakámdmḱmm Bo (north of Taylorsville)
Genesee Valley	Yetámeto Ḱoyó, Yetámeton
genesis	ḱabḿḱ - start (n), beginning (n)
genitals (men's)	báno, wosó
genitals (women's)	hésboiyoiyo, pmsí, wosó
gentle	chḿitimen - tender, soft
geography	ḱódoi - area
geology	ḱódoi - area
germs	cheméni
get	mé
get (someone to do)	make (someone do), force, cause: MMG p. 56, -ti infix on verb
get a move on	wilék - hurry (v)
get across using a cane-like implement	bití'ukitmsitopin
get ahead	mwála - go past
get all the way down	mpéḱanuhanpin/mpéḱanohánpin
get away	wadá; let someone get away: sówono; be away (from someone): tmtḿ
get away with (bad behavior)	hesámakati
get back	get something back: memé; get someone back: hóiwi'okit; get back to where one started: hasíp, mdíknoweḱoi
get back at	yámmotopai - retaliate
get bigger	tetébe - get larger
get busy	botópai
get caught	without getting caught: hesámakati
get closer to	yḿ'aswopai
get even	yámmotopai; get even with: yámmoto
get here	okít; almost get here: okítpoto
get home	hunhépinkit
get in	lmkḿnno - enter, go in
get into (car, etc)	mmít, mmítkapin, wonó
get lost!	cháinapi - get out!
get mad	wasóso - get angry
get on a road	mmít
get on in years	nenó - grow old
get on something (as smoke)	súkpai
get on top	yoťá
get out	get something out: hésbapin; exit quickly: wḿssasip; get out of a bad situation: hónsu; get out! cháinapi! or chái'mḱoi; to bad spirits: hesápḱoi
get over (feelings)	chedá - rest, take a break

English	Maidu
get rid of	wiyéti or wiyéti - cause to be missing/gone - make someone leave
get the hang of	makít - understand
get things together	hésbomoto, hésbobopai
get to (a place)	ꟽdíkno, towóikit; plural subject: ꟽdíknotoye
get to one's feet	tꟽ́sdoi - rise, stand up
get up	otó; get up from sitting: tꟽ́sdoi, tꟽ́skadoi; stand up: sꟽwékadoi, sꟽwéwedoi, sꟽwéwikadoi; get back up: pátkadoi
get well	wodá; perhaps not get well: wadámenhelu
getaway (n)	ꟽḱóida - departure
get-together (n)	ꟽ́mmotope
ghost	ꟽswálulu/uswúlulu
gigantic	tetéluťi
giggle	núksasa
giggle	nuk - laugh
gills	huhú - lungs
gimpy (lame)	wósdotno, ťát
girl	kꟽlém pꟽ́be; pet name for girl: písto, pístobe; adolescent girl: yúpu
girlfriend	kꟽlé - woman
give	méi; hand to: hapíno, bohú'isito; really give: méiluť; be reluctant to give: me'ókole; without giving to: méimenkꟽ
give a hand (applaud)	má wátdan - clap the hands
give a job to	woiyó - hire
give a sermon	hꟽhwé, wewéi, túwei - make a speech
give a speech	wewé - deliver a speech
give a talk	hꟽhwé, wewéi, túwei - make a speech
give away (for free)	méiti
give back	méiyewe, yewé
give birth	puk, té bísti, tékꟽ, ꟽháiye; be born: púkti; keep on giving birth: téťꟽ́tꟽ́ kꟽ'ꟽ́ye
give food to	pewó
give off light	ékdadoi - shine, twinkle
give something out	méito
give thanks	héwwonoye, hó - say "it is good," say "ho"
give up	yasáno
glad	yahát hubúktipe - pleasant
glance	hiníswopai; glance back: hóicheche
glance (barely touch)	pukétkakachono - brush, touch going by
glance over	hiníswopai - glance at, catch a glimpse of
glare at	chepánu, bátꟽtꟽnkinu; stand around glaring at: sꟽ́nchetutumoto
glass	wólek bosó; window glass: momím chetókꟽ; drinking glass: mokꟽ́m loló, mom loló
glasses	hínchekoikꟽ, hiniwáchikkꟽ, hínsolokꟽ, yepaisolo
glean	hꟽ́ - collect, gather
glide	hásno - slide, ski
glimpse	ḱꟽ́iche, oḱꟽ́i
glob	okꟽ́nꟽni
global	yꟽwáitokꟽdi - everywhere the world extends
globe	kódo - area
globular	pꟽlꟽ́lꟽmpe - spherical
glove	matakúpno, takúpno
glow	ékdadoi - shine, twinkle; banáḱdoi
glower at	chepánu, bátꟽtꟽnkinu; stand around glowering at: sꟽ́nchetutumoto
glue	dak
gnash	chawái - chew
gnat	dídik
gnaw	éskocho; gnaw something soft to cut it: wétꟽk; run around gnawing on things: éskochowekoi; keep tearing with the teeth: wétetepdaw
go	ꟽkói, yꟽ́; go (plural subject): kóko; go as footprints: ꟽdá; start to go: ꟽnónoi; tell someone to go: ꟽkóiwo; keep going: ꟽkói'ebís; want to go: ꟽnóyaha; where one wants to go: ꟽnóyahape; go all over the land: kódo ꟽ́mmoto
go a little ways	ťíktetepin, ťíktetekoi
go across	ꟽsíto, yꟽ́sito/yꟽsíto, ꟽ'íto; travel across: ꟽ'ásito; go/crawl across: luksíto; go across over towards: ꟽchópin; go across with something: hasítoye

345

English	Maidu
go after, chase	yáhpat, bínmeye, hédatpai; run after (in anger): bínmedoi; go after in anger: yáhpatchono; keep going after: hédakpai; go off after: yáhpatkoi; take off after: yáppatdoi; go after someone, to kill them: sohúnbmk, sohúnbmkmsipin; one who does not go after people: bínmenmímenkm
go along	mnó, ymno; go along on the side of a hill: leléchopin; go along ascending: mdóino; cause to go along ascending: mdóinoti; go along doing: ha'mkói; go along the trail (like footprints/tracks): bówodaw
go along doing	along (going): MMG p. 56, -no infix on verb
go around	mnóye, ymnóye; wander around: mnói; go around out and about: konói, wéido; go all around: mmóto; go around stealthily: ká'mnoye; make a circuit going around: wónmidoikapin; go all around inside: msítoye; go around (in dancing): mchóno; go all around the land: kódo mmmoto
go around doing	around (going): MMG p. 56 -noye infix on verb
go around with (someone)	mhénoye, mhékoi
go away	chái'mkoi; to a dog: wmsmkoi; leave: mkói; go away from: cháinada, mkóida; go away angry: wasmkoi; go away (plural subject): mkókoitoye; go away (plural subject) to different locations: mkókoiyetoye
go AWOL	wi'íye - not be there, be missing
go back	yewé; go back home: hepínkoi, sa yewé; go back taking something: haiyéwe; go back to where one came from: mkói'mye; go back the same way one came: myéwe
go backwards	kíwna bényewei - walk backwards
go beyond	waláw - exceed
go by (time)	wosíp
go call/get someone	yakói
go carrying	mahákoi
go down	mt, mtno, mnno; go down a mountain: hmtpin; go down as sun: ba'á'aidaw, hínchono, hínpupu, kmchono; the sun is going down: ókpai ochónodom, ókpai wochónodom; go down towards: mtpin; come down towards: mchópin; go down a hole: pmdónu; continue to go down a hole: kumpmdónu; go down into: mmítkapin, in'ínno, ymnno
go down (in numbers or strength	tibíbew, wmsuisúikit - dwindle, get fewer, deflate
go farther	m'áswodaw; go off farther: ym'áswokoi; go far across: kikí'usito; go farther uphill-ish: ym'áswodoi
go fast	mlék, bmlék, wilék; hurry up!: wilékleki! mlékleki!; Go very fast: támpipítkoi, koháno; go along fast: mléklekno; rush past: mlémno, mlém, mlélemchono, mlélem; rush up and over towards: mlékwochopin
go full speed	koháno - go at utmost speed
go get	hóiwikoiti, sohún, máno; go get (someone): hóiwikoi, hóiwinotiyá, yakói; go get (water): henó, hewíno; go and bring: hekóitoye, mahá, hólsip; go get and bring in: sohúnpin; go get (firewood, for example): sóiyo, sóyo, sówikoi, sóiwino
go get	sóiwino, sóiyo - fetch
go hungry	pemén - not eat
go in	lmkmno; go down into: in'ínno
go in with	km'ídi - share
go into hiding	ká'ukkinu - crouch down and hide
go off	hit the road: bodí mkói; go off (plural subject) in different directions: mkókoi, káwhehekokoi; go off (plural subject) one after another: káwhehekoi; trudge off in all directions, kicking up dust: káwheiheikokoi; go off secretly: ka'mkói; go off (plural subject) towards: mnótoye; go off farther: mkóiye; go off downhill: mdáw; start going off/go off uphill: mdóino; go off angry: wasmdaw; go off kicking up the dust: káwheikoi
go off (blow up)	pópti - explode
go off (leave)	mkói - go away
go on a rampage	yáhpatchono, wasóhati - go after someone in anger, bring wrath down upon
go on forever	wónomen - be immortal
go out	ymsip; go out (plural subject): tisíp; go out as a fire: bukúi, bukúibos, bukúkuikit
go out (of a door or building)	lmksip - climb or crawl out of a building
go over (a mountain, etc.)	mchóno, obúschono, wochóno; go over fast: mlékwochopin
go over to attack	yáhpatchono
go past	mwála; go past quickly: mlém, mlémno, mlélemchono
go see	chekói, chenókoi

English	Maidu
go slow	winú - be slow
go somewhere else!	cháinapi - get out!
go tell about	yekói
go through	hachóno
go towards	ᴍyé; go towards loudly: wᴍtᴍ́swoye
go underground	ká'ukkinu - crouch down and hide
go up	ᴍdói, bᴍlélek; reach the top: bᴍlélekdoichoi; go along ascending: ᴍdóino; go up fast: támpipidikno
go visit	chenᴍ́koi, cheno'ukoi
go with	ᴍhé, ᴍhéi, ᴍkói'idi; go along with: ᴍhéino; start going somewhere with: ᴍhédoi; go along together with: ᴍhéto; go around with: ᴍhékoi, ᴍhénoye
goal	bodíknokᴍ, tawálihape
goat	mountain goat: om sᴍmí
God	kódoyakᴍ - Creator
going on, happening (questions)	what is going on?: hesáka?, bei hesádom/bei hesádom?; what could be going on?: hesádowet mayákken?; what is really going on here?: hesádom píkno mayákken?
gold	ódo
Gold Lake	Chítani Pakáni
gold pan	ódom piláto, piláto
golden currant	nunholwa
golden eagle	moluku
goldfinch	mukédewowe
good	yahá, yá, yahápe, wené; good (for plural noun): yaháha; good tasting: hanána; be good: yahá; very good: yaháhaluťi; it is good: yahákan; are things good?: yahá'ade?; for good: yahádi; make something good/better: yaháti; make (food) taste good: hanána yahátidom; well/good (adverb): yahát; be good weather: kódom yahádom; good enough: ámbᴍkbᴍ; sound for "good job!": chúkchuk; do good (in the world): yahánu
good at	be good at: yahámakit
good job!	hés ekáw - (how wonderful)
good luck	yú - luck
good Samaritan	bené'ekᴍ - helper
good!	héw!, yahákan!
goodbye	hehé, hew; may you go well: yahát ᴍkóipada; may you stay well: yahát bíspada; until I see you again: che ma'akas min; until I hear from you again: pin ma'akas min
good-for-nothing	ᴍ́spa - rascal
good-looking	yaháchetipe, yahátcheno
goods	wasása - stuff; hadó - load
goose	ló; snow goose: lúlukᴍ/lᴍ́lᴍku, wuluku; lesser snow goose: wawi
gooseberry	yᴍhémi, yunemi, me'ahemi, pamíni
gopher	hemé (RD, WS), hisoche (PM-M)
gopher snake	ho'ém/howém
gorgeous	ekáwchetipe - beautiful
goshawk	lᴍ́ksu'ano
gossip	to gossip: símmak, símmakto; gossip about: chewéto; a gossip: símmaksa, wéyenoyesakᴍ
governor	yepóni - chief
grab	dón; grab at: yelápwo; grab at and miss: sitái; grab at a certain place (like the tail): nak dó; grab by the arm: yímdi dón; start to grab: méhyodoi; grab out of the air: óidon; reach out and grab: yelábito; reach up and grab: yelálapdoi; lunge and grab: méhyo; jump at to grab: méyodoi; spring down onto and grab: méhyotno; while grabbing in the hand: chᴍ́doiťonum
grab hold	dónwika; reach down and grab hold of: dónwikatno
grab up	sódoi; grab something up in the hand: chᴍ́doi; grab something and pull it up: dónwikadoi; grab up something quickly and run: sówekadoi; grab up something in the arms and run: sówikadoi
grade (hill)	léyi - slope
grammatically correct	yahát wéye húkeskinudom - using correct speech
granary	kúmmenwi
grandchild	pei/peyí; son's son: sáka; granddaughter: peyím kᴍlé
grandfather	ópa; paternal: sᴍkᴍ

English	Maidu
grandmother	kotó, kotóto; great grandmother: hóyyam mᴍkóto, bónom kolókbe; a pair including a grandmother/grandchild: kotókᴍto; paternal grandmother: sᴍssᴍ
grant (v)	méi - give
grape	pímmili/pímeli
grasp with the hand	widók; grasp and hold tight: siťíw; grasp and pull up: widókdoi
grass	sᴍpó/sopó; dry grass: popó; native blue grass: ókwa
grass game	sᴍpó helá/sopóm helá; shorter version of grass-game: láda; grass-game songs: sopóm helám solí; sing grass-game songs: sopóm helám sól
Grass Valley	Wakᴍdat
grasshopper	tᴍlí; brown grasshopper/locust: chike; grasshopper stew: tᴍlím homí
grassland	ḱoyó - meadow
grave (n)	tánkᴍ - burial ground
graveyard	tánkᴍ - burial ground
gravy	homá - soup
gray	balbalpe/bawbawpe (FC), kówkow (WS); dull grayish: púppup, wipúppu; get gray: kowkowtiche; be dull and gray (sky): yáku; getting gray (as hair): púppupmape; grayish: ekókow
gray fox	yóskope, yóskopem hawí
gray hair	óśkoni; gray-haired: óśkonpe; getting gray (as hair): púppupmape
gray pine	towáni; gray pine tree: towánim chá
gray sage	lupúpu
gray squirrel	sáwwali/sáwali
gray willow	chupí, hísdom chupí
graze (barely hit)	pukétkakachono - brush, touch going by
graze (feed)	ḱedé; go from grazing: ḱedéhepinḱoi ḱedé, ḱedéno; graze around together: ḱedétonoye
grease	hᴍťi/húti
great	great!: yaháḱan; be great: yáhálut́
great grandmother	hóyyam mᴍkóto
Great Horned Owl	mᴍkkᴍlᴍsi/mᴍkᴍlúsi
greatest	yaháhaluťi - the best
grebe	kówukᴍ (HM), wakdᴍ (PM-M)
green	tít, títtit, títtitpe; greenish: etítit, etítitpe; become green (as plants in spring): yótitdoi; greens (to eat): sawí
Greenville	Kótasi
greetings	hehé - hello
grieve	lól; go around grieving: lólnino; feel sad: wasát hᴍbᴍ́k
grin (v)	núkcheche - smile (v)
grind	yók; grind underfoot: ťeťálak; grinder (rock roller): walátkᴍ; grinding rock: áli (portable), pᴍlᴍ́, yókkᴍm 'ó
grinder	mill: áli - portable grinding rock
gristle	paḱ
grizzly bear	páno, kapá
groan (v)	ᴍháiye
grope	bamák
grosbeak	pine grosbeak: bám chiti; black-headed grosbeak: sewíspolotkᴍ
grouch	wáschᴍ - quick-tempered
grouchy	be grouchy: wasósa
ground squirrel	hiló, súpa; type of ground squirrel: ḱoyóm títtitkᴍ; Belding squirrel: títtitkᴍ
ground, dirt	ḱawí; to the ground: ḱawná
groundhog	sᴍpa/supú, kawí yudútkᴍ
group	bomó, pí; out of the whole group: bomómdi'im
grouse	hᴍ́kwo; sage grouse: kohíkwᴍ
grow	dí; be growing up: tetébe; growing in the rocks: ódi dídom; grow through: dísito
grow up	dí - grow; díbos - be fully grown
growl	tᴍ́n/tún, wás
grown	be fully grown: díbos
grub	pekᴍ́ - food
gruel	bukúm yokó
guardian angel	ḱákkini - spirit guide
guess	húpai, hónno, húti; guess wrong: sitái; guesser: húpaikᴍ; guess at: húpapai
guide (n)	ḱákkini - spirit guide
guide (v)	hóiwiháno - lead, escort (v), usher (v)

English	Maidu
guideline	ma - law (n)
guilty (not)	not guilty: hesámenkm
guitar	wéppenkm
gull	kolókm
gullible	tǐkchelelepe, mpékani tǐkchelelepe (easily believing anything)
gum	chaká; chewing gum: chakámin, wólem chakámi
gums	chikím smmí
gun	pándaḱa, mmskmt
gunnysack	púmsalawim wadápi
gush	yonó, opín - gush forth, gush out
gush out	yonó, opín
gut (v)	to gut (an animal): pitḱol
guzzling (adj)	mosápe - one who frequently drinks
habitually	by nature, always (doing): MMG p. 56, -sa infix on verb
hack (cough)	ḱepm
had (helping verb "had done" or "had been")	MMG p. 65 -wono on verb
haft	íntas - base (n), hilt
hail	bokm, kók chmlmlm, kóm chmlmlm
hair	butú; hair of the head: onóm butú; male pubic hair: kósbu; female pubic hair: pmsbu; hairy: butúipe; covered with hair: butúitapope; lose hair: kam; hairball: butúweh
hairdresser	wmkmstokmm máidm - barber
half and half, equal	mmyákbebe; exactly half: mmyákdmbe mmyákbe
half gone	be half gone/half as much as before: hehépai
halfway	go halfway/be halfway: éswo; be halfway to: éswoḱoi; be about halfway to: éswowo, éswowoḱoi; be halfway into: éswomit; put halfway into: éswomitti; get halfway up (a hill): lelédikno; get about halfway up: éswowodiknoitimáldoi; be about halfway down: éswowokit; be about halfway out of: éswowosipin; halfway down: éswowotpindi
halt	yesáno/yosáno
Hamilton Branch	Naḱám Sewí
Hamilton Mountain	Yakmki/Yakúki
hamlet	bískmm ḱódo, hmbóboto - village
hammer (v)	tómdan - hit making a sound; wó, wódato - hit with an instrument
hand	má; hand to: hapíno, sóye, hápye; hand over: hápsip; hand over to: hápno, bohú'isito, hápsipto, sówono; hand across to: hápsito; hand down: hápdaw; make someone hand over: hápsiptoti; open up the hand: má leléwaito; wave the hand: má welék, má weléknoye; clap hands: má wátdan; have something stuck in the hand: mábo; take someone by the hand: madí dón; grasp with the hand: widók; grasp with the hand and pull up: widókdoi; have the hand under someone: tókno; one-handed: ma smtikm; hand-in-hand: widóktotonu
hand (v)	soyá - pass (by hand)
hand game	sútto
hand out	méi - give
handgun	pístola - pistol
handkerchief	hindákm/hundákm, paper handkerchief: híkmdakmm papéli; cloth handkerchief: híkmdakmm chi
handle (n)	íntas - base (n), hilt; doorknob: oḱéli - knob
handle (v)	katí - do to (with negative connotations)
handle (v)	feel (with hands): pukét - touch (v); smnóye - work with things
handler	baṭánokm - driver
hands	hold hands: widóktoto/widmktotó; shake hands: madóntoto; grasp hands: má dóntoto
handsome	yaháchetipe, yahátcheno
handy (close by)	hedénna - nearby
hang	la (hang by itself); hang something up: wehétkit; hang multiple things up: wehétyo
hang around	téte - hang out; lanóye
hang back	tókdati'us - lag behind
hang down (like cord)	píubokiti; let something hang down: píubonpinti
hang onto	dónbis
hang out (like a tail)	opíninu

English	Maidu
hang out (like friends)	téte
hang out with	ohé - mix in (with people), be in a crowd
hang over (something)	opíninu - hang out, stick out
hang up to dry (meat)	sikéyo
hanging	be hanging/hung up: wehétkinu; be likely to be hanging up: wehétyonutohelu; be hanging up from: yodótpanuto
happen over and over	madóm ṃpéḱadom - repeat
happen to be	mahélu
happy	yahát hubúktipe; make oneself happy: hṃbṃ́kti'us
harass	héi, yáhpat - chase, follow, pursue, go after
harbor (v)	kilé - hide (something)
hard (like "work hard")	too much, a lot, excessively: MMG p. 55, -luṫ infix on verb
hard liquor	sudákṃ, sudákṃm momí
hard, tough (substance)	chṃ́iti
harder (rain)	tetétbewto
hardship	wehépti - misfortune
hardy	épti - tough, strong
harebrained	húkesmen - foolish, stupid; hokótisape - ridiculous
harm (v)	chemhúsem; not harm: chemhúsemmen; harmless: hesátimenkṃ
harmonica	sóltotokṃ, símni sóltikṃ
harvest (v)	hṃ́ - collect, gather
hassle (tr)	hokótito - argue with
hat	olé; netted hat: wiká; put on a hat: olékṃ; coonskin cap: akíchanam onúknokṃ
hate (v)	ṗiṫúk
haul	hanṃ́n, hanṃ́nno, hánno
have	kṃ/kú; keep on having (children, for example): kṃ'ṃ́ye; not have: wi'í
have (helping verb "have done" or "have been")	MMG p. 65 -wono on verb
have a bite	dómaki - have a taste
have a mind to	húyeti - intend to
have compassion for	bomṃ́mṃkno - pity (v), feel sorry for
have confidence in	húno - rely on, back
have goose bumps	hínchesem - feel strange toward
have mercy on	bomṃ́mṃkno - pity (v), feel sorry for
have no end	wónomen - be immortal
have on (wear)	chí - put on clothes
have one's hands full	botópai - get busy
have one's period	ṃdáw, chos - menstruate
have one's way	yahádom ma'aḱán - do as one wants
have something (in one's current possession)	hadónu
have something done	woḱói
have to	ought to, should, need to: MMG p. 49 -s on verb, "I ought to, " -we on verb, "we ought to, " -yaha on verb, "you ought to" or use commands on p. 48-9
have to (do)	be forced, force oneself: MMG p. 54 and 56, -ti infix on verb for being forced to do, use -ti'us (ti + 'us infixes) on verb for forcing oneself
have to (do)	really want to: MMG p. 55 and 57, -yaháluṫ (yaha + luṫ infixes on verb)
have what it takes	ṫotimén - be strong
having	kupé/kṃpé
hawk (n)	red-tailed hawk: búklakkṃ; sharp-shinned: báku; Cooper: túptupe; sparrow hawk: kélikliki; fish hawk: cháutata; marsh hawk: málbṃ; night hawk: sṃ́mpupa/súmpupa; sound of a hawk: buk buk buk
hawk (v)	sél - sell
hawthorn	wahíkṃ
hay	ṗopó
haywagon	ṗopóm kaléta
he	mṃmṃ́m
head	onó; be on the head: onó; shake the head: onó o'ṃ́'ṃlṃm; bump the head: onó bṃnó; slap water on the head: onóspatpatto; incline/bow the head: olé; having the head bowed: olékinu; having the head always hanging/bowed: olékinusa; having the head always more or less hanging: olékinuhudansa; head of (for example, a penis): oḱéli; the head only: onódṃkṃ; be headed somewhere; sṃ́nwoḱoi
head (v)	sṃ́nwoḱoi - be headed (a certain way)

English	Maidu
head (v)	papái, hóiwiháno - lead
head man (n)	yepóni/yopóni, yepónim máidm
head out	mdói
head someone off, herd	kachík
head towards	mkóiye, smnwokoi
headache	have a headache: opók; cause a headache: opókti; massage to treat a headache: onó smkáw
headband	owólakkm
headdress/headstall (regalia)	pálak
headlights	toyákmtipe
headman	yepóni - chief
heal	hmkmpti, húiti
health	wadá, hmkmpi, hmkmp; healthy: hmkmpkupe, wadá; be healthy: húikmp, épti; heal/make healthy: hmkmpti, hónhukupti; be healthy enough: basáp; make oneself healthy: hónhukupti'us
hear	pín; hear someone out: pinwéye; hear of/hear about: pínmakit; hear across a distance: pinhássito; let someone hear/tell someone about: pínti; not want to hear about: pínokole; don't let someone hear about: píntimen; hear wrong/mis-hear: pintái; be heard in the distance: pínkenutihadáw
hear it for	má wátdan - clap the hands
hearing aid	píntikm - radio
hearse	holóhadóikmm kaléta
heart	honí; soft-hearted: honím lelépe; beat (as the heart): halmk
heat (v)	to heat (as a fire): láino; heat basketry sticks before splitting: modá
heat up (food)	pewíhakit - cook, prepare food
heat up (tr) (warm)	láino - heat, warm (tr)
heave at	batáp - throw at
heaven	epínim koyó, epínim kódo, kódom kíwdi; target land: kódom bodíkdi, kódom bodíknokm; deathless land: wónomenkmm kódo
heaviest (rain)	tetédmkm
heavy	wmhúlpe, hek, hehékpe; be heavy: wihml; be heavy to lift: mil
heavy drinking (adj)	mosápe - one who frequently drinks
hectic pace	hútudom
hedge (n)	dm - bush
heedless	pínmenpe
heel	páisuku, sukú
hellgrammite	óm kmikm
hello	hehé, ho
help	bené'e
help oneself to food	áisiye, áiye
helper	bené'ekm
helping	pená - serving, portion
hemlock (plant)	butchiwi
hemp	pu/pu'u
hen	né
henceforth	uní wóinan, uní woyím
her	MMG p. 40, as object of sentence - mm or mmmm. as possessive (belonging to her) - mmkí
herb (minty)	osókmm bukúikm, yamánim bmkúike
herd	bomó; to herd: kachík
here	uní, unídi; around here: unínante; in this area: unínandi; all around, here and there: ántenantenántedi
hermit	dmkkm - loner
heroic	betéi - legendary
heron	mmkahúlkm; blue heron: mmlokm; night heron: po wáksi
herself	mmmmt; by herself: mm'úsi; to herself: mmwet
hesitate	etúdede - wait a little bit; chedá - rest (v)
hey	si, hei, sásaka
hi	hei, hehé, ho, sásaka
hibernate	kúmlai
hiccup	kepm
hide (n)	po

351

English	Maidu
hide (v)	hide oneself: ḱá'u, ḱá'uk, ḱá'ukkinu; go and hide: ḱá'ukḱoi; hide something: kilé (RD)/kᴖlé (WS); hide something for a reason: kiléda; hide oneself out of modesty: múi; be unable to hide something: kiléchᴖi; not let someone see something: chetímen
high	hadá; high up: hadádoi, mántedoi
highway	kalétam bó, bᴖ́wom kalétam bó
highway patrol (n)	dónkᴖm máidᴖ - police (n)
hijack	pedáyeto, soháḱoi - kidnap
hill	yáhni, yamánbe, ḱᴖsí; get halfway up a hill: lelédikno
hillside	yan, leléimpini; go along the side of a hill: leléchopin
hilt	íntas; to the hilt: íntasluťna
him	MMG p. 40 - objective, mᴖ or mᴖmᴖ
himself	mᴖmᴖ́t; by himself: mᴖ'úsi; to himself: mᴖ́wet
hint (n)	tibínak - a little bit
hinterland	cham ḱódo - the woods
hip	máwa; hipbone: máwam bᴖmí
hire	woiyó, woyó
his	MMG p. 40 - possessive, mᴖḱí
hit	wó, wó'a; hit others/hit with something: wódato; hit with something: bopókno, wokᴖ́chono, wopók; hit with the hand: yo, waťán; hit someone on the back: kíwwo; get ready to hit: yomá; hit the target: bodíkno, yodá, yodúk; hit all around: wóyo, wopókno; hit a container to make something come out: wotók
hit the jackpot	thrive, be successful, prosper, flourish: yahát yatí'us - do well for oneself
hit the road	bodí ᴖḱói
hit the sack	túikit - go to sleep
hitch (v)	yodótpai - fasten
hoard	méibono
hobble	hobble around: bᴖpói; hobble along: páiḱᴖtḱᴖt
hobnob	ohé - mix in (with people), be in a crowd
hobo	hᴖbó wi'ípe - homeless person
hoist (v)	wiwó - lift, raise
hoist onto the back	áp/háp; hoist up on one's back: ápdoi/hápdoi, hadói
hold	dón, doníno, ménu; hold in the hand: chᴖ́donu; hold for someone: bísdodo; hold with the hand: widók; hold each other's hands: widᴖktotó/widóktoto, má dóntoto; hold in the mouth: dódoi; holding hands: widóktotonu, widókpe; dance in a circle holding hands: widóktotopepe; hold on tight: ḱídumchekín, siťíw; hold onto: donínu; hold something back: yaché; being held (event): ᴖ́mmotope
hold a meeting	ᴖ́mmoto - assemble, come together
hold off (tr)	etúti - cause to wait
hold one's head high	ᴖḱáwche'us - have self confidence
hole	beḱel, pᴖ́nno, pᴖ́no, pᴖ́nḱel; hole in the ground: ḱumí, ḱumpᴖ́nno; grinding hole: pᴖlᴖ́; dig a hole: ḱumbe; perforate: wikél; make a bunch of holes: ḱumtapoti; have many holes: píkitpᴖnḱelpe; be full of holes: ḱumtapo
holler	pelíp - shout
hollow (n)	pᴖ́nno - cavity
home	sá (fire); return home: sa yewé
homebody	lᴖ́ksipbodᴖkkᴖ
homecoming	okítkᴖ
homeless	hᴖbó wi'ípe
homely	wasá'ape, wasachetípe - ugly; yahátchetiboduk - not very good-looking
homeowner	hᴖbókᴖpe
Homer Lake	Chám Sᴖ́dom, Chamsudonim Pakánim (FR), Chám Sidom (LM), Pepépem Cham (FR1)
homesick	hᴖbó húkitmen
honestly	tetét, ha'ái - really
honey (term of endearment)	ᴖťᴖ́ťᴖibe - term of affection; oiᴖ́paipe - beloved
honey (to eat)	hané
honey bee	hániyakᴖ, hanéyakᴖm epéni
Honey Lake	Hanᴖ́leke (RD), Hanílek (WS), Tetém Mómdanni (LM)
honk (as goose)	yo'ó
honor (tr)	heyáwe, ťíkche - support a cause or person by action
hood (clothes)	onúknokᴖ; put on a hood: onúkno

English	Maidu
hoof	bichí, páibichí
hook (fishing)	lumí
hook (v)	yodótpai - fasten
hop	mhém, wósdok; hop along: mhémno, túpno; hop around: tmpnoye/túpnoye, wósdoknoye; hop on one foot: wósdot; hop around on one foot: wósdotnoye; hop out: beťéksip; keep hopping out: beťéksipwew; hop and skip: wmskmtḱmt; that which makes someone hop around: túpnoyetikm
hope (v)	yomó - wish for, pray for, invite
hope for	tetétluťi yahá - so want to (verb before yaha)
hope to	húyeti - intend to
hopefully	ha'ái
hopper basket	wapḿn
horizontal (adj)	bátbatpe - flat, planar
horn (of animal)	yónno
hornet	tái'epeni
horrible	wemtichḿktiti; sounding horrible: wemchichmkpintipe
horribly	tetét - very
horse	kawáyu/kowáiyo, lḿkťakmm sḿ; pair of horses: kawáyucho; horse rider: lḿkťakm; come on horseback: lḿkťaye
horseshoes	kawáyim bolóḱo; have shoes put on a horse: bolóḱtiwoḱoi; play horseshoes: sḿmpaito
horsetail	hḿskmm sawí
hose (n)	lumí - tube
hose bib	oḱéli - nozzle
hosiery	íschomi - socks
Hosselkus Creek	Pupuwelim Sewí
hot	ṗilís; hot weather: ṗilái; be hot: ṗilís; be excessively hot: ṗilísbos
Hot Springs Mountain	Pólpolim Yamánim
hotel	hutél
hot-tempered	wáschm - quick-tempered
hours	áwasi
house	uyí, uiyí, hmbó; bark house: hḿ; dwelling house: ḱumhḿm hmbo; at my house: níkdi; inside the house: hḿm ḱanáidi; towards the house: úyina; have a house: hmbóḱm; have a bark house: ḱumhḿkm; might have a house: hmbóyákḱen; housebound person: lḿksipbodmkkm
household (adj)	bískmm - residential
hover	yéidíkno; soar, take flight, be airborne: yéi, kai - fly (v)
how	hesádom, hesása; just how: hesápiknodom; that's how it is: amápem kmḱán; how much?: Hesánbe?; How are you?: hesásaḱa?, sásaḱa? How are things/how are they/how is it?: Hesáḱade, hesásaḱade?; How have you been?: hesasawéẃka? How about...(suggestion): hesátidom; how to do: hesánudom; that's how much: ka'ánte
however	achét, amám ma'át
howl	wó, pelíp, howáwa, wo'ó; howl at: pelíppai
hub	ésto - middle
hubbub	yohón - noise
huckleberry	anána; huckleberry oak: katukpu
hug (v)	lulúmwochono, sitápin; hug each other: sitápintoto; hug as part of foreplay: smkásai
huge	tetéluťi
hull (n)	posála - shell
hum	ḱásolto, ḱámmmmwet sól
human race	wónom máidm - mankind
human(s)	wónom máidm
humanity	wónom máidm - mankind
Humbug Valley	Tásmam Ḱoyó; Humbug Valley village: Tásma
humiliate	yepíti - cause shame
hummingbird	hómṗilisto/húmṗilisto; what hummingbird says: ṗíyuno
humor (someone)	ḱuidakwiyakka - sort of like
hunch the back	poḱḿs; hunchbacked: poḱḿsnu
hundred	máischoḱom máischoḱo/máschoḱom máschoḱo
hung up	at the place where things were hung up: wehétyodi
hunger	óksa; be hungry: ók; cause hunger: ókti; die of hunger: okówono; hungry season/time: óktipem ḱódo; get hungry: ókda

English	Maidu
hunker down	tᴧikiti
hunt (look for)	hatám/atám; hunt all over: hatámyekinu; look all over for/hunt down: hatámᴧchono
hunt for food	hun; hunt with guns or arrows: múhun; hunt deer: sᴧmhún; go hunting: húnḱoi, húnmodaw, mᴧhúnḱói, muhúnḱói; go hunting (plural subject): múhunkoḱói; go off hunting: húnmoḱoi, húnᴧdawtoye; go off hunting (plural subject): húnḱokoi, húnmodawtoye, mohunkoḱói; go hunt deer: sᴧmhúnḱoi; go off to hunt deer: sᴧmhúnḱokoi; come back from hunting together: múhunepínimoto; be on a hunting trip: húnḱoido; hunt for food: húnbᴧk; arrive to hunt: hunóḱit; hunt all over: hatámyekinu; hunt here and there: húnyeto; go down into the valley to hunt: muhúnmitno; hunt something specific on a regular basis: hunyéhto; go around hunting: húnmoye; a place to do a little hunting: húnmokitpepé
hurry	wilék, ᴧlék, hᴧlíslisno, sᴧlékwono; hurry up!: wilékleki; speed up!: hᴧlilisno, ᴧlékleki; hurry around: wiléknoye; hurry past: ᴧlélem, ᴧlémno; hurry along: bᴧlék, ᴧléklekno; hurry and bring: hapyekáka
hurt	ítu (by itself); hurt someone/cause hurt: ítuti; get hurt: ílaḱitó
husband	yepí; second husband: muli; marry a husband/have a husband: yépkᴧpe; marry a second/subsequent husband: yépkᴧlele
hush (i.t.)	kelémbo - become silent
hush up (tr)	chetímen - not let (someone) see
hushed (adj)	kelé - quiet (adj)
husk (n)	posála - shell
hustle (v)	wilék - hurry (v)
hypothesize	huhéye - imagine
I	ni; I, of course/I, as usual: ní hapá; I alone: ní'usi; I myself: niníwet, ni hápte; I, being...: ni hai
I don't care	nik mením kᴧkán - it doesn't matter to me
I hope (someone) does	let (someone do), may (someone do): MMG p. 49, -ta forms of the verb (depends on subject)
ice	eyᴧ, chumíliti; be icy: eyᴧkit; be covered with ice: chumilitimotó
ice-skate (v)	hásno - ski, skate
idea	huhéye; a good idea: yahá; this was your big idea: mínḱi huhéyedi
identify	chesáḱ - recognize
idiot	húboḱoisape - one who is witless
idiotic	húboḱoipe - witless; húkesmen - foolish, stupid
if	"if" is expressed by the -mᴧni suffix on verbs (see Lesson 11 in Mountain Maidu Grammar); if he/she goes: ᴧḱoimᴧni; if I go: ᴧḱoismᴧni; if you go: ᴧḱoinímmᴧni
if (if...then...)	whether: MMG p. 85, 87, -mᴧni or -chet suffix on verb
if only	hap
ignite	sátodep; be ignited: chópai
ignite	bolákdoi - catch on fire, blaze up
ignoring	mᴧná'anwet, mᴧnámenwet
ill	be ill: ítu; start to be ill: ítudoi; lie around ill: ᴧhákinu; rather ill: ítuhtu; sickly: ítudedes, ítusa, ítusape; illness: ítum ḱódo
illegality	wasá - evil
illegitimate (child)	hálbis
illness	ítu, ítukᴧ; weakness/illness: ťoiyí; illness-causing, disease-carrying: ítukpe; cause a little bit of illness: ítuhtuti
illuminate	toyá
illumination	banáḱ - light (n)
imagine	huhéye; imagine something into being: hukít
imbibing (adj)	mosápe - one who frequently drinks
imitate	yakka - do like
immerse	hamít; immerse a bunch of things: hamítyo; go immerse in water: mómni hítpaino
immobilized	be immobilized: wálukinu
immorality	wasá - evil
immortal	wónomen; that which is immortal: wónomenkᴧ
implant	yᴧmᴧchono - put into
implement	ma'ákᴧ - doer
imply	ḱái, mái - mean (v)
impossible	be impossible: hayahámen
impotent	be impotent: wálukinu; powerless: etósmen - weak

English	Maidu
impregnate	tékᴍti
impression	be under the impression: machókito (WS), maichákito (RD)
imprison	bístikíye - confine, restrict
improper	wasá - wrong
improperly	wasát - badly
impropriety	wasá - evil
improve (something)	yaháti - make (something) good
in	at, on, to (place): MMG p. 23, -di on noun or pronoun
in addition	kiú - also, as well
in doing	because of, due to: -di on abstract noun - see huhéyedi in Dictionary.
in error	wasá - wrong
in exchange	wonóto - in trade for
in order to	intending to, to (do): MMG p. 87, -madom or -mapem suffix on verb
in return	wonóto - in trade for
in spite of	although, even though: MMG p. 87, -wet suffix on verb
in the distance	ántena - that way
in the future	amákan - later, after that
in there	di'ím
in transit	ᴍnókᴍdi - on the way going along
inaccurately	wasá
incapable	wasá
incapacitated	be incapacitated: wálukinu
incarcerate	bístikíye - confine, restrict
incense cedar tree	maním chá
inception	k̓abᴍ́k̓ - start (n), beginning (n)
incessantly	ᴍpék̓ape - always, continuously
inch along	winú - be slow
inclination	bó - way
incline (n)	léyi - slope
include	sín - contain (as ingredient)
include	yᴍ́mmoto - enclose, encircle
incorrectly	wasát - badly
increase (v)	multiply (i.t.): dí (intrans), díti (trans) - grow
incredible	ek̓áw - wonderful
indebtedness	humusma - debt
Indian	ínyana (object of sentence), ínyanam máidᴍ, ínyanam (adj or subject of sentence)
Indian Creek	Bᴍmᴍ́k̓ᴍm Sewí, Tosí K̓oyóm Sewí (near Taylorsville)
Indian Falls	K̓oyóm Bukúm Sewíno, Hᴍnkᴍ, Hᴍnkᴍ Sewím
Indian Heights, Susanville	Súmbili
Indian paintbrush	ínyanam yó
Indian Valley	Nadam K̓oyó; north part of valley: Dókochom
Indian Valley people	tosáidom máidᴍ
indicate	mái; indicate with hand motions: hewakaktímoto
individually	sᴍ́titi - for each one
indoors	hᴍ́m k̓anáidi - inside the house
inebriated	hudásu - drunk
inequity	wasánu - evil
infant	konó, konóbe; newborn infant: béidᴍk̓ᴍm té, bíspem té
infect	ítuti - cause sickness
infer	k̓ái - refer to, mean
infinitesimal	núktiluti - very tiny
inflatable boat	hínnotikᴍm yak̓á - boat
inflate	witái - exaggerate
inflexible	ᴍ́hᴍ - stubborn
inflict pain	ítu - hurt (tr)
influential	ᴍhᴍ́ - powerful
inform	mamá - advise, tell
informant	mákpapaitikᴍ - teacher
informed	makítpe
infrequent	helú, helúto - a few, a very few
infuriate	wasósati
infuse	ohéti

English	Maidu
-ing	MMG p. 29-30, -dom for nouns and verbs. p. 73-74, -pem for adjectives, p. 36, -ing in questions, -dom
ingest	pe - eat
ingredients	wasása
inhabit	ᴍbis - occupy
inhale	hónyewei
initial (adj)	hínwom - ahead
initiate	hukít - create using thought
inject	yᴍmᴍchono - put into
injure	ítuti; get injured: ílakitó
injustice	wasánu - evil
inn	hutél - hotel
innards	pítkololo - guts
inning	ónkoḱoito - contest (n)
innocent	hesámenkᴍ; good: yahá
innovate	púḱsito - bring about
inquire	hónmaknoye
inquisitive	pekúla; ask a lot of questions: pí epínsa
insect	kapí
insert	ḱapól, sᴍ, bó, wohópmit, sᴍhópḱoi, yohóp; insert into an orifice (nose/ears): sᴍḱói; insert as ear ornaments: bonó sᴍháwkit, sᴍyáwkito; insert as plug: ḱadópchik; insert something into something: yohópḱoi; insert down into: yohópmit; try to insert/almost insert: wohópmithudódoito
inside of	in'ínno; inside the house: hᴍm ḱanáidi
insides (n)	innards, entrails, bowels: pítkololo - guts
insight	húkesi - wisdom
inspect	chehéiheino
inspiration	hónhulu
instead (of doing)	expressed by verb 1 in -menwet followed by verb 2 in imperfect. Emphasizer 'as may come after -menwet. Instead of x, I was doing y "without x--ing, I was doing y"
institute	sᴍkúl - school
instruct	mákpapaiti, mákpaiti
instructor	mákpapaitikᴍ
instrument (musical)	sóltikᴍ
instrument (tool)	ma'ákᴍ - doer
insult (v)	kᴍléweye; always insulting/insulting by nature: kᴍléweyesa
Intake Tower (L. Almanor)	Choldino
integrate	wᴍkdi maháye - bring together in unity
intelligent	húkes - smart, clever
intend to	húyeti, mápem
intending to	to (do), in order to: MMG p. 87, -madom or -mapem suffix on verb
intensely	do intensely: búsno, yépcheti
intentionally do/cause	matí; what was the intention?: hesátimadom?
inter	tam - bury
interacting with	to (someone): MMG p. 5, -to infix on verb
intercom	píntikᴍ - radio
interfere with	wasáyati - make things bad for
interior	in'ínno
intermission	chedá - break (n)
interpret	mákpapaiti - explain, teach
intersect	ḱótwochono - crisscross, go back and forth across
intestines	pítkololo
intimidate	hᴍstaye - scare away
intoxicated	hudásu
intuition	húkesi - wisdom
inundate	mombóno - to flood, flow
invalid, sickly	ítusa
invent	púḱsito - bring about
investigate	hónmak, hónmaknoye
invisible	chewúsuktipe, chehéhechonope, chechᴍisape
invite	yé; invite someone to go: yéḱoi; invite someone to come: yé'okít; get someone to come: yaḱói, yomó; invite to go along: ᴍnówochoi; invite/summon: ái

English	Maidu
invocation	túweye - prayer
invoke	bókweye
iPod	píntikṃ - radio
irate	wasó - angry
iris	debá
irrelevant	it is irrelevant: mením kṃkán
irritated	be irritated with: wáskato
is	kakán; that's the way it is: ma'ákṃm
island	ónkṃsdobe
isolate	yotótchik - divide, separate (tr)
it	MMG p. 40, as subject - mṃm, as object - mṃ
it doesn't matter	mením kṃkán - it is irrelevant
itch	wimúmu, wimú, sukúi/sṃkṃi
item	hesí; point, unit: sṃti - one
its (belonging to it)	MMG p. 40 - possessive - mṃkí
jack in cards	yáskakno, yepónim te
jackass	sekés
jacket	kapóťa
jackrabbit	chínkuťi, kowékesi/kówekkesi
Jacuzzi pump	mómpoldoitikṃ
jail (v)	bístikíye - confine, restrict
jamb	hṃmtṃti - beam (n), rafter
Janesville	Widóikṃm
jaw	chawá, chawám bṃmí
jay	scrub jay: si'ítku (HM), cháitakṃ (FC-E); pinyon jay: aiyak; Steller's jay: káieskṃ (FC), kaihískṃ (WS), káieskṃm máidṃ
jealousy	to fight from jealousy: wókit
Jeffrey Pine	bṃbṃ; Jeffrey pine tree: bubúm cha (JD)/bṃbṃm cha
jelly	soťálkṃ
jerk (n)	ṃspa - rascal
jerk (v)	wilók - twitch
Jerusalem Cricket	si'ṃne
Jesus	chísas
jewelry	wearing jewelry: kúilaimape
job	tawáli - work, tawálihape; get a job/have a job: tawálkṃ
Job's Coffin constellation	hémuimu
jock	tókdatokṃ - racer
jog	welé - run (v)
John Meadows	makáchipa
join a gathering	úmmoto
joist	hṃmtṃti - beam (n), rafter
joke (n), joking	mínono - in fun, kidding
jolt (n)	yanánaito - earthquake
journalist	male journalist: papélkṃm máidṃ; female journalist: papélkṃm kṃlem
journey	ṃkoi
jump	tṃp, talóp; jump by itself/pop: pṃp; jump across: tṃpsito; jump around: tṃpnoye, bolópchono; jump away: pátkoi; jump in: tṃpmitno; jump into: beťékda, beťékeno; jump into quickly: beťék'inno; jump quickly: beťék, tákakabo; jump and run: bolóp; be about to jump: beťékdapoto; jump over: jump over: beťékchono, dónwikachono; jump back in: bolóp'inno; jump to one side: sṃhékachono; jump at to seize: méyodoi; jump onto and grab: méhyotno; jump down in: betékmitpin, tṃpmitpin; come jumping down/jump off: tṃpínpin; jump out: beťékdaw, beťéksip, bolópsip, bosíp, talópsip; jump/pop out like popcorn: pṃpsip; jump out of water: yodói; jump towards: tṃppin; jump off towards: tṃpchopin; jump up: sṃwéikadoi; jump and make a tapping sound: ťákkaka; jump/pop abruptly (like popcorn): pṃpkoi
jump on	méhťakit - assault, rape
junco	tetékṃ, pachititi
juniper	ťápṃ; juniper tree: ťápṃm cha
just	pikno, kánte, hesátmet, dṃkṃ
just (adj)	yahá - good
just as	just as (something was about to happen): bédukan; just like: ṃpé
jut out	sṃ, sṃdáw - protrude

English	Maidu
juvenile (adj)	yʌ́pe - young people
juveniles	yʌ́pe - young people, teenagers
katydid	tilítili
kayak	yakʌ́ - boat
Keddie Peak	Yakʌ́m Yamáni
Keddie Ridge	Chiwítbem Yamáninom (FR), Yot'im Yamáni (WS)
keep	mayá, yaché - save back conserve
keep away from	wadá - dodge, get away
keep close to	wodák - stick close to
keep doing	awébisim; kept doing: kawé'am
keep doing	keep on: MMG p. 54, 56, 57 - -nu,-bis, -webis, or -ebis infix on verb
keep secret	kilé - hide (something)
keep time (rhythm)	benhúye
keep watch	chenú - watch
kerchief	owólakkʌ - scarf
Kettle Rock	Óm Lolóm Yamáni (FC-E)
key	kí
kick	ísyo; keep on kicking: ísyoda; kick angrily: wás'isyo; kick away: ísdotdoi, íswawakoi; kick backwards: t'eyó, t'eyóyewei; kick downhill: ísdotmitno; kick over: ísdotchono
kick oneself	yepí - be ashamed
kickoff (n)	kabʌ́k - start (n),beginning (n)
kid (n)	te - child
kidding around	mínono
kidnap	sohákoi, pedáhakoi; habitually kidnap: pedá'ʌkinu; kidnap (children): pedáyeto
kidney	chúmlo
kill	wónoti; kill many: hénoti; want to kill: wónotiya; be obliged to kill: wónotiwe; kill each other: wónotito; kill one by one: wi'ítisa; kill oneself: wónoti'us; kill for food: húnbʌk; keep killing: wónotiew; not be killing: wónotimeninu; killer: wónotikʌ; something killed: wónotiwono
killdeer	kowʌ́t'ʌt'ʌtkʌ, kuwitiktikʌ
killer	wónotikʌ - murderer
kind (nice)	yahá; be kind: yahá; be kind to each other: yamáitototi
kind (of thing)	some kind of: wasása; that kind: ka'ápe, ka'áwini; this kind: eyáwini, ma'ápe; what kind of? hesáwinim? That's the kind: ka'ápe 'as
kindling	t'ʌ́t'ʌ, t'ʌkt'ʌk, chópaitikʌ
king in cards	dópaski, yepónim máidʌ
king size	tetébe - largest
kingdom come (n)	wónomenkʌm kódo - heaven
kingfisher	wékweke, chált'át'api
kingsnake	t'íyani, yopónim húskʌ
kink (n)	wʌ́nt'et'enoye - curl
kinky	onotʌ́itʌikʌ - curly-haired
kiss	chobót; kiss someone: chopótpot; kiss each other: chobóttoto
knapsack	hadó - backpack
knead	bʌ́mheloto - rub, massage
knee	pokósi
kneel	pokósyokit, pokósyokinu
knife	chámmi (WS, FC), chúmmi (RD)
knit hat	olé, wiká - hat, netted cap
knob	okéli
knock	bókkok/bʌkkʌk/bukkuk; knock something (like seeds) into something: wóhʌ, wodótmit; knock a lot of things into something: wodótmityo; knock as a shaman: betéiboko; a knock: bókkoko; knock something off: susúpdoi; knock something out of a container by hitting it: wotók; knock over: wopókno
knock (someone) down	wopókkit
knock down	knock down: wʌdʌ́m; knock down a tree: kaití, wʌdʌ́minnokakínu; go along knocking down trees: kaití'ʌno; knock over: wopókno
knot	púnya; tie knots: pun; knotted string for day-counts: púnyapem walási, walási
know	makít/mákkit, yákkit; know about by hearing: pínmakit; want to know: mákkityaha; pretend to know: makítkukus; not know: yákken/yátken; not know much about: mákmakitmen; not understand a situation: hínchesem; without you even realizing it: mayákkeno; without my knowledge: mayákkes

English	Maidu
know nothing about	mákmakitmen - not know, not know much about
know-it-all	be a know-it-all: húkesyopaida
knowledge	húkesi
knowledgeable	makítpe, pi makítpe
Konkow	tái'i, tái'im máidᴀ; Konkow people: táiyima
lack	wi'í; not lack: wi'ímen
lacking	without (on nouns): use -wi'ípem on noun
ladle out	ái - dish up, serve
lag behind	tókdati'us
laid out (as dead body)	be laid out: wónokinu
lake	mómdani/mómdanni
Lake Almanor	Nákam Mómdanni
Lake Tahoe	Nem Tonna, Tetém Mómdanni
lame	wósdotno, t́at
lamp	toyákᴀ, toyá
land (n)	ḱawí, ḱódo; have a land: ḱódoikᴀ; learn about the land: ḱódoi mákpai
land (v)	land as birds or aircraft: hánpi, ᴀpéḱanohánpin, kái'inpin; land somewhere after being thrown: héyumit
landscape (n)	ḱódoi - area
language	wéye; different language: cháitikkapem wéye
lantern	toyákᴀ - lamp
lard	hᴀt̓i - fat (n)
large size	tetébe - largest
larger	tetébe; be a little larger: tetébew; get a little larger: tetébe
last (of all)	kaní, kaním; the last one: hóipai, batásono; the last house (on the road): batáskinum úyi; last (former): hóiyᴀ, last (year, month, etc): hóiyᴀmmen; the very last one (in a series): hóipaidᴀkᴀ; at last: kaníwonom
last (v)	ᴀbis - remain, endure
last (year or time)	hóiyᴀmmen
last forever	wónomen - be immortal
latch	dᴀchik - lock up, close up
late (deceased)	yat̓a, ísḱayat̓a
lately	béidᴀktonanna, béidᴀkmen
later	cháimen, héki, hóipaidi; then later/after that: amánkan, amákan
latter	the latter (refers to someone previously mentioned): amám; that one (just mentioned, object of sentence): amá
laugh	nuk, núksa; laugh! nukí! always laugh/laugh a lot: núksasa; laugh and say: núkdowéye; laugh at: núkpapai; laugh very hard: núkbosno, núkbusno; laugh very hard about: núkbusto
laugh at	hokót - ridicule
lava	yamánim sedém
lavatory	pit̓ím uyí - bathroom
law	ma
law enforcement	dónkᴀm máidᴀ - police (n)
lawmaker	mákupe
laxative	sumpiti
lay into	méht̓akit - assault, rape
lay something (down)	yᴀmᴀ́; lay something down: sówokit, wowóchono, yᴀmᴀ́kit, yᴀmᴀ́kitcho, yaiyóno; forcefully lay someone down: hánwokit; a place where one has forced someone down: hánwokitkᴀ; lay something down on top of something: wot̓á, wowót̓a; lay things in something (like suitcase): wowómit; go along laying things down: hekítᴀkoi
lay things out (like food)	sówot̓a; lay a lot of things out: sówot̓ayo
layer (v)	húl, ban - spread, put over, cover over
layman	yomímeni
lazy	okólesa, okólesape; be lazy: okóle; cause laziness: okóleti; be not very lazy: okóleboduk
leach acorns	bᴀmi; be leached: pis; leaching festival: wípe
lead	hóiwiháno, hóiwiha, papái; bring somewhere by leading: hóiwihaye, hóiwihayeti; lead someone all the way somewhere: hóiwihadikno; lead someone across: hóiwihasito; lead someone by the hand: widókhaḱoi; lead around by the hand: widóknoye; lead out by the hand: hówihasip; lead away from: hóiwihasip; lead up/upstairs: hówihadoi; be led up to: hóiwihadoinu
lead astray	héwwelek - seduce

English	Maidu
leader	yepóni (RD, FC), yopóni (WS)
leader of a secret society	húku
leaf	botó
leaf out	sáwdoi, sáwsip, yótitdoi
leaky	látpe; always leaky/be leaky: látsape
lean (adj)	ťoť - thin, skinny
lean against using hands	mái'odikno
leap	tmp
learn	mákpapai, mákpai, mákkitdoi; want to learn: mákkityaha; learn about the land/nature: kódoi mákpai; start to learn: mákwonohóiye; learn songs: sólmakito; learn together: makítto
leather	wolósi; leather string: wolósim kukú
leave	mkói, bodí mkói; leave (plural subject): kóko; leave quickly: wmssa, koháno; leave one after another: káwhehekoi; leave (plural subject) going various ways: káwhehekokoi; pull up and leave/move: néndoi; leave someone alone: tmtm; leave for good: mkóida; leave something/someone: bísti, utí, wodáwti; make people leave/evacuate: wiyéti; make someone leave again: mmyákwiyeti; leave people behind in a race: tókda; leave something behind: kmpyeti, úkit; where I left (something): bístisma
leave a dangerous area	wmssasip - leave, be forced to leave
leave the ground	káidoi - fly up
leave undone	mtai - miss, overlook
leaving	mkóida - departure
lecture (v)	to lecture: túwei; lecture someone: héwa; take the floor, address (v), give a speech: wewé - deliver a speech
lecturer	wewéyekm - speaker
leech	mólbiti
left behind	be left behind: okm, o
left over	leftovers: léwo; be left over: okm; be left over/extra (as a person): awónom
left side	yímduku, dakú; to the left: dakúna, yímdukna
leftover (adj)	léwom - some
leg	tolí; have the leg twitch: páiwilok; straddle with the legs: mósťapin; between the legs: máwam pulúmto; put one's legs over someone: mósťapinhanóye
legend	betéi - story
legendary being	betéi
leisure	mpé bísdom - doing nothing
Lena Benner	díchulto
Lena Benner's Mother	che'ésta
lend	dámmai
length of time	ebmm - a long time
lengthen	ťéstimen - prolong
lengthy	lalám - long
leopard lily	lokómini
less	tibína; be a lot less: hehépaiwiyáka; be less/be half gone: hehépai
let (someone do)	may (someone do), I hope (someone) does: MMG p. 49, -ta forms of the verb (depends on subject)
let go	woiyókoi - send (someone) away
let someone go	sówono
let's	MMG p. 49, let's (the two of us) -pm'm on verb, let's (3 or more) -pe'e on verb
letting someone down (after carrying them)	ápokite
level (adj)	bátbatpe - flat, planar
level (in a building)	polówa - floor
level (n)	bénno - step
level (v)	wi'íti - destroy
Lewis Woodpecker	chitátati
lexicon	wéye - speech
liability	humusma - debt
liable to be	bíshelu - likely to be
liar	hálkm, halím máidm, hálhudanpe; habitual liar: hálsa, hálsasape
liberate	sówono - let someone go
lice	head lice: dí; body lice: pedési; be covered with lice: dítapope, pedésťapope
lichen	chám símpani/sam símpani

English	Maidu
lick	énto
lid	wᴧsᴧtikᴧ, hónbakᴧ; put a lid on: hónba
lie around	tᴧinoye; lie around moaning: ᴧhákinu
lie down	tᴧi, tᴧikit, ḱachó, ḱachókit, yoḱós; make someone lie down: yoḱósti; lie down outstretched: yoḱóskit; be lying down: tᴧikinu; still be lying down: lᴧkabis; lie down like a log: kai; lie on the back: yoḱóskinu; lie down together: yoḱóskinuto; lie face down/lie on belly: wusútkinu; lie with one's back to the fire: ḱiwsukinu; don't make someone lie down: yoḱóstimen; lie down between: yoḱósmit; lie down close to: yoḱóspanúto
lie in wait for	ḱahúkit
lie low	ḱá'ukkinu - crouch down and hide
lie on someone/something	lie on something: tᴧ'itánu; lie on someone: hópmit, yoḱóschononu; be lying on top of: yoḱóstonu; lie all over someone: yoḱóstaheyto
lie prone	wusútkinu - lie face down, lie on the belly
lie, tell a lie	hal, hálpapai; lie to oneself: halsa'us; always lie: hálsa; lying: hálhudanpe
life	hónwe'i; come (back) to life: pokᴧkinu, wimík
lifetime	hónwe'i - life
lift	wiwó, sódoi; lift up (with hands): sówodoi/sówwodoi, wiwódoi; keep lifting: sódoiyew; lift (someone): sowiḱado; lift onto the shoulder: sódopai, sódoipai; lift onto the back: áp, háp, hápdoi; lift and carry over the shoulder: sówiḱachono; lift and carry all the way (somewhere): sówiḱadikno; lift out with the hand: sóisup; lift (as fog): wᴧsdoino; lift up one's skirt: wiḱéidoi, wiḱéiḱeidoi
lift off	ḱáidoi - fly up
light (bright)	a light (fixture): toyá, toyákᴧ; lights/headlights: toyákᴧtipe; to light (fire/cigarette): ṕipaiti; to light a lamp: toyá, toyákit; get light (sky): banánaḱ; start to get light (sky): yodádalchopin; light a fire: sa ku, sa wó, sa yá; light switch: toyákᴧtikᴧ; be lighted (lamp): toyákᴧ; be lit (sky, anything lit from another source): banáḱno; cigarette lighter: hᴧṕáikᴧ
light (weight)	wᴧhúlmenpe, wihᴧlmenpe
light-colored	edáldalnope
lighter (cigarette)	hᴧṕáikᴧ
lightning	wiṕíli; be lightning: wiṕíl; give a stroke of lightning to: witᴧmtᴧm mé
Lights Creek	Hópnom Sewí
like (adverb)	yákkat/yakát; like this (showing with hands): ándᴧkbe, ántᴧtᴧ; like this: eyáwei; like that in size: ka'ándukbe; be like: ayá, eyá, mᴧyák, yak, yáka; seem like/look like: yakbé, yakánu; be just like: yákdᴧkbe; It's not going to be like that: ka'ámenmapem kᴧḱán; sound like: yakṕinti; feel like: yákhubᴧk; become like: makᴧno; stay like: eyánu; do like: ka'á, eyádom, ayáti, ka'áhuyeti, yákka, eyáweyeti, ka'átido; doing like me: níḱ yákkadom haṕá; doing like you: min yákkadom haṕá; someone who would do like that: ka'ámape; you should not do it like that: ka'ámenmapem kano; make it like: ayáti; things like that: ka'ápepe; say like this: eyái, eyáiwei; do likewise: do likewise: mᴧyáka
like (v)	ḱúidak, yahátche; admire: ᴧḱáwche; like better: sᴧssᴧ; not like much: sᴧssᴧmen, wasám chewé; like to do: yahá; likeable: yahácheti; to sort of like: ḱúidakwiyakka
like better	would rather (have or do), favor (v): sᴧssᴧ - prefer
like to	want to: MMG p. 57, -yaha infix on verb
likely	ha'ái; likely to be: bíshelu
lilac	chᴧṕátim dᴧ/chepátim dᴧ, yaṕáti (JD); squaw carpet: ḱawíbano; white lilac: hébe
lily	mountain lily: ᴧswelenom yó; mariposa lily: wuiléspuikᴧm yo
limb	ṕaḱá; low-limbed: tíswili
limit (edge)	batás; outer limit: woi; to the limit: batáschono
limit (mobility)	bístikíye - restrict, confine
limp (v)	wósdok; drag oneself around, injured: bᴧṕói, bᴧṕóipoi; walk with one leg short: wóspoi, wóspoino; limp along: ṕaikᴧtḱᴧt
line (cord)	ḱuḱú - rope
line of work	tawáli - work
lip	símpo, símimpo; upper lip: obᴧdoyim símpo; lower lip: ḱanáyim símpo; smack the lips: sím watámchik
liquefy	ḱómchú - thaw
liquid (n)	momí - water
liquor	hútum sudáka - whiskey

English	Maidu
listen	pínkinu/pínkenu, pínheiheino; listen to: pinwéye; listen carefully: pínluť; listen for: pinhéye; keep listening: pinópininu; be listening from a distance: pinwoyénu; be heard in the distance: pínkenutihadáw; not listen: pinhéhenon; one who doesn't listen: pínmenpe
lit up (as the sky)	banákno
little	tibí
little bit	a little bit: núkti, tibínak; only a little bit: helúto, helú
live	bis (stay); live (be alive): hónwe; live beyond: bísyekoi; live over (a hill): bíschoi; live somewhere else: bísekoi; be still living/alive: hónwehelu; make a living by doing: hónwe'inu; live/have a house (somewhere): hᴍbókᴍ; might live/have a house (somewhere): hᴍbóyákken; live through (something hard): honwéyepati; live together: bístoto
live oak	óm hámsim cha, babákᴍ cha, wihám cha
liver	kᴍlla
living (adj)	hónwe'inu - alive
lizard	pítchakᴍ, óm pítchaka; small brown lizard: umpétillilla; big green lizard: móilompani
load	a load: hadó; to load onto the back: hadói, hadóipai; load up a container: hedói
loaf (v)	téte - hang out
loaf bread	wólem maháti
loan (v)	dámmai - lend
loathe	piťúk - hate (v)
lobelia	sumbíli
local (adv)	hedénna - nearby
location	kokó; at a location: yᴍdi; be located: ú
lock (v)	dᴍchik - lock up, close up; close up a house: hᴍbᴍchik; be unable to lock (something): dᴍchikchᴍi
lock horns	wokótito - quarrel (v)
locust	chike
lodgepole pine	welé; lodgepole pine tree: wálim cha/wálum cha/welém chá
lodging	túimape
lofty	hadádoi - high up
log	kai, kayyí; rotten log: holó; a very big load of logs: tetét yahám kayí
logger	chá hunékᴍ - lumberjack
logging truck	holóhadóikᴍᴍ kaléta
loincloth	wosóťa; wearing only a loincloth: wosóťadᴍk
loiter about	téte - hang out
lonely	dᴍkkᴍ, húkit; lonely by nature/a loner: húkitsa; be lonely: hukítimen, húkitmen
long ago	hóiya, hóiyam kódodi, hadám kódoidi, hésmen
long time	a long time: ebᴍm; be a long time: ebᴍdom, ebᴍbᴍ
long, be long	lalám, lam, lalámpe; long-legged: lalámpem tólkᴍpe/lalám tólkupe; rather long: lámlam
look across	chesíto; look across at: chehéiheikoi
look after	bísdodo - stay with and take care of; stand by (someone), stick up for: húno - support
look around	chehéhenoye, chehéyeno; look around at: chehéyenoye; look around for: hatámnoye; go take a look around: chenói'noye, chenónoye; look around across: chehéhesito; look around down into: chehéhemitno; look and check everywhere around: ᴍscheheyenoye; look around in bewilderment: ᴍscheheiye; stand up and look around: chehéwodoi; while looking around: chehéhekoido, hat'dá; without looking around: chehéhenonwet
look at	chehéiheino; have a look at: chebᴍk, chenóno, cheťá; look down at: ᴍchékinu; look around at: chepípitino; keep looking at: cheyénu; turn the head towards and look at: sᴍche; go along looking at (several things): chehéye'ᴍno; around looking at (several things): chehéye'ᴍnoye; look at repeatedly: chekákasip; look at steadily: chekón, chenú; go right up and look at: okᴍkoidikno; without looking at: hehénomenwet; look at secretly: cheká, chekáto
look back	hóiche; look back around: chehéyewew; look back at: sᴍnchewono
look behind (someone)	hóichenu
look closely	chebós; look closely at: chekíno
look down	ᴍchékinu; peek down secretly: ka'okᴍkᴍino; look down at: chehéiheikit; look down in: okᴍkᴍinpin; look down into: sᴍwéwe
look elsewhere	cháichekonu; pretend to be looking elsewhere: cháichekonukukus

English	Maidu
look foolish	yepí - be ashamed, embarrassed
look for	hatám, atám; look for someone: ᴍpé, chenóno, chenó'ohe; look for/expect: chebóye; go look for: hatámḱoi, opéḱoi; go wandering around looking for: hatámᴍnóiye; go all around looking for: wochíkimoto, ᴍpéno, ᴍpé'ᴍnoye; look for/follow tracks: wochík, pai wochík, hanó'ono; look all over for: hatámᴍchono
look forward to	tetétluťi yahá - so want to (verb before yaha)
look forward to (doing)	húyeti - intend to
look forward to (something coming)	chehéiye - expect (someone to arrive)
look good	yahácheti
look in	okᴍ́kᴍino; gaze into: chemínu
look in on	chenóḱoi - visit (v)
look into	hónmaknoye - investigate
look like	mᴍyákchetipe, yakbé, yákcheti; look just like: yákchetiluť; look more and more like: yakawéw
look out	be on the lookout: sikáta; on lookout: chenúdi
look that way	cheḱónu
look through	chetól
look through	chesíto - look across
look toward	sᴍ́ncheye, sᴍ́nche; look in the direction of: chehéiḱoi, chehéiheiye; look down towards: sᴍ́nchechopin
look up	chehéhedoi, yehéhedoi; be looking up: epínchedónu; stand up and look: chehéwodoi; look up at: chedónohanoi
look within	e'uschenu
look/appear	chetí; how someone looks/what they look like: hesáchétipe; look the same: chenóno'us
looking out towards	chepítwono - facing towards
looks	mussú - face
loose	come loose: hépᴍt, hé; come loose and fall: hédakdaw
lord	yepóni - chief
lose	bokóiti, wonó; lose a contest: ónḱoiti; lose hair/fur/feathers: kam, kámda; lose momentum: wusuisuikit
lose a charge (battery)	tibíbew, wᴍsuisúikit - dwindle, get fewer, deflate
lose color	píbáw - fade (i.t.)
lose one's temper	wasóso - get angry
lost	be lost: ᴍ́sbokoi
lot (n)	ḱawí - land
lots of, a lot	pí; a huge amount: píluťi; be a lot: yépcheti, wéhyakbedom; what I have a lot of: píkᴍsma; make a lot of noise: yepéinti
loud	be loud: yohónto, mohᴍ́twono, mohᴍ́twonowiḱoi; be very loud: yepíntiti, yepínti; talk in a loud voice: hᴍ́hwepai; louder: mohᴍ́hᴍt; do something louder: mohᴍ́hᴍtnoti, mohᴍ́hᴍtdoi; by being loud: tetédᴍḱᴍ; loudest (weather event): tetédᴍḱᴍ; loudly: wᴍtᴍ́swoye
loudspeaker	píntikᴍ - radio
lounge around	míknoye, téte - hang out
louse	head louse: dí; body louse: pedési
love	love someone: oi'ᴍ́pai, hᴍbᴍ́kto; love each other: hᴍbᴍ́ktoto; fall in love: hoi'ᴍ́pai; love in a light-hearted way: oyᴍ́pai; a couple in love with each other: hᴍbᴍ́ktotopecho; the beloved: oi'ᴍ́paipe
lovely	yahácheti̇pe - pretty
low	nᴍs, nus, hadádoiboduk; lower down: obᴍ́nno
lower (v)	reduce, curtail, cut down, diminish (tr), trim, scale down: tibíti - make smaller
lucid	be lucid: hówikᴍp
luck	yú; lucky: bodáwsa; bad luck: yépti; good luck charm/amulet: ómsulu, oméiyi, oméikᴍ, óm sulú, heláyim oméiyi, helám oméiyi, heláikᴍᴍ oméiyi; experience terrible luck: hesáiluť; get out of a disastrous situation with good luck: hónsu
ludicrous	hokótisape - ridiculous
lug (v)	hanᴍ́n - haul
luggage	hadóikᴍ - suitcase
lumberjack	chá hunékᴍ
lunacy	hútudom
lunatic	hútukᴍ
lunch	piné, ékpe; fix lunch: pinéti

English	Maidu
lunchmeat	bá sᴍmí
lunchroom	pekᴍ́m uyí - restaurant
lung, lungs	huhú; lung illness: huhúm ítu
lunge and grab	méhyo; make a lunge for and grab: méhyodoi
lupine	pukᴍ́
lure (v)	héwwelek - seduce
luscious	dóchekᴍ - delicious
-ly (adverb ending)	MMG p. 75, -ni, -t. -dom on verbs can express adverbs
lying (somewhere)	wowókinu, wowó; be lying on top: wowóťanu
lynx	boksᴍkᴍla, inchépi
lyrics	adóm sóldom; what do the lyrics say/mean?: adóm sóldom máiḱade?
machine	mᴍsín, bᴍsín
machinery	mᴍsín - machine
mad (angry)	wasó, wáschᴍ
made	yawónope
madrone	lillil cha
maggot	wem
magic	yómpa - sorcery
magpie	at'áte
mahala mat	humchi
maidenhair fern	lopípi, lepípi
Maidu	ínyanam máidᴍ, máidᴍ; Maidu language: ínyanak wéye, máidᴍk wéye
mail (v)	ᴍkóiti - send
mail man	papéli hanᴍ́nokᴍm máidᴍ
main	tetébe - bigger, largest
make	ma, ya, sikés, tawál; make food: hesbáp, sikés; make with ingredients: sín; make something for (someone) yatí; you ought to make something: hesátiyahá
make (someone do)	force, cause, get (someone to do): MMG p. 56, -ti infix on verb
make a bed	húlnoye, bánkoi
make a circuit	wᴍnᴍ́doi - travel in a circle
make a fire	sakᴍ́
make a getaway	bosíp, wadá - escape (v), get away
make a plate for	ái - dish up, serve
make amends	koyó - make up for, pay for
make an appearance	chebᴍ́k, chebᴍ́kdoi - appear
make an effort	mák, mákwono - try, try to
make an exit	yᴍ́sip - go out
make food	pewíhakit - cook, prepare food
make it	ᴍdíkno - arrive, reach
make love	héiyeto - have sex with
make off with	pedá - steal; hijack, seize, abduct: pedáyeto, sohákoi - kidnap
make sense of	makít - understand
make trouble	matí - cause, do (something) to
make up (lie)	hal - tell a lie
make up for	koyó
male	yepí; males: yepsᴍ́
mallard duck	óbᴍno/óbunu, wátkᴍ
man	máidᴍ, yepí; young man: pᴍ́be; old man: waisí; legendary man: yépsabe, máidᴍbe; become a man: máidᴍ
manage	yaháti - organize things
manager	papélim yepóni
manager	yepóni - chief
mandarin	owánchi - orange (fruit)
mandolin	wétpeikᴍ - banjo
manipulate	máni
mankind	máidᴍse, wónom máidᴍ
manner	papáyi, bó - way
manufacture	yatí - create
many	pí, hesánbe, helúmeni, lokó, yépchetikᴍ; a huge amount: píluťi; too many: píto; however many there are: mᴍséwet; as many: hesándᴍkbe ma'át; so many times: píninu; be very many: yépcheti, wéhyakbedom; be quite a few: yépchetiti; that which I have many of: píkᴍsma; not very many: píboduk

English	Maidu
manzanita	epɨ́m/ebm; larger kind: ékpm; red manzanita: láklakpem ékpm; large black manzanita: síwsiwpem ékpm; greenleaf manzanita: dadakasi, whiteleaf manzanita: tátum cha; low-growing pinemat manzanita: ḱawídano; low-growing high-elevation manzanita: ḱawí dóndom tótto, tótto/tɨ́mttm, yamánim tótto; low-growing red manzanita: láklakpem tótto
manzanita berry	epɨ́m hiní
manzanita powder	epɨ́m tm
maple	dapí; big-leaf maple tree: dapím chá; Torrey maple: líllilta
marathon	tókdato - foot race
mare	kmlém kawáyu
margarine	soťálkm - butter
margin	wehé, wohó, waťá
mariposa lily	wuiléspuikmm yo
mark (v)	bal
market (place of trade)	méitokmm hmbó - store, shop
market (v)	sél - sell
marmot	supwa
married	married couple: kmlékmto; married (man): kmlékmpe; married (woman): yépkmpe
marrow	bapál, bmmím bapáli
marry	marry/come together as one: wmkdímoto; marry a woman: kmlékm, kmlékmto, kmlépeto; marry a man: yépkm; marry another man/marry again (as women): yépkmlele
marry again	púli
marsh	osóḱm - bog
marsh hawk	málbm
marten	sásasi
marvel (v)	mkáwche - admire
marvelous	eḱáw - wonderful
Marysville	Táisida
mash	wobúno, yolók
mask (tr)	kilé - hide (something)
mass, glob	okɨ́nmni
massacre (v)	hénoti
massage	bɨ́mheloto; massage the head for headache: onó smḱáw; massage the head to shape it: smlát
master (n)	lord: yepóni - chief
master, pet owner	mutútu
masticate	chawái - chew
masturbate	smkála'us/smkúla'us, máni tawál'us
match (for fire)	wosó, hmpáikm; matches: méchms
match (n)	ónkoḱoito - contest (n)
matched, similar	mmyákaka
mate (v)	mate (male animals): búpaito, ápbonno; mating season: búpaitomenkmmeni
materialize	chebɨ́k, chebɨ́kdoi - appear
materials	wasása
mates	wosíkmtoto - cousins, associates
matter (no matter...)	no matter what: hesíma'at, hesímma'at, hesánudowet; no matter what cause: hesádowet ma'át; no matter who: homónim ma'áti; no matter what! (after telling someone not to do something): wíyepada!
matter (what's the matter?)	what's the matter?: hesádom?; What's the matter with you?: hesádom maḱá?; What's the matter with all of you? hesádom mínsmm maḱá?; What's always the matter with you?: hesádom mawéwḱa?
mature (adj)	developed: ḱap - ripe
mature (v)	dí - grow, díbos - be fully grown
may (someone do)	I hope (someone) does, let (someone do): MMG p. 49, -ta forms of the verb (depends on subject)
maybe	ai sm'mi, ma'át, hápte; maybe this, maybe that: hesíwetim hesíwetam; maybe or maybe not: wínit
me	nik; me first: níkuni; not me: níḱmeni
meadow	ḱoyó; into a meadow area: ḱoyóm upedi; walk along the edge of a meadow: ḱoyówaťa'mno
Meadow Valley	Eyolim Ḱoyó
meadowlark	díchulto, kowɨ́tɨ́mtkm, chiwíspolótkm, chí'uluťchono

English	Maidu
meager	píboduk - scarce
meal	pená; lunch: ékpe, piné; breakfast: chedá; dinner: ḱaipe, ḱaipekm
mean (v)	kái, mái, máiye; if that's what you mean: ka'áinimmni; be meaning/trying to get (an idea) across: máiyew; what do you mean?: hesí máiḱa?; What do the lyrics mean?: adóm sóldom máiḱade?
mean to	húyeti - intend to
meander	mnói - wander
meaningless	be meaningless: mením kmḱán
meanwhile	achét, amánkan
measure (n)	ma - law (n)
measure (v)	womákti; measure a distance: bomákti; take various measurements: womáktichonoye
meat	smmí, waḱá; animal carcass: sm; roast meat: ítus, ítusyo; to dry meat: wáḱda
median	ésto - middle
medicinal plant	wenépmkm; a plant for chest colds: bmtchmwi
medicine	wené; medicinal fluid rubbed on: yútokmm wené
medley	cháitikkape - different ones
meet (i.t.)	mmmoto - assemble, come together
meet (n)	ónkoḱoito - contest (n)
meet (tr)	chenó, odá, odáto; meet each other: odátoto; meet by chance: mchák, mdémmai, mlémmai, mdémťa; nearly meet by chance: mdémťahudoi; wherever one meets people: yúmotokmdi
meet halfway	ťikche - go along with, trust
meet together	úmmototo/mmmototo
meeting (n)	mmmotope - event, get-together
melody	solí - song
melt	melt as ice: chu, chumí, chumú; melt as butter or fat: píchuchu; something meltable: chumíliti
membrane	pumi, púmpumi
men	máidmse, yepśm; a couple of men: yeṕkmto
mend	tawáldmkdmk, yadmkdmḱ - repair (v)
menopause	ympmhekiti
menstrual hut	chos'úyi, dómim uyí, kapúmim hmbó
menstruate	mdáw, chos; have the first menstrual period: ympm; start one's menstrual period: ók; be menstruating: pemén; be isolated in menstruation: chosbís, chóspe
mention	yawí
mentor (v)	mamá
merchandise	wasása - stuff
mercury (element)	mmkmli
merganser (duck)	bowakno
merge with	pin; merge with and let it carry up: wmkkánuhadóino
mesh	biní - net
mess up	wasáti, wasáyati, wíhya, ; mess things up for oneself: wasát yatí'us/wasáyati'us
message (n)	wewé - speech; brief message: wéyebe
message (v)	mḱóiti - send
metal	mílda
mete out	km'ídi - share
meteor	sátoyo - falling star
method	papáyi, bó - way
metropolis	máidmm pípenak - city
Mexican	smnpánymtim máidm, pámyoli
microbe	cheméni - bacteria, germs
microphone	talk into a microphone: nákweye
microscopic	núktiluťi - very tiny
midday	ekím ésto; toward midday: ekím éstona
middle	ésto; in the middle: éstodi; in the middle of the land: ḱódo éstodi; right smack in the middle: éstoluťi; come down in the middle of: éswomit; put something in the middle: éstoti
Middle Fork of Feather River	Wuwáyonoktom Sewí
middle-aged	neyé
midget	dímenkm - dwarf
mid-life (adj)	neyé - middle-aged
midnight	pó'esto; at midnight: pó'estodi

English	Maidu
might	hápte, ai sᴍ'ᴍi, ha'ái, ma'át, mayákḱen; might be: mayáikḱen, yákkatcheti; might or might not: wínit; "might" verb constructions include the kᴍ infix, the -bᴍ verb mode, and the -nache verb mode (see Mountain Maidu Grammar, Lessons 8 and 12 for more details)
might ("may it be so")	should (future meaning), will : MMG p. 94, use -tabᴍ verb suffixes (depends on subject)
might ("possibly" or "maybe")	MMG p. 93, ma'át + mᴍni on verb, or ma'át + future ma on verb
might (be or do - present tense)	MMG p. 55, -kᴍ infix on verb with present tense
might (because of something)	would (future meaning): MMG p. 95, use -nache verb suffixes (depends on subject). This is used with -bᴍ forms in the other clause "in case" (p. 94), to show the predicted result if the "in case" part should come true.
might do (predicting)	MMG p. 94, use -bᴍ verb suffixes (depends on subject), means "might" in the main clause
might do (warning + predicting)	MMG p. 94, use -bᴍ or bᴍni verb endings (depends on subject)
mighty	ᴍhᴍ - powerful
milk	miní; to milk (an animal): minťáp; drops of milk: mínmini
milk snake	tíyani
milkweed	pumí; purple milkweed: ómpu
Milky Way	láidamlᴍlᴍm bo
mill (n)	áli - portable grinding rock
Mill Creek Indians	ḱómbom máidᴍ, bo kómbom máidᴍ
mind (doing)	okóle - be reluctant, be unwilling
mind (n)	húmit; having in mind: húweyepepe, húdan; lose one's mind: honí wi'í; having nothing in mind: húweinonwet
mindless	húboḱoipe - witless
mine (my)	niḱi
mine for gold	ódo tawál
miner's lettuce	wadákdakᴍ, yawi
mingle with	ohé - mix in (with people), be in a crowd
mining (hard rock)	ó chawáidom
mink	ṗichádaito
minnow	hálbaḱu/hálbukkᴍ; minnows: makóm tétᴍte
minor (n)	te - child
minors	yᴍ́pe - young people, teenagers
mint	osóḱᴍm bukúikᴍ, osákᴍ, hisamsaw
mirror	hínchetokᴍ
misbehave	wasá - be bad
mischief-maker	ᴍ́sṗa - rascal
miserly	méiťisa, méibonosa, húlissa
misfortune	wehépti, yehépti, yépti
mislead (seduce)	héwwelek - seduce
mislead (trick)	hálpapai - deceive, trick
misplace	boḱóiti, wonó
miss (v)	overlook: ᴍtái, betái; grab at and miss/miss a shot: sitái; be missing: wi'íye, wíye; nearly meet someone but miss each other: ᴍdémťahudoi; not miss/overlook/skip doing: wonómen
miss, yearn for	chebá, húheye; suffer the loss of: wonó
mission (target)	bodíknokᴍ - goal, target
mission, job	tawálihape
mis-speak	wéyetai
mist	ťiw
mistaken (wrong)	wasá - wrong
mistakenly	wasá
mistreat	bomᴍ́titi, katí
misunderstand	pintái
misuse	wahéno - waste (v)
mittens	matakúpno - gloves
mix (ingredients)	sín, motó; mix by hand: maní sínto; mix something in: ohéti
mix in (with people)	ohé

English	Maidu
moan	hónsap, tás; wak - cry; make someone moan (with pleasure): tásti; lie around moaning: ᴍhákinu
mob (n)	bomó - bunch, group
mobile home	uyúkkᴍm kaléta - RV
moccasin	ískal, ískalki, ískalno, bolókom soló; buckskin moccasins: wolósim 'ískali, wolósim 'ískalki, wolósim ískalno; as place name on Indian Creek: Chiwísi
model (n)	yahóiyape - first one created
modern	béidᴍk'i/béduki
Modoc	bᴍdom máidᴍ
mole	yútduli, yúnunu, yúnunukᴍ
molest	bomᴍtiti - mistreat
molt	kam, kámda
moment	tibína
momentum	lose momentum: wᴍsuisúikit
mommy	mími
money	liáni/líyani
monkey	chátchatkᴍ
monologue	deliver a monologue: wewéyebis
monsoon	kóh'bono - a great rain, storm
monster	uswúlulu - devil
month	pokó
moon	kulúm pokó, pokó, póm pokó
more	béitapo, teténa; more than: waláwdᴍkbe, waláwti; a little more than: batáschono; be more than: waláw; become a little more: béwkinu; give a little more (effort): béitapoti; some more of it: béitope; more or less: teténak tibínak; no more/no longer: tíkbe
more (comparing)	MMG p. 74
morning	béneki; earlier morning/dawn: ékda, ékdakoi; in the morning: bénekto, bénektodi; towards morning: bénektonana; the next morning: chái'im bének; get to be dawn/morning: ékdaye; start to get light (sky): yodádalchopin; to be doing at dawn: ékda; to be nearly dawn: ékdadakit
morning star	ékdam lᴍlᴍ
moron	húbokoisape - one who is witless
moronic	húkesmen - foolish, stupid
morsel	kachémeni - crumb
mortal	wónokᴍ
mortal beings	wónom máidᴍ
mortar	yókkᴍm 'ó
mortgage	humusma - debt
mortify	yepíti - cause shame
mosquito	sᴍhᴍli/suhúli
Mosquito River	Sᴍhᴍlim Sewí
moss	sosó/sᴍsᴍ; black moss: chám simí, chám siwí, eluku; green or blue-green moss: chám sosó
most	"most" is expressed by the -luť- infix on the verb (see Appendix 2) or by adding the word waláwpe "exceeding;" most of all: ᴍpékanbe... waláwpe
motel	hutél - hotel
moth	kulúm kapúslele, chí pekᴍm kápuslele, yómetsusu; woodland moth: kápuslelem mᴍkkᴍlusi
mother	né (always preceded by mᴍ, nik or min); mothers: mᴍnéwoli; bereaved mother: komám kᴍlé; parent: téťmťᴍkᴍpe; a pair including a mother: nécho; mother-in-law: péti, pétim kᴍlé; mother and daughter pair: pókᴍto, pókᴍtoto/pókitoto; doing with one's mother: nékᴍto
Mother Nature	yawónope - that which is created
motherland	hóyyam kódo - ancestral land
motivate	ma'áti - cause to do
motor	mᴍsín - machine
motorhome	uyúkkᴍm kaléta - RV
mound	yáhni - hill
mount (stairs)	ᴍdói - ascend, go up
mount for intercourse	animals only: ápbonno; humans only: yoťá
mountain	yamáni; small mountain: yamánbe; mountains: yamánmanto, yamándato; along in the mountains: yamánnodi; mountain range: yamánmanto; mountain ranges: yamánmantono; behind the mountain/at the back of the mountain: yamánim kiw

English	Maidu
mountain goat	om sɷmí
mountain lion	pekúni
mountain mahogany	siwím cha
Mountain Meadows	Óm Willium Kasdoi
mourn	lól; put soot and pitch on the cheeks as a sign of mourning: chakámti'us
mourning dove	wuiléspuikɷ
mouse	chúmbɷ; field mouse: yossó; jumping mouse: dálkumsɷmi
mouth	simí; having a big mouth: teté sínkɷpe; have the mouth hanging open: símdadaptonu, dóbabak; have the mouth closed primly: símbachaminu; have a big ugly mouth: dótʼɷinope; big mouthed: wesiki
move	tʼiyɷk, yɷ; move/change place of residence: nénkoi, nénokoi, néndoi; move or slide (as a door): kahás; move a little: tʼiyɷymk; move away from: kaʼáskoi; move something (like a door): kaʼás; move forward in a board game: ɷkóino; a move (in a game like checkers): kaʼási; move something a little bit towards: kaʼáswosipin; make something move around: tʼiyɷkti; move around a certain way: sinóyewew; move something aside for: héiyuwaito; move close to: yɷʼaswopai; move close to each other: yɷʼáswodikno; move over in a sitting position: lápsito; move down and off: yɷʼasdaw; move down across: nenasíno; move past: lélemchono; always moving/changing abodes: nénnoyesape; seldom moving/changing habitats: nénnoyebokuk
mp3 player	iPod: píntikɷ - radio
Mt. Dyer	Náka Yani, Chiwítbem Yamáni
Mt. Hough	Hunanasim Kódom
Mt. Jura	Payím Yáhni
Mt. Lassen	Tái Yamáni
Mt. Lassen Ridge	Kóm Yamánim
much	tetét, píknona; that much: kaʼánbe; not much: tĭktein, helú; be much: yépcheti
mucus	huní
mud	kúmpiťi
mud hen	bústoye
mug (v)	méhtakit - assault, rape
mugwort	múnmuni/mɷnmɷni, múnmunim sawí
mule deer	ínkayi
mule's ear	túmbakɷ; stalks of mule's ear plant: latomi
mull over	húni - consider
multiply (i.t.)	dí (intrans), díti (trans) - grow
murder (v)	wónoti - kill
murderer	wónotikɷ
muscle	waká
muscular	etóspe
mush	homá
mushroom	wá; mushroom types: poisonous: yowa, panak wa (red, groups of 4), muntu (red), ɷswálulum wá, ɷʼɷ wa; edible mushrooms: bɷchekchekɷ/be chekcheke (small, yellow, tastes sour), inkasati (big and brown, eaten in November), kolewa (small, slimy, white, eaten in November), kumle (brown, eaten in fall), polko (brown, eaten in spring), pulkati, tipi (eaten in fall), wa dáte (large, tender, white, tastes like pork), wa wuku (shelf fungus on white fir and black oak trees), welele wa/wilíliwa (cottonwood mushroom), yomén wa (eaten in spring)
music	solí - song
musical instrument	sóltikɷ; stringed instrument: wéppenkɷ
musician	sóltikɷ
muskrat	hechíhene
mussel	odóko, kodókoki
must be (future tense)	MMG, p. 95: use the -nache verb forms (depends on subject).
must be	áikate - translates as "I figure, I guess."
must be (no future meaning)	seems to be: MMG p. 95, use -yakke verb suffixes (depends on subject).
must be (present tense)	MMG p. 55, use -kɷ infix "might"
mustache	símpani
mute	be mute: wéyechɷi
muzzle	híkɷ
my	niki; by myself: níwet; at my house: níkdi
my	MMG p. 40 - possessive, nik(i)

English	Maidu
myth	betéi/betéyi
mythological	betéi - legendary
mythology	betéi - story
nab	dón - catch, dónhun - capture
nag (v)	wokótito - quarrel
nail (finger/toe)	bichí
naive	tĭkchelelepem - gullible
naked	chí wiyi, chíwi'ipe; stark naked: chíwi'iluťpe; be naked: chíwi'i
name	yá, yawí; to name someone: yakɱti; what is your name?: hesí yákupem maká? be named: yakɱ
napkin	cloth napkin: símdakɱm chi; paper napkin: símdakɱm papéli
narcissistic	yaháchetí'uspe; eḱáwche'uspe - uppity
narrate	recite, retell: betéi - recount
narrow	hadáwaitoboduk
nation	ma'a - people
nationality	ma'a - people
native land	hóyyam ḱódo - ancestral land
nature	Mother Nature, the wild: yawónope - that which is created
naughty	wasá - bad
nauseating	wemtichúti; feel nauseated: wém memé
navel	beték, ḱamím betéke
near	hedén; near/nearby: hedénna, hedénto, hédeden, ínḱidi, nak; near here: héden mɱdí, unína hedénna; from the nearby country: naḱám ḱódo; in the vicinity of: papáidi; be nearby: éswoye; get close to: ḱa'ó
neck	ḱui/ḱuiyí/ḱuyi; throat/neck: ḱulúlumi
necklace	ḱúila; wear a necklace: ḱúilai; put a necklace on someone: ḱúilaiti; necklace-wearing: ḱuilái ḱúilaipe; seashell necklace: wókkolom ḱúila
need (v)	require, do without: wi'í - lack
need to	have to, ought to, should: MMG p. 49 -s on verb, "I ought to, " -we on verb, "we ought to, " -yaha on verb, "you ought to" or use commands on p. 48-9
needle	pɱyékɱ
negate	hálcheche - contradict
neglect	ɱtai - miss, overlook
neighborhood	in one's neighborhood: yɱnóyedi; neighboring: ínḱiki; be in the neighborhood of: wochóno
nephew	kamí; nephews: kamím wolí/mɱkámimwoli
nest	ťɱťɱ/ťuťú; build a nest: ťɱťɱti
net	biní, témbini; to fish using nets: momhɱ; catch fish in nets: humín, momhɱ́koḱoi; go fishing with nets: momhɱḱói (RD)/momhɱ́ḱoi (WS); to stretch a net across to catch (animals): mikchíkti; net trap: támbini
Nevada City	Ustumá, Tetema
never	"never" is expressed by verb + men + kɱm with the verb kɱḱán.
never (have done)	MMG p. 65, "usually" forms of the verb with -men infix
never (is or does)	use -menkɱ infixes on verb or -menkɱm adjective suffix, túimenkɱm ni - "I am one who never sleeps"
nevertheless	awét ma'át, amám ma'át
Nevis (under Lake Almanor)	Chám Bokini, Si'ápkɱ/Sihápkɱ
new	béidɱk'i
newfangled	béduki - modern
news item	wéyebe - brief message
next	chái'im; the next day: mɱm bének; you go next: míḱuni; next door: obɱ́chopindi
next to	lédi; next to each other: ínḱiki
nick, cut by nicking	kadés
niece	kamím kɱlé
night	pó, kulú, kulúm ekí; last night/tonight/at night: kulúdi; middle of the night: kulúm ésto; every night: kakánim po; all night long: pótapo; get to be night time: kulúnanna
night hawk	sɱ́mpupa/súmpupa
nightfall	kulúnanna
nightgown	túichikɱ
nightingale	píyutkɱ
nine	mámchuiyi

English	Maidu
nipple	miním onó, miním óschumi
Nisenan	tánkm, tánkmma, tánkmm máidm
nitwit	húbokoisape - one who is witless
no	wíiye/wíye; say 'No': wíyekana
no matter when	hesántenuwet - sometime
nod off	túiwopno
noise	yohón; make noise: yohón, héwpinti, yohónto, mohḿtwono; make a lot of noise: mohḿtwonowikoi, yepínti, yepíntiti; make noise as children playing: héwkinu; with a loud noise: tetédmkm; not let children make noise: héwkinutimen; resume activity making more noise: mohḿhmtdoi; do more noisily: mohḿhmtnoti; noisily make one's way somewhere: wmtḿswoye
nomadic	nénnoyesape
none	wi'í - not exist
none, no one	sḿtim (with negative verb): sḿtim pínmenkan "no one heard."
non-native bush	wólek dm
nonsense	húbokoi; nonsense!: hokóttisa!
normal	be normal: ma'áwew
normally	ekm - usually
north	chan, kódom chánna, bḿda, kódom beléw, tosí (FC), nóto (SP); to the north: beléwdi, tosína, kódom chándi, kódom chanantedi; northern: bḿdam máidm; northern people: msítopinim máidm, notom ma'a; north wind: bḿdawi
North Arm	Hópnom, Hópnom Koyó
northwest	chan, kódom chánna, kódom chándi; to the northwest: kódom chanantedi, kódom chánna
nose	híkm
nosebleed	híkm póp
not (do)	MMG p. 56, -men infix on verb
not comply	cháitika - be different
not feel like	okóle - be reluctant, be unwilling
not guilty	hesámenkm - innocent
not make sense	húbokoi - make no sense
not pass (a test)	wi'íye - fail
nothing	hésiki (with negative verb), iská; sitting around doing nothing: mpé bísdom; it is nothing: wíyekan mpé, mením kmkán; nothing of any kind: hesím beté (with negative verb); nothing but: hesátimwet; do for nothing: mpékayew; I have nothing to say: wéye wí'ikas bei
notice	notice and comment: chewé; be noticing: aichénew
noun	yá - name
nourish	pekḿti - feed
now	bei, béiki, béidmk; right now: béidmktapo; nowadays/even up to now: udó; by now: achéknu; from now on: uní wóinan, uní woyím, unínan; up to now: achéki
nozzle	okéli - hose nozzle
nucleus	ésto - middle
nude	chí wiyi - naked
nudge	hmkḿsto; nudge with elbow: hmkḿs
number	written number(s): hemmák balím; a certain number of: ka'ánbenini; that number of: ka'ándukbe
nurse (as a baby)	mintáp
nuthatch	hékekkm
nuts	kokó/kókkm
nylons	íschomi - socks
oak tree	útim cha; black oak: hámsim chá; scrub oak: busúlim hámsi; blue oak: chakom cha; valley oak: chakom cha, wáksapem hámsim chá, lóm cha; live oak: babákmm cha, wihám cha, óm hámsim cha; huckleberry oak: katukpu
object (n)	wasása - thing
objective (goal)	bodíknokm - goal, target
obscure (v)	kilé - hide (something)
observe (holiday)	bmyím motó - celebrate; wéda - celebrate the big time
obsidian	bosó; sharp obsidian: tókpem bosó; worked obsidian: ínyanam bosó; to work obsidian: bosó tawál
obsolete	hésmeni; kéi - old
obstinate	ḿhm - stubborn
obstruct	etápti, yosánoti - stop something

English	Maidu
obtain	méito - buy; mé - get, take
occasion	mmotope - event
occasionally	léiwonini - sometimes, once in a while
occupy	mbis
occur to, realize	húni, húmit - recall
occur, happen	mahélu
ocean	tetém mómdanni, tetétluťim mómdanni
oddball (n)	ka'ámenim máidm - strange person
odd-looking	cháichetipe
odor	scent: híssa - smell
of	possessive ending, belonging to, 's: MMG p. 23 -k or -ḱi on noun
of course	hapá
off (as in "go off")	MMG p. 55, -daw or -ḱoi infix on verb
offbeat	cháitikapem
officer	dónkmm máidm - police (n)
off-white	edáldalnope - light (colored)
often	píninu
ogle	cheḱón - gaze at
ointment	yútokmm wené - liniment
OK	héw, héwma'aḱan, su; is it OK?: héwma'aḱade? yahá'ade?
OK (adj)	ámbmḱbm - good enough
old	old (of people): nenó, nenópe; old man: waisí; old woman: kmlókbe; elderly: nenóhno; old (of things): kéi, hésmen, héda; get old (women): kmlókbekbedoi; get old (people): nenó; How old are you: hesánbem ḱúmmenim okítpem maḱá? be old (things): ebmdom; be somewhat old (things): hédada; old man coyote: wépam wáisi; older (of siblings): hínwonope, hínwono; oldest: hínwono, nenóluť; get older (as a child): tetébe
olden times	beté; in the olden times: hóyyam ḱódodi, betémemenkmdi, betémen; people from the olden times: hóiymm máidm, kéi'im máidm; old-time (adj): betéitodi'im; be in the olden times: betémen
old-fashioned	betéi'i - ancient (adj)
OMG, oh my god!	hes ha'ái!
on	"on" is expressed by the -di suffix on nouns or the -ťa suffix on verbs: tébmldi "on the table," bénťa "step on;" be clustered on (as flies): halúḱup
on	to (place), in, at: MMG p. 23, -di on noun or pronoun
on (doing on)	MMG p. 56, -ťa infix on verb
on occasion	léiwonini - sometimes, once in a while
on the way	mnókmdi - on the way going along
once	"once" (meaning "after" or "since" in a subordinate clause) is expressed by the -chet suffix on verbs: "once he had finished leaving...": mḱóiboschet; "one time:" smtibe, smttini; once long ago: hóyyam, hóiyam ḱódodi; once upon a time there was: ḱan bíschoi'a; only once: smttim dmḱm; once in a while: léiwonini; even once: smtunima'át (with verb in -men means "never once"); once you do (it): anímchet
once	after, since (something happened): MMG p. 85, -chet or -weten suffix on verbs. -chet changes the subject in the next clause, -wet keeps the same subject
one	smti/smtti; as one: wmkdi; the very one: tené; one time: smttini; one of you: mínsmm smti; all but one: bóschet smti; every single one: smtim ma'át; for each one: smtiti; one who is not: maméni
oneself	by oneself: mm dmḱm, dmḱm; do something all by oneself: ka'ádmtm; look inside oneself: uschenu
oneself	do to/for oneself, self-: MMG p. 54, -'us infix on verb
onion	papuli/papmle, edi; a type of onion, eaten raw: chanputi, wolabmkm
only	pikno (especially for prepositional phrases and adverbs like tetét), dmḱm (especially for nouns and verbs), mpé, hesátmet; only then: mmmméndmḱm
oops!	ni!
open	púl, hupék, púlkit; open a place in the fire: héyuwaito/héiyuwaito; open up a place: yuwáwaito; open a door: púlkm púlkitpi, ka'áskoi, ka'áspin, kaháspin; open the hand: má leléwaito, smwáiti/sowáiti, tókwaito; open the eyes: wikmkmi; open the eyes a little: wilmlwo'aito; be left open (door): púlkinu; open up (hand): smwái, benékwaito
open space	ka'ásḱoikm
opening (n)	mnó - function or run
operate (i.t.)	batánokm - driver
operator	

372

English	Maidu
oppose	ónkokoi, ónkokoito - compete, disagree with each other
opposite	obmasito, obmchono, obm'asdoino, u; opposite from: obm'aschono; the opposite side: ucháni; in the opposite direction: cháinantedi; on the opposite side: obmchopindi; to the opposite side: obmi'chonodi
or	ma'át...ma'át..., ai sm'mi... ai sm'mi..., ai
orange	owánchi
orate	túwei, wewéi
orator	túweykm
order	order (someone) to do: mákpaiti; get things in order: yaháti; ápe - ask for
ordinance	ma - law (n)
ordinarily	ekm - usually
Oregon grape	pompomi
Oregon junco	pachititi
organize	yaháti; file (v), put away, pack up, put back: hésbopai - pack things up, put back in its place
orgasm (v)	pópti - ejaculate
orientation	bó - way
orifice	ka'áskoikm - opening (physical)
originate (tr)	púksito - bring about; hukít - create using thought
oriole	sewíspolotka
Oroville	Koyómkawi
orphan	kulái/kolái, kúlupem té; orphans: kuláiwoli; orphan girl: kúlusa; be orphaned: kúlu
oscillate	dmymym - shake, tremble (i.t.)
ostracize	batásip - drive out, chase out
other	chái/chái'i, kayí; others: chacháyi; other side: batás, michan; on the other side: chánaki; other place: u
otherwise	hesámet - on the contrary, or húkoi - still, yet
otter	mompáno
ought to	you ought to: yahá (suffix on verb); I ought to: -s or -si suffix on verb; you ought to make something: hesátiyahá; you ought to go: mnóyaha; I ought to go: mnósi
ought to	should, need to, have to: MMG p. 49 -s on verb, "I ought to, " -we on verb, "we ought to, " -yaha on verb, "you ought to" or use commands on p. 48-9
ounce	kachémeni - crumb
our	MMG p. 40 - possessive, depends on how many people are involved in "our"
our people	niséma
out	out of: MMG p. 56, -sip infix on verb
outdo (beat)	ónkoi - come out on top, beat, outsmart
outdo (exceed)	waláw - exceed
outer space	lmlmm máidmdi - at the home of the star men
outfit (n)	chí - clothes
outfox	ónkoi - come out on top, beat, outsmart
outhouse	pitím uyí, tibím uyí
outmaneuver	ónkoi - outsmart
outreach	wéyetodom
outrun	tókda; outrun each other (be tied in a race): tókdatoto; be outrun: tókdati'us
outside	púiyadi, púidi; the place outside: pui; towards the outside: púiyana; from the outside: púiyanan
outsider	obmdaw; foreigner: koyói - stranger
outskirts	wo'áswono - on the outskirts
outsmart	ónkoi, ónkoito; outsmart multiple people: ónkokoito
outstanding	yaháhaluti - the best
outstrip	waláw - exceed
outwit	ónkoi - outsmart
oven	ótokma
over (above)	epíni
over (action over something)	around (action going over or around an obstacle): MMG p. 55, -chono infix on verb; go down over: mchópin
over (going over/across)	across (going across): MMG p. 56, -sito infix on verb
over and over	madóm mpékadom; do over and over: awébisim, mpékanu
over one's head	hadá - deep
overcast	be overcast: yáku
overcome	ónkoi, ónkoito; overcome several obstacles: ónkokoito

English	Maidu
overcooked	k̓ápsito
overflow (v)	mómbochono - flow over
overhang (v)	hang over (something): opíninu - hang out, stick out; sm, smdáw - protrude
overlay (v)	húl, ban - spread, put over, cover over
overlook	mtái, betái; not overlook/miss: wonónomen, mtáimenwet
overlooking	chepítwono - facing towards
overnight	stay overnight: uyúk/myúk
overnight bag	hadóikm - suitcase
overpass	yakm̂ - bridge
overpriced ($)	hélmono - expensive, high in price
overshoot	sitái - miss a shot, grab at and miss
overtake	batápai
overthrow	ónk̓oi - come out on top, beat, outsmart
overturn (i.t.)	wmpm̂lamto - roll over
owe	hmm̂smanu
owl	great horned owl/big owl: m̂kkmlmsi/mmkmlúsi; screech owl: popópkm; burrowing owl: kúk̓ú; pygmy owl: wáspololo
owner	expressed by the noun + kupe or kmpe: kalétakupe "car owner;" mutútu - master (of a pet)
pace	bilísi - speediness
pack (bundle)	a pack: hadó; pack belongings: yaháhati, hésbopai, hésbobopai; pack in bundles for carrying: hákwowopapai; pack in a sack: hayápapai
pack (group)	bomó - bunch, group
pack up	hésbopai - pack things up, put back in its place
package	pékuchi, budú
packet	budú - package
pain	ítu; give pain: ítu; a pain in the side: chichím bmmím 'ítu; cause a little pain: ítuhtuti; the cause of pain: ítunok
paint	to paint: bal, dóbap; paint designs or pictures: bálti; paint stripes: kólokito; paint white stripes: smdáldalino; put on white ceremonial paint: sidádalino; white paint: dúbat, dúbap; balikm - dye (n)
Paiute	tólomma, t̓olómmam máidm, t̓oló eskochim máidm
pajamas	túichikm - nightgown
palm, sole	t̓át̓a; palm of hand: mám t̓át̓a
pan for gold	ódo tawál
panhandle	hápe, ápe - ask for
panic	to cause panic by making noise: wisétyahátpinti
pansy	pmkkm̂
pant (as dog)	léhle
pants	páitolo; put on pants: páitolo
pantyhose	íschomi - socks
papa	táta
paper	papéli; use paper: papélni; write on paper: papélkit; paper shredder: papélim wa'áitikm
paradise	epínim koyó - heaven
paragraph	léiwo - part
parboil	hom - boil, stew
parcel (land)	k̓awí - land; k̓oyó - field
parcel (load)	hadó - load
parcel (package)	budú - package
parch	p̓ik̓álti - dry (tr)
pardon (v)	sówono - let someone go
pare	pum, yat̓a - peel (v)
parent	tét̓m̂t̓mkmpe; be a parent: tét̓m̂t̓mkm; parent and child pair: tékmto
park (i.t.)	hakínu - be parked, be in a place
parsnip	mowasó (RD), momwasó (JD)
part of	léwo/léiwo; part of the world: k̓ódom beléw; become part of something and let it carry up: wmkkánuhadóino
partake	dómaki - have a taste
particle	kachémeni - crumb
particles	cheméni, p̓ibáwi
particular	sm̂ti - certain
parting (n)	mk̓óida - departure
partition	én - wall

374

English	Maidu
partner	bené'ekm - helper
partners	wosíkmtoto - cousins, associates
party (dance)	wetém - dance (n)
party, group	bomó
pass (n)	a pass in the mountain or river: msíto, bówochono
pass (time)	wosíp - spend (time)
pass (v)	mwála; pass quickly: lélemchono, mlém, mlémno; pass over quickly: mlélemchono
pass away	wónoda
pass something to	soyá, sóye
past (in distance)	wodóino - beyond, other side of
past tense	-ed ending: MMG p. 28, 63-67 - depends on tense and subject
past times	hóiya - formerly
paste	dak - glue
pasture	koyó - meadow
patch (n)	wmndm
path	bó, wochóno, papáyi; on the path of: mnókmdi; next to the path: bóminki
pathetic	bommtipe - pitiful
pattern	yahóiyape - first one created
pause (n)	etúweti; recess, intermission: chedá - break
pause (v)	take a break: chedá - rest (v); hesitate: etúdede - wait a little bit
Paviotso	ťolómmam máidm
paw	má; to paw at someone: bamák
pay	pakál; pay back: pakályewei; pay restitution for (crime): koyó
pay a visit	chenókoi - visit (v)
pay attention	not pay attention to: pinhéhenon; paying no attention: ánwet
pay attention to	chikáta - focus on, watch intently
pay back	reimburse, refund (v): pakályewei - repay
pay no attention	chenúkoimen - not pay attention
payload	hadó - load
peaches	píchms
peak (n)	chuchúi - summit, top
peak of bark house	oťámoto
pear	péya
peas	pís
pebble(s)	óbeťmťm; good-luck pebble: ómsulu
peck	bó; peck each other: bókito; peck as woodpecker: bódato; peck out (eyes): bókkol; peck a hole through: bepélkoi
peddle	sél - sell
pedestal	tébmli - table
peek	kḿi; take a peek: kḿiche; peek in: okḿkmino; peek down in: okḿkminpin; peek through: okḿi, okḿisito; peek out of (an opening): okḿkmsip; peek down through: okḿkmin; peek down secretly: ka'okḿkmino
peel (n), peeling	pumi, púmpu, púmpumi
peel (v)	pum, yaťa
peep-hole	pḿmbel, pḿnkeli
peer at from close range	okḿkoidikno
pelican	hinumi; white pelican: ehómi
pellet (ammo)	nokó - arrow
pelt	po - hide, skin
pelt down (rain)	taiyái'aluť
pelvis	máwam bmmí - hipbone
pen	bálkm, papélkm, papélkítkm
pencil	bálkm, papélkm, papélkítkm
penis	kosí, chuchúkm, ḿhm; child's term for penis: chúmbmbe; get rid of a penis: ḿhwono; head of the penis: kosím 'okéli
pennyroyal	bukúikm/bmkúikm, bmkḿkmm sawí
people	máidm, máidmmnono (subject), máidmnono (object), ma'a, máidmse
pepper	teťép, titipi
peppermint	tímsawi, lukúm tímsawi
Pepsi	súda - soda
perceive	hmbḿk - feel
perched on	be perched on: lápťanu
percussion instrument	wátdakm - clapper stick

English	Maidu
perforate	sᴍháw - pierce; wiḱél
perform	ma - accomplish
performance	sú
performer	ma'ákᴍ
performer (music)	sóltikᴍ - musician
perhaps	ai sᴍ'ᴍi
period (menstrual)	ᴍdáw
permanently	ᴍpéḱnudom - continually
permit (v)	méi - allow
perpetual	wónomen - immortal
perpetually	ᴍpéḱnudom - continually
perpetuate	yaché - keep, save back
persecute	yáhpatchono, yáhpatwéḱoi - go after to attack; bomᴍtiti - mistreat
person	máidᴍ
personal property	wasása, hesí - things
pester	wokótito - quarrel; sᴍkála - bother
pestilence	ítukᴍ
pestilential	ítukpe
pestle	álim o, sᴍné/suné, suném o
pet	sᴍ́; keep as a pet: sᴍ́don, sᴍ́ya; to pet affectionately: báslem
petite	nᴍs - low (adj)
petroglyph	hóiyam máidᴍm ódi balí
petticoat	ḱanáyim ínkᴍl
pew (n)	bísťakᴍ - bench
phantom	uswúlulu - ghost
phoebe (bird)	pam beché'okᴍ
phone call	míldan ḱúḱ; make a phone call: míldan ḱúḱti
physique	lulú - body
pick (guitar)	wéppem - strum
pick a fight	hokótito - argue with
pick up	pick something up: yᴍmᴍ́doi; pick someone up: sowíḱado; pick up off the ground: méwiḱadoi, chᴍ́wikadoi; start to pick up (something): bᴍyᴍ́kdoi; pick up and carry off: sódoi, soháoino; pick up onto one's back: ápdoi
pick up	sóiwino, sóiyo - fetch
pick, select, gather	hᴍ́, hᴍ́ye; pick/choose a person: woiyó; pick out: bᴍyᴍ́ksip; go pick: hᴍ́ḱoi; go pick for: hᴍ́noti, hᴍ́ḱoiti; go around picking: hᴍ́noye, hᴍ́no; go off to pick for a while: hᴍ́ḱoiyew; I'm not picking you: mínmeni ka'as
pickpocket	pedákᴍ - thief
pickup truck	hadóikᴍm kaléta - truck
picnic (n)	bᴍi - feast (n)
picture (v)	huhéye - imagine
picturesque	eḱáwchetipe - beautiful
piece	okᴍ́tno; small piece: okᴍ́tnobe; a cut-off piece: hudáwdo; to cut up in small pieces: tibíbitidom wiyᴍ́l; cause to be in many small pieces: tibíbiti
pied-bill grebe	wakdᴍ
pierce	bihít, sᴍháw, bó; pierce with needle-like object: bidít; pierce the earlobe: bonó sᴍháwkit, sᴍháwkit; thrust/pierce: hil; pierce the nose: híkᴍ sᴍháwkit
pig	ᴍskᴍ/óski, kóchi
pigeon	háni, ahóni
pigment	balikᴍ - dye
pile	a pile: wulúti; to pile: wulút, wutúl; pile stuff together: hésbohamoto; pile stuff up: wu, wulútdoi; pile up a bunch of things: wutúlyo, yaiyókit/yayókit, yaiyókitye; pile up firewood: chá wulút; pile things by throwing over: yáiyochopin
pileated woodpecker	mákmakᴍ, lákono
pilfer	pedá - steal
pillage	wasáti - mess up, ruin
pillow	oḱénkᴍ, ḱanáikᴍ; feather pillow: yem oḱén; pillow case: oḱénkum wadápi
pilot light	toyákᴍtikᴍ
pimp	witáḱam máidᴍ, witáḱana yépsᴍ hóiwihayetikᴍm máidᴍ
pimple	pᴍní; pimply: pᴍ́ntapo
pin	cháwo; to pin something on: bidítpai
pinch (v)	ḱí; pinch something closed: ḱídumchekín; pinch affectionately: sᴍkásai
pinch (n)	kachémeni - crumb

English	Maidu
pincushion	bidítpaikʌ, pʌyékʌ bidítpaikʌ
pine cone	hínkakala
pine grosbeak	bám chiti
pine nut	lilí; sugar pine nut: sumú
pine squirrel	tʌlʌlʌ/tulúli
pine tree	bʌbʌ́m chá, watoktiti; ponderosa or Jeffrey pine: bʌbʌ́, bʌbʌ́m chá; sugar pine: sumú; lodgepole pine: wálum cha, welé, welém cha; gray pine: towáni, towánim cha
pinemat manzanita	ḱawídano
pintail duck	tulúpi, likʌ
pint-sized	nʌs - low (adj)
pipe (plumbing)	lumí - tube
pipe (smoking)	pánpetokʌ
piss ant	pʌchʌ́mi, hísampʌno
pistol	pístola
pit (n)	ḱumí - hole; ḱumpʌ́nno - hole in the ground
Pit River (tribe)	kóm máidʌ, odókpepe, odókpepem máidʌ
pitch (n)	chaká; pitchy: chakámni, chakámdʌḱdʌ́kpe; just pitch: chakámdʌḱʌ; put pitch on oneself in mourning: chakámti'us; get pitch on (something): chakámpai; get pitch on oneself: chakámpaiti'us; get something covered with pitch: chakámťapoti
pitch (v)	wʌdʌ́m - throw
pitiful	bomʌ́ti, bomʌ́tipe; very pitiful: bomʌ́titi
pity (v)	bomʌ́mʌkno
pivotal	tetébe - bigger, largest
place (location)	ḱódo/ḱódoi, ḱokó, uní, naḱí; dwelling place: bisí; this place: uní, nada; in this place: upédi, unídi; at a place: yʌ́di; from a place: yʌ́nan; from this place: unína; in the same place as before: mʌkándi; in the place where one travels: yʌnóyedi; in the place one was told about: mákpaitipedi; in a place a certain distance away: tǐkteḱóidi; a very beautiful place: chelúťnak; a place where someone was: bisyéwonope; in the place where they were made to live: bískʌmtikoidi; to/in a faraway place: ántedi; to that place (previously mentioned): amána; from that place (previously mentioned): amánan, amánankan; from that place: anínan; in that place: anídi; to that place: anína; the place where someone wants to go: ʌnóyahape; be in a place: hakínu, bís, u
place (v), put	hayá
place to live	hʌbó - house
Placerville	Indak
plain (looking)	be not so good-looking: yahátchetiboduk
plan	have a plan: makkíti; plan something together: húsemweteyo
planet	poḱó - heavenly body
plant	linó; small edible plants: pʌkʌ́; green plants: sawí; plants in the carrot family: chuluwa piwí, solamwene, buchiwi; varieties of Queen Anne's lace (WS): pʌlʌ́t, sokóm; unidentified berry plants: waihá, seléwwa, yupúppupi; unidentified plants whose roots are boiled and eaten: ḱé, wáipolo; a mountain herb: yamánim bʌkúike; redbell: púsle; a part of plants, possibly the stalk: latumi; See also individual plant, e.g. rose, lilac, etc.
plastered	hudásu - drunk
plastic	pilástiki/pʌlástiki
plate	waťá; maple basketry plate: daṕím waťá
platform	yaḱʌ́ - bridge
play (adult) games	gamble: helái, heláiye; play handgame: sútto; be seated and ready to gamble: halémmemmoto; play horseshoes: sʌ́mpaito
play (as children)	téte; go play: tétekoi, téteno; play around: teténoye; make noise while playing: héwkinu; playmate: tibíbe; be hearing children play: téteweḱoiyew
play a trick on	hálpapai - trick, deceive
play hooky	wi'íye - not be there, be missing
play it safe	óḱket - be careful
play music	play music or a musical instrument: sólti; play the flute: yálulu; play the flute on and on: yáluluwebis; play the violin: ílimto; not be able to play (an instrument) well: sóltiwasa
play the fiddle	ílimto - play violin
plead loudly	pelíptonu
pleasant	yahát hubúktipe
please (do)	hénte

English	Maidu
please (do)	MMG p. 48-49 verb forms
please oneself	yahát hubúkti'us
pleased	yahát hubúktipe
pledge (v)	méi - give
Pleiades constellation	dótodoto
plenty	wém
plot (n)	ḱawí - land
plot to	húyeti - intend to
pluck	wipól
plug (n)	wusutikɷ - stopper
plug (v)	insert as plug: ḱadópchik
plum	ḱasi, pɷlɷ́m; plum tree: ḱasím cha
plume (regalia)	díhyo
plunge (v)	yókit - dive down; ɷ́n, ɷ́t - descend
plural	pi - many
pneumonia	hóntustusi - coughing sickness
poach	hom - boil, stew
pocket	wólsa
pod	ḱokó - seed
point (n)	sɷ́ti - one
point (of time)	mɷmén - at that point in time
point of departure	ḱabɷ́ḱ - start (n), beginning (n)
point the way	héw - point in the right direction
point with the finger	sɷḱét/siḱét; point here and there: sɷḱétnoye; point down at: sɷkéketkit; point around at things (while explaining): hewakátnoye; point around in different directions/point things out: héwakátnoye; point out surrounding areas: hewakaktímoto; point in the right direction (guide): hew
pointed (adj)	ťok - sharp
poison	petí (noun); to poison: wasóiti/wasóti; get poisoned: wasói; poisoner: wasóitikɷ
poison oak	small spriggy kind: chutáḱa/chiťóḱ, bushy kind: popósi, posí; poison oak bush: popósim pá; have the poison oak rash: chiťóḱ
poke	bɷyóti; keep poking: bɷyódatoti; perforate: wiḱél; poke around in things: hésbonoye; fire poker: sɷsɷ́
poker game	put chips in: wótnoti
pole (beam)	hɷ́mtɷti - beam (n), rafter
police	dónkɷm máidɷ, máidɷ donkɷ
politician	yepóni - chief
pomegranate	kulanabeli
pond	pakáni
ponder	áiḱaḱat
Ponderosa Pine	bɷbɷ́; ponderosa pine tree: bɷbɷ́m chá/babɷ́m cha/bubúm cham
pool	pakáni
poorly	MMG p. 57, use -was infix on verb
pop (v)	póp, pópti, pɷ́pḱoi; pop out: pɷ́psip; pop up: pɷ́p
pop (n)	súda - soda
pop in on	chenóḱoi - visit (v)
pop up	chebɷ́k, chebɷ́kdoi - appear
poppy	California poppy: tapɷ́kɷ
populated area	máidɷm pípenak
porcupine	choní/chaní, sɷ́pa; pet porcupine (or woodchuck): sɷ́pam sɷ
pork	kóchi - pig
porridge	bukúm yokó
port (USB, etc.)	pɷ́nno - cavity
portion (food)	pená - serving
portion (part)	léiwo - part of
position (n)	tawáli - work
position (v)	position (someone): tɷ́sdiknoti
possess	kɷ/ku
possessions	wasása - stuff
possessive ending	belonging to, of, 's: MMG p. 23 -k or -ḱi on noun
possibly	ma'át - maybe
post (building support)	main post of the dance house: sɷdóko (RD)/sudoḱo (WS)
post (message)	ɷkóiti - send

English	Maidu
post (v)	chewéto - testify about
post office	papélim uiyí
postcard	papélimbe - playing cards
post-contact times	wóleimen
posterior	kíwdi - at the back; ínno - buttocks
postman	papéli hanᴧnokᴧm máidᴧ
postpone	etúti - cause to wait
pot roast	ítus - roast (n)
potato	wólem poyó, potéto; Indian potato: wai, wuiléspuikᴧm yo
potent	ᴧhᴧ́ - powerful
potluck	bᴧi - feast (n)
pound (as the heart)	wi'íhudai
pound (v)	tómdan -hit making a sound; wó, wódato -hit with an instrument
pound into a powder	yók, hihí; pound up fine: hihíluť
pour	pour down into: wádᴧmit; pour (liquid) in: hítkit; pour dry material into: wámit; pour dry material out of: wásip; pour water on/over: momwasipťa; pour towards by magic power: wáiwotopin
pour in (i.t.)	mombomít - flow, flood (v), flow down into
powder	tᴧ, dus, baťí
powerful	ᴧhᴧ́; be powerful: épti
powerless	etósmen - weak
powwow	ᴧ́mmotope - event, get-together
practice (v)	wéyetoti
prairie dog	chichikᴧ, kitkitkᴧ
praise	penóweye
prance around	tóihlalaino
prawn	tulí - shrimp
pray	túweye
pray for	yomó - hope for
prayer	túweye; one who says a prayer: túweykᴧ
preach	túwei
preacher	túwei - preach
precaution	take special precautions: ókketwono
precipice	síteḱ
precipitation	ḱadíki - rain (n)
precisely	haṕá
predict	ayáwe
prefabricated	yabóspe
preface (n)	hínwonope - ahead, in front of
prefer	sᴧ́ssᴧ
pregnant	tékupe, potáyamno; be pregnant: téha, téhadoi, téku/tékᴧ, tékᴧma; get someone pregnant: tékᴧti
prehistoric times	betéihuki - the ancient world, after humans were created
pre-made	yabóspe
prepare (something)	sᴧkéswo, yaháti; prepare food: yaháti, sikés/sᴧkés, hesbáp, pewíhakit, pewíkakit; prepare food for: sikéstido; prepare meat (skinning, drying, etc): sikéyo, yaháhati; be prepared (food)/cooked: yaháhanu
prepare oneself	yaháhati'us - get ready
prepared (adj)	ḱáptipem - ready, ripe
preposterous	hokótisape - ridiculous
presage	húpai - foresee
present, attending	be present: okítnoye
present-day (adj)	béduki - modern
presently	tibínak - soon
preserve (v)	yaché - keep, save back; mayá - save back conserve
president	yepóni - chief
presumably	áite, áiḱate
pretend to	"pretend to" is expressed by the -ḱuḱus infix on verbs (see Appendix 2): pretend to know: makítḱuḱus
pretty	yaháchetipe, yahátcheno; very pretty: ᴧḱáwchetipe/eḱáwchetipe
prevent	wás - forbid
previous	hínwom - ahead
previously	hóiya - formerly
price (n)	yawí - cost

English	Maidu
pricey	hélmono - expensive, high in price
prick (something)	bᴍhᴀ́k, bᴍhᴀ́m
prickle	íchem - sting (i.t.), tingle
primarily	hesátmet - just, only, nothing but
prime (adj)	hínwom - first, ahead of, older (adj)
principal (n)	yep̓óni - chief
prior	hínwom - ahead
probably	ha'ái; probably be: bíshelu
probably be	bíshelu - likely to be
problem	misfortune: yépti, wehépti; any problem: hesáte; intentionally cause problems: matí
procreate	puk̓ - give birth
procure (buy)	méito - buy
procure (get)	mé - get, take
prod (v)	bᴍlók, bohóp - shove
produce (v)	yatí - create
produce offspring	puk̓, kᴍkít
producer	ma'ákᴍ
profound	hadá - deep
progenitor	hóyyam máidᴍ - ancestor
prohibit	wás - forbid
project (v)	sᴍ, sᴍdáw - protrude
projection	bichí - thorn
prolong	t̓éstimen
prom	wetém - dance (n)
prong (n)	p̓aká - branch
propaganda	polópokanda
propagate	púk̓sito - bring about
propel	bᴍlók, bohóp - shove
proper	betéitodi'im- traditional, one who is traditional; correct (adj): yahá - right (adj)
property	tract, lot, real estate, acreage, plot (n), parcel: k̓awí - land
prophesy (v)	ayáwe - predict; húpai - foresee
pros and cons	hónsaweye - argument
prosper	yahát yatí'us - do well for oneself
prostitute	witáka, witákam kᴍlé, welénokᴍm kᴍlé, héiyetokᴍm kᴍlé
prostrate ceanothus	humchi
prototype	yahóiyape - first one created
protrude	sᴍ, sᴍdáw; be protruding: sᴍsínu; be protruding like porcupine quills; be sticking out: opíninu
provide	méi, méito - give, give out
provide food for	pekᴀ́ti
provoke	matí - cause, do (something) to
pry open	hédas - crack open
puberty	reach puberty (girls): yᴀ́pᴍ; reach puberty (boys): máidᴍ; girls' puberty rites: mak̓á, dónkato, yᴀ́pᴍkato; girls' puberty rites song: mak̓ám solí, yᴀ́pᴍm solí; a girl who has just reached puberty: dómi; be the age for the puberty dance: wetémhoiyapa
pubic hair	female pubic hair: pᴍsím butú, pᴀ́sbu/pᴀ́sbᴍ; male pubic hair: kosím butú, kósbu
public speaker	túweykᴍ - orator
pull	wipól; pull a long, stem-like object: wiháp; pull something flat and cloth-like: widán; pull at: wikú; pull along: hak̓ói; sort of pull on: wikúku; pull down: héchapdaw, wichápdaw; pull loose: widák; pull off: widókdaw, héchap; pull out: wikᴀ́pdoi, wipólsip; pull up over: wihúl; pull something over oneself: wihúlt̓a'us; pull up clothes: húldoi; pull up: widói, wihúldoi; pull up something (like a blanket): widándoi; pull up a long, stem-like object: wihápdoi; pull up from a flat surface: wibákdoi; pull someone up by grabbing under the arms: hánwidoi
pulsate	as the heart: halᴀ́k, lᴀ́kwebis
pulse	feel the pulse: sᴍk̓áw
pulverize	yók, hihí - grind to powder
pumice	yamánim sedém - lava
pump (n)	mómpoldoitikᴍ
puncture (v)	sᴍháw - pierce

380

English	Maidu
punish	wasáyati - make things bad for
purchase (v)	méito - buy
purpose (goal)	bodíknokɱ - goal, target
pursue	héi, yapát, héidoi, hédatpai, bínmeye; pursue persistently: hédakpai; pursue in water: yo'ɱhésitoye; pursuer: bínmedoipe; one who does not pursue people: bínmenɱímenkɱ
pus	kopé; to ooze pus: kopé, kopékit
push	bɱlók, ḱadót, ḱatá; push with the hand/arm: widót; push against: ḱadótdikno; push into: sɱpól, sɱpólno; push out: hasíp, sidópsip; push along: haḱói, ḱatáno; push apart: ḱatáwaito; push away: ḱadótḱoi; push something back: sóyewe; push under: ḱadútkit; push something all the way in: bɱlókdikno; push something all the way into: bɱlókdiknoti
pussy-whipped man	pɱskusum máidɱ/pɱskusim máidɱ
put	yɱmɱ́, kɱ́, utí, utíyo, hayá; put something into: heyá, bóno, hedói, wowómit, yɱmɱ́chono; put in fire: sakɱ́nno, sakɱ́ṭa; put in an orifice, like pierced earlobes: ḱapól, sɱḱóiti, sɱyáwkito; put under/behind (a belt): yehétchono; put down: wokít, hekít, bɱsɱ́p, yɱmɱ́kit; put down into: hápmit, wákit, yɱdɱ́mitno, yɱmɱ́tno; put things down: yayókit; put something back: hésbopai; put something back in: heyá; put something over (like a blanket): ban; put over on the other side: yɱmɱ́'asito; put together: motó; put something under the head while lying down: onúk; where it was put: utípedi; where you put it: mínḱi utípedi; put out a fire: bukúitida; put out food (for people): wokíkit; put (wood) on (the fire): momít
put aside	yaché - keep, save back
put away, put back	hésbopai - pack things up, put back in its place
put down	hokót - ridicule
put in order	yaháti - organize
put off	etúti - cause to wait
put on (the body)	put on clothes: chí; put on shoes: soló, put shoes on someone else: bolóḱtiwo; bolóḱti; put on a hood: onúkno; put on pants: páitolo; put on bands (regalia): bopóṭati; put on full regalia: hesúpai; put on feather ornaments: silépai; put feather ornaments on someone else: silépaiti; put on a netted cap: wiká
put on the market	sél - sell
put out (fire)	bukúiti - extinguish
put out (tr)	wiyéti - force someone out
put to death	wónoti - kill
put up for sale	sél - sell
put up with	ḱuidakwiyakka - sort of like
pygmy	dímenkɱ - dwarf
pygmy owl	wáspololo
quail	yúhyu, yúyu, yúyulu; valley quail: hánpai
quake	earthquake: yanánaito; to quake: yanái, yanáinaito, yanáito, wisɱ́sɱ
quaking aspen tree	sililikɱm cha, wilílim chá
quantify	womákti - measure (v)
quantity	ka'ánbe - that much, that many
quarrel (v)	wokótito
queen in cards	yepónim kɱlé, nawáspe
question	epín; ask a question: epín; ask a lot of questions: pí epínsa, pekúla; question words: epíndom wéye
quibble (v)	hálchetoto - disagree with each other
quick	bilísno; quick! ɱlékleki; very quick: támlep; quickly: wilékleknini, wilékni; move quickly: beṭék; do quickly: sɱlékwono; do very quickly: támlelep; go as fast as possible: koháno
quick-tempered	wasósape - hot-tempered
quiet	kelé; keep quiet: ka'ánuwewol; become quiet: kelémbo; keep the children quiet: héwkinutimen
quiet down	kelémbo - become silent
quilt	pumlénki
Quincy	Silóm, Silóm Ḱoyó, Nukuti
Quincy people	Silóm ma'a
quit	hékit
quiver (v)	wilíl - flutter, tremble
quiver for arrows	noká, nokóm noká, buhúpyokɱ
quiz	welé - test, trial run

English	Maidu
quote (n)	yawí - cost
rabbit	wékkesi; jackrabbit: chínkuťi, kowékesi/kówekkesi; cottontail: wipélki, téloli, telólele, tibím kówekkesi; brush rabbit: pám wékkesi, tallóli; snowshoe rabbit: kóm wékkesi, kowékesi; a kind of rabbit (WS): wipélno
rabbit sage	lᴧpúpu/lapúpu
rabbit skin	saláwi
rabbit skin blanket	chínkuťim saláwi, saláwi
raccoon	akíchana, patátaka, monkoba
race	foot race: tókdato; to race against/run a race: tókdato; one who runs in a race: tókdatokᴧ
race (n)	ma'a - people
racehorse	tókdatokᴧm kawáyu
racer snake	bidípno, hásnom húskᴧ
racket (noise)	yohón - noise
radiance	banák - light (n), brightness
radio	píntikᴧ, píntikᴧm wasása, solí solé'uskᴧ wasása
raft	yakᴧ, hínnotikᴧm yaká - boat
rafters	hᴧmtᴧti
rag, cloth	witᴧťmino
rage (v)	wasóhati - go after someone in anger, bring wrath down upon; wasó'ituti - be sick from anger
railway	train - train
rain	kadíki; a light rain: kadíkim pibáwi; a heavy rain: kóh'bono; to rain: kadík kít; to pelt down rain: taiyái'aluť; to rain torrentially: yᴧ'aswono; harder (as in raining harder): tetétbewto; rain cloud: tumímya
rainbow	ókmolaka, ókwilaka; stretch down as a rainbow: ókmolakkit, ókwilakkit
rainbow trout	palíki
rainfall	kadíki - rain (n)
rainstorm	kóh'bono - a great rain, storm
raise	tókdoi, wiwó; raise the arms: bekúkuk; raise a child: hᴧbís; raise dust: sukdóiti; raise up: wiwódoi; raise/lift oneself up: hakélwodoi; raise/lift oneself up a little bit: hakélwodoikato
raisin	pímmilim pikáli
rake (v)	linóditi
ram in	buhúp, buhúpno, bu'úpu; something used to ram things in: buhúpnokᴧ; a ramrod for a gun: bu'úpukᴧ
ramshackle	kéy'i
ranch (n)	kawí - land
rancheria	lanchelía
range (as animals)	ᴧnói
rant (v)	yáhpatchono, wasóhati - go after someone in anger, bring wrath down upon
rap (n)	bókkoko
rape (v)	hédastoti, húnbᴧk, méhťakit
rapids	pólpolchenopem momí, sewíno
rare	helú, helúto - a few, a very few
rare, underdone	kamák, kápmeninu
rarely	bᴧdᴧk
rascal	ᴧspa
raspberry	pani'ini, widópo, láklakpem hiní, húlupiti
rat	sápa; wood rat: óm sápa, tela; bushy-tailed rat: chám sápa
rate (of speed)	bilísi - speediness
ratify	héwwo, húno - be verbally supportive
rationale	ma'ámᴧni - reason why
rattle	rattlesnake rattle: chhatátakakatikᴧ; ceremonial rattle: sokóti; deer-hoof rattle: yókolkᴧ; one who carries the rattle: yowáwi; to rattle: chhatáta
rattlesnake	chhatátaka (WS)/chitatakᴧ (PM-M), chhatátakam húskᴧ, chílwa (FR)/chuluwa (JD), búksiukᴧ (FC), sokótkᴧpem húskᴧ (RD) - note that the word chhatátaka or chitatakᴧ should not be pronounced except at the bear dance ceremony.
rattlesnake root (to ward off rattlesnakes)	chuluwa piwí/chílwam piwí
ravage	wasáti - mess up, ruin
raven	popoka, pulpkᴧ
ravioli	lawióli

English	Maidu
ravishing	ekáwchetipe - beautiful
raw food	k̓amáka
ray	ókpayi - ray of sunshine
raze	wi'íti - destroy
razor	wmk̓mstokm
reach (i.t.)	piúbonpininu - extend down (as a rope)
reach (with the hand)	reach for: yaláp; reach out and grab: yelábito; reach up and grab: yelálapdoi; reach down in: yelápwo'mheno; reach up: yalálapdoi
reach, get to	mdíkno, towóikit; reach a good sum in cards: mdík; reach the top: bmlélekdoichoi; reach the goal: bodíkno; reach by crawling: lmkdikno; almost reach: okítpoto; reach under: tókno; reach the halfway point up a hill: lelédikno; reach the final destination: kaníwoi'mdikno; reach a place from a distance: ka'ántekit; be unable to reach: dónchmi; reach the end of (tracks) after following: hádikno; make something (like a rope) reach down: píubokiti; after reaching a place from a distance: ka'ántekitchet; out of reach/far: hadádaw
react	pedáto - reply, answer
read	chekíno, yawí, chebmk; pretend to read: yawík̓uk̓us
ready	ready (to eat, as food): k̓áptipe, smtápó; be ready/ripe: díbos; get something ready: yaháti; get oneself ready (to go out): yaháhati'us
real (adj)	lút̓i
real estate	k̓awí - land
reality	ma'ákm - the way it is
realize	makít - understand; hónmak, mákpai - find out; without your even realizing it: mayákk̓eno
really	hai'í; really/very: tetét; really (emphasizing previous word): ás
really	a lot, extremely: MMG p. 55, -lut̓ infix on verb
really want to	have to (do): MMG p. 55 and 57, -yahálut̓ (yaha + lut̓ infixes on verb)
rear (adj)	k̓íwdi - at the back; ínno - buttocks, butt
reason	the reason why (someone did something): ma'ámmni; for what reason: hesádom? do for no reason: mpék̓ayew
reason (why)	expressed by -tipe on the verb "that which causes..." nik̓i mk̓óitipe "the reason why I left"
rebound	pmpyewei/pmpyewe
rebound (v)	pokmkinu - come back to life
recall	húmit, huhehé, húkinu; be unable to recall: húmitchmi
receive	mé - get, take
recently	béidmkmen, béidmktonanna
receptacle	loló - container
reception	bmyím motó - festive gathering
recess	chedá - break (n)
recite	betéi - recount
reckon	áik̓ak̓at - figure, surmise
recline	t̓mi, yokós
recluse	dmk̓k̓m - loner
recognize	chesák, chebós, tisák; now recognize: chesákew; be unable to recognize: chebók̓oi, chesákmaka; recognizable: chesákti
recoil	myéwe - go back
recollect	húmit - recall
recommend	mamá - advise, tell
recompense	pakál - pay (v)
record (v)	papélkitti
recount traditional stories	betéi, betéito, túwei
recover from (illness, death)	wadá, recover from: chedá; recover from illness: wodá; recover consciousness: wimík
recover something, get something back	memé
rectify	yadmkdmk̓, tawáldmkdmk
rectum	pit̓ík̓m
recuperate	wadá, wodá - get well; ámbmk̓bm - get better
recur	madóm mpék̓adom - repeat
recycle	yewé'iti
red	láklak, láklakpe; very red: láklaklut̓pe; turn red: wilák, elákk̓oi; reddish: elálak, elálakpe

383

English	Maidu
Red Ants Valley	Wóslum Ḱoyóm
red berry	láklakpem hiní
red fir tree	tutukmm cha
red fox	yóskope, yóskopem hawí, yóspem hawí
red maids (plant)	chiwemyo
red manzanita	láklakpem ékpm
redbell	púsle; redbell flower: púslem yo
redbud	lmlí/lilí/lulí
redhead duck	ohaibuldm
redress (v)	koyó - make up for, pay for
red-tailed hawk	búklakkm
reduce (tr)	tibíti - make smaller
reduce to powder	yók, hihí - grind to powder
red-winged blackbird	monkmlío/monkolí'o
refer to	kái, máiye
reflect on	húni - consider
refund (v)	pakályewei - repay
refuse (v)	wíye, wíyekana
refute	hálcheche - contradict
regalia	types of regalia: headstall: bátchawi/báchawi, pálaḱ; tremblers: wiléle; feather plume stick: díhyo; bands: póti; put on regalia: smlépai'i, bihíp, hesúpai; put on feather regalia: smlépaiti'us, silépai/smlépai; put feather regalia on someone else: silépaiti; put on bands: bopóťati; wearing necklaces: ḱúilaimape; a man wearing feathers: smlépaipem máidm
regarding	halíle
regards	hehé - hello
regiment	bomó - group
register (v)	papélkitti, womít - record (v)
regress	kíwna bényewei - walk backwards
regret (v)	yepí - be ashamed
regularly	mpéḱanbem ekí - every day; ekm - usually
regulate	yaháti - organize things
reimburse	pakályewei - repay
reinforce	etósti, chḿititi - strengthen
reject	a reject: yahámeni; to reject an idea: hálche
relative, friend	héskm; relatives: héskmto
relax	lie around: míknoye; chedá - rest
release (n)	wewé - speech
release (tr)	sówono - let someone go
relish (v)	dómaki - have a taste
relocate	nénḱoi, nénoḱoi; relocate something: utí
reluctant to	be reluctant: oḱóle; be reluctant to hear: pínokole; be reluctant to see: che'ókole; I am reluctant to: oḱóleḱas
rely on	húno
remain	bis, ḿbis; be left: okḿ; remain like that: ka'ánu
remark (n)	wéyebe - brief message
remarry	marry another man: púli
remember	húkinu, húmit, huhehé; remember a person: makít; be unable to remember: húmitchmi
remote (adj)	hadá - distant (adj)
remove	wiyéti - cause to be missing/gone, make leave; mahá'uḱoi - take away
remunerate	pakál - pay (v)
Reno	Líno
renounce	hálche - reject (v)
repair	yadḿkdḿḱ, tawáldmkdmk; what I have repaired: yadḿkdmkisma
repay	pakályewei/pakályewe
repeat (adj)	béibmm - again
repeat (n)	pedáto - echo, reply
repeat (v)	mmyákati - do the same thing again
repeat (what someone says)	yakka - do like
repeat (what you said)	béibmm wéyep
repeatedly	madóm mpéḱadom; do repeatedly: awébisim, mpéḱanu
repeatedly do (tr)	matíwe - always do, keep causing (problems)

English	Maidu
reply	pedáto
report (n)	my (upcoming) report: nikí wéyemasma; his/her (upcoming) report: mmkí wéyemape; (already-given) report: wéyewonope
report (n)	wéye - speech
report (v)	wéye - tell
reporter	epínnoyesakmm máidm
reproduce	puḱ
repudiate	hálcheche - contradict; hálche - reject (v)
request (something)	ái; request a donation, request giving: méiwo
require	wi'í - lack
research (v)	hónmak
resemble	yak, yakánu, yákanudo, yakbé, yákcheti; resemble someone more and more: yakawéw; resembling: yakchetípe; mmyákchetipe
reserve (v)	yaché - keep, save back
reside	mbis - occupy
residential	bískmm - residential
residential area	bískmm ḱódo
resign	yasáno - give up
resin	chaká
resistant	épti - tough, strong
resolve	húkes - figure out
resounding	yakwéto; resoundingly: pintitinini
respectable	yahá - good
respond	pedáto - reply, answer
rest (v)	chedá, wokócheda
rest, left over	the rest: léwo
restaurant	pekḿm uyí
restitution	pay restitution: koyó
restrict someone's movements	bístikíye
restroom	piťím uyí - bathroom
result	as a result: mayákḱen
retain	yaché - save, keep; mayá - save back conserve
retaliate	yámmotopai
retch	tás, wémmuk
retell	betéi - recount
retire (go back)	myéwe - go back
retirement	mpé bísdom - doing nothing
retreat (v)	myéwe - go back
retrieve someone	hóiwi'okit
return	yewé, haiyé; return home: hepínḱoi, sa yewé; return in a vehicle: hányewei/hányewe; return to the starting place: mdíknowēḱoi, mḱói'mye, hasíp; return from hunting: húnhepinye, hunhépinḱoi; return back the same way: myéwe; return towards: ḱótchonokachopin; return carrying: sohá'okit; return/give back something: méiyewe; in return: yewé
reunion	ḿmmotope - get-together; bmyím motó - festive gathering
reveal	wéye - tell
revenge	get revenge on: yámmoto, katída
revert	ḱíwna bényewei - walk backwards
review (v)	chekíno, yawí, chekíno - read, examine, look closely at
revise	yadḿkdmḱ, tawáldmḱ; revised: what I have revised: yadḿkdmkisma
revolting	wemtichḿktiti
revolve	wmpḿlmmnoye - whirl oneself round and round
rework	rewrite: tawáldmkdmk - revise
rhubarb	chḿchmḱ/chuchúkm; wild water rhubarb: momtátati
rhythm of walking/stepping	benhúye
rib	ḱowóm bmmí, chichím bmmí
rice	láisi
rickety	kéy'i
ride a horse	lḿkťano, lḿkťa, yúťa; horseback rider: lḿkťakm
ride over/through	come riding over/through in a vehicle: hachóno

English	Maidu
ridge	kʌsí, kʌswo; little ridge: ónkʌsdobe; ridge top: kʌsdo; along a ridge: kʌswo, kʌswowono; along the top of the ridge: kʌswowóno, kʌswodoinodi; at the top of the ridge: kʌswodoidi; down at the lower part of the ridge: kʌswonnodi; go along a ridge: kʌswonó
ridicule (v)	hokót; someone who ridicules others: hokótsa
ridiculous	hokótisape, hokót'isa, hokóttipe
rifle	pándaka
rig (n)	hadóikʌm kaléta - truck
right (adj)	yahá - good
right (side)	right hand: yímluťi; right side: yímdʌkʌ; to the right: lúťna, yímluťna, yímdʌkna
right before	MMG p. 85, -meninupe verb ending
right, agreed	that's right: yahát hapá, áihisáwonoman, he'é, ho - yes
right, enough	just right: wémťikluťpe, wémťikpe
rigid	chʌiti - hard, tough
ring (as a bell)	kolulunti
ring (n)	wichákʌ - belt; (wichák means encircle); jewelry ring: monkʌdati
rip	rip by itself: widás, widásdo, yʌťʌi, wʌťʌi; rip (something) apart: wʌťʌiwaito; rip (something): hédas; rip (something) open: hédasto, yʌťʌito; rip wide open: yʌťʌiwaito; rip to pieces: wʌťʌikitbos
ripe	kap, káptipe; completely ripe/overripe: kápsito; be ripe: díbos; get ripe: kap, kápti; start to get ripe: kapdói; be almost ripe: káppoto
rise (fog)	ťiwdoi
rise (smoke)	súkdoipeti
rise (sun)	háhadoi, wochóno
rise (water)	móm, mombudúťkoi
rise above	waláw - exceed
rise, arise	ʌdói - ascend, go up; from sitting to standing: tʌsdoi; as fish coming to the surface, or a balloon rising: héyudoi; come up to the surface in water: yódoi; get up in the morning: otó
risk (v)	helái - gamble
river	sewí; go to the river's edge: sewí'ʌno; rivers: séwsewto
river bed	sewím bo, piní, séwbonpini, séwwonpini; a rocky river bed: om sewówokit
river hawthorn	wahíkʌ
river-dwelling	séwsewtodi biskʌ
road	bó; street/road for cars: kalétam bó; on the road: bódi; along the road: bóno; next to the road: bóminki; to wind along (as a road): bówono; to wind into the distance (as a road): bówokoi
roadkill	bódi wónotiwono
roam	ʌnói - wander
roast	a roast: ítus, ítusyo; to roast: ítus, kápti; roast in ashes: wulúi
robber	pedákʌ - thief
robbery	pedá'i - theft
robin	chístatakʌ, wistátak, chí'uluťchono (RD), chiwíspolótkʌ (RD)
rock (n)	ó; rocks: óm bomó; portable grinding rock: áli; hole in a rock: ómpʌnno; growing in the rocks: ódi dídom
rock (v)	to rock (back and forth): núwunto/nʌwʌnto; keep rocking: nʌwʌntowebis; rocking chair: nʌwʌntokʌm bísťakʌ
rockslide	kóyekini
rocky	óm yʌyʌ́ko, ótoto
Rocky Mountains	Óm Yamáni (WS)
roe	chak
rogue	ʌspa - rascal
roll	kʌlʌ́; roll on the ground: wʌpʌ́pʌlamto; roll material to make rope: pán; roll a cigarette: lemít; roll along (by itself): kʌlʌ́no; roll as thunder: kʌlʌ́lʌ; roll something along: kʌlʌ́noti; roll around (by itself): kʌlʌ́noye; roll something around: kʌlʌ́noyeti; roll under the hand or foot (to smash): wobúno/wubúno; roll away (by itself): kʌlʌ́koi; roll something away: kʌlʌ́koiti; roll over (like an animal): wʌpʌ́lamto; roll towards (by itself): kʌlʌ́ye; roll something towards: kʌlʌ́yeti; roll something up: witúl; roll something up and tie it: witúlkit; roll several things up: witúlyo; roll things up and tie them: witúlkityo; roll back and forth: nʌwʌnto; a roll (of tape, etc): wólek yodáwi
roll (n)	wanʌ́n - roll of basketry materials; yodáwi - coil
roll eyes	mʌ́l; roll the eyes up in anger: mʌ́ldoi

English	Maidu
roller	walátkṁ - rock roller
roller skate (v)	hásno - ski, skate
roof (slanted)	leléimpini
room	lúmi
rooster	wokḿm chhikíni, yepím chhikíni
root (n)	piwí; bag of roots: piwímduki
root around	yudút
root for	má wátdan - clap the hands
rope	ḱuḱú; a tie rope (noun): yodótpaikṁm ḱuḱú; to make rope: ḱuḱú, pán, ḱuḱú pán
rose (plant)	lílchiche, chḿlchṁkṁ, yéltutu; rose flower: chḿlchṁkṁm yó
rotate (i.t.)	wṁpḿlṁmnoye - whirl oneself round and round
rotten	holóko, ťṁn; be rotten: ťṁnti; rotten log: holó
rotund (adj)	pṁlḿm - round (adj)
round (adj)	pṁlḿm, pṁlḿlṁmpe; disk-shaped: waťám chetípe
round (boxing)	ónkoḱoito - contest (n)
round (n)	a round/go-round in dancing: motópe
round house	ḱumhḿ
round people up	yeḱói
Round Valley	Hunódim
Round Valley Reservoir	Hunódim Mómdanni
route	along the route: ṁnókṁdi
routinely	ṁpéḱanbem ekí - every day
row boat	yakḿ - boat
rowdy (adj)	wasá - bad
rub	ḱa'úwa; rub on: yú, bḿmheloto, sṁḱói, sṁḱóiti; rub in: yúto; rub the head to shape it: sṁlát; rub in the hands: máni
ruddy	wiláknope
ruin	wasáti, wíhya; ruin things for oneself: wasát yatí'us
rule (n)	ma - law
rumble	ḱṁlḿplṁlṁp; be rumbling: ḱódom ḱṁlḿplṁlṁpdom
run (n)	tókdato - foot race
run (with legs)	a trial run: welé; to run: welé, weléno/wiléno; start running: beťékdoi, wiléḱoi; run holding something: hánwele; grab and run: sóweḱadoi/sówiḱadoi; run a race: tókdato; run uphill: wilédoino; run across somewhere: welésito/wilésito; run after: bínme, yáhpat, bínmeḱoi, bínmedoi; start running after: yáhpatdoi; run off after: chudáwileno; run along: wiléwkit; run around: ṁchónowei, weḱói, welénoye; run around behind something: bolópchono; run uphill/upstairs: welédoi, welédoino; run up to: wilediḱno; run back to where one started: weléye/wiléye; run downhill: witḿmino; run down towards: witḿmit; run into (a room): sṁlékwopin; run off holding something: hánweleḱoi/hánwileḱoi, hánwileḱoiye; go running off: weléḱoi; run off towards: wiléḱoiye; come running to: binmé'okit; rush out: sṁlékwotpin; run out and away: wilédaw; be running: wiléw; runner: welénokṁ; run away: welé'ṁkoi, witḿm; run away (plural subject): wiléḱoiḱoi; run away from: welédaw; run away from someone chasing: héḱoi; keep running away; hénu; flee wildly in all directions: koháhaḱoi; flee wildly: koháḱoi; go running away (plural subject): witḿmkoḱoi; run away holding something: hánbeťek, hanbeťékchono; bolt and run away holding something: hanbeťékdoi
run against	ónkoḱoi, ónkoḱoito - compete, disagree with each other
run as a machine	ṁnó, sol; make (a machine) run: ṁnóti, sólti
run as nose	hunpapus; runny nose: hunpapuspe
run down, as sap	héyuye
run into	ṁchák, chenó - chance upon, meet; odáto - meet, encounter
run out (like a liquid)	opín
run out (tr)	batásip - drive out
run ragged	wokóti - tire out (tr)
rural district	ḱódo - area
rush (v)	wilék - hurry (v), hṁlíslisno; bolóp; rush around: wiléknoye; rush in: sṁlékwopin; rush out: bolópsip, sṁlékwotpin
rut (v)	to rut in mating season: búpaito; rutting season: búpaitomenkṁmeni
RV	uyúkkṁm kaléta

English	Maidu
-s plural noun ending	MMG p 12 and 17, plural usually not expressed on noun. p. 42 -woli plural with kinship terms. p. 57 -yo on verbs for plural object. p.58-59 reduplication on verb to express plural subject or object. p. 75, optional endings such as -nono, use of bomó and pim to express plural
sack	dúki, wadápi; put things in a sack: wadápyo; go along carrying a sack: wadápmno
Sacramento	Sekumne
Sacramento Valley	Ḱódom Bónnodi
Sacramento Valley people	tḿkmma
sad	wasát hmbḿkpe; feel sad: wasát hmbḿk; make someone sad: wasát hmbḿkti; make oneself sad: wasát hmbḿkti'us
saddle	síya
safe	be safe: yahát bis; safely, in a safe manner: yahátupe, yahádi
sage (plant)	bupupu/bmpupu; rabbit sage: lmpúpu/lapúpu/lupúpu
sage (wise person)	húkespe - wise, clever
sage grouse	kohíkwm
said	being said/as someone was saying: adóm 'as; was said/had been said: awónom, ḱáiwono
sail (v)	hásno - slide, ski
sailboat	hínnotikmm yaḱá - boat
saint	ḱákkini - spirit
salamander	wowáka, mómi wowáka
salesperson	méitowokm
saliva	yaká, yakán
salmon	maihí (WS), maiyí (RD), mayhí (FC); male salmon: pama
Salmon Falls	Yatim
salt	bá; salt as ingredient: bám wasása; salt tule: bám kúpkm; to get salt: bá
salve	yútokmm wené, yútokmm wené - liniment
same	the same: mmyákape, mmyák; the same one: tené; the same thing: mmkáni, mpéḱa; the same kind: ka'áwini; the same one as before: mmkán(im); be the same as each other: mmyákkḿti; be exactly the same: mmyáktitiluťi; be the same as before: mapém mmkan; do the same: mmyáka, ka'áhuyeti; do the same (thing again): mmyákati; in the same place as before: mmkándi; in the same way: mmyákat 'as; keep doing the same old thing: mpéḱahúyeti; the same eating place: ka'ápepem upé; the same amount (in dividing up): mmyákbebe; the same portions (in dividing up): mmyákdmkbe mmyákbe
sample (v)	dómaki - have a taste
San Juan Ridge	San Wan Ḱmsí
sand	bmmḿkm, ḱmm'ḿk
sand bar	ónḱmsdobe, ḱḿsi, sem ḱḿsi
sand hill crane	wóldokkm, kodoko
sandpiper	mmmbmdmnkm
sap	chaḱá; sap as gum: chakámin; get sap on something: chakámpai; get sap on oneself: chakámpaiti'us; get something covered with sap: chakámťapoti
saplings	witóktmtm
sapsucker	chatúti'i, chówanoti
Sasquatch	kombḿ
sass	hokótito - argue with
sated	be sated/full: idát
satellite dish	tiwí waťá
satisfied	yahát hubúktipe - feeling pleasant
Saturday	sáteki
sauce	homá - soup
save	yaché, mayá; save food (for someone): peyáche; that which was saved: yachépe
savor	dómaki - have a taste
savory	sudábe
saw (cut)	a saw (for cutting wood): hunékm, chá hunékm; to saw: huné
saxophone	yálulu - elderberry flute

English	Maidu
say	wéye, a/há, we; say (often referring to what people used to say): mái, kái/ka'ái; say in a speech: wewéi/wewé; say a word: yawí; say to each other: atóto; say like this: eyái, eyáiwei; always say: a'ᴧye; keep saying: máiyew; let them say: atá; he said to me: akán nikí; they will say about me: amákan nikí; being said ("as I told you before"): adóm 'as; what I will say/would say: wéyemasma; say 'ho': hó; say 'uh': íska adóm; say pitifully: bomᴧtiweye; be the way (someone) says it: ha'ái ka...; not say anything: wewémen; not say such things: ka'áimen; without saying anything: aménwet
say	what did you say?: hesí aká?; What are you saying (trying to say)?: hesí máika?, hesádom máika?; What are you/they talking about?: hesí wéyedom?; How do you say 'child?:' 'child' hesáika?
say grace	túweye - pray
saying	adóm; after saying this: wéyeto
scab	pikálchiki
scaffold	yakᴧ - bridge
scale (v)	kam - shed (v)
scale down	tibíti - make smaller
scamper	scamper across or around: lᴧksitoye
scanty	píboduk - scarce
scar	díchikwonomi
scarce	píboduk
scare	wisétti, húse; scare (people/animals) away: hᴧstaye; go around scaring (people/animals) away: hᴧstanóye; scare everyone away: hᴧstakobós; to scare with noises: wisétsetpinti; one who scares people: wisétikᴧ; make someone run away: wiléwkittikoi; one who makes people run away: wilémkoitikᴧ
scared	wisét, wisétpe, wisétset; a bunch of scaredy-cats: wisétsapem kilím bomó; not be very scared: wisétboduk
scarf	owólakkᴧ
scary	yehéptuyetipe, épti; to sound scary: yehéppinti
scatter (something)	wᴧkᴧk, wokᴧkᴧsitoye; be scattered around: woyónute; lie scattered around: wowói'onuto
scaup (duck)	kówukᴧ
scene, scenery	kódo - place
scent	híssa - smell
school	yawítikᴧm hᴧbó, mákpapaitikᴧm uiyí, sᴧkúl; go to school: sᴧkúlkoi
scissors	pekᴧtikᴧ, wᴧkᴧskᴧ
scoop	scoop something like dirt: chᴧwikadoi; scoop up a liquid: supút, supúttonu; be scooping up a liquid: supútputtonu; be scooping around in a liquid: supútsitoye
scoop up (food)	ái - dish up, serve
scoot over	lápsito
scorn (v)	hokót - ridicule
Scotch broom	wólek dᴧ
scoundrel	ᴧspa
scowl at	bátᴧtᴧnkinu, chepánu
scram!	cháinapi - get out! chái'ᴧkoi - go away! to a dog: wᴧskoi!
scramble (v)	hᴧlíslisno, wilék - hurry
scrap (n)	hudáwdo, okᴧtno - a cut-off piece
scrape stems for basketry	ihé, wa'á
scraps of food	bᴧtᴧmi
scratch	scratch an itch: sᴧkᴧi/sukúi; scratch the ground: bewés, bawá; scratch oneself: sᴧkᴧi'us; go along scratching oneself: sᴧkᴧi'no; scratch each other: sᴧkᴧitoto; scratch as chickens: kedé; scratch with claws: chᴧwak; scratch noisily with claws: bákocho; scratch on something, like a match: hᴧpái; scratch up dirt: chᴧwikadoi
scrawny	toť - thin
scream	kobébek, chat; make someone scream: kobébekti, kobébeknoti; something that causes screaming: kobébebekchᴧti
screech (v)	kobébek - scream
screech owl	popópkᴧ
screen (n)	chᴧlᴧ - strainer
screen (n)	wᴧsuitakᴧ - shade (n)
screw up (v)	wasáti - mess up, ruin
scrotum	pálam wadápi
scrub jay	cháitakᴧ, si'ítku

English	Maidu
scrub oak	busúlim hámsi
scrutinize	chehéiheino - inspect; chebós - look closely
seagull	kolókm
seal up	yuťúi, yuťúchik, yuťúichik; dḿchik - lock up, close up
search for	hatám; search as one goes along: atámmkinú; search for someone: mpé; go around searching for someone: mpé'mnoye, mpéno/opéno; go search for someone: opékoi; go all around searching for: wochíkimoto; in searching: hat'dá; searcher: opékoipe
season	ḱódo, méni; same season: yaktekít
seat (chair)	bmdóiťakm
second (2nd)	pepéne
secondhand	héda - used
secret	keep a secret from: ḱáwono
secure (lock)	dḿchik - lock up, close up
secure (v)	chḿititi, secure one end: yodótpai; be secured/attached: yodótpanu
securely	yahádi
seduce	héwwelek
see	che; see/meet: chenó; be able to see: chekít, ḱḿiche; have a chance to see: chehéyenoyetiti; see well: cheyákan; be unable to see: chechḿi; be unable to see well: chebókoi, cheḱóiboḱói, chewás; want to see: cheyáha; so want to see: tetétluťi cheyáha; be wanting to go see: chenóḱoiyahawew; go and see: chenóno, cheḱói; be reluctant to see/not want to see: che'ókole; pretend not to see: cheménḱuḱus; fail to see: chewátai; see every single thing: chemtaimén; see through a hole: wébelbel
see through	chesíto - look across
seed	ḱomí, seméni, hiní, ḱoḱó; large seed/pit: ḱmm; full of seeds: ḱómtapope; go to seed: sáwno, sáwwono; seed-beater (basket): lóksu
seed	sperm: ow - semen
seek	atám/hatám, chenó'ohe
seem(s) to be	must be (no future meaning): MMG p. 95, use -yakke verb suffixes (depends on subject).
seems	appear to be: chetí; it seems: ha'ái, ai sm'mi; seems like: yakwé; seems to me: yákkasma; always seems: kawéwkm; seem to be: yákka; seem to cause: yákati; "seems" is expressed by adding the km infix or the -yakken suffix to verbs. See Mountain Maidu Grammar, Lessons 8 and 12.
seep up	míkyosippin
seesaw	péwmnto
seethe	wasó'ituti - be angry till it hurts
see-through (adj)	chehéhechonope - transparent
segregate	yotótchik - divide, separate (tr)
seize	méyodoi; seize someone and carry off: dónwikanu; seize someone as an evil spirit: mépbo
seize (kidnap, hijack)	pedáyeto, soháḱoi - kidnap
seize up (muscles)	widú
seldom	bmdḿk
select	bmyḿksip; select/hire someone: woiyó; select a few from many: bmyḿksipdomhehe
self-	oneself, do to/for oneself: MMG p. 54, -'us infix on verb
sell	méitoti, sél
sell for	yawí - cost (v)
semen	ow
semi (truck)	hadóikmm kaléta - truck
senator	yepóni - chief
send (letter, message, pkg.)	mkóiti - send
send (someone) for, send someone to do	sódoiwo, woiyó/woyó, woyóḱoi
send (someone) inside	woyóno
send (someone) out	woyósip
send away	batásip - drive out; woiyóḱoi/woyóḱoi
send fast	támlepti
send packing	woiyóḱoi - send (someone) away
send-off (n)	mkóida - departure
senior (adj)	nenó - old
senior citizen	nenópe - old (person)

English	Maidu
sense (not having)	húboḱoipe; always lacking common sense: húboḱoisape
sense (v)	hᴍbḿk - feel
separate (v)	ᴍwáito (intransitive); to separate things: ᴍwáitoti, yotótchik; separate from each other: yúnototo; separate/divorce: yḿno/yúno; a separation: úno
separation	úno - divorce (n)
serve	yaháti - make (something) good
serve (food) to	ái, ḱaipeti, ḱaipewo
serviceberry	sobá
serving (n)	a serving (of food): pená
set (as the sun)	hínchono, ba'á'aidaw, hínpupu; be almost set: hinháhadikno
set (something) back	sóyewe
set (something) down	hekít, sókit, sówwokit, yᴍmḿkiti; set down a load: háwokit; set someone down: ápokite; set down for someone (like food): sókiti, wokíkit; set in place/set down during creation: bᴍsḿpkit
set (something) out	sówoťa, set out many things: sówoťayo; set out (food) for: wokíkit
set a trap	ťúye; set a fish trap: yemík
set fire to	tochóno; set fire to: topái; set fire to the countryside (as a controlled burn): ḱodo topái
set free	sówono - let someone go
set up	bᴍsḿpkit - set in place
setting (n)	ḱodo - place
setting out	ᴍkóida - departure
settle (i.t.)	hakínu - be parked, be in a place
settle (v)	hánpi - land on the ground
settlement (houses)	hᴍbóboto
seven	sáichoḱna sḿti, sáichoḱom sḿti, máwᴍkḿm péne, tapewe, tebíbe
sew	pᴍyé/púya
sexual intercourse	have sex with: héiyeto/héyeto, hóiwito, hᴍpéto, hᴍpé, hᴍchḿ; have sex with each other: hóiwitoto; have sex with repeatedly: héyetoibisim; go have sex with: hᴍpétoḱoi; want to have sex: hᴍchḿtoya; mount for sex (animals): ápbonno; mount for sex (humans): yoťa; thrust the hips during sex: ínwok; one who is having sex: héyetope
shade	yamái; a shade: wᴍsuiťakᴍ
shadow	yamái; be in someone's shadow: yamáichik
Shaffer Mountain	Túmbakᴍm
shaft (n)	ḱumí - hole
shake	shake (as a person): yḿkkᴍk, dᴍyḿyᴍ, ťiyḿk; shake (as the earth): wisḿsᴍ, ťiyḿyᴍk; shake the head: onó o'ḿ'ᴍlᴍm, o'ḿ'ᴍlim; shake something: dᴍyḿyᴍti; shake hands: madóntoto
shall be	it shall be so: mabó; you shall be: mamánkano
shaman	yomé/yomí, yomím máidᴍ; a shaman who blows to cure: bḿdam máidᴍ; shaman who calls the spirits: betéibok'i; female shaman: yomím kᴍlé; to practice shamanism: yom
shame (tr)	yepíti - cause shame; shameful: yepísape
shape (health-wise)	hᴍḱmpi - health
shape (n)	lulú - body
shape (v)	ya, yatí, yánto, ya'ati - create
share (n)	léiwo - part of
share (v)	kᴍ'ídi
sharp	ťok, ťókpem
sharp (tasting)	chuchᴍkpe - sour
sharpen	ťókti; sharpen a little: ťóktiti
sharp-shinned hawk	báku
shave	símpani wᴍḱmsto
she	mᴍmḿm (subject); mᴍmḿ, mḿ (object)
shears	wᴍḱmskᴍ - scissors
shed (n)	uyí
shed (v)	kam, kámda
sheep	chípi
sheet (for bed)	kodál, chínukᴍ, túichinukᴍ
shell (n)	posála; shell punched with a hole (for necklace): wókkolo; shell necklace: wókkolom ḱuila
shell (v)	chísᴍl, ḱisᴍl
shelter (v)	shelter each other: yamáitototi

English	Maidu
shelter (willow)	yamáichik k̓umhm̓
sheriff	dónkm̓m máidm̓ - police (n)
shimmer	momyodádanu
shinbone	tolím bm̓mí
shine	ékdadoi, banák̓doi; the sun is shining: ókpai wakítdom
shiner (fish)	hálbak̓u
ship (n)	yak̓m̓ - boat; sailboat, raft, inflatable boat: hínnotikm̓m yak̓á - floating boat
ship (v)	m̓k̓óiti - send
shipment	hadó - load
Ship's Creek, NV	Bam Héli
shirt	kamísa; women's shirt: chít̓akm̓
shitepoke (bird)	mm̓kahúlkm̓
shiver	dúwuwu
shock (n)	yanánaito - earthquake
shoe/shoes	soló, bolók̓o, solóm bolók̓o; put on shoes: bolók̓ti, soló; put shoes on someone (or a horse): bolók̓tiwo
shoo!	chái'm̓koi - go away! to a dog: wm̓sk̓oi!
shoot	shoot something: mú/mm̓; shoot a gun: pópti; keep shooting: mm̓dato; shoot at each other: m̓m̓kito; shoot all ammunition: yutúp; shoot almost all one's ammunition: yutúpotonan; aim to shoot: sm̓'á'asdoi; go shoot a gun: póptino; to sound like shooting: póptiwek̓oi; shoot through (something): mm̓sito; shoot entirely through something: mm̓sap
shoot ahead	m̓wála - go past
shoot out/emerge suddenly	póp
shoot up (grow)	dí - grow
shooting star	sátoyo - falling star
shooting stars (flower)	duk̓ulemyo
shop	a shop: méitokm̓m hm̓bó, méitokm̓m uiyí, méitom hm̓bó; to shop/go shopping: méitok̓oi
shoplift	pedá - steal
shoplifter	pedákm̓ - thief
shore	wat̓á; from the shore: wat̓ánan
shore up	etósti, chm̓ititi - strengthen
short	t̓es, t̓espe, nus/nm̓s; a short time: ebm̓webismenwet; after a short time: t̓iktenaki; a short distance: t̓ikte, t̓iktete; after a short distance: t̓iktetedoinodi; shortish/rather short: t̓ésnono
shortage (of food)	óktipem k̓ódo
shortening	hm̓t̓i - fat (n)
shortly	tibínak - soon
short-tempered	wasósape - hot-tempered
shot (n)	mokm̓ - beverage
shot (n)	nokó - arrow
shotgun	pístola - pistol; m̓m̓skm̓t - musket
should	you should: yahá (suffix on verb); I should: -s or -si suffix on verb; you should make something: hesátiyahá; you should go: m̓nóyaha; I should go: m̓nósi
should	need to, have to, ought to: MMG p. 49 -s on verb, "I ought to, " -we on verb, "we ought to, " -yaha on verb, "you ought to" or use commands on p. 48-9
should (future meaning)	will, might ("may it be so"): MMG p. 94, use -tabm̓ verb suffixes (depends on subject)
should (someone) have done...?	was (someone) supposed to...? : MMG p. 64, use question forms for the imperfect, with sm̓'m̓i
shoulder	dadáka; shoulders: dadákase
shoulder to shoulder	in'ánto - side by side
shout	pelíp; talk in a shouting voice: hm̓hwepai; shout at: pelíppai
shove	bm̓lók, sidóp, k̓adót, bohóp; shove (someone) with the hand or arm: widót; shove someone aside: widótk̓oi; shove forward: sidópsip; shove in: bohópmit; keep shoving in: k̓apólyo; shove into (something): k̓apólk̓oi; shove someone against: k̓adótdikno; shove something all the way in: bm̓lókdikno, bm̓lókdiknoti
shovel (n)	t̓oló
shovel (v)	k̓áwba, sut - dig a hole, dig
shoveler duck	k̓áwmm̓kkm̓
show (performance)	sú

392

English	Maidu
show (v)	chebᴧkti, yapái; go show (someone something): yapáiḱoi, yapáino; show around inside: yapáisitoye; show by pointing down at: sᴧkéketkit
show up	chebᴧk, chebᴧkdoi - appear
show up at	ᴧdíkno, okít - arrive at, arrive
shower head	oḱéli - nozzle
shred (v)	hutᴧkityo
shredder	papélim wa'áitikᴧ
shrew (animal)	héchiudᴧ
shriek (v)	screech (v): ḱobébek - scream
shrike (bird)	kéike
shrimp	tulí
shrink back	ᴧyéwe - go back
shrub	dᴧ - bush
shuffle cards	maní sínto
shut	bᴧkúiti/bukúiti; shut the door: púlkᴧ bukúitipi; shut up/seal: yuťúi, yutúchik; shut up a house: hᴧbᴧchik; shut up a house with brush: dᴧchik
shut up (be quiet)	etápkinu
shy	be shy: yehéptoye; be shy of someone: chesém
sibling	sámboye
sick	be sick: ítu, ťoi; start to get sick: ítudoi; lie around sick: ᴧhákinu; rather sick: ítuhtu; sickly: ítudedes, ítusa, ítusape; sickness: ítum ḱódo
side	side of the body: chichí; side (of the land): beléwi, chan, ḱódom beléw; beside/alongside: beléw, chan, lédi, ínḱi, hénante, sᴧhehéhno/sᴧheheino, sᴧhehéinodi; one side: chánwono; on one side then the other: cháni...bei cháneki, chánan... chánan; going from one side to the other: chanyᴧno; the other side: obᴧchopindi, kiwí; the other side of the world: ḱódom chándi; on either side: in'ánto, in'ántodi, in'ántokit; the other/opposite side: ucháni, uchándi, ú'ichan, obᴧasito, obᴧ'asdoino, ú'ichan...ú'ichan; on that side: ikún; go alongside of: sᴧhehéikoi; spring to one side: sᴧhékachono; the other side of the fire pit (away from the door): sáwono; do something on the side (as a side job): cháinakḱenu; at the side of the road: bómhededi
sidestep	wadá - dodge, get away
sidewalk	bó - path
Sierra Buttes	Chíťakam Yamáni
Sierra currant	yupupi
Sierra Nevada Mountains	Óm Yamáni
Sierra Valley	Kéhemheli Ḱoyó
sieve (n)	chᴧlᴧ - strainer
sift	báť, behék
sigh	húmu, sigh deeply: húmusip
sight	be in sight: che; clear sight: hinchesmeni
signify	kái, mái - mean (v)
silent	kelé; silent with wonder: eḱáwkinu; become silent: kelémbo; be silent: ḱáwono
silk tassel bush	chowó
silly (foolish)	hokótisape - ridiculous; unwise: húkesmen - foolish, stupid
silly (fun)	núkyahape; be silly: núksasa
silver	sílwa; silvery: silsilwape
Silver Lake	Hayino Pakáni
silvertip bear	pusúne
silvertip fir tree	tutukᴧm cha
similar	be similar: mᴧyákaka
simmer	hom - boil, stew
sin (n)	wasá - evil
since	since you do: anímchet; "since" meaning "after" or "because" is usually expressed by the -chet or -dom suffix on a verb. -dom is used when the subject is the same, while -chet is used when the subject changes in the next clause.
since	since then: amá wóinan; ever since: udó
since (something happened)	once, after: MMG p. 85, -chet or -weten suffix on verbs. -chet changes the subject in the next clause, -wet keeps the same subject
sinew	paká
sinful	wasá - bad

English	Maidu
sing	sol; ask someone to sing: sólwo; make someone sing: sólti; start singing: sóldoi; sing about: sólpai; keep singing: sólebisim; keep on singing: sólwebis; be singing away: sólekoi; sing together: sóltoto; sing quietly: kásolto; sing badly: sólwasa; sing wildly/emotionally: sólbusno; sing with (someone): sól'idi; hire someone to sing: sólwoyo; sing grass-game songs: sopóm helám sól; sing to someone's step: ɱnósol; sing lyrics: mái; ceremonial singers: yowáwi
singe	piyúti; singe off: piyútidaw; get singed: piyú; smell of singeing: piyúhissa
single	sɱti; even a single one: sɱtim ma'át
single man	kɱléwi'ipe
single-handedly	ka'ádɱtɱ
sink (v)	hínchuku, hínchukudaw; under water: hínkit; as the setting sun: kɱchono
sip (n)	mokɱ - beverage
sip (v)	mo - drink
sister	mɱ sámboyem kɱlé/sámboyem kɱlé; younger sister: ká; little sister: kábe; older sister: éti/ati; a pair including a sister: étikɱto
sister-in-law	mási, másim kɱlé, epi
sit	bɱdói, hakínu; keep sitting: bɱdói'ebis, bɱdóikinu; sit down: bɱdóikit, lápkinu, wólkit; sit down close to: bɱdóihékit, láptikinu; sit on the butt with legs stretched out: lap; sit around: bɱdóinoye; sit around (plural subject): bɱdói'ɱno; sit in a row: wólťanutono; sit on: bísťa, bɱdóiťa, wólťa; sit on (something), covering it: lapchikínu; be sitting on: wólťanu; be sitting down: wolkinú; sit astraddle: mósťapin; not just be sitting around: bɱdóikinu'ebismen; from where they were sitting: wólkinudompenan
site	kokó
site	kokó - location, uyí - site
situation	be in a situation: bisɱkínu
six	sáichoko/sáchoko; máwɱkɱm sɱtti; six times: sáichokonini; the sixth (one): sáichokninima
size	be the right size: wémťikdɱkbe; one that size: ka'ándukbe
skate	hásno; skate away: háskoi; go skating: hásnoyekoi
Skedaddle Mountain Range	Pólpolim Yamánim
skedaddle!	chái'ɱkoi - go away!
skein	wanɱn - roll of basketry materials
ski	a ski: chuwá; to ski: hásno; go skiing: hásnoyekoi, hástokoi; ski off: háskoi; ski wax: chuwám yúkɱ
skid around	hásnoye
skilled	one who is skilled at: yahámakitpe; be skilled at: yahámakit
skim (v)	hiníswopai - glance at, catch a glimpse of
skimpy	píboduk - scarce
skin	posála; animal skin: wolósi, po; skin/membrane: púmpu, púmpumi; to skin (an animal): kós; to skin a vegetable: yaťa
skinny	ťoť, yɱnó; skinny man: yáskakno
skip (hop)	wɱskɱtkɱt
skip (not do)	skip doing something: wonó; not skip doing something: wonómen
skip (tr)	ɱtai - miss, overlook
skip out	wadá - escape (v), get away; take off, leave: ɱkói - go away
skirmish (n)	hómpaito - fight (n)
skirt (n)	nawási, ínkɱl, wosó, wosóťa; lift up one's skirt: wikéidoi, wikéikeidoi
skirt (v)	to skirt (a meadow, etc): wehé'no, wohó'ɱno
skunk	wai'ó, woiyó
skunk cabbage	poyoli
sky	epínim koyó, epínim kódo
slap	waťán; slap in the face: waťánchik, simí waťánchik
slapping motion	pát
slash (v)	wɱkɱ́s - cut
sleep	túi; go to sleep: túikit, túitoye; go off to sleep: túitoyewékoi; go off somewhere to sleep: túikoi; nod off: túiwopno; go to sleep sitting up: túiyiwol; sleep overnight somewhere: uyúk; sleep lightly: túiboduk; sleep soundly: túibosno; be sound asleep: túibusno; sleep with: túiyidi; talk in one's sleep: ɱsweye; walk in one's sleep: ɱs'ɱno; cry in one's sleep: ɱswak; be sleeping: túikinu; sleep talker: ɱsweyesa; sleep walker: ɱs'ɱnosa; a place to sleep: túimape; a light sleeper: wimíkhudanpe; go around half-asleep: túichenotoye

English	Maidu
sleepwear	túichikm - nightgown
sleepy	sleepy person: túikmm máidm; be sleepy: tḿi, túimei, tuiyím mé; be somewhat sleepy: túimehme
sleet	chulm, kóm chmlḿlm, kók chmlḿlm
slender	ymnó - thin, slim
slice	wmkḿt, wmkḿtyo
slice (v)	wmkḿs - cut
slick	dip/dmp, bidípnope, pómolmoli
slide	slide on the feet: has, hásno; slide as a door: ḱa'ás/kahás, kahásḱoi/ḱa'ásḱoi; slide down: héyap, hassíno, héyappin; slide down off: hé'asdaw, hekíwno; slide down one by one: héyapyapto, héyappinpin; slide around: hásnoye; slide away: hásḱoi
slight (adj)	ťoi, etósmen - weak
slim	ymnó
slimy	pómolmoli
sling (v)	wehétkit - hang up
slip (undergarment)	ḱanáyim ínkml
slip (v)	to slip (on the feet): has; slip and lose balance: hásdoi, ťedís; start to slip: ťedísdoi; almost slip: hásdoihudoi; almost slip while going up towards: ťedisdoihudódoiye; slip down: hassíno, ťedisdaw; slip down (as pants): héyupkit; cause someone to slip and fall: wmdáktemáldoi; let something slip and fall: susúpdoi; ťedísim: slipping: ťedísim
slippery	dmp/dip, dḿpdmp, pómolmoli
slit (v)	wmkḿs - cut
slither down into	smwéweimpin
sliver	tibím chábe; stick into (as a sliver): smdétno, smhóp; get a sliver: sidétno
slope	léyi
slough	kam - shed, molt
slow	eyḿsape; be slow: winú; slowly/with difficulty: wúni
slow-witted	húboḱoipe - witless
slurp	hup
smack the lips	sím watámchik
small	tibí; small ones: tibíbi, tibíbinono; the smallest: tibíluťi; although small: tibíma'at; make something small or smaller: tibíti; get smaller: tibíbew; small (according to SPB): wedaka
smallpox	pmním 'ítu
smart	húkes, húkespe; the smartest: húkeswaláwpe; be smart: húkes
smart (v)	íchem - sting (i.t.), tingle
smash	wobúno
smear	bmmhélo; smear on: bḿmheloto
smell	smell (something): hí; smell (good or bad): híssa; always smell (good or bad, but usually bad): híssasa; cause to smell: híti; good smelling: yahát hísatipe; something/someone that is always smelly: híssasakm; stinker/stinking: hísatikm; smelly/fragrant: hísatipe; always smelly/fragrant: hísasape
smile	núksa, núkcheche
smoke	smoke (noun): súku, sam sukú; to smoke, as a fire: súk; make smoke: súkda; get on someone/something (as smoke): súkpai; drift away (as smoke): súkdawi; smoky: suklí; to smoke (something): pe; to smoke tobacco: pánpe; be smoking tobacco: pepánu; smoke tobacco together: pepánototo; chain smoker: pánpesape; smoking pipe: pánpetokm
smoke hole	ólolokó, súksipmape; top of the smoke hole: ólolokóm chuchúi
smother	kún
smug	húkesyopaida
snail	sokólwolwoli
snake	húskm, húsbillaito, palo; king snake: tíyani; gopher snake: ho'ém, howém; water snake: húselíkm, momím húskm; racer snake: bidípno, hásnom húskm; rattlesnake: chhatátaḱa(WS)/chitatakm (PM-M), chhatátaḱam húskm, chuluwa/chílwa (JD), búksiukm (FC), sokótkmpem húskm (RD); great (legendary) snake: paláwaikm - note that the word chhatátaḱa or chitatakm should not be pronounced except at the bear dance ceremony.
Snake Rock (Indian Creek)	Mínminim Om
Snake-eater Man	sáwwonom máidm
snakeroot	chílwam piwí/chílwam piwí
snap	break by snapping: wisóp, wisópti, yabát, yabátyo; snap fingers: bichí yohónti; snap someone with the fingers: dmkḿ, dmkḿtomsito, híkm dmkḿ

English	Maidu
snare (n)	ḱení
snatch	wisúp; snatch and carry off: dónwikanu; snatch away from: wisúpno; snatch suddenly: méhyotno
sneak	sneak around: ḱa'ᴍnoye; sneak off: ḱa'ᴍḱói; sneak up: loḱétdoi, loḱétḱoi; sneak up on: ḱálᴍkpai; sneak underneath: ḱakánaipin; sneak crawling: ḱálᴍk, yedúdutkit, yedúwokit
sneeze	hachís, hatĭchem
snicker	awéḱoi
sniff	híbᴍk; go sniffing around: híloye; sniff along (like a dog): hítuktukno
snipe (bird)	soduwᴀ́pkᴍ
snobbish	eḱáwche'uspe; be snobbish: eḱáwche'us; act snobbish: eḱáwche'us húweye
snoop (n)	símmaksa - gossip (n)
snore	dóskol
snot	huní
snotty	eḱáwche'uspe - uppity
snout	híkᴍ - nose
snow	snow (noun and verb): kó; it is snowing: kó kítdom
snow goose	lᴀ́lᴍku/lúlukᴍ; lesser snow goose: wawi; white snow goose: wuluku
snow plant	ᴀ́swelenom yó
snowberry	sum pekim yehi; snowberry bush: tatókum cha
snowboard (v)	hásno - ski, skate
snowshoe	chuwá, kóm soló
snowshoe rabbit	kóm wékkesi, kowékesi/kówekkesi
snowslide	kohekíwno
snuff out	bukúiti - extinguish
so	adónkan; so/and: amᴀ́ni, awét mᴍyí; so/then: amᴀ́nikan, amánkan, sa'á; so far: ka'ánte, ma'ánte; so much: tetét, tetét píkno
soak (something)	hamít, hamítyo; be soaked: hítape
soaproot	heḱékumsa, ho, po
soar	yéi, kai - fly (v)
social gathering	bᴍyím motó - festive gathering
society (n)	wónom máidᴍ - mankind
socket	pᴀ́nno - cavity
socks	íschomi
soda	beverage: súdi, súkam momí; baking soda: súda, súdam wasása, salwétas
Soda Rock	Bam Ólasi (near Keddie), Chuchúdom O, Chuchúkᴍm O, Chuchúyem Bam (on Indian Creek near Indian Falls)
Soda Springs	Chuchúye
soft	chᴀ́itimen, mútmutpe
soft drink	súda - soda, súkam momí
soil	ḱawí
soil-building	ḱáwyadom
sojourn (v)	uyúk - stay overnight
soldier	hódesi - fighter
sole (foot)	ťáťa, paiyím ťáťa/payím ťáťa
solicit	méiwo - ask to give
solitary	húkitsa
solve	húkes - figure out
some	léiwo/léwo, homó
somehow	mᴀ́méntapo, mayákḱen
someone	hamóniwet
someone else	chái'i
something	hesí, hesíwet, hésdiwet, hesíwi
something else	chái'i
sometime	hesántenuwet
sometimes	léiwonini, sᴀ́tᴍni
somewhat	káina, núkti, wiyák, teténak tibínak
somewhere	ántenántenan
somewhere else	chái, cháidi, chaina
son	té
song	solí, sólkᴍ; a different song: sólwet; a song that was sung: sólwon; gambling song: helám solí; grass game song: sopóm helám solí; songfest: solím motó; learn songs: sólmakito; what do the words of the song mean/say? adóm sóldom máikade?
son-in-law	péti

English	Maidu
soon	tibínak, wéttito; pretty soon: wi'ínit
soot	put soot on the cheeks for mourning: chakámti'us
sop up	supút, supúttonu, supútput, supútputtonu
sorcery	yómpa
sorry	oops, sorry!: ni!; sorry/pitiful: bomʌ́tipe; feel sorry for: bomʌ́mʌkno
soul	honí
sound	to sound (good/bad): pínti, píntiti, ma'ái; to sound wonderful: ʌkáwpinti; sound like: pínnoti, yakpínti, yakwé; make a loud sound: yohónti; make a scary sound: howówo; dislike the sound of: wisótpin; the sound of dancing: ťaťákam wétemi; -sounding: píntitini; sounding like: yakwéto
soup	homá, kok; make soup: hómti
sour	chuchúk, chuchʌkpe, sáwa
sour dock	chuchúku, waťokťoko
source (n)	mákpapaitikʌ - teacher
south	komó; to the south: komóna; in the southern area: komónantedi; from the southern area: komónantenan; in/to the southwest: ḱódom bónnodi
space (in a board game)	bénno
space (outer)	lʌlʌ́m máidʌdi - at the home of the star men
space out	híscheno
spacious	hadáwaito - wide
spandex	wihʌ́pkʌ - elastic (n)
Spaniard	sʌnpányʌtim máidʌ, sʌpányeti, pámyoli
Spanish Creek	Silóm Sewí
Spanish Creek Canyon	Bʌ́wom Luḱú
spank	kíwwo - beat, whip
sparkle	ékdadoi - shine, twinkle
sparks	ṗoṗún; make sparks: ṗoṗúnti; drop sparks: ṗoṗúnḱoi
sparrow	golden-crown sparrow: kúchilili; chipping sparrow: pámbiche'okʌ
sparrow hawk	kélikliki
sparse	píboduk - scarce
spawn (salmon)	hínya, sapí
speak	wéye, we, wewé; begin to speak: wewéyeḱoi; keep up a speech: wewéyebis; make a speech: hʌ́wepaito; speak about: mái; speak louder: wewém sʌdói; speak through a hole: wébelbel; mis-speak: wéyetai; speaking (to): wéyeto, yapáitodo; without speaking: wewémenwet, aménwet
speaker (person)	wewéyekʌ, wéyekʌm máidʌ; lecturer, public speaker: túweykʌ - orator
speaker (sound)	píntikʌ - radio
spear	bʌhʌ́nkʌ, muso/mʌ́so, yakka; to spear: mʌ́, bʌhʌ́m
spearhead (v)	papái, hóiwiháno - lead
special (adj)	sʌ́ti - a certain
specific	sʌ́ti - a certain
speck	kachémeni - crumb
specter	uswúlulu - ghost
speculate	huhéye - imagine
speech	wéye, wewé, hónwe; start to give a speech: wewéyedoi; make a speech (to): hʌ́wepaito, hʌhwé; keep up a speech: wewéyebis; deliver a speech: wewé
speechless	be speechless: wéyechʌi
speed	bilísi; move at a great speed: támlelepno, támlepluť, támṗiṗítḱoi
speed up	wilék - hurry (v); hʌ́lilisno; speed up!: wiléklеki!
spell (v)	bal - write
spell out (clarify)	mákpapaiti - explain, teach
spellbound	be spellbound: eḱáwkinu
spells (n)	yómpa - sorcery
spend the night	uyúk, uyúkkit
spend time	wosíp
sperm	ow - semen
spherical	pʌlʌ́lʌmpe
spice	titipi
spider	makáťi, chu'ʌkʌ
spider web	húsbini, makáťim hʌbó
spiked	ťok - sharp
spill	wáno; spill out: wádamino
spill over	mómbochono - flow over

English	Maidu
spin (i.t.)	wᴧpᴧlᴧmnoye - whirl oneself round and round
spin a web	hᴧyá
spine	kiwím bᴧmí
spiral	wᴧnťeťenoye - curl
spirit	betéboki, ḱákkini, honí; spirit person: kulúm máidᴧ; spirit land: kulúm ḱódom
spit	ťuṕ, chᴧṕ, chᴧṕkit; spit on: ťuṕpai; spit on each other: ťuṕpaito; spit out: ťuṕsip
splinter (n)	tibím chábe
split	wiyᴧ́t, widásdo; split by itself: póyᴧt, póyᴧtwaito; split a long object: wadásto; split a sucker for basketry: wa'áiti, yodá; split something open: wiyᴧ́tto; split/divide up: wiyᴧ́i; split up/divorce: yᴧ́no
split (leave)	ᴧḱói - go away
split (n)	úno - divorce (n)
split (v)	kᴧ'ídi - share
spoil (something)	wíhya
spokesperson	wewéyekᴧ - speaker
sponsor	húno
spooky	bᴧ́de - weird, evil
spool	wanᴧ́n - roll of basketry materials
spoon	ťoló, pekᴧ́m ťoló
sport (v)	chí - put on clothes
spot (n)	ḱoḱó - location
spouse who was previously married	pulí
sprawl	be sprawled out on: lápťanu
spray (as skunk)	mᴧ́dato
spread (n)	a spread (like butter): soťálkᴧ, huťólpi; to spread on (butter, etc): huťól
spread (n)	bᴧi - feast (n)
spread (tr)	spread out a blanket or other linen: ban, bánkit, húlnoye
spread apart	spread legs apart: mósda, mósdada; spread the legs wide apart: mósdawaito; spread someone else's legs apart: mósdadati; spread someone else's legs wide apart: mósdawaitoti
spread out	spread things out: chat, hésboye, yaiyókityo, hésbonoye; be spread out: bató; to spread out as a search team: witípwai
spring (jump)	beťék, talóp; spring down: méhyotno; spring into: beťékʔinno; spring out: beťéksip; spring over the edge: beťékchono; spring to one side: sᴧhékachono
spring (season)	yóhmeni, ókmeni, ókmenkiti; in the springtime: yókmenkitdi, yókmendadi; be almost spring: yóhmendapoto; become spring: yóhmenda; spring festival: yóm wéda
spring of water	paḱáni/pᴧḱáni, osóḱᴧ, luḱú, bosóḱ; springs: paḱánkanto, osóḱsokto; little spring: osóḱbe; spring water: luḱúm momí
spring tea	osóḱᴧm buḱúiḱᴧ/asalḱᴧm bᴧkuiḱᴧ
sprinkle	sprinkle something dry around: wᴧkᴧ́k, wokᴧ́kᴧsitoye; sprinkle (as rain): ḱadíkim pibáwi
sprint (v)	wilék - hurry; welé - run (v)
sprout (v)	chebᴧ́k; begin sprouting: chebᴧ́kdoi
spruce	báso; spruce tree: básom chá; spruce tips: básom chípbᴧ
spur (n)	bichí - thorn
spurn	hálche - reject (v)
spy (v)	cheḱá, ḱᴧi; spy around: okᴧ́inoye; spy on: ḱáchenu
squabble (v)	wókit
squabble (v)	wokótito - quarrel (v)
squad	bomó - group
squander	wahéno - waste (v)
squat (adj)	nᴧs - low (adj)
squat (v)	ínyambóno; squat down on the balls of the feet: boḱᴧ́lkinu, boḱᴧ́l; squat down: tᴧ́ikiti
squaw carpet	ḱawíbano, humchi, demtatoko
Squaw Peak	Om Chatim Yamáni
Squaw Queen Creek	Om Chatim Sewí
Squaw Valley (Plumas)	Om Chatim Ḱoyóm
squeak (v)	chat, chátnoye
squeeze	kapíl, ḱítap
squint	híncho; squinting: wikútui

English	Maidu
squirrel	gray squirrel: sáwali/sáwwali; ground squirrel: hiló, súpa, ḱoyóm títtitkṃ; flying squirrel: káinokṃm tṃlṃ́lṃ, chabába; pine squirrel: tṃlṃ́lṃ/tulúli; Douglas squirrel: hindakono; Belding squirrel: títtitkṃ; "squirrel foot" basket design: sáwalim payí
St. John's wort	wululutikṃ
stab	bṃhṃ́k, wó, bṃhṃ́m, yohóp
stable	be stable: hétilkit, petílkit
stack	wulút, wutúl, yaiyónpin; stack things: wutúlyo; stack wood: chá wulút
staff (for walking)	bṃsákṃ; basá - cane, walking stick; use a staff to get across: bití'ukitṃsitopin
stage (n)	polówa - floor
stagecoach	sṃtéchi
stagger	stagger around: ya'ṃstaino, wunúnoye; stagger and fall: pṃ́ksalew
stain (n)	balikṃ - dye
stair	bénno - step
stake (n)	léiwo - part of
stalk (of plant)	latomi, lumí - stem
stallion	búlim kawáyu, yepím kawáyu; stud stallion: héiyatokṃn kawáyu
stand (i.t.)	tṃs, tṃ́sweye, tṃ́skinu; stand around: tṃ́swonoye; stand/be standing as a tree: pa, panú, wodónu; stand in a certain place: tṃ́sdikno; stand someone somewhere: tṃ́sdiknoti; stand as a permanent object: tṃ́swoye, kolóikinu, yṃdónu; stand by or on: tṃ́sbokit; stand leaning against with the hands: mái'odiknonu; stand around glowering at: sṃnchetutumoto; be standing at: tṃ́sda; stand on: tṃ́sťa, tṃ́sboťa; stand still: tṃ́skit; remain standing (as a plant): wodónbis; be continually standing by: tṃ́sdanu; stand up: sṃwédoi, sṃwékadoi, sṃwéwedoi; stand up from sitting: tṃ́sdoi, tṃ́skadoi; stand up and watch for: tṃ́sbokitno
stand (tr)	honwéyepati - survive something, bear (v), endure
stand by	wodák - stick close to
stand by (someone)	húno - support
stand for	mṃyákkṃ́ti - be the same as each other
stand guard	chenú - watch
star	lṃlṃ́; falling star: sátoyo
stare	chenú; stare at: cheyénu, cheḱónu, sṃnchedónu; stare off in the distance: cháicheḱonu; one who is always staring off into space: ṃ́schenusape
start	a start/the start: ḱabṃ́k; to start: ḱabṃ́k; start on (something): mépai; start to go: ṃnónoi, ṃdói; start going (with someone): ṃhédoi; start off going: ṃdóino; start up (by itself): ṃnódoi; start something up: ṃnódoiti; having started: ḱabṃ́kṃm; from the start: wonónan; where one had started from: ṃnódoiwono, wónṃidoiwonope
start (a project)	hukít - create using thought
starve	okówono (RD), ókwono (FC)
stash (tr)	kilé - hide (something); store (v): yaché - save
state (n)	ḱódo - district, area
state (situation)	be in a state, be in an emotional state: bisṃkínu
state (v)	wewé - speak
statement	wewé - speech
station	ḱoḱó - location
station wagon	lalám kiwíkupem
statute	ma - law (n)
stay	bis, ka'ánu; stay like this: eyánu; make someone stay: bístikíye, bishúkit; intending to stay: bísmadom; be staying: wowó; stay here! ká'anupi! stay with: bísidi; stay with while going: ṃhéto; stay with and take care of: bísdodoi; stay with and care for temporarily: bísdodo; stay together: bístoto; stay back: hadádadi'ebis; stay away: tṃtṃ́; always staying away: ṃpéka wiyétidom
stay near	wodák - stick close to
steadfastly	ṃpéḱnudom - continually
steady	be steady: petílkit
steak	hudáwdo - a cut-off piece
steal	pedá; go around stealing: pedáyeto; bring together what was stolen: pedáhamoto; in order to steal: pedáḱoido
stealing (n)	pedá'i - theft
steam (v)	pólpol
steep (tea leaves) (v)	hamít - soak
steer clear of	wadá - dodge, get away
steer to	héw - point in the right direction

English	Maidu
Steller's Jay	kaieskɱ/kaihískɱ/káyeskɱ, kaieskɱm máidɱ
stem	lumí
step (n)	bénno - step
step (v)	step (noun): bényepe, bénno; take a step: bén, bénye; take steps: bénno; step on: bénťa; step across: bénsito; step around: bénnoye; step down: bénkit; step into (something): ťehús; step into water: pɱ́tno; step out of: bénsip; step through: bénsitoye; step up: béndoi; step in the rhythm (of someone else): benhúye; sing to the beat of someone's step: ɱnósol
stepping stone	bénno - step
sterile, non-reproducing	walú
stew (n)	homá, to stew (food): hom
stew (v) in anger	wasó'ituti - be angry till it hurts
stick (n)	chá, ṕaká; fire poker stick: sɱsɱ́; gambling sticks: démi; a big stick/club: wókɱ
stick in (v)	bó, bihít, bidít, bɱhɱ́k, bɱhɱ́m; stick something into: ḱapólno, sɱhópḱoi, yohópḱoi; stick things in: buhúpḱoyo, buhúpyo; stick into an orifice: sɱḱói, sɱḱóiti; stick in a belt: yehétdoi; stick into as a sliver: sɱhóp, sɱdétno, sidétno, bihít'inno; stick feathers in the hair: sɱlépai; stick something down into: yohópmit; stick something into a hole to close it: wohópno; stick something on someone (like a pin): bidítpai; stick something through something: ḱapólsito
stick on (something sticky)	dáḱpai, yu; stick something on: dáḱpaiti, pulót, bidítpai
stick out, stick up	sɱ, sɱdáw; be sticking out (like quills): sɱsínu, sɱdáwwinu; be sticking out (like a tail): opíninu; be sticking out like this: eyádawinu; stick up vertically: bɱ́donu, sɱdói
stick up for	húno - support
sticker (n)	bichí - thorn
sticky substance	daḱ; sticky tape: dáḱpai'im
stiff	yóiyoi
still (adj)	kelé - quiet (adj)
still, up to now	húḱoi, huḱóino, húḱoinum; still doing: huḱóido, still do: huḱói
sting	sting (by itself): íchem; sting someone: yo, yu; keep stinging: yudáto; stinging insect: yokɱ́m kapí
stingy	méiťi, méiťipe, méibonosa, húlis, méiťisa
stink	híssa, hísatipe; always stinky: híssasa; stinker/stench-causer: hísatikɱ (note that without the adverb wasát, these terms could mean "fragrant" rather than "stinky," but usually the implication is "stinky")
stink beetle	búchɱli
stint	tawáli - work
stir	yaw; stir around: yáwsitoye; stir a small quantity: wichúmɱl; stir a large quantity: hóweye; stir a large quantity round and round: hóweyesitoye; stir up dust: sukdóiti, súknoti
stir up trouble	wasásoti; make trouble, provoke, cause problems: matí - cause, do (something) to
stitch (v)	pɱyé - sew, púya
stock (n)	wasása - stuff
stockings	íschomi
stoic	be stoic: hóntos
stolen property	bring together stolen property: pedáhamoto
stomach	ḱamí; have a stomach ache: ḱamílák; lie on the stomach: ḱámnak
stomp on	ťéhul, tétyol
stomping ground	in somebody's stomping ground: yɱnóyedi
stone (n)	ó
stool (n)	pew, bench: bísťakɱ - bench
stoop	a'ái; be stooped over: yɱnɱ́s, yɱnɱ́skit; be stooped way over: hadá ma'át yɱnɱ́skit
stop (n)	batásluťi - the extreme end
stop (v)	etáp, hékit/húkit; stop moving: yesáno/yasáno/yosáno/yɱsáno; stop/wait! étu; stop something/someone: etápti, yosánoti (stop a vehicle or animal from moving); stop (plural subject): hékikit; stop raining: ḱadíkhekit; stop and stand still: tɱ́skit, tɱ́sbokit, kolóibokit; stop little by little: etátapkit; not stop doing: etápmenchono; where they had stopped: tɱ́skitwonodi
stop over (v)	uyúk - stay overnight
stop up (something)	wohópno; a stopper: wusutikɱ
storage bin	sukun
store (n)	méitokɱm hɱbó, méitokɱm uiyí, méitom hɱbó

English	Maidu
store (v)	yaché - save
storm	kóh'bono
story	betéi/betéyi; what is being told (a story): betéipe; tell a story: betéi, túwei; tell a story about (someone): betéitai; when telling the old stories: betéidom amᴧni; storyteller: túweykᴧ; what goes along with a story (like songs): betéinakḱenupe
story (in building)	polówa - floor
stove	óm sá; stovepipe: óm sá bodóitikᴧ
Stover Mountain	Kúduidᴧm
straddle	yoḱósťaheyto
straggle	tókdati'us - lag behind
straighten up	tᴧsdoi - rise, stand up
strain (v)	gag, retch: tás; strain while defecating: hónkui, hónku
strainer	chᴧlᴧ; baskets used as strainers: chᴧlkᴧm woló, chᴧlchᴧl woló
strange	strange people: ka'ámenim máidᴧ
stranger	ḱoyói, ḱoyóyo; not strangers: chaicháimeni
strangle	kum, ḱíloschik, bichís; strangle someone: bichísti, ḱadóschik
strap	haḱ; strap a child in a cradleboard: laḱít
strawberry	húluρiti, hulópichi
streak (n)	ókpayi - ray of sunshine
stream (n)	momí, sewí, sewí luḱú
stream (v)	yonó, opín - gush forth, gush out
street	bo, kalétam bó; in the street/on the street: bodí; street light: bom toyakᴧ
strengthen	strengthen something: chᴧititi; strengthen oneself: éptito'us; strengthen someone: etósti; strengthen each other: éptitoto
stretch	wi'áswaito, pulót; stretch a rope: píuboḱoiti; completely stretch a rope: píuboḱoitibos; stretch by pulling: wihᴧp, wihᴧpḱoi; stretch things out: yaiyókityo; stretch a net over to catch something: mikchíkti, húhuchik; stretch with the foot: ťe'áswaito, ťehᴧp, ťehᴧpḱoi; stretch gradually with the foot: ťehᴧhᴧpḱoi; stretch all the way with the foot: ťedátdikno; stretched out (skin): bató'ono
stretch (i.t.)	piúbonpininu - extend down (as rope)
stretch (oneself) out	kachó
stretch the truth	witái - exaggerate
stretch to	extend to: towóikit
stride (n)	bénno - step (n)
stride (v)	take longer strides: tóllalaino
strife	hómpaito - fight; cause strife: wasásoti
strike back	yámmotopai - retaliate
string	ḱuḱú; make string: pán; counting string: walási
stringed instrument	wéppenkᴧ
strip (v)	strip off clothes: husíp; strip a place of vegetation: podáti; be virtually stripped of vegetation: pódatihudoi
stroke (v)	stroke affectionately: báslem
strong	physically strong: etósi, etóspe; mentally/spiritually strong: épti, éptito; strong like a piece of cloth that doesn't tear: chᴧiti; be strong: épti, hóntos, ťotimén; be stronger: etóswalaw; be not very strong: etósboduk; be strong enough: basáp; being strong: ťotimenwetí
structure (n)	uyí - building (n)
struggle (n)	hómpaito - fight
strum	wéppem, strum away: wéppemto
stub one's toe	íswolo
stubborn	ᴧhᴧ
stuck	get stuck: daḱ; get stuck to: dáḱpai, be stuck to: dáḱpanu; get stuck onto: dáḱdikno; be stuck together (animals): yedát, yedáttoto, ṕákchik; get all of them stuck in: buhúpnobos; have something stuck in the hand: mábo
stuck up	eḱáwche'uspe; be stuck up: eḱáwche'us; act stuck up: eḱáwche'us húweye
stud (n)	hᴧmtᴧti - beam (n), rafter
study (v)	chekíno, yawí, chekíno - read, examine, look closely at
stuff	wasása
stumble	yolós, yolósno; stumble and fall: pᴧksalew; stumble around: yásmaye, yásnoye; pretend to stumble: yolósḱuḱus
stump (n)	osḱúni
stunned	ᴧs - dazed
stunning (adj)	eḱáwchetipe - beautiful

English	Maidu
stupid	húkesmen, huní wi'ípe
sturgeon	hulmayi
stylist	wᴍkᴍ́stokᴍm máidᴍ - barber
subsequently	hóipaidi - afterwards
subside	chedá
subsidize	húno - sponsor (v)
subsidize	heyáwe - support by doing something
substance	wasása - ingredient
subtract	mahá'uk̓oi - take away
suburbs	wo'áswono - on the outskirts
succeed (do well)	yahát yatí'us, wi'íyemen; it succeeded: yahát 'as
succeed (follow)	hóipai - follow
such, such a	ka'át, ati; in such a way: ka'átik
such-and-such	ka'áwini
suck	as an infant: miní; not as an infant: dútdut, dut, dútap; suck in curing: dúttap, yómkit; to doctor by sucking: yówwochik, bodóiti; hire a doctor to suck illness out: dútwoyo
sucker fish	tahohoni, t̓ohóni, t̓átate, wᴍ́slᴍ, yami'i
suckle	miníti
suddenly	kétetebodom, mayákk̓en; move suddenly: kétetebo
suffer	bomᴍ́mᴍti
sufficient	t̓ík; be sufficient: wémt̓ikiti
sugar	súka, sudák; sugar pine: sumú
sugar pine	sumú; sugar pine tree: sumúm chá
suggest	wéye; refer to, mean: kái
suitcase	hadóikᴍ
summer	láimeni, elák, láimenkit
summit	chuchúi; at the summit: chuchúidi
sun	ekím pok̓ó, pok̓ó, ékdam pok̓ó
sunburned	wiláknope - ruddy
Sunday	súneki/sᴍneki
sunflower	túmbakᴍ, wólek túmbakᴍ, tú, bukᴍ
sunglasses	hiní wichíkkᴍ
sunlight	ókpai/ókpayi; come in/down as sunlight: ókpayim pín
sunny	it is sunny: ókpai wakítdom
sunrise	ékdadoi, kᴍdói
sunset	the sun is setting: ókpai wochónodom, ókpai ochónodom; be almost sunset: hínk̓iknopoto; where the sun sets: hínk̓oikᴍmnantedi, pok̓óki kᴍ́chonokᴍnantedi
sunshine	ókpayi/ókpai; ókpai wákitdom: sunshine is coming down
superb	superb one: yahádikᴍ
supernatural being	k̓ákkini - spirit
supersede	hóipai - follow
supervisor	yep̓óni - chief
supplant	hóipai - follow
supply (v)	méi, méito - give, give out
support (v)	húno, penóweye; lend support by providing or doing something: heyáwe; give verbal support: pepáno, héwwonoye, héwwo
support (v)	heyáwe - support by doing something
suppose	maichákito; supposing that...: hesámet
surely	hai'í, tetétse, yahátkana
surface (n)	púidi - outside
surface (v)	chebᴍ́k, chebᴍ́kdoi - appear
surmise	áik̓ak̓at
surmount	ónk̓oi - outsmart
surpass	waláw - exceed
surprisingly	mayákk̓en - unexpectedly, somehow
surrender	yasáno - give up
surround	yᴍ́mmoto; surround someone to catch them: k̓achík; completely surround: k̓achíkimotobos
surroundings	k̓ódoi - area
survey (v)	chebós - look closely

English	Maidu
survive	hónwehelu, hónwenu; keep surviving: hónhuluk; continue to survive: hónhulu; survive by doing: hónwe'inu; survive all this time by doing: hónwenuwéw; survive it/live through this/be brave: honwéyepati; cause someone to survive: hónhulukti; those who survive: honwépepe
Susan River	Pam Sewím
Susanville	Súmbili
Susanville area	sumbilnandi, Pam Sewím Ḱódom
Susanville people	kulúma/kulómu
suspect (v)	ókket - doubt
suspend (v)	wehétkit - hang up
sustain	heyáwe - support by doing something
sustain	t̓éstimen - prolong
Sutter Buttes	Éstom Yamáni
swallow (bird)	kampíchulapi/kómpichilip̓/ḱumpichilipe, píchilipe
swallow (v)	ḿnnoti, ḿtnoti
swamp	pakáni
swamp	osókɱ - bog
swan	wóldokkɱ
sway (as a branch)	wíslai
swear, cuss	wásweye; swear at: wáswewe; swear at oneself: wáswewé'us, waswéye'us
sweat	lḿpkitti; to sweat: lḿpkit; make someone sweat: lḿpkittiti; sweat and dance: ḱumlái; sweathouse: ḱumhḿ
sweep	hɱbás/hebás; sweep out: hebássip; sweeper/broom: hɱbáskɱ
sweet (tasting)	sudákpe, sudák, sudábe
sweetheart	ɱt̓ḿt̓ɱibe - term of affection, oiḿpaipe - beloved
sweet-smelling	yahát hísatipe - fragrant
swell (v)	swell up: pú; swell shut: púchik
swerve	wḿndoi - turn aside
swim	swim as humans: piyéto/pi'eto/pɱyéto; swim as fish: yá; swim across: pesíto/pisíto; swim alongside: pepáno; swim around (humans): pinóye; swim around (fish): yánoye; swim away: piḱói; swim down across: pesítopin; swim downstream (as humans): pínno; swim downstream (as fish): yánno; swim out: pisíp; swim upstream (as fish): yáno; swim upstream (as humans): pinó; swim up to the surface: yódoi; swim routinely: hehepiyétono
swing (n)	a child's swing: nḿwɱntokɱ; to swing on a swing: nḿwɱn
swing while dancing	side to side: kodéle'émto; swing arms while dancing: yíwoye; swing round and round: wḿnt̓et̓enoye/wánt̓et̓enoye
swipe (v)	pukétkakachono - brush, touch going by
swipe (v)	pedá - steal
swirl as water	hínnoyeti, mómpoldoi
swish the tail	wíslai
switch on (v)	toyákit - turn on (light)
swoop	támp̓it; swoop down: támp̓it̓in, ḱái'inpin; swoop down towards: támp̓it̓inpin; swoop upward: yéiwodoi
symbolize	mɱyákkḿti - be the same as each other
sympathize with	bomḿmɱkno - pity (v), feel sorry for
tab (n)	humusma - debt
table	pewót̓akɱ, tébɱli
tacos	takósi
tadpole	óspo
tail	bukú
tailbone	kiwím buḱú
taillight	kalétam toyákɱtipe - headlight
tailor (v)	pɱyé - sew
take	mé; take something that is handed: médato; take from (someone): méda; take something over or across: méno; take someone somewhere: hóiwihaḱoi; take away: donínoḱoi, mahá'uḱoi; take someone along (down in something like car or boat): hóiwihatno; take something down: hápdaw; take down something hanging: wehétda, wehétdaw; take down something hanging and carry across: wehéthachono; take down something hanging and carry to another place: wehéthachopin; take something back: memé, haiyéwe; take something back out: yewékit; take (someone) up/upstairs: hówihadoi; take food from the fire: áisiye, áiye, yo'ái; take something out: hasíp; take out by hand: sówwosip; take out of a pocket: wihópdoi; take off clothes: husíp

English	Maidu
take (someone) out	hóiwi'ai - lead someone somewhere
take a chance	helái - gamble
take action	hesáti - do something
take advantage of	hᴍhá - use
take care	ókket - be careful
take care of	bísdodoi; take care of something for someone: bísdodo
take exception	hálcheto - disagree
take flight	yéi, kai - fly (v)
take for granted	huhéhenomen - not think twice about
take into account	húni - consider
take it easy	rest after exertion: wokócheda - rest (v); relax, ease up: chedá - rest
take no notice	chenúḱoimen - not pay attention
take off	káidoi - fly up
take off	ᴍkói - go away
take off after	héi, yáhpat - chase, follow, pursue, go after
take one's leave	ᴍkói - go away
take out	wikᴍ́p - extract (v)
take pity on	bomᴍ́mᴍkno - pity (v), feel sorry for
take place	mahélu - occur, happen
take pride in	ᴍkáwche - admire
take the floor	wewé - deliver a speech
taking off (n)	ᴍkóida - departure
talented	yahámakitpe; be talented at: yahámakit
talisman	óm sulú, oméiyi - good-luck charm (n)
talk (n)	yapáito; talking/speech: wewé
talk (v)	wéye, wewé; talk to: yapáito; make someone talk: wéyeti; talk like this: eyái; start talking away: wewéyeḱoi; talk together: yapáitoto; talk to oneself: wéye'us, yapáito'us; talk as if: yákwei; talk in one's sleep: ᴍ́sweye; talk pitifully: bomᴍ́tiweye; talk through (an opening or crack): nákweye; talk into a microphone or talk on the telephone: nákweye; start talking: wéyedoi; keep talking: wéyebis; be unable to talk: wéyechᴍi; one who talks like that (inappropriately): ka'áimapem; don't talk like that/say such things: ka'áimen; a big talker/one who goes around talking all the time: wéyenoyesakᴍ
talk about	máiye, chewéto; what are you/they talking about?: hesí wéyedom?; What could he/she/they be talking about?: máiyewyakḱen?
talk back to	hokótito - argue with
talk nonsense	húboḱoi wéyedom - make no sense
talk out of	héwa, mamámen - warn not to do
tall	teté, hadá, lam, hadádoi; look tall: hadádoiwiyakka
tambourine	wátdakᴍ - clapper stick
tame (tr)	sᴍ́don - make a pet of
tanager	táwlikkᴍ
tangerine	owánchi - orange (fruit)
tap (v)	bódato
tape (n)	dáḱpai'im - sticky tape
target	bodíknokᴍ
tart (adj)	chuchᴍkpe - sour
tarweed	yómpom sawí
task (n)	tawáli - work
taste	taste (something): dó; taste (good or bad): dóti, dótipe; have a taste: dómaki; tasting good: hanána yahátidom; tasty: dóchekᴍ, dóchema, sudábe; be tasty: sudá
tasty	luscious: dóchekᴍ - delicious
Taylor's Creek	Am Sewí
Taylorsville	Tosí Ḱoyó/Tosím Ḱoyó/ Tasíḱoyo, Ḱᴍsdu
tea	tí'i
teach	mákpapaiti; teach school: yawíti
teacher	yawítikᴍ, mákpapaitikᴍ; male teacher: yawítikᴍm máidᴍ; female teacher: yawítikᴍn kᴍle
teal (duck)	líki, olupkᴍ
team	bomó - group
tear (v)	widás, yᴍtᴍ́i, widásdo, wᴍt́ᴍ́i; tear open: yᴍtᴍ́ito; tear apart: wᴍt́ᴍ́iwaito; tear to pieces: wᴍt́ᴍ́ikitbos; tear wide open: yᴍtᴍ́iwaito; keep tearing with the teeth: wétetepdaw

404

English	Maidu
tear down	wi'íti - destroy
tears (n)	wobí, wom; tearful: wobítapo
teenagers	yᴍpe
teeth	chawá; grind the teeth: chikí ƙᴍƙᴍƙᴍsti
telephone (v)	míldan ƙúƙti - make a phone call
telephone wire	míldan ƙúƙ
tell	a, káiye, wéye; keep telling someone: wowéw, kaiyéw; tell someone to go: ᴍkóiwo; as was told ("as I told you before"): adóm 'as; tell each other: wéwetoto; tell someone to do: wo; I have to tell you: wéyes min; tell a story: betéi, betéito; tell stories about: betéitai
tell oneself	wéye'us - talk to oneself
tell the truth	wémťiki kai - tell the truth
temblor	yanánaito - earthquake
temper	hot tempered: wasósape, wáschᴍ; lose one's temper: wasóhati; regain one's temper: wasácheda
temperature	ƙódom - weather
tempest	kóh'bono - storm
temporarily	núktina, ťíktenaki - for a little while, for a certain time
temporarily could not	couldn't: MMG p. 55, use -men infix on verb + imperfect verb ending (p. 64)
tempt	héwwelek - seduce
temptation	resist temptation: hóntos
ten	máschoƙo, máchoƙo, máischoƙo, sᴍttim máschoƙo
tend	bísdodo - stay with and take care of
tender (as meat)	chᴍitimen
tense (present or past)	ƙódo - time
term	yawí - word
terminate	etápti - stop (something)
terminology	wéye - speech
terminus	batásluťi - the extreme end
terribly	tetét - very
territory	my territory: ᴍnó'esma; in my territory: ᴍnó'esmadi; in his/their territory: ᴍnópedi
territory	ƙódo - district, area
terrorize	yáhpatchono, yáhpatwéƙoi - go after to attack
test (n)	welé
test (v)	mákwono - try to
testicles	kosím ṗála, ṗála
testify about	chewéto
textiles	saláwi - cloth, blanket
than	dᴍƙᴍ; more than: waláwdᴍkbe, waláwti
thank (v)	give thanks: héwwonoye, hó - say "it is good," say "ho." Thank you: nik yaháti'ankano, or hew
that	mᴍ/ mᴍm, mᴍyé; that one: héwi, mᴍwéti; that distant (one): ayápe, aní/aním; that one (just mentioned) amá, mᴍyím; that same one: mᴍhéwi; that way/direction: anína; at that time: akᴍmen; in that place: ayápedi, mᴍídi; from that place: mᴍína
that	MMG p. 41, various forms depending on meaning
that's right	he'é, ho - yes
thaw	kómchú
the	MMG p. 12, 41 mᴍm or left off
the Almighty	ƙódoyakᴍ - Creator
the country	ƙódo - area, country
the one before	hínwom - ahead
the past	hóiya - formerly
the wild	yawónope - that which is created
the world over	yᴍwáitokᴍdi - everywhere the world extends
theft	pedá'i
their	their (2): mᴍchóƙi; their (3 or more): mᴍséƙi, mᴍyéƙi
their	MMG p. 40 - possessive, depends on how many people are involved in "their"
them	them (2): mᴍsá, máicho, máisᴍ; them (3 or more): mᴍsé, máise
them	MMG p. 40 - objective, depends on how many people are involved in "them"
themselves	mᴍséwet

405

English	Maidu
then	ḱan, bei, awetén, amánkan; then/so then (with focus shift to the other character): amɤ́ni, amɤ́nikan, amákan, achét; then (without focus shift): ánkanim, amápem, adóm, apém, amét; then/subsequently: mayákḱen; then (during that season): yaktekítpedi; then/at that point in time: mɤmén; only then: mɤmméndɤḱɤ; then, because of that (already discussed): amám; just when (one thing happened), then (something else happened): kan... kan
theorize	huhéye - imagine
there	mɤdí, aní, mɤyí; to there/to that place: mɤná, anína; in there: anídi; from there: mɤnán, anínan, mɤnándi; in that same place: mɤídi; from that same place: mɤína; right there: makán, hedéndi, ɤpéḱanupe; and in that place: amádikan; in/to that place (previously mentioned): amádi, amána; from that place (previously mentioned): amánan; in that direction: amának, ántedi; to/in a faraway place: ántena; from somewhere in the distance: ántenántenan
thereafter	amá wóinan
therefore	amét, ánkan, ánkaninkan
these people	uním bomó
these two	unícho
they	they (2): mɤsám, máichom, máichem; they (3 or more): mɤsém, máisem
thick (consistency)	ehɤ́s; make thick/thicken: ehɤ́sti
thick (dimension)	kówwil
thicket	dɤ́, pá, sémkɤs
thief	pedákɤ; habitual thief: pedása, pedásape
thievery	pedá'i - theft
thigh(s)	máwa; between the thighs: máwam pulúmto
thimbleberry	dálkɤ
thin	thin as a person/tree/animal: ḱa'ók, yɤnó; thin in dimension: ťoť, ťóťťoť; be thin: banhɤ́tanu; make something thinner (more watery): momchúiti, mómwiyakti
thin out	mómwiyakti - make more watery
thing	hesí, wasása; little thing: hesísi; "thingy:" íska
think	húweye/hɤwéye, húni; do some thinking: húheiye; give a thought to: húheihei; think it all the way through: húweyebos; think as one goes along: huhéye'ɤno; start to think about: húweyedoi; have in mind: húdan; think/wonder: áikaḱat; think/be under the impression: maichákito; think about: húheye, huhehé, húweyepai; think about/plan together: húsemweteyo; having something in mind: húweyepepe; What do you think you're doing?: makɤḱá?; not think twice about it: huhéhenomen; without thinking about it: huhehénonwet; not think about: húťamen; one who doesn't think: húweyemeni; not thinking of anything in particular: húweinonwet
thirsty	momsík
thirty	sápɤ máischoḱo
this	uním, hedénim; this kind of: ánťɤťɤ, ayáwinim; in this kind of place: ayápedi; this same: mɤkán(im); get this far: ma'ántekit
this	MMG p. 41, various forms depending on meaning
this group	uním bomó
this time	about this time: achéki; by this time: achéknu; "all this time" is expressed by the -wew- infix on the verb.
Thompson Peak	Widóikɤm Yamánim
thorn	bichí, bití; covered with thorns: bichítapope
those	MMG p. 41, various forms depending on meaning
those (3 or more)	máisɤ, mɤyésɤ, mɤ́m bomó; those people there: mɤséna, aním bomó; those things: mɤhéwi
those two	máicho, mɤpéne, mɤchó; those two by themselves: mɤchó'us
thoughts	húweye
thrash someone	kíwwo
thread	pɤyékɤm ḱukú
three	sápɤ, sápwi; three times: sápɤinini
thrive	yahát yatí'us - do well for oneself
throat	ḱuilulumi/ḱulúlumi/ḱɤilulumi; to clear the throat: ḱepɤ́
throughout	throughout a time period: bísto; throughout the land: pípem ḱódo

English	Maidu
throw	a throw: wʌdʌ́m/wadʌ́m; to throw: wʌdʌ́m/wadʌ́m, bó', boḱói; throw a lot of things/materials: wá, wádʌm; throw something pliable: waťák; throw something at: batáp; throw towards: wʌdʌ́mdo; wʌdʌ́msito/wadʌ́msito; throw (something) across towards: wadʌ́msitopin/wʌdʌ́msitopin; throw a lot of things across: wádʌmsito; throw (a pliable thing) across towards: waťáksitopin; toss back and forth: yodʌ́msito, yodʌ́msitopin; go along throwing (something): wʌdʌ́mno; throw (something) along after (someone): wʌdʌ́m'ʌheyno/wadʌ́m'ʌheyno; throw (things) along after: wádʌm'ʌheyno; throw at and miss: watáito; while throwing (something) across: yʌdʌ́msitodo, yodʌ́msitodo; throw (a pliable thing) towards: waťákye; throw (something) upwards: bodói; throw something up to: wodíkno
throw (someone) off balance	wʌdáktemáldoi
throw away, throw out	wʌdʌ́mḱoi/wadʌ́mḱoi, wádʌmye; throw a lot away: wádʌmḱoi; throw a pliable thing away: waťákḱoi; throw out: wádaw; throw (a lot) out: wádʌmdaw
throw down	throw (someone) down: hánokiti, hawíkakit; throw (something) down: wʌdʌ́mdawto, wʌdʌ́mkit/wadʌ́mkit, wákit; throw a lot down: wádʌmkit; throw down from a tree: héyunpintiyo; throw down an incline: wʌdʌ́mḱoino, wʌdʌ́mmitno, wadʌ́mḱoino, wadʌ́mmitno; throw in a downhill direction: bónno; throw down into: wánpin, waťákmit, wádʌmit, wʌdʌ́mino, yayónpin, héyumit, wʌdʌ́mit; throw down cards (in a game): wudúmkit; throw in the water: wáyo; be thrown down: wákinu
throw in, throw on	throw on: wáťa; throw over into: wáchopin; throw onto: wádikno; throw (a lot) on: wádʌmpai; throw something into: wʌdʌ́mmit/wadʌ́mmit, throw things in: yayópin, wáiyo, wádʌmmit; throw in (as firewood): yaiyónpin; throw in the water: wáyo; throw into a pile: wutúlkit
throw off	throw (something) off: wʌdʌ́mdawino, wadʌ́mdawino; throw (this and that) off: wʌdʌ́mdadawino, wadʌ́mdadawino; throw (something) off (as clothes): wadʌ́mdaw, wʌdʌ́mdaw; throw off (as a horse): wʌdʌ́mchono, wadʌ́mchono
throw off (emit)	hónwesip - exhale
throw up	wé - vomit
thrust	hil; thrust (something) into (something): sʌpól, sʌpólno; thrust many sharp things into: hílpai; thrust secretly: ḱáwok; thrust in sexual intercourse: ínwok, yepésto
thumb	tem chipbʌ, tetém mám chípbʌ
Thumb Rock	Tetém Mamchipbʌm Om
thunder	wʌtʌ́mtʌmi/witʌ́mtʌmi/witúmtumi/wutúmtumi; to thunder: yohón; to roll/rumble as thunder: ḱʌlʌ́lʌ, ḱʌlʌ́plʌlʌp; be thundering: ḱódom kʌlʌ́plʌlʌpdom, ḱódom kʌlʌ́lʌdom; thundering: wʌtʌ́mi
tic (twitch)	have a eye tic: hínwilok
tick (bug)	tení, ťíḱ
tickle	chhʌḱʌ́, chhʌḱʌ́chhʌkʌ; tickle each other: chhʌḱʌ́chhʌkʌtoto, go tickling each other: chhʌḱʌ́chhʌkʌtoḱoi; tickle as foreplay: sʌkásai
tie (n)	ḱuḱú - rope
tie (v)	to tie: dol, ṕúnto, wiṕún, yodót; tie a knot: ṕúnye; tie knots: ṕun, dólyo; tie in a bundle: budú; tie things together: dolím motó; tie something around: dólchono, dólsitoye; tie down: wiṕúnkit; tie onto: dólpai, widátpai; tie up: dólkit, budúti; tie up (something) for (someone): yodótpaititi, yodótpaitino; tie onto the head: owólak; tie shut with: wʌkʌ́mchik; tie with lacings: witámmoto; tie and cinch a bunch of things: witáyeyo; not know how to tie anything: dólwasa; tie rope: yodótpaikʌm ḱuḱú; be tied around: widúmmoto; be tied to: yodótpanuto
tier	polówa - floor
tiger lily	loḱóm, loḱómini; tiger lily flower: loḱómim yó
tight	tight (like shoes): ťát; be tight (like a belt): bʌḱʌ́w
tighten	chʌ́iti, bʌḱʌ́wti; be tightened (as a rope): hétilkit; tighten a belt: witám, witámto, witámdoi
tightwad	húlissa - cheapskate
timberland	cháchato - woods
time	time period, as year or season: ḱódo/ḱódoi, méni; the same time of year: yaktekít; for a short time: tibína, ťíktenaki; at some point in time: mʌméntapo; what time is it?: hesánte kítade?; at the time: achékmen; by this time: achéknu; in a short time: yaktekítpedi; a long time: ebʌ́m; be a long time: ebʌ́dom, ebʌ́bʌ
timeworn (adj)	betéi'i - ancient (adj)

English	Maidu
tingle	íchechem
tiny	núktiluťi
tiny ones	tibíbi, tibíbinono
tip, end	chípbm, óschumi, óschumnaki
tipsy	hudásuhsuh
tiptoe	go on tiptoe: loḱét, loḱétḱoi; stand on tiptoe: lánḱeḱét; sort of tiptoe: loḱéḱet; tiptoe across: loḱétsito; tiptoe around: loḱétnoye; tiptoe into: loḱéťinno
tip-top (n)	chuchúi - summit, top
tire someone out	wokóti
tired	wokópe; be tired: wokó; get tired: wasádoi; being too tired for something: wohadóimakat
tissue (for wiping)	híkmdakm papéli, hundákm
to	"to" (meaning "towards") is expressed by the -na or -di suffix on the noun; "to" (on verbs as infinitives) is expressed by the -dom suffix; "to" (meaning "in order to") is expressed by the -madom or -mapem suffix; all the way up to: ínkina
to (+ verb "infinitive")	MMG p. 29, -dom, such as wéyedom "to speak"
to (do)	in order to, intending to: MMG p. 87, -madom or -mapem suffix on verb
to (someone)	interacting with: MMG p. 5, -to infix on verb
to a place	towards: MMG p. 23, -na or -di on noun or pronoun. p. 57, -ye infix on verb
to one's surprise	mayákḱen - unexpectedly, somehow
toad	hawáni, awaní
toadstool	wá; poisonous toadstool: petím wá
tobacco	paní; smoke tobacco: pánpe; be smoking tobacco: pepánu; smoke tobacco together: pepánototo; chew tobacco: paní chawái
today	bey'ím 'ekí, bey'í
toe	pái'im chípbm, payím chípbm
toenail	pái'im bichí, páibichí
tofu	dópu
together	smtidi, pu'u, úm, wmkdi; bring together: mpimoto; come together: mmmoto
together	MMG p. 56, -moto infix on verb
toilet paper	índakmm papéli
tolerable	OK: ámbmḱbm - fair (adj)
tolerate	ḱúidakwiyakka - sort of like
Tom Young	hánchibmi
Tom Young's brother	núsnusi, wabálto
tomato	tmmétm, tumétu
tomb	tánkm - burial ground
tomorrow	béneki
tongs	smsm - fire poker
tongue	éni
tonight	bey'ím kulú, bey'ím kulúdi, uním kulúdi, kulúdi, bey'ím po
too (also)	béibm, ú
too much (do too much)	a lot, excessively, hard (like "work hard"): MMG p. 55, -luť infix on verb
too much, excessively	tetét píkno
tool (n)	ma'ákm - doer
tooth	chiḱí
tooth (of machinery)	bichí - thorn
toothache	chiḱí 'ítu; have a toothache: chiḱí 'ítu
toothpick	chísbmhmlkm
top	óschumi, chuchúi; to/at the top: oschúmdi, chuchúidi; at the very top: óschumluťdi; top of a (pointed) house: oťámoto; top of the head: óskoko; top part (of something flat): óidi; on top: obúdoidi; be on top: mťá; get on top: mdóiťa; get to the top: bmlékwodoi, bmlélekdoi; reach the top: bmlélekdoichoi; be almost to the top: bmlélekdoipoto; a top (for a container)/lid: hónbakm
top (clothes)	chíťakm, kamísa - blouse, shirt
topography	ḱódoi - area, country
torment (v)	yáhpatchono, yáhpatwéḱoi - go after to attack
torrential rain	be a torrential rain: ym'aswono
Torrey maple	líllilta
torso	lulú, lulúmi
torture (v)	bommtiti

English	Maidu
toss	wṁdṁm; go along tossing: yṁdṁmno; toss around: wílliw; toss away: wṁdṁmdaw; toss across (back and forth): yodṁmsito, yodṁmsitopin; toss debris: wṁtṁmwidótnoye'ṁno; toss a lot of things: wáyo; toss the head: owílliw
tot (n)	te - child
totally	finishing off, completely: MMG p. 54, -bos infix on verb
touch	pukét, bṁyó; touch (someone) while going by: pukétkakachono; almost touch (someone) while going by: pukétkachono; get up against (someone)/be touching: ḱa'ódato
touch down (v)	hánpi - land on the ground
touch lightly	pukétkachono - almost touch, brush over
tough	tough (as a person): épti; tough (as meat): chṁiti
toughen	etósti, chṁititi - strengthen
tour (n)	ṁḱóido - traveling, ṁḱói - journey
tournament	ónkoḱoito - contest (n)
tow (v)	hanṁn - haul
towards	"going towards" is expressed by the -ye- infix on the verb and/or the -na suffix on the noun. go towards: ṁyé; towards the mountain: yamánna; turn the head towards: sṁche
towards	to a place: MMG p. 23, -na or -di on noun or pronoun. p. 57, -ye infix on verb
towel	hindákṁ
towhee	to'éskṁ; brown towhee: kapáduwa
town	bískṁm ḱódo, hṁbóboto; in town: towndi
toxin	petí - poison (n)
toyon	lolosi
trace (n)	tibínak - a little bit
trace (v)	hutiyo
track (n)	bó - way
track (v)	pahádaw, pahánoye, pahéḱoi, pai háchono, wochík, pai wochík; to follow tracks going along: paháno; find by tracking: pai chekátḱoi; be unable to find by tracking: pai hánochṁi
tract	ḱawí - land, ḱoyó - field
trade	wonóto; trade for: wónotodo
traditional	betéitodi'im; traditional story: betéi, betéyi
tragedy	yehépti, wehépti, yépti
trail	bó, wochóno; deer trail: sṁmbó; around the trail: bówochono; by the trail: bóminki; on the way going: ṁnókṁdi; on the trail: bódi; to wind along (as a trail): bówono; to wind into the distance (as a trail): bówoḱoi; to go down the trail: bówodaw
trail behind	tókdati'us - lag behind
train (animal)	sṁdon - make a pet of
trainer	mákpapaitikṁ - teacher
transient (n)	hṁbó wi'ípe - homeless person
transit	ṁḱóido - traveling
translate	símmolus/chímolus, betá, hesái; What do you call it?: hesí betámaḱa?; how do you translate..?: ...hesáiḱa?
transmit	ṁḱóiti - send
transparent	chesítope, chewúsuktipe, chehéhechonope
transport (v)	hanṁn - haul
trap	ḱení, chedṁk, ťúno; fish trap: míkki; to set a trap: ťúye; set a fish trap: yemík, míkkit; make a trap: ḱénkiti; fix a trap: ťúyeti, ťúyetiti; stretch a net as a trap: mikchíkti; be caught in a trap: wó
travel	ṁnó, ṁyé; want to travel: ṁnóyaha; travel around: ṁnóye, nénnoye; travel the world: ḱódo ṁmmoto; travel side by side: chanṁno; travel in groups: hehé'ṁno; travel while tracking: háno; travel around in a circle: wṁnṁdoi; travel back and forth: wṁnṁinṁichono; be traveling: ṁḱói'ukinu; travel as a spirit: wóno'ṁḱoi; travel while doing: ṁní; where one travels: ṁnókṁ; where one wants to travel: ṁnóyahape; traveling: ṁḱóido; my departure: ṁnódoisma; their departure: ṁnódoipe
travel (n)	ṁḱóido - traveling
traverse	ḱótwochono - crisscross, go back and forth across
tray	patá, waťá; maple tray: daɒím waťá; using a tray: patáimi; on a tray: patáidi
treat (a patient) shamanistically	yómkit, ítutawal, mokúla; treat patients while traveling: wene'ṁnó

English	Maidu
treat (v)	katí - do to (with negative connotations)
tree	chá; small tree: chábe, potókbe; limby/bushy tree: paktapopem chá; tree root: chám piwí; trees: cháchato; young trees: witóktmtm
trek (n)	mkóido - traveling
tremble	ymkkmk, dmymym, wilíl; as the earth: yanái, yanáinaito, yanáito
tremblers (regalia)	wiléle
tremendously	teté
trespass	no trespassing area: mpé'mnoyemenkm
trestle	yakm - bridge
trial (challenge)	ónkokoito - contest (n)
tribe	ma'a - people
trill (v)	wolólo
trim (v)	tibíti - make smaller
trip (n)	mkói
trip (v)	ískadak; trip and fall: beké'chono
tripe	kampúmpu
trivia	tibíbinono - small ones
troop	bomó - group
trot	yáchaichai; trot along: yáchaichaino; trot down towards: yáchachái'inpin
trouble (tr)	smkála - bother
trout	palíki
truck (n)	hadóikmm kaléta
truck (v)	hanmn - haul
trudge off	káwheikoi, káwheiheikokoi
true	it's true: ma'ákmkan, yahát hapá
truly	tetét, ha'ái - really
truly (emphasis)	ás (follows the word it is emphasizing)
trunk (tree)	lumí - stem
trust	tikche; don't trust/not trust: ókket
truth	wemtiki; "I'm telling the truth:" wemtiki káikás
try	mák; try to: mákwono; try to do: húyeti; try!: mákwonopi!; start to try: mákwonohóiye; want to try/ought to try: mákwonoyaha; try (some food): dómaki; try on shoes: ískoi mákwono; try to say: máiyew
try out	mákwono - try to
try to figure out	húpai - try to figure out
T-shirt	chitakm, kamísa - blouse, shirt
tube	lumí
tuberculosis	honé, honém 'ítu; someone with tuberculosis: honépe, honépem máidm
tucked in	be all tucked in: túikitbos
tug at	wikú
tule	kúpkm; small tule: sokúmbibi
tumble over and fall	beké'chono
tune (n)	solí - song
tune out	pinhéhenon
tunnel	óm kumí, ómpmnno - cave
turkey	kolókolo
turn	a turn: kmdawe; "your turn:" mi kún kmdawe, míkuni; to turn: wmn; turn and face toward: kótwoye; turn and face away: kótwokoi; turn one way and then another: kótwochonoye; turn off the road/turn aside: wmndoi; turn around: wmnnoye, wmnnmnmi; turn around towards: wmnnmnmikoi, kótchonokachopin, turn (something) around (as a vehicle): wmnnoyeti; turn (something) around toward (something): wmnnmnmikoiti; turn around and around (as a windmill): wmnnmnminoye; while turning from side to side in dancing (adv): kotwélemtodo; something that turns: yenmnnokm; turning off place/a turnoff: wmndoikm; turn upside down: smnchewodoi; turn the head towards: smche; have the head turned towards: smnwokoi
turn (something) off	bukúiti/bmkúiti
turn (something) on	turn on a light: toyákit, toyákm toyákmti; turn on the TV: tiwitati
turn down (say no)	wíye - refuse (v)
turn in	túikit - go to sleep
turn out (tr)	wiyéti - force someone out
turn out to be	makm; if it turns out to be: makmmmni
turn over (i.t.)	wmpmlamto - roll over

English	Maidu
turn pale	píbáw - fade (i.t.)
turn up (show up)	chebᵐk, chebᵐkdoi - appear
turnip	tᵐnᵐp
turtle	ó 'opánokᵐ, ómkanai
tusk	chikí - tooth
tutor (n)	mákpapaitikᵐ - teacher
TV	tiwí, chikínokᵐ
tweet	sol - sing
twelve	máischokna péne
twenty	pénem máschoko
twice	péneinini
twig	t́ᵐt́ᵐ/t́ᵐtt́ᵐ
twilight	ḱai; at twilight: kulúmeni; in the twilight: tái'idi; get along toward twilight: yo'ᵐ'ᵐsḱoi, yo'ᵐ'ᵐsno
twine	kuḱú
twine	ḱuḱú
twinkle	ékdadoi
twirl	wílliw
twist	wᵐchadai; twist around something: ḱuiwitubil; twist together: wilíliwimoto; twist on: witúbil
twitch	wilók; have the arm twitch: yímwilok; have the leg twitch: páiwilok; have the mouth twitch: símwilok; have the eye twitch: hínwilok
two	péne; those two: mᵐpéne; two children: pénemte; by twos: pénene
two-by-four (n)	hᵐmtᵐti - beam (n), rafter
tyke	te - child
type	that type: ka'ápe, ka'áwini; this type: eyáwini, ayáwini, ma'ápe; what type of?: hesáwinim?; That's the type: ka'ápe 'as
typing	balí - writing
ugly	wasá'ape, wasachetípe, wemtichᵐkti, wemtichúti, wasáchetípe; be ugly: wasát chenó, wasácheti; be not very good looking: yahátchetiboduk
uh	adóm, íśka
ukulele	wétpeikᵐ - banjo
ultimately	eventually: MMG p. 65, -wono on verb
umbilical cord	betékbono, betékem ḱuḱú
unable	be unable: chᵐi; not know how to: húboḱoi
unattractive	wasá'ape, wasachetípe - ugly
unbeknownst	unbeknownst to you: mayákḱeno; unbeknownst to me: mayákḱes
uncle	bonóno, bonó
uncommon	helú, helúto - a few, a very few
uncommon	ka'ámenim - unusual, strange
unconventional	cháitikapem
under	ḱanáidi, ḱanái'im; the place underneath: ḱanái; crawl under: ḱanáidi lᵐktik; where it goes underneath: ḱanáiwositodi
under the influence	hudásu - drunk
underarm	ḱowó
undercooked	ḱamák, ḱápmeninu
undershirt	ḱanái'im kamísa
underside	ḱanái
understand	makít, pín; understand for oneself: makiti'us/makkítti'us; have an understanding: makítsa
underway	get underway: wonó
undress	husíp
unearth	wikᵐp - extract (v)
uneasy	be uneasy: yehéptoyehye
unexpectedly	mayákḱen - unexpectedly, somehow
unfamiliar	uncommon: ka'ámenim - unusual, strange
unicorn	sᵐti yónnope, yónnowᵐkᵐ
unify	wᵐkdi maháye - bring together in unity
unit	sᵐti - one
unite	wᵐkdímoto
universal	yᵐwáitokᵐdi - everywhere the world extends
universally	yᵐwáitokᵐdi - everywhere the world extends
universe	ḱódo - area, world

English	Maidu
unknowingly	mayákḱen - unexpectedly, somehow
unless	MMG p.87, -menmᴍni ending
unmarked bone in gambling	híndukᴍ, tállala
unmarried	unmarried woman: yepíwi'ipe, hálbisi; unmarried man: kᴍléwi'ipe
unrecognizable	chesáktimen; be unrecognizable: chesáktin, chetínti
unripe	ḱamák, ḱápmeninu
unseen	cheméni
unsightly	wasá'ape, wasachetípe - ugly
unsure	be unsure: yákḱen; be unsure about: hínchesem
unsurpassed	yaháhaluti̇ - the best
untie	pᴍ́n, pᴍ́t, pᴍ́tye, hésbapin; untie a pack: hadóidi pᴍ́tye; come untied: hépᴍt; be all untied: bosíp; untie a knot: pᴍ́twaito; untie several knots: pᴍ́tyo
until now	udó - to this day
unusual	unusual person/people: ka'ámenim máidᴍ
unwilling	be unwilling: okóle; I am unwilling: okóleḱas
unwise	húkesmen - foolish, stupid
unwittingly	mayákḱen - unexpectedly, somehow
up (do upwards)	MMG p. 55, use -doi infix on verb
up to	not be up to (an activity): wohadóimakat
up to now	udó - to this day
upbeat	yahát hubúktipe - pleasant
upcoming	be upcoming: machói
update (tr) (with news)	chewéto - testify about
uphill	make something go uphill: ᴍdóinoti; go farther uphill-ish: yᴍ'áswodoi; start going off/go off uphill: ᴍdóino; run uphill: wilédoino
uppity	eḱáwche'uspe
upright	yahá - good
uproot	wopóldoi, wopólno
upset (tr)	sᴍkála - bother
upside down	sᴍ́nchewodoi
upstream	sewí ᴍdói
up-to-date	béduki - modern
urban area	máidᴍm pípenak
urinate	chuchú, dékti; urinate as a dog: hás, hásdoi; urinate against: chupai, háspai; go urinate: chuchúno, déktino, chuchúḱoi; urinate all over: chuchúsitoye; feel like urinating: chuchúmme; urinate scantily: chúmbitbit
urine	chu, chuchú, chumí
us	nisé; us two: nisá; us two alone: nisá'usi; us two ourselves: nisáwet
use	hᴍhá; use up half: hehéti; add -ni + verb endings to a noun to express using it: papélnip! "use paper!"
use up	wahéno - waste (v)
used (things)	héda, hédada
used to (do)	MMG p. 65, verb form depends on person and number.
used to be	ka'úsan
usher (v)	hóiwiháno - lead
usual	as usual: ḱá'usan
usually	ka'úsan, ekᴍ; usually be: ma'áwew; it usually is: ma'áwewḱan
usually do	MMG p. 65, verb form depends on person and number.
uterus	tém uyí
utter (v)	ḱái - refer to, mean
utterance	wewé - speech
vacuum (n)	wi'ípe - empty, abandoned
vagabond	hᴍbó wi'ípe - homeless person
vagina	pᴍsí, pᴍsím ḱumí; have a large vagina: pᴍ́stapo; have an inflamed vagina: pᴍstᴍ́
vagrant	hᴍbó wi'ípe - homeless person
vain (adj)	eḱáwche'uspe
valley	ḱoyó; in a valley: ḱoyódi; to a valley: ḱoyóna; into a valley: ḱoyóm upedi
valley oak	valley (white) oak: lowí, lowím chá, wáksapem hámsim chá, lóm cha; valley (blue) oak: chakom cha
valley quail	susu
van (n)	kaléta - vehicle
vanish	wi'í - disappear
variety	cháitikkape - different ones

English	Maidu
various	chacháyi
various things	hésboyoyo
vary (v)	cháitika - be different
veer	wᴧndoi - turn aside
vegetation	sawí, linó
vehicle	kaléta
veil	owólakkᴧ - scarf
vein	sedém paká
venison	ínyanam sᴧmí
venom	petí
ventilate	wéllep - fan (v)
venue	kokó - location
Venus	kai pakáni
verbalize	kái - refer to, mean
vertical	be vertical: yᴧdónu
very	tetét, yahát, yát
very much	tetét píkno; by very much: tetét pídom
vest	sállaito
veto (v)	wíye - refuse (v); hálche - reject (v)
vibrate (i.t.)	dᴧyᴧyᴧ - shake, tremble (i.t.)
vibrate (tr)	dᴧyᴧyᴧti - shake something
vice (n)	wasá - evil
vicinity	nak; in the vicinity: papáidi, wochónodi; be in the vicinity: wochóno
victim	play the victim: ónkoiti'us
vigilant	be vigilant: ókketwono
vigor	hᴧkᴧpi - health
vigorously	perform vigorously: wó'ᴧhanoye, wó'ᴧhadoito
village	bískᴧm kódo, hᴧbóboto
vindicate	sówono - let someone go
violet	tᴧsape, pᴧkᴧ, sila
violin	bailín, ílimtokᴧ; play the violin: ílimto
virtuous	yahá - good
visible	chetípe; be visible: cheyáha
visit	go visit: chenókoi; come visit: chenó'okit; go visit relatives: heskᴧtokoi
visit (v)	yapáito - chat (v)
visualize	huhéye - imagine
vivid	yopípilipe- bright
vocabulary	wewé, wéye - speech
vocation	tawáli - work
voice breaking	have the voice break at puberty: kúilulumim pú
void (n)	wi'ípe - empty, abandoned
vomit	wé, wem; make someone vomit: wéti; vomiter: wékᴧ; bad vomit-causing man: wémchᴧchᴧkti
voodoo	yómpa - sorcery
vote in	woiyó - select, pick for a job
voyage (n)	ᴧkóido - traveling
vulture	miní'usi, mihasi, husi, wékᴧm kutí
wade	pó; wade around: pónoye around; wade across: pósito; wade into: pódaw; wade out: pokᴧkinu, pósip
wag (tail)	búkwislai, wíslai
wager (v)	helái - gamble
wagon	kaléta
wail	go around wailing: wáknoyesa; moan, bawl: wak - cry
waist	ínkᴧl, lulú, lulúmi, lumí; pants waistband: páitolom lulúmi
wait	wait! étu; wait a little bit: etúdede; wait for (someone): bócheye, chebóye; wait in expectation: chekínu; lie in wait (to assault someone): bókachik
wake up	wake up (intransitive): wimíkekoi, túicheno; wake somebody up: túichenoti; wake-up time: túichenonomᴧni
walk	ᴧnó; walk around: ᴧnóye; make someone walk: ᴧnóti; want to walk: ᴧnóyaha; go for a walk: ᴧnóyekoi; walk a child: ᴧnóyeti; start to walk towards: benínpin; walk backwards: kíwna bényewei; walk in one's sleep: ᴧs'ᴧno; walk off towards: ᴧnótoye; be hardly able to walk: ᴧnówasa; one who walks: bénnokᴧ
walk out on	wasᴧkoi - go away angry

English	Maidu
walking stick	bᵐsákᵐ/basákᵐ, basá; make a walking stick: basá; use a walking stick to get across: bití'ukitᵐsitopin
wall	én; near the wall: énnan
wall off	dᵐ́chik - lock up, close up
wallop (v)	kíwwo - beat, whip
wallow in	yokósťaheyto
wander around	ᵐnói, ᵐnóye; wander around calling someone: yomó'ᵐnoi; wander around in the forest: chacháinoye; wander around in a downhill direction: ᵐ́nnoye, ᵐ́tnoye; not wander far off: ᵐnóibodᵐk; don't wander (far) off: ᵐnóimenwet, ᵐnóibodᵐkwet; ᵐnóibenmap; don't let (someone) wander off: ᵐnóibenmapa
want to	like to: MMG p. 57, -yaha infix on verb
want, want to	yahá, kái; "I don't want you" mínmeni ka'as; doing what one wants: ka'áyahádom; where someone wants to go: ᵐnóyahape
war (n)	hómpaito - fight
war (v)	make war: wónotito
warble (v)	sol - sing
warm	lái; be warm (person): lᵐp; be warm (weather) lái; be warm (fire): láino; get warmed up (meat): p̓ikókolauk̓oi
warn	ayáwe; warn not to do: héwa, mamámen
warrior	hódesi, hudési; a man wearing feathers: sᵐlépaipem máidᵐ
wart	pᵐt̓
was	ka'án, kᵐkán, kᵐ'ᵐm ma'ám; apparently was: machói'a, machói'am (this tense is used if the speaker was not present during the action)
was	past tense of "is": MMG p. 29, use the same verb forms as "I am," "he is," etc. for recent past or a state of being. For other past tenses, see p. 63-67.
was (someone) supposed to...?	should (someone) have done...?: MMG p. 64, use question forms for the imperfect, with sᵐ'ᵐi
was unable to	couldn't: MMG p. 55, use -chᵐi infix on verb with a past tense ending (p. 63-66)
was/were doing	past tense of "is doing.": MMG p. 64, use the imperfect verb tense. Verb forms depend on person.
Wasám Pool	Paláwaikᵐnundun
wash	chukú/chuk̓út, go wash: chuk̓útno; wash someone (like a child): lakít
Washo	cháisᵐ; Washo person: cháisum máidᵐ
washroom	pit̓ᵐ́ uyí - bathroom
wasp	pᵐchᵐ́lale/puchᵐlule/búchilale; black wasp: ustabaku
waste (v)	wahéno
wasted (adj)	hudásu - drunk
wasteful	wáiheno; habitually wasteful: wáihenosape
wasteland	podá - desert
watch	chenú; sit around and watch: chenúno; watch (as TV): chek̓íno; watch secretly: k̓áchenu, chek̓áto; not want to watch: che'ókole; watch and wait: chek̓áta; watch for: chebóye; stand up and watch for: tᵐ́sbok̓itno; watch intently: chik̓áta; watch together: chek̓íttoto
watch out	watch out (especially of people): ók̓k̓et; watch out (especially for snakes, poison oak, etc.): éssem; be on the lookout: sik̓áta
water (n)	momí; move through water: yó; under water: mómdo
water (plants)	dékti, moti; go water: déktino
water bug	mówinᵐnkᵐ
water down	dilute: mómwiyakti, momchúiti - make more watery, thin up
water hemlock	butchiwi
water lily	momím yó
water ouzel	mompíspisto, momípispisto
water snake	húselíkᵐ, momím húskᵐ
watercraft	yak̓ᵐ́ - boat
watercress	mómkiwi
waterfall	sewíno, tetém momíki yochónonupe, pólpolchenopem momí
waterleaf	makalúsim sawí
waterless	p̓ik̓álpe - dry (adj)
watermelon	taméli, momím taméli
waterway	sewí - river, creek
watery	make more watery: momchúiti, mómwiyakti
wave (in hair)	wᵐ́nt̓et̓enoye - curl
wave (something)	welék; wave the hand: má welék, má weléknoye

414

English	Maidu
waver (v)	wilíl - flutter, tremble
wavy	onotmitmikm - curly-haired
wax (n)	chaká, yúkm
wax currant	nunholwa
way	bó, papáyi; on the way: mnókmdi; (do) this way: eyádom, eyáweyeti, ka'átido; in some way or other: hesánudowet, hesíwet; in such a way: ka'átik; that way (direction): anína, ántena, mmná; that's the way it is: ma'ákmm
waylay	ḱahúkit, ḱanúkit
ways (distance)	a ways (some distance): t̓íkteno; a little ways: t̓íktete; be a little ways out: t̓iktetéye
we (2)	nisá; we (2) alone: nisá'usi; we (2) ourselves: nisáwet
we (3 or more)	nisé; we (3 or more) alone: nisé'usi; we (3 or more) ourselves: niséwet
weak	etósmen, t̓oi; be weak: t̓oi; not be up to (a physical challenge): wohadóimakat; weakness: t̓oiyí; don't be weak!: t̓otimén; without being weak: t̓otimenwetí
wear	chínu, hadónu; wear a necklace: ḱúilai; be wearing jewelry: ḱúilaimape; wear a hood: onúkno; wear a hat: olékm, wiká; make someone wear a necklace: ḱúilaiti
wear (v)	chí - put on clothes
wear out (tr)	wokóti - tire out (tr)
weary	be weary: wokó
weasel	wíbusi
weather	ḱódom; being good weather: ḱódom yahádom
weave	his; weave a contrasting pattern: bal
wedlock	out-of-wedlock: hálbis
weed out	wi'íti - destroy
weep	wak, wob, wom; weep with grief: lól; go out weeping: lóleḱoi; weep as one goes: lólmḱoi; weep continually: wómbusno
weigh	wihḿl - be heavy
weird	bḿde
weirdo	ka'ámenim máidm - strange people
welcome!	yínpin
well (adverb)	yahát, yát
well (healthy)	hmḱḿpkupe, wadá
well (n)	ḱumí - hole
well done!	hés eḱáw - (how wonderful)
well, now	adóm bei
well-behaved	yahá - good
were	they were: ka'án, kmkán, km'mm ma'ám; apparently were: machói'a, machói'am (this tense is used if the speaker was not present during the action)
were	past tense of "are.": MMG p. 29, use the same verb forms as "you are," "they are," etc. for recent past or a state of being. For other past tenses, see p. 63-67.
west	tái, poḱóm hínkitkmdi, hínḱoikmmnantedi; downhill country: ḱódom bónnodi; toward the west: táina, poḱóki ḱmchonokmdi, hínchonokmnántedi; in the western area: poḱóki ḱmchonokmnantedi
Westwood	Siápkm
Westwood Mill Pond	Siápkmm Ḱoyóm
wet	dékpe, déktikm; to wet something: dékti; be wet: dek
what	hesí (object of sentence), hesím (subject of sentence); what kind of: hesápe; what? (if you don't hear): hai'i?, hesí aḱá?; What now?: hesím béi?; What is that/what was that?: hesím adé?; What next?: hesúwa?; What am I doing?: hesádom maḱádes?; What on earth?: hesím beté; what kind of creature: hesím máidmwet; whatever: hesíwet; whatchamacallit: ísḱa
what	MMG p. 35, hesím (subj) or hesí (obj) in questions only. MMG p. 73 and 81 - for non-questions, expressed by adding -pe(m) to verb, as "that which"
wheel	yenḿnnokm, wíl
wheelbarrow	wílba
wheelbarrow (v)	hanḿn - haul
when	because, while: MMG p. 84, 86, -mmni or -dom suffix on verbs. -mmni changes the subject in the next clause, -dom keeps the same subject.
when	MMG p. 35, hesánteni in questions only. P. 87 -mmni "if/when" for non-questions
when (non-questions)	right when: bédukan; "when" is expressed by adding the -mmni suffix to verbs for non questions: okítmmni: when he arrived; when I do: ásmmni; when he does: ámmni; Alternatively you can use the -chet suffix, which means "once/after:" when he had arrived: okítchet; when you do that: anímchet (see Mountain Maidu Grammar, Lesson 11 for more details)

415

English	Maidu
when?	hesánteni
whenever	hesántenuwet - sometime
where	MMG p. 35 homóndi in questions only. p.73, 81-83 for non-questions, use -pe(m) on verb
where (questions)	homó, homón, hamóndi/homóndi; to where: hamóna/homónna/homóna; from where: hamónan/homónnan; where in the world: homónte; whereabouts: hesápedi; I wonder where they could be?: hesáyakḱen áite nik
where (the place where)	for non-questions, "where" (= the place where) is expressed by the -pe, -kᴍ, or -ma suffix on the verb, often with a postposition like -di after that: where it was put: utípedi; where it was dark: banákmenpedi; where there was no one: wi'ípedi; where the sun comes up: ékdadoikᴍdi
wherever	homómondiwet, homónmondiwet, hesím betéwet; wherever one goes: yunókᴍdi; going wherever: ᴍsáwet
whether	if (if...then...): MMG p. 85, 87, -mᴍni or -chet suffix on verb
which (non-questions)	to express "which" for non-questions, use the -pe or -kᴍ suffix on the verb: "which keeps dripping:" látsape; "his rabbit-skin blanket, which was belted on, was wet:" saláwi mᴍkí, wachákinupe, déktikᴍm
which (questions)	homó, homómo; whichever: hesáwet
while	a short while: béidᴍkto; a long while (many months): pím poḱó; after a while: bísyet, adá, núktina; in a little while: bedukto; once in a while: sᴍ́tᴍni; be a while: ebᴍ́bᴍ
while	when, because: MMG p. 84, 86, -mᴍni or -dom suffix on verbs. -mᴍni changes the subject in the next clause, -dom keeps the same subject.
whimper	úk'uk
whine	whine (as a dog): úk'uk
whip (v)	kíwwo
whippoorwill	ṕoléwḱuti, palíkukuté
whirl (oneself) around	wᴍpᴍ́lᴍmnoye, wᴍpᴍ́lam, wᴍpᴍ́lamnoye
whirl around	wᴍpᴍ́lamnoye
whirlwind	hákalulu, hákkalulu
whiskbroom	hebásdawkᴍ
whiskers	símpani - beard
whiskey	hútum sudáka, sudákᴍ, sudákᴍm momí
whisper	ḱáweye; go around whispering: ḱawéyenoye; whisper to each other: ḱawéyetoto
whistle	huk, húkḱel; whistle tunes: húkḱeltete; signal by whistling: húkpai; make a whistling sound as air rushes out of something: chówowo
white	dáldal, dáldalpe, kókkok; whitish/light color: edáldalnope; be white: dáldalno; white paint: dúbap, dúbat; put on white (ceremonial) paint: sidádalino
white (Caucasian)	wóle; white man: wólem máidᴍ; white woman: wólem kᴍlé
white fir	písum cha/pichum cha, nowim cha
white oak	lowí; white oak tree: lowím chá
whiteboard	dáldalpem bóadi, bóadi; whiteboard spray: dáldalbene wasása
whitefish	buchí
white-headed woodpecker	chotúti
whiteleaf manzanita	tátum cha
whitewash (v)	chetímen - not let (someone) see
who (non-questions)	"who" (meaning "one who") is expressed by adding the -pe or -kᴍ suffix to the verb: one who doesn't listen: pínmenpe; one who lives in the rivers: séwsewtodi biskᴍ; one who believes anything: ťíkchelelepe
who (questions)	homónim (subject of question), homóni/hamóni (object of question); who is it?: hamónim makáde?; I wonder who it is?: homónim aité; no matter who: homónim ma'áti
whole	ᴍpéḱandᴍkbe; the whole of it: kan, kaní
whooping cough	hóntustusi - coughing sickness
whose (questions)	hamónik
why	hesádom/isádom, hesá; what was your plan/what were you thinking: hesátimadom
why not do...	hesátimet
wicked	wasá - bad
wide	hadáwaito
widow	ḱúli, ḱúlu, ḱuluibe; pitch-covered widow: chakámťapopem ḱúli; be widowed: ḱúl
wield	welék - wave (tr)
wife	kᴍlé; legal wife: kᴍléwťi; someone to lie down on: ḱachókitkᴍ

English	Maidu
wildcat	ínsep; bobcat: baksakala/boksmkmla, ťolóma
will (do or be)	future tense: MMG p. 47, -ma on verb + verb endings
will (v)	might ("may it be so"), should (future meaning): MMG p. 94, use -tabm verb suffixes (depends on subject)
Willard Creek	Bmlmkm
Willards Ranch Meadows	Papáikmdi, Papá
willow	pá, pám cha, pam dm; gray willow (for basketry): chupí, hísdom chupí; red-barked willow: yamánim chupí; willow branch: pámchmkm; willow shelter: yamáichik kumhm; gray willow tree: chupím chá
willpower	have willpower: hóntos
wilt	lachḿi
win	bodáw, halé; win a song competition: solónkokoito; almost win (a game): haléhudoi
win (v)	bodáw - win games
win (v)	ónkoi - come out on top, beat, outsmart
wind	bḿwo/búwo; north wind: bḿdawi; cold wind: bḿhewi; the wind blew: kódom bḿwochoi'a
wind along	wind along (as a trail): bówono; wind off in the distance: wokói, bówokoi
Wind Hole (on Indian Creek)	O Buwuwum Kumí
wind something on	witúbil
wind up at	mdíkno, okít - arrive at, arrive
windfall	yú - luck
window	momím chetókm
wine	pímelim sudákm, sudákm
wing	wing of an insect: yé; wing of a bird: yémba
wink	hiníswiki
winnow	báť, walét; winnowing basket: walétkm
winter	kúmmeni; wintertime: kúmmenkit; through the winter: kúmmen; wintering over: kúmmen bísdom; in preparation for winter: kúmmenna; become winter: kúmmenda; be winter: kumménchik; winter house: kúmmenowet; end of winter: kúmmenhekit
Wintu	wínťu; Wintu person: wínťum máidm, budawim máidmm
wipe	dá; wipe off: dádaw
wipe out (destroy)	wi'íti; wiping out: wi'ítida
wire	kukú; metal wire/telephone wire: míldan kúk
wisdom	húkesi
wise	húkes, húkespe; be wise: húkes
wise person	húkespe - wise, clever one
wish for	yomó
witch	wasám yomén kmle
witchcraft	yómpa
with	to express "with" use the -ni, -idi, or -kan suffix: kmléni, kmlé'idi, kmlékan all mean "with the woman;" hei "go with"
with (doing with)	along with: MMG p. 55, -idi on verb
with (someone else)	and (along with), accompanied by: MMG p. 23, -kan on the first noun
with (using)	MMG p. 23, -ni on the noun
with a view of	chepítwono - facing towards
withdraw	myéwe - go back
withheld	what was withheld: yachépe
withhold	yaché
within	di'ím, in'ínno
without	wi'ípe; be without: wi'í; go without: wi'íwo'us; "without doing" is expressed by adding -menwet to verb
without (doing)	MMG p. 87, -menwet suffix on verb
without (on nouns)	lacking: use -wi'ípem on noun
without stopping	mpékape - always, continuously
witless	húbokoipe, húbokoisape
witness (v)	chewé
wolf	helí'eni, helíyene
Wolf Creek	Kótasim Sewí, Helí'enim Sewí

417

English	Maidu
woman	kᴍlé; women: kᴍlóknono/kolóknono; two women: kᴍlécho; old woman: kᴍlókbe; little old lady: kᴍlókbeto; old women: kᴍlókbeťᴍťᴍ; with the two women: kᴍléchoni; act like an old woman/be an old woman: kᴍlókbechu
womb	tém uyí - uterus
wonder	áikakat; I wonder: áite nikí; I wonder how: hesádom aité; I wonder what (they) will do: hesáhelu; I wonder what that could be: hesí mayákken áite?
wonder (at)	marvel (v), be astonished: ᴍkáwche - admire
wonderful	ᴍkáw/ekáw; look wonderful: ᴍkáwcheti/ekáwcheti; sound wonderful: ᴍkáwpinti
wood	chá; wood chips: ťᴍťᴍ; stack wood: chá wulút
wood rat	óm sápa; tela
wood tick	ťík, tení
woodchuck	kawí yudútkᴍ, sᴍ́pa; pet woodchuck: sᴍ́pam sᴍ
woodpecker	Lewis woodpecker or sapsucker: chitátati/chatúti'i; red-shafted woodpecker: chiťúť; white-headed woodpecker: chotúti; red-breasted woodpecker: chówanoti; pileated woodpecker: lákono, mákmakᴍ, tetém panáka; acorn woodpecker: panáka
woodpile	chám wulúti
woods, forest	cháchato
woof (v)	wákpai - bark (like a dog)
word	yawí; words: hónwe, wéye; by saying that word: yawíd; what do the words (of the song) mean?: adóm sóldom máikade?; I have no words: wéye wí'ikas bei; without a word: ánwet
words	wewé - speech
work	tawáli; to work: tawál; go around working: tawálnoye; finish all the work: tawálbos, tawálhekitbos; get working on something: botópai; work on something: sikés; work one's way outward: tawálᴍsip; work with (things): sᴍnóye; work something over/fix it: tawáldᴍkdᴍk, yadᴍ́kdᴍk
work (v) (machine or device)	ᴍnó - function or run
world	kódo; lower/other world: kanái'im kódo
world	kódo - area
World Maker	kódoyakᴍ, kódoyape
world without end	wónomenkᴍm kódo - heaven
Worldmaker	kódoyakᴍ - Creator
world-wide (adj)	yᴍwáitokᴍdi - everywhere the world extends
Worley Mountain	Húskᴍm Yamánim
worm	kaihí, kaise; roasted earthworms: kaihím ítusi
wormwood	múnmuni/mᴍ́nmᴍni; wormwood leaves: múnmunim sawí
worn out	worn-out (things): héda, hédada; get worn out/tired: wasádoi
worried	be worried: yehéptuye; be a little worried: yehéptoyehye
worry (v)	yehéptuye - be afraid or worried
worst case scenario	experience the worst case scenario/have the worst luck: hesáiluť
worthy	yahá - good
would	MMG p. 88, -ma + verb endings on verb = future in the past
would (future meaning)	might (because of something): MMG p. 95, use -nache verb suffixes (depends on subject). This combines with -bᴍ forms in the other clause "in case" (p. 94), to show the predicted result, if the "in case" came true.
would rather (have or do)	sᴍ́ssᴍ - prefer
would rather not	okóle - be reluctant, be unwilling
wound (tr)	ítu - hurt (tr)
wrap	a wrap (for warmth): saláwi; to wrap up: bánchonoi, budú; wrap up in a net: húhudoi; wrap around and cover: bánchonoye; completely wrap up: bánchonoibos
wrap (v)	bánchonoi - wrap up
wreck (v)	wasáti - mess up, ruin
wren	chékchekkᴍ; canyon wren: ómtitiwi
wrest (v)	wikᴍ́p - extract (v)
wrestle	hómpaitododó; hómpaito, hómpaitoto
wriggle (as salmon)	hin'á
wring out	witᴍ'ú
wrist	mákulu; wrist bone: mákulum bᴍmí
write	bal, papél, papélkit; write down: bálkit; make someone write down: papélkitti; writing: balí
wrong	wasá

English	Maidu
wrong (n)	wasánu - evil
wrongly	wasát - badly
yack	yapáito - chat (v)
Yahi or Yana Indians	kómbo, bo kómbom máidṃ; bokombo, kómbom máidṃ, kómbom máidṃ
yampa	papá, papám piwí, palúťi
yank out	wikṃ́p - extract (v)
Yankee Hill	Komchu
yap (v)	wákpai - bark (like a dog); yip as a dog or coyote: wáiyuyuk
yard	ḱoyó - field
yarrow	wíslam bukú, wíslam yo
yawn	háiyum/háyum; yawn a lot: háiyuyum/háyuyum
year	ḱódo, ḱódoi; years old: yókmeni (if born in spring), ḱúmmeni (if born in winter)
yearn for	chebá
yell	pelíp; yell at: políppai
yell	pelíp - shout
yellow	chulálak, chulálakpe
yellow fritillaria	muiyukṃ/muyuko
yellow star tulip	muku
yellow warbler	sáwinkotutu
yellowhammer	mákmakṃ (but this word mainly refers to the pileataed woodpecker). see also "flicker"
yellowjacket	epéni
yelp (v)	wákpai - bark (like a dog); yip as a dog or coyote: wáiyuyuk
yelp with pain	wayṃ́yṃk
yerba santa	yómpom saiwi
yes	he'é, héw, hó
yesterday	kulúdi, ṃ ekídi, yesterday morning: kulúm bénekto
yet	achéki
yew tree	pándaḱam cha, bubúti, yolílim cha
yield (v)	puḱ - give birth
yip	yip as a dog or coyote: wáiyuyuk
yonder	ántena - that way
you	mi (subject), mín (object); all of you: mínchṃ, mínsṃ (object), mínsṃm (subject); you alone: míwet, mi'úsi; you first/next: míḱuni; it was you: mí haṕá; I mean YOU: min káiḱasi; doing like you: min yákkadom haṕá; and you? adóm mí?; every one of you: ṃpéḱnim; not you: mínmeni, mínmeni ka'as; someone other than you: min chai'í; you yourself/yourselves: mimíwet, mínchṃwet
you two	mínche, míncho; you two yourselves: mínchewet, mínchowet
young	nenómen, béidṃk'i; younger (sibling): hóipai; young man: máidṃbe
young people	yṃ́pe, teťṃ́ťṃ
youngster	te - child
your	MMG p. 40 - possessive, depends on how many people are involved in "your"
yours	mínḱi; using yours: mínḱini
youth	yṃ́pe - young people
Yuba	Yupu
zero	wi'í - not exist

APPENDICES

Appendix 1: Maidu Sense of Time

Time of Day:

Maidu	English
ékda	dawn, earliest morning
béneki	morning
ekím ésto	mid-day
ékpe hékitdi	afternoon
ḱai	evening, dinner time
kulúnanna	evening, as it gets dark
pó	night time
pó'esto	middle of the night

Months

Maidu Months, according to Roland Dixon (1905), are as follows. See the dictionary entries for Dixon's attempts at translating them. Names of months are notoriously hard to analyze (take English months, for example). More study needs to be done. Although Dixon says these begin in autumn (indeed, the first "month" actually means "autumn moon"), he did not say what months these correspond to in English. I suspect, since there are only nine months given, that the first month may actually be an entire season. However, other sources show that the summer months can all have the same name.

Sémenim Póḱo
Tem Chám Pawtom Póḱo
Tetém Chám Pawtom Póḱo

Ḱanái Pinom Póḱo

Bóm Hinchulim Póḱo
Bó Ekmen Póḱo
Bóm Tetnom Póḱo
Kónom Póḱo
Kɱlókbe Pinem Póḱo

Seasons:

Maidu	English
seméni	autumn
ḱúmmeni	winter
yóhmeni/yókmeni	spring
láimeni	summer

Year:

The words "year" or "time" can be expressed by ḱódo or méni.
Last year/last month/last time: hóiyɱmmen
When telling how old someone is, count the number of seasons (depending on the season in which they were born): sápɱm yókmeni "three years old" for someone born in spring.

Appendix 2: Building Blocks of Maidu Words

Maidu words are made up of roots, optional infixes and grammatical suffixes. Infixes can be stuck between a word root and a suffix. They can be used in combination (several infixes in the same word) to flavor the meaning. The following chart shows some common infixes. For more information on these and the grammatical suffixes, please see Mountain Maidu Grammar.

Infix	Meaning	Examples
bmk	try to do	don: catch, dónhunbmk: try to catch; sohún: go get, sohunbmk try to get; che: see, chebmk: peer at (try to see)
bew	a little more, become more	wéye: talk, wéyebew: talk a little more; teté: big, tetébew: get a little bigger
bis	keep doing	don: catch, dónbis: hang on; wéye: talk, wéyebis: keep on talking
boduk	not very much	túi: sleep, túiboduk: not sleep much; ḱúidak: like, ḱúidakboduk: not like very much; wisét: be frightened, wisétboduk: be not very frightened
bokit	stop, stand still	tḿs: stand, tḿsbokit: stop in one's tracks
boḱoi	fail to, lose	che: see, cheboḱoi: fail to see
bos	completely, totally	pe: eat, pebós: eat all up; bánchonoi: wrap up, bánchonoibos: completely wrap up; bukúi: go out (as a fire), bukúibos: go out completely
busno	do intensely and continuously	nuk: laugh, núkbusno: laugh hard; sól: sing, sólbusno: sing wildly; túi: sleep, túibusno: be sound asleep
chmi	be unable to	mno: go/walk, mnochmi: be unable to go/walk; dḿchik: lock, dḿchikchmi: be unable to lock; dón: grab, dónchmi: be unable to reach; húmit: remember, húmitchmi: be unable to remember
chik	over/into, closing over	ťú: fence/dam, ťúchik: dam up; húkit: remember, húkichik: forget; waťán: slap, waťánchik: slap in the face; yamái: shadow, yamáichik: cover someone's shadow
choi	up over the edge, around from behind	che: see, chechói: find; bís: live, bíschoi: live over the hill; bmlélekdoi: get towards the top, bmlélekdoichoi: reach the top
chono	do in a circle, to the limit, over edge (choi+no)	wetém: dance, wetémchono: dance in a circle; beťék: jump, beťékchono: jump over; bolóp: jump, bolópchono: jump around behind; dm: brush, dḿchono: cover with brush; dól: tie, dólchono: tie around; hatám: search for, hatámchono: search all around for; hín: float, hínchono: float down over the horizon
dmkbe/dukbe	just, exactly	yák: be like, yákdmkbe: be just like; mpéḱa: the same thing, mpéḱandmkbe: the whole thing; ka'ánbe: that much, ka'ándukbe: exactly that much
da	do passively, be in the process of doing, do as a result of	bo: throw, bodá: drop; ḱa'ó: get close to, ḱa'ódato: get up against; katí: do to someone, katída: get back at someone; kilé: hide something, kiléda: hide something for a reason; ḱúmmen: through winter, ḱúmmenda: become winter; mé: take, méda: take from someone; súk: smoke (as fire), súkda: make smoke
daw	down and away	da: wipe, dadáw: wipe off; welé: run, welédaw: run away from; wicháp: dislodge, wichápdaw: pull down from above; beťék: jump, beťékdaw: jump out; haláp: drag, halápdaw: drag down and out
dikno	reach, arrive	hóiwiha: lead someone, hóiwihadikno: lead someone all the way; ḱadót: shove something, ḱadótdikno:

do	do to or for someone	shove something against; lᴧk: crawl, lᴧkdikno: reach by crawling; mahá: bring, mahádikno: arrive carrying pelíp: shout, pelípdo; shout to; sikés: prepare, sikéstido: prepare for (someone)
dodo	do with someone	wetém: dance, wetémdodo: dance with; bís: stay, bísdodo: stay with and take care of;
doi	upward, start to	tᴧs: stand, tᴧsdoi: stand up; chebᴧ́k: sprout, chebᴧ́kdoi: begin sprouting; chó: burn, chódoi: flare up; dó: bite, dódoi: bite off or start biting
donu	keep doing, do continually	wodák: stick close to, wodákdonu: keep close to; yehétdoi: stick in the belt, yehétdonu: be carried under the belt; bᴧ́: blow, bᴧ́donu: stick up (like hair); chᴧ́doi: grab something in the hand, chᴧ́donu: hold something in the hand
epini/hepin	come back from	múhun: hunt, múhunepínimoto: come back from hunting together; hún: hunt, húnhepinye: come back from hunting; ḱedé: graze, ḱedéhepinḱoi: come back from grazing
ew, wew, yew	do for a while, keep doing, "by now;" with negative (-menew), means "not doing anymore"	chemén: not see, cheménew: not see anymore; -ew follows consonants; -yew follows -i with same meaning, or if not following -i, means "keep doing towards (or to a person)." -wew follows other vowels.
hehe	each and every, one after another, time after time	ḱáwheiḱoi: go off kicking up the dust, ḱáwheheḱoi: leave one after the other; cheḱói: go see, chehéheḱoi: look around in all directions; bᴧyᴧ́ksip: select, bᴧyᴧ́ksipdomhehe: select a few from many
hekit	stop doing	tawál: work, tawálhekitbos: finish up and stop working; yᴧ́pᴧ: start having periods, yᴧ́pᴧhekiti: stop having periods (menopause); ḱadík: rain, ḱadíkhekit: stop raining
helu	possibly, probably, likely	wadámen: not get well, wadámenhelu: perhaps not get well; wehétyonuto: hang things up, wehétyonutohelu: be likely to be hanging up; bís: be (there), bíshelu: be likely to be (there); hónwe: survive, hónwehelu: be likely to survive
hudoi	almost do, not quite do, come close to doing (but end up not doing)	wóno: die, wónohudoi: almost die; halé: win (a game), haléhudoi: almost win (a game); hásdoi: slip and lose balance, hásdoihudoi: almost slip and lose balance; okít: arrive, okíthudoi: barely succeed in arriving
idi	do with someone	bis: live, bísidi: live with someone; sól; sing, sól'idi: sing with someone; túi: sleep, túiyidi: sleep with someone
inno/ᴧnno	into	kai: to fly, kái'inno: fly into; beťék: to spring, beťék'inno: to spring into; bihít: to stick, bihít'inno: stick into; bolóp: jump or dash, bolóp'inno: jump or dash into; loḱét: tiptoe, loḱéťinno: tiptoe into
kᴧ	might be (present/future tense), at that time, "had done" (past tense)	pínmen: not hear/understand, pinmenkᴧchoi'a: had not understood; tókdato: race, tókdatokᴧ'ankano: (it looks like) you might be racing
kinu	be doing, lasting action (kit+nu)	pin: hear, pínkinu: listen (be hearing); olé: incline the head, olékinu: have the head inclined; ónḱoi: beat someone, ónḱoi'ᴧkinu: beat someone and keep going; púl: open, púlkinu: be left open; túi: sleep, túikinu: be sleeping
kit	down or reaching a destination	túi: sleep, túikit: go to sleep; ú: be somewhere, úkit: be left somewhere; uyúk: camp, uyúkit: camp for the night; wᴧdᴧ́m: throw, wᴧdᴧ́mkit: throw down; wiléw: be running, wiléwkit: run along arriving; wipún: tie something, wipúnkit: tie something down
ḱoi	away, go off to do	wodót: fling with a stick, wodótḱoi: fling away with a stick; woiyó: send someone outside, woiyóḱoi: send someone away; yapái: show, yapáiḱoi: go show; yé: invite, yéḱoi: invite someone to go; ᴧnóye: walk

424

ḱukus	pretend to	chemén: not see, cheménḱukus: pretend not to see; konókm̥: baby, konókḱukus: pretend to be a baby
lek	hurriedly, fast	wilé: run, wiléklek: run quickly; sm̥: insert, sm̥lékwopin: rush in/come rushing in
luť	exactly, fully, extremely	pin: hear, pínlut: comprehend (hear fully); yákcheti: look like, yákchetiluť: look exactly like; batás: the edge, batásluťi: the very edge; chíwi'ipe: naked, chíwi'iluťpe: completely naked; ésto: in the middle, éstoluťi: right smack in the middle; hm̂ťi: fat, hm̂ťluťi: the fattest one; hihí: pound up, hihíluť: pound up fine
maka	be unable to	hesá: something, hesámaka: be unable to do anything; chesák: recognize, chesákmaka: be unable to recognize; chemáka: be unable to see
men	time	hóiym̥: last, former, hóiym̥men: last year/time; kulú: evening, kulúmeni: evening time; lái: warm, láimeni: summer (warm time)
men, n	not (be), not (do). -n- sometimes is the negative, for example after ti or no and before -wet.	pin: hear, pínmen: not hear; húkes: smart, húkesmen: foolish/stupid; húweye: think, húweyemeni: one who doesn't think; ka'ái: say, ka'áimen: don't say (it); ḱuidak: to like, ḱuidakmen: to not like
minu	mit+nu: down onto, down into	che: look, chemínu: gaze down into
mit	down on to, down into	m̥: morpheme meaning "motion," m̥mit: get into (e.g. a car); wm̥dm̂m: throw, wm̥dm̂mit: throw down in; waťák: throw, waťákmit: throw down into; witm̂m: run away, witm̂mit: run away down towards; wodót: fling with a stick, wodótmit: fling down into (a container) with a stick
moto	together, encircling/enclosing	m̂pin: approach, m̂pimoto: bring together; dí: grow, dímoto: grow around something; hm̥yá: build a house, hm̥yámoto: build a house together; mahá: bring, mahámoto: bring together
n/t	downstream, downhill, SW	m̥: morpheme meaning "motion," m̥tnoye: wander around downhill-ish; méhyo: lunge and grab, méhyotno: lunge down onto and grab; sohá: carry in the arms, sohátno: carry downward in the arms
no	along, go along and do	téte: play, téteno: go play; túp: hop, túpno: hop along; wm̥dm̂m: throw, wm̥dm̂mno: go along throwing
noḱoi	go along doing	che: see, chenóḱoi: visit; donínο: hold, donínoḱoi: carry off
noye	around	nuk: laugh, núknoye: have a good time (laugh around); m̥nó: walk, m̥nóye: walk around; okm̂i: spy/peek, okm̂inoye: spy around; okít: arrive, okítnoye: be present; sm̥ḱét: point with the finger, sm̥ḱétnoye: point around with the finger
nu/inu	keep on doing, lasting action or state	che: see, chenú: stare, watch; mé: take, ménu: hold; pokm̂s: hunch the back, pokm̂snu: hunchbacked; wónotimen: not kill, wónotimeninu: not be killing
okole	be reluctant to do/not want to do	tawál: work, tawálokole: not want to work; pín: hear, pínokole: not want to hear/be reluctant to hear; che: see, che'ókole: be reluctant to see/not want to see; me: give, me'ókole: not want to give
pai	against, up against, up, towards, "by interacting"	mak: know, mákpai: learn; pelíp: yell, pelíppai: yell at; sódoi: lift up, sódoipai: lift against oneself; súk: smoke, súkpai: get smoke on (someone); túichenono: wake up, túichenonopai: be alert to; ťúṕ: spit, ťuṕpai: spit on; wák: cry, wákpai: bark at
panu	pai+nu: onto	yodót: tie, yodótpanu: be attached to; dáḱ: get stuck, dáḱpanu: get stuck to
pin	do toward	wm̥dm̂msito: throw something across, wm̥dm̂msitopin: throw something across toward
poto	be almost	ḱap: be cooked/ripe, ḱappoto: be almost cooked/ripe; bm̥lélekdoi: reach the top, bm̥lélekdoipoto: almost

		reach the top; batápai: catch up with, batápaipoto: almost catch up with; beťékda: jump, beťékdapoto: be just about to jump
sa	always, by nature	nuk: laugh, núksa: always laughing; bodáw: win in games, bodáwsa: always win/be lucky in games; chechɱi: be unable to see, chechɱisape: invisible; eyɱ: freeze, eyɱsape: freezing
sip	out, out of	háp: lift, hápsip: hand over; hebás: sweep, hebássip: sweep out; hóiwiha: bring by leading, hóiwihasip: lead away from; hónwe: breathe, hónwesip: exhale; lɱk: crawl, lɱksip: crawl out
sito	sip+to: across, through	ɱ: general motion, ɱsito: go across; ben: step, bensito: step across; láp: sit on the buttocks, lápsito: scoot over on the buttocks; loḱét: tiptoe, loḱétsito: tiptoe across; mɱ: shoot, mɱsito: shoot through; okɱi: peek, okɱisito: peek through
ťa	on top of, do something <u>on</u>	ben: step, bénťa: step on; sakɱ: make a fire, sakɱťa: put wood on a fire; tɱs: stand, tɱsťa: stand on top of
ti	cause, make do	pin: hear, pínti: sound (good, loud); tékɱ: be pregnant, tékɱti: get (someone) pregnant; tetébew: be a little larger, tetébewti: make a little larger; túi: sleep, túiti: put (children) to sleep
tino	go cause to do	dék: be wet, déktino: go water (something); opít: fill up, opítino: fill up by going down into; póp: shoot off by itself, póptino: go shoot (a gun); yodótpai: tie something to, yodótpaitino: tie something up for someone
to	to/for something or someone	wéye: talk, wéyeto: talk to; yapái: chat, yapáito: chat with; hɱbɱk: have feelings, hɱbɱkto: have feelings for
toto	to each other	yapái: chat, yapáitoto: chat with each other; hɱbɱk: have emotions, hɱbɱkto: love someone, hɱbɱktoto: love each other; hálche: refuse to believe, hálchetoto: disagree with each other; hómpaito: fight someone, hómpaitoto: fight each other; ḱáweye: whisper, ḱawéyetoto: whisper with each other
toye	go off to	húnmoḱoitoye: go off to hunt; túi: sleep, túitoye: go off to sleep
us	do to oneself	wéye: talk, wéye'us: talk to oneself
wai, waito	apart	mósda: spread open, mósdawaito: spread open wide; póyɱt: split, póyɱtwaito: split apart; wɱťɱi: tear, wɱťɱiwaito: tear apart; hadá: far, hadáwaito: wide; ḱatá: push something, ḱatáwaito: push apart
was	forbid, not allow	hei: hunt, héiwas: not allow hunting
wasa	do badly, not be able to do	pin: hear, pínwasa: hear poorly; sólti: play an instrument, sóltiwasa: play an instrument badly; ɱnó: walk, ɱnówasa: be hardly able to walk
webis/ebis	keep doing, do on and on	sol: sing, sólwebis: keep singing; a: do, awébisim: keep doing over and over; ɱḱóiye: go towards, ɱḱóiyebisim: keep going towards; yálulu: play the flute, yáluluwebis: play the flute on and on; bɱdói: sit, bɱdói'ebis: keep on sitting
wew	keep doing, "up to now, by now" See -ew above, which is a variant. -wew follows all vowels except -i.	hesásaḱa?: how are you?, hesasawéwḱa?: how have you been?; beťéksip: hop out, beťéksipwew: hop out every time; chenóḱoiyaha: want to see, chenóḱoiyahawew: keep wanting to see; wónoti: kill, wónotiwew: keep killing
wo	tell someone to do; go winding off	yɱ'ásdaw: move down and off, yɱ'áswodaw: move farther off; ɱḱói: go, ɱḱóiwo: tell someone to go; duschikínu: close one's eyes, duschikínuwo: tell someone to close their eyes
wono	be done, had done	ḱái: say, ḱáiwono: had said; píťápḱít: burn down, píťápḱítwono: was burned down; púḱ: produce offspring, púḱwono: be born; tetébetɱtɱ: get a little

yaha	want to do, like to do	bigger, tetébetm̩tm̩wono: had gotten a little bigger ɱkói: go, ɱkóiyaha: want to go; ɱnó: travel, ɱnóyaha: want to travel; betéi: tell a story, betéiyaha: want to tell a story; mákkit: know, mákkityaha: want to know
ye	over here, towards (a person or location)	haláp: drag, halápye: drag towards; paháno: follow tracks, pahánoye: follow tracks towards; p̬ún: tie knots, p̬únye: make a knot for each one; sm̩nche: look in a direction, sm̩ncheye: look towards
yenu	keep doing towards	che: look, cheyénu: keep looking towards
yewe/yewei	back	lm̩k: crawl, lm̩kyewei: crawl back; méi: give, méiyewe: give back; pm̩p: bounce, pm̩pyewei: bounce back; pakál: pay, pakályewei: pay back
yo	do to several things	ya: do, yáyo: do with several things; wadápi: sack, wadápyo: put things in a sack; wáṭa: throw on/cover up, wáṭayo: throw on a bunch of things/cover with a bunch of things; witúlkit: roll up and tie something, witúlkityo: roll up and tie a bunch of things

Appendix 3: Changes Made From Original Sources

Dixon and Shipley used their own specific orthographies (ways of writing the words), as did the other sources when transcribing Maidu words. In the Source Spelling column (Maidu-English section), I show how the source spelled the word. In the left-most column, I have transcribed their orthography into fish-head. It was easy to do this for Shipley, who was relatively consistent. It was somewhat easy to do this for Dixon, who distinguished more vowels (and vowel quality) than Shipley, but fewer consonants. The other sources were more difficult, usually trying to fit the Maidu words into the English alphabet. I did my best to transcribe these, but I encourage the student to check the Source Spelling column and draw your own conclusions.

I have listed many words with different spellings, based on various sources. I believe the different spellings must reflect a certain natural variation in the language, since even the same speaker (for example Tom Young) seemed to pronounce the same word differently from time to time (based on Dixon's transcription of his speech). I had access to written notes of our teacher, Farrell Cunningham, dating back to the 1990s, where he wrote the same words many different ways, and at one point developed an entire alphabet for Maidu, which I was able to decipher. By the time he had started teaching our class in 2008, he had standardized his spelling somewhat (the fish-head orthography being his invention), but most of the classes were done orally, so the students sometimes came away with different spellings. Use the various spellings as a clue to the pronunciation. For example, note that Dixon spelled máidɷ as mai'dü most of the time. The ü symbol is the same one he uses to spell bis (RD büs). Sometimes he spells máidɷ as mai'dö, the ö symbol being the one that usually transcribes as ɷ. This is a clue that that the final vowel of máidɷ is possibly a little different from most ɷ sounds, and a little closer to a short /i/ sound, as in Maidu bis, or English "sit." But there was also variation, so sometimes it was pronounced ɷ as well.

I value Dixon's transcriptions of Maidu in that he meticulously records the vowels as he hears them, including vowel length (drawing out the sound of a vowel), which we know is common in Konkow and Nisenan. If it hadn't been for Dixon writing the vowel length, this information may have been forever lost. I appreciate that Dixon did not try to regularize spelling (sometimes spelling the same word various ways even on the same page), but wrote what he heard, so that we can get a better picture of the variation[4]. On the other hand, Dixon seldom wrote the glottalized consonants and glottal stops, so we have Shipley to thank for carefully recording these.

I appreciate Shipley's ear for glottalization, and have transcribed Dixon's words with glottalized letters if a clearly related word in Shipley had the glottalized consonant. Shipley is also careful to write double consonants where he hears them, while Dixon and Cunningham often wrote them as single consonants. You will find among the spelling variations in this dictionary that sometimes the same word is spelled both with and without double consonants.

Changes Made to Shipley's Dictionary Entries

This dictionary includes all the words from William Shipley's dictionary, but Shipley wrote his dictionary for linguists, so the orthography is very hard to read for everyday use. Our dictionary is for people who want to learn to speak the language. Here are the changes I made to Shipley's entries, with this in mind:

---

[4] "It will be noticed that in the text the same word is often spelled in different ways, or given differing stress. It has seemed best to record these different forms just as they were heard at the time, rather than to try to reduce them to a single, normal form." (Dixon 1912:2)

1. I converted his orthography to "fish-head" (see the Introduction) for easier reading. Initial glottal stops are removed with a small number of exceptions. Glottal stops are represented by an apostrophe /'/.
2. Shipley's original orthography is shown for each word in the "Source Spelling" column.
3. Shipley arranged words by word root. I arrange the words in alphabetical order for ease of finding the word. Also, since he writes all words starting with a vowel as really starting with the glottal stop, the initial-vowel words are (in his dictionary) at the end of the alphabet under the glottal stop. I do not write the initial glottal stop, so the words starting with a vowel will also be found in alphabetical order.
4. In addition to real words in the language, Shipley lists "morphemes" which are not words on their own. Morphemes are certainly interesting, but to avoid confusion, I have removed the morphemes that are not real words. In cases where I was not sure, and the morpheme was possibly a full word, I left it.
5. Infixes which are not words on their own are taken out of the dictionary and moved to another list, in Appendix 2. They are important word-building elements, but to avoid confusion, I have removed them from the dictionary word list itself.
6. His alternate spellings are listed in a separate column instead of in the main entry with ~ as he has them in his dictionary. As in his dictionary, I also list the word under an alternate spelling in many cases.
7. Shipley routinely left off the final vowel on nouns. That final vowel is important to know, although it is optional when the noun is the object of the sentence (WS yamán vs. FC yamáni, WS ḱadík vs. FC ḱadíki). When a noun is the subject of a sentence, the final vowel is needed: yamánim hadán kmkán. In all cases where I could find the final vowel from other sources or other words, I entered that as the main spelling, and relegated his form to "Other Spellings" in column 6.
8. I updated his English translations where his term is obsolete. Example: "thou" becomes "you," and "hither" and "thither" are expressed in other ways. whither -> to where, whence -> from where, thou thyself -> you yourself.
9. I changed his translations to better-known, more colloquial words: hasten -> hurry, creel -> fish catching basket, be loath to see -> hate to see, bedclothes -> bedding, disbelieve -> refuse to believe, hawk up -> cough up, kerchief -> scarf, thrice -> three times, hereabouts -> around here, ill-looking (meaning bad looking) -> bad-looking; for Achomawi I added added Pit River.
10. I changed his translation where I considered it to be incorrect: hither-> towards. Verbs in -ye or -pin are not necessarily coming towards the speaker. They do mean going towards something, which is obvious in the context. chetínti "unrecognizable" -> be unrecognizable (RD 98:3 shows it to be a verb). Nik "I, me" -> me (nik never means "I"). Yellowhammer -> flicker. Blue racer (not a California snake) -> racer snake. Hudáw "take up a burden" really should be "a cut off piece" as in the Dixon translation of the same story (a cut-off piece: hudáwdo). Related words hukót, etc. all have to do with cutting. Shipley also changes all -do suffixes to -dom in his transcriptions of Dixon's Maidu Texts. I have gone back to -do wherever this has been noticed. kamím wolí: nephew -> nephews and ḱuláiwoli: orphan -> orphans (-woli is a plural suffix for humans). Shipley translates komó as "north" while Dixon translates it as "south." This word is also "south" in Nisenan. He lists ḱut as generic for small animals but it can also be for large animals including deer (in the stories of Maidu Texts). tóttimen "use all available spiritual power" is clearly ťotimén based on ťoi "be weak," thus my translation: "don't be weak." Shipley echoes Dixon in translating puk as "be born, come into being, be conceived." I translate it as "give birth, produce offspring," which makes sense in the context of all the texts. The smche "look upon with affection" definition seems wrong. smche is to turn one's forehead or face towards. No affection is implied. Wosó "female genitals" -> genitals, since a wosóťa is also a man's loincloth. ympm, for pubesce (girls), seems to mean "menstruate," since menopause is ympmhekit. Shipley translates smḱói as "rub on" for the story about the bear dance, but I add "insert" since the wormwood can be inserted in the nose and ears at the bear dance. He translates pet as "son-in-law." I found no instances of this in other sources, but péti means "mother-in-law," according to Shipley's Grammar. It could be that péti is a reciprocal term for both "mother-in-law" and "son-in-law." On page 64 in Maidu Texts, Shipley translates pepanudom as "egging them on" where it looks like "smoking tobacco" to me. hesíki he translates as "nothing," where it seems to mean "anything." It only means "nothing" when used with a negative verb.
11. I assumed the following to be typos: page 70:4 ejawje should be ejawej, page 54: 24 widykpe should be widokpe.

12. I removed his etymologies, which seemed English-centric and were distracting: "woman boy," "brain snot" "forehead see," "stick in-er," "sit on-er," etc. Again, my objective was to remove confusion.
13. Awkward constructions: Where he has a verb specific to a certain subject, he lists it as, for example, "smoke to come out." I changed these to "come out (smoke)," etc. I changed things like "the beside place" to "the place beside."
14. When there is more than one related meaning for a word, I changed his numbered meanings to words separated by commas: 1) spruce. 2) fir -> spruce, fir. Unrelated meanings are separate entries.
15. Nouns and verbs are separated out on different lines. Part of speech is noted where ambiguous: step -> step (verb), spring -> spring (verb)
16. I changed his format: butter From English -> butter (from English)
17. "From English" (or Spanish) - I sometimes removed this comment if there is a possibility these words are native, for example: hudásu, tawál.
18. Intransitive vs. transitive: WS often writes "in the intransitive sense." I write (intransitive) or (i.t.) when a verb cannot take a direct object. In the English-Maidu section, I often write "by itself" or (i.t.) to mean "intransitive." For transitive verbs, (something) or (someone), or (tr) lets the reader know it takes a direct object.
19. "severally" is replaced by "plural subject."
20. Punctuation changed - removed most periods, put additional info and examples in parentheses.

Changes Made to Dixon's Translations

Since Dixon did not create a dictionary, getting words and their translations from his texts was much more difficult than getting the words from the Shipley dictionary. Dixon transcribed multiple stories as spoken by Tom Young around 1903. Shipley took Dixon's work and transcribed it into his own orthography for Maidu Texts and Dictionary, and surprisingly, changed many of the original words and constructions. He apparently read the stories to Maym Gallagher, and she suggested other words if she was not familiar with the word Tom Young used 50 years before. It was a delight to find so many words in Dixon's texts that were not in the Shipley dictionary, but some guesswork was involved in determining the best translations. For each word extracted from Dixon, I have entered some sample page numbers where that word can be found in Dixon's Maidu Texts, so readers are encouraged to check these words in context and see if they agree with my translation.

I treated the following as typos (in Dixon's Orthography):

Page	Dixon typo	Should be
14	kummenchikom	kummenchikdom
38	wösi	wösip
38	wusi	wusip
50	nöni	möni
62	ösékinu	ötsékinu
104	awet'em	awet'en
110	yakatidom	yahatidom
110	pi	pe
116	dek'tikom	dek'tiköm
116	hestihemiki	hetsihemiki
126	öket	oket
136	astset	atset
148	ökoibem	ökoiben
160	wīn'oti	wōn'oti
160	tsekau'ni	tsakam'ni
168-70	möpo'tsoiam	möpo'tsom
176	yedisdaw	tedisdaw
186	okit'boto	okit'poto
204	yemái	yamái

210	yahā′nati	yahā′hati
214	wisetyahatpinteweam	wisetyahatpintiweam
216	manāñ′kano	mamāñ′kano
222	betē′man	betē′men
228	wēmtsitsök′titi	wēmtitsök′titi
228	kökus	kökas
230	kuloi′kinu	koloi′kinu

Dixon loosely translated many of the texts, and in some cases, didn't translate words or phrases at all. There are some instances where I have come up with a different translation than he did. The following are a few examples of how I interpreted words and phrases differently from Dixon:

p. 174 hesásakade: Dixon translates "How are you?" but the form is third person, and should be translated "How are things?" The answer (on the same page) is Yahákan, "They are fine."

p. 150, 202, 234 and many other pages: machói'am - Dixon translates as "they say." I translate as "apparently remained/did." Although Shipley and Dixon understood there was something speculative about this verb form, it is the form itself (-choi'a or choi'am ending) that is speculative. The verb is ma: "do." It is consistently the main conjugated verb of the sentence, not a side note "they say." If the translation of "say" were correct, Shipley and Dixon would have to put it in the past tense, "they said." I disagree with their translation of this verb. See Mountain Maidu Grammar, Lesson 9.

Dixon does not translate the aman construction in the second person as I do. It always appears in a quote, and I interpret it as "who are you" or "why did you do x?" The person asked is always out of earshot in these constructions: aman = ámano. My interpretation is the same for matíwe'aman and mawé'aman. Dixon translates these as 3rd person "I wonder why he…," "I wonder who it is," etc. Grammatically -an is short for -ano, 2nd person.

Dixon translates the verb root puk as "be born" which makes no sense in the story contexts. I translate it "give birth." See pages 10 and 14 in Dixon's Maidu Texts (1912).

On p. 76, in the story of Coyote and his "baby," Dixon translates sḿche as "play with." Shipley translates it "look at affectionately." While sm implies turning the head towards to look, they were not necessarily looking at Coyote's baby with affection or playing with it. In fact, they were commenting that it didn't quite look like a baby at all. Of course, it turned out to be Coyote's penis.

In several cases (for example, page 19 and 24), Dixon hears "mam" and thinks an /a/ might be missing, so he writes (a)mam. My interpretation is that the mam is a suffix for the previous word, for example: uním sowonowonosmam, "that which I have left" (Dixon 1912:19), and yadmkdmkismam, "that which I make over" (Dixon 1912:24).

Sometimes Dixon interprets animmni as anim "a far off place" + mmni "when" (Dixon 1912:19) so his translation does not make sense. My interpretation is: a "do" + nim "you" + mmni "if," meaning "if you do." This makes sense in all cases.

Appendix 4: About Some of the People who Preserved the Language

Indian Valley Informants:

- Tom Young, whose Maidu name was Hanchibmyim, was from Genesee in Indian Valley. He was about 30 years old when he recited Maidu stories for Roland Dixon in 1902-1903. Dixon wrote the stories phonetically, just as he heard them from Young, and we are very fortunate to have this very extensive and early example of Maidu in Dixon's Maidu Texts (abbreviated throughout this dictionary as RD), which was published in 1912. Tom Young was said to a master story teller, so we not only have these stories preserved in Maidu, but in the elegant language he used. For this dictionary, over 1300 words have been added solely from Tom Young's stories. Tom Young was no longer living when Shipley did his work on Maidu in the 1950s and early 60s. Shipley re-transcribed some of Young's Coyote stories from RD in his 1963 volume (WST). Shipley's 1991 work (WS-MM) is all translations of Tom Young's stories, but these are re-translated from Dixon's Maidu Texts. None of Tom Young's stories were received first-hand by Shipley.

- Herb Young, the son of Tom Young, was born in 1894 and grew up on Hosslekus Ranch in Genesee Valley. His mother died when he was young and his father remarried his mother's sister, Selena Jackson, a famous basket maker. In the 1960s, Herb Young worked with Dorothy Hill and Francis Riddell and recorded songs, prayers and stories in Maidu. He also provided many important place names and Maidu words for plants and animals. He married Lilly Baker's sister Jennie (born in Indian Valley around 1896). They lived in Palermo near Oroville. He was a shaman, taking over from Shim Taylor. When he made his recordings in 1967, he was living in Feather Falls (Konkow area).

- Farrell Cunningham grew up in Genesee. Although born in 1976, he learned Maidu from the elders who babysat him while his parents worked. They spoke Maidu around him thinking he wouldn't understand, until one day he commented in Maidu himself. As a teenager and young man, he made an effort to learn more Maidu, and worked with elders such as Lilly Baker to expand his vocabulary. After teaching Maidu in Plumas and Lassen counties, He had a teaching opportunity in Nevada County starting in late 2008, which is when the author began taking his class. He taught Maidu in the Nevada City area from 2008-2012, and had a large following. He went back to Plumas county in early 2013 to work for the Susanville Rancheria, and passed away in Susanville in August, 2013. It was due to his efforts and his dream of revitalizing the Maidu language that this dictionary has been written.

American Valley Informants:

- Tom Epperson was born Apr 4, 1886 in Crescent Mills, CA. He was living with his wife Nellie in Indian Township, Taylorsville, CA (Plumas County) in 1910 (U.S. census information). Although he was born in Indian Valley, he grew up living with his grandparents in American Valley (just north of Keddie), according to Francis Riddell (FR1). Epperson provided valuable place name information as well as plant and animal names to several informants: Francis Riddell, Mary E. Dunn, John Duncan, and James McMillan.

- Dan Williams, shaman and Shipley informant during the 1950s, was at that time living in Quincy in American Valley. He died before Shipley's work was published. I was not able to determine where his original home was, but he had family in Susanville, and did doctoring in Janesville, according to HLME.

Big Meadows, Butt Valley and Mountain Meadows Informants:

- Maym Gallagher was living in Paynes Creek at the time she was William Shipley's main informant in the 50s and early 60s, but she was from Butt Valley. She recorded her reminiscences for Shipley, with many stories from her childhood. She provided the largest recorded (both on tape and written) volume of Maidu language since Tom Young more than 50 years earlier.

- Lena Thomas Benner was Maym Gallagher's mother, and a Shipley informant herself. She was born in Butt Valley, as was her father. Her mother was a Pit River Indian. She is recorded by Shipley telling some traditional stories. She died before his work was published.

- Lilly Baker was born on land overlooking Honey Lake around 1911. Her father, Billy Baker, was a full-blooded Maidu from Genesee. After her father's death in Susanville in 1924, the family moved to Salem Ranch at Big Meadows. Her mother, Daisy Baker, and her mother's mother were originally from Prattville, Lake Almanor. Lilly Baker went to high school in Westwood, being the only Indian in a white school. The book Picking Willows was written about her. She provided many plant and animal names for John Duncan (JD) and James McMillan (PM-M). She was also a mentor for Farrell Cunningham (FC).

- Marie Potts was born around 1895, a descendant of Big Meadows Bill. She was also one of Shipley's informants, living in Sacramento at the time she shared her words with him. Her contributions are listed as source WS-MP when coming through Shipley. But she was also an informant for Francis Riddell (FR-MP). She is the author of the book The Northern Maidu.

Susanville and Honey Lake Valley Informants:

- Roxie Peconum was born in Susanville around 1851 and died in 1958. Her daughter was Leona Morales (1900 - 1958), and her son was George Peconum (1877-1972). They were all Shipley informants. Mrs. Peconum's Reminiscences (which are recorded with Shipley's work) provided valuable words for this book (WST-RP).

- Leona Peconum Morales was born around 1900, and lived in Susanville all her life. She is the source of much of the creation story and Maidu geography on the HoneyLakeMaidu.org site, with much valuable information about place names, not only in the Honey Lake area but throughout the Mountain Maidu world. Her voice is on the Shipley recordings with her mother.

- George Peconum (1877-1972), son of Roxie Peconum, was also one of William Shipley's informants. He lived in Susanville. His voice can also be heard on Shipley's recordings. In addition, he supplied important place information for the HLME source.

Non-Maidu Sources: People who Wrote it Down:

- Roland Dixon (1875-1934) was Franz Boas's first doctoral student at Harvard. He worked closely with Alfred Kroeber and collaborated on some articles. He was a professor at Harvard after 1916. He published Maidu Texts in 1912, and also published a short grammar as well as a book about Maidu culture: The Northern Maidu (see the bibliography for more information).

- Stephen Powers (1840-1904) was an ethnographer who traveled around learning about native cultures and writing about them for the *Overland Monthly* journal. Later they were published in *The Tribes of California* (1877). Powers did not distinguish the Mountain Maidu from the Konkow, so it is not clear whether his words come from a Maidu or Konkow informant, but some of them are noticeably different from all other sources. For example, he lists mama instead of ma as "hand." His word for "woman," which he spells catee, is likely the word for "aunt," kati. In the 1877 work, we have place names captured by Powers, all in Konkow areas. Powers' work is of interest because it is our oldest source for any written Maidu. Unfortunately, he does not name informants.

- C. Hart Merriam (1855-1942) was a zoologist and ethnographer who studied at Yale and Columbia University (where he earned an MD degree), and taught at Harvard. In 1904, he published <u>Indian Names for Plants and Animals among California and Other Western North American Tribes</u>, which included many entries in Mountain Maidu. It is not known who his informants were.

- Alfred Kroeber (1876-1960) was an anthropologist who received his PhD under Franz Boas at Columbia University in 1901 and later taught at UC Berkeley. He contributes several Maidu place names from his 1925 work, <u>Handbook of the Indians of California</u>. Unfortunately, we do not know his informants.

- John Whitfield Duncan wrote <u>Maidu Ethnobotany</u> for his Master's Thesis at California State University, Sacramento, in 1963. He contributed many plant names to our knowledge, as well as cultural knowledge. He lists his informants, but not per each word given. See the "Sources" list before the Maidu-English section.

- Francis Riddell (1921-2002) was an archaeological field researcher with the California Department of Forestry. He was a champion of preserving Native American sites. He recorded place names in Mountain Maidu in the late 1960s, and names his Maidu source for each one.

- William Shipley (1921-2011), a linguist, was a student of Alfred Kroeber and Mary Haas at UC Berkeley. He began studying Maidu, working with native speaker Maym Gallagher, in 1953 and wrote the <u>Maidu Texts and Dictionary</u> as part of his PhD studies. Later he taught at UC Santa Cruz. He also wrote a grammar, and in 1991 wrote <u>The Maidu Indian Myths and Stories of Hánc'ibyjim</u>, re-translating the Tom Young stories that Dixon had recorded in 1902-3.

MAPS

Appendix 5

Maps and Place Names of the Mountain Maidu Areas

The place names for traditional Mountain Maidu areas have been gathered from many sources and brought together here. There are some wonderful maps and resources on the internet, as well as scholarly papers and hand-drawn maps that have been written over the years. Please see the bibliography for sources.

The maps included here are not exact, but should give the reader an idea where villages were and what the mountains, rivers, and valleys were called. The two reference maps show how modern-day landmarks correspond to pre-contact landmarks. The reference maps are followed by five maps without modern highways or reservoirs. Map 1 shows the overall Mountain Maidu area. Map 2 zooms in on American Valley (Quincy area). Map 3 focuses on Big Meadows, which is now Lake Almanor, and the northwestern part of Mountain Maidu territory. Map 4 shows the Honey Lake and Susanville area, and Map 5 features Indian Valley. Each map has numbered places with a corresponding key. For more details about any of these places, find them by their Maidu names in the dictionary.

Meanings of Place Names

In the map keys, there is a "Meaning, if Known" column, where the meaning of the place name is sometimes given. In many cases, I have listed what a similar word means, without knowing if the similar word is related to the place name. Maidu readers are invited to figure out the place name meanings based on traditional knowledge of that area. What natural resource or activity was that area known for? Here are some guidelines for figuring out place name meanings:

- There are certain words, whose meanings are known, that we often see in place names: sewí (river or creek), yamáni (mountain), o (rock, canyon or mountain), ḱoyó (valley or meadow), pakáni (lake, pool, or spring), mómdanni (lake), and ḱódo (country). These are some elements we are sure of.
- If you are unfamiliar with the Maidu language, you may wonder why a word is sometimes spelled with an -m at the end and sometimes without it. For example, Om and O are exactly the same word, and yamáni is the same as yamánim. The -m at the end is like "the" - it is optional.
- Another spelling puzzlement to those unfamiliar with Maidu is that when the /m/ sound falls before a /k/, the result is an "ng" sound. Some people writing down place names actually write "ng" (like Silongkoyo for American Valley) but it is exactly the same as Silom Ḱoyo, which is spelled to show the word Silom. Both spellings are pronounced the same (silong ḱoyo).
- The glottalized /ḱ/ sounds like a /g/ to some people, so when a word is spelled with a g by the source, it is probably a /ḱ/.
- Shipley spelled the /y/ sound as a j. If you see the word jamáni, it is really pronounced "yamáni." Some sources used both orthographies in one place name, for example "Joskopem Yamani," which should either be Yoskopem Yamani or Joskopem Jamani. In this dictionary's orthography, the y is always used for the /y/ sound.
- To confuse things even more, some people wrote the /ch/ sound as j, for example Jambokinee for Cham Bokini.
- Some native speakers of Maidu pronounced /s/ as /sh/. This seems to be a natural variation in Maidu pronunciation. So some place names originally written sh- are written in this dictionary as s-. On the other hand, a place name here and there was written with an s- when it should have been ch-. An example is Sitakam Yamani for Chítakam Yamáni. The only way I knew this was chítakam was that another source called it "beargrass mountain" and the word for beargrass is chítaka.
- -to and -tono are plural endings that can change a mountain into a mountain range, for example. In addition, the doubling of a syllable can make it plural. yamáni is mountain, yamánmanto is mountains or mountain range, and yamánmantono is "mountain ranges." -no, -non and -nom, as well as the word pinem or pinim, refer to a mountain "top to bottom."
- Unstressed vowels are often written various ways. For example, the word for Genesee is written by various sources as follows: Yetámeto/Yoťámmoto/Yatámoto/Yṁtámoto. As you can see, the stressed vowel á is easy to hear, and most of the sources agree on that. But the first vowel, which is unstressed, is harder to hear, and thus people hear it four different ways. This makes it harder to figure out the word's meaning. Both -ťa and -moto are Maidu word building blocks (see Appendix 2), with -ťa meaning "on" and -moto meaning "together." ťa is used on verbs, for example ben is

"step" and bénťa is "step on." So we assume the first syllable in the word for Genesee is a verb, but which verb? ya means "build, make, do." ye means "invite." yɨ means "go." yo can mean "cure." When trying to figure out a word's meaning, you may have to look through the dictionary at words that have the same consonants but different vowels. Particularly misspelled is the ɨ sound, which was often written as u because there is no corresponding vowel in English. Shipley wrote this as y.

- The letter and sound /h/ can be left out, or replaced by a glottal stop /'/ if between vowels. Again, this is a natural variation in the language. Words that start with h- (especially ha-) often have a "double" that starts with a-. So look under both h- and a- in the dictionary for meanings.
- the letter and sound /y/ is sometimes not heard. Words that start with yɨ- often have "doubles" starting with just ɨ-, so keep this in mind while searching the dictionary. Within a word, -ye- is often heard as -e-.

It is very difficult to figure out, without hearing the spoken words, what the spelling "should" be to reflect how the word was pronounced, without already knowing the meaning of place names. However, if you know the history of a place, you have a better chance of figuring out the meaning.

In all cases, you can look up the place name in the Maidu-English section of the dictionary for more information, including the original spellings of all the sources. In some cases, there is additional information about the location (for villages), the importance of the place, and what other people have said about its meaning.

Reference Maps

Post-Contact Maidu Country:

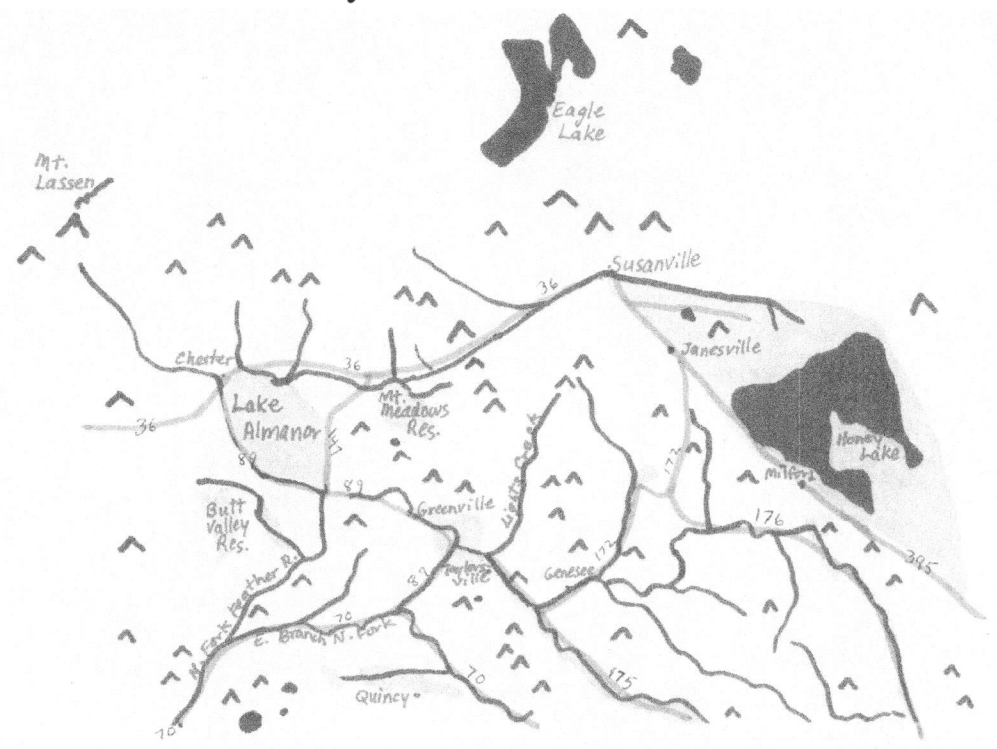

Pre-Contact Maidu Country (see following pages for sub-maps):

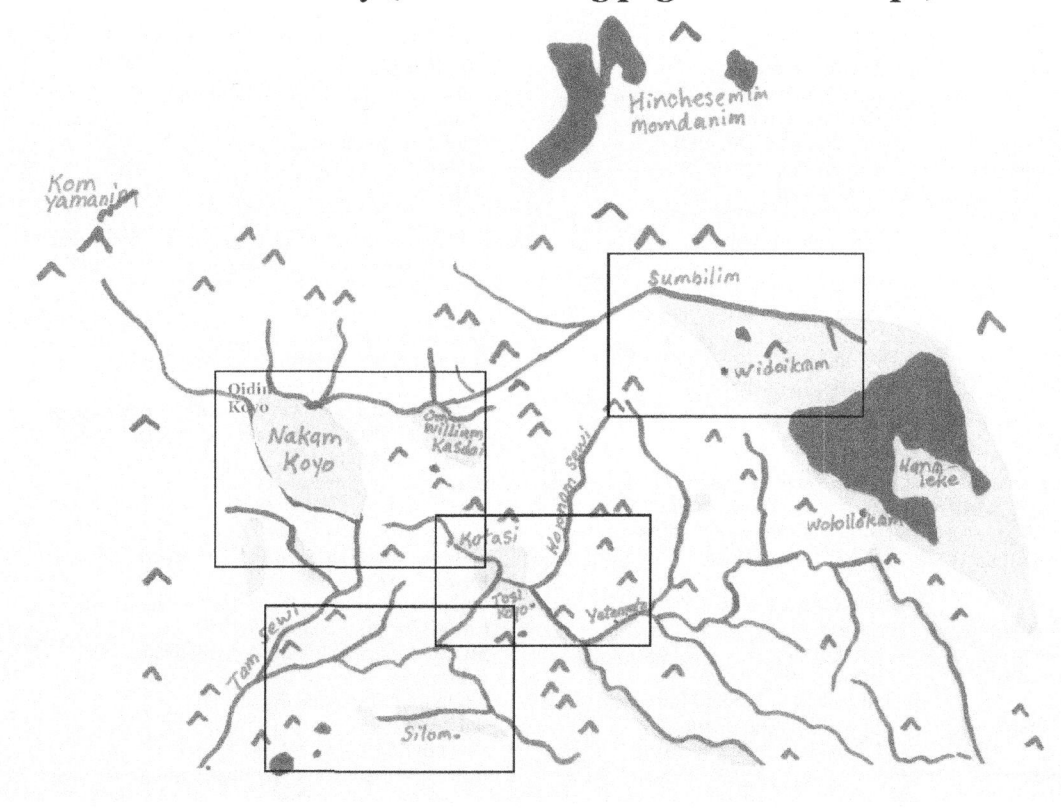

MAP 1: Mountain Maidu Country

Key #	Current Name	Maidu Name	Meaning, if Known[5]
1	Lassen Ridge, Mt. Lassen	Kóm Yamánim or Tái Yamáni	snow mountain or west mountain
2	Eagle Lake	Hínchesemim Mómdannim	strange-feeling lake
3	Antelope Mountain	Óm Yepónim Yamánim	chief rock mountain
4	Shaffer Mountain	Túmbakmm	sunflower
5	Susan River	Pám Sewím	willow river
6	Clear Creek (town area)	Óm Yawken or Yot'im	
7	Coppervale Mountain or Fredonyer Mountain	Óm Kulúdoiwem	kulúdoi means "starting to get dark;" or kulu may be a reference to Susanville (see kulumam in the dictionary)
8	Big Springs	Besapenim or Wisótpinim or Basíkmm	
9	Susanville	Súmbilim or Pam Sewím Ḱódom	lobelia or willow river country
10	Janesville	Widóikmm	that which is pulled up
11	Humbug, Humbug Valley	Tásma, Tásmam Ḱoyó	
12	Big Meadows	Naḱám Ḱoyó, Óidim Ḱoyó	Noḱám means "a quiver for arrows." nak means "area." In Nisensan, nak means "reflect." Óidi means "the top part."
13	Hamilton Branch	Naḱám Sewí (through Big Meadows), Yot'ím Sewí (through Clear Creek); Yoti was a village near Hamilton Branch.	see above (Big Meadows)
14	Mountain Meadows	Óm Wíllium Kasdoi	wilílim means "cottonwood" or "aspen," kmsdoi means "up the ridge"
15	Coyote Peak	Ot'a Yaḱm Yamáni or Yaḱmm O	be-left-on-top canoe mountain or canoe rock
16	Hamilton Mountain	Yaḱmki	canoe's, or "of/by canoe"
17	Diamond Mountain	Óm Lulmlm	Mt. Shimmering, likely related to lmlm, "star"
18	Honey Lake Valley	Ḱoyóm	valley
19	Honey Lake	Hanmleke or Tetém Mómdanni	tetém mómdanni means "big lake"
20	Butt Valley Reservoir	Ḱáwbat'im Mómdanni	flat ground lake
20	Butt Valley	Ḱáwbat'im Ḱoyó or Ḱáwwati	flat ground valley
~~21~~	~~Dyer Mountain~~	Chiwítbem Yamáni or Náka Yáni	little clover/grass coming up mountain (for ideas

[5] If the meaning is not known, some similar words may be given, in the format "x means y." This is not to say this word is related to the place name, but only to give ideas to others who are trying to figure out place name meanings.

			on Náka, see Big Meadows above). Yani means "hill."
22	Keddie Peak	Yakm̂m Yamáni	Yakm̂m Yamáni is "canoe mountain"
23	Keddie Ridge	Chiwítbem Yamáninom or Yoťim Yamáni	Chiwítbem: little clover/grass coming up
24	North Arm	Hópnomi or Hópnom Ḱoyó	river canyon valley
25	Wolf Creek	Helí'enim Sewí or Kótasim Sewí	wolf creek or Greenville creek
26	Indian Valley	Nadam Ḱoyó	Ḱoyó is "valley"
27	Mt. Jura	Payím Yáhni	foot mountain
28	Genesee	Yoťámmoto	yaťamoto means "build on together"
29	Genesee Valley	Yoťámmoto Ḱoyó	
30	Lights Creek	Hópnom Sewí	river canyon creek/along the creek creek
31	Indian Creek	Bm̂mm̂km̂m Sewí	sandy creek
32	Kettle Rock	Óm Lolóm Yamáni	rock basket mountain
33	Thompson Peak	Widóikm̂m Yamánim	pulled up mountain
34	Milford	Wolóllokm̂m	flicker
35	Homer Lake	Chám Sm̂dom or Chám Sm̂dom Pakáni	cham sm̂dom pakáni means "protruding tree pool"
36	Stover Mountain	Doldinom or Kuduikm̂m	
37	Humbug Mountain	Doldinom	
38	Canyon Dam	Chítakam Yamánim	beargrass mountain
39	Greenville	Kótasi	on the snow, snowline
40	Feather River	Tam Sewí	tam means "burial," while táim means "west"
41	Buck's Lake	Yakani Pakáni	yakáni pakáni means "saliva pool"
42	Crystal Lake	Otem Pakáni	pakáni is "pool" or "spring"
43	Silver Lake	Hayino Pakani	pakáni is "pool" or "spring"
44	Gold Lake	Chítani Pakani	pakáni is "pool" or "spring"
45	Taylorsville	Tosí Ḱoyó or Ḱm̂sdu	tosí means "north," while tosai means "tall-standing." km̂sdo means "ridgetop." These were possibly separate villages at Taylorsville
46	unidentified mountain near Belden	Helám Púksakm̂m Yamáni	gambling birthplace mountain
46	unidentified mountain near Belden	Paním Bisím Yamáni	tobacco living mountain
46	unidentified mountain near Belden	Yók'olťanum Yamáni	flag-on-top mountain
47	Mt. Hough	Hunanasim Ḱódom	hananasi means "chokecherry place"
48	Meadow Valley	Eyolim Ḱoyó	yolílim ḱoyó means "yew tree valley"
49	American Valley	Silóm Ḱoyó	
50	Quincy	Silóm	silam means "violets"
51	Dixie Peak	Óm Chumi; Also in this area: Siwim Yamáni and Tuwilitum Yamáni	Mt. Urine or urine canyon; Siwim means digging stick
52	Skedaddle Range and hot springs	Pólpolim Yamánim, Pólpolpolim	bubbling mountain, bubbling
53	none	Homlukbe	lukbe is "little spring of water"
54	none	Kunabe	
55	Willards Ranch	Papá or Papáikm̂di	yampa, where there is yampa (edible bulb)
56	Devils Corral	Pichilipem	swallows (birds)
57	Bald Mountain	Yóskope or Yóskopem Yamánim or Óskm̂pe	Yóskope means "fox," Óskm̂pe means "having a bald head"

MAP 2: American Valley and Indian Creek below Indian Valley[6]

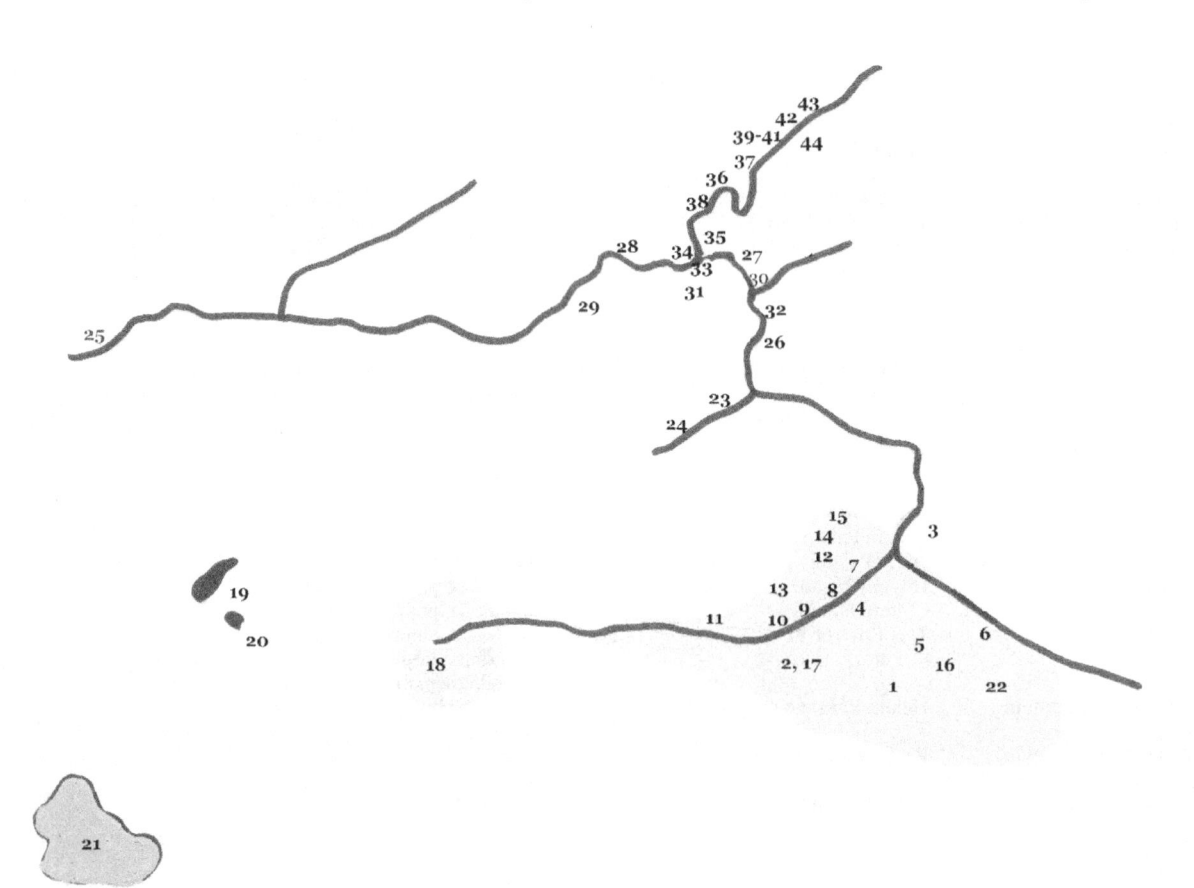

Key #	Current Name	Maidu Name	Meaning, if Known[7]
1	American Valley	Silóm Ḱoyó	
2	Quincy	Silóm	sila means "violet," silo means "poison oak" in Konkow.
3	none	Sátkini or Sátkini Waťám Ḱumhú	Sátkini Waťám Ḱumhú means "roundhouse at the edge of Sátkini"
4	none	Chakám	pitch
5	none	Bábe	little salt
6	none	Ḱawa	
7	none	Pitelim	pi tᴍlim means "a lot of grasshoppers"
8	none	Pecháma	
9	none	Bukúlisa Ínkomi	bukúlusi means "ant," ḱumí is "hole"
10	none	Chílwam Ínkomi	chilwam is "rattlesnake," ḱumí is "hole"
11	none	Dasím Yodá	daṕím yodá means "split maple suckers"
12	none	Wépam Momí	coyote water
13	none	Opᴍle or Boléiwi	o pᴍlᴍ is grinding hole rock, bo léiwo is "part of the road"
14	none	Wépam Momí Ustu	coyote water cemetery
15	none	Wépam Momím Chaťá Hᴍbé	coyote water - hᴍbe could be "small house" chata may mean "flat area"
16	none	Om Hᴍbe	stone little house
17	Quincy	Nukuti or Silóm (see #2)	núkti means "small"

---

[6] Since the first edition of this book, new place names have been found (source: Lilly Baker, in Farrell Cunningham's notes):
Spanish Creek: Silóm Sewí, Dublin Jack Ravine (flowing into Spanish Creek near #11 on the map): máidᴍ homím sewí, meaning "people-cooking creek," Middle Fork of the Feather River: Wuwáyonoktom Sewí

[7] If the meaning is not known, some similar words may be given, in the format "x means y." This is not to say this word is related to the place name, but only to give ideas to others who are trying to figure out place name meanings.

Key #	Current Name	Maidu Name	Meaning, if Known[7]
18	Meadow Valley	Eyolim Ḱoyó	
19	Silver Lake	Hayino Pakáni	
20	Gold Lake	Chítani Pakáni	
21	Buck's Ranch	Yakani	
22	none	Bᴧmi	bone
23	Butterfly Creek	Húntulam Sewí	
24	Butterfly Valley	Húntulam Ḱoyó	
25	North Fork Feather River	Tam Sewí or Tetém Sewí	tam means "burial" while tái'im means "west." tetém sewí means "big river"
26	Keddie	Bam Ólasi	bam is "salt"
27	none	Púislam Ḱoyó	white camas valley
28	none	Tohánom	ṫohóni is "sucker fish"
29	none	Nokóm Pino	many arrows
30	none	Túm Ḱoyó	sunflower meadow
31	none	Wóslum Ḱoyóm	wíslam is "chipmunk" or "yarrow," LM calls this place "red ants"
32	none	Bᴧwom Luḱú	wind brook
33	none	Luwú Humenim	luwú is "eel," humín is "catch fish in nets"
34	Oak Flat	Ḱowówtayi or Ḱawawtai	kaw means "land," tai means "west"
35	Soda Springs	Chuchúye	urinate across
36	Soda Rock	Chuchúyem Bam or Chuchúkᴧm O or Chuchúdom O	urinating across salt or urinator rock or urinating rock
37	Indian Falls	Hᴧnkᴧ or Ḱoyóm Bukúm Sewíno	thundering or valley tail waterfall
38	Buzzard Rock or Snake Rock	Miníhusim O or Mínminim Om	buzzard rock or milk rock
39	Wind Hole Rock	Búyem Ḱumí or O Buwuwum Ḱumí	wind hole or wind hole rock
40	Thumb Rock	Tetém Mamchipbᴧm Om	thumb rock
41	Split Rock	O Wichono	
42	Wasám Pool	Paláwaikᴧnundun	paláwaikᴧ means "great snake"
43	Moccasin	Chiwísi	clover place
44	Indian Creek	Bᴧmᴧkᴧm Sewí	sandy creek

MAP 3: Big Meadows/Lake Almanor[8]

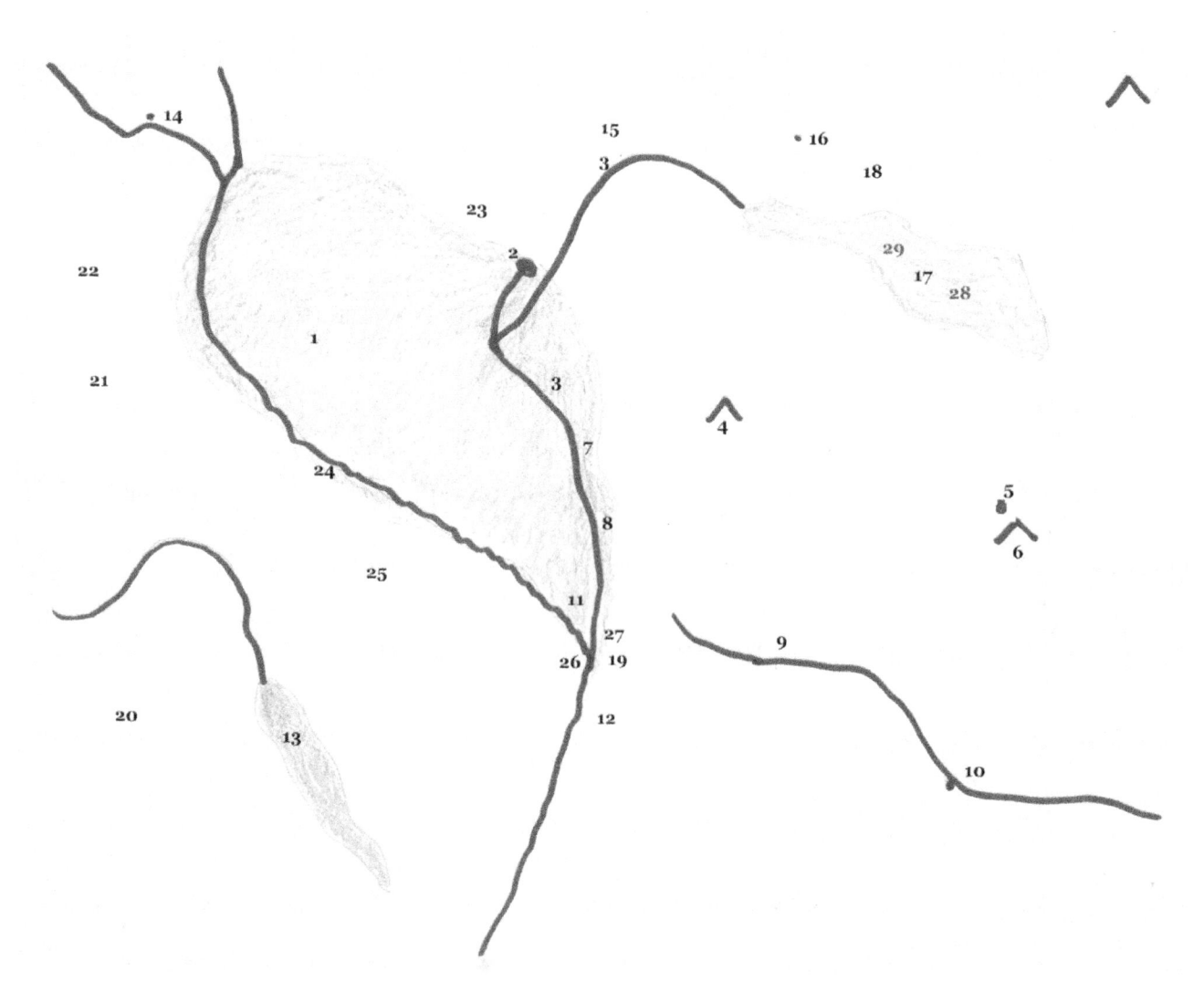

Key #	Current Name	Maidu Name	Meaning, if Known[9]
1	Big Meadows/Lake Almanor	Nakám Ḱoyó	
2	Big Springs	Besapenim (LM) or Wisótpinim (RD) or	
3	Hamilton Branch	Nakám Sewí (through Big Meadows), Yoṱím Sewí (through Clear Creek)	
4	Dyer Mountain	Chiwítbem Yamáni or Náka Yáni	chiwítbem: little clover/grass coming up mountain
5	Homer Lake	Chám Sᨆdom or Chám Sᨆdom Pakáni	cham sᨆdom pakáni means "protruding tree pool"
6	Keddie Peak	Yoṱím Yamáni or Yaḱᨆm Yamáni	Yaḱᨆm Yamáni is canoe mountain
7	Bill's Place (Big Meadows)	Poidowin	
8	none	Wélkeṱim O	frog rock
9	Wolf Creek	Helí'enim Sewí or Kótasim Sewí	
10	Greenville	Kótasi	

[8] Since the first edition of this book, new place names have been found (source: Lilly Baker, in Farrell Cunningham's notes): Basíkᨆ - place name, west of Lake Almanor Inn, Ḱáwwati - place name for Butt Lake Valley (Ḱáwbati being between Humbug Valley and Big Meadows), Choldino - Intake Tower, Náka Yáni - Mt. Dyer, Tᨆldino - Prattville, Wiyekᨆm - Almanor Inn area, Kúduidᨆm - Stover Mountain, Yóiti - Big Springs Village, Basíkᨆ - place name, west of Lake Almanor Inn.

[9] If the meaning is not known, some similar words may be given, in the format "x means y." This is not to say this word is related to the place name, but only to give ideas to others who are trying to figure out place name meanings.

11	Nevis Island	Cham Bokini	
12	Salmon Falls (waterfall near Seneca)	Yatim	
13	Butt Valley	Ḱáwbaṯim Ḱoyó	flat-ground valley
14	Chester	Óidim Ḱoyó	
15	Clear Creek (town)	Óm Yawken or Yotim	
16	Westwood	Sihápkᴍm	
18	Westwood Mill pond area	Siápkᴍm Ḱoyóm or Sihápkᴍ	
17	Mountain Meadows	Óm Wíllium Kasdoi	wililim means "cottonwood" or "aspen," kᴍsdoi means "up the ridge"
19	Canyon Dam area	Chítakam Yamánim	beargrass mountain
20	Humbug Valley	Tásma, Tásmam Ḱoyó	
21	none	Chatamoto	
22	none	Cham Bukúnayim	
23	none	Kólyem	
24	North Fork Feather River	Tam Sewí or Tetém Sewí	tam means "burial," while tái'im means "west." tetém sewí is "big river"
25	Prattville	Táldinom or Tᴍldino	
26	none	Potádi	
27	none	Maním Báldᴍkᴍ	bal is "paint," maní is "with the hand," dᴍḰᴍ is "only"
28	none	Wépam Yamáni	coyote mountain
29	none	Pepépem Ḱum	

MAP 4: Honey Lake and Susanville Area[10]

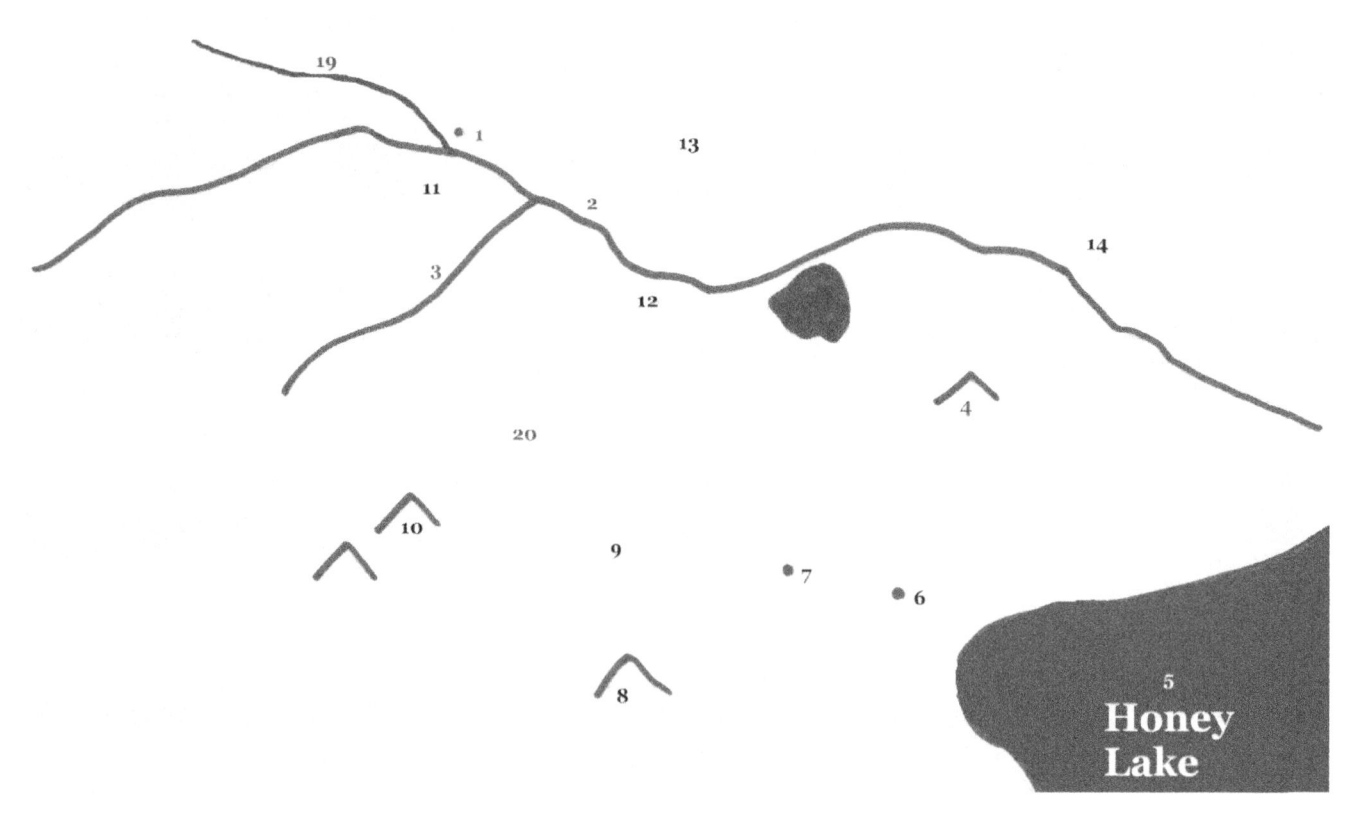

Key #	English	Maidu	Meaning, if Known[11]
1	Susanville	Súmbilim (Indian Heights area) or Pám Sewím Kódom (Inspiration Pt. area)	súmbili is "lobelia," pám sewím kódom is willow river country
2	Susan River	Pám Sewím	willow river
3	Gold Run Creek	Dákpem Sewím	sticky river
4	Bald Mountain	Yóskope or Yóskopem Yamáni or Óskmpe	fox or fox mountain, or "having a bald head"
5	Honey Lake	Hanmleke or Tetém Mómdanni	
6	Buntingville's Baxter Creek	Hanánim Sewím	chokecherry river
7	Janesville	Widóikmm	pulled up
8	Thompson Peak	Widóikmm Yamánim	pulled up mountain
9	Elysian Valley	Bmwopo or Bmwom Bom Páidi	bmwo is "wind" bmwo bo is "wind road"
10	Diamond Mountain	Om Lulmlm	Mt. Shimmering
11	none	Kasím Yamánim	plum mountain
12	Sand Slough	Wetáyim	
13	none	Supóm or Smpám	groundhog, woodchuck or porcupine
14	Honey Lake Valley	Koyóm	valley
15	Antelope Mountain	Om Yepónim Yamánim	stone chief mountain
15	natural amphitheater nearby	Ómpmnno	rock hole
16	Worley Mountain and meadow	Húskmm Yamánim and Húskmm Koyóm	snake mountain and snake meadow
17	Rice Canyon	Bukom	meaning is "sunflower" according to sources
18	Porcupine Hill	Choním Yamánim	porcupine hill
19	Piute Creek or Smith Creek	Tibím Sewím	little creek
20	none	Wetáyim (different from #12)	

---

[10] Since the first edition of this book, more place names have been found (source: Lilly Baker, in Farrell Cunningham's notes): Willard Creek: Bmlmkm

[11] If the meaning is not known, some similar words may be given, in the format "x means y." This is not to say this word is related to the place name, but only to give ideas to others who are trying to figure out place name meanings.

MAP 5: Indian Valley[12]

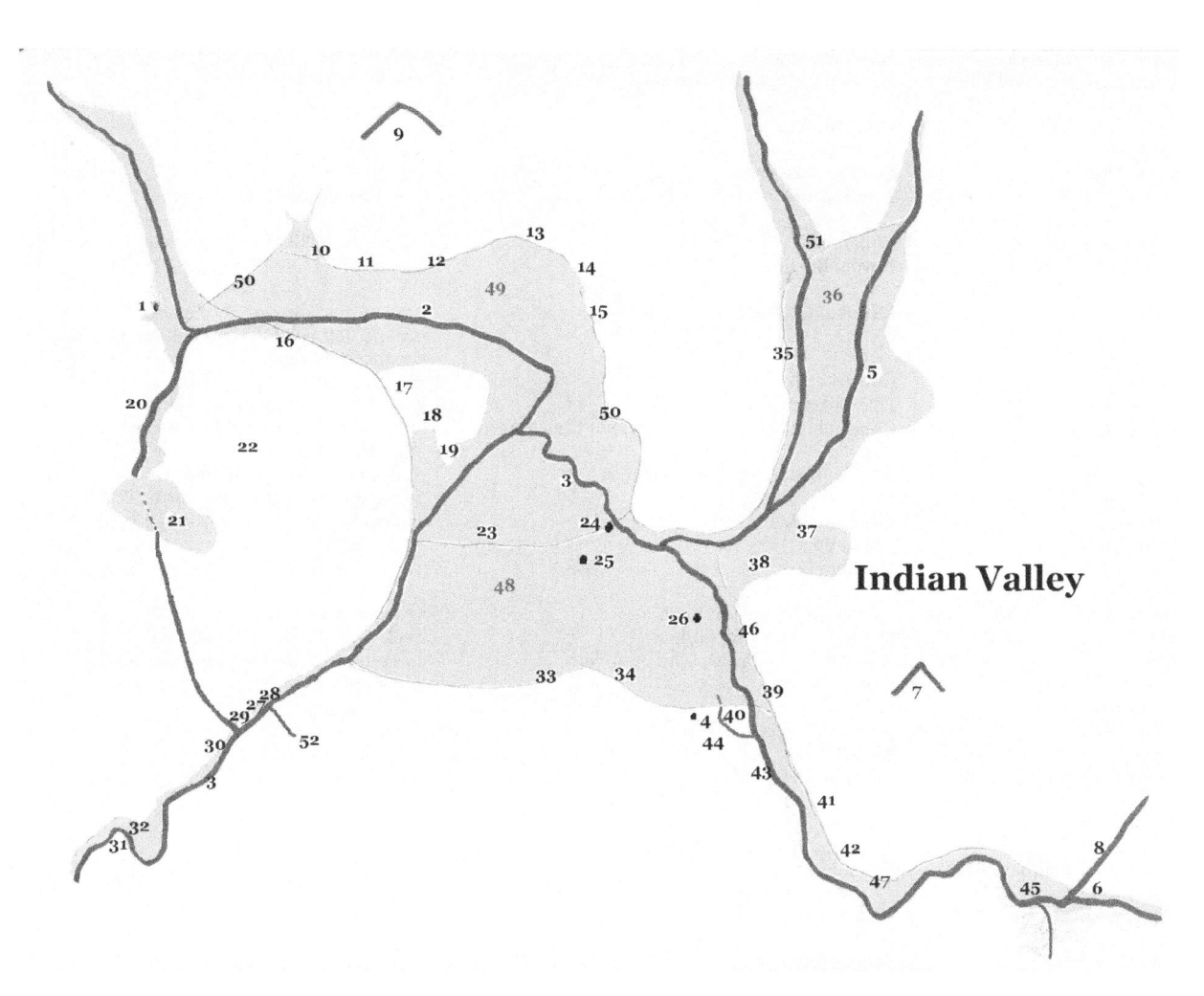

Key #	Current Name	Maidu	Meaning, if Known[13]
1	Greenville	Kótasi	on the snow, snowline
2	Wolf Creek	Helí'enim Sewí or Kótasim Sewí	wolf creek or Greenville creek
3	Indian Creek (SW)	Bɷmɷ́kɷm Sewí	sandy creek
4	Taylorsville	Tosí Ḱoyó	tosí means "north," tosái means "tall standing"
5	Lights Creek	Hópnom Sewí	river canyon creek
6	Genesee	Yetámeto	
7	Mt Jura	Payím Yáhni	foot hill
8	Hosselkus Creek	Pupuwelim Sewí	
9	Keddie Peak	Yakɷ́m Yamáni	canoe (yakɷ́m) or cloudy (yakum) mountain
10	none	Kóbatas Doyím	going up to edge of snow
11	none	Kówkowki Yakum	
12	none	Kókitpe or Kokitbe	snowy or little snowfall
13	none	Bunúk	
14	none	Dakḱa	sticky
15	none	Dókochok Doyím	Dókochom's (north Indian Valley) entrance
16	none	Olílimbe	

---

[12] Since the first edition of this book, new place names have been found (source: Lilly Baker, in Farrell Cunningham's notes): Babcock Peak: Bɷmɷ́kɷm Yamáni Pinem, Squaw Valley (Plumas County): Om Chatim Ḱoyóm, Squaw Queen Creek: Om Chatim Sewí, Squaw Peak: Om Chatim Yamáni

[13] If the meaning is not known, some similar words may be given, in the format "x means y." This is not to say this word is related to the place name, but only to give ideas to others who are trying to figure out place name meanings.

17	none	Wépam Momí	coyote water
18	none	Okóno	
19	Forgay Point	Ochó or Úho or Cholcholum	o means "rock," cho means "burn out"
20	North Canyon Creek	Hunódim Sewí	
21	Round Valley, Round Valley Reservoir	Hunódim, Hunódim Mómdanni, Hébe	hébe means "white lilac"
22	Green Mountain?	Hunódim Yamáni	
23	Stampfli Ln.	Kusim Bo	road to Kusim
24	Kusim Hill	Kusim or Kusimen	kᴀsí means "ridge"
25	Tankusim Hill	Tam Kusim/Tankusim	tam means "bury," kᴀsí means "ridge"
26	Wapunbem Hill	Wapúnbem	wapᴀnbe is "little hopper basket"
27	Crescent Mills, or golf course area to Moccasin Creek	Ḱoyóm Bukúm	valley tail
28	none	Ḱáwokum Púlumtom	ḱáw means "dirt/ground," okᴀ means "left behind," and púlumtom means "between."
29	Moccasin	Chiwísi	clover place
30	Wasám Pool	Paláwaikᴀnundun	paláwaikᴀ means "great snake"
31	Soda Rock	Chuchúdom O or Chuchúkᴀm O or Chuchúyem Bam	urinating rock or urinator rock or urinating towards salt
32	Indian Falls	Ḱoyóm Bukúm Sewíno or Hᴀnkᴀ	valley tail waterfall or hᴀnkᴀ: noise made by an approaching storm (TE)
33	none	Chílwam Ínkomi	chílwam is "rattlesnake" kumí is hole
34	Arlington Rd.	Tosím Bo	north road
35	Diamond Mountain Rd. and possibly North Arm Rd.	Hóṕnom Bo	river canyon road
36	North Arm	Hóṕnomi or Hóṕnom Ḱoyó	river canyon valley
37	none	Óm Ḱoyó or Óm Ḱoyódikno	rock valley, arriving at rock valley
38	none	Yodáwim or Yodáwim Ustu or Yodati	basketry coil, basketry coil cemetery
39	none	Chakámdᴀḱᴀ	pitch only
40	Taylorsville	Ḱᴀsdu	kᴀsdo means "ridge top"
41	none	Konók Wusúpa	konók is "infant's"
42	none	Kóm Ḱoyó	snow meadow
43	Indian Creek (Taylorsville area)	Tosí Ḱoyóm Sewí	
44	Taylor's Creek	Am Sewí	
45	Genesee Valley	Yoťámmoto Ḱoyó or Yoťámmoton	
46	Genesee Rd, south of Taylorsville	Yoťámmotom Bo	road to Yetameto
47	Genesee Rd, north of Taylorsville	Chakámdᴀḱᴀm Bo	
48	Indian Valley	Nadam Ḱoyó	this-place meadow
49	North Indian Valley	Dókochom	
50	North Valley Rd.	Ḱoyóm Bo	valley road
51	none	Benwawikdowen	
52	Moccasin or Dixie Creek	Hébem Sewí	white lilac creek

About the Author

Karen Lahaie Anderson was born and raised in California. She holds a degree in French language and literature from UC Berkeley and a master's degree in linguistics from Stanford University. Her specialties at Berkeley and Stanford were historical linguistics, Indo-European linguistics and African languages. Maidu is her first Native American language, and she hopes to study others. Karen is also the author of Mountain Maidu Grammar and Modern Maidu.
The fish-head font and spell-check are available on request by email.
To contact the author with questions, comments, and corrections, please email her at: karen87659@yahoo.com.

Bibliography

#	Sources:			
	Anderson, Karen Lahaie	2014	*Mountain Maidu Grammar*	San Bernardino, CA: CreateSpace Publishing.
1	Cunningham, Ben	n.d.	Notes, in possession of the author	
2	Cunningham, Farrell	1996-2012	Notes, in possession of the author	
3	Cunningham, Farrell	2008-2013	personal communication	
4	Cunningham, Farrell and BethRose Middleton	2007	*Proposed Maidu Summit Lands*	Maidu Mapping Consortium.
5	Dixon, Roland B.	1912	*Maidu Texts*	Leyden: The Netherlands.
6	Dixon, Roland B.	1905	*The Northern Maidu*	New York: Bulletin of the American Museum of Natural History 17(3): 119-246.
7	Dixon, Roland B.	1910	*Maidu, An Illustrative Sketch*	Washington: Government Printing Office
8	Duncan, John	1963	*Maidu Ethnobotany*	
9	Dunn, Mary E.	1962	*The Maidu Indians of Plumas County*	*Plumas Memories: The Maidu Indians of Plumas County*. The Plumas County Historical Society, Number 8 (1962), 2002 reprint
10	Fariss and Smith, eds.	1882	*Illustrated History of Plumas, Lassen, and Sierra Counties*	San Francisco: Fariss and Smith.
11	Kroeber, A.L.	1925	Handbook of the Indians of California	*Bureau of American Ethnology Bulletin 78*. Washington, D.C.
	Lindgren-Kurtz, Pat	2011	Picking Willows: with Daisy and Lilly Baker, Maidu Basket Makers of Lake Almanor	iUniverse Publishing.
12	Manning, Danny	2015	Personal Communication	
13	McMillan, James H.	1969	*The Northeastern Maidu*	*Plumas Memories: The Maidu Indians of Plumas County*. The Plumas County Historical Society, Number 34, 2002 reprint.
14	Merino, Thomas	1998	*Maidu Sense of Place* Map	Greenville, California. Maidu Cultural and Development Group.
15	Merriam, C. Hart	1904	*Indian Names for Plants and Animals among California and Other Western North American Tribes*	Socorro, New Mexico: Ballena Press. Assembled and annotated by R.F Heizer. 1967 reprint.
16	Powers, Stephen	1877	*Tribes of California*	Berkeley, California: University of California Press, 1976 reprint.
17	Powers, Stephen	1886	*Meidoo* word list attributed to Stephen Powers	The Native Races, ed. H.H. Bancroft. Volume III, p. 652. San Francisco: A.L. Bancroft & Company, Publishers
18	Rathbun, Robert	1973	*Coyote Man, The Destruction of the People*	Berkeley, California. Brother Willliam Press.
19	Riddell, Francis A.	1968	Ethnogeography Of Two Maidu Groups	Masterkey 42 (2): 45-52.
20	Riddell, Francis A.	1978	Maidu and Konkow	in *Handbook of North American Indians*, Vol. 8, California, ed. Robert F. Heizer, pp. 370-386.

	Ruhlen, Merritt	1991	*A Guide to the World's Languages, Volume 1: Classification*	Stanford University Press, Stanford, CA. Originally printed 1987
21	Shipley, William S.	1963	*Maidu Texts and Dictionary*	Berkeley and Los Angeles: University of California Press
22	Shipley, William S.	1964	*Maidu Grammar*	Berkeley and Los Angeles: University of California Press
23	Shipley, William S.	1991	*The Maidu Indian Myths and Stories of Hanc'ibyim*	Berkeley, California: Heyday Books.
24	Simmons, William S., Ron Morales, Viola Williams and Steve Camacho	1997	Honey Lake Maidu Ethnogeography of Lassen County, California.	*Journal of California and Great Basin Anthropology 19:2-31*
25	Theodoratus Cultural Research	1985	Cultural Resources of the Indian Creek Water Power Project, Plumas County, California	Theodoratus Cultural Research, Fair Oaks, California.
26	Tolley, Sara-Larus	2006	*Quest for Tribal Acknowledgment, California's Honey Lake Maidus*	Norman, Oklahoma. University of Oklahoma Press.

Recordings:

27	Potts, Edytha	n.d	Roundhouse Recordings	Greenville.
28	Worth, Sarah Potts	n.d.	Roundhouse Recordings	Greenville.
29	Young, Herb	1967	unknown sponsor	Feather Falls, California.

Web Pages:

30	Morales, Leona and Steve Camacho	1994	www.honeylakemaidu.org/creation.html	*The World of Ko'domyeponi* map.
31	unknown	n.d.	http://indianvalleychamber.snappages.com/an ancient trail - A Maidu Auto Tour.htm	Indian Valley Chamber web site.
	Manlove, Robert	2009	www.sierravoices.com/2009/08/the-mountain-maidu-bear-dance/	*The Mountain Maidu Bear Dance*, News from Native California, Vol. 22 #3
	unknown	n.d.	www.drumhop.com	

Maps for Location Details:

AAA map	2014	Northern California	
Forest Service Map	1985	Plumas National Forest	U.S. Government Printing Office
Google Maps	2015	www.google.com/maps	
Keddie, Arthur	1892	www.loc.gov/resource/g463p.la000033a	Keddie's map of Plumas County, California, Library of Congress.

Made in the USA
Middletown, DE
28 January 2024